MODERN
INTERNATIONAL
ECONOMICS

Wilfred J. Ethier

UNIVERSITY OF PENNSYLVANIA

MODERN INTERNATIONAL ECONOMICS

W · W · NORTON & COMPANY · NEW YORK · LONDON

Photograph Credits
Historical Pictures Service (6)
Warder Collection (51, 289)
Swedish Information Service (90)
Wide World Photos (134)
New York Public Library (289)
Harvard University Archives (345)

First Edition

Library of Congress Cataloging in Publication Data
Eithier, Wilfred.
    Modern international economics.
    Includes bibliographies and index.
    1. International economic relations.   I. Title.
HF1411.E824   1982   337   82-14122
ISBN 0-393-95250-9
W. W. Norton & Company, Inc. 500 Fifth Avenue, New York, N. Y. 10110
W. W. Norton & Company Ltd. 37 Great Russell Street, London WC1B 3NU

1 2 3 4 5 6 7 8 9 0

In Memory of My Father

Contents

Part Three

International Monetary Theory and Applications   285

Preface

"Beware of a thick book."—RICHARD WAGNER

THIS BOOK is intended for conventional undergraduate courses in international economics of either one or two semesters in length. The full line of usual topics is included, and the discussion is almost entirely verbal and geometric. More advanced or specialized material is provided by starred sections labeled *EXPLORING FURTHER*. These sections contain no algebra or advanced mathematics, but do on occasion make intensive use of geometry. They can all be skipped without loss of continuity. The mathematically trained student is directed to Appendix I, which provides a technical treatment of international trade theory, keyed to Part One of the text. A typical one-semester course would cover the unstarred sections of the core chapters (1–4, 8, and 9) together with whatever the instructor wishes from other chapters. A one-year course might cover the entire text and supplement it with readings. Appendix I is suitable for graduate students and more sophisticated undergraduates.

The majority of sections are followed by a selection of problems. The problems are arranged more or less in order of increasing difficulty, and especially challenging problems are distinguished by asterisks. Students should at least attempt the unstarred problems before going on to the next section. Appendix III provides the answers to a selection of problems.

Acknowledgments

THE FOLLOWING economists read various parts of the manuscript and provided many very useful suggestions.

ARTHUR I. BLOOMFIELD
University of Pennsylvania

AMY H. DALTON
Virginia Commonwealth University

ALAN V. DEARDORFF
University of Michigan

JORGE A. BRAGA DEMACEDO
Princeton University

JONATHAN EATON
Yale University

ELIZABETH GOLDSTEIN
University of Pennsylvania

THOMAS GRENNES
North Carolina State University

PETER KENEN
Princeton University

RICHARD MARSTON
University of Pennsylvania

STEVEN MATUSZ
University of Pennsylvania

ASSAF RAZIN
Tel Aviv University

MICHAEL SCHMID
University of Mannheim

EDWARD TOWER
Duke University

DONALD S. LAMM and SUE LOWE, of W. W. Norton & Company, provided valuable editorial help. The manuscript was efficiently prepared by JEANNE ETHIER, ISABELLE GIBSON, and JENNIFER GOLDENBERG.

Introduction

"International trade meaning in plain English trade between nations, it is not surprising that the term should mean something else in Political Economy."

—F. Y. EDGEWORTH

EVERYONE KNOWS what international economics is all about. It is about international trade and whether we should restrict imports of Japanese automobiles or Korean shoes. It is about nagging balance of payments problems and spectacular foreign exchange crises. It is about the gnomes of Zurich, the sheikhs of Araby, and the millions of poor migrants who are trying to find better jobs by leaving southern Europe for the north or the Far East for the Middle East or by paying someone to smuggle them into the United States. It is about multinational corporations larger than countries, fuel bills that seem huge to those who must pay them, and automobiles that look smaller than ever before. It is about European complaints that interest rates are too high in America and American complaints that Europe is not charging us enough for her steel.

This book is about all these things and many others as well. We discuss them by developing the basic ideas of international economic theory and then putting those ideas to work. What makes international economic theory distinct from general economics? Is it perhaps really the same, except for a more cosmopolitan terminology and distinctive practical applications? To a large extent the answer is yes. The basic tools, ideas, and modes of thought of general economics are basic to this book. But there are two key aspects of the subject that make international economic theory distinct.

1. *In the world economy some markets are national while others are international.* The most important example of this feature is the assumption

that the factors of production—land, labor, and capital—are perfectly mobile within nations but completely immobile between nations (national factor markets), whereas commodities can be traded both nationally and internationally (international commodity markets). This assumption has characterized international trade theory since its development by the classical economists, and the assumption will be basic to the first three chapters of this book. But of course the assumption is not true. We can all think of exceptions. Capital flows into projects around the globe—but perhaps not into certain blocks in your town. No North American student can be blind to international human migration, yet families often refuse to leave depressed areas for more favorable regions of the same country. Our assumption, then, is not a literal description of reality, but an abstraction of an underlying tendency. As such, the assumption is useful for thought but we must not make a religion out of it. International factor mobility is consequently examined in detail in Chapter 7 and is mentioned elsewhere in the book, as are still other departures from the assumption.

2. *National sovereignty influences the character of economic activity.* This point first arises in Chapter 4, where we examine the effects of national expenditure policies that directly influence aggregate demand in one country but not in others. Chapters 5 and 6 study commercial policies that tax or otherwise impede commodity exchanges between countries but not within countries. Almost every nation has its coin of the realm, so that transactions between nationals involve a common currency whereas transactions between residents of different states require one type of money to be exchanged for another. A large part of this book is concerned with issues related to the existence of indpendent national monetary systems.

The two features are not independent. International factor movements are certainly inhibited by national policies and by the reluctance of factor owners to expose themselves or their wealth to foreign jurisdictions.

This book first examines—in Parts One and Two—those issues that do not involve money, and then—in Parts Three and Four—those that do. In each case we first develop the basic theory (in Parts One and Three respectively). The theory is presented as a few fundamental ideas, which are developed gradually in the light of basic characteristics of the modern international economy and are linked together. Parts Two and Four respectively further exploit and apply the theory. In conclusion, Part Five serves as an overview, incorporating both monetary and non-monetary issues.

MODERN INTERNATIONAL ECONOMICS

Part One

The Pure Theory of International Trade and Applications

THE pure theory of international trade gives answers to three sets of questions. First, why do nations exchange goods and services, who exports what to whom at what prices, and which countries produce which goods? In other words, it explains the pattern of international trade and production. Second, there are the welfare implications of such trade: is international trade a good thing for the world, and, if so, how are the gains distributed among nations? Do all benefit, or are some countries made better off at the expense of others? Last are the implications of trade for the domestic economy: how does trade affect the internal allocation of resources and the distribution of income? The level of unemployment and the rate of inflation?

As we study this theory, it is advisable to have in mind a perspective of actual international trade. The figure below shows the network of world trade in 1979.

Each number gives exports plus imports as a percentage of world exports plus imports. Thus Japanese exports to Western Europe plus Western Europe's exports to Japan equaled 1 percent of all goods exported by all nations plus all goods imported by all nations. Trade among the countries of Western Europe likewise accounted for 34 percent of world trade. Altogether, 70 percent of world trade is accounted for in the figure (the remaining 30 percent is accounted for by the forty-three trade flows that round off to 0 percent, plus the countries, such as Australia, that are excluded).

If you study the figure for a few minutes, your mind should begin to concoct hypotheses about geographical, political, and historical influences on trade flows. Note in particular the very large part of world trade accounted for by exchanges among industrialized market economies (North America, Western Europe, and Japan), the small part of world trade accounted for by the communist countries (USSR, Eastern Europe, and China), and the peripheral role played by the non-oil-exporting, less developed countries (Latin America, Africa, and Other Asia), whose modest trade tends to be concentrated with particular parts of the more developed world.

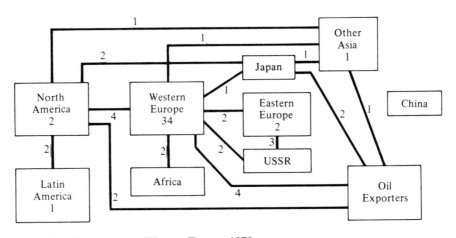

THE NETWORK OF WORLD TRADE, 1979

SOURCE: IMF, *Direction of Trade*

Our perspective on world trade can be broadened by looking at the characteristics of specific countries. The table below lists ten countries ranked according to the amount of trade they do. Examination of the first column shows little relation between national size, as measured by population, and trade: India, the most populous country, trades the least. When size is instead measured by the gross national product, it correlates more closely with trade, but there are exceptions. Large, continental countries (U.S., USSR, Brazil) tend to trade proportionally less than smaller countries, with the European industrial nations the heaviest traders. Thus, 26 percent of the United Kingdom's national income is spent on imports, compared with 9 percent for the United States, and the average German spends almost three times as much on imported goods as does the average American. The country in the table with the least trade relative to GNP is the USSR; communist countries generally trade less than half as much as do noncommunist countries with similar characteristics.

CHARACTERISTICS OF SELECTED COUNTRIES, 1979

Country	Population (millions)	GNP* ($ billions)	Imports ($ billions)	Exports ($ billions)	Imports per capita ($)	Imports as % of GNP	Imports as % of World Imports
U.S.	221	2412	219	182	991	9	14
W. Germany	61	766	160	172	2623	21	10
Japan	116	1011	110	102	948	11	7
U.K.	56	403	103	91	1839	26	7
USSR	255	1350	58	65	227	4	4
Canada	24	222	57	58	2375	26	4
Brazil	119	199	20	15	168	10	1
Singapore	2	9	18	14	9000	200	1
India	651	118	9	7	14	8	0.6

SOURCE: IMF, *International Financial Statistics*

The table contains two apparent anomalies. Canada is geographically large, like the United States or Brazil, but trades more than they do relative to GNP. The reason is twofold: because most of Canada's economy is close to the American border, it trades much with the United States; and since the Canadian economy is only about one-tenth the size of the American, this trade is relatively much more significant for Canada. The strangest entry in the table is Singapore, which exports more than it produces and imports goods worth about twice its own GNP! How does Singapore do it? Singapore is an *entrepot:* large quantities of goods are imported and then, perhaps after some processing, reexported to final buyers. Singapore serves as a middleman.

Contemplation of the figure and the table is suggestive, but it does not give us answers to our three sets of questions. This is why we need the theory, which consists of four basic ideas. These, in order of decreasing generality, elegance, and importance, are *comparative advantage, reciprocal demand,* the *factor-endowments* basis of comparative costs, and the *foreign trade multiplier.* Each of the four chapters of Part One is devoted to one of these ideas. The first two form the basis of the classical theory of international trade developed by the nineteenth-century English classical economists. The last two ideas are twentieth-century developments, the third basically an extension of classical thought and thus sometimes described as neoclassical or modern. The fourth, on the other hand, is distinct: the application of the Keynesian revolution to international trade. In contrast to the other three, it is macroeconomic in nature rather than micoreconomic and concerned more with short-run disequilibrium than long-run equilibrium.

Chapter 1

Comparative Advantage

"No real Englishman in his secret soul was ever sorry for the death of a political economist."
—W. BAGEHOT

THE PRINCIPLE of comparative advantage is one of the great ideas of economics: simple and elegant, applicable under very general circumstances, and central to an understanding of a host of different phenomena. The basic idea was developed in the early nineteenth century by the English classical economists and is attributed primarily to David Ricardo.

We first illustrate comparative advantage in a very elementary framework, called the simple Ricardian model, and then discuss it under more general circumstances. As we develop the theory, you might want to consider how it relates to two interesting phenomena.

1. *International wage differences.* Wage rates vary dramatically over the globe. For example, in September of 1980 average hourly wages in manufacturing in three countries were

United States	$7.42
South Korea	1.63
Malawi	.44

What accounts for these differences? How can countries like these compete with each other and profitably trade? Can they?

2. *The Great Tomato War.* During the winter, tomatoes and other fresh vegetables reach American tables from producers in Florida and Mexico. Field hands in Mexico are paid a wage about one-third of that

received by their Florida counterparts. Mexican growers have been gradually expanding their share of the market at the expense of Florida growers, and they have now captured about one-half of the total market for winter vegetables. Farmers in Florida have reacted to this with demands—thus far unmet—for protection from unfair Mexican competition. What should U.S. policy be?

DAVID RICARDO (1772-1823)

David Ricardo was the son of a Jewish financier who had migrated to London from Holland. The family was of Portuguese origin. At the age of twelve David went to work for his father, but he was disowned when he converted from Judaism to marry a Quaker. Ricardo made a fortune on the London stock exchange and retired young. He purchased an estate and a seat in Parliament, from which he would on painful occasion expound his views. Ricardo's estate—Gatcombe—is now the residence of Princess Anne.

Despite his fabulous practical success as a businessman, as an economist Ricardo emphasized abstract theory. He analyzed growth and income distribution and was a major architect of the classical system of thought, from which both Marxism and modern conservative economics have developed.

1. The Simple Ricardian Model

Suppose that in two countries, say France and Germany, there can be produced but two goods, machines and wine. Each cask of wine produced in France requires exactly two units (say, man-hours) of labor for its manufacture. Table 1.1 shows the amounts of labor necessary to produce one unit of each of the goods in each of the two countries.

Table 1.1.   A SIMPLE RICARDIAN MODEL: LABOR REQUIRED IN
EACH COUNTRY TO PRODUCE ONE UNIT OF EACH GOOD

	Machines	*Wine*
France	6	2
Germany	1	1

It is evident that from Table 1.1 that both goods require more labor for their manufacture in France than in Gemany.

Suppose that initially each country is producing some of both goods, and consider the following experiment. France cuts back her production of machines and uses the labor released from the machine industry to produce more wine, which is sent to Germany. The Germans can then cut back on their wine production and use the labor released from the wine industry to produce more machines, which can in turn be sent to France. What would result? If the French produce one less machine, six units of labor will be released, which will be able to produce three additional casks of wine. If this wine is sent to Germany, enabling the Germans to reduce their wine production by three casks, three units of German labor will be released. Now only one unit of German labor is required to produce the machine necessary to replace the original French cutback. Therefore France and Germany are now able to produce together just as much wine and machinery as before, and in addition there are now two units of German labor left over with which to produce two more machines, or two more casks of wine, or some combination of wine and machinery. Table 1.2 shows the final result if these two Geman laborers are divided equally between the wine and machine industries. This additional output can be divided between the two countries, making both of them better off.

Table 1.2. A SIMPLE RICARDIAN MODEL: POSSIBLE RESULTS OF THE EXPERIMENT

	Additional Machines	Additional Wine
in France	−1	+3
in Germany	+2	−2
in World	+1	+1

Be sure that you understand fully the above reasoning. It is the heart of the principle of comparative advantage and will be made use of again and again in this book, under many different guises and for many different purposes. To test yourself, show that if France instead shifts labor from the wine industry to the machine industry, exporting machinery to Germany for wine, France and Germany will together become worse off.

Clearly this experiment can be repeated, and the two countries together can be made even better off. That is, additional French labor can be shifted from the machinery industry to the wine industry, and the trade of French wine for German machines extended. This process can continue until either the entire French labor force is producing wine, the German labor force is specialized in machines, or both countries are specialized.

Thus only these three final possibilities are compatible with an efficient pattern of world production.

KEY CONCEPT

An *efficient pattern of production* is one for which it is impossible to increase the production of any good without reducing the output of some other good.

Reviewing our reasoning, we see that this result depends not at all on the *absolute* levels of the four labor requirements in Table 1.1, but only on the *ratios* of the requirements within each country. For example, if excessive wine consumption caused French labor to become much less efficient so that both numbers in the first row were multiplied by 100, say, we would still get exactly the same result. Similarly both German labor requirements could be multiplied by any positive number at all, and none of the conclusions would be changed. Everything depended only on the fact that 6/2 is greater than 1/1. More generally, letting a_W^F denote the labor necessary to produce one cask of wine in France, and so on, everything depended upon the fact that

$$\frac{a_M^F}{a_W^F} > \frac{a_M^G}{a_W^G}. \tag{1.1}$$

You should verify that if this equality were reversed, efficient world production would call for France to produce machines and Germany to produce wine.

These ratios also help to shed further light on our result. They are expressed in the following units:

$$\frac{a_M^F}{a_W^F} = \frac{\text{labor/machine}}{\text{labor/wine}} = \text{wine/machine}.$$

Thus each ratio tells us the cost, in terms of wine, of producing one more machine in each country. The inequality says, then, that the world must sacrifice more wine to build a machine in France than to build one in Germany. Hence, the conclusion that as many of the world's machines as possible should be produced in Germany.

The inequality in (1.1) can equivalently be written

$$\frac{a_W^G}{a_M^G} > \frac{a_W^F}{a_M^F}. \tag{1.2}$$

In this form the inequality says that the cost in terms of machines of producing one cask of wine is greater in Germany than in France. Hence as much of the world's wine as possible should be produced in France. When we speak in this way of the cost in terms of wine of producing a machine, we are referring to what are termed *opportunity costs.* That is, a machine is obviously not produced by using up wine, but, rather, the true cost of the machine to the economy is the wine that *could* be produced by the labor that is actually used to make the machine, *if* that labor were instead used by the wine industry.

KEY CONCEPT

The *opportunity cost* of a good to an individual or to a society is the amount of some other good that must be forgone in order to obtain one unit of it. Suppose you have five dollars and want to buy a five-dollar pizza and five dollar's worth of gas. You obviously cannot afford both and so must choose. The *opportunity* cost of the pizza is the gasoline, and the *opportunity* cost of the gasoline is the pizza. The *money* cost of each is five dollars.

When the labor requirements are in the relation (1.2), we say that "France has a comparative advantage over Germany in wine relative to machines." Just as the inequality could be written in two equivalent forms, this statement is equivalent to the statement, "Germany has a comparative advantage over France in machines relative to wine." These two sentences are completely interchangeable; each implies the other. The important point to note about each is its double-barreled relativity; we speak of nothing in absolute terms but of wine *relative to* machines, of France *over* Germany.

What conclusions can be drawn in this simple Ricardian world directly from a knowledge of the pattern of comparative advantage? Notice that we cannot tell *exactly* what the pattern of production would be. If, to take an extreme example, everyone in the world wants only wine and has no use for machines, then both countries will produce only wine and international trade will be pointless, regardless of the pattern of comparative advantage. Or, to take a more realistic case, if the world wants more wine than France is capable of producing, Germany must produce some wine also. But comparative advantage narrows things down by distinguishing between efficient and inefficient patterns of production. In terms of our example, France should never produce any machines if Germany is producing some wine, and Germany should never produce any wine if France is making some machines. For these are precisely the situations to which we can apply the reasoning used at the beginning of this section to show that by exploiting the pattern of comparative advantage, the world can have more of both machines and wine.

Thus comparative advantage tells us something about the pattern of production. Its implication for the pattern of international trade is even simpler: if trade takes place, a country should export that good in which it has a comparative advantage and import that good in which it has a comparative disadvantage. In the example of Table 1.1, France should export wine and import machines.

PROBLEMS

1.1 Suppose that in England five man-hours of labor are required to produce each cask of wine and five man-hours are required to produce each bolt of cloth, whereas in Portugal one man-hour of labor is required for a cask of wine and four man-hours for a bolt of cloth. (Except for the choice of numbers, this is the example used by Ricardo to discuss comparative advantage.)

   a Who has a comparative advantage in what and why? Make two equivalent statements.

   b Prove that your answer to **a** is correct by showing in detail that when both countries are producing both goods, the world can be made better off by allowing England and Portugal to reallocate labor and trade in accordance with the pattern of comparative advantage. Derive the analog of Table 1.2.

   c Now suppose that it becomes possible to move labor between the two countries. What should be done?

1.2 In the context of the above problem, suppose there is also a third country, France, where one man-hour of labor can produce either one bolt of cloth or one-half cask of wine. What statements can you make about comparative advantage? Which patterns of production and international trade are efficient?

1.3 An executive in a certain firm happens to be an excellent typist but he is, nonetheless, given a typist, who in fact types more slowly than the executive.

   a Formalize this situation in terms of our discussion of comparative advantage and show explicitly how this assignment of people to jobs could be efficient from the firm's point of view. (Hypothesize that each individual can either type so many pages or make so many decisions in one hour—make up your own numbers.)

   b Suppose instead that this job assignment reflects only sexist discrimination. Use the idea of comparative advantage to show that the firm is paying a cost for this discrimination.

2. Efficiency in the Simple Ricardian World

The previous section showed that if the pattern of trade and production conflicts with comparative advantage, it is possible to increase world output of all goods through increased trade and international specialization. Now we shall reexamine this conclusion from a slightly different point of view, both to further drive home the basic point and to introduce some concepts and techniques of use later on.

Let us first look at the various possible total outputs of both goods that can be produced by each country. To do this, we need to know not only the productivities of labor, but also how much labor is available. Assume that France has a total labor supply of 600 units, and Germany a total labor supply of 500 units. Then if France devotes its entire labor force to the machine industry, it can produce $600/a_M^F$, or, in view of Table 1.1, 100 machines; if it specializes in wine, it can produce $600/a_W^F$, or 300 casks of wine; if it divides its labor equally between the wine and machinery industries, it can produce 50 machines and 150 casks of wine; and so forth. The various possibilities are depicted by the line in Figure 1.1 (a). This line, known as the French production possibility frontier, can be precisely thought of as the collection of all alternative feasible French outputs of the two goods having the property that the output of one good can be increased only by lowering the output of the other. That is, it depicts all possible French outputs that are efficient. Point C involves more of both wine and machinery than does A, but C lies outside the production possibility frontier and thus requires more labor resources than France possesses. Point B, on the other hand, is inefficient; it lies inside the production possibility frontier and involves less of both wine and machinery than does A. If the French economy is producing the outputs denoted by B then some French labor must be either idle or employed in a wasteful manner. Point D, like A, is efficient; it involves less wine output than does A but more machines. In similar fashion we can derive Germany's production possibility frontier, which is depicted in Figure 1.1(b).

KEY CONCEPT

The *production possibility frontier* of a country, or other entity, shows the alternative combinations of various goods that the entity can produce, given its technology and its stock of productive factors, such as labor.

The slope of the French production possibility frontier is

$$-\left(\frac{600}{a_W^F} \middle/ \frac{600}{a_M^F}\right) = -a_M^F/a_W^F.$$

Thus the slope of the production possibility frontier is determined *only* by the labor input requirements, whereas its distance from the origin depends upon the size of the French labor force. (Verify that if France's labor supply triples, say, the French production possibility frontier will be shifted outwards by a factor of three but will retain the same slope.) Thus inequality (1.2), which determined the pattern of comparative advantage, translates geometrically into the French production possibility frontier being steeper than the German. We usually term a_M^F/a_W^F, the negative of the slope, the

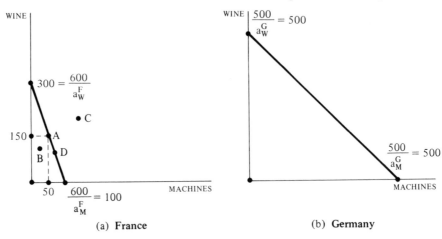

(a) **France**   (b) **Germany**

Figure 1.1. PRODUCTION POSSIBILITY FRONTIERS

"marginal rate of transformation of wine for machines," denoted MRT_{WM}
It tells us the quantity of wine that must be foregone in order to produce
one more machine, that is, the opportunity cost of a machine in terms of
wine. Similarly it tells us the amount of extra wine that France could produce if it reduced its machine output by one unit.

KEY CONCEPT

The *marginal rate of transformation* of one good for another is
the amount by which production of the first must be reduced in
order to free enough productive factors, such as labor, to produce one additional unit of the second.

We thus have a second method of determining comparative advantage: if the MRT_{WM} in France is greater than it is in Germany, France has a
comparative advantage over Germany in wine relative to machines. This
method is conceptually distinct from the earlier method of using ratios of
labor productivities. But clearly in the simple Ricardian world the two must
be equivalent.

The production possibility frontier is intimately connected with the
question of efficiency in a country *by itself*, but we are also interested in the
efficiency of the world as a whole. Clearly the world will not be operating
efficiently unless each country is, that is, unless each country is operating on
its production possibility frontier. But is this all that is necessary for world
output to be efficient? No. For we saw in section 1 that unless comparative
advantage is followed, world output is not as high as it could be. Let us

therefore examine efficient world output patterns, that is, the *world* production possibility frontier.

Suppose that France is specialized in wine production. Then world output will be equal to whatever Germany happens to be producing plus the 300 casks of French wine. These possibilities are given by the line AB in Figure 1.2(a). For example, at point A France produces 300 casks of wine, and Germany 500; at B France produces 300 casks of wine, and Germany 500 machines. When Germany is specialized in machinery, world output will equal whatever France is producing plus the 500 German machines. This gives the line BC in Figure 1.2(a). The world production possibility frontier is then ABC.

But note that we could have proceeded differently. If Germany is specialized in wine then world output equals France's output plus the 500 casks of German wine; this gives AD in Figure 1.2(b). Similarly DC is obtained by supposing that France specializes in machinery. Clearly ADC lies inside ABC. That is, except for A and C where both countries specialize entirely in the same good, any pattern of world output on ADC is inefficient because more of both goods can be obtained at some point on ABC.

What is the difference between these two attempts to find the world production possibility frontier? In the first case, we looked at what world output would be for all patterns of production compatible with comparative advantage. But in the second case, we were looking at situations that violated comparative advantage. At D, for example, Germany is specialized in wine, and France in machinery. The world production possibility frontier, then, illustrates in geometric terms the meaning of comparative advantage.

Points A, B, and C on the world production possibility frontier correspond to complete specialization in both countries. At A both specialize in

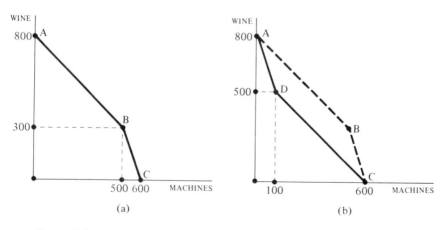

Figure 1.2. THE WORLD PRODUCTION POSSIBILITY FRONTIER

wine; at *B* France produces only wine, and Germany only machines; at *C* both specialize in machinery. Between *A* and *B* France is specialized in wine, while Germany produces both goods. Here the world marginal rate of transformation of wine for machines equals that in Germany. This reflects the fact that if world output is to change, it must come about through changes in Germany; France remains specialized in wine. Between *B* and *C*, however, the situation is reversed. France produces both goods, while Germany is specialized in machines, and the world marginal rate of transformation equals that in France. Note that at *B* it makes no sense to talk about *the* world marginal rate of transformation. Here the world opportunity cost of wine in terms of machines is not simply the reciprocal of the world opportunity cost of machines in terms of wine. (Why?)

Where on the world production possibility frontier should the world produce? We cannot say. That depends upon world tastes for the two goods, about which we as yet have said nothing. This reflects the conclusion in the previous section that comparative advantage does not tell what world production should be: it specifies the efficient alternatives.

PROBLEMS

1.4 Consider, as in Problem **1.1**, that in England five labor are required for each unit of wine and each unit of cloth, while in Portugal one labor produces one wine and four labor produce one cloth. Suppose also that each country has 100 man-hours of labor available.

    a Draw the production possibility frontiers for England, Portugal, and the world. How do they change if England's labor force increases to 1,000?

    b If everyone in the world always consumes exactly one cask of wine for each bolt of cloth, what should each country produce and what should the direction of trade be?

    c Draw the world production possibility frontier if the labor is *internationally* mobile.

1.5 In the above problem, suppose that in France one labor can produce one cloth while two labor are required for one wine, and, in addition, that France has 200 man-hours of labor. Draw the world production possibility frontier. Who is producing what at various points along it? Depict the inefficient patterns of specialization.

3. The Economics of the Simple Ricardian World

The previous two sections discussed what the pattern of international trade and specialization *should* be but said nothing about what it actually *would* be. This distinction is important; for example, one might conjecture on the basis of Table 1.1 that both French industries would be driven out of business by more efficient German competition, and this would surely not be efficient for the world as a whole. Also, our discussion has so far dealt entirely with production; we have as yet said nothing about the economics of international trade. It is time to turn to these questions.

Suppose initially that we can observe the French economy in an *autarkic* state, that is, free of any economic relations with the rest of the world. Then the French must supply their own wine and machinery. Suppose that the (autarkic) wage rate in France is w^F, expressed in some unit of account (say dollars, or francs, or casks of wine). Then if the labor market is competitive, all French firms must pay w^F for each unit of labor they use, and since labor is the only input required in either industry, the cost of producing a cask of wine in France must be $a_W^F w^F$ and the cost of a machine must be $a_M^F w^F$. These must, in fact, be the actual prices, P_W^F and P_M^F, if the wine and machines are competitive and *if* both wine and machines are produced. If $P_W^F > a_W^F w^F$, for example, then French wine producers are earning a profit that will, ultimately, be bid away by competition. If $P_W^F < a_W^F w^F$ then wine producers are receiving less for their product than it costs them to produce it and so will eventually close down if the inequality persists.

Since France cannot trade, the French economy will be in equilibrium only when demand equals supply in all three markets (labor, wine, and machinery). Suppose this occurs at point A in Figure 1.1(a). If w^F is equal to one, for example, we have $P_W^F = a_W^F = 2$ and $P_M^F = a_M^F = 6$. The 150 units of wine produced at A are thus worth 300, and the 50 machines are worth 300, so that the value of national output is 600. Similarly the total wage bill (that is, national income) is 600. There are three markets and three prices here, but note that only *relative* prices really matter, in the sense that if all prices change in the same proportion, no one will act differently, so that the economy will remain at A. Suppose, for example, that $w^F = 2$. Then $P_W^F = 4$ and $P_M^F = 12$. The prices faced by each individual have doubled, but so has his income. He will behave no differently.

Let us, then, look at the relative price of machines in terms of wine: $P_M^F/P_W^F = a_M^F w^F / a_W^F w^F = a_M^F / a_W^F = 3$, the marginal rate of transformation of wine for machines. That is, P_M^F/P_W^F can be unequal to the marginal rate of transformation of wine for machines only if France specializes completely to one of the goods. But that is very unlikely in autarky, when the French must produce both goods in order to consume both.

If we examine Germany, we arrive at similar conclusions. The German autarkic relative price of machines in terms of wine, P_M^G/P_W^G, must equal the German marginal rate of transformation of wine for machines, a_M^G/a_W^G (again, unless all the Germans do completely without one of the goods). We thus have a third method for determining the pattern of comparative advantage: if the autarkic relative price of machines in terms of wine is greater in France than in Germany, France will have a comparative advantage over Germany in wine relative to machines. This third method is conceptually distinct from the other two. They both depended upon technological parameters, whereas this method depends upon economic data: autarkic market prices. But in this simple Ricardian world, all three methods must give the same result.

What will happen if France and Germany begin to trade with each other? Suppose that, initially, both French prices are higher than both German prices; for example, w^F and w^G both equal 1, so that the numbers in Table 1.1 are the initial prices. Then German firms will be deluged with customers and will try to hire more workers, thereby bidding up wages and thus costs—and German inflation will take place. French firms, on the other hand, being undercut in world markets, will begin laying off workers, thereby causing French wages and costs to fall, relative to German at any rate. This state of affairs will persist at least until German costs rise sufficiently relative to French costs so that some French good becomes competitive in world markets. Suppose for simplicity that French prices do not fall at all, so the relative change in costs consists entirely of German inflation. Then German wages must rise by at least 100 percent (in which case, German costs will be as indicated in the second row of Table 1.3); otherwise, no French firm can compete on world markets, and the inflation must continue. With 100 percent inflation, the table shows that French wine can compete, but French machines cannot. France must specialize in wine production, while both goods may be produced in Germany: world output must be somewhere along the line AB in Figure 1.2. Use $p = P_M/P_W$ to denote the international relative price of machines in terms of wine that is established when the countries trade. With 100 percent German inflation, $p = 2/2 = 1$, the German relative autarkic price.

Table 1.3.   Wages and Costs of Production When Trade Takes Place

	Machines	Wine	Wages
France	6	2	1
Germany (after 100% inflation)	2	2	2
Germany (after 200% inflation)	3	3	3
Germany (after 500% inflation)	6	6	6

The German wage can rise by no more than 500 percent (in which case, German costs are given by the bottom row of Table 1.3); otherwise, all German firms would cease to be competitive, and the process would be repeated in reverse. With 500 percent German inflation only German machinery will be competitive, while France may produce both goods: world output must be somewhere on the line BC in Figure 1.2, and $p = 3$, the French autarkic relative price.

If German wages rise by more than 100 percent but less than 500 percent, Germany must specialize in machines, and France in wine: world output will be given by point B in Figure 1.2, and p will lie somewhere between 1 and 3, the autarkic relative prices. The third line of Table 1.3 illustrates such a case.

All this sheds light on the phenomenon of international wage differences, pointed out on page 1. First of all, wage differences tend to reflect general differences in labor productivities between countries. In Table 1.3, German labor is two to three times as productive as French labor, and, as we have seen, the German wage will be two to three times as large as the French wage. Thus international differences in wages actually make it possible for countries to compete with each other. Secondly, and more subtly, the actual degree of wage difference depends upon world demand. In our example, if world demand for machinery is high, the wage in Germany will be fully three times as high as the French wage, forcing the Germans to specialize in machines, where their productivity advantage is greatest. A high world demand for wine, on the other hand, results in a German wage only twice as high as the French wage, forcing the French to specialize in wine, where their productivity disadvantage is least.

When the economics of the simple Ricardian world are spelled out, all the conclusions of section 1 about what trade and production patterns should be are, in fact, guaranteed by the international economic mechanism. Comparative advantage is not merely a prescription for how international trade should be organized, it is also an explanation of how such trade is determined. In addition, it tells us something about the international price p: it must lie somewhere between the two autarkic relative prices inclusive. We have thus been able to substantially answer the first of the three basic questions presented at the beginning of Part One as the purpose of a pure theory of trade. But we cannot tell exactly what p will be, or exactly what the pattern of production will be, until we know something about world demand, that is, how the world values the two goods.

PROBLEMS

1.6 We have seen that the pattern of comparative advantage can be determined by comparing relative prices in the two countries when free trade is restricted. When the restriction is removed, trade proceeds according to comparative advantage, and prices in the two countries are driven toward common international prices. But if prices are the same everywhere, why would anyone bother to trade?

1.7 Suppose, in the context of Table 1.1, that $w^F = 1$ and $w^G = 1$. Then both French prices are higher than both German prices, and, as we saw in section 3, international competition will cause the French wage to fall if the two countries trade. Does this not indicate that free trade will hurt the French working man?

1.8 In Problem **1.4(b)**, what will be traded, and what will all prices be? Do both countries gain as a result of trade? By how much? If the world suddenly decides it will consume one cask of wine for every *two* bolts of cloth, how will your answers change?

1.9 The discussion in the text supposed that wages and prices in France and Germany adjusted themselves to each other entirely through inflation in Germany. Suppose instead that it happens entirely through French deflation, with German prices constant. Restate the argument of the text and write down the analog to Table 1.3.

1.10* *The Exchange Rate.* French prices are expressed in francs (fr), and German prices in marks (DM). If the French wage equals fr1 and the German wage is DM1, what are the costs of production of both goods in both countries with the technology of Table 1.1? The exchange rate is the price of one currency in terms of another: it allows us to compare prices in the two countries. With an exchange rate of one franc per mark, compare the costs of the two goods in the two countries. Suppose that, unlike the discussion of this section, there is no inflation or deflation in either country, so that the wage rates do not change, but that the exchange rate can adjust. What must the exchange rate equal for both countries to be able to compete? Derive an analog to Table 1.3 for different values of the exchange rate. Can you think of any economic mechanism that would tend to alter the exchange rate to make it appropriate?

4. The Gains from Trade

We are now in a position to answer the second basic question: are there gains or losses resulting from international trade, and, if so, how are they distributed? Section 1 demonstrated that free trade is beneficial to the world as a whole. But how are the benefits distributed among the two countries? Is it possible for France to be harmed while Germany greatly benefits?

To answer this question, look again at each country's production possibility frontier, reproduced in Figure 1.3. The production possibility frontier depicts the various alternative combinations of the two goods that a country in question can consume in autarky, as anything that is to be consumed must be produced at home. If free international trade takes place, the relative price p of machines will be somewhere between the two autarkic relative prices, or equal to one of them. Suppose that $p = 2$. Then France will specialize in wine, producing 300 casks. The French can consume all or some of this wine, receiving one machine in exchange for every two casks of wine they export. The dotted line in Figure 1.3(a) depicts all such consumption possibilities. It is now easy to see that France must benefit from free trade. The dotted line lies outside the production possibility frontier, so that every possible autarkic consumption pattern, such as *A*, is dominated by some free-trade consumption pattern, such as *B*, featuring more of both wine and machinery. Only if the French do without machines and always consume 300 casks of wine will this not be true. But in that case,

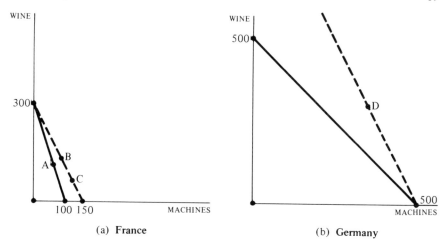

Figure 1.3. CONSUMPTION POSSIBILITIES IN AUTARKY AND WITH FREE
INTERNATIONAL TRADE

France will never enter the international market at all. Two things should
be noted about these gains from trade, unambiguous though they are. First,
France will not *necessarily* consume more of both goods under free trade
than it would under autarky. Consumption could take place at *C*, for
example, which involves more machinery but less wine than *A*. But the
point is that in this case the French have simply chosen to spend their
incomes on *C* in preference to *B*, which costs the same. Second, we are
arguing that France as a whole gains from trade, not that every individual
Frenchman does. The Ricardian model is too simple to adequately discuss
the internal distribution of income, which we will come to later in this book.
But for now, we can say that the gainers gain more than any losers lose, and
France as a whole gains: it is possible to give each French citizen more of
both goods than in autarky.

What is the reason for these gains? They occur because the world
relative price *p* differs from the autarkic relative price. In France, the autarkic relative price is higher than *p*, so France specializes in wine. Then
exporting one unit of wine gives France more machines as imports than it
could obtain by producing one less unit of wine and using the labor to
produce machines itself. The dotted line in Figure 1.3(a) is flatter than
France's production possibility frontier. From Germany's point of view, the
opposite is the case. The autarkic relative price is lower than *p*, so Germany
specializes in machines, and Germany can obtain more wine for a single
machine by exporting the machine than by not producing it and using the
labor to make its own wine. The dotted line in Figure 1.3(b) is steeper than
the German production possibility frontier. Germany must gain from trade
in the same sense as France does.

KEY CONCEPT

The *terms of trade* measure the number of units of exports a country must sacrifice for each unit of imports. Thus p is France's terms of trade, and $1/p$ is Germany's. The terms of trade can be taken as an index of the gains from trade. The more favorable (that is, the lower) the terms of trade, the more a country gains.

The distribution of the gains from trade should now be clear. If a country's autarkic relative price is the same as the international price, it will not benefit from trade and all the gains will go to the partner country. The more the international price differs from the autarkic price, the more it gains from trade (and the less the partner country gains). But under no circumstances will trade actually harm either country. In terms of Figure 1.2(a), along AB all the gains accrue to France, and Germany is no better off; along BC Germany obtains all the gains; at B the gains are divided among the two countries, in a way that depends upon what value p has.

PROBLEMS ───

1.11 As in Problem **1.4**, suppose that England has 100 labor and requires 5 to produce each unit of wine and of cloth, whereas Portugal has 100 labor units, with 1 required to produce each wine and 4 to produce each cloth unit. If the world relative price of wine in terms of cloth is one, what will be the pattern of trade and production; what will be the prices in each country; and who will gain from trade?

1.12 Discuss the gains from trade in relation to Problem **1.3.**

1.13 Use the framework of the simple Ricardian model to discuss the Great Tomato War. Should the United States restrict imports of Mexican vegetables? Does the model help explain why Florida growers in fact want these imports restricted?

1.14 How would you explain the gains from trade to an unemployed New England textile worker?

1.15 Suppose that when trade opens, France for some reason is forced to continue producing at point A in Figure 1.3(a), instead of specializing in wine. How is the argument in the text altered? Compare this situation with both autarky and the case where France specializes.

1.16* From 1792 to 1900, the United States was legally on a *bimetallic standard:* the dollar was defined in terms of both gold and silver. As a result of the Coinage Act of 1792, the U.S. mint stood ready to convert gold or silver into coins, at the prices in the first line of the table below, for anyone presenting either metal. Alexander Hamilton, Thomas Jefferson, and Robert Morris were chiefly responsible for this act (while its essential features were readily adopted by Congress, there

Mint Prices of One Ounce of Gold and Silver,
Representative of 1803–1834

	Gold	Silver
U.S.	$11.60	$ .77
France	fr60	fr3.87

was intense debate over whose likeness should appear on the coins). France was also on a bimetallic standard from 1803 until 1874, and the bottom line contains French prices illustrative of the early part of this period.

From the first line of the table, we see that the official U.S. relative price of an ounce of gold in terms of silver was $11.60/$.77 = 15 ounces. Similarly the French price of gold in terms of silver was fr60/fr3.87 = 15½ ounces.

a Use the logical structure of the simple Ricardian model to deduce what happened after passage of the 1792 act. France was economically much larger than the United States in those years.

b The U.S. mint ratio was changed in 1834 and 1837 to about 16 silver ounces per gold ounce. The world price ratio by and large remained near 15½ to 1. What do you think happened from 1834 to 1862 (the U.S. government abandoned metallic standards in the Civil War)?

5. Case Study: Unequal Exchange

As we saw at the start of this chapter, wage rates can differ greatly from country to country. The wage in the United States, for example, is many times larger than that in Malawi. This means that, when the two countries trade, the product of one hour of American labor exchanges for the product of many hours of Malawian labor. Such a situation has been called *unequal exchange* by the Greek Marxist Arghiri Emmanuel, of the University of Paris. Unequal exchange in this sense is typical of trade between the prosperous industrial countries and the poorer, less developed nations.

We can use a simple Ricardian model to illustrate the essence of the idea. Suppose that the United States and Malawi can produce tobacco and steel subject to the labor requirements indicated in Table 1.4. Clearly the United States has a comparative advantage over Malawi in steel relative to tobacco. Suppose that, with free trade, the U.S. terms of trade are 5:1; five units of steel exchange for each unit of tobacco. Five units of steel require 20 units of U.S. labor for their production, while 1 unit of tobacco requires 20 Malawi labor units. Thus the produce of each hour of Malawian labor exchanges for the produce of one hour of U.S. labor: a case of *equal exchange* in Emmanuel's terminology.

Table 1.4.   A SIMPLE RICARDIAN MODEL: LABOR REQUIRED IN
EACH COUNTRY TO PRODUCE ONE UNIT OF EACH
GOOD

	Steel	*Tobacco*
United States	4	10
Malawi	40	20

Now suppose that technical progress takes place in America so that only 1 U.S. labor unit is necessary to produce a unit of steel, and suppose that the terms of trade change to 10 steel for 1 tobacco. The 10 steel require only 10 U.S. labor units to produce, but the tobacco still requires 20 units of Malawi labor. This is an example of unequal exchange: Malawi must use up two hours of its labor to pay for the fruits of each hour of U.S. labor that it purchases.

Such unequal exchange is sometimes regarded as international exploitation. But note that it is consistent with our discussion of the gains from trade. Even after the technical improvement, Malawi can obtain a unit of steel for only 2 units of labor, if the labor is used to produce tobacco to trade for the steel, whereas 40 labor would be required to produce the steel directly. Although the technical improvement did move Malawi from equal exchange to unequal exchange, it nevertheless made the country better off because its terms of trade improved: each labor unit devoted to the production of tobacco for export was able to obtain twice as much steel as before, even though this greater amount of steel was produced by only half as much U.S. labor.

PROBLEMS

1.17 Does your answer to Problem (1.11) show unequal exchange taking place?

1.18* In the discussion of the simple Ricardian model, we were concerned with trade in commodities. But in a sense, the two countries were actually exchanging their labor services, because a unit of each good is actually an embodiment of the labor that produced it. This viewpoint came up in our discussion of unequal exchange. Define the "factoral terms of trade" to be the number of units of labor a country must give up in order to purchase one unit of foreign labor in this sense. What is the precise relation between the factoral terms of trade and the commodity terms of trade? What values can the factoral terms of trade possibly assume? What condition must the factoral terms of trade satisfy for a country to gain by trade? Suppose that France becomes more efficient in its export industries (say a_W^f falls from 6 to 3) and thus exports more, causing the world relative price p to rise. What will happen to the factoral terms of trade? Which terms of trade do you think is a better index of gains? Why?

6. Empirical Testing of the Simple Ricardian Model

The Ricardian model is useful for explaining and manipulating basic ideas of international trade and for understanding related complex phenomena. But is it also relevant in the much narrower sense of explaining actual trade flows in terms of relative labor productivities? This question was addressed in a famous study by the English economist G. D. A. MacDougall. He examined 1937 data for twenty-five U.S. and U.K. industries and compared for each industry the ratio of American and British output per worker with the ratio of British and American exports to third countries. (He used exports to third countries, that is, to all countries except the United States and United Kingdom, rather than exports to each other, because in 1937 the two countries exported relatively little to each other and because they imposed differing tariff barriers to imports, whereas British and American firms competed in third markets on terms of relatively more uniform equality.)

MacDougall found that, in twenty of the twenty-five industries, the United States had a larger share of the export market than did the United Kingdom whenever American labor was more than twice as productive as British labor, and a smaller share otherwise. American wages were about twice as high as British, so that American labor had to be twice as productive to give equal labor costs. These findings were taken as support for the view that comparative advantage can in fact be explained by labor productivities.

A further striking fact emerged from MacDougall's data: there seemed to be a significant, functional relationship between relative labor productivity and relative exports. When MacDougall's twenty-five observations were plotted on a graph, as in Figure 1.4(a), they seemed to cluster by and large around a curve, which was a straight line when the axes were measured in a logarithmic scale. Such a relationship is not implied by the Ricardian model. Theory suggests that whenever American productivity is

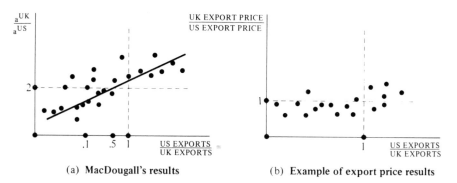

(a) MacDougall's results　　　　　　(b) Example of export price results

Figure 1.4. Empirical Tests of the Simple Ricardian Model

less than twice British, the British firms would produce at lower cost and capture the entire market. The United States would have the entire market whenever its labor productivity was more than twice Britain's, and the two countries would perhaps share the market of a single good produced at equal cost in both countries. One can think of many complications, ignored in the simple model, that could muddy the waters and account for the departure from theory. For example, each of the twenty-five industries is, in fact, an aggregate of related products; thus even if Britain has a productivity advantage in footware, on the average, the United States might still be able to produce some kinds of shoes more cheaply. Or there could be quality differences: if British cars are perceived by consumers as different from American, some people will continue to buy them even if they cost more. Or transportation costs and other trade barriers could be significant: even if woolen clothing costs more to produce in the United States than in the United Kingdom, American firms might be able to undersell British in those markets "closer" to the United States. These reasons, and others like them, would lead us not to expect the simple all-or-nothing result that comes from the theory in its elementary form. But neither would they necessarily cause us to expect to find a systematic functional relation between relative productivity and relative exports across different industries.

A number of subsequent investigations, using different data and covering different periods, have obtained results similar to MacDougall's. Thus the empirical evidence seems to be at least consistent with the view that trade patterns are largely determined by relative labor productivities. Of course, some other theory might perform even better. In principle we would like to consider all the factors that could possibly influence trade patterns and to test for their relative importance. The procedure of instead looking to see whether a specific simple theory is consistent with the data is a more practicable, but second-best, alternative.

In section 3, we saw how comparative advantage could be expressed in terms of relative autarkic prices. MacDougall and other economists have also inquired whether trade patterns could be explained in terms of relative prices. But in order to do this, two problems need to be faced. First, data on actual, internationally comparable transaction prices are very hard to come by. Economists have had to make do instead with quoted values of aggregates of commodities (ignoring, for example, quality differences). The second, more fundamental, problem is that comparative advantage depends on relative *autarkic* prices, and trade establishes a single international price in each market. Since we observe countries trading with each other, it is impossible, even in principle, to measure what autarkic prices would be. Economists have attempted to deal with this problem by comparing British and American export prices (that is, prices at the point of export rather than in the market where actually consumed). Transport costs and other barriers prevent these prices from being completely equalized by trade.

MacDougall found that, in twenty-one of twenty-three industries, the country with the lower export price had the larger share of the third-country export market. Similar results have been obtained, on balance, by other researchers. However, economists have not found a significant functional relationship between relative export prices and relative exports. (MacDougall did find such a relationship, but it failed to turn up in subsequent investigations.) This is illustrated in Figure 1.4(b). Such a relation is not predicted by the basic theory, but we do not know why it turns up with relative labor productivities but not with relative prices.

MacDougall in effect tested the *joint hypothesis* that comparative advantage is determined by labor productivities *and* that comparative advantage determines trade. The economist H. Glejser, of the University of Brussels, focused on the latter by itself. In 1957 six European countries agreed to form the Common Market and gradually eliminate tariffs and other restrictions on mutual trade. Glejser compared relative prices in 1958, before the agreement took effect, with trade flows in 1966, when considerable tariff reduction had been implemented. He found that low relative prices tended to be correlated with large market shares. This supports the view that comparative advantage determines trade, independently of whether the simple Ricardian model adequately describes reality.

7. Comparative Advantage in More General Circumstances

The first four sections examined comparative advantage in the simple Ricardian model. The remainder of this chapter tries to make clear that the concept is an extremely general one, quite independent of the specific technology.

The Ricardian world is obviously simplified in many ways. Some of these simplifications perhaps seem very palatable. As regards the assumption of just two goods and two countries, for example, machines and wine can be taken as proxies for 'aggregate imports' and 'aggregate exports,' France and Germany as proxies for the 'home country' and the 'rest of the world.' In any case many of the specific problems caused by a multiplicity of goods and of countries can be dealt with as they arise. Still other simplifications, such as ignoring transportation costs, or such as the clear-cut distinction between domestic markets, where labor is perfectly mobile, and international trade, where labor is completely immobile, seem desirable in order to focus on the essential nature of the problem while avoiding unnecessary details. But other assumptions ought not to be accepted so readily. The special technology of the Ricardian model appeared to be the crux of comparative advantage, so it is precisely the role of the technological assumptions that must be examined.

We supposed that the production of a unit of each good entailed simply the use of a certain amount of homogeneous labor. But in reality many factors beyond 'raw labor,' such as various types of capital equipment, labor skills, natural resources, and entrepreneurial ability, all play varying roles. Thus a simple description of the technology, such as that in Table 1.1, is not possible. But at least one of the technological concepts of the preceding sections can still be used. The various factors of production are available only in limited amounts, so that there is a basic scarcity of resources, and the economy must still decide among alternative patterns of production. We can still talk about the production possibility frontier, although it will not in general possess the simple properties discussed in section 2.

More general production possibility frontiers for France and Germany are depicted in Figure 1.5. These frontiers are of course downward sloping, since if an economy is producing efficiently, the only way to increase production of one good is by decreasing production of the other. But these curves are also bowed outward, rather than inward or some combination of the two. Why? Suppose France is producing at a point such as *B*, which calls for most of its resources to be devoted to wine production. Then if it wishes to reduce wine output somewhat in order to produce more machines, this can be done by shifting from the wine industry to the machine industry those factors, such as skilled industrial workers, that are not very suited to wine making but quite productive when working on machinery. If, on the other hand, France is producing mostly machinery, such as at point *C*, then the only way to decrease wine output and increase machine output still more is by transferring from wine to machines factors of production, such as grape pickers or peasants with big feet, that are actually

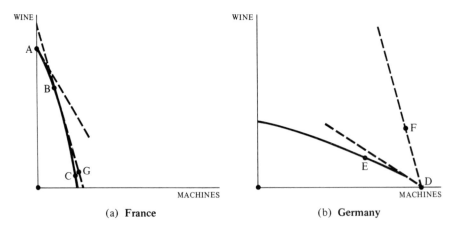

(a) **France**   (b) **Germany**

Figure 1.5. Production Possibility Frontiers Displaying Increasing Opportunity Costs

much better suited for the wine industry. The production possibility frontier will therefore be flatter at B than at C. In other words the MRT_{WM} increases as we move along the production possibility frontier from the wine axis to the machine axis; there is increasing opportunity cost to shifting the pattern of production.

Although the labor requirements that we originally used to determine the pattern of comparative advantage are no longer available, the marginal rate of transformation still is; but its value will depend upon the actual pattern of production. The marginal rate of transformation of wine for machines is still equal to minus the slope of the production possibility frontier at the point in question. If France is producing some of both goods, it must be that the relative price of machines in terms of wine is equal to MRT_{WM}. Why? Suppose, for example, that $P_M^F/P_W^F > MRT_{WM}$. Then $P_M^F > P_W^F MRT_{WM}$. This means that the value of one additional machine is greater than the value of the reduction in wine output necessary to produce it. Thus entrepreneurs will increase machine output and reduce wine output, and, as a result, MRT_{WM} will increase. This process will be repeated until either France specializes entirely in machinery or the marginal rate of transformation becomes equal to relative prices. Thus if France is producing at point B, say, then the dotted line through B depicts all those combinations of wine and machines that cost the same as the output at B, and the negative of the slope of this line must be the relative price of machines in terms of wine.

The problem now is to be able to speak of comparative advantage, despite the facts that we can no longer rely on the simple labor requirements originally used for this purpose and that the marginal rate of transformation and the autarkic price ratio are no longer simple parameters but can assume many possible values. Suppose initially that the French and German production possibility frontiers bear the simple relationship to each other depicted in Figure 1.5: *each* point on France's production possibility frontier is steeper than *every* point of Germany's, that is, the slope at point A in Figure 1.5(a) is steeper than the slope at D of Figure 1.5(b). Then the marginal rate of transformation of wine for machines must always be greater in France than in Germany. Regardless of what the autarkic patterns of production are (say C in France and E in Germany), it must be the case that $P_M^F/P_W^F > P_M^G/P_W^G$. The experiment of section 1 can now be repeated for this case, with exactly the same result. (If there is any doubt in your mind, work through the reasoning again in the context of this section.) Indeed, we will obtain all the conclusions of sections 1 through 4 about the gains from trade, about the efficiency of world output, and about how the international economy will bring about patterns of trade and production compatible with comparative advantage. If, for example, the international relative price is equal to minus the slope of the line BG in Figure 1.5(a), then France will produce at B, and Germany at point D, specializing in machines. French consumption will be given by some point on the dotted line, say *G*. Then German consumption will be given by *F* (the line *FD* has the same slope and length as *BG*). Both countries gain from trade, and the amount of the gain depends, as before, on how favorable the terms of trade are, that is, on how much the international relative price differs from what the autarkic relative price would be. Note that a country must gain if these two relative prices differ, regardless of whether the country actually specializes or not.

Thus all our earlier conclusions about comparative advantage remain valid in this case of increasing opportunity costs. But suppose that the two production possibility frontiers do not have the simple relationship assumed above but are instead as in Figure 1.6. We can no longer say that one is unambiguously steeper than the other. For example, the marginal rate of transformation at point *A* on France's production possibility frontier is the same as at *B* on Germany's. Even in this case we can talk about comparative advantage if we define it, as before, in terms of actual autarkic relative prices. If, for example, autarkic French production and consumption of the two goods are given by point *E*, and German by point *F*, then the autarkic relative price of machines in terms of wine is higher in France than in Germany and so France has a comparative advantage over Germany in wine relative to machines. But if, on the other hand, France is at point *C* in autarky and Germany at *D*, then it is Germany whose comparative advantage lies in wine.

The experiment of section 1 can now be repeated here as well. That is, if the autarkic positions are given by *E* and *F* respectively, world output can be made more efficient if France shifts resources from machinery to wine and Germany does the reverse (verify that if the countries are originally at *C* and *D* they should shift resources in the opposite direction). We can once

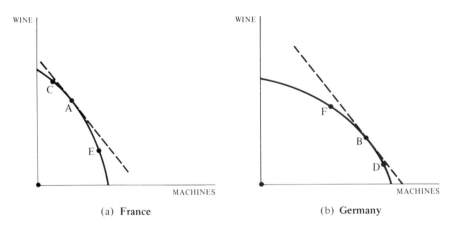

Figure 1.6. INCREASING OPPORTUNITY COSTS AND INCOMPLETE SPECIALIZATION WITH FREE TRADE

again arrive at the same results concerning both world efficiency and what will happen if free international trade commences. If you are at all troubled, you should work this out in detail. There are, however, two differences between this case and our previous examples. First, and most fundamentally, comparative advantage cannot be deduced on the basis of technology alone. In the earlier cases we could tell which country had a comparative advantage in which good simply by looking at the two production possibility frontiers. But now we must also know exactly *where* on those frontiers each country would produce in the absence of free trade, that is, we must know something about domestic demands. In addition, one of our earlier conclusions must be slightly altered: it is no longer certain that at least one country will be driven to complete specialization under free trade. If, for example, France at point E in Figure 1.6(a) shifts resources from machinery to wine and Germany at point F does the reverse, the French marginal rate of transformation will fall and the German will rise. It is now quite possible that they will actually become equal before either country specializes completely. This is illustrated in Figure 1.6, where France produces at A and Germany at B under a common international price. Thus, in general, it is true only that a country will increase the production of that good in which it has a comparative advantage and decrease the production of the other good once trade begins. With the exception of this minor alteration, all of the conclusions concerning comparative advantage in the simple Ricardian world remain true in quite general situations.

PROBLEMS

1.19 Recall that in section 1 we considered the experiment of shifting labor from machines to wine in France and the reverse in Germany, recording the result in Table 1.2. Do the same now, in the context of increasing opportunity costs, and derive a table analogous to Table 1.2.

1.20* Suppose that France exports wine to Germany in exchange for machinery under increasing opportunity costs. Neither country is specialized. Now suppose that the cost of transporting one machine from Germany to France equals 50 percent of the (German) cost of producing the machine. The cost of transporting wine, however, is so low that it can be ignored. What must be the free trade relationship between the prices of each good in the two countries? Suppose that a "transportation revolution" is expected to reduce by one-half the cost of shipping a machine within the next four years. Can you predict anything about the likely effects of this on international trade and upon the pattern of production in both countries?

8. Tastes as a Determinant of Comparative Advantage

The previous section emphasized that comparative advantage is quite general and does not depend upon a special technology. We shall now drive

home this point even more by showing that we can talk about comparative
advantage even when there is no production structure at all. Suppose that
France and Germany each possess 100 casks of wine and 100 machines.
This is depicted in Figure 1.7, where A and B denote these endowments of
the two goods. Since these endowments cannot be altered, we can no longer
speak of the marginal rate of transformation. But we can still use autarkic
relative prices to define the pattern of comparative advantage. If each
country were in autarky, prices would be determined at which the domestic
demands for the two goods equal the (fixed) domestic supplies. The lines *FF*
and *GG* in Figure 1.6 are drawn with slopes equal to minus these relative
autarkic prices. Clearly, $P_M^F/P_W^F > P_M^G/P_W^G$. Then we say that France has a
comparative advantage in wine relative to machines with respect to Germany. But what does that mean in this case?

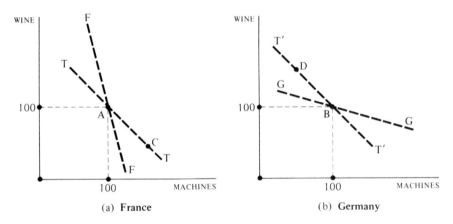

Figure 1.7.   Comparative Advantage in the Absence of Production

---

KEY CONCEPT

An individual's *marginal rate of substitution* of one good for
another is the largest amount of the first good that the individual
would willingly sacrifice to obtain one more unit of the second.

In order to answer this question, let us first look at the situation from
the point of view of an individual (French) consumer, say Marie. By the
"marginal rate of substitution of wine for machines," denoted MRS_{WM}, we
mean the amount of wine that must be given to Marie in order to exactly

compensate her for the loss of one machine. Or, equivalently, the amount of wine that must be taken away from her to leave her just as satisfied as she was originally if she is given one more machine. Each individual's MRS_{WM} depends upon her own tastes. But it also depends upon her pattern of consumption (just as the marginal rate of transformation depends upon the pattern of production). Suppose, for example, that a consumer has a very large quantity of wine but very few machines. She will then find an additional machine a good deal more useful, and the loss of one unit of wine considerably less irksome, than she would if she had, instead, many machines and only a little wine. In other words: a consumer's MRS_{WM} normally diminishes as she substitutes wine for machines. Now any consumer, facing given market prices for two goods, will always spend her income in such a way as to make her MRS_{WM} equal the relative price of machines in terms of wine, P_M^F/P_W^F. Why? Suppose, for example, that she instead spent her income so that $P_M^F/P_W^F > MRS_{WM}$, or $P_M^F > P_W^F MRS_{WM}$. This means that the money she would save by purchasing one less machine is greater than the cost of the wine necessary to compensate her for the loss of the machine. This excess could be spent on both goods, making her better off. Similarly if $P_M^F/P_W^F < MRS_{WM}$, the consumer could make herself happier by spending less on wine and more on machines. We are not imagining the consumer to be a calculating machine, always computing her MRS: if she spends her income in the way she most prefers, she must be causing her MRS to equal the relative price she faces, whether she is aware of the concept or not. Since all French consumers face the same relative prices, P_M^F/P_W^F equals the MRS_{WM} of *every* French consumer. This does not mean that they all spend their incomes in the same way. Different individuals have different incomes and different tastes and will purchase different assortments of goods. But if they face the same prices, they must have the same MRS_{WM}. Similarly each German consumer will spend his income so that his MRS_{WM} equals the autarkic relative German price. These conclusions are valid regardless of the structure of production in both countries.

Since $P_M^F/P_W^F > P_M^G/P_W^G$, it must be that in autarky the MRS_{WM} of each French consumer would exceed that of each German consumer, that is $MRS_{WM}^F > MRS_{WM}^G$. Suppose now that one machine is taken from some German consumer, say Fritz, and given to Marie. Marie will be just as well off as she was originally if MRS_{WM}^F units of wine are also taken from her. But only MRS_{WM}^G units of that wine need to be given to Fritz to compensate him exactly for the original loss of one machine. Thus there is wine left over that can make both of them better off. Notice the precise formal similarity between this reasoning and that of section 1. We have come to exactly the same conclusion, that trade according to the pattern of comparative advantage can benefit all. Only now we are doing this not by making world output more efficient but by making the world distribution of goods more efficient.

> **KEY CONCEPT**
>
> An *efficient pattern of consumption* is a distribution of goods among individuals for which it is impossible to redistribute the goods to make someone happier without making someone else less happy.

What will actually happen if these countries trade? Initially $P_M^F/P_W^F >$ P_M^G/P_W^G. Then in Germany a machine costs (P_M^G/P_W^G), units of wine. This much wine can be obtained in France for $P_W^F(P_M^G/P_W^G)$, which is less than P_M^F, the amount the machine can be sold for in France. Thus there is profit to be made by exporting French wine for German machinery. The relative price of machines in terms of wine will fall in France and rise in Germany until a common international relative price p is determined. This is depicted by the lines TT and $T'T'$ in Figure 1.6; France consumes at C, and Germany at D.

Thus the principle of comparative advantage leads to the same conclusion as before about the pattern of trade, and again both countries gain from trade. And, again, the gains from trade accruing to a country depend upon how favorable its terms of trade are, that is, upon how much the international relative price differs from what the autarkic relative price would be.

This example is also instructive in that it makes it clear that the gains from trade do not result solely from altering the world pattern of production. There is, to be sure, a *production gain* from trade: as the previous sections demonstrated, free trade causes world output to be on the world production possibility frontier. But we have now seen that there is in addition a *consumption gain:* free trade ensures that the actual assortment of goods produced will be distributed efficiently among the world's consumers.

9 *Exploring Further:* **Indifference Curves**

AN INDIVIDUAL'S INDIFFERENCE CURVES

An individual's tastes can be described by a collection of indifference curves. This is done in Figure 1.8 for Marie, our typical French consumer. Point A indicates a consumption bundle consisting of 5 wine and 2 machines. The curve through A, labeled I, shows all combinations of wine and machines that Marie regards as neither better nor worse than A. Thus if the bundle A were replaced by E, Marie would not care. The actual shape of such an indifference curve is subjective, reflecting Marie's individual tastes. But some general conclusions can be drawn. For example, an indifference

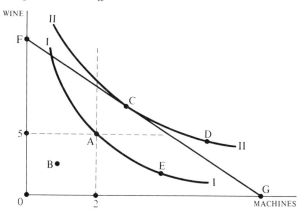

Figure 1.8. Marie's Indifference Curves

curve must have a *downward* slope, because more wine compensates for fewer machines. Indifference curves further from the origin depict better alternatives. In Figure 1.8, bundle *C* must be better for Marie than *A*, because *C* has more of everything; likewise *B* is worse than *A*. Thus the indifference curve through *C* (labeled *II*) lies outside that through *A*, and the curve through *B* would lie inside if that curve were drawn. Bundle *D* lies on a higher curve than does *A*, so Marie prefers *D* to *A*. If we did not know the shape of these curves (that is, Marie's tastes), we would not be able to compare *A* and *D*, because one bundle has more wine, but the other has more machinery.

The MRS_{WM} at any point is given by the slope of the indifference curve at that point (more precisely, by *minus* the slope, since the latter is a negative number). Thus if Marie consumes the bundle *C*, her MRS_{WM} will equal OF/OG. The "bowed-in" shape of the indifference curves reflects the property of diminishing marginal rate of substitution: MRS_{WM} falls as more and more machinery is substituted for wine, that is, as we move downward and to the right along an indifference curve.

Suppose that the relative price of machines in terms of wine equals OF/OG, and that Marie's income enables her to buy OG machines or OF wine. Thus she can purchase any bundle in the triangle OFG. She will buy the bundle that puts her on the highest indifference curve. This will be at a point, such as *C* in Figure 1.8, where an indifference curve is just tangent to the edge of the triangle. Thus Marie will choose a bundle that makes her MRS_{WM} equal to the relative price of machines in terms of wine: the conclusion we reached in section 7.

COMMUNITY INDIFFERENCE CURVES

We have used indifference curves to describe the subjective tastes of an individual Frenchwoman. Presumably distinct collections of indifference curves describe the tastes of all other French (and German) residents. Many parts of trade theory can be conveniently treated with community indifference curves: a set of curves describing the collective tastes of a nation as a whole. It is not generally possible to derive such curves from individuals' indifference curves in a wholly satisfactory way, and one would not want to use them when considering problems involving the internal distribution of income or other issues where differences between individuals matter. But in other cases community indifference curves can be heuristically convenient.

In that spirit, then, suppose that the tastes of the French nation as a whole are summarized by one set of community indifference curves, and German tastes by another. Each country is characterized by two types of information: objective supply conditions, described by the production possibility frontier, and subjective tastes, described by the community indifference curves. Figure 1.9 shows this information for both countries. If a country cannot trade, it will produce and consume at that point on its production possibility frontier lying on the highest community indifference curve: point A in France and B in Germany. At such a point, the two curves are tangent, with the common slope reflecting the autarkic price ratio. Thus in France the relative autarkic price of machines in terms of wine (P_M^F/P_W^F) equals OC/OD $(= MRT_{WM}^F = MRS_{WM}^F)$, while in Germany $OE/OF = P_M^G/P_W^G = MRT_{WM}^G = MRS_{WM}^G$.

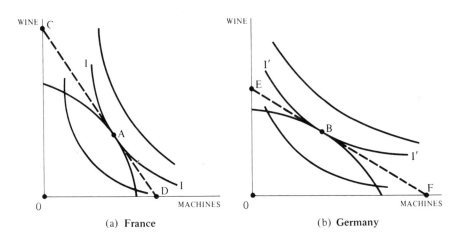

(a) France   (b) Germany

Figure 1.9.   Autarkic Equilibria

Figure 1.10 shows a free-trade equilibrium. France produces at point H and exports HJ $(= H'J')$ units of wine to Germany in exchange for JK $(= J'K')$ units of machinery. Thus France consumes at point K on the indifference curve II. Under autarky, France produced and consumed at A

on the lower indifference curve *I*, so France has gained from trade. Likewise Germany, now producing at *K'* and consuming at *H'*, has gained from trade by moving from the indifference curve *I'* to the higher *II'*.

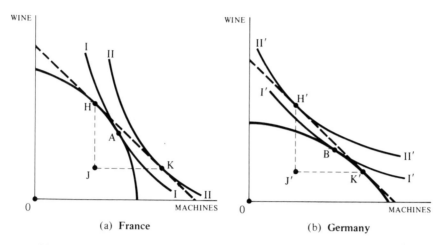

(a) **France**   (b) **Germany**

Figure 1.10. FREE-TRADE EQUILIBRIUM

PROBLEMS

1.21 Prove that, for a single individual, two distinct indifference curves can not intersect.

1.22 Draw community indifference curves in Figure 1.7 to show that international differences in tastes can serve as a basis for mutually beneficial trade.

1.23 Go through the discussion in section 3 of the gains from trade, using indifference curves.

1.24 Draw the community indifference curves that depict the tastes described in Problem **1.4b**: everyone always wants to consume equal numbers of bolts of cloth and casks of wine.

10. North-South Trade

How does comparative advantage measure up in terms of actual trade? We now take a detailed look at world trade.

One natural way to idealize the world, in terms of the two-country examples considered in the previous sections, is to view it as divided into two blocks: the developed countries (also called the "North" or the "Center") and the less developed countries (the "South" or the "Periphery"). And commodities can be classified into two groups, manufactured goods and primary products. One would expect the developed countries as

a group to have a comparative advantage over the less developed countries
in manufactured goods relative to primary products.

This accounting convention is used in Table 1.5, which shows the
pattern of world exports in various years. The first number in each entry
gives the value of the appropriate exports in billions of U.S. dollars, and the
number in parentheses shows what percentage that value is of total exports
for that year. DC stands for the developed countries as a group, and LDC
for the less developed.

Table 1.5. TRADE OF DEVELOPED AND LESS DEVELOPED
NON-COMMUNIST COUNTRIES IN SELECTED YEARS
(BILLIONS OF DOLLARS)

(a) 1953
Exports from

Exports to	*DCs*	*LDCs*	*Total*
DCs	$29 (42%)	$18 (26%)	$47 (68%)
LDCs	16 (23)	6 (9)	22 (32)
Total	45 (65)	24 (35)	69 (100)

(b) 1973
Exports from

Exports to	*DCs*	*LDCs*	*Total*
DCs	$294 (63%)	$ 80 (17%)	$374 (80%)
LDCs	69 (15)	23 (5)	92 (20)
Total	363 (78)	103 (22)	466 (100)

(c) 1979
Exports from

Exports to	*DCs*	*LDCs*	*Total*
DCs	$734 (59%)	$187 (15%)	$ 921 (74%)
LDCs	228 (18)	99 (8)	327 (26)
Total	962 (77)	286 (23)	1248 (100)

SOURCE: GATT, *International Trade*

Three striking characteristics of world trade are immediately apparent from these figures. First,

> *The largest part of world trade is that among the developed countries themselves, rather than between these countries and the less developed.*

We would expect differences in comparative costs and tastes to be much more marked between the two groups of countries than between individual developed countries. The fraction of world trade accounted for by trade between the less developed countries themselves is minor.

A second salient fact is the very rapid growth in world trade in the period 1953–79. Indeed this growth has been rapid relative to world output.

> *International trade has grown more rapidly than world production in nearly every year since the Second World War.*

That this rapid growth has, however, not been balanced is the third feature revealed by Table 1.5.

> *Trade among the DCs has increased much faster than trade in general and thus accounts for an increasing proportion of total trade.*

Thus trade among the DCs rose from 42 percent of total trade in 1953 to 63 percent in 1973. But by 1979 this figure had receded somewhat, to 59 percent. This reflects the dramatic rise in the price of oil since 1973–74. The oil exporters are grouped in with the LDCs, so the rise in oil's price has inflated the value of the exports of these countries (and also enabled them to afford to import more). This has the effect of reducing the relative size of intra-DC trade. If the oil exporting countries are simply excluded, trade among the DCs in 1979 accounted for 69 percent of all trade.

What about the commodity composition of trade, the exchange of manufactured goods for primary products? Table 1.6(a) reveals that the DCs do, on balance, export manufactured goods to the LDCs in exchange for primary products, as expected. (The number in parentheses in each entry shows what percentage of total trade between the two groups of countries consisted of trade in manufactures.) Trade among the DCs themselves also involves, to an increasing degree, manufactured goods. Since Table 1.5 revealed that trade between these countries was increasing more rapidly, we would expect trade in manufactures to be accounting for an increasing fraction of total trade. That this is indeed the case can be seen in Table 1.6(b).

Table 1.6. INTERNATIONAL TRADE IN MANUFACTURES

(a) *The Pattern of Trade in*   (b) *Relative to Total Trade*
    Manufactures, 1978 (billions
    of dollars)

Exports to	Exports from DCs	LDCs	Year	Value ($ billion)	As % of Total Trade
DCs	$463 (75%)	$45 (21%)	1928	12	39
LDCs	171 (82)	23 (32)	1953	32	45
			1973	350	61
			1979	943	58

SOURCE: U.N., *Monthly Bulletin of Statistics*

> *The DCs, on balance, export manufactures to the LDCs in ex-*
> *change for primary products. The DCs also exchange manufac-*
> *tures among themselves.*

Thus the most significant part of world trade is the exchange of similar goods (manufactures) between similar economies (DCs).

Such aggregate statistics mask some significant developments. We have already mentioned the rise in the price of oil. Another important trend is the rapid rate at which LDCs have increased their exports of manufactures since the sixties. World trade in manufactures grew at an average annual rate of 8.9 percent from 1960 to 1975, with the DCs expanding their exports at 8.8 percent while LDC exports of manufactures grew at 12.3 percent—the most dynamic part of world trade. (The fact that the global growth rate was so much closer to the DC's rate reflects the latter's large absolute share.) Table 1.6(a) shows that LDC exports of manufactures in 1978 totaled $68 billion, or 9.6 percent of world manufactured exports. This is a modest share, to be sure, but in 1960 it had been only 4 percent.

> *LDC exports of manufactures are the fast-growing part of world*
> *trade, although their absolute share is still small.*

Much of this growth is accounted for by a small group of "transitional" LDCs, such as South Korea, Taiwan, Hong Kong, Singapore (sometimes called the "Gang of Four"), and Brazil. These countries have experienced rapid growths in incomes while expanding their exports of manufactures such as shoes, textiles, and steel.

The general pattern of the exchange of manufactures and primary products seems quite natural from the perspective of comparative advantage theory. But the latter does force attention toward one feature: the fact that the lion's share of world trade consists of the exchange of manufactures among DCs, whereas the large differences in relative autarkic prices would presumably be between the DCs and LDCs. The disproportionate share of intra-DC trade need not indicate that this trade is not due to comparative advantage. The DCs have much larger market economies than do the LDCs (this is, after all, what development means) and would therefore be expected to trade more. Also the DCs as a group are much less inclined than the LDCs to limit their trade with taxes, controls, and other protectionist devices. Nevertheless, we cannot rule out the possibility that the huge volume of trade among the DCs is due, at least in part, to reasons quite different from comparative advantage.

This possibility is somewhat enhanced by a final characteristic of world trade. Bela Balassa, Herbert Grubel, Peter Lloyd, and others have demonstrated that the rapid expansion of trade among the DCs has not taken the form of increased specialization, as comparative advantage would lead one to expect, but rather of a simultaneous increase by all countries of their exports of most industries.

> *Trade among the DCs features a large and growing volume of intra-industry trade, both absolutely and relative to inter-industry trade.*

Thus France exports steel and automobiles to Germany while also importing both goods (intra-industry trade) instead of just exporting one and importing the other (inter-industry). It might seem senseless to both import and export automobiles, but there are several good reasons for doing so. *Product differentiation* is one: French and German automobiles are not quite the same, so trade gives consumers more choice. *Division of labor* is another reason: parts of the car might be built in France and other parts in Germany, so that trade in automobile parts is necessary to assemble complete cars. Intra-industry trade need not, therefore, be different in principle from inter-industry trade. What makes it interesting is that, since roughly similar goods are exchanged, comparative cost differences are unlikely to be large between countries. This again suggests the possibility that something beyond comparative advantage is at work.

PROBLEM

1.25 Since the Second World War, the DCs have substantially lowered trade barriers, but the LDCs have not. Explain how Table 1.5 seems to be consistent with comparative advantage. What would you expect to be true of the relative *gains* from the various trade flows, as distinct from their sizes?

11. International Trade of the United States

A second way to split the globe is between the United States and the rest of the world. This trade is summarized in Table 1.7. The three most important trading partners of the United States are Canada, Japan, and the European Economic Community (EEC) as a whole. Trade with the oil-exporting countries has, as we would expect, increased very rapidly in the last decade and is quite unbalanced. Trade with Eastern Europe has also increased substantially but remains a small fraction of the total. The United States trades more with other DCs than with the LDCs. International trade accounts for a relatively low proportion of the United States' GNP but, due to the size of the American economy, is nonetheless a substantial fraction of total world trade.

Table 1.7. INTERNATIONAL TRADE OF THE U.S. IN 1980 (BILLIONS OF DOLLARS)

(a) Direction			*(b) Composition*	
Partner	*Exports*	*Imports*	*Commodity Group*	*Exports-Imports*
DCs	135	127		
Canada	39	42	Food	17.4
EEC	54	36	Fuels	− 75.1
Japan	21	31	Other raw materials	11.9
LDCs	83	119	Capital goods	43.2
OPEC	17	56	Automotive	− 10.2
Other LDCs	66	63	Other consumer	
			goods	− 18.0
Eastern Europe	4	1		
TOTAL	222	249		
As % of U.S. GNP	8.5%	9.5%		
As % of World Trade	12.0%	13.4%		

SOURCE: *Survey of Current Business*

The United States appears to have a comparative advantage in temperate-zone agricultural products (notably wheat, corn, and soybeans) and in high-technology manufactured goods (such as capital goods). On the other hand, America is a net importer of low-technology manufactured products (such as consumer goods) and of mineral fuels (notably oil), though on balance it exports other crude materials. All this seems consistent enough with what one would guess relative autarkic prices to be, considering the nature of the American economy.

PROBLEM _____

1.26 What reasons can you think of for the pattern of comparative advantage apparently indicated by Table 1.7(b)?

12. Case Study: The International Trade of Canada

Canada is the largest single trading partner of the United States, accounting for about 20 percent of the total U.S. trade. But since the Canadian economy is only about one-tenth the size of the U.S. economy, this trade is even more important for Canada. As is clear from Table 1.8, about 70 percent of all Canadian trade is with the United States. On balance, Canada exports raw materials and imports manufactures. The large two-way trade in automotive products reflects the fact that Canada and the United States basically share a common automobile industry. A 1965 agreement between the two countries eliminated all tariffs on shipments of auto parts by G.M., Ford, Chrysler, and American Motors.

Table 1.8. CANADA'S INTERNATIONAL TRADE, 1979 (BILLIONS OF U.S. DOLLARS)

Commodity Group	Exports to		Imports from	
	U.S.	Others	U.S.	Others
Food	1.6	4.7	2.0	1.8
Fuels	6.2	1.1	1.9	3.0
Other primary	7.4	6.0	2.3	0.8
Capital goods	5.6	2.1	12.8	2.7
Automotive	8.7	0.9	10.7	0.9
Other				
Manufactures	7.8	2.9	7.8	5.2
Total	37.5	17.6	37.9	14.7

SOURCE: GATT; *Direction of Trade*

PROBLEM _____

1.27 What reasons can you think of for the pattern of comparative advantage apparently indicated by Table 1.8?

13. Alternatives to Comparative Advantage: Scale Economies

Sections 10, 11, and 12 revealed trade patterns consistent with ideas of comparative advantage, except possibly for the large volume of intra-industry trade in manufactures between the DCs. This trade could also be generated by comparative advantage, but it might reflect something entirely distinct. What difference does it make? Comparative advantage implies that gains are likely to be greatest for trade between economies that are least similar. Thus one might conclude that expansion of DC-LDC trade is relatively important, whereas changes in the already-extensive trade among DCs are relatively unimportant. This policy conclusion becomes questionable if trade is significantly due to some other cause.

A distinctive feature of the theory of comparative advantage is its generality: most reasons for trade turn out to be special cases of comparative advantage. (Chapter 3 looks at such cases in detail.) Of those few reasons that are quite distinct from comparative advantage, the most important involve increasing returns to scale—the idea that production is most efficient when conducted at a large scale. The simple Ricardian model, by contrast, assumes *constant returns to scale:* varying all inputs in proportion causes output to vary in the same proportion. In Table 1.1, for example, *each* machine produced in Germany required 1 unit of labor, so that 2 units of labor produced 2 machines, 3 units produced 3 machines, and so on.

KEY CONCEPTS

A technology has *increasing returns to scale* if an equiproportional increase in all inputs increases output in greater proportion, *constant returns to scale* if it increases output in the same proportion, and *decreasing returns to scale* if it increases output in a smaller proportion.

To see the effects of scale economies, consider a simple example in which France and Germany are identical: same size, same technology, same tastes. This rules out comparative advantage as a cause of trade. Now suppose that the technology for producing machines from labor is as described in Table 1.9, in each country. Thus the first machine produced requires 3 units of labor, the second machine requires 2 additional units, and each machine beyond the second requires 1 additional unit.

Suppose for simplicity that wine technology resembles machine technology (and so is also described by Table 1.9 in each country), that France and Germany each possesses ten units of labor, and that consumers in both countries always consume equal amounts of wine and machinery.

If France and Germany do not trade, each country will divide its

Table 1.9. TECHNOLOGY FOR MACHINE PRODUCTION IN EACH
COUNTRY (INCREASING RETURNS TO SCALE)

To Produce This Many Machines	Requires This Much Labor
1	3
2	5
3	6
4	7
5	8
6	9
7	10

labor force equally between the two industries. Thus in France 5 units of labor produce (from Table 1.9) 2 machines, and the other 5 units of labor produce 2 wine. Germany, likewise, has 2 machines and 2 wine. Since the countries are identical, they must have equal relative autarkic prices, so neither country has a comparative advantage in anything. But there is still good reason to trade. Suppose France specializes to wine, and Germany to machines. Then, from Table 1.9, the 10 units of German labor produce 7 machines, and France produces 7 wine. If the French trade 3.5 wine to Germany for 3.5 machines, each country can consume 3.5 of each good, compared to 2 of each good in autarky. Note two features of this trade.

Increasing returns to scale furnish a basis for trade independent of comparative advantage.

This simple example abstracted entirely from comparative advantage.

The pattern of trade tends to be indeterminate if the cause of trade is increasing returns to scale.

Suppose that instead France had specialized to machinery and Germany to wine. We would have obtained the same consumption pattern (3.5 units of each good in each country) with the opposite pattern of trade! Since the two countries are identical in this example, their roles are interchangeable, and no theory can prescribe or predict the pattern of trade.

Suppose next that, as in section 7, we admit the possibility of more factors of production than just labor. The production possibility frontier of a country could look like Figure 1.11. The "bowed-in" shape, or *decreasing opportunity costs*, illustrates the increasing returns that can be captured by specialization in either commodity, that is, by producing close to either axis. Suppose, again, that the two countries are identical, so that Figure 1.11

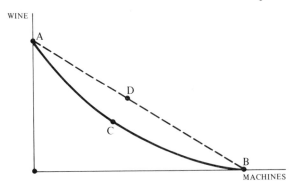

Figure 1.11. DECREASING OPPORTUNITY COSTS

applies to each. Then in autarky each country must produce and consume
at a point such as *C.* If the two countries trade, one can produce at *A* and
the other at *B,* and each can consume at a point like *D.* Again, trade and
specialization pay. Recall that in section 7 incomplete specialization became
more likely when labor was no longer the sole factor. But now complete
specialization is still called for.

> *Trade is likely to be characterized by complete specialization if it
> is due to increasing returns to scale.*

Increasing returns might arise at the level of the individual firm if a
larger output allows the use of a larger, more efficient plant, or longer
production runs in a plant of irreducible size. They might also arise at the
industry level, if, for example, a larger industry causes the populace to
adopt the skills, habits, and attitudes appropriate to working in that industry.
   Such scale economies can give an entirely different perspective to
DC-LDC trade than does comparative advantage. For if the former explains this trade, LDC exports of primary products are basically a result of
historical accident: the DCs simply specialized to manufacturing first. Such
a view of the role of LDCs in the world economy has sometimes been used
to justify policies of protecting manufacturing in the hope of realizing scale
economies as the industry grows. We will return to this in Chapters 2 and 6.
   But the anomalous aspect of world trade is the large volume of intra-
industry trade among the DCs. This does not seem to fit in well with our
discussion of scale economies. At the industry level, such economies imply,
as we have seen, extensive industrial specialization and inter-industry trade,
just the opposite of the nonspecialization and intra-industry trade we actually observe. At the plant level, the larger DCs seem sizable enough generally to support efficient-sized plants irrespective of changes in trade policy.

PRODUCT DIFFERENTIATION AND THE DIVISION OF LABOR

But scale economies can work in other ways. One of the most important reasons for scale economies at the industry level is that a larger market permits a greater division of labor. Take Adam Smith's example of the pin factory: if each worker produces entire pins from scratch, productivity is much less than if pins are produced in assembly-line fashion, with each worker specialized to an individual step in the process. The key requirement is that the market for pins be large enough so that enough workers can be employed to specialize in different crafts: the division of labor is limited by the extent of the market. This sort of thing is obviously central to modern industry. A final good such as an automobile is built from thousands of special parts, each of which is in turn produced by many workers with specialized crafts and equipment.

Scale economies resulting from the division of labor differ in one crucial way from the scale economies we considered earlier. The former required *geographical concentration* of production: to exploit the advantages of large plant size, production must take place *at* the plant; to imbue a population with industrial skills, industry must be sizable *where* the population is. But this is not true of Smith's pin example. If each worker concentrates on a distinct part of pin making, there must be enough work concentrated where each worker is to keep him fully employed, but the workers themselves need not be concentrated in the same factory, city, or nation, provided that it is not too difficult to ship pin parts from worker to worker. Likewise all the parts that go into an automobile need not be produced in Detroit in order to profit from the division of labor. These scale economies are *international*: they depend upon the size of the world market rather than upon the amount of geographical concentration of production.

If geographical concentration does in fact take place, with all stages of pin production performed in Britain and all constituent parts of the automobile produced in Detroit, then trade will be inter-industry, as Britain exports finished pins and America exports whole cars. But otherwise we will observe intra-industry trade, with unfinished pins shipped from one country to another for further processing and automobile parts exchanged internationally. (We noted in the previous section the existence of such trade within the joint Canadian-American automobile industry). What determines which will happen? Here comparative advantage returns. If countries are quite different, each is likely to have an advantage in most of the stages of production of certain industries. Trade will be inter-industry. But similar countries are unlikely to have such advantages and so will tend to share industries: there will be much more intra-industry trade. Thus such international scale economies are consistent with the basic anomaly we uncovered in section 10 and even give comparative advantage a central role.

If scale economies are due to the division of labor, countries with substantial comparative cost differences will specialize, and trade will be largely inter-industry. Countries without substantial cost differences will be nonspecialized at the industry level, and trade will be intra-industry.

Product differentiation can also help explain the facts. Suppose that the technology for producing wine in France is as described in Table 1.9, and that France has 20 units of labor. Suppose that in autarky 10 of these labor are allocated to wine. Then they can produce 7 wine, from Table 1.9. But perhaps the French would prefer to consume two kinds of wine—red and white, say—rather than just one, or perhaps some French consumers prefer red wine while others prefer white. Then instead of allocating all 10 wine workers to a single wine-making operation, the French might establish two operations, with 5 workers each, to make two varieties. From Table 1.9, they could thereby produce 2 white wine and 2 red wine. Suppose that the French would, in fact, rather have this combination, in preference to 7 of a single wine type, and do therefore conduct two operations. Suppose, once again, that Germany is identical to France, and that therefore Germany also produces and consumes 2 red wine and 2 white wine in autarky.

Now suppose that France and Germany trade. We could then have all red wine produced in France (7 units, by Table 1.9), and all white wine in Germany. If France exports 3.5 red wine and Germany 3.5 white wine, each country can now consume 3.5 of each type. Alternatively, the two countries could now differentiate wine even more. For example, France could continue to produce 2 red and 2 white, as in autarky, while Germany produces 2 aperitif and 2 dessert wines. In this case the two countries together produce the same amount of wine as without trade (8 units), but each consumer can choose from four varieties rather than two.

Regardless of whether trade causes an increase in output or an increase in variety, the result has been intra-industry trade: wine is exchanged for wine. If, instead of assuming that France and Germany were identical, we had allowed one to be relatively more efficient than the other, then all wine types would have been produced in that country. Thus we would have had inter-industry trade: all wine varieties exchanged for machines. Thus product differentiation, like the division of labor, enables returns to scale to shed light on the apparent anomaly observed in section 10.

With product differentiation, countries with substantial comparative cost differences tend to each produce all varieties of different goods so that trade is inter-industry. Countries without substantial cost differences will be nonspecialized at the industry level and trade will be intra-industry.

PROBLEMS

1.28 If France has 10 labor units, and if Table 1.9 describes the technology of both the wine and machine industries, draw France's production possibility frontier.

1.29 Suppose Germany is identical to the France of Problem **1.28**. Draw the world production possibility frontier.

1.30 Industries are sometimes described as having *decreasing* returns to scale: increasing all inputs in proportion increases output in a smaller proportion. Try to deduce the consequences of such scale diseconomies for international trade.

1.31 Economists sometimes distinguish between those scale economies that are *internal* to the firm and those that are *external*. Internal economies can be realized by a single firm as it varies its size. External economies depend on the size of the whole industry, and an individual firm would not expect to profit significantly from them simply by increasing its own size. This section described several types of scale economies. Which are likely to be internal, and which external? Can you think of further examples of each type?

1.32 Can you think of any reasons why it matters whether scale economies are internal or external, as defined in Problem **1.31**?

1.33 Suppose that scale economies are due to the division of labor, and that there are two countries. Discuss the relation between the production possibility frontiers of the two countries and of the world.

14. Summary

1. The basic reasoning underlying the principle of comparative advantage was presented in section 1. It is essential that the logic of the example in section 1 be thoroughly understood. The balance of this first chapter has been devoted to exploring the actual economic implications of comparative advantage and to emphasizing the very general nature of the idea.

2. If some interference with free international trade causes the relative price of machines in terms of wine to be higher in France than in Germany, we say that France has a comparative advantage over Germany in wine relative to machines, or, equivalently, Germany has a comparative advantage over France in machines relative to wine.

3. If trade is liberalized, then (a) each country will tend to increase the output of that good in which it has a comparative advantage and will tend to decrease the output of that good in which it has a comparative disadvantage; (b) each country will export the good in which it has a comparative advantage and import the other; (c) world output will tend to become more efficient; (d) each country will gain from free trade relative to autarky; and (e) the gains enjoyed by a country will be greater the more favorable its terms of trade, that is, the greater the difference between relative prices before and after trade is liberalized.

4. The actual world relative price and the actual pattern of production in

each country cannot be deduced from comparative advantage alone. Detailed knowledge of world demand for the two goods is also necessary.

5. The DCs on balance export manufactures to the LDCs in exchange for primary products, but the largest part of world trade is the intra-industry exchange of manufactures among the DCs themselves.

6. Economies of scale that are due to the division of labor, or that are accompanied by product differentiation, imply that trade between economies with modest comparative cost differences will be largely intra-industry, and that trade between economies with substantial comparative cost differences will be largely inter-industry.

PROBLEM

1.34 Write down as many reasons as you can think of why two countries should trade with each other. For each reason, indicate either (a) it has absolutely nothing to do with comparative advantage, or (b) it helps to determine what the pattern of comparative advantage is. Justify your answers.

SUGGESTED READING

Balassa, B. *Trade Liberalization Among Industrial Countries.* New York: McGraw-Hill, 1967.

Bhagwati, J. "The Pure Theory of International Trade: A Survey." In *Surveys of Economic Theory.* New York: St. Martin's Press, 1967. Pages 159–72 contain a discussion of the Ricardian theory and a critique of statistical tests of it.

Cooper, R. *The Economics of Interdependence: Economic Policy in the Atlantic Community.* New York: Columbia, 1980. A discussion of the development of the postwar international economy.

Emmanuel, A. *Unequal Exchange.* New York: Monthly Review Press, 1972.

Ethier, W. "Internationally Decreasing Costs and World Trade." *Journal of International Economics* 2, 1979. Scale economies and the division of labor.

Glejser, H. "Empirical Evidence on Comparative Cost Theory from the European Common Market Experience. *European Economic Review,* 1972.

Grubel, H. G. and Lloyd, P. J. *Intra-Industry Trade.* New York: John Wiley, 1975.

Haberler, G. *The Theory of International Trade.* New York: Macmillan, 1937. See chapter 10 for a good discussion of comparative costs.

Jones, R. W. "Comparative Advantage and the Theory of Tariffs: A Multi-Country, Multi-Commodity Model." *Review of Economic Studies,* 1961. The basic statement of comparative advantage in the general case of many goods and countries.

Lancaster, K. "Intra-industry trade under Perfect Monopolistic Competition," *Journal of International Economics* 2, 1980. Scale economies and product differentiation.

Leontief, W. "The Use of Indifference Curves in the Analysis of Foreign Trade." In *Readings in the Theory of International Trade.* Edited by H. S. Ellis and L. A. Metzler. Homewood: Irwin, 1950.

MacDougall, G. D. A. "British and American Exports: A Study Suggested by the Theory of Comparative Costs." In *Readings in International Economics.* Edited by R. E. Caves and H. G. Johnson. Homewood: Irwin, 1968.

Matthews, R. C. O. "Reciprocal Demand and Increasing Returns." *Review of Economic Studies,* 1949/50. Geographically concentrated scale economies.

Ricardo, D. *The Principles of Political Economy and Taxation.* Baltimore: Penguin, 1971. Ricardo's treatment of comparative advantage is found in chapter 7.

Samuelson, P. "The Gains from International Trade." In *Readings in the Theory of International Trade.* Edited by H. S. Ellis and L. A. Metzler. Homewood: Irwin, 1950.

Samuelson, P. "Social Indifference Curves." *Quarterly Journal of Economics,* 1956. When community indifference curves exist.

Chapter 2

Reciprocal Demand

"A movement along an offer curve of international trade should be considered as attended with rearrangements of internal trade; as the movement of the hand of a clock corresponds to considerable unseen movements of the machinery." —F. Y. Edgeworth

"The produce of a country exchanges for the produce of other countries, at such values as are required in order that the whole of her exports may exactly pay for the whole of her imports.
—J. S. Mill

Comparative advantage explains the pattern of trade. It also furnishes a strong argument for trade gains and tells much about production and the terms of trade. But to explain the actual pattern of production, or the exact terms at which one country's products exchange for those of another, we also need detailed knowledge of demand. In this chapter we explore these further problems and answer completely the first two of the questions posed at the outset of Part One: What explains the pattern of international trade and production? What are the welfare implications of international trade?

You may recall from elementary economics how demand and supply curves describe how price is determined. We want to do the same now for international trade. But the situation is complicated: we have at least two goods, imports and exports, and two market participants, the home country and the rest of the world, who are both simultaneously buyers and sellers.

This is a problem of general equilibrium. The key idea used for this problem, that of reciprocal demand, is due to John Stuart Mill. Comparative advantage and the law of reciprocal demand constitute the two basic building blocks of the classical theory of international trade. As we develop the theory, you might consider how it relates to the oil crises of the seventies, which changed everyone's life. The prime feature there was a dramatic change in the terms of trade of the oil exporters. Why did this happen? Why did it happen then?

JOHN STUART MILL (1806–1873)

John Stuart Mill survived an unusual educational regime imposed by his father, the economist James Mill, to become a great philosopher and economist, and one of the major intellectual figures of his day. In his writing and (briefly) his speeches in Parliament, he was also a major exponent of the liberal viewpoint on such issues as reform and women's rights. He was apparently much influenced by Harriet Taylor, with whom he had a relationship for about twenty years before the death of her husband allowed marriage. Incidentally, Mill was the friend at whose home the only copy of the manuscript of the first part of Carlyle's *The French Revolution* was inadvertently destroyed. Mill's *Principles of Political Economy* was published in the revolutionary year 1848—also the year of the publication of *The Communist Manifesto*—and became the supreme statement of classical economics and, for nearly half a century, the standard textbook.

---

1. There's No Such Thing as a Free Lunch

Imagine a single economy in isolation: say the French economy of the last chapter. Recall that there are but two commodities, wine and machines. Anyone who wishes to buy a machine must offer for sale an equal-valued amount of wine, and the only reason wine is ever offered for sale is to purchase machinery. This elementary observation is universally true: if I agree to purchase an $8,000 car then I am simultaneously offering to sell $8,000, that is, to sell my right to $8,000 worth of goods. The demand for the car and the offer of $8,000 worth of goods are one and the same thing. In the French economy as a whole, then, the value of the total demand for wine plus the total demand for machinery must always equal the value of the total supply of wine plus the total supply of machinery. That is, it is *always* true that $P_W^F D_W^F + P_M^F D_M^F \equiv P_W^F S_W^F + P_M^F S_M^F$, or

$$P_W^F(D_W^F - S_W^F) + P_M^F(D_M^F - S_M^F) \equiv 0, \tag{2.1}$$

KEY CONCEPT

Walras's Law: For any individual, group, country, or the entire world, the sum total of the values of the excess demands for all goods, services, and assets is always equal to zero.

---

where D_W^F denotes the total French demand for wine, and so forth. In other words, the values of the economy's excess demands (the excesses of demands over supplies) of the two goods always sum to zero. This property is known as Walras's Law, after the French economist Léon Walras (1834–1910). Walras's Law is quite general: if there were ten thousand goods in this economy instead of two, the same reasoning would imply that the values of the excess demands in the ten thousand markets would always sum to zero. Two other aspects of Walras's Law deserve emphasis. First, it is an identity that always holds, quite apart from whether the economy is in equilibrium or not; this is the meaning of the three-barred equality sign in (2.1). If the French economy is in autarkic equilibrium so that demand equals supply in each market, then (2.1) must hold since each term in parentheses is itself equal to zero. But Walras's Law will continue to hold even outside of equilibrium. We deduced (2.1) directly from the fundamental meaning of "demand" and "supply" and never said anything about equilibrium. Secondly, Walras's Law is a statement about the relationship *between* the two markets and tells us nothing about the markets individually. For example, it does not say whether the wine market is in excess supply ($S_W^F > D_W^F$), has excess demand ($D_W^F > S_W^F$), or is in autarkic equilibrium. But it does imply that *if* the wine market is in equilibrium, then the machine market *must* be in equilibrium also; if there is an excess demand for wine, then there must be an excess supply of machinery, and so on.

PROBLEMS

2.1 Suppose that in addition to wine and machinery there are 9,998 other markets in the French economy. Then what does an excess demand for wine imply? If the other 9,999 markets are in equilibrium, what must be true of the wine market? If the answers to these questions do not come to you at once, go back to the beginning of this section and rededuce Walras's Law directly for an economy with 10,000 markets.

2.2 Fill in the blanks in the following table.

Price of Wine in Terms of Machines	Excess Demand for Wine	Excess Demand for Machines
1/10	1000	
1/5		− 80
1/2		− 20
2/3	0	
1	− 10	
3/2		30
2		50
5		100
10	− 15	

2.3 A man sold a bond for $10,000, bought a $7,000 automobile, and put the remaining $3,000 in the bank. Since the value of the bond supplied exceeded the value of the car demanded, did he not (heaven forbid!) violate Walras's Law? What if you give a bum fifty cents for a cup of coffee?

2. Offer Curves

Suppose the French can trade at the international prices of wine and machines. If there is an excess French demand for machinery, this excess is the net French demand for machine imports. By Walras's Law there must simultaneously be an excess supply of wine, that is, a net supply of exports of wine, of equal value at the international prices. So define $M^F = D_M^F - S_M^F$ and $X^F = S_W^F - D_W^F$ and rewrite (2.1) as $-P_W X^F + P_M M^F \equiv 0$, or

$$pM^F \equiv X^F, \tag{2.2}$$

where $p = P_M/P_W$, the French terms of trade. Note that (2.2) is nothing more than (2.1) rewritten in such a way as to emphasize the role of international trade. It simply says that the French demand for imports is always equal in value to the French supply of exports; this is always true whether or not world markets are in equilibrium, that is, whether or not the rest of the world is willing to satisfy the French demand for imports and to purchase the French supply of exports.

An offer curve (sometimes called a "reciprocal demand curve") summarizes the various possible roles a country can play in the world economy. In Figure 2.1 the horizontal axis is measured in units of machinery and will be used to depict the excess demand for machines, while the excess supply of wine will be marked off on the vertical axis. Any point in this plane thus represents specific values of M^F and X^F. Point *A*, for example, indicates a demand for (machine) imports of *OB* and a supply of (wine) exports of *BA;* point *E* represents a demand of *OJ* for (wine) imports and a corresponding supply of *EJ* of (machine) exports.

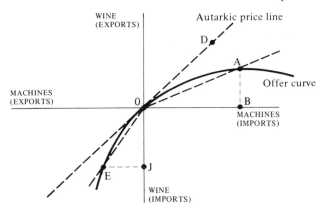

Figure 2.1. THE FRENCH OFFER CURVE

A country's offer curve records how much of one good that country is willing to pay (export) in order to buy (import) each quantity of the other good. Thus the fact that point *A* is on France's offer curve in Figure 2.1 means that the French are willing to pay *AB* wine in order to obtain *OB* machines; similarly, they would pay *EJ* machines for *OJ* wine.

From Walras's Law, seen in (2.2), $p = X/M$. Thus at any point in Figure 2.1 the demand for imports and supply of exports are given by the coordinates, while the relative price of machines in terms of wine equals the slope of the line through that point and the origin. At point *A*, for example, $p = BA/OB$. Walras' Law implies that the offer curve must be contained in the NE and SW quadrants (why?). The French autarkic equilibrium price, P_M^F/P_W^F, is given by the slope of the line *OD;* at this price domestic demand will equal domestic supply in both markets, and the offer curve passes through the origin, *O.* If the world relative machine price *p* is less than p^F, say that indicated by the line *OA*, then comparative advantage indicates that France will import machines and export wine, as discussed in Chapter 1. This is illustrated by point *A* on the offer curve. On the other hand, if *p* is above the autarkic price, the French export machines and import wine, as at *E*, and the offer curve is in the SW quadrant.

Three important features of the offer curve should by apparent. First, it is a general equilibrium concept; if the international price changes, the offer curve indicates the effect on the demand for imports and supply of exports as the *entire* economy adjusts: both consumers and suppliers, both import markets and export markets. Second, the offer curve is itself relevant *only* to the French economy. We had to know nothing about Germany to derive it, and it itself tells us nothing about Germany. Finally, we need not know what the international price actually is, because the offer curve indicates how an economy *would* behave under all *hypothetical* values of this price. (Just as a normal demand curve does not tell us the price and what quantity will actually be demanded, but rather how much would be demanded at each hypothetical price.)

PROBLEMS

2.4 Why does Walras's Law imply that the offer curve is restricted to the NE and SW quadrants?

2.5 Graph the observations in the completed table from Problem **2.2** and "connect the dots" to draw an offer curve.

2.6 Suppose France has 100 casks of wine and no machines. The French tastes are such that the country would wish to behave as follows:

If P_M/P_W is:	The French wish to:
greater than 3 W/Ma	consume only Wine
3 W/Ma	export 60 Wine Casks
not more than 2 W/Ma	consume 20 Wine Casks

Use Walras's Law to deduce M^F and X^F for each case. Draw the French offer curve by graphing the observations and connecting them.

2.7 Suppose you have the following data for Germany:

P_M/P_W	Ma demand	Ma supply	W demand	W supply
4		120	140	20
4/3	80	110		30
1	100	100	50	
	140	80	45	85

Fill in the blanks. Draw Germany's offer curve by graphing the observations and connecting the dots.

2.8* Suppose that in England five units of labor are required to produce either a bolt of cloth or a cask of wine, that England has 100 units of labor, and that each Englishman always consumes one cask of wine for each bolt of cloth that he consumes. What can you say about his marginal rate of substitution? Derive England's offer curve exactly. (Hint: draw England's production possibility frontier. What is the autarkic price? For each value of the relative price ask yourself: what will England produce; what will it consume? Record the differences to draw the offer curve.)

2.9* Suppose that in Portugal 4 units of labor can produce a bolt of cloth, 1 labor unit can produce a cask of wine, 100 labor units are available, and each Portuguese always spends one-half of her income on each good. Derive Portugal's offer curve exactly.

2.10* Suppose Germany has a production possibility frontier displaying increasing opportunity costs, and that each German always consumes one machine for each cask of wine that he consumes. What does Germany's offer curve look like?

2.11* Trade in commodities can be regarded as indirect trade in the services of the primary factors embodied in the goods. Derive the exact shapes of the "factoral" offer curves for the English and Portuguese economies described in Problems 2.8* and 2.9*.

3.* *Exploring Further:* Income and Substitution Effects

The offer curve in Figure 2.1 is drawn so that a fall in the price of imports causes a rise in M. But the curve also has another, unexplained characteristic: it eventually "bends backwards", that is, over part of the curve M increases while X falls. Such a shape is indeed a distinct possibility and is worth pausing to investigate. A change in relative prices can be thought of as exerting its influence upon M and X in two logically distinct ways. First, there is what can be termed a *substitution effect:* a fall in the relative price of machinery, say, will induce consumers to substitute machinery for wine. Also, if the economy is not already specialized to wine production, there will be a movement along the production possibility frontier so that wine output is substituted for machine output. The net result is an increased excess demand for machines and an increased excess supply of wine, that is, M and X both tend to rise. But there will also be an *income effect:* the fall in the relative price of machines means that the income of wine exporters has in fact risen, that is, the wine that they are exporting will now buy more machinery. (By the same token the income of machine sellers has fallen.) For example, if in Figure 2.2 the relative price of machines falls from AB/OB to HB/OB, the French need export only HB units of wine, rather than AB, to buy OB machines. This increase in income will normally cause the French to consume more of both goods (although there are some goods, such as gruel and secondhand clothes, that we consume less of as our income rises). The income effect, then, usually causes M to rise and X to fall, as the only way to consume more of the export good is by exporting less of it. In this case, the improvement in the terms of trade will necessarily increase M but may cause X to rise or fall, depending upon whether the substitution or income effect is dominant. The offer curve will then bend backward if the income effect eventually becomes dominant. At point O the substitution effect necessarily dominates since the income effect is zero—the fact that our exports are worth more cannot help if we are not exporting. But as we move away from O along the offer curve the income effect becomes more important, and it *may* eventually dominate, causing the curve to bend downward.

An illustration may prove of use at this point. Suppose you are a pea-picker working as long as you want at a certain wage. Then you are essentially 'exporting' your labor in order to 'import' the goods you pur-

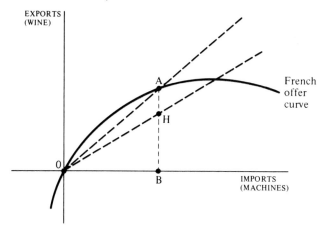

Figure 2.2. An Improvement in the French Terms of Trade

chase with your wages. If your wage increases, your income will rise, and you will perhaps respond by working more. But if your wage increases again and again, you decide there is more to life than picking peas and you will begin to cut back on your labor so as to have more leisure in which to enjoy your new-found affluence. That is, the income effect will eventually dominate. There is nothing farfetched about this example: labor unions frequently take part of their wage increases in the form of a reduced work-week, and the average work-week has indeed tended to fall over the years as incomes have risen. An offer curve that eventually bends downward is thus a distinct possibility and need not imply anything unusual either about the tastes of the country under consideration or about the goods imported or exported.

PROBLEM

2.12 Discuss the roles of income and substitution effects in Problems **2.8***, **2.9***, and **2.10***.

4. The Volume and Terms of Trade

The French offer curve summarizes how the French economy will behave under all possible relative prices. To analyze world markets we need similar information for Germany, that is, we need Germany's offer curve as well.

In deriving the French curve we arbitrarily called machinery imports and wine exports. This did not reflect a prediction about what the actual trade pattern would be; the NE and SW quadrants of the figures represent the two possibilities. But regardless of what the actual pattern is, it must certainly be that Germany exports whatever France imports and vice versa. Therefore, define M^G to be the German excess demand for wine and X^G as the excess supply of machines; that is, simply reverse the roles played by the wine and machine axes, and then proceed just as for France. French and German offer curves are shown in Figure 2.3.

If you find it difficult to remember which axes represent imports for which countries, the following device will be helpful: imagine an offer curve to be a "bowl" that contains its imports. Thus in Figure 2.3 the French "bowl" contains the positive part of the machine axis and the negative part of the wine axis, while the German "bowl" contains the positive part of the wine axis and the negative part of the machine axis.

We are now equipped to understand the basic idea contributed by Mill. The intersection of the two curves reveals the world relative price and the pattern of trade. This is the law of reciprocal demand. In Figure 2.3 France will import AD machines from Germany in exchange for OD wine; the international price of machines in terms of wine is OD/AD, the slope of the straight line through the origin and point A. Only at A, the intersection of the two curves, can both world markets be in equilibrium. If, for example, the international relative price were as indicated by the line through O, B, and C, then the German demand for imports of wine and supply of

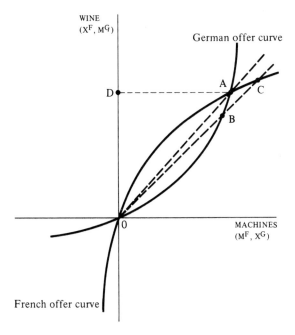

Figure 2.3. THE TERMS OF TRADE

exports of machinery would be given by *B* while the French supply of exports of wine and demand for imports of machinery would be indicated by *C*. There would thus be an excess world demand for machines and an excess world supply of wine. Only at *A* do the desired exports and imports of the two countries just match.

Note that at the origin the German offer curve is flatter than the French. This indicates that the German autarkic price of machines in terms of wine is lower than the French, that is, France has a comparative advantage over Germany in wine relative to machines. If the French curve were instead the flatter, they would intersect in the SW quadrant, indicating that France exports machines and Germany wine. Thus the offer curves illustrate the principle of comparative advantage.

PROBLEMS

2.13 Draw Figure 2.3 as it would look if France had the comparative advantage in machines.

2.14 Suppose that France and Germany, as described in Problems **2.6** and **2.7**, enter into free trade. By drawing their offer curves, find the terms of trade and the volume of goods exchanged.

2.15* England has 100 labor units, of which 5 are required to produce either a cask of wine or a bolt of cloth. Each English resident always consumes the two goods in equal quantities. Portugal also has 100 labor units with 1 required to produce a cask of wine and 4 to produce a bolt of cloth; each Portuguese always consumes quantities of wine and cloth equal *in value* to each other. What will the terms of trade between these countries be? Who exports how much of what? What are the wages and prices in the two countries? Now suppose that England's labor force increases to 1000 units and nothing else changes. Which curves shift? What are the new terms of trade and pattern of trade? What size must England's labor force be if that country is to export wine?

5. Elasticity

Because it summarizes how the economy would react to any international price, the offer curve is one of the main tools of international trade theory. And the shape of the offer curve is a basic characteristic of the economy. One measure of this shape is the elasticity of import demand, measured by the formula

$$e = \frac{\text{percentage rise in } M}{\text{percentage fall in } p}. \tag{2.3}$$

A great virtue of the elasticity concept is that it gives you a pure number reflecting a fundamental property of the economy: the value of *e* does not depend upon whether *M* or *p* is measured in pounds, ounces, gallons, or quarts.

KEY CONCEPT

The *elasticity of import demand* is the percentage increase in the demand for imports resulting from a 1 percent improvement in the terms of trade, that is, a 1 percent fall in *p*.

Since an increase in *p* implies a decrease in *M*, *e* will always be positive. Import demand is elastic or inelastic if *e* > 1 or *e* < 1 respectively. If *e* > 1, a 1 percent fall in the price of imports increases the volume of imports more than 1 percent. Thus the total amount spent on imports increases. An improvement in the terms of trade will, therefore, cause the economy to increase its expenditure on imports if import demand is elastic and to decrease such expenditure if import demand is inelastic.

You may have met with the notion of demand elasticity before, and perhaps even learned a method of reading it off a demand curve. That method cannot, however, be applied to an offer curve, where the axes represent imports and exports rather than imports and their price. To find the value of *e* at, say, point *A* on the offer curve of Figure 2.4, proceed as follows. Draw a straight line through *A* tangent to the offer curve at *A* and extend it until it intersects the *X*-axis (as at *C* in Figure 2.4). Then the value of *e* at *A* will be given by *OB/OC*, where *B* is the point on the *X*-axis directly across from *A*, that is, *OB* equals the volume of exports indicated by point *A*.

Verifying that this procedure does indeed yield the true value of *e* is a largely manipulative affair. But a feel for elasticity can be obtained by a closer look at the geometry. First of all, notice that the value of *e* given by this procedure depends upon the exact point at which the elasticity is measured; *e* does not have the same value at all points of the curve. Elasticity is intended to tell us how the economy will respond to a change in a given situation. It is only natural that this response should depend upon the situation.

Second, if the offer curve is elastic and *p* falls by 1 percent, then *M* increases by more than 1 percent, so that the total amount spent on imports (price times quantity) rises. But exports are what are spent on imports. Thus if *e* exceeds 1, a fall in *p* raises *X:* the offer curve is upward sloping. Similarly the downward-bending portion, where *X* falls as *p* falls, must be inelastic, and the borderline point, *D* in the figure, where *X* does not change as *M* rises, must have *e* = 1. All of this is reflected by our geometric procedure for finding *e*. If *A* is between *O* and *D*, as illustrated in Figure 2.4, *C* must lie below *B* so that *e* = *OB/OC* > 1. If *A* were beyond *D*, the tangent line would slope downward so that *C* would be above *B*, while if *A* were at *D*, *B* and *C* would coincide. All of this does not prove that our method is correct, but it is at least compatible with common sense.

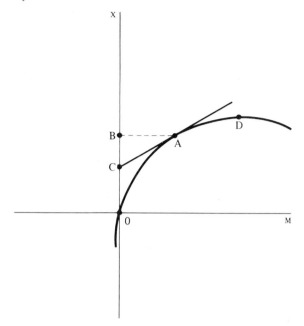

Figure 2.4. FINDING THE ELASTICITY OF IMPORT DEMAND

THE ELASTICITY OF EXPORT SUPPLY

We have investigated the elasticity of import demand, but it is just as natural to look at the elasticity of export supply, f, which is the percentage increase in the supply of exports resulting from a 1 percent improvement in the terms of trade:

$$f = \frac{\text{percentage rise in } X}{\text{percentage fall in } p}.$$ (2.4)

Since the offer curve is both a demand curve for imports and a supply curve of exports, e and f must be two ways of looking at the same thing; given the value of one we should be able to calculate the other. The relation is simple. If p falls by 1 percent, M rises by e percent and X by f percent. Now a 1 percent fall in p reduces the cost of imports by 1 percent, so that the total spent on imports (that is, exports) rises by $e - 1$ percent. Thus

$$e - 1 = f.$$ (2.5)

It is now easy to see how to read f off an offer curve. In Figure 2.4 the value of e at A is OB/OC. Thus $f = e - 1 = (OB - OC)/OC = BC/OC$. Using this formula, observe that along the upward-sloping part of the curve, from O to D, f is positive, at D it is zero, and beyond D it is negative.

THE ELASTICITY OF EXPORTS WITH RESPECT TO IMPORTS

The offer curve relates M, X, and p. We have expressed its shape alternatively as the elasticity of M with respect to p and as that of X with respect to p. The final possibility is the elasticity, g, of X with respect to M:

$$g = \frac{\text{percentage rise in } X}{\text{pecentage rise in } M}.$$ (2.6)

From formulas (2.3), (2.4), and (2.6),

$$g = f/e.$$ (2.7)

In Figure 2.4 the value of g at A is given by $g = f/e = (BC/OC)/(OB/OC) = BC/OB$. Thus g is positive from O to D, zero at D, and negative beyond.

PROBLEMS

2.16 Suppose you have the following observations:

p	M	X
100		100,000
99	1,030	

Fill in the blanks. Calculate e, f, and g for the change from the first observation to the second.

2.17 In Problem **2.2** calculate e, f, and g for each pair of successive observations, using the definition of each elasticity. Also calculate f and g from your values of e using the relationships derived above. Try to explain any discrepancies.

2.18 Look at Figure 2.4. What is the geometric method for finding e in the SW quadrant? For finding the import elasticity of the German offer curve? For finding f and g in these cases?

2.19* What can you say about the elasticities of the curves you derived in Problems **2.8***, **2.9***, and **2.10***?

2.20* Prove that the geometric technique for finding the value of e is correct. Prove the relations between e, f, and g.

6. Some International Economic Problems of the Less Developed Countries

The offer curve is useful to explore the international economic situation of the less developed countries (LDC). As we saw in the previous chapter, these countries as a group export primary products to the developed countries (DCs) for manufactures. Many assert that the demand of the

DCs for primary product imports is quite inelastic, reasoning that because these goods are often necessities, demand for them cannot vary much in response to price changes. Also the supply of primary products by the LDCs is often asserted to be inelastic, at least in the short run, since this supply depends upon past planting, mining exploration, and so forth, and can be varied only after a substantial time lag. Such a situation is depicted in Figure 2.5, which shows international equilibrium *A,* where the elasticities are small.

THE ISSUES

Three distinct areas of concern to the LDCs follow from this description.

1. *Fluctuations of export earnings.* Natural events such as crop failures, the business cycle, inventions, taste changes, and so forth cause these curves to shift around year by year. With low elasticities fairly minor shifts can cause substantial variations in the terms of trade, and therefore substantial year-by-year fluctuations in the export earnings of individual countries. For example, in Figure 2.5, if the LDC offer curve shifts slightly to become curve *L'* the terms of trade change substantially, from the slope of *OA* to that of *OB.* Low elasticities mean that substantial price changes cause small quantity changes; therefore a moderate quantity change requires a large price change to be effected.

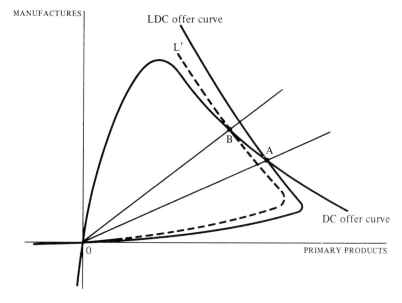

Figure 2.5. TRADE BETWEEN DEVELOPED COUNTRIES (DC) AND LESS DEVELOPED COUNTRIES (LDC)

2. *Terms of trade.* If the DCs' offer curve is inelastic, the LDCs face less favorable terms of trade than need be. For suppose the LDCs as a group were permanently to trade less with the DCs. This means that they permanently shift their offer curve toward the origin, say to L' in Figure 2.5. This permanently improves their terms of trade. The LDCs would be using their position as a monopolist in the primary product market (and monopsonist—or sole buyer—in the market for manufactures) to restrict supply (demand) and thereby force price up (down). This process cannot be pushed too far, because we saw in Chapter 1 that autarky is worse than free trade: it matters not how favorable the terms of trade are if a country does not trade much. But if the DCs' demand is inelastic, the LDCs would be better off by trading less. In Figure 2.5, for example, the LDCs are clearly better off at B than at A because they are importing more manufactures while sacrificing fewer primary product exports. By the same token the DCs are worse off. Inelastic offer curves, then, furnish the LDCs a potentially powerful motive to abandon free trade, even though such a move would be inefficient for the world as a whole.

3. *A secular decline in the terms of trade.* Spokesmen for the LDCs often argue that their terms of trade are steadily worsening. This is asserted to be due to many causes; the two that concern us are low elasticities and a tendency for the LDCs' offer curve to shift outward, relative to the DCs', as the world economy grows. The argument is that as income grows a smaller fraction of it is spent on necessities, such as food, and a larger fraction on manufactured goods. Also development itself requires large imports of manufactured goods. Finally, the DCs are constantly developing new products, such as plastics, that substitute for primary products. Figure 2.5 illustrates the implication. Suppose in some time period the LDCs' offer curve shifts outward from L', while the DCs' offer curve expands hardly at all. Then equilibrium shifts from B to A, and the LDCs experience a decline in their terms of trade. The assertion is that this is in fact the long-term trend.

THE LDC RESPONSE

The picture that emerges from the above is one of steadily worsening LDC terms of trade with wide short-run fluctuations and a strong temptation to forsake free trade. More generally, there are obviously huge disparities in real incomes between the DCs and LDCs. Consequently the latter share a dissatisfaction with their present role of providers of primary products. This has had two basic results.

Import substitution. Many LDCs have tried to limit dependence on the world economy by shifting resources from traditional export sectors to the production of goods they have imported; thus they have attempted to shift their offer curves toward the origin. Such "import-substitution" policies have been forcefully implemented in the past by many Latin American countries and others.

The New International Economic Order. In recent years groups of LDCs have come together to demand, and sometimes attempt, a restructuring of the world economy. The frustrations and aspirations of these countries have been expressed in resolutions of the United Nations General Assembly, and further expression was given in 1964 at the first U.N. Conference on Trade and Development (UNCTAD), attended by 122 nations—about 90 of them LDCs. UNCTAD was subsequently made into a permanent agency of the United Nations, with a staff in Geneva and subsequent meetings at three- and four-year intervals.

From such sessions and meetings has emerged a demand for a "New International Economic Order." The more important proposals in this program include the following:

1. an "integrated" program to stabilze and support the prices of a group of primary products in terms of manufactures,
2. increased development aid,
3. the expansion in the LDCs of various manufacturing activities now located in the DCs, and
4. the transfer of advanced technology from the DCs to the LDCs independently of private firms.

THE EVIDENCE

Before examining various attempts and proposals, let us look at the evidence.

Indications of low elasticities abound, and many primary product prices have in fact fluctuated markedly relative to prices of manufactures. Table 2.1 illustrates quarter-by-quarter changes in the indices of selected commodity prices and compares them with the behavior of the U.S. wholesale price index. Since many LDCs concentrate their exports in only a few products, they must have experienced significant fluctuations in their terms of trade. But beyond this the evidence is unclear.

Consider the first issue: export earnings. Calculations of export earnings of groups of LDCs frequently show only moderate fluctuations. The reason is simple. Suppose a bad crop shifts the LDC offer curve to L' in Figure 2.5. The decrease in quantity and consequent rise in price cancel each other at least in part; export earnings fluctuate less than the terms of trade. But the situation of individual LDCs is more complicated, and the reason is a good illustration of the care required in using offer curves. A frost in Brazil that decimates the coffee crop may have only a moderate

Table 2.1. Indices of Selected Commodity Prices and of U.S. Wholesale Prices (1975 average = 100)

Quarter		Coffee	Copper	Groundnut Oil	Sugar	Superphosphate	Tin	U.S. Wholesale Price
	II	82	132	58	46	41	96	76
1973	III	88	164	67	45	56	75	80
	IV	89	178	76	52	56	83	82
	I	90	191	123	94	105	107	85
1974	II	95	226	128	112	146	135	88
	III	85	140	123	148	169	125	95
	IV	85	110	129	230	173	103	98
	I	89	103	121	160	155	108	98
1975	II	90	102	88	90	102	103	99
	III	105	100	101	83	77	98	101
	IV	116	95	90	66	66	93	102
	I	139	101	83	69	49	98	103
1976	II	175	124	78	68	41	111	104
	III	185	126	90	51	45	120	105
	IV	225	104	95	38	44	120	106
	I	163	153	113	40	58	212	128
1979	II	197	160	108	39	64	221	133
	III	246	159	103	45	71	223	137
	IV	258	172	90	67	86	236	142
	I	248	212	87	99	96	254	148
1980	II	255	166	84	136	85	252	151
	III	253	171	105	153	82	252	156
	IV	255	161	125	176	84	231	159
	I	267	149	130	121	96	206	164
1981	II	268	142	135	81	81	192	168
	III	182	140	129	70	69	213	169
	IV	187	135	93	61	69	236	169

SOURCE: *International Financial Statistics*

effect on the earnings of coffee exporters in the aggregate. But Colombia, unaffected by the frost, will experience only the sharp rise in price whereas Brazil will itself have to bear the full decline in quantity.

Even if individual LDCs do experience large swings in earnings this need not hamper development. Such fluctuations will be expected and recognized as transitory and perhaps adjusted for. The few studies that exist of the effect of such fluctuations on LDC development largely fail to reveal any significant impact.

The evidence for a secular decline in the LDCs' terms of trade is even more sketchy and has received abundant criticism. Relevant price indices are hard to find and do not adequately account for changes in the quality and variety of manufactures. Also a decline in the terms of trade would not in itself imply a deterioration in the LDCs' position, since it could be due to an increased ability to export. The position of LDC spokesmen on this issue is the opposite of that of the classical economists, who believed that the pressure of a growing world economy on a limited stock of arable land and mineral resources would inevitably drive up primary product prices. This view has found modern expression in the concerns of conservationists and neo-Malthusians over the "limits to growth."

THE REMEDIES: INTERNATIONAL COMMODITY AGREEMENTS

Despite the ambiguous evidence, the general position of the LDCs has guaranteed policy measures. The most natural would be for the LDCs to control their offer curves with export or production quotas or purchases and sales of primary products. Such measures could apply to all three issues.

Individual LDCs have in fact followed such policies. Brazil has restricted coffee exports to hold up prices, and Cuba has even burned part of its sugar crop. But single countries can at best achieve only transitory success in this way. If some LDC restricts exports, a competitor will step in to fill the gap so that the restriction will result in a loss of market share rather than a higher price. Thus Brazil's restriction of coffee exports allowed other Latin American countries to increase their markets and helped stimulate the development of coffee cultivation in East Africa. Geometrically, although the producers (and potential producers) of a primary product may *in the aggregate* face an inelastic foreign offer curve, any individual producer faces a much more elastic curve because, from its point of view, the rest of the world includes competitors as well as customers.

There is thus good reason for LDCs to join together, in what is called a "producer cartel," for multilateral action. There have in fact been many such attempts. Most of these have had little success. One basic problem is the temptation to cheat. If export restrictions are binding and price is being held up, individual countries will be tempted to violate their quotas (and this can often be done with little fear of detection). The temptation would be enhanced by a suspicion that other countries are cheating or by dissatisfaction with the quota allotment. Similarly new producers have little incentive to join the agreement rather than taking a "free ride." Thus such agreements have proved unstable. LDCs have sometimes tried to deal with this by involving the DCs in the agreement, essentially as enforcers. The International Coffee Agreement involves both producer and consumer nations, with the United States, as a large consumer, in a key position. This brings up a second problem. While both the LDCs and the DCs may desire stable prices, and so be in basic agreement over the issue of price stabilization, the interests of the two groups clearly conflict with respect to the issue of improving LDC terms of trade. Even if the agreement is limited to price stabilization, the participants must agree where the price should be stabilized. The International Coffee Agreement has broken down in the past because of such producer-consumer variance. Further DC reluctance is due to a belief that commodity agreements, whatever their aims, tend in practice to respond more to the needs of producers than to those of consumers. The United States has long opposed such agreements, although the opposition has gradually eroded in recent decades.

Some agreements feature a *buffer stock*. An international agency is endowed with a fund and a stock of the commodity. The agency then attempts to control price by selling from the stock in the face of upward pressure and adding to it when prices soften. There is a basic twofold problem. The international agency will find its funds or its stock exhausted unless it both stabilizes at the true long-term equilibrium price and possesses sufficient resources to deal with the actual disturbances that arise. The size of both can only be guessed. The International Tin Agreement uses both a buffer stock and export quotas. This agreement is widely regarded as the most successful of the various stabilization attempts, simply because it has continued in existence for over twenty-five years. But its buffer stock has been depleted several times, and the agreement has had at most only modest success in limiting price fluctuations.

Many economists are skeptical of stabilization agreements because of the ambiguous evidence for their need and the proven difficulty of implementation. There is a third reason as well. Private speculators can play a stabilizing role. If the price of tin were to fall below its "normal" level, speculators would purchase tin to sell later at a profit and thereby limit the price decline. A commodity agreement could be justified if there were reason to believe that its managers would be more effective than professional speculators would be. Otherwise the efforts of the agreement would simply displace those of speculators, and the agreement could succeed in limiting price fluctuations only if its activities were more extensive than those the speculators were willing to undertake. This means that an effective stabilization program could require larger resources and substantial costs. Many economists question the wisdom of using scarce LDC resources in this way.

Nevertheless, spokesmen for the LDCs argue for redoubled efforts, as with an "integrated" fund to stabilize a number of commodity prices at once. Perhaps part of the reason for this is the success of the Organization of Petroleum Exporting Countries (OPEC). OPEC has been concerned not to stabilize oil prices, but to keep the price of oil up, that is, achieving favorable terms of trade. Exporters of other primary products have tried to emulate OPEC but with little success. (We will examine the world oil market in greater detail in the next section.)

CASE STUDY: The Integrated Program for Commodities

On June 27, 1980, representatives of 101 nations agreed to establish the Common Fund Under the Integrated Program for Commodities. The Common Fund is to consist of two accounts. The First Account will be used to lend to participating international commodity agreements for stockpiling. Since all commodity prices do not move together (see Table 2.1) some commodity agreements are likely to need financial resources to add to stockpiles at the same time as other agreements are selling from their stockpiles. Thus the Common Fund could allow a more efficient use of financial resources than would separate funds for the individual agreements. The First Account is to consist of $470 million of subscriptions from the participating countries, plus contributions from the commodity agreements that join the program, plus whatever the Common Fund borrows in private capital markets. Of the subscriptions, 62 percent are to come from the DCs, 19 percent from the LDCs, 14 percent from the Soviet bloc, and 5 percent from China.

The Second Account is to be used to finance primary-product research and development. This account is to consist of $70–150 million from the First Account plus $280 million in voluntary contributions from participating nations (the United States has announced it will not contribute). The Common Fund is to come into existence when formally approved by 90 states accounting for two-thirds of the subscriptions to the First Account and half of those to the Second. As of April 1981, over 30 countries accounting for over 55 percent of the First Account subscriptions and almost 85 percent of the Second Account contributions had agreed, and preparatory work on the Common Fund was under way. But for the Fund to work, international commodity agreements must be established, and they must enter into association with the Fund. Originally, agreements were envisaged for ten commodities—coffee, tea, cocoa, sugar, copper, tin, hard fibers, cotton, jute, and rubber—and others could be added later. But agreement has actually been reached only on rubber, although some earlier agreements—such as those on cocoa and tin—remain in force.

THE REMEDIES: IMPORT SUBSTITUTION AND TARIFF PREFERENCES

Import substitution. Many LDCs have followed import substitution policies. These countries cannot effectively deal with the three issues for the same reason that attempts by individual countries to control prices are ineffective. But import substitution does insulate an LDC from external fluctuations by reducing the role of world markets. Such a reduction has also often been desired for noneconomic reasons. The cost should be obvious after Chapter 1: such a country is forsaking the benefits of comparative advantage. Significant import substitution requires that some goods be produced domestically at higher opportunity cost than that at which they could be purchased abroad. These programs have lost much of their appeal in recent years as awareness of their inefficiency has spread. This awareness is due both to the success of some LDCs, such as Taiwan and South Korea, that have relied on foreign trade and to recent studies documenting the cost of import substitution. (Of course single-country studies will miss any terms-of-trade improvement due to many LDCs simultaneously pursuing import substitution.)

Generalized Systems of Preferences (GSPs). In UNCTAD the LDCs have pressed for *tariff preferences* on manufactures, that is, lower DC tariffs on imports from the LDCs than on similar goods imported from other DCs. Note that this contrasts sharply with import substitution in emphasizing trade rather than limiting it. The hope is to foster the development of light manufacturing industry in the LDCs (and so deal with the three issues indirectly). The European Community instituted a preferential tariff system in 1971, Canada in 1974, and the United States, after initial opposition, began such a program in 1976. Other DCs also have GSPs. These schemes have significant limitations. Benefits have thus far been limited, although in recent years the LDCs have expanded manufactured exports to the DCs faster than world trade has grown, as we saw in section 10 of Chapter 1.

PROBLEMS ———————————————————————————————————

   2.21 The alleged secular decline in the LDCs' terms of trade was explained by low elasticities and the relative shifts of offer curves. How would the argument be affected by elastic curves? What is the role of elasticity?

   2.22 Unilateral action is unlikely to be effective, because an individual LDC faces a much more elastic offer curve than do LDCs in the aggregate. But if so, how could the three issues ever arise for individual countries?

   2.23 The International Monetary Fund (about which more will be said when we come to international monetary economics) has a facility to lend to LDCs with temporary shortfalls of export earnings. What are the pros and cons of such a measure? Compare it to commodity agreements.

   2.24 The LDCs are sometimes urged to follow *export diversification*. If they exported many primary products rather than just a few, fluctuations in individual prices would tend to cancel so that the overall terms of trade should be more stable. Discuss this proposal and compare it to import substitution.

2.25 Suppose that the LDCs succeed in improving their terms of trade. This makes the DCs worse off. Suppose the latter are considering using foreign aid as a bribe to induce the LDCs to return to free trade. Is it possible for the DCs to offer a tempting bribe, that is, one large enough so that the LDCs are at least as well off as they are now but not so large that the DCs are worse off? Why?

7. Case Study: The International Economics of Energy

The most important economic event of the seventies was the dramatic rise in the price of oil. The oil market is the world's largest, and oil is the most prominent internationally traded good in terms of both tonnage and value. The commodity is important to us all—directly, to fuel our automobiles and heat our homes; indirectly, for the energy essential to modern industry.

DEVELOPMENT OF THE WORLD OIL MARKET

The petroleum market began after the discovery of a well at Titusville, Pennsylvania, in 1859; international trade in the commodity began two years later when it was exported to Europe from Philadelphia. The development of the automobile created a large demand for crude oil, and the first three decades of this century witnessed the exploitation of major oil fields in the American southwest and the Middle East, as well as the development of what were to become the seven large international oil companies, or "majors" (Exxon, British Petroleum, Royal Dutch/Shell, Texaco, Mobil, Gulf, and Standard of California). Despite much contemporary talk about Big Oil, these companies no longer dominate the international oil market as they did before the sixties. Prior to the Second World War, the majors constituted a producer cartel. For years these companies sat on reserves of easily extractable oil that must have seemed almost limitless and certainly overshadowed demand. This combination of oil company solidarity and large supply forced the countries that actually possessed oil into a passive position for many years in their relations with the majors. This was dramatically illustrated in 1951 when a radical government in Iran nationalized foreign oil interests. The majors simply refused to buy Iranian oil. They could do this because the plentiful world supplies allowed them to get the oil they needed elsewhere; the Iranians could not sell their oil to anyone else because the majors controlled the world market. Thus Iranian oil earnings disappeared, and in 1954 a CIA-assisted coup in Iran ousted the regime and returned the shah to power.

Figure 2.6 shows the situation faced by an individual oil exporter in these years. The large supply of oil available at a fixed price meant that such a country faced a straight-line offer curve such as *OC*. Any attempt to seize control of production and shift its own offer curve would fail to influence price and so only reduce the amount of imports it could buy, from *AB* to *DE* in the figure.

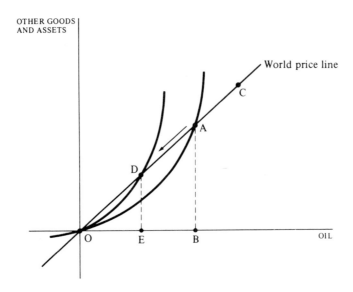

Figure 2.6. RESTRICTION OF OIL SALES BY A SINGLE SUPPLIER

The price of oil was kept high enough relative to (the low) costs to earn the majors healthy profits, yet low enough relative to other energy sources to make oil attractive. The long availability of plentiful oil had two major results: the industrial economies became dependent upon cheap energy, and oil became the most important source of that energy. The automobile conquered America; postwar reconstruction in Europe and Japan produced an industry dependent upon oil rather than coal. An insignificant source of energy at the start of this century, oil accounted for 45 percent of world energy supplies by the end of the sixties. Natural gas contributed almost 20 percent more, and the share of once-dominant coal had fallen to less than 30 percent.

The dominant position of the majors has deteriorated since the fifties. Competition has come from other companies (the "independents") that previously limited themselves to a share of the domestic American market but then went international, and from many companies (such as Italy's E.N.I. and France's C.F.P.) set up by national governments. In addition the producer countries have been increasingly successful at gaining control of the petroleum resources within their borders.

OPEC AND THE OIL CRISIS

The Organization of Petroleum Exporting Countries (OPEC) was founded in 1960 in response to a reduction in oil prices (and thus in producer country revenues) brought about by a glut in the market. Throughout the sixties OPEC had only a modest impact, but individual producer countries were becoming stronger relative to the majors, and membership in OPEC grew from the original five nations to thirteen. By 1977 OPEC accounted for about one-half of world oil production and two-thirds of world reserves. In 1970 the OPEC countries gained control of decisions on how much oil was to be produced within their borders and at what price it was to be offered for sale. Oil prices began to rise (see Table 2.2). This rise reflected in part the emerging power of OPEC, but it also reflected a fundamental change in market conditions that would itself also strengthen OPEC's position: world demand was overtaking supply. This is not to say that the world was suddenly confronted with the specter of an imminent depletion of its oil stocks. Rather, the rapid rise in demand—itself the product of decades of cheap oil—made it clear that supplies were not inexhaustible and would become tighter in the decades ahead. The realization of this future would cause prices to begin to rise immediately. (The pricing of an exhaustible resource is discussed below.) But in late 1973 and early 1974 OPEC was able to restrict supply and effect a fourfold rise in oil's price. This is shown in Figure 2.7, where a (rather modest) shift in OPEC's offer

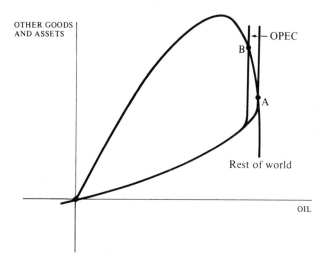

Figure 2.7. A Rise in the Price of Oil

Table 2.2.   PRICE OF CRUDE OIL (ARABIAN LIGHT) (DOLLARS PER BARREL)

					First Shock			*Second Shock*		
year	1960	1964	1969	1971	1973 (Aug)	1974	1977	1979	1980	1981
price	$1.91	1.74	1.51	2.49	3.03	11.65	13.66	23.50	28.00	32.00

curve causes equilibrium to shift from *A* to *B* and dramatically increases the price of oil. There are two key ingredients: the ability of OPEC to control supplies and the low elasticity of the rest of the world's offer curve.

Pricing an Exhaustible Resource. The cost of a barrel of oil includes its cost of production (extraction, processing, marketing, and so forth), as with any good. But oil is different in that once a barrel has been used up it no longer exists and can never be replaced: oil is an *exhaustible* resource. To see what effect this has on pricing, imagine that you have an oil well, that it costs you $2 to produce a barrel of oil from this well, and that you can sell the barrel for $32. You are trying to decide whether to sell one more barrel. If you sell the barrel you will be richer by $30, whereas if you do not, you will still have one more barrel of oil than otherwise. Thus your decision is basically whether to keep a part of your wealth in the form of oil or to put it into a financial form (this is exactly the decision that countries like Saudi Arabia must make on a grander scale). Your choice depends upon which form will give you the greater rate of return. The $30 can give you the going rate of interest if you save it. The oil in the ground earns no interest, of course, but if the price of oil is expected to be higher next year than now, the rate of return of holding on to the oil is just this price increase. Thus you will produce and sell the barrel of oil if the rate of interest exceeds the rate at which the price of oil is rising, and you will hold on to the oil in the opposite case. The general tendency in the oil market as a whole will be to supply oil to the world in amounts that will cause its price to rise at the rate of interest, so that oil will steadily become more expensive relative to other goods. This tendency reflects not a lack of competition, but the fact that the world's oil stock is being exhausted as it is used.   □

During the next five years the price of oil continued to rise, but at a modest rate and even declined, on balance, relative to the prices of other goods. But in 1979 the market tightened up, partly in response to the revolution in Iran, which choked off oil supplies from that country and engendered fears of other future disruptions, and OPEC was again able to dramatically raise the price (the second "oil shock"). Table 2.3 shows the

Table 2.3. TERMS OF TRADE (IMPORT UNIT VALUES ÷ EXPORT UNIT
VALUES) (1972 = 100)

	First Shock						*Second Shock*	
	1972	1973	1974	1975	1976	1977	1978	1979	1980
Oil Exporters	100	87	37	38	37	36	41	32	23
Other LDCs	100	93	100	111	108	104	109	111	112
DCs	100	101	114	111	112	114	110	114	120

SOURCE: IMF *Annual Report*

effects on indices of the terms of trade of blocs of countries. Note that the terms of trade of the oil exporters vary more dramatically than do those of the other blocs; this is because the former mainly trade oil for other goods, whereas the latter also have very much trade not involving oil. Note also the modest movements between the two shocks; indeed, the position of the oil exporters had deteriorated by 1978 relative to 1975. Finally note the different responses of the other LDCs and the DCs to the first shock: the latter's terms of trade deteriorated at once, whereas the former's displayed a delayed reaction. This is for two reasons, First, in the early seventies markets were tight for many primary products other than oil; this resulted in boom conditions because of the low elasticities in these markets. Since the other LDCs on balance exported primary products, this tended to offset the effect of more expensive oil on their terms of trade, until the primary-product boom ended. (The DCs, by contrast, were worse off on both counts.) Second, the LDCs buy oil directly from the oil exporters, of course, but they also buy it indirectly since the manufactures that they purchase from the DCs are produced by means of oil. This means that the LDCs suffer a delayed deterioration in their terms of trade when the DCs pass along their increased costs.

RESPONSE TO THE SHOCKS

By 1981 the oil market had loosened up and prices fell a bit. People began to speculate that OPEC was losing its grip. Two influences now seem to be at work.

The effect of higher oil prices in the importing countries. Individuals have responded to the high oil prices by conserving energy overall and by switching to non-oil sources of energy. Examples of the former are fuel-efficient automobiles and appliances, increased insulation, and so forth. Aggregate effects are reflected in Table 2.4. The three countries in the table are in different positions. Japan is the most vulnerable to increases in the oil price—99 percent of Japan's oil is imported. The United States imports less than half its oil, and Canada, the only country of the three to increase its energy intensity, has adequate supplies of its own (as well as a government policy of keeping energy prices low).

Table 2.4. Energy Consumed per Million Dollars of GNP (at 1979 U.S. prices), in Terms of Equivalent Barrels of Oil

Country	1960s Average	1979
U.S.	6,500	5,800
Canada	6,700	7,000
Japan	3,600	3,200

Other energy sources that are replacing oil include coal and (in some countries) nuclear power. Synthetic fuels do not yet supply a sizable portion of our energy needs. The basic conclusion is that although the demand for oil is very inelastic in the short run, as depicted in Figure 2.7, the long-run elasticity is quite a bit higher.

The difficulty of maintaining a cartel. As OPEC has restricted output, other oil supplies have been developed and OPEC's share has declined. The solidarity of the cartel has deteriorated, with the uniform price policy abandoned for years at a time and with two charter members (Iran and Iraq) even going to war. In addition to the problems inherent to any cartel—discussed in the previous section—OPEC has a distinctive problem of its own. Some members (notably Saudi Arabia) have vast reserves and shallow populations. The Saudis will be selling oil for a long time and so do not want to spoil the market for the long term by stimulating the large-scale development of synthetics. But other OPEC members, such as Iran and Nigeria, are selling off their oil rapidly and have large present-day revenue needs. It is in the interest of these countries to exploit to the full the short-run inelasticity of the demand for oil, regardless of the long-term consequences.

Speculation as to the future of the oil market is hazardous, especially in light of the political volatility of the Middle East. It may or may not be true that OPEC's days as an effective cartel are numbered. Indeed it may be possible that today's oil price is not greatly different from what it would be had OPEC never existed. But, nevertheless, the organization was able to unify and to take advantage of short-run inelasticity to capture for itself hundreds of billions of dollars during the seventies. This makes it history's most successful cartel.

8. "Elasticity Optimism" and "Elasticity Pessimism": Empirical Estimates

In our discussion of the LDCs, high elasticities were generally good and low elasticities bad. This is true of other applications as well. The classical theory is basically a story of adjustment through relative price changes. If elasticities are high, substantial quantity adjustments can be effected by moderate price movements and the process can be expected to work well; low elasticities spell trouble. Thus those who believe that elasticities are in fact high are called "elasticity optimists", and those who doubt this are called "elasticity pessimists." The former tend to have considerably more faith in the efficiency of the price system.

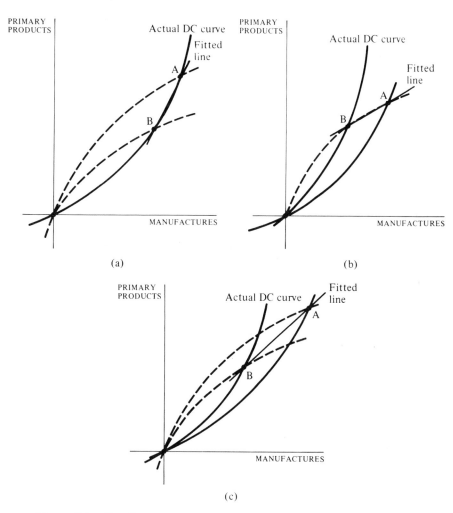

Figure 2.8. THE INDENTIFICATION PROBLEM

Economists have made many attempts to measure trade elasticities. At first the estimates were low and much pessimism was generated. But more careful methodology has subsequently led to higher estimates.

There are many reasons why good estimates are hard to come by. Satisfactory data are a big problem. Another can be illustrated by Figure 2.8. Suppose the economist wishes to estimate the shape of the DCs' offer curve. She will have a set of observations of actual prices and quantities traded at various times; points *A* and *B* in each panel represent two such observations. The natural way to proceed is to fit a curve to the data, for example, to connect *A* and *B* in this case. This will be appropriate if the movement from *A* to *B* (and to the other observations) was in fact due to a shift of the LDCs' offer curve, as depicted in panel (a). But if the data were in fact generated by shifts of the DCs' offer curve, as in (b), or, more likely, by shifts of both curves, as in (c), the procedure will not work. This is known as the *identification problem*. The way to deal with it is to use additional information about the determinants of the offer curves to estimate both simultaneously. (You will perhaps think of yet another problem. We have assumed that the data are observations of equilibrium positions—intersections of the curves. If the observations are in fact of transition between equilibria they need not lie on either curve.)

Table 2.5. ESTIMATES OF LONG-RUN PRICE ELASTICITIES OF
AGGREGATE IMPORTS

Country	Number of Estimates	Range of Estimated Values	'Best' Estimate of Home Demand	'Best' Estimate of Rest-of-World's Demand
United States	21	.41–3.00	1.66	1.41
Canada	7	.60–1.59	1.30	.79
Japan	5	.77–1.47	.78	1.25
France	6	.39–1.53	1.08	1.31
West Germany	8	.24–1.48	.88	1.11

SOURCE: Stern, Francis, and Schumacher, *Price Elasticities in International Trade*

Table 2.6. PRICE ELASTICITIES FOR U.S. IMPORTS OF SELECTED
COMMODITY GROUPS

Crude Materials	.18
Crude Foodstuffs	.21
Semimanufactures	1.83
Finished Manufactures	4.05

SOURCE: *Houthakker, H.S. and S.P. Magee, "Income and Price Elasticities in World Trade"*

Table 2.5 provides a summary of the estimates obtained by econo-mists of import elasticities of some major countries. For each country, the 'best' estimate of the home elasticity of import demand plus that of the rest of the world sum to more than unity. Table 2.6 shows some estimated price elasticities for the U.S. demand for imports of specific commodity groups. Note the low primary-product elasticities.

9. Summary

1. A demand is by its very nature a supply of something else of equal value. This leads to Walras's Law: the total value of excess demand in all markets always equals zero.

2. An offer curve shows the amount of exports a country is hypothetically willing to supply for each quantity of imports.

3. The picture of international equilibrium as the intersection of the home and foreign offer curves illustrates Mill's *law of reciprocal demand:* the relative international price will be determined at that level at which the domestic demand for imports and (equal valued) supply of exports simultaneously equal the foreign supply of exports and demand for imports.

4. The elasticity of an offer curve measures the responsiveness of quantities to price changes. High elasticities usually imply a smoothly functioning price sys-tem, whereas low elasticities spell trouble.

5. The LDCs are generally thought to have, and to face, low elasticities, because of the nature of their exchange with the DCs of primary products for manufactures. This is the source of many LDC policy issues.

6. Thus far we have examined two ideas, comparative advantage and recip-rocal demand, which suffice to give answers to the first two of the three questions posed at the beginning of Part One: What explains the pattern of trade? What are its welfare implications? The pure theory of trade up to this point was essentially developed by the nineteenth-century English economists and is accordingly fre-quently referred to as the Classical Theory. The next two chapters deal with twentieth-century developments and are addressed to the remaining question with which we began: what are the domestic implications of international trade?

10. *Exploring Further:* How to Derive an Offer Curve

An economy's offer curve depends upon all conditions of production and consumption in that country. This section shows how the offer curve can be explicitly derived from the production possibility frontier and com-munity indifference curves. We do this in two steps, using a technique developed by the Nobel laureate James Meade, of Cambridge University.

TRADE INDIFFERENCE CURVES

First we derive the country's trade indifference curves, showing the community's tastes with regard to trading opportunities. Figure 2.9 has the

same axes as Figure 2.1. France's community indifference curves are drawn
in the SE quadrant of the figure—curves *I* and *II* are simply curves *I* and *II*
in Figure 1.10(a) rotated 90° degrees clockwise (curve *I* in Figure 2.9 shows
all combinations of wine and machines the French regard as equivalent to
OD machines plus *DC* wine). *AHJ* is the French production possibility
frontier—the same frontier as in Figure 1.10(a), but turned upside down.
Now slide the production possibility frontier *AHJ* along the indifference
curve *I*, keeping the two curves tangent, as in the figure. Then the corner *A*
traces out the curve U_I. This curve shows possible trades France regards as
equivalent.

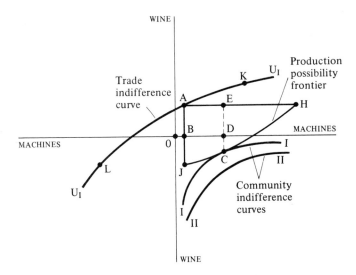

Figure 2.9.   DERIVATION OF TRADE INDIFFERENCE CURVES

Point *A*, for example, indicates machine imports of *OB* and wine
exports of *AB*. If France trades in this way, the country will also produce
AE machines and *EC* wine, thereby consuming *OD* (= *AE* + *OB*) machines and *DC* (= *EC* − *AB*) wine. Thus France consumes as indicated by
C and is on the community indifference curve *I*. The slope of U_I at *A*
necessarily equals the common slope of *HJ* and *I* at *C*. The trade indifference curve U_I shows all trades that enable France to consume on the indifference curve *I;* the French regard the trades indicated by points *L* and
K as neither better nor worse than *A*. A distinct trade indifference curve
corresponds to each community indifference curve. For example, sliding
AHJ along *II* would trace out a curve U_{II}, and so forth. All such trade
indifference curves are positively sloped, and moving in a southeasterly
direction moves us onto better curves.

THE OFFER CURVE

We now use France's trade indifference curves to derive her offer curve. Figure 2.10 has the same axes as before, and suppose that France's trade indifference curves have been traced out. Three such curves are drawn: U_A, U_I, and U_{II}. Recall that the slope of a straight line through the origin indicates the relative price of machines in terms of wine. Thus the straight line through O and A, for example, shows all trades for which the wine traded is equal in value to the machines traded if $p = AE/OE$. At that price, the French will choose the trade on this straight line that puts them on the highest trade indifference curve (that is, the curve that is farthest to the southeast). This is at point A, where trade indifference curve U_I is tangent to the straight line OA. Thus A must be on France's offer curve, because it will trade at A when $p = AE/OE$. The entire offer curve can then be found by rotating this straight line through the origin and tracing out its points of tangency with the trade indifference curves. This generates the graph $BAOCD$: France's offer curve.

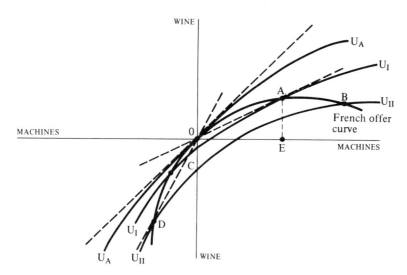

Figure 2.10. DERIVATION OF THE FRENCH OFFER CURVE

INCOME AND SUBSTITUTION EFFECTS

We can use the relation between the offer curve and trade indifference curves to demonstrate the role of income and substitution effects. France's offer curve is the graph through points O, A, and B in Figure 2.11. If $p = AE/OE$, France trades at A, on the trade indifference curve U_A. From our construction, we know that, at A, U_A must be tangent to the straight line OA. If France's terms of trade improve to BD/OD, France will change its trad-

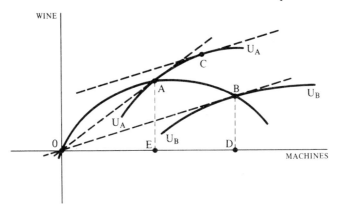

Figure 2.11. INCOME AND SUBSTITUTION EFFECTS

ing to B, on the trade indifference curve U_B. The movement from A to B can be decomposed into income and substitution effects as follows. Shift the straight line OB vertically upward until it is just tangent to U_A; this happens at point C. The movement from A to C shows the substitution effect: how the French trading changes if the terms of trade alter but *real* income is held fixed, in the sense that France is allowed to remain on U_A. The movement from C to B is the income effect: how French trading changes if its budget line improves at constant terms of trade (the slope of U_A at C equals the slope of U_B at B). Because of the curvature of the trade indifference curves, the substitution effect necessarily increases both imports and exports. But the impact of the income effect depends upon the relative positions of U_A and U_B.

THE GEOMETRY OF INTERNATIONAL EQUILIBRIUM

We can derive trade indifference curves and an offer curve for Germany, as we did for France, from Germany's production possibility frontier and indifference curves. But it is convenient to reverse the roles of the axes. Thus Germany's indifference curves are drawn in the northwest quadrant. This is done in Figure 2.12, which shows full international equilibrium in its full geometric glory.

France's offer curve is OAF and Germany's is OAG. They intersect at A, so that $p = AE/OE (= OE'/E'A)$, and France is on the trade indifference curve U_F while Germany is on the trade indifference curve U_G. France produces AB machines and imports OE from Germany, consuming OD. Germany produces $C'B'$ machines, exporting $D'B' (= OE)$ to France and consuming $C'D'$ itself. (Describe what the two countries do with wine.) France consumes at C on indifference curve I, and Germany consumes at C' on I'.

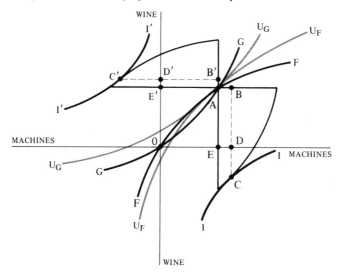

Figure 2.12. FULL INTERNATIONAL EQUILIBRIUM

PROBLEMS

2.26 Show geometrically that the income effect is very small near the origin on the offer curve.

2.27 Suppose that in England 5 units of labor are required to produce either a bolt of cloth or a cask of wine, that England has 100 units of labor, and that each English resident always consumes one cask of wine for each bolt of cloth. Use the techniques of this section to derive England's offer curve.

2.28 If you know what a Giffen good is, show how Figure 2.11 looks if wine is such a good. If machinery is a Giffen good.

2.29 Using trade indifference curves and offer curves, show that:
a free trade is always better for a country than autarky;
b free trade is efficient in the sense that it is impossible to make one country better off without harming the other; and
c limited trade may be better than, or worse than, free trade for a single country.

2.30 Draw and explain Figure 2.12 with equilibrium in the SW quadrant.

11. *Exploring Further:* Stability of International Equilibrium

Section 3 showed how international equilibrium was determined by the intersection of offer curves. Only at this equilibrium will demand equal supply in both markets. Thus the international economy can settle down at no other place. But this is not the same as saying that the economy must

actually settle down there. Suppose, for example, that in Figure 2.13 the
world relative price is as indicated by the line *OBC*. Then there will be a
world excess demand for machines and a world excess supply of wine. The
world must either eventually move to point *A* or remain indefinitely in flux.
But nothing has been said to indicate which. The problem can be posed
somewhat differently. Suppose the world is in equilibrium. We all know,
however, that the economy is never frozen in position, forever repeating
itself. Rather, it is subject to frequent shocks and disturbances, the curves
will sometimes shift, and so on. This leads to the following question: will a
deviation from equilibrium cause the economy to automatically return
there, so that the economy is in fact nearly always at or near equilibrium, or
will the deviation feed upon itself, causing the economy to move farther and
farther away from *A?*

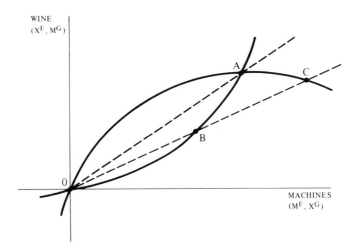

Figure 2.13. EQUILIBRIUM AND DISEQUILIBRIUM PRICES

An equilibrium is said to be *stable* if the economy will automatically
return there after a slight deviation. Otherwise the equilibrium is unstable.
A common physical analogy is useful. A bowl can hold an egg in two
distinct ways. Either you can rest the egg at the bottom inside the bowl, or,
with much more skill and patience, you can balance the egg on top of an
overturned bowl. Both situations represent equilibrium, but a gentle flick of
the finger reveals that while the first is stable, the second is not.

It should be clear that the question of stability is important. It does us
no good to determine the equilibrium world price if that price will never be
attained. And any analysis of international economic problems based on
the assumption that world markets are in equilibrium is not worth much if
that equilibrium is unstable.

But how can we tell whether an equilibrium is stable or not? At this point we cannot say, because stability depends upon how markets behave out of equilibrium, and we have not investigated this. Something must be added to our present equipment. There is an appealing assumption about market behavior that we can add. Suppose that the wine market has excess demand. Then at the going price all sellers can find more than enough buyers, but some buyers will inevitably be disappointed. We would certainly expect to see the price of wine rise. We are therefore tempted to make the following assumption:

Disequilibrium Hypothesis: *If a market is in excess demand, price will be rising and if in excess supply, price will be falling.*

Note this disequilibrium hypothesis is compatible with Walras's Law. If wine is in excess demand so that its price is rising, then by Walras's Law the machine market is in excess supply so that its price is falling, and a rise in the relative price of wine is the same thing as a fall in the relative price of machinery.

Armed with this assumption it is easy to argue that the equilibrium depicted by point A in Figure 2.13 is in fact stable. Suppose something were to cause p to fall below its equilibrium value, say to that implied by OBC. Then there is an excess demand for machines and an excess supply of wine. By our disequilibrium hypothesis this will cause p to rise, that is, to return toward equilibrium. Verify that if p were pushed above its equilibrium value, the assumption would imply that p must fall back down.

It is important to realize that the hypothesis does not constitute an assumption that markets are stable. This is illustrated in Figure 2.14. Here there are three possible international equilibria represented by A, B, and C. It is easy to show, just as above, that A and C are stable. But B is not. Suppose, for example, that the world economy is initially at B and that some shock causes p to fall, say to the value determined by ODE. Then the demand for imports indicated by D falls short of the foreign supply of exports indicated by E, that is, there is a world excess supply of imports. Then by our assumption p must fall, thus moving even further away from equilibrium. (To test yourself, examine the stability of A, B, and C by looking at the X market instead.)

What is it that determines whether a market is stable or not? In view of our disequilibrium hypothesis a market will be stable if *a fall in price below equilibrium calls forth an excess demand.* For then the hypothesis implies that the price will be forced back up.

Let us return to the example of France and Germany and look at the machine market. World excess demand for machines is $M^F - X^G$, the excess of French demand over German supply. Then the market will be stable if a fall in p causes M^F to rise relative to X^G. Now suppose p falls by

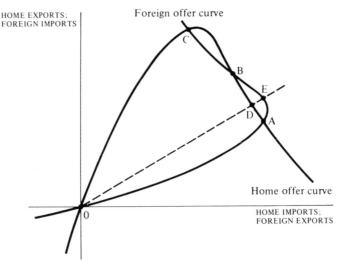

Figure 2.14. Unstable International Equilibrium

1 percent. Then M^F rises by e^F percent and X^G *falls* by f^G percent (because a fall in p is a *worsening* of the German terms of trade). Thus the world excess demand for machines increases by $e^F - (-f^G) = e^F + f^G = e^F + e^G - 1$ percent. Stability requires that it rise rather than fall, that is, that $e^F + e^G > 1$. Thus if we accept the disequilibrium hypothesis, an international equilibrium will be stable if the elasticities of the two offer curves sum to more than one. In Figure 2.14, for example, this condition is met at both A and C, where in each case at least one of the curves is actually elastic, whereas at B both are very inelastic.

The condition $e^F + e^G > 1$ is known as the Marshall-Lerner condition, after the great English economist Alfred Marshall (1842–1924), who developed the offer curve technique in the last century, and twentieth-century economist Abba Lerner, who also contributed to trade theory. Once again we find that high elasticities are good, and low elasticities bad. Note that, although low elasticities were important in the issues discussed in sections 6 and 7, the diagrams we used all satisfied the Marshall-Lerner condition.

PROBLEMS

2.31 Express the Marshall-Lerner condition in terms of the f's; the g's.

2.32 What can you say about the stability of an equilibrium in which one of the countries has the offer curve you derived in Problem **2.8***?

2.33 Suppose the disequilibrium hypothesis of this section is *not* true and that an equilibrium can be stable even if the Marshall-Lerner condition fails. Draw Figures 2.5 and 2.7 with the condition violated. How does this effect the discussion of policy issuses in sections 6 and 7?

2.34 Suppose that in Problem **2.9*** each Portuguese instead always consumes one cask of wine with each two bolts of cloth. Derive the Portuguese offer curve. Suppose that England has the offer curve of Problem **2.8***. For what sizes of Portuguese and British labor forces does an unstable equilibrium exist?

2.35* Derive the Marshall-Lerner condition algebraically. Those familiar with calculus should use it to formulate a precise definition of e and to derive the condition. (You can check your answer by reading section A.3 of Appendix I.)

SUGGESTED READING

Balassa, B. et al. *The Structure of Protection in Developing Countries.* Baltimore: Johns Hopkins University Press, 1971. Empirical studies and assessment of policies.

Behrman, J. N. *International Economic Order and Commodity Agreements.* Reading: Addison-Wesley, 1978.

Bhagwati, J. N., ed. *The New International Economic Order: The North-South Debate.* Cambridge: M. I. T. Press, 1977.

Bhagwati, J. N. and Srinivassan, T. N. "Trade Policy and Development." In *International Economic Policy.* Edited by R. Dornbusch and J. Frenkel. Baltimore: Johns Hopkins University Press, 1979. A useful survey.

Dixit, A. K. and Norman, V. *Theory of International Trade.* London: Cambridge University Press, 1980. See chapters 2, 3, and 5 for an advanced treatment.

Houthakker, H. S. and Magee, S. P. "Income and Price Elasticities in World Trade." *Review of Economics and Statistics* 2, 1969.

Jones, R. W. "Stability Conditions in International Trade: A General Equilibrium Analysis." *International Economic Review* 2, 1961. Contains a detailed algebraic treatment of elasticity.

Krueger, A. *Foreign Trade Regimes and Economic Development: Liberalization Attempts and Consequences.* Cambridge: Ballinger, 1978. An assessment of LDC policies; part of a large project.

Leamer, E. and Stern, R. M. *Quantitative International Economics.* Boston: Allyn and Bacon, 1970. See chapters 2, 3, 6, and 7 for a treatment of problems in empirical work.

Marshall, A. *Pure Theory of Foreign Trade.* London: London School of Economics and Political Science, 1930. The first (1879), and still one of the best, offer-curve treatments.

Meade, J. E. *A Geometry of International Trade.* London: George Allen and Unwin, 1952. A thorough treatment of the geometry of offer curves.

Meier, G. M. *The International Economics of Development.* New York: Harper and Row, 1968. Trade problems of the LDCs.

Mill, J. S. *Principles of Political Economy.* Edited by W. J. Ashley. London: Longman, 1909. Contains a statement of Mill's theory of international values.

Newbery, D. and Stiglitz, J. *The Theory of Commodity Price Stabilization.* Oxford: Oxford University Press, 1981. A recent and insightful theoretical approach.

Odell, P. R. *Oil and World Power.* 5th ed. Harmondsworth: Penguin, 1979.

Stern, R. M.; Francis, J.; and Schumacher, B. *Price Elasticities in International Trade.* London: Macmillan, 1976. A comprehensive bibliography of estimates of price elasticities from 1960–1975.

Chapter 3

The Basis of Comparative Advantage

"Generally, abundant factors are relatively cheap, scanty factors
are relatively dear, in each region. Commodities requiring for
their production much of the former and little of the latter are
exported in exchange for goods that call for factors in the opposite proportions. Thus indirectly, factors in abundant supply are
exported and factors in scanty supply are imported." —B. OHLIN

THE FIRST two chapters developed two concepts, comparative advantage
and reciprocal demand, to explain the classical theory of international trade
and to answer the first two of the three questions posed at the outset. We
now seek to uncover the effect of trade upon the domestic allocation of
resources and distribution of income.

In order to do this we must take a closer look at the internal workings
of the economy. Up to now we have taken the production possibility frontier as given. True, in the simple Ricardian model different marginal rates
of transformation were a consequence of different labor productivities. But
this was mainly an illustration, and the different productivities were not
themselves explained. We now probe below the surface to discover why
production possibility frontiers have the slopes they do. More generally still,
we wish to explain the pattern of comparative advantage.

This is difficult because there are obviously many different reasons for
countries to trade. Anyone can see that tropical countries have a comparative advantage over temperate zones in tropical fruits relative to fir products

because of climate. Geographical proximity plays a role: New England and New York are closer to much of Canada than to most of the United States, and trading patterns have historically been sensitive to the location of waterways and to changes in transportion. As we saw in section 8 of Chapter 1, tastes can help to determine comparative advantage. In this chapter we first focus on one particular explanation: factor endowments. The United States, for example, is highly endowed with physical capital—factories, equipment, and so forth—whereas India relies much more on labor power. The importance of capital relative to labor in most other countries is somewhere in between, with Western Europe closer to the U.S. end of the scale, and the less developed world closer to the Indian. It is precisely on these differences that we shall focus.

The theory we shall examine was advanced in the first half of this century and is frequently referred to as the Heckscher-Ohlin theory, after the Swedish economists Eli Heckscher and Bertil Ohlin, who developed it. The theory has been refined and elaborated by many economists, a process that still continues. This theory is also sometimes called the modern theory of international trade, to distinguish it from the classical theory, of which it is a logical extension.

With all the conceivable explanations of comparative advantage, why focus on this particular one? There are a number of reasons. First, different factor endowments seem to be one of the more important (if not the most important) explanations, although the extent to which this is true is still a point of lively debate among economists (and one to which we shall return). Second, this particular approach will link international trade to the domestic allocation of resources and distribution of income. Also a country's factor endowment is itself determined in part by economic phenomena: the present capital stock is determined by past behavior, and the present state of the economy will determine what the future capital stock will be. Thus it becomes possible to examine the relationships between international trade and economic development and growth and between international trade and international capital movements. Finally, the factor endowments approach can be made conceptually general enough to include many other possible explanations. That is, we can regard climate, technical secrets, patents, location, and so forth as themselves factors of production. We can do this either by complicating our analysis with a very large number of factors or by defining "capital" and "labor" in a very general fashion. Of course the further we pursue this road, the more cumbersome or vague our conclusions become and the more difficult they are to apply to real situations. A theory that explains everything really explains nothing at all.

The factor-endowments approach is a powerful and useful one. Nevertheless, it is far less general than either of the other two concepts we have developed.

ELI. F. HECKSCHER (1879–1952)

The Swedish economist Eli Heckscher is probably best known to English-speaking economists for his book *Mercantilism,* a study of the economic doctrine that preceded classical thought and viewed the power of the nation-state as a policy objective. Much of Heckscher's work was devoted to a monumental study of Swedish economic history, but he also devoloped the essentials of the factor-endowments theory of international trade in a short article published in Swedish in 1919 and translated into English thirty years later.

BERTIL OHLIN (1899–1979)

Heckscher's follower Bertil Ohlin developed and elaborated the factor-endowments theory and was responsible, through his writings, for the wide exposure that the theory received, beginning in the thirties. In addition to holding a professorship at Stockholm, Ohlin was a major Swedish political figure. He served in the Riksdag (Sweden's parliament), headed the Liberal party for almost a quarter of a century, and was Minister of Trade during the Second World War. In 1979 Ohlin was awarded (jointly with James Meade of England) a Nobel prize for his work in international economic theory.

1. The Heckscher-Ohlin-Samuelson Model

The vehicle we shall use for presenting our theory is called the Heckscher-Ohlin-Samuelson model. (Paul Samuelson of M.I.T. was instrumental in developing the structure of this model.) As in the previous chapters, suppose there are two countries—called France and Germany respectively—and two goods, wine and machines.

THE ASSUMPTIONS

The Heckscher-Ohlin-Samuelson model consist of four basic assumptions.

1. There are two countries, two goods, and two factors of production (call them capital and labor).

We need at least two factors in order to study the role of relative factor endowments; limiting the number to two makes the model as simple as possible.

2. The two factors are available in fixed amounts in each of the two countries, are fully mobile between industries within each country, but are immobile between countries; all markets have free and perfect competition.

This assumption establishes the difference between international trade and domestic trade, just as in the classical theory.

3. The two countries are alike in every respect except for their endowments of the two factors. In particular, the technologies for producing wine and machines are available to both countries, and they have identical tastes in the sense that if they face identical prices for wine and machines they will consume them in identical proportions.

The purpose of this assumption is to ensure that our conclusions reflect only differences in factor endowments and not a mish-mash of many causes.

4. For each of the two goods there is a given technology (available to both countries) indicating how capital and labor can be combined to produce output. This technology possesses constant returns to scale (varying both capital and labor in the same proportion will vary output in that proportion).

These assumptions are made for two distinct reasons. Assumptions 1, 2, and 4 try to make the theory as simple as possible. If they do not correspond to reality, the arguments that follow from them may have to be made more complex, but the basic idea of the factor-endowments basis of comparative advantage will not be challenged. Assumption 3, on the other hand, ensures that our theory reflects only the latter, and so its realism is connected to the basic idea that trade is due to different factor endowments. This assumption can be defended directly. Technology is really just knowledge, which is not constrained by national boundaries; tastes for broad aggregates should reflect basic human needs rather than national peculiarities. But whether these arguments are relevant at an operational level is an empirical question. We make assumption 3 simply to focus on the effects of different factor endowments.

SOME DEFINITIONS

According to assumption 3 the only difference between France and Germany is in their endowments of capital and labor. A little jargon is appropriate to describe this difference. Denote the French endowments of capital and labor by K^F and L^F and the German by K^G and L^G. We shall use the following definition.

KEY CONCEPT

France is said to be *capital abundant* relative to labor compared to Germany if:

$$K^F/L^F > K^G/L^G.$$

Notice that this definition has a double-barreled relativity as does that of comparative advantage, in Chapter 1. It is interchangeable with the following:

Germany is *labor abundant* relative to capital compared to France if

$$L^G/K^G > L^F/K^F.$$

For concreteness we shall call the capital-abundant country France and the labor-abundant country Germany.

In each country wine firms and machine firms employ labor and capital to produce their products. The wages and rents they pay for these factors constitute the firms' production costs. All wine and machine firms in the same country must pay the same wages and rents, since they compete with each other in factor markets. But since the two goods are different, they will not use capital and labor in equal proportions. Thus we need another definition.

KEY CONCEPT

The wine industry is said to be *capital intensive* relative to labor compared to the machine industry if, at identical wages and rents, the wine industry employs more capital per worker than does the machine industry.

This definition also has the by-now-familiar double-barreled relativity and so is completely equivalent to the following:

Machines are labor intensive *relative to capital compared to wine if, at identical wages and rents, the machine industry employs more workers per unit of capital than does the wine industry.*

We shall assume that wine is always the capital-intensive industry and that machinery is the labor-intensive industry.

These are the two definitions suggested by the assumptions of the model. Factor *abundance* classifies the two countries since, by assumption 3, they differ in no other respect. Factor *intensity* classifies the two industries; it applies to both countries because they share the same technology.

PROBLEMS

3.1 Recall the discussion of U.S. trade patterns in section 11 of Chapter 1. Try to explain the apparent U.S. comparative advantage in terms of relative factor endowments (do not confine yourself to capital and labor; try to think of other relevant factors). Do the same for trade between the DCs and LDCs.

3.2 Suppose that England has 100 workers and 160 units of capital, whereas Portugal has 100 workers and 70 units of capital. Also suppose that each cask of wine requires 4 workers and 1 unit of capital to produce, whereas each bolt of cloth requires 5 units of capital and 2 workers. Apply the definitions of factor abundance and factor intensity.

3.3 What do you think is true regarding the relative factor abundance of the following countries: United States, France, Israel, Taiwan? The relative factor intensity of the following industries (in the United States): steel, wheat, research, street cleaning, teaching?

2. A Basic Relationship

In each country capital and labor are hired to produce outputs, and firms use no other inputs. Firms must pay a wage in order to hire labor and a rent in order to hire capital. Thus the wage and the rent in a country fully determine the costs of producing wine and machines in that country. Consider a change in relative factor prices, say an increase in the wage with the rent remaining constant. This increases costs in both industries. But the two industries will not be affected the same way. Since the machine industry is labor intensive, its costs will be increased proportionally more than costs in the wine industry, where labor is not as important. A rise in the wage relative to the rent increases the cost of the labor-intensive good (machines) relative to that of the capital-intensive good (wine). This relation is shown in Figure 3.1. (Actually we can say more, but we postpone until section 4 a detailed discussion of the relation between relative factor prices and relative commodity costs.)

Three features of this curve deserve emphasis. First, it is a *technological relationship;* its slope depends on relative factor intensities.

Second, because the curve is a technological relationship, and because the two countries have the same technology, the curve applies to *both* countries. Since factors are not internationally mobile and French labor does not compete with German labor, wages and rents in France need not

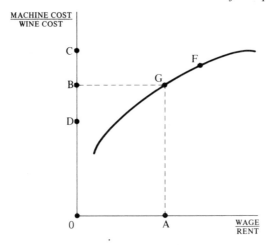

Figure 3.1. RELATIVE FACTOR PRICES AND RELATIVE COSTS

equal those in Germany. Thus the two countries may be at different points
on the curve; for example, France could be at *F* in Figure 3.1 and Germany
at *G*. But both countries must be somewhere on the *same curve* as long as
they have the same technology.

Finally, there is the relation between the costs of machines and wine
and the prices of these goods. If a good is produced in a country, its price
must equal its cost in long-run equilibrium: if cost exceeds price, no one will
wish to produce it and the industry will close down; if price exceeds cost, the
profit will induce competition forcing the two into equality. Thus if the
wage-rental ratio in Germany equals *OA* in figure 3.1, and if wine and
machines are both produced in Germany, then *OB* must equal the relative
price of machines in terms of wine. But if a good is not actually produced,
cost could exceed price (the reason, after all, for not producing it). Thus if
Germany is specialized to wine, the relative price of machines in terms of
wine could equal *OD*, for example. Or if Germany is specialized to machinery, the relative price could equal, say, *OC*.

PROBLEMS

3.4 Draw Figure 3.1 in the case where machine production is capital intensive. What would the curve look like if, by a fluke of nature, machines and wine
used exactly the same technique of production?

3.5 Derive a curve like that in Figure 3.1 if each cask of wine requires 4
workers and 1 unit of capital to produce and each bolt of cloth requires 2 workers
and 5 units of capital. What could you conclude about English production if the
wage and the rent in England both equaled 1 and the price of cloth in terms of wine
was 2?

3.6 Suppose that, as a result of some innovation, it is now possible to produce machines with fewer workers per unit of capital than before. No change occurs in wine technology. What is the effect on the curve in Figure 3.1?

3.7* What would the curve in Figure 3.1 look like if machines were relatively capital intensive at low wage-rental ratios but relatively labor intensive at high wage-rental ratios, with wine and machines using exactly the same technique at some intermediate wage-rental ratio? What circumstances could cause two industries to have this relation?

3. The Heckscher-Ohlin Theory: Comparative Advantage and Factor Prices

The model described in section 1 is used to develop four basic propositions, all of which have frightening names. We discuss two of them in this section and two in the next.

THE HECKSCHER-OHLIN THEOREM

This proposition explains the pattern of comparative advantage in terms of factor endowments.

> *A country has a comparative advantage in the good that is relatively intensive in the country's relatively abundant factor.*

Thus in the present case France will have a comparative advantage in wine and Germany in machines. Note that the theorem is consistent with the definitions of the last section: it will not claim that both countries have a comparative advantage in the same good.

Once the Heckscher-Ohlin theorem tells us the pattern of comparative advantage, we can apply the results of the previous chapters: France will export wine to Germany in exchange for machines, and so forth.

The Heckscher-Ohlin theorem is easily proved using the curve discussed in the previous section and reproduced in Figure 3.2. Recall that the curve applies to both countries. Suppose that France and Germany are both in autarky. The relative labor abundance of Germany will be reflected in a lower autarkic wage-rental ratio (equivalently, the relative capital abundance of France will be reflected in a lower rental-wage ratio, that is, a higher wage-rental ratio). This is shown in Figure 3.2, where *OG* denotes Germany's autarkic wage-rental ratio and *OF* denotes France's. In autarky each country must produce both goods for itself, so *OB* denotes the German autarkic price of machines in terms of wine, and *OA* the French autarkic price. The relative autarkic price of machinery is higher in France than Germany: Germany has a comparative advantage in machines, and France in wine.

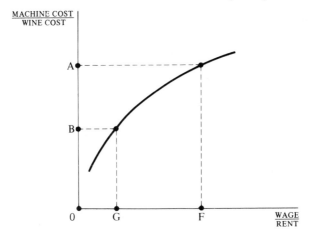

Figure 3.2.   THE HECKSCHER-OHLIN THEOREM

Figure 3.3 shows the same production possibility frontiers for France and Germany as does Figure 1.6. France is the relatively capital-abundant country and therefore is better equipped to produce the capital-intensive good, wine. This is reflected in the figure by the generally steeper slope of France's curve. (The next section will demonstrate why this is so.) Since the two countries are assumed to have identical tastes, autarkic equilibrium in France (at *A*) will feature a steeper slope than autarkic equilibrium in Germany (at *B*). Thus, without trade, wine is relatively cheaper in terms of machines in France than in Germany.

The greater the dissimilarity in French and German relative factor endowments, the greater the dissimilarity in their production possibility frontiers. If the two countries had identical endowments of capital per worker, their frontiers would have identical shapes—the frontier of the larger country would be simply a blow-up of that of the smaller country. If,

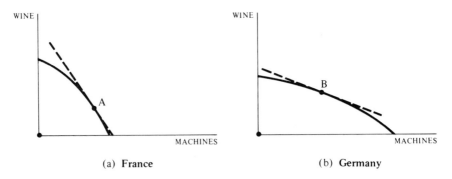

Figure 3.3.   PRODUCTION POSSIBILITY FRONTIERS

on the other hand, France's relative capital abundance exceeded Germany's by enough, each point on France's frontier would have a steeper slope than every point on Germany's (as was true of Figure 1.5). In this case, you will recall, free trade must cause at least one country to specialize completely. This bring us to the second basic proposition.

THE FACTOR-PRICE EQUALIZATION THEOREM

Free international trade between two countries will cause factor prices in the countries to become more equal. If both countries continue to produce both goods with free trade, their factor prices will actually be equal.

Thus if France and Germany each produce both wine and machines while freely trading, the French wage will equal the German and the French rental will also equal the German. This proposition can be proved with the aid of Figure 3.4. Suppose that German and French autarkic wage-rental ratios equal *OG* and *OF* respectively, so that relative autarkic prices in Germany and France equal *OB* and *OA*. If these countries engage in free trade, world prices must be somewhere between the autarkic prices, say equal to *OC*. If each country produces both goods, then *OC* also equals relative costs in both countries, and *OH* must therefore equal the wage-rental ratio in both France and Germany. Since relative factor prices are therefore equal, absolute factor prices must be equal also. Otherwise one country would have uniformly higher factor prices than the other, and so costs—and thus prices—could not be the same.

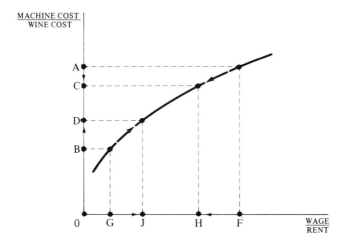

Figure 3.4. Factor Price Equalization

If either country specializes, factor prices need not be completely equalized because costs need not equal international prices and therefore each other. Suppose, for example, that Germany specializes to machines while France produces both goods. Then French costs equal relative prices, *OC*, but German costs could be somewhat less, say equal to *OD*. Then the German wage-rental ratio equals *OJ* while the French equals *OH*. Factor prices are not completely equalized by trade, but they are more nearly equal than they would be in autarky.

The factor-price equalization theorem reflects the basic presumption of the Heckscher-Ohlin approach: trade is due to different factor endowments because factors cannot be moved from country to country. Suppose that France and Germany freely trade and that both countries produce both goods so that their factor prices are equalized. If some revolutionary development were to enable labor and capital to move freely between countries, just as they can move within a country, nothing would happen! With equal factor prices, no factor has any incentive to move. Free trade has been a complete substitute for international factor mobility. If specialization prevents complete factor-price equalization, trade in goods is only a partial substitute for factor mobility.

PROBLEMS

3.8 Refine your answers to Problem **3.1** in light of the discussion of this section.

3.9 Agricultural trade between the United States and Europe is not free. The yield per acre on a French farm is typically much higher than on an American farm devoted to the same crop. Does this indicate relative American inefficiency or backwardness? Explain in terms of the theory. What would you expect to be true of relative French and American prices of the relevant factors? What do you think would be the effect of a movement to free trade?

3.10 Suppose that when each cask of wine produced requires 4 labor units and 1 capital unit and each bolt of cloth requires 2 and 5 units respectively of labor and capital, the wage and the rent each equal 100. What is the cost of wine and cloth? Suppose the wage and the rent both increase to 110. By what percentage have they risen? What are the new costs of the two goods, and by what percentages have they changed? Answer the same questions if instead the wage increases from 100 to 120 and the rent from 100 to 105. If instead the wage falls from 100 to 90 while the rent rises from 100 to 120.

3.11* Discuss in detail the Heckscher-Ohlin and the factor-price equalization theorems in the context of Problem **3.7***.

3.12* Suppose that we retain all of the assumptions of the Heckscher-Ohlin-Samuelson model, *except* that we assume that all French citizens have a much greater relative preference for wine consumption than all German citizens (who therefore have a much greater relative preference for machine consumption). How is the Heckscher-Ohlin theorem affected?

4. The Heckscher-Ohlin Theory: Income Distribution and Growth

We now discuss the remaining two of the four basic propositions of the Heckscher-Ohlin theory.

THE STOLPER-SAMUELSON THEOREM

This proposition links international trade to the domestic distribution of income. The curve in Figures 3.1, 3.2, and 3.4 implies that if both goods are produced, an increase in the relative price of the labor-intensive good (machines) increases the wage relative to the rent, so that labor's income rises relative to capital's. But in 1941 an even stronger result was obtained by Paul Samuelson and Wolfgang Stolper, now at the University of Michigan.

> *An increase in the relative price of the labor intensive good will increase the wage rate relative to both commodity prices and reduce the rent relative to both commodity prices.*

If an increase in the relative price of machines raises the wage-rental ratio, laborers gain relative to capitalists. But they need not thereby gain absolutely: if the wage rises less than the price of machinery, any worker who spends his income mainly on machines will be worse off in spite of the wage increase. The theorem asserts that this will not happen. Wages rise relative to *both* commodity prices, so workers are better off no matter how they spend their incomes; rents fall relative to both commodity prices, so capitalists are unambiguously worse off.

By combining this result with the Heckscher-Ohlin theorem, we can see how trade affects domestic income distribution. A country has a comparative advantage in the good intensive to its relatively abundant factor. Free trade will increase the relative price of that good and so, by the Stolper-Samuelson theorem, increase the real income of the relatively abundant factor and reduce that of the relatively scarce factor. Since the country as a whole gains from trade, the abundant factor gains more than the scarce factor loses. The former could in principle compensate the latter for its losses and still gain. A sufficiently elaborate political system might undertake such compensation. Otherwise there will be a class in the economy permanently harmed by free trade, even though the country as a whole gains.

For example, the United States in its early history had an abundance of land and scarcity of capital relative to Europe. The farmers of the West and South (who owned land) favored free trade, whereas the businessmen of the Northeast (who owned capital) favored restrictions on trade.

■ *Proving the Stolper-Samuelson Theorem.* The theorem is easy to prove. Suppose, for example, that the price of machines rises by 10 percent and that of wine remains unchanged, both goods being produced. Then the cost of a machine rises by 10 percent and this cost consists of the cost of labor and capital. The wage and rent cannot both rise by exactly 10 percent because Figure 3.4 indicates that wages rise relative to rents. They cannot both rise by more than 10 percent because then the cost of a machine would have to rise by more than 10 percent; similarly the wage and rent cannot both fail to rise by at least 10 percent. Thus one rises more than 10 percent and one does not. As wages rise relative to rents, it is the wage that rises more than 10 percent, and thus increases relative to both commodity prices.

The price of wine, and so its cost, has not changed. But the wage has increased. Thus the rent must actually fall, since otherwise the cost of wine would have to increase. Therefore the rent falls relative to both commodity prices. ∎

THE RYBCZYNSKI THEOREM

While still a student, T. M. Rybczynski, now chief economist at La-zard Bros. Co., Ltd., in London, proved a proposition relating trade and economic growth. The latter will be reflected in changes in a country's endowments of the factors. Like the Stolper-Samuelson theorem, this proposition applies when both goods are produced.

> *At constant prices, an increase in one factor endowment will increase by a greater proportion the output of the good intensive in that factor and will reduce the output of the other good.*

Suppose, for example, that the French capital stock increases by 10 percent, the labor force remaining constant. Then the theorem asserts that French wine output will increase by more than 10 percent and French machine output will actually fall. This is illustrated in Figure 3.5. The increase in capital must shift the French production possibility frontier outward. In the figure it shifts from curve *ABC* to *DEF*. Suppose France is initially at *B*. Then the Rybczynski theorem asserts that point *E* on the new production possibility frontier, which has the same slope as *B* on the old (thus the same MRT_{WM}, and corresponds to the same relative price), lies to the northwest of *B*, as illustrated.

By combining this result with the Heckscher-Ohlin theorem, we can see how economic growth affects a nation's trade. If a country's capital stock increases by, say, 10 percent, national income will rise by some smaller proportion, because only part of national income comes from the earnings of capital. This increased income will normally be spent on both goods, so that, at constant prices, national *demand* for both goods will rise by less than 10 percent. The Rybczynski theorem tells us that the *supply* of the capital-

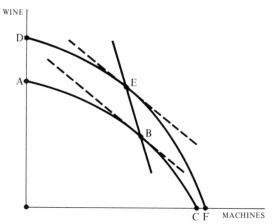

Figure 3.5. THE RYBCZYNSKI THEOREM

intensive good (wine) rises by more than 10 percent while the supply of machines falls. Thus wine supply rises relative to demand, and machine demand rises relative to supply. If the country is capital abundant, the Heckscher-Ohlin theorem tells us that it exports wine and imports machines, so that the growth of capital causes the country to trade more at each price: its offer curve shifts outward. If the country is instead labor abundant, its offer curve shifts inward. The general conclusion, illustrated in Figure 3.6, is that economic growth that accentuates a country's relative factor abundance (and so makes the country less like the rest of the world) shifts its offer curve out; growth that moderates the country's relative factor abundance shifts the offer curve in.

■ *Proving the Rybczynski Theorem.* The Rybczynski theorem is proved with exactly the same logic as the Stolper-Samuelson theorem. Suppose the capital stock increases by 10 percent and the labor force is unchanged. If both goods continue to be produced, factor prices will not change, by the factor-price equalization theorem, and so the techniques of production will not change either. The output of both goods cannot rise by 10 percent, since this would require 10 percent more labor, and the labor force has not increased. Similarly, the output of both goods cannot rise by more than 10 percent. They cannot both fail to rise by 10 percent either, or else the increased capital stock could not all be utilized. Thus the output of one good rises by more than 10 percent and that of the other does not. Since wine is capital intensive, it must be wine output that rises by more than 10 percent. The labor force has not changed, but the wine industry has expanded and so increased its use of labor. Therefore, the output of machines must actually fall. ■

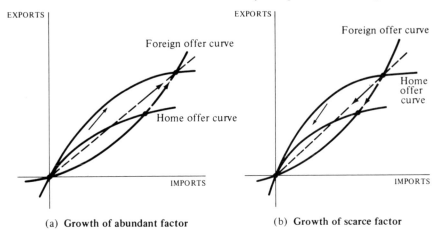

(a) **Growth of abundant factor**   (b) **Growth of scarce factor**

Figure 3.6. THE EFFECT OF ECONOMIC GROWTH
                ON INTERNATIONAL TRADE

PROBLEMS

3.13 What do you think is the consequence of the historic rise in the American wage, relative to other factor prices, on the cost of a university education? On the cleanliness of city streets? Specifically relate your answers to the theory.

3.14 Show how your answers to Problem **3.10** illustrate the Stolper-Samuelson theorem.

3.15 The savings rate in Japan after the Second World War has been much higher than in most other countries. What is the likely effect on relative Japanese factor abundance? Use the theory of this section to predict the likely consequences.

3.16 Suppose that some country, where a cask of wine requires 4 and 1 units of labor and capital respectively and where a bolt of cloth requires 2 and 5 units respectively, produces 200 casks of wine and 200 bolts of cloth. How much capital and labor is this economy using? Suppose wine output falls to 80 casks. What are the changes in percentage terms? How much capital and labor is now required? What are these changes in percentage terms? How does this illustrate the Rybczynski theorem?

3.17 Calculate the outputs of wine and cloth in Portugal and England if the countries have the technology described in Problem **3.16**, if England has 100 workers and 160 capital units, and if Portugal has 100 workers and 70 capital units. (Do this either by trial and error or by setting up and solving two simultaneous equations in two unknowns.) Show how a comparison of Portugal and England illustrates the Rybczynski theorem. Show how it also demonstrates the Heckscher-Ohlin theorem, if the two countries are freely trading.

3.18 Using the results of this section, describe the possible effects of economic growth upon the terms of trade. Upon internal income distribution.

3.19* The Stolper-Samuelson and Rybczynski theorems apply to situations in which both goods are actually produced. Suppose instead that France specializes completely in the production of wine. How would French wages and rents be affected by a rise in the price of wine? By a rise in the price of a machine? How are *real* wages affected? How would French outputs respond to a change in factor endowments, with the prices of wine and machines unchanged?

3.20* The Stolper-Samuelson theorem assumes that both factors are freely mobile between industries within a country. But in fact this is not true, at least for substantial time periods. Suppose, for example, that labor is freely mobile between wine and machine production but that capital is immobile, so that each industry's capital stock is fixed. Discuss the Stolper-Samuelson theorem in this case.

5. *Exploring Further:* Analysis of the Heckscher-Ohlin-Samuelson Model—the Firm

Consider the behavior of a single firm—say a French producer of wine. The firm has two decisions to make: how much capital and labor to hire and how much wine to produce. That is, it must determine its technique of production and its scale of operations. Its problem is illustrated in Figure 3.7.

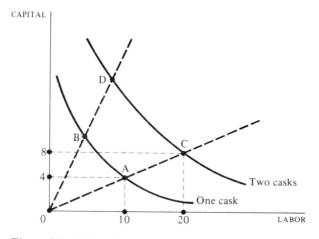

Figure 3.7. WINE INDUSTRY ISOQUANTS

The curved line through points A and B gives the various alternative combinations of capital and labor that can be used to produce one cask of wine. This curve, called an *isoquant,* must slope downward, since the only way to continue producing the same output with less capital is by adding more labor. A distinct isoquant corresponds to each level of output, and larger outputs correspond to isoquants farther from the origin. The negative of the slope of an isoquant is called the marginal rate of technical substitution of capital for labor and is denoted $MRTS_{KL}^W$.

> **KEY CONCEPT**
>
> The *marginal rate of technical substitution* of capital for labor is the amount of additional capital that must be employed to keep output unchanged if one fewer worker is employed.

The isoquants in Figure 3.7 are 'bowed inward,' that is, $MRTS_{KL}^W$ increases as successive units of labor are replaced by capital. Why? At a point such as A the cask of wine is produced by a very low capital-labor ratio, that is, many workers are employed per machine. If one worker is laid off, she will hardly be missed and there will be little loss of output; only a small amount of capital need be added to maintain output at one cask. But at point B there are fewer workers per machine; one less worker implies a substantial loss of output, and one more unit of capital a relatively slight gain. Thus $MRTS_{KL}^W$ must rise as we go from A to B, that is, the isoquant is bowed inward.

Suppose now that the firm has somehow decided to produce exactly one cask of wine. The firm knows its scale of operations and presumably knows what it must pay for capital and labor; the question is which technique to employ. What point on the isoquant costs the least?

Suppose first that the firm were to spend exactly fr100. If the full fr100 were spent on capital, fr100/r units would be employed where r denotes the rent; if only labor were hired, fr100/w units would be employed where w denotes labor's wage. By dividing the fr100 between capital and labor, any combination on the line FC in Figure 3.8 can be employed. Thus FC denotes all combinations of capital and labor that cost exactly fr100 at the given rental and wage rates. The slope of FC if given by

$$-\frac{OF}{OC} = -\frac{fr100/r}{fr100/w} = -\frac{w}{r}.$$

Therefore the slope of this "budget line" reflects the ratio of wages to rents and nothing else. The total amount spent determines how far the budget line is from the origin. If the budget were reduced from fr100 to fr50, for example, the line FC would shift to DE, which has the same slope but is only half as far from the origin as FC. (How would FC be affected if instead the wage rate were to double?)

The firm's problem of finding the least-cost technique to produce one cask of wine is the geometric problem of pushing the budget line FC as close to the origin as possible while still touching the one-cask isoquant. This must occur at a point of tangency, such as A in Figure 3.8. The firm will always produce at least cost if it uses capital and labor in such proportions as to cause the $MRTS_{KL}^W$ to equal w/r, the wage-rental ratio.

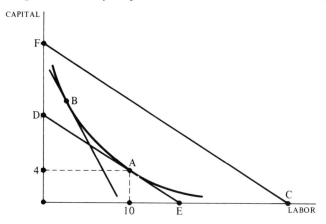

Figure 3.8. FINDING THE TECHNIQUE OF PRODUCTION

So, the wage-rental ratio determines the technique of production once the firm knows which isoquant to produce on. But what determines the scale of operations? This problem is simplified by the assumption of constant returns to scale, which means that an equi-proportional change in *both* capital and labor will always change output by that same proportion. Doubling the amount of capital and labor used by a wine firm, for example, will exactly double its output of wine. Constant returns to scale are more relevant the more long run our point of view, because in the short run it is simply impossible to vary all inputs. Since we are interested in long-run questions such as the allocation of resources, this is no problem.

The one-cask isoquant now tells us everything we need to know about the technology of producing wine. If for example, the wage-rental ratio is equal to the $MRTS^W_{KL}$ at point A on the one-cask isoquant in Figure 3.8, so that the cheapest way to produce one cask of wine is by using 10 units of labor and 4 of capital, then the cheapest way of producing two casks of wine is to use the same technique at twice the scale, that is, to employ 20 units of labor and 8 units of capital. In other words, point A is the technique that should be used for *each* unit of wine, regardless of how much wine is produced. Constant returns to scale ensures that the problem of choosing the technique of production is entirely independent of the problem of choosing the scale of operations.

Suppose now that the wage-rental ratio increases, say to the value indicated by the slope of the straight line through B in Figure 3.8. The least-cost technique for producing wine is now given by point B, where the $MRTS^W_{KL}$ equals the new wage-rental ratio. Firms will substitute capital for labor so that each unit of wine will now be produced by technique B, regardless of how much total wine continues to be produced. In this way we can use the one-cask isoquant to determine the technique of production, that is, the ratio of capital to labor employed in the wine industry, for each value of the wage-rental ratio.

PROBLEMS

3.21 Suppose that the production of each cask of wine requires 4 (or more) units of capital together with 2 (or more) units of labor. Draw the one-cask isoquant. What can you say about the $MRTS_{KL}^W$ in this case? What technique of production would a wine producer choose if $w/r = 5$? If $w/r = 1$? For other values of w/r ?

3.22 Suppose that each bolt of cloth requires 1 unit (or more) of capital plus 4 units (or more) of labor to produce. Answer the same questions as in Problem **3.21**.

3.23 Suppose that any quantity of cloth can be produced either as described in Problem **3.22** *or* by using 7 (or more) units of capital plus 1 (or more) units of labor. Answer the same question as in Problem **3.21**.

3.24 Suppose that K units of capital plus L units of labor can always produce $(KL)^{1/2}$ units of wine. Answer the same question as in the above problem.

6. *Exploring Further:* **Analysis of the Heckscher-Ohlin-Samuelson Model—the General Equilibrium of Production**

Suppose that the prices of wine and machinery, P_W and P_M, are given. These might be free-trade prices determined by reciprocal demand, or they might be autarkic equilibrium prices. It matters not; we take them as starting points.

The wine technology, as we have seen, can be completely described by any single isoquant, and so can the machine technology. Figure 3.9 shows the isoquant that produces one franc's worth of wine and that which produces one franc's worth of machines. For example, if a cask of wine costs one-half a franc, the isoquant that has been drawn is that which shows how to produce two casks of wine.

Each firm, regardless of how much it produces, will use the point on its isoquant where the $MRTS_{KL}$ equals the wage-rental ratio. The line $CABD$ in Figure 3.9 has been drawn tangent to both curves. If the wage-rental ratio is equal to minus the slope of this line *(OC/OD)*, the cheapest way to produce one franc's worth of wine is to employ technique *A*, and the cheapest way to produce one franc's worth of machinery is to use technique *B*.

If both goods are produced, each franc's worth of wine will be produced by *A*, and so the total amounts of capital and labor employed by the wine industry will lie somewhere on the ray through *O* and *A*. Similarly, the total capital and labor devoted to machinery must lie somewhere on the ray

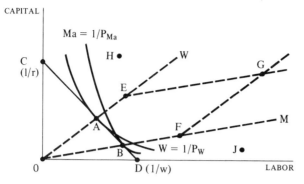

Figure 3.9. THE GENERAL EQUILIBRIUM OF PRODUCTION

through O and B. Suppose that G denotes the amounts of the two factors available to the economy as a whole. Then this total must be divided between wine production and machine production in just such a way as both to give each industry the factor proportions indicated by its respective ray and to add up exactly to G. To see this geometrically, complete the parallelogram formed by the two rays and by points G and O in Figure 3.9; draw a line *(EG)* through G parallel to OB and another line *(FG)* through G parallel to OA. The completed parallelogram is $OEGFO$. Point E indicates the total capital and labor used in the wine industry, and F shows the factors allocated to machine production. EG is parallel to, and the same length as, OF. Thus adding OE and OF together is the same as adding EG to OE or adding FG to OF; we end up at G.

Since A shows the capital and labor required to produce one franc's worth of wine, E will produce OE/OA francs' worth of wine. For example, if E is twice as far from the origin as A, then two francs' worth of wine is being produced (or four casks, at a price of one-half a franc per cask). Likewise, OF/OB francs' worth of machinery is being produced.

Figure 3.9 also reveals what factor prices must be in equilibrium. The line $CABD$ is the common tangent to both one-franc isoquants and therefore shows the combinations of capital and labor that cost exactly one franc. Thus C shows the amount of capital that can be hired for one franc: $1/r$ units. The rent is therefore $r = 1/OC$. Similarly, D shows the labor that can be hired for a franc, $1/w$, so that $w = 1/OD$.

PROBLEMS

3.25 Suppose each wine cask requires 4 units of capital and 2 of labor while each bolt of cloth requires 1 unit of capital and 4 of labor. What will be produced if the economy has 10 units of labor and 6 of capital? What will factor prices be if the price of wine is fr2 and that of cloth is fr1?

3.26 What will happen to the outputs of the two goods if, in Problem **3.25**, the capital stock increases to 8 units? What happens to factor prices if the price of cloth increases to fr2?

3.27 The discussion in this section assumed that the economy-wide capital-labor ratio was between the least-cost capital-labor ratios in the two sectors, that is, that G in Figure 3.9 was between the rays OA and OB. What would happen if instead the economy's endowment were as indicated in Figure 3.9 by point H? By J?

3.28* How do your answers to Problem **3.25** change if a bolt of cloth can be produced *either* by the technique described in that problem, *or* by 7 units of capital plus 1 of labor.

3.29* Use isoquants to illustrate, in a diagram like Figure 3.9, the situation described in Problem **3.7***.

3.30* Suppose that an economy is producing both goods, as in Figure 3.9. Now introduce a third good, cloth, with its own distinctive isoquants. If the prices of wine and machines do not change, under what circumstances will cloth actually be produced instead of one of the other goods? When will all three goods be produced? Complete the parallelogram in this latter case.

7. *Exploring Further:* Analysis of the Heckscher-Ohlin-Samuelson Model—Basic Propositions

RYBCZYNSKI THEOREM

In Figure 3.10 the ray OW indicates, as in Figure 3.9, the least-cost technique for producing wine, and the ray OM the least-cost technique in the machine industry. The economy's endowment is indicated by G, so that

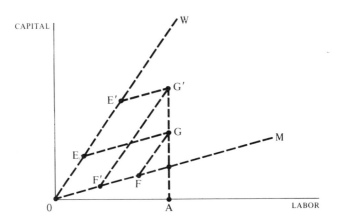

Figure 3.10. THE RYBCZYNSKI THEOREM

OA units of labor and AG units of capital are available. E and F indicate the allocations to the wine and machine industries respectively, so that wine output is proportional to the distance OE and machine output is proportional to OF.

Now suppose that the capital stock increases in the amount GG', the labor force and all prices remaining unchanged. Then the endowment point moves from G to G'. Completing the new parallelogram, we see that the allocations to the wine and machine industries are now E' and F' respectively. It is clear from the geometry that the output of the labor-intensive good, machinery, must fall (in an amount proportional to FF') and the output of the capital-intensive wine must increase. Furthermore, the proportional rise in wine production, EE'/OE, exceeds the proportional increase in the capital stock, GG'/AG.

THE STOLPER-SAMUELSON THEOREM

In Figure 3.11, point A again shows the capital and labor required to produce each franc's worth of wine, and B the requirements for one franc's worth of machinery. The wage is $1/OD$ and the rent $1/OC$. Now suppose that the price of machinery increases, that of wine remaining unchanged. Since machinery is worth more, fewer machines correspond to a franc's worth: if the price of machinery rises from one-third of a franc to one-half, for example, the number of machines worth a franc drops from three to two. Thus the one-franc isoquant for machinery shifts inward; in Figure 3.11 the isoquant through B shifts to that through H, the quantity HB/OB reflecting the proportionate rise in the price of machinery. As the price of wine is unchanged, the one-franc isoquant for wine stays put.

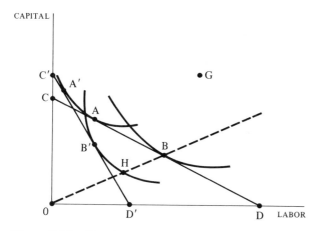

Figure 3.11. The Stolper-Samuelson Theorem

The new common tangent to both isoquants is the line $C'A'B'D'$. Since $1/OC'$ is less than $1/OC$, the rental has fallen, and the wage has risen because $1/OD'$ exceeds $1/OD$. Furthermore, $D'D/OD$ exceeds HB/OB: the proportionate rise in the wage exceeds that in the price of the labor-intensive good (machines). Thus we have the Stolper-Samuelson theorem: an increase in any commodity price produces a proportionately greater increase in the price of the factor intensive to that good and a fall in the price of the other factor.

Note that the change in factor prices induces both industries to alter their techniques of production. The machine industry replaces the technique H by B', and the wine industry replaces A by A'. Both industries respond to the rise in the relative cost of labor by switching to more capital-intensive techniques. How is it possible for *every* firm in the economy to become more capital intensive if the overall amounts of available capital and labor do not change? The labor-intensive industry (machines) must expand, and the capital-intensive (wine) must contract. The *intra*-industry substitution of capital for labor must be accompanied by an *inter*-industry substitution of machines for wine so that the total employment of capital and labor does not change. You can see this in Figure 3.11 by completing the parallelograms from the endowment point G for both pairs of techniques.

THE FACTOR-PRICE EQUALIZATION AND HECKSCHER-OHLIN THEOREMS

In proving the Stolper-Samuelson theorem we have shown that the wage-rental ratio is positively related to the cost of the labor-intensive good. This justifies Figure 3.1, which was used to establish the Heckscher-Ohlin and factor-price equalization theorems. But we can add to our understanding of these propositions by looking at them again from a slightly different point of view.

Consider first the Heckscher-Ohlin theorem. In Figure 3.10, point G' can represent the endowment of the capital-abundant country, and G that of the labor-abundant country. Clearly the former must have a greater output of capital-intensive goods, relative to labor-intensive goods, than the latter. By assumption, the two countries consume the two goods in the same proportions. Since imports and exports equal the differences between production and consumption, the capital-abundant country must be exporting the capital-intensive good, and the labor-abundant country must be exporting the labor-intensive good. If point G' is moved up (or G is moved down) enough to cross the ray from the origin, and thus cause specialization to the good intensive in the relatively abundant factor, this argument will not be changed.

We turn next to factor-price equalization. For given international commodity prices we can proceed, as in Figure 3.9, to find the budget line corresponding to production of both goods and, thereby, the factor prices that must hold and the techniques of production that must be used if both goods are produced. Suppose these techniques are as indicated by the rays OW and OM in Figure 3.10. Then any pair of countries with endowments (such as G and G' in the figure) between these rays will in fact produce both goods and have identical factor prices, and use identical techniques, provided that the countries engage in free trade at the given international commodity prices. If, on the other hand, a country has an endowment that is not between the two rays, free trade will cause that country to specialize completely in the production of one of the goods and to have factor prices different from those in the other country.

PROBLEMS

3.31 Using the technology described in Problems **3.21** and **3.22**, illustrate the four propositions with specific numerical examples.

3.32 In Figure 3.11 complete the parallelograms from point G to find the allocations of capital and labor to the two industries both before and after the price change. Compare the two situations.

3.33* Illustrate the Rybczynski theorem, if possible, in the case described in Problem **3.30***, when all three goods are produced.

8. Case Study: The International Wheat Market

This and the following two sections illustrate the factor-endowments theory.

One would expect, in accord with that theory, that countries relatively well endowed with the lands and climate so important for wheat cultivation would have a comparative advantage in the crop. This is indeed the case, as the major wheat exporters are the United States, Canada, Argentina, and Australia. Historically, Eastern Europe, with its plains, has had a comparative advantage over Western Europe in wheat. The difficulty of transporting the crop formerly limited trade but did not eliminate it: ancient Greece imported wheat from southern Russia, and for centuries Western Europe has imported the crop from the East. In the latter part of the nineteenth century, Australia and the Western Hemisphere were opened up to wheat cultivation, and transportation costs dropped dramatically. The crop now enters international trade on a large scale, and patterns of trade and production are as suggested by our theory. But it is also true that much of the industrial world heavily protects its agriculture. Trade in wheat is far from free; Western Europe, formerly an insignificant exporter, continues to be a large producer of wheat; trade and specialization has not been allowed to proceed as far as it would in a free market.

Table 3.1 shows data about wheat production and trade for selected countries. Several features emerge from the table. First, there are substantial differences in yields, even among those countries with broadly similar economic structures and between whom trade is otherwise quite free: compare yields in the United States and Canada with those in the three West European countries. Our theory predicts that, if trade is free and if countries do not specialize completely, they will have equal factor prices and therefore will employ the same techniques of production. But the absence of free trade in wheat prevents this from being as true as it otherwise would be. A second notable feature of the table is the fact that the countries with a comparative advantage in wheat (the United States and Canada) have *lower* yields than those with a comparative disadvantage. This seems strange, since comparative advantage is associated with relative efficiency. But our theory explains such a state of affairs. The United States and Canada, because they are relatively land abundant, employ more land-intensive methods, that is, each farmer works a larger quantity of land than does a farmer in France, Germany, or the United Kingdom, where the high yields reflect a large input of labor per acre. The United States is also a capital-abundant country and employs capital-intensive methods of farming; otherwise the U.S. entry in Table 3.1 would be even lower.

Table 3.1. WHEAT PRODUCTION AND TRADE OF SELECTED
COUNTRIES

	Yield, 1980 (metric ton/hectare)	*Production, 1980 (million metric tons)*	*Net Exports, 1979 (million metric tons)*
U.K.	5.7	8.1	− 2.5
France	5.2	23.5	6.8
West Germany	4.9	8.1	− .6
U.S.	2.2	64.5	33.4
Canada	1.7	19.1	11.7
USSR	1.6	98.1	− 6.7

SOURCE: *Food and Agriculture Organization*, Monthly Bulletin of Statistics

Two countries look a bit strange in Table 3.1. We have said that France is not a relatively efficient producer of wheat, but the third column reveals that country as the third-largest wheat exporter in the table. The reason is that French agriculture is protected by the Common Agricultural Policy (CAP) of the European Economic Community (EEC), so France, which is an efficient wheat producer relative to the rest of the EEC, can sell the crop in a market shielded from the rest of the world. Thus the large French exports do not reflect free international trade but, rather, just the reverse. We shall examine the CAP further when we study the EEC in Chapter 12.

The USSR has both the lowest yield and the highest production in the table yet is a hefty importer. With a large endowment of suitable lands, the nation employs land-intensive methods, as indicated by the low yield. Russia has historically been a major exporter of wheat and has a comparative advantage over much of the world in the crop, although her wheat-growing areas are less desirable and have a more unpredictable climate than those of the United States and Canada. Also the USSR is a large wheat *consumer*. Thus the country has often been a large net importer during the last decade, even though she remains the world's largest producer and still exports the crop to Eastern Europe. In Chapter 12 we will examine U.S.-USSR grain transactions.

PROBLEMS

3.34 On the basis of Table 3.1, what can you conjecture about the relative sizes of the prices of wheat cropland in the various countries, relative to other factor prices?

3.35 Suppose that the countries in Table 3.1 were to all adopt completely free international trade—including wheat. How do you think the various entries in the table would be affected?

9. Case Study: Relative Wage Movements

As pointed out in Chapter 1, trade in manufactured goods between developed countries has expanded rapidly since the Second World War. This expansion has been accompanied by (and partially caused by) a significant lessening of trade barriers: tariffs and transportation costs have fallen, businessmen have become more internationally minded, communications have become more efficient, firms have gone multinational, and so forth. If the expansion is interpreted as a movement toward free trade, the theory implies that factor prices and production techniques should become more similar across countries. Such developments have taken place, as any international traveler can attest. Table 3.2 provides an illustration. The table clearly shows that between 1959 and 1979 wages in the various countries converged in dramatic fashion. (The mean of the eight entries rose from 43 to 88, while their standard deviation fell from 29 to 17.) This is illustrative but should not be interpreted as "proof" of the theory. Other influences have also been at work: for example, capital and labor have become increasingly mobile internationally, and agriculture has remained protected.

Table 3.2. HOURLY WAGES IN MANUFACTURING IN SELECTED
COUNTRIES AS A PERCENTAGE OF THE U.S. WAGE

	1959	*1979*
Canada	82	95
Japan	11	82
Sweden	39	109
France	27	60
Italy	23	72
West Germany	29	107
U.K.	29	76
U.S.	100	100

SOURCES: International Financial Statistics; *U.N.* Monthly Bulletin of Statistics

10. Case Study: South Korean Experience with Export-Led Growth

As noted in Chapter 2, South Korea has differed from many LDCs by
relying on foreign trade to help stimulate economic development, a policy
known as *export-led* growth. In recent years, Korea has accumulated capital
at a rapid rate, both absolutely and relative to the rest of the world. The
Korean experience has been examined in detail in various studies, and
Table 3.3 contains a few calculations from one of these studies. The first
column shows the increase in the capital-labor *(K/L)* ratio for the Korean
economy—about 115 percent between 1966 and 1975. Note that the overall
capital-labor ratio is between the capital-labor ratios in the two sectors,
manufacturing and agriculture.

The second column shows that the wage has increased substantially;
in fact, wages have risen relative to rents (not shown in the table). As a
result, capital has been substituted for labor in both sectors, as revealed in
the third and fourth columns. But the increases in the capital-labor ratios in
the two sectors are not large enough to accommodate the overall increase in

Table 3.3. SOUTH KOREAN EXPERIENCE (K/L RATIOS IN THOUSANDS
OF DOLLARS PER LABORER)

Year	*(1) Overall K/L*	*(2) Wage Index*	*(3) K/L in Manufactures*	*(4) K/L in Agriculture*	*(5) K/L in Exports*	*(6) K/L in Non-Competing Imports*	*(7) Total Exports ($ million)*
1966	.7	100	1.8	.3	1.0	6.5	250
1975	1.5	183	3.0	.7	3.1	16.7 (1972)	5,081

SOURCE: *Wontack Hong*, Trade, Distortions and Employment Growth in Korea,
1979 (Seoul: Korea Development Institute)

the capital stock per worker indicated in the first column. Thus there must have been the sort of reallocation of resources from the labor-intensive sector to the capital-intensive sector that is predicted by the Rybczynski theorem. This is revealed in the last column, where exports are shown to have increased dramatically—Korea exports both primary products and manufactures, but the latter accounted for most of the export increase. The fact that the fifth column resembles the third much more closely than the fourth is indicative of the relative importance of manufactures in exports. Indeed Korean exports changed from consisting mainly of ores and other raw materials to manufactures such as textiles, shoes, steel, and electronics. A comparison of columns five and six furnishes support for a factor-endowments explanation of trade: exports are much less capital-intensive than noncompeting imports—goods that are imported and not produced at all at home.

The illustrations in this and the preceding two sections demonstrate the use of the Heckscher-Ohlin theory and lend that theory support. But they are far from formal tests of verification.

11. The Leontief Paradox

The Heckscher-Ohlin-Samuelson model leads to powerful and interesting results, as witnessed by the four propositions discussed in sections 3 and 4. But the model itself also makes stringent assumptions, as discussed in section 1; in this respect, it contrasts sharply with the more general ideas of comparative advantage and reciprocal demand. Empirical investigation is called for.

Such investigation could concern two questions: the general one of whether factor endowments are important determinants of comparative advantage, and the more specific one of whether the Heckscher-Ohlin-Samuelson model is an adequate description of reality. It is natural to start with the latter question, since a positive answer implies a positive answer to the former as well.

In 1953 Wassily Leontief published the results of one of the most famous empirical investigations in economics, an attempt to test the consistency of the Heckscher-Ohlin-Samuelson model with U.S. trade patterns.

Leontief wished to measure the capital-labor ratio actually used in the production of U.S. exports and imports. One complication is the existence of inter-industry flows. The automobile industry, for example, uses as inputs not only factors such as capital and labor but also steel and other *intermediate goods* (that is, goods that are used to produce goods). The steel industry also uses intermediate goods, including motor vehicles! Leontief (who received a Nobel Prize for the development of input-output analysis) used a 1947 input-output table for the U.S. to cut through these circular flows and calculate the total use (both directly, and indirectly in the form of intermediate goods) of capital and labor in various industries.

Leontief then calculated, on the basis of the U.S. pattern of trade in 1947 (and, in a subsequent recalculation, in 1951), the capital-labor ratio embodied in a representative collection of U.S. exports, and also that embodied in a representative collection of U.S. import-competing goods. He had to calculate the factor requirements of import-competing goods, rather than those of actual imports, because he had only U.S. data. Thus he ignored imports that were not also actually produced in the U.S.—notably coffee, tea, and jute. Also ignored were those sectors, mainly services, that did not enter into international trade at all.

Leontief found that U.S. exports used a capital-labor ratio of $13,991 per man-year, whereas import substitutes used a ratio of $18,184 per man-year. Given the presumption that the U.S. is relatively capital abundant, this is just the reverse of what the Heckscher-Ohlin theorem predicts! Thus it is called the Leontief Paradox.

This type of test differs from MacDougall's study discussed in Chapter 1 and the elasticity estimates discussed in Chapter 2 in that it does not examine a large number of observations in the hope of discovering regularities. Instead it is basically a description of a single observation—U.S. trade in 1947. Thus it raises the question of whether that observation is nonrepresentative; for example, 1947 was right after the Second World War, when the United States was the only major industrial economy free of devastation. Leontief's calculation has therefore been repeated, by Leontief and others, using different data. The Paradox has been found to be an enduring feature of U.S. trade. The same type of calculation has also been made for other countries and regions, and similar paradoxes have sometimes (but not always) been found.

The Leontief Paradox has stimulated a huge amount of both empirical and theoretical research, and still does: anything this glaring calls for an explanation. The rest of this chapter can be regarded as at least partially a response to the Paradox.

PROBLEMS

3.36 Discuss in detail the compatibility of Leontief's procedure with each of the assumptions made in section 1.

3.37 Review the discussion in Chapter 1 of the commodity composition of U.S. trade and your answer to Problem **3.1**. How reasonable do you think it is to try to fit the United States into the Heckscher-Ohlin-Samuelson model on the basis of capital and labor as the two factors?

12. Possible Explanations of the Leontief Paradox

This and the following two sections discuss suggestions that have been made to explain the Leontief Paradox. This section considers two possibilities suggested by the Heckscher-Ohlin-Samuelson model, section 13 deals with extensions of the factor-endowments approach, and section 14 looks at alternatives to factor endowments.

FACTOR INTENSITY REVERSAL

In section 1 we noted that the two industries (wine and machinery) would not normally use capital and labor in identical proportions, and so we defined the capital-intensive industry to be the one that uses a greater amount of capital per worker. But it is quite conceivable that under some circumstances wine might be relatively capital intensive while under other circumstances machinery might be.

Suppose, for example, that the machine industry is very inflexible: one unit of capital plus one unit of labor can produce one machine, and there is no other available method. Suppose, on the other hand, that capital and labor are easily substituted for each other in the wine industry: there are many methods of producing a cask of wine. If the wage-rental ratio is very high, wine producers will choose a capital-intensive method so as to economize on the use of expensive labor, and wine production will be capital-intensive relative to machine production. If the wage-rental ratio were to fall, wine producers would substitute labor for capital, but machine producers, hampered by the inflexible technology, would have to continue using one unit of capital with each unit of labor. Thus the capital intensity of the wine industry would decline relative to that of the machine industry. If wages fall enough, relative to rents, the capital-labor ratio in the wine industry could fall all the way to that in the machine industry and below. Thus at low enough wage-rental ratios, the wine industry would be labor intensive relative to machinery. Such a switch in the pattern of relative capital intensities is called a *factor intensity reversal*.

How can such a reversal affect the Heckscher-Ohlin theorem? Suppose that France is capital abundant relative to Germany, and that the two economies are in autarky. France thus has a higher wage-rental ratio than does Germany, and each French industry employs more capital per worker than does its German counterpart. Now suppose that the two countries are separated by a factor intensity reversal, with wine, say, relatively capital intensive in France but relatively labor intensive in Germany. Then the Heckscher-Ohlin theorem would predict that, if free trade were to commence, the capital-abundant country (France) would export its capital-intensive good (wine), and the labor-abundant country (Germany) would export its labor-intensive good (wine). This is nonsense: the theorem predicts both countries export the same good. Thus the presence of a factor intensity reversal nullifies the Heckscher-Ohlin theorem, which must be violated by one of the countries.

The Leontief Paradox can therefore be due, in principle, to a factor intensity reversal between the United States and the rest of the world. Unfortunately, testing for a reversal on the basis of existing technological data is extremely difficult. Economists have come to varying conclusions about the likely practical importance of such reversals. We cannot say that there is in fact very strong empirical evidence indicating that the Leontief Paradox is due to factor intensity reversals.

DEMAND REVERSAL

The assumption of identical tastes in the two countries ensures that the labor-abundant country has the lower autarkic wage-rental ratio. Suppose that we drop this assumption, and suppose further that each country has a strong preference for the good intensive in that country's relatively abundant factor. Thus in our example the Germans have a stronger preference than the French for machines and a weaker preference for wine. Then it is possible that Germany, despite her larger endowment of laborers per unit of capital, could have a higher wage-rental ratio than France, if the demand for labor to satisfy the greater desire for labor-intensive goods is sufficiently pronounced. Such a situation is called a *demand reversal.* In this case Germany would have a comparative advantage in the capital-intensive good (wine), and France in the labor-intensive good (machinery).

A demand reversal could potentially explain the Leontief Paradox. If the United States has a sufficiently great desire for capital-intensive goods, it could be led to import them from the rest of the world, despite the possession of more capital per worker.

Is this the case? One can find examples where a country has a marked preference for a good that it is relatively well endowed to produce. The French do in fact like their wine. But international comparisons of consumption patterns have failed to reveal substantial systematic differences in tastes. Thus there is no empirical support for the suggestion that the Leontief Paradox is due to demand reversals, and the assumption of identical tastes seems pretty good. This is really what we would expect: the same casual empiricism that makes us sure that the United States has more capital per worker than the rest of the world also makes us just about as sure that the United States would have a higher autarkic wage-rental ratio.

We have examined two possibilities, suggested by the Heckscher-Ohlin-Samuelson model, to account for the Paradox. Although these cases increase our understanding of the theory, they do not have strong empirical support. We must look elsewhere for an explanation of the Paradox.

PROBLEMS _____

3.38 Draw a diagram showing the relation between the wage-rental ratio and the ratio of machine cost to wine cost if a factor intensity reversal is present. If the relative factor intensities of the two industries reverse themselves twice.

3.39 If the Leontief Paradox were indeed due to a factor intensity reversal, what would Leontief have found if, instead of calculating the capital and labor used to produce a bundle of U.S. import substitutes, he had calculated the capital and labor actually used in the rest of the world to produce a bundle of U.S. imports? What would he have found if he had performed his actual calculation for the rest of the world rather than for the United States?

3.40* What can you say about factor-price equalization if a demand reversal is present?

3.41* Discuss the factor-price equalization, Rybczynski, and Stolper-Samuelson theorems in the presence of a factor intensity reversal.

13. Extensions of the Heckscher-Ohlin-Samuelson Model

In this section we consider a number of suggestions that depart substantially from the Heckscher-Ohlin-Samuelson model but, nevertheless, share the basic view that trade can be explained by relative factor endowments.

NATURAL RESOURCES

Some economists have argued that it is inadequate to limit consideration of factors to capital and labor, and that natural resources should also be included, thus restoring the traditional triad of capital, labor, and "land." Those, such as Jaroslav Vanek of Cornell University, who think that this point helps explain the Leontief Paradox employ a two-part argument. It is alleged, first, that many natural resources have become relatively scarce in the United States and that it imports natural resource–intensive goods. Second, natural resources and capital could be "complementary," that is, those goods whose production requires large quantities of natural resources could also require large quantities of capital. This combination of circumstances could potentially explain the Paradox. According to this story, the United States does indeed import capital-intensive goods, not because capital is scarce but because capital-intensive goods are also natural resource–intensive and natural resources are scarce. For example, the United States imports crude oil, which requires a large capital investment for extraction and transportation, so that the services of this capital are also imported. But the trade is due to an American shortage of oil, not of capital.

Empirical investigations have found that natural resources have become increasingly relatively scarce in the United States over the last century, and they have presented evidence that this is a significant determinant of trade patterns. Thus this consideration seems to have some power.

HUMAN CAPITAL

Nations and individuals invest in their future not only by accumulating physical capital, such as plant, equipment, and inventories, but also by spending on education, training, and other investments that are embodied in human form, that is, human capital. A portion of total wages is in fact a return to human capital rather than a payment for simple labor services. A neglect of human capital could potentially account for the Leontief Paradox if export industries used more human capital than did import-competing industries. It is known, from the work of Irving Kravis, at the University of Pennsylvania, that export industries do in fact tend to pay higher wages.

Measuring human capital is difficult because there is no explicit market for it. Methods of calculation have varied. For example, some studies have assumed that all wages, above the wage paid for unskilled labor, are a return to human capital; others have tried to construct measures directly by means of data on the costs of education, training, and so forth. The various studies have together established that human capital is significant and that U.S. exports are human capital–intensive, so that the phenomenon is an important determinant of trade. Indeed one study (by Peter Kenen, now at Princeton) even calculated that the Paradox could be reversed by adding human capital to physical capital.

Once they have been calculated, measures of human capital can be employed in two ways. The quantity of human capital can be added to that of physical capital to obtain a measure of total capital. If this is done, the basic Heckscher-Ohlin-Samuelson model remains intact, and the issue is solely one of measurement. Alternatively, human capital can be treated as a distinct factor, like labor and physical capital. In this case the model is substantially altered because the number of factors increases from two to three. Empirical studies have employed both methods, and, although some economists have concluded that it is better to treat human capital as a separate factor, the evidence is not conclusive on this point.

LABOR SKILLS

A nation's labor force is far from homogeneous but rather consists of many skill groups. Some economists, such as Donald Keesing, previously at Stanford and now working for the World Bank, have sought the explanation of trade patterns in endowments of skills. Various studies have established a connection between the skill mixes of national endowments and the mixes embodied in imports and exports, and some studies have also established an influence of skill mix on the trade status of specific commodities.

Since this approach essentially treats different types of skilled labor as distinct factors, it departs from the basic Heckscher-Ohlin-Samuelson model by increasing the number of primary factors beyond two. In some cases the departure also involves increasing the number of goods.

Taking account of labor skills is obviously closely related to taking account of human capital, and so the question arises whether this approach actually contributes anything additional. Some studies have accordingly employed both human capital measures and indices of skills. The conclusion appears to be that the latter do in fact have explanatory power beyond that contributed by human capital.

PROBLEMS

3.42 Sometimes human capital is added to physical capital to obtain a measure of total capital, and sometimes the two types of capital are treated as separate factors. Now physical capital itself can take many forms (different types of buildings, different equipment, inventories of different goods), and the form it takes depends upon the sector in which it is employed. If the purpose of the theory is to explain trade in a long-run perspective where capital is completely flexible, how should the two types of capital be treated (added together, or separate)? What difference does it make? Can you think of any reasons to distinguish between human and physical capital but not between forms of the latter?

3.43 Suppose you were to discover that in nearly all countries wages are generally higher in export industries than in import-competing industries (there is some factual support for this). What would this imply about the empirical relevance of the human capital explanation? Would this cause you to prefer one method of measuring human capital over another?

3.44 Specific skills are due in part to innate ability and in part to training (or human capital). If innate abilities are distributed in about equal proportions in the populations of different countries, should the skill groups and human capital explanations be distinct?

3.45* Some commodities, because of high transportation costs, do not enter into international trade at all. Personal services are often of this sort. Suppose we alter the basic model by adding a third, nontraded good. Does this change the model in any way beyond increasing the number of goods from two to three? If nontraded goods consist mainly of service industries, what effect would they have on calculations such as Leontief's? Try to deduce the implications of the presence of a nontraded good on the four basic propositions of the Heckscher-Ohlin theory.

14. Alternatives to Factor Endowments

The previous section considered possibilities that depart from the basic Heckscher-Ohlin-Samuelson model but still preserve a factor-endowment viewpoint. Recent years have also seen the development of theories that focus on entirely different considerations. Some of these theories are inconsistent with a factor-endowments basis of comparative advantage, whereas others are consistent with and complementary to factor endowments. In this section we discuss several of these alternative approaches.

TECHNOLOGICAL CHANGE

We saw in Chapter 1 that the United States exports technologically advanced manufactured goods. This fact has stimulated many studies, the common element of which is that the United States has a comparative advantage in research and development (R&D) itself. Thus goods that are relatively costly to produce at home might, nevertheless, be exported because of the R&D that they embody, and the actual export mix would have to constantly change in order for R&D, in the form of "advanced" products, to continue to be exported.

This approach could in principle be reduced to a form of the factor-endowments theory, if one were to hypothesize that factor endowments explain the comparative advantage in R&D. The main modifications to the simple model would once again be increases in the numbers of factors and goods (and perhaps also an explicit dynamic element). But empirical investigations have not followed this path. Rather, they have attempted the more rudimentary task of relating exports to various industry characteristics thought to reflect the importance of research activities: the proportions of scientists and engineers in employment, the first trade date (to indicate the newness of a good), expenditure on R&D, the degree of product differentiation, and the like. Results have been mixed. Some studies have confirmed the importance of R&D for U.S. trade flows (as one would expect), but no clear framework of cause and effect has emerged.

This influence of technological advance upon trade is sometimes described in terms of a *product cycle*. According to this scenario, a new product is developed in the United States because of that country's comparative advantage in R&D. The product is initially produced at home for the domestic market because direct communication between producer and customer is essential to the development of the good. As that development proceeds and the good is perfected, production expands and an export market develops. Eventually the good becomes standardized, or familiar, and constant communication between buyer and seller declines in importance relative to the consideration of producing where costs are lowest. Production therefore begins abroad. At first, foreign production is small, as a learning process takes place abroad, and the foreign output is sold only on the local market, displacing some U.S. exports. Foreign production then gradually increases, and U.S. exports gradually fall, until the good is finally imported into the United States and foreign output supplies the entire world market. In the meantime, the U.S. firms have developed still newer products that are being introduced and will subsequently experience the same cycle. This sort of story obviously lends itself more readily to case studies than to aggregate empirical testing, and a number of such case studies have been made, notably in motion pictures and electronics.

Explanations of American imports and exports as trade in technology raise further questions. First, what is the source of the hypothesized U.S. comparative advantage in R&D? As noted above, the factor-endowments and alternative explanations presumably could enter here. Second, if the United States does in fact have a comparative advantage in R&D, what determines whether this causes exports of new goods rather than the direct export of research services for foreign customers or for U.S. firms with productive capacity abroad? This question will arise again in Chapter 7, where we examine international investment and the multinational firm.

TARIFFS AND OTHER DISTORTIONS

All nations use tariffs and other measures to interfere with their international trade, and all experience at least some distortions in domestic markets as well. We saw in Chapter 2 that many LDCs have policies that extensively influence trade flows away from those dictated by comparative advantage. In many of these countries the domestic markets likewise have been influenced to depart substantively from what would have come about in a purely competitive environment. Such measures are much less pronounced in the developed countries, but these do nonetheless impose tariffs. In some sectors, especially agriculture, the degree of protection from international competition can still be large. Some economists, notably William Travis, have suggested that the Leontief Paradox might be due largely to tariffs and other forms of protection. There is evidence that, in the United States and some other DCs, industries, such as textiles and footwear, that are relatively intensive in unskilled labor are relatively heavily protected. Investigations have shown that tariffs might contribute to the Paradox, but that protection is not a major factor, at least as far as the DCs are concerned.

INCREASING RETURNS TO SCALE

The basic Heckscher-Ohlin-Samuelson model assumes constant returns to scale. We saw in Chapter 1 that scale economies could provide a basis for trade entirely independent of comparative advantage, and therefore also independent of factor endowments, which work through comparative advantage. For example, suppose that France and Germany have identical factor endowments (so that the Heckscher-Ohlin theorem would predict no trade), and therefore identical production possibility frontiers, but that geographically concentrated scale economies cause that common frontier to be "bowed inward," as in Figure 1.11. Then, as we saw, there is a basis for trade and specialization not predicted by comparative advantage or, therefore, by factor endowments.

All this applies to *national* scale economies, which require the geographical concentration of production. What if the scale economies are *international*—a result of the division of labor—or if product differentiation is significant? Then, as we saw in Chapter 1, *inter-industry* trade will still be based upon comparative advantage, and countries that are relatively similar, and so have minor comparative-cost differences, will engage mainly in *intra-industry* trade. Now the factor-endowments theory hypothesizes that countries with large differences in factor endowments have large differences in comparative costs, whereas those with similar endowments have similar comparative costs. If this is so, two conclusions follow.

1. Trade between countries with similar endowments is largely intra-industry, whereas countries with dissimilar endowments engage in largely inter-industry trade.
2. International scale economies do not vitiate the factor-endowments theory.

Factor endowments are of course much more similar between the DCs than they are between the DCs as a group and the LDCs. Thus these conclusions are consistent with the trade patterns discussed in Chapter 1.

The fundamental message of the Heckscher-Ohlin theory is that trade and factor mobility are *substitutes* for each other. The presence of international scale economies does not alter this conclusion as far as inter-industry trade is concerned. But they cause intra-industry trade and factor mobility to be *complements*. If factors were to become more mobile between countries, this movement would reduce comparative cost differences, thereby reducing inter-industry trade but increasing intra-industry trade.

LINDER'S HYPOTHESIS

Yet another theory has been proposed by the Swedish economist Staffan B. Linder, who assigns a central role to demand. Linder's theory is intended to apply only to manufactures, with trade in primary products presumably explained by endowments of crucial natural resources. The theory has two components.

1. *Potential exports are those goods for which a domestic market exists.* This assumption is defended by the same sort of alleged information requirement central to the early part of the product cycle: the knowledge of how to develop, produce, and market a product cannot be acquired without a local market with which to interact. The assumption is asserted as a general tendency, and the existence of counter-examples, such as the Korean export of Christmas decorations to the United States, is acknowledged. Since a country would never import a good without a local market, this assumption implies that a country's potential trade is limited to those goods having a domestic market. It also implies that the potential trade between any two countries is limited to those goods for which markets exist in *both* countries.

2. *The range of goods for which domestic markets exist is determined by per capita income.* This amounts to assuming that income is the dominant determinant of tastes.

The two assumptions together imply that the amount of potential trade between countries is greater the more nearly equal are their per capita incomes. According to the second assumption, countries with greatly different incomes will have domestic markets for different types of goods, so that only comparatively few goods will have markets in both countries. But the first implies that only those goods with markets in both countries are tradeable; thus there will be little trade between countries with greatly dissimilar incomes.

Linder's theory leads to conclusions quite different from those of the factor-endowments approach. Countries with high per capita incomes also have much capital per resident. Linder's theory accordingly predicts that the volume of trade will be the greatest between countries with similar capital-labor ratios and therefore similar per capita incomes. The Heckscher-Ohlin theory leads to precisely the opposite conclusion: countries with similar capital-labor ratios will have similar comparative costs and thus little basis for mutual trade. Nevertheless, there is some scope for complementarity between the theories. Linder's theory predicts which goods are potentially tradeable but says nothing about the pattern of trade in those goods, that is, which will be imported and which exported by any particular country. Presumably this can be explained by other theories, such as that of Heckscher and Ohlin.

Linder's theory is in rough accord with the facts: the lion's share of world trade is among the DCs, with broadly similar per capita incomes, rather than between the DCs and LDCs. However, detailed empirical support for the theory has not been found, and tests of propositions thought to reflect Linder's theory have not given it much support.

15. The Factor Content of American Trade

A 1971 study by Robert Baldwin of the University of Wisconsin examined the international trade of the United States. Table 3.4 shows some of his results pertaining to the 1962 pattern of trade.

The first entry in the table indicates that the (physical) capital-labor ratio employed in the production of a typical $1 million of U.S. import substitutes was 1.27 times as large as the capital-labor ratio used in the production of a typical $1 million of U.S. exports. This is the Leontief Paradox once again, and not much different from the ratio Leontief had obtained earlier (1.30). The second table shows that when natural resource–intensive industries are ignored, the ratio falls to 1.04. Thus the natural resources explanation seems to be quite important in practice, though not important enough to entirely account for the Paradox by itself. That the same is true of human capital is revealed by the third entry, showing that the ratio drops from 1.27 to 1.14 when human capital is added to physical capital. Taking into account both the natural resource and human capital explanations does eliminate the Paradox in the fourth entry. These conclusions are reinforced by the last two numbers, which show that

Table 3.4.   CHARACTERISTICS OF U.S. TRADE, 1962

Variable*	Ratio of M Variable to X Variable
PK/L	1.27
PK/L (−NR)	1.04
(PK + HK)/L	1.14
(PK + HK)/L (−NR)	.97
S & E	.74
S & E (−NR)	.62

* PK/L: ratio of physical capital to labor; (PK + HK): physical capital plus human capital calculated as the cost of education of labor; (−NR): indicates that industries intensive in the uses of natural resources are excluded; S & E: proportion of employees who are scientists and engineers.

SOURCE: *Baldwin, R. E., "Determinants of the Commodity Structure of U.S. Trade,"* American Economic Review, *1971*

Table 3.5.   RELATIVE IMPORTANCE OF SKILL GROUPS IN IMPORT-COMPETING AND EXPORT EMPLOYMENT

Skill Group	M/X Ratio
Farmers and Farm Laborers	.7
Professional and Technical	.85
Craftsmen, Managers, and Foremen	1
Sales and Clerical	1.01
Operatives and Laborers	1.25

SOURCE: *Baldwin,* op. cit.

scientists and engineers are proportionally less pronounced in import-competing employment than in export employment, and that the disparity widens when natural resource–intensive industries are dropped. The importance of labor skills is further elaborated by Table 3.5. The last entry, for example, means that the fraction of total employment used to produce a typical $1 million of import-competing goods that are operatives and laborers was 1.25 times as great as the fraction used for a typical $1 million of exports.

PROBLEMS

3.46 Compare the discussion of the factor content of U.S. trade (this section) with the discussion of its commodity composition (Chapter 1). Discuss whether the two seem intuitively consistent.

3.47 What do you think would be the consequences of a U.S. abandonment of liberal trade on the domestic distribution of income between factors?

3.48 If farmers and farm laborers are simply workers who happen to work on farms, does the relative intensity of such workers in imports and exports tell us anything about whether relative factor endowments *cause* the pattern of trade, as the Heckscher-Ohlin theorem asserts? Answer the question with regard to other skill groups.

16. Case Study: The Factor Content of Canadian Trade

The international trade of the United States is most often the object of study, but it is instructive to look at things from the other side of the fence also. The economist D. Wahl found that in 1949 Canada, the most important single trading partner of the United States, exported goods with a higher capital-labor ratio than its import substitutes. This was generally regarded as consistent with the presumption that Canada is capital abundant relative to the rest of the world, but inconsistent with the presumption that Canada is capital scarce relative to the United States, its dominant trading partner. But it was consistent with Leontief's result.

Table 3.6 shows results of a study by Harry Postner. Canadian exports are most strongly intensive in natural resources, which accords well with prior expectations, and are also intensive in physical capital and labor with at most an elementary-school education. Human capital would appear to be scarce. These results dovetail nicely with our discussion of U.S. trade. This can also be seen in Table 3.7, which focuses on the trade between the United States and Canada alone. The basic picture that emerges is like that of Table 3.6, except that now even elementary labor is relatively more intensive in imports, and exhaustible natural resources are now the most export intensive.

Table 3.6. FACTOR CONTENT OF CANADIAN TRADE, 1970

Factor*	M/X	M − X
RNR	.46	−83
ENR	.61	−86
PK	.82	−531
Elementary L	.91	−3.1
Secondary L	1.07	3.8
University L	1.14	1.3
Total L	1.02	1.9

* RNR: renewable natural resources (such as forest products); ENR: exhaustible natural resources (such as minerals); PK: physical capital; Elementary L: labor with an elementary school education only; M: factor content of a typical $1 million of import substitutes; Labor is measured in man-years, and capital and resources in thousands of dollars.

SOURCE: *Postner, H.* Factor Content of Canadian International Trade, *1975 (Ottawa: Economic Council of Canada)*

Table 3.7. FACTOR CONTENT OF BILATERIAL U.S.-CANADIAN TRADE, 1967

Factor*	M/X	M − X
RNR	.70	− 35
ENR	.55	−105
PK	.81	−579
Elementary L	1.06	2.3
Secondary L	1.17	9
University L	1.14	1.2
Total L	1.12	12.5

See note to Table 3.6. M refers to *Canada's* imports.

SOURCE: *Postner*, op. cit.

PROBLEMS ───

3.49 Compare the discussion of the factor content of Canadian trade (this section) with the discussion of its commodity composition (Chapter 1). Discuss whether the two seem intuitively consistent.

3.50 What do you think would be the consequences of a Canadian abandonment of liberal trade on the domestic distribution of income between factors?

3.51 What do you think would be the consequences for U.S.-Canadian trade of a large-scale disinvestment of capital in the United States and investment in Canada?

17. *Exploring Further:* Many Goods and Factors

The previous sections lead to two conclusions. First, the simple Heckscher-Ohlin-Samuelson model is inadequate to satisfactorily explain world trade. Second, the factor-endowments approach in general is quite useful for such an explanation. Nearly all the suggestions that had explanatory power could be thought of as simply the addition of more goods and factors to the basic Heckscher-Ohlin-Samuelson model. Our four basic propositions, on the other hand, were developed on the assumption of just two goods and factors. Thus we must ask whether these propositions retain any validity when the numbers of goods and factors rise. This question is discussed in section A.5 of Appendix I. Here we simply sketch out how the propositions fare if the numbers of factors and goods are equal but greater than two, and if in other respects we adhere to the description of the Heckscher-Ohlin-Samuelson model given in section 1.

FACTOR-PRICE EQUALIZATION

The firms in each of the (possibly many) industries face market prices for each of the factors, and they choose the least-cost technique: that collection of quantities of the various factors that can produce one unit of output at minimum cost. Because of constant returns to scale, this technique can be operated at any level, so each industry will employ the various factors in the same proportions in which they are required by the least-cost technique. These requirements and the factor prices determine the cost of production of each good, and, if the commodity is actually produced, this cost must equal its price. When world prices equal these costs, any country, whose endowment consists of factors in proportions between the proportions required by the various industries' least-cost techniques, will produce all goods and will have the corresponding factor prices. Thus all such countries must have equal factor prices when freely trading with each other.

THE HECKSCHER-OHLIN THEOREM

Suppose that free trade takes place with factor-price equalization. Jaroslav Vanek has shown that, in these circumstances, much of the Heckscher-Ohlin theorem continues to hold. Because all countries have identical factor prices, they use identical techniques, so that the quantities of the various factors used to produce a unit of any good are the same regardless of where that good is produced. Therefore the assumption that all countries consume goods in identical proportions implies that all countries "consume factors" in identical proportions. For example, if some country's national income were 10 percent of world income, then the goods that it consumed would together require for their production exactly 10 percent of the world endowment of each factor. Thus the country's exports would together require more of any factor for their production than would the country's imports when the country possessed more than 10 percent of the world endowment of that factor, and any factor for which the country's endowment accounted for less than 10 percent of the world endowment would be imported in the same sense. More generally, we can say that a country is relatively abundant in any factor for which the country possesses a greater fraction of world supply than the fraction of world income that the country accounts for, and that the country is relatively scarce in the factors for which it possesses a smaller fraction. Then each country's exports will, in the aggregate, use a greater quantity of each of its abundant factors and a smaller quantity of each of its scarce factors than will its imports in the aggregate. This argument does not say whether any particular good will be imported or exported (unless there are only two goods), but it does justify aggregate calculations of the Leontief type. Indeed, James Williams of McMaster University and Edward Leamer of the University of California, Los Angeles, have argued that when the presence of additional factors is recognized, U.S. trade patterns need not imply that the country is abundant in labor relative to capital. Leamer has in fact pointed out that Leontief's figures are actually consistent with the reverse.

STOLPER-SAMUELSON AND RYBCZYNSKI THEOREMS

The reasoning employed in section 4 to prove the Stolper-Samuelson and Rybczynski theorems can still be used when there are many goods and factors, and substantial parts of those two propositions remain true. Consider the Stolper-Samuelson theorem. Suppose again that the price of machines rises, say by 10 percent, that the prices of all other goods are unchanged, and that machines and at least one other good continue to be produced. All factor prices cannot rise by more than 10 percent, or the costs of all goods would rise by more than 10 percent and nothing could be produced; all factor prices cannot rise by exactly 10 percent, or all costs would rise by 10 percent and no goods with unchanged prices could still be produced; finally, all factor prices cannot fail to rise by at least 10 percent, or the cost of machines could not rise by the 10 percent increase in price. Thus at least one factor price rises by more than 10 percent and at least one factor price does not rise as much as 10 percent. If all factors were to rise in price or remain unchanged, the costs of all goods would increase, so at least one factor price must fall for a good with unchanged price to experience no change in costs.

We conclude then, that an increase in any commodity price, with the prices of other commodities held constant, will cause a greater than proportional rise in *some* factor price and an absolute fall in *some* factor price. Thus the real income of the first factor unambiguously increases, and that accruing to the latter factor unambiguously falls.

The Rybczynski theorem can be similarly extended. An increase in the endowment of one factor, with all other factor endowments and all prices constant, would cause the output of some good to increase in greater proportion and would cause the output of some other good to actually fall.

PROBLEMS

3.52 What does the version of the Heckscher-Ohlin theorem deduced in this section imply about the validity of the natural resources explanation of the Leontief Paradox if factor-price equalization takes place?

3.53. Go through the reasoning of section 7*, as best as you can, if there are three goods and two factors. If there are two goods and three factors.

18. Summary

1. This chapter has investigated the basis of comparative advantage, the most prominent explanation of which is the factor-endowments theory: countries tend to have a comparative advantage in those goods whose production makes relatively intensive use of those factors with which the country is relatively abundantly endowed.

2. The factor-endowments theory is given explicit form in the Heckscher-Ohlin-Samuelson model, which hypothesizes a world of two goods, two factors, and two countries that are identical in all respects except factor endowments.

3. The Heckscher-Ohlin-Samuelson model yields four basic propositions that explain the pattern of comparative advantage and establish links between international trade and domestic factor markets, income distribution, and growth.

4. Leontief's finding that U.S. exports tend to use less capital per worker than do U.S. import substitutes, and similar calculations by others, have undermined faith in the two-good, two-factor, Heckscher-Ohlin-Samuelson model as an adequate vehicle for the analysis of trade.

5. Theoretical and empirical investigations have studied alternative approaches. The approaches that have been most successful have typically exploited a factor-endowments explanation requiring more than two factors and goods. Those suggestions, such as demand reversals, tariffs, national increasing returns, and Linder's theory, which abandon the factor-endowments approach, have received less empirical support. Consequently it is important to know whether the four basic propositions derived from the Heckscher-Ohlin-Samuelson model are crucially dependent upon the assumption of just two goods and two factors.

6. A central core of the four propositions does remain valid in the presence of many goods and factors.

7. The Heckscher-Ohlin theory studied in this chapter is one of the two basic ideas of the pure theory of international trade developed in this century. It is basically an extension of the classical theory, which it both builds upon and complements. Thus it is sometimes referred to as the neoclassical, or the modern, theory of international trade.

SUGGESTED READING

Balassa, B. "The Changing Pattern of Comparative Advantage in Manufactured Goods." *Review of Economics and Statistics*, no. 2, 1979.

Baldwin, R. E. "Determinants of the Commodity Structure of U.S. Trade." *American Economic Review*, no. 1, 1971. An empirical test.

Dixit, A. K. and Norman, V. *Theory of International Trade*. London: Cambridge University Press, 1980. Chapters 1 and 4 discuss the factor-endowments theory with many goods and factors.

Ethier, W. "National and International Returns to Scale and the Modern Theory of International Trade." *American Economic Review* 2, 1982. Scale economies, intraindustry trade, and the factor endowments theory.

Ethier, W. "Some of the Theorems of International Trade with Many Goods and Factors." *Journal of International Economics* 2, 1974. The fate of the basic propositions with more than two goods and factors.

Heckscher, E. "The Effect of Foreign Trade on the Distribution of Income." *Readings in the Theory of International Trade*. Edited by H. S. Ellis and L. A. Metzler. Homewood: Irwin, 1949. The original article in English translation.

Hufbauer, G. C. "The Impact of National Characteristics and Technology on the Commodity Composition of Trade in Manufactured Goods." In *The Technol-*

ogy Factor in International Trade. Edited by R. Vernon. New York: National Bureau of Economic Research, 1970. An empirical study.

Johnson, H. G. *International Trade and Economic Growth.* Cambridge: Harvard University Press, 1965. Chapter 1 contains an alternative geometric treatment of the factor-endowments theory.

Jones, R. W. "Factor Proportions and the Heckscher-Ohlin Theorem." *Review of Economic Studies,* Oct., 1956. A basic treatment of the Heckscher-Ohlin theorem.

Jones, R. W. "The Structure of Simple General Equilibrium Models." *Journal of Political Economy* 6, 1965. An algebraic treatment.

Keesing, D. B. "Labor Skills and Comparative Advantage." *American Economic Review* 2, 1966. The empirical relation between trade patterns and skill groups.

Kenen, P. B. "Nature, Capital and Trade." *Journal of Political Economy* 5, 1965.

Leamer, E. E. "The Leontief Paradox, Reconsidered." *Journal of Political Economy* 3, 1980. The United States is capital abundant after all.

Leontief, W. "Domestic Production and Foreign Trade: The American Capital Position Re-examined." In *Readings in International Economics.* Edited by R. E. Caves and H. G. Johnson. Homewood: Irwin, 1968. The Leontief Paradox.

Linder, S. B. *An Essay on Trade and Transformation.* New York: Wiley, 1961. Linder's theory.

Ohlin, B. *Interregional and International Trade.* Cambridge: Harvard University Press, 1933. The classic statement.

Postner, H. H. *Factor Content of Canadian International Trade.* Ottawa: Economic Council of Canada, 1975.

Rybczynski, T. M. "Factor Endowment and Relative Commodity Prices," *Economica* 88, 1955. The Rybczynski theorem.

Samuelson, P. A. "International Factor-Price Equalization Once Again," *Economic Journal* 234, 1949. The factor-price equalization theorem.

Stern, R. M. "Testing Trade Theories." In *International Trade and Finance.* Edited by P. B. Kenen. Cambridge: Cambridge University Press, 1975. Surveys the empirical contributions.

Stolper, W. F. and Samuelson, P. A. "Protection and Real Wages." *Review of Economic Studies* 1, 1941. The Stolper-Samuelson theorem.

Travis, W. P. *The Theory of Trade and Protection.* Cambridge: Harvard University Press, 1964. The effects of tariffs.

Vanek, J. "The Factor-Proportions Theory: the N-Factor Case." *Kyklos* 4, 1968. The Heckscher-Ohlin theorem with many goods and factors.

Vanek, J. "The Natural Resource Content of Foreign Trade, 1870–1955, and the Relative Abundance of Natural Resources in the United States." *Review of Economics and Statistics* 2, 1959.

Vernon, R. "International Investment and International Trade in the Product Cycle." *Quarterly Journal of Economics* 2, 1966.

Wahl, D. F. "Capital and Labor Requirements for Canada's Foreign Trade." *Canadian Journal of Economics and Political Science,* 1961.

Williams, J. R. "The Resource Content in International Trade." *Canadian Journal of Economics* 2, 1970.

Chapter 4

National Income and International Trade

"Where wealth and freedom reign, contentment fails,
And honour sinks where commerce long prevails."
—O. GOLDSMITH

"In the long run we are all dead."   —J. M. KEYNES

WE NOW come to the last of the four basic ideas in the theory of international trade. This chapter, like the preceding one, deals with twentieth-century developments. But whereas the Heckscher-Ohlin theory is a modern extension and development of the classical theory, the present chapter proceeds in a different direction: the application of Keynesian national income analysis to international trade.

The preceding chapters showed how international economic adjustment is effected by changes in relative prices. Thus "elasticity optimists" and "elasticity pessimists" have differing views on the practical usefulness of such relative price changes. To the extent that they do not bring about international adjustment, whether because they are ineffective, or only slowly effective, or because sufficient relative price changes do not occur, or occur only slowly, adjustment will be brought about in other ways: through changes in incomes, employment, and other aggregates. This is the subject of the present chapter.

To put matters in clear relief suppose that relative prices remain fixed. Thus we can speak unambiguously of the total output of all goods, or gross national product. This will depend upon the extent to which the economy's resources are actually employed. In the preceding chapters relative prices were flexible, but the level of resource employment was fixed (output was always *on* a given production possibility frontier): now the situation is just the opposite.

This chapter introduces the macroeconomic issues of unemployment and inflation as related to international trade. Chapters 8 and 9, on international monetary theory, develop these issues more fully. The present chapter serves as a bridge between the pure and monetary aspects of the subject and, in addition, supplies us with just enough macroeconomic equipment for the policy discussions in Part Two. We begin with the elementary macroeconomics of a country in autarky.

JOHN MAYNARD KEYNES (1883–1946)

The foremost economist of this century was, like John Stuart Mill, the son of an economist and, like Ricardo, made a fortune in financial speculation. After a brilliant career at King's College, Cambridge, Keynes joined the India office and, in addition, became a major figure in the Bloomsbury group (which included the literary figures Virginia and Leonard Woolf, the historian Lytton Strachey, and the art critic Roger Fry). He served in the Treasury during the First World War and was the Treasury's representative at the Versailles peace conference. His denunciation of the settlement in *The Economic Consequences of the Peace* was an influential popular success. Between the wars, Keynes was a prominent critic of economic policy but, as a member of the minority Liberal party, removed from power. He also pursued many outside activities, continued his financial speculation, and conducted a prominent academic career at Cambridge. The latter culminated in *The General Theory of Employment, Interest and Money,* the classic work of the Keynesian revolution. During the Second World War he was an adviser to the government, and he negotiated with the United States over war finance and the structure of the postwar international monetary system.

1. Basic Income-Expenditure Theory

EQUILIBRIUM

An economy is in equilibrium if the demand for the nation's output equals supply. Let Y denote total national output of all goods (since relative prices are fixed, they can be used to make the outputs of distinct goods, such as wine and machines, commensurable). Then Y is both the supply of goods and the level of national income. Demand has two components. First is the demand for goods for consumption, denoted C. Consumption depends upon Y because if output increases then so does income, and part of the increase will be devoted to consumption. The second component, denoted I and called investment, is autonomous demand: private investment and government expenditure. Thus for supply to equal demand,

$$Y = C + I.$$

This can also be written $Y - C = I$. Now. $Y - C$ is that part of income not spent on consumption, that is, national savings, and so is denoted S. Then the equilibrium condition can also be expressed:

$$S = I. \tag{4.1}$$

In this form the condition says that total injections I (that is, expenditure not due to income) must exactly replace total leakages S. Equilibrium is depicted in Figure 4.1. Y_0 indicates the value of Y that solves (4.1). Since I does not depend on Y, it is drawn as the horizontal line through A and B. The S curve, on the other hand, slopes up because part of an increase in income will normally be saved. The slope is called the *marginal propensity to save (MPS)*. Thus in Figure 4.1, $MPS = BC/AB$.

KEY CONCEPT

The *marginal propensity to save* is the fraction of an additional unit of income that a country will save.

Thus far nothing has been said about full employment output, that is, the value that Y would have if all resources were employed at desired levels. If this is greater than Y_0, such as Y_1 in Figure 4.1, the economy must have unemployed resources. If, on the other hand, it is less than Y_0, the economy cannot actually produce Y_0, at least not for long, and inflationary pressures will build up.

THE MULTIPLIER

Suppose now that I is increased in the amount $I_1 - I_0$ in Figure 4.1, that is, the I_0 line shifts to I_1. Then the intersection moves from A to C and national output is increased by $Y_1 - Y_0$. Now from the figure it is apparent that $(I_1 - I_0)/(Y_1 - Y_0) = BC/AB = MPS$. Thus

$$Y_1 - Y_0 = (\frac{1}{MPS})(I_1 - I_0).$$

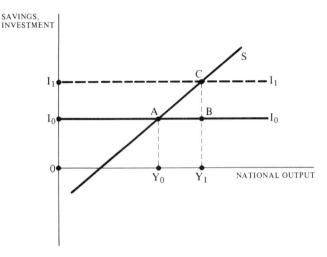

Figure 4.1. Equilibrium National Output

The number $1/MPS$ is called the *multiplier* because the initial change in I is multiplied by it to find the resulting change in Y.

KEY CONCEPT

The *investment multiplier* is the amount by which a unit increase in investment will increase equilibrium national income.

We can look at this in an alternative way, less direct but more illuminating. Suppose that firms increase their investment in new plant by $I_1 - I_0$. Then there will be a "first round" increase in Y in the amount $I_1 - I_0$ in order to meet this demand. Thus the total wages, profits, rents, and so forth increases by $I_1 - I_0$. Of this increased income, $(MPS)(I_1 - I_0)$ will be saved and the rest, $(1 - MPS)(I_1 - I_0)$, will be spent on consumption, giving rise to a "second round" demand for this much additional output. This in turn generates a "third round" demand in the amount $(1 - MPS)$ $(1 - MPS)(I_1 - I_0)$, and so forth. The total demand for new output, including all successive rounds, is thus

$$Y_1 - Y_0 = (I_1 - I_0) + (1 - MPS)(I_1 - I_0) + (1 - MPS)^2(I_1 - I_0) + \ldots$$

$$= [1 + (1 - MPS) + (1 - MPS)^2 + \ldots](I_1 - I_0)$$

Now the term $[1 + (1 - MPS) + (1 - MPS)^2 + \ldots]$ is an example of a *geometric series* and equals $1/(1 - (1 - MPS)) = 1/MPS$, which is the multiplier.

PROBLEMS ————————————————————————————

4.1 Suppose in England that consumption equals 100 units plus three-fourths of the English income. What is the English multiplier? What is English income if investment equals 200 units? How much does income increase if investment increases to 300? Answer this by the method of successive rounds, calculating the increase in income after 6 or 7 rounds.

4.2* We can investigate the *stability* of the equilibrium in Figure 4.1. Suppose that investment is OI_0 but that income is OY_1, so that saving exceeds investment. Then some output is not being sold, so we would expect firms to cut back production. This suggests the disequilibrium hypothesis: Y is falling when S exceeds I and rising when I exceeds S. Is the equilibrium in Figure 4.1 stable? Draw an unstable equilibrium. What is the stability condition?

2. The Demand for Imports

Suppose now that the autarkic economy begins to trade with the rest of the world. How do things change?

EQUILIBRIUM

Equilibrium still requires that the demand for national output equal its supply, or that total injections equal total leakages. Now exports constitute an injection of demand for domestic output just as does investment, and expenditure on imported goods constitutes a leakage from expenditure on domestic goods as does saving. Thus the equilibrium condition (4.1) must be revised to read

$$S + M = I + X. \tag{4.2}$$

The first three chapters examined commodity trade and largely ignored international borrowing and lending, that is, the sale and purchase of foreign assets. Walras's Law then implied that the value of import demand always equaled export supply. If we were to do the same now, we would have $X = M$ and (4.2) would be no different from (4.1): no international issues would emerge. Since we are in fact interested in such issues, we shall no longer assume that there are only two markets (imports and exports) but allow a third market—assets. An asset is a promise to pay in the future, such as a bond or bank account. A sale of an asset, that is, a promise to pay in the future, constitutes borrowing, and a purchase of an asset is lending. Now M need not equal X, and Walras's Law implies that the trade balance $X - M$ can increase if there is an equal increase in net purchases of foreign assets.

We have now met both of the key assumptions that distinguish the present chapter from the three previous ones: (1) Relative prices are rigid and employment is variable; and (2) International capital movements are not assumed away.

IMPORT DEMAND

What determines $X - M$? We could alternatively ask what determines capital movements, but the Keynesian theory regards the trade balance as the active component to which international lending passively adjusts as required by Walras's Law.

The demand for domestic exports is of course the same thing as the foreign demand for their imports. Thus we need know only what determines M—the same principles applied to the rest of the world will explain exports.

The demand for imports, like that for any good, depends upon prices and income. But prices are constant, so national income assumes the strategic role. Figure 4.2 depicts a curve showing the demand for imports at various levels of Y, if all other determinants (such as relative prices) do not change. The curve slopes up because as income increases, consumption increases, and part of the increase will normally be spent on foreign goods.

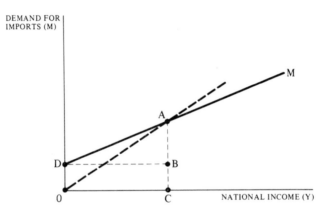

Figure 4.2. THE DEMAND FOR IMPORTS

PROPENSITIES AND ELASTICITY

The import curve is a crucial link between the domestic and foreign economies. Thus its properties are important. The term "average propensity to import" (APM) refers to M/Y. In Figure 4.2 the APM at point A is thus AC/OC. The APM at any point on the import curve is equal to the slope of a line through that point and the origin.

The "marginal propensity to import" (MPM) is the slope of the import curve. Thus at A in Figure 4.2 the MPM equals $AB/DB (= AB/OC)$.

The "income elasticity of imports" (η) is the elasticity of the import curve; $\eta = MPM/APM$. Thus in Figure 4.2 the value of η at A is $(AB/OC)/(AC/OC) = AB/AC$.

KEY CONCEPTS

The *average propensity to import* is the fraction of total national income that is spent on imports. The *marginal propensity to import* is the fraction of a unit increase in national income that would be spent on imports. The *income elasticity* of imports is the percentage by which the demand for imports would increase if national income increases by 1 percent.

PROBLEMS

4.3 Suppose that English imports always equal 50 units plus one-fourth of English income. Draw the English import function, and calculate MPM, APM, and η.

4.4 Portugal always spends one-half of its income on imports. Draw the Portuguese import curve and calculate MPM, APM, and η.

3. Case Study: Mexico, France, and Other Countries

Some examples can clarify the above concepts. The contrast between Mexico and France is instructive.

Mexico has a large, fairly underdeveloped economy, and so the foreign sector is not very large: in 1978 about 8 percent of Mexican gross domestic product was devoted to imports, that is, $APM = .08$. But these imports include capital goods, necessary for growth, and "luxury" consumer goods, the demand for which is sensitive to income. In 1978–79 the increase in Mexican imports was 16 percent of the increase in income. If this is taken as indicative of the MPM, then $MPM = .16$ and $\eta = .16/.08 = 2$, that is, each percentage increase in Mexican income was accompanied by a 2 percent increase in imports.

France, on the other hand, is an open economy with more extensive trading relations. In 1977 the French $APM = .19$, that is, almost one-fifth of national income was spent on foreign goods. In 1977–79 the increase in French imports was about 19 percent of the increase in French income. If this is taken as indicative of the French MPM, then $MPM = .19$ and $\eta = .19/.19 = 1$. Thus while the French APM is about two and one half times as large as the Mexican, Mexico appears to have almost as large an MPM and a larger elasticity. It therefore actually appears more open on a marginal criterion. These properties are reflected in the curves in Figure 4.3.

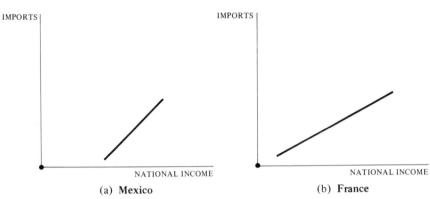

Figure 4.3. IMPORTS AND INCOMES

ESTIMATION

These back-of-the-envelope type of calculations are helpful in under-standing the concepts involved. But they should be used with care. There is no problem with the *APM:* one simply divides observed imports by ob-served income. But *MPM* and η are more difficult. They refer to import changes that would result from income changes with *other things constant.* Our calculations, however, involved actual changes during a period when other things, including relative prices, were indeed changing. Accurate es-timation of *MPM* and η is therefore difficult and is analogous to that of estimating price elasticities, discussed in Chapter 2.

A good example of these difficulties is seen in Table 4.1, which shows the relevant data for France in 1978 and in 1979.

The oil-price rise in 1979 inflated the value of imports relative to income because the French import oil. Thus we see that the *APM* in 1979 was .19 if actual imports are divided by actual income. but .17 if the data

Table 4.1. FRENCH IMPORTS AND INCOME

	1978	1979	*Change from* 78–79
(1) Imports (billions of francs)	369	455	86
(2) Income (GNP in billions of francs)	2140	2445	305
(3) Imports at Constant Prices	369	411	42
(4) Income at Constant Prices	2140	2437	297
(5) (1) ÷ (2)	.17	.19	.28
(6) (3) ÷ (4)	.17	.17	.14

SOURCE: International Financial Statistics

are adjusted for the price changes. Which measure is correct? They *both* are. The *APM* depends upon the units of measurement, and the two numbers differ because these units have changed; with accurate price indices, either number can be converted to the other. If we now try to estimate the *MPM* as above by dividing observed import changes by observed income changes, the contrast is even greater; we obtain a value of .28 when actual data are used and .14 with price deflated data. Which is correct? Neither! The first number is, of course, much larger than the second because the rise in oil prices inflated imports relative to income. But the relative price change caused the French to alter their spending patterns; the import curve shifted down. Thus both numbers reflect a combination of a shift in the curve with a movement along it; consequently neither is a good indicator of the *MPM*, which refers only to the movement along the curve.

SOME ESTIMATES OF INCOME ELASTICITIES

The Houthakker-Magee study mentioned in Chapter 2 also contained estimates of income elasticities. Several of these are presented as illustrations in Table 4.2.

Table 4.2. INCOME ELASTICITIES OF THE DEMAND FOR MERCHANDISE IMPORTS

Country	η
Australia	.9
Japan	1.2
U.S.	1.7
U.K.	1.5
Canada	1.2

SOURCE: *Houthakker and Magee*, op. cit.

NORTH AMERICAN EXPERIENCE

The *United States* has a large self-sufficient economy and, thus, a relatively low *APM*. Also as the economy developed during the nineteenth and twentieth centuries, it became less dependent on foreign imports, so the *APM* tended to fall. From a value of .1 near the beginning of this century, it steadily declined to about .03 after the Second World War. But recent behavior has been different. The *APM* has been rising for some time, and in 1979 was about .09. Note that the estimate of the U.S. income elasticity in Table 4.2 is above unity. This estimate is also the largest in the table, so that the United States seems quite open by this criterion, although the *APM* of .09 is relatively low.

Since we have looked at both Mexico and the United States, a few words about *Canada* will complete a cursory survey of North America. Canada, unlike the United States, did not become a relatively closed economy as it developed: in 1980, about one-fourth of Canadian GNP was spent on imports. The elasticity estimate in Table 4.2 is, however, less than that for the United States. But the estimate does exceed unity and, indeed, the Canadian *APM* has tended to rise in recent years.

PROBLEMS

4.5 Describe the effect of each of the following on a country's import curve.
a The country imposes a tax on imports from abroad.
b The country's residents decide to save less, thereby boosting income and imports.
c The country establishes an import quota, prohibiting imports in excess of a certain amount, $\overline{M}$.
d The rest of the world imposes a tax upon its imports from this country.

4.6 Using the 1979 U.S. *APM* of .09 and the estimate of the U.S. η, shown in Table 4.2, calculate an estimate of the U.S. *MPM*. Calculate the actual increase in U.S. imports for 1979–80 as a fraction of the actual U.S. increase in GNP (see Appendix II for data sources). Compare the two results. List all the reasons you can think of why they might differ from each other and from the true *MPM*. Do the same for Canada.

4. The Simple Foreign Trade Multiplier

EQUILIBRIUM

Let us now once again consider a country—say, France—trading with Germany. Using equation (4.2), French equilibrium income is determined by

$$S + M = I + X. \tag{4.3}$$

Now French exports X are simply German imports, which depend upon German income. From the French point of view German income is exogenous, and thus so is X. Therefore the right-hand side of (4.3) is exogenous; the left-hand side depends upon Y. The equilibrium level of income is that which equates the left-hand side to the right-hand side. This is shown in Figure 4.4.

The parallel with Figure 4.1 should be obvious; the picture is the same, only the labels have been changed. The distance *OD* now represents the sum of investment and exports; and the upward-sloping line shows how savings *plus* imports depend upon income. Its slope, *BC/AB*, thus equals *MPS* + *MPM*. Equilibrium French income is *DA*, determined by the intersection of the two curves.

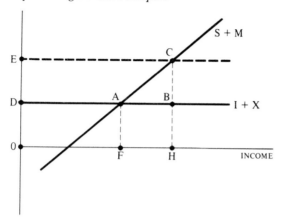

Figure 4.4. EQUILIBRIUM FRENCH INCOME

FOREIGN TRADE MULTIPLIER

Suppose that French investment plus exports increase, say by the amount DE in Figure 4.4. This could be an increase in I, or in German imports, or any combination of the two. Then equilibrium moves from A to C and French income increases by AB.

Thus the increase in income AB is related to the increase DE in autonomous expenditure by

$$AB = \left(\frac{1}{MPS + MPM} \right) DE.$$

The term $1/(MPS + MPM)$ is called the foreign trade multiplier because it must be multiplied by the increase in autonomous expenditure to find the resulting increase in income.

KEY CONCEPT

The *foreign trade multiplier* is the amount by which the equilibrium national income of an open economy will be raised by a unit increase in investment or in exports.

A slightly different picture of equilibrium is also useful. Rearranging (4.3) we obtain

$$S - I = X - M. \tag{4.4}$$

The left-hand side is the excess of saving over domestic investment; in a closed economy, it must be zero. The right-hand side is the *trade balance,* or excess of exports over imports. Each side of (4.4) is graphed in Figure 4.5. $S - I$ has a positive slope, because an increase in income raises S and leaves I untouched; $X - M$ slopes down because the income increase raises M but not X. Equilibrium is at point T. This graph has the advantage of explicitly showing the two major variables that are determined in equilibrium: national income (equal to OH here) and the trade balance (TH).

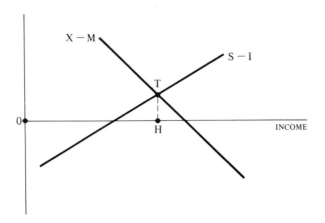

Figure 4.5. Equilibrium Income and the Trade Balance

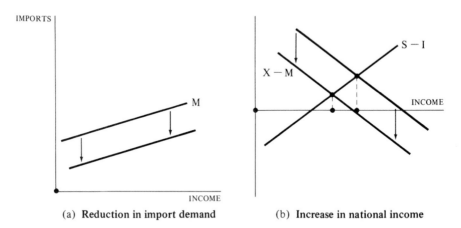

(a) **Reduction in import demand**   (b) **Increase in national income**

Figure 4.6. A Shift in Import Demand

Several important conclusions emerge from our discussion of the foreign trade multiplier.

First, the multiplier is smaller than if the economy were closed because the denominator has increased by *MPM*. An increase in I will thus cause a smaller increase in income than if foreign trade were absent. This is because some of an increase in demand leaks onto foreign goods. This may not matter much for the United States, which spends only a small fraction of extra income on foreign goods, but it is crucial for an open economy such as Belgium, which spends over half its GNP on imports.

Second, the international sector now becomes another source of disturbances influencing income. An increase in exports causes the same multiplied increase in income as an increase in investment. Also national income can be influenced by changing import demand. The import curve can be shifted downward by tariffs, quotas, or other restrictions on the

---

CASE STUDY: The Macroeconomic Impact of the Oil-Price Rise on the United States

Let us look—through Keynesian, demand-side, glasses—at the macroeconomic effect of the 1973–74 oil price rise. In 1974 U.S. crude petroleum imports of 1,162 million barrels were only slightly above the 1973 level of 1,011 million barrels, but the average price had climbed from $3.33 to $11.01 because of the first OPEC shock. Thus the 1974 cost of $12.8 billion would have been only $3.9 billion at 1973 prices—a difference of $8.9 billion. The increase in their oil revenues enabled the OPEC countries to import more: their 1974 imports from the United States of $6.8 billion exceeded their 1973 imports by about $3.1 billion. However, the United States also purchased considerable petroleum and petroleum products from non-OPEC countries, and the oil-price rise also increased the cost of these imports—by about $9 billion. If we assume that this generated an increase in U.S. exports of $4.1 billion (basically a guess—it is very difficult to trace out the exact effect), we have the following direct effect of the first oil shock on total U.S. $X - M$:

Increased bill for OPEC oil	$-$8.9 billion
Increase in exports to OPEC	3.1
Increased bill for other oil products	$-$ 9.0
Increase in other exports to other sellers	4.1
Net effect on $X - M$	$-$10.7 billion.

Thus the first shock shifted the U.S. $X - M$ curve downward by about $10.7 billion in 1974. This was a contributing factor to the 1974–75 recession, the most severe since the Second World War. The overall trade balance $X - M$ fell by $6.2 billion, from $.9 billion in 1973 to $-$5.3 billion in 1974.

import of specific goods; with aggregate consumption unchanged, such measures switch demand from foreign goods to domestic goods. This is depicted in Figure 4.6(a). Then the exports-minus-imports curve will shift up by a like amount, producing the increase in national income depicted in Figure 4.6(b).

Third, policies that influence national income will also influence the trade balance, itself frequently a matter of concern for policy makers. Suppose the French increase I, causing income to rise from Y_0 to Y_1 in Figure 4.7. Then the trade balance falls, as the figure shows. Similarly a reduction in I will increase the trade balance. The implication is that in making expenditure policy, the authorities will wish to consider its effects on the trade balance as well as on national output.

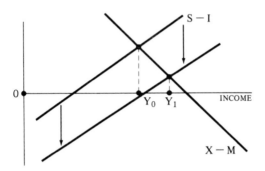

Figure 4.7. AN INCREASE IN INVESTMENT

PROBLEMS ――――――――――――――――――――――――――――

4.7 Use the method of successive rounds to derive the foreign trade multiplier.

4.8 Find the multiplier for England if consumption equals 100 units plus three-fourths of English income and if imports equal 50 units plus one-fourth of income. What is English income if investment equals 200 units and exports 100? If investment increases to 300? Suppose instead that investment remains at 200 but trade policy is used so that English imports now equal 40 plus one-fifth of English income; calculate the effect on income.

4.9 Suppose that the Portuguese always save one-quarter of their income and spend one-half on imports. Calculate the multiplier. What is Portuguese income if investment equals 50 and exports 100?

4.10 Calculate a formula for the term that must be multiplied by a change in I to obtain the effect on the trade balance $X - M$.

4.11 The discussion in the text assumed that autonomous expenditure was all devoted to domestic goods. Suppose instead that the fraction MPM of an increase in I is spent on imports. Calculate the formula for the multipler in this case. How would your answer to Problem **4.10** change?

4.12 The discussion of trade policy assumed that the reduction in M for any Y was all spent on domestic goods, that is, that trade policy switched expenditure from foreign goods to domestic ones. Suppose instead that the income no longer spent on foreign goods is simply saved. How would trade policy affect income and the trade balance in this case?

4.13 The CASE STUDY in this section supposed that the oil price rise translated into an increase in M, since Americans had to pay more for their oil. But oil is an intermediate good. So paying more for it would reduce the income of importers. How would our discussion change if the direct effect of the oil price rise were a reduction in Y rather than a rise in M? Depict both cases geometrically.

5. Policy Dilemmas

INTERNAL AND EXTERNAL BALANCE

Policy makers will be concerned about both the level of national income (internal balance) and the size of the balance of trade or net foreign lending (external balance). If the only available policy tool is expenditure policy (control of I), it could be impossible to pursue both goals. Suppose the authorities wish to attain certain target levels of both Y and $X - M$. If income in fact exceeds its target level while the trade balance falls short, there is no question as to the proper policy—contraction (that is, a reduction of I) will move the economy closer to both targets. Similarly, if Y falls short of its target while $X - M$ exceeds its target, expansionary policy is called for on both counts. But if Y and $X - M$ both exceed their targets, or, alternatively, if both fall short, there is a conflict between internal and external balance. Any change in I intended to approach one target will move the economy away from the other. Furthermore if the authorities do succeed in approaching both targets, such a conflict will almost certainly emerge, because our theory has given no reason to expect that the exact value of I that will equate Y to its target will also happen to cause $X - M$ to just equal its target.

Suppose, using Figure 4.8(a), that the authorities wish income to be given by point B and that they also desire balanced trade: $X = M$. But the latter goal requires income to be at A. If the authorities pursue their external balance target and land at A, income falls short by AB; if instead internal balance is aimed at and achieved at B, the trade balance is negative in the amount BC.

If expenditure policy is the only available tool, the authorities must therefore ultimately choose between internal balance and external balance and hope that the other will take care of itself. American authorities, for example, have generally directed their efforts toward achieving internal balance. The British experience after the Second World War of "stop-go" growth can be viewed as a case of alternating concern with external and

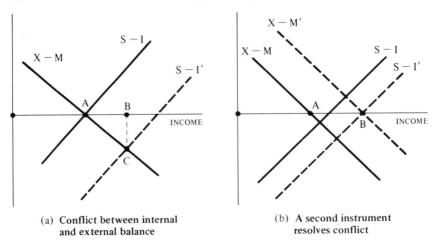

(a) **Conflict between internal
and external balance**

(b) **A second instrument
resolves conflict**

Figure 4.8. INTERNAL AND EXTERNAL BALANCE

internal balance: British authorities have depressed aggregate demand to improve external balance ("stop") until concern with unemployment has caused them to switch gears and stimulate the economy ("go"), until deteriorating external balance has prompted another reversal, and so forth.

Escape from this dilemma is possible if a second policy tool can be found. We have seen that trade policy can also be used to influence Y and $X - M$. Thus the proper combination of expenditure policy and trade policy can in principle achieve both internal and external balance, as illustrated in Figure 4.8(b). But variations in trade policy involve movements away from free trade and therefore long-term inefficiencies, as comparative advantage makes clear. Also it is not a very flexible tool as it tends to have concentrated impact on special interest groups. For these reasons many economists question the wisdom of using trade policy for the short-run objectives of internal and external balance.

INTERNATIONAL INTERDEPENDENCE

The options faced by national policy makers are also influenced by the international interdependence caused by trade. To understand this interdependence, introduce Germany into the discussion. German income is determined in the same way as French income; it must be such as to equate leakages to injections, as in (4.5). We now use superscripts to distinguish the two countries. German exports are of course French imports: $X^G = M^F$.

$$S^G + M^G = I^G + X^G. \tag{4.5}$$

Suppose now that France increases I^F, causing a multiplied rise in Y^F. As we have seen, this will increase M^F. Thus the Germans experience a rise in the right-hand side of (4.5), and so German income will increase by this amount multiplied by the German foreign trade multiplier. So an increase in I^F raises Y^G as well as Y^F; similarly an expansionary policy in Germany will stimulate both economies. This is simply the other side of the coin from the "leakage" we observed when deriving the French foreign trade multiplier.

A change in investment in any country constitutes a change in world investment and stimulates all countries. International trade is the mechanism for transmitting the stimulus from country to country. Likewise for a decrease in investment. Thus the Great Depression spread from the United States to the rest of the world. American recessions and booms greatly influence our major trading partners, and most other countries are affected indirectly as well as directly. For example, an American recession will produce a deflationary effect in Australia by reducing the American demand for imports of Australian goods. But it will also reduce demand in Japan, a major trading partner of the United States; since the Japanese import much from Australia, this will in turn reduce Australian demand also.

Trade policy likewise has international ramifications, but of a different sort. Suppose the French shift their import curve down and so raise Y^F, as in Figure 4.6. The downward shift decreases M^F. This will be partially offset by the stimulating effect on imports of the rise in Y^F, but only partly as otherwise French income could not in fact rise. Thus M^F on balance falls. This will cause a multiplied reduction in German income. Thus trade policy produces an *opposite* effect in foreign countries. Similarly an upward shift in the French import curve would stimulate German income while depressing French.

A change in trade policy in any country switches aggregate world demand from the products of one country to those of another. Thus during the Great Depression many countries tried to stimulate their economies at the expense of their partners by restricting imports with tariffs and quotas. Such attempts are sometimes called "exporting unemployment," and the policies used to implement them "beggar-thy-neighbor" policies. To the extent that several nations all attempt this at once, whether for offensive or defensive purposes, their efforts will tend to cancel, but world trade will shrink, with accompanying inefficiency. That is what happened in the thirties.

INTERNATIONAL POLICY CONFLICTS

Suppose the French authorities desire a certain level of aggregate demand, say Y_D^F, and the Germans desire Y_D^G. These are represented by point D in Figure 4.9. If the world is at D, all is well. Otherwise there are four possibilities, indicated by the quadrants in the figure.

For example, if the world is in quadrant I, say at point A, both coun-

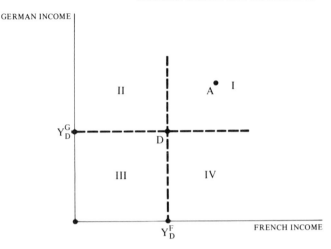

Figure 4.9. POSSIBLE POLICY CONFLICTS

tries wish to reduce demand. If expenditure policy is the tool in each country, they both decrease I and these actions are mutually reinforcing. Similarly, if the world is quadrant *III*, France will increase I^F and Germany will increase I^G, and each country's action will reinforce that of the other. But in quadrants *II* and *IV* the goals of the two countries conflict. One will increase I while the other reduces it, and each country's action will frustrate the other. In a perfect world the two countries could simply adopt the values of I^F and I^G that would allow both to reach their desired incomes. But in reality the authorities can never be sure of what result will follow from their policies, or even of what policy will actually follow from their attempts, and these attempts cannot be smoothly altered. Thus the possibility of policy conflict is very real.

Suppose instead that France and Germany use trade policy. Then in quadrant *I* each country will attempt to shift its import curve up to reduce aggregate demand. But this will stimulate demand in the other country. Likewise in quadrant *III* each country's attempt to solve its own problem will make things worse for the other. Quadrants *II* and *IV* now represent the cases where policy actions in France and Germany are mutually reinforcing.

CASE STUDY: Project LINK

If one were to estimate the actual values of MPM^F and MPS^F, expression (4.3) would become a rudimentary *econometric model* of the French economy: the economist could use it to obtain a forecast of what French income and imports would be if investment and exports equaled certain hypothesized values. Of course this would be a very simple model indeed. All productive sectors are lumped together and asset markets, the monetary sector, price changes, and so forth are ignored completely. Similarly expression (4.5) would become a rudimentary model of the German economy for an economist with estimates of MPM^G and MPS^G.

Now the forecast that each economist would obtain with his model would depend on what he assumed exports to be, so that each economist would be forecasting one of the variables that the other economist was guessing at. Obviously there is an incentive to link the two models together to increase the accuracy of each and to allow for consistent global forecasts.

Econometric modeling of national economies has developed rapidly in recent decades, and elaborate models now exist for all major economies, as well as for many smaller ones and some groups of small economies. Some of these models contain hundreds of equations and variables. Project LINK is an international research project attempting to develop connections between econometric models of about thirty countries, including seven centrally planned economies. The project is an ongoing one both in that the individual models and the links between them are continually being refined and in that additional links are being forged. Table 4.3 shows the results of some dynamic simulations with the LINK system. Each row contains four multipliers showing the percentage by which, in terms of deflated dollars, the incomes of each of the four countries would have risen in 1982, per percent increase in the government spending of the country identified on the left, starting in 1978.

Table 4.3. LINK SIMULATIONS OF EFFECTS ON 1982 INCOMES IN VARIOUS COUNTRIES OF HYPOTHESIZED INCREASES IN GOVERNMENT SPENDING STARTING IN 1978.

Source of Shock	Effects of Shock			
	U.S.	Germany	Japan	Canada
U.S.	2.64	.45	.24	.75
Germany	.18	2.54	.18	.16
Japan	.03	.07	1.26	.04
Canada	.05	.03	.01	1.40

SOURCE: *V-Filatov, B. G. Hickman, and L. R. Klein, "Long-Run Simulations with the Project LINK System, 1978–85"*

6. *Exploring Further:* General Equilibrium

In this section we examine repercussions between two trading economies. This amounts to a simple theoretical treatment of the issues Project LINK addresses econometrically.

The simple foreign trade multiplier expresses the direct link between the domestic and international economies. But there are indirect links as well. For example an increase in French investment will cause a multiplied increase in French income, and this will increase imports as indicated by the French import curve. This increase in French imports is an increase in German exports, so there will also be an increase in German income as determined by the German foreign trade multiplier. Now the increase in German income will bring about an increase in German imports from France, which will induce a "second round" increase in French income. And so through successive "rounds."

These repercussions reflect the fact that the French and German incomes are not independent but are jointly determined. This is explicit in (4.6) and (4.7):

$$S^F + M^F = I^F + M^G \tag{4.6}$$

$$S^G + M^G = I^G + M^F \tag{4.7}$$

Expression (4.6) says that French income depends upon German income (through M^G), and (4.7) that German income depends upon French income (through M^F). Neither can be determined independently of the other. Just as in Chapter 2, we are confronted with a problem of general equilibrium.

To see how the two national incomes are jointly determined we must first see how each depends on the other. This is done in Figure 4.10, which shows how French income depends upon German income. Suppose German income is equal to Y_0^G, as shown on the vertical axis in Figure 4.10(b). Then this determines German imports from France, and the French equilibrium income is determined as in section 4. This is shown at point A in Figure 4.10(a) so that French income is Y_0^F. In other words, if German income is Y_0^G then French income must be Y_0^F; this is recorded in Figure 4.10(b) at point B. Now if German income increases from Y_0^G to Y_1^G, German imports from France will increase by $MPM^G(Y_1^G - Y_0^G)$. The intersection in Figure 4.10(a) then shifts from A to C, French income increasing from Y_0^F to Y_1^F. This is recorded in Figure 4.10(b) as a movement from point B to D. By the foreign trade multiplier the increase in French income must be

$$(Y_1^F - Y_0^F) = \left(\frac{1}{MPS^F + MPM^F}\right) MPM^G(Y_1^G - Y_0^G).$$

The curve Y^F in Figure 4.10(b), then, shows what French income must

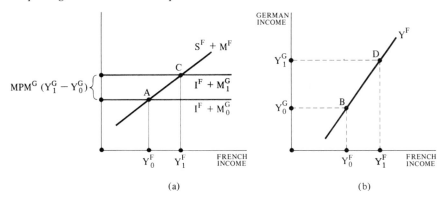

Figure 4.10. How French Income Depends upon German Income

be for each level of German income; it has a slope of $(MPS^F + MPM^F)/MPM^G$.

In similar fashion a curve Y^G can be derived showing what German income must be for each level of French income. This curve is depicted in Figure 4.11. To test yourself, show exactly how this curve is derived and demonstrate that it must have a slope of $MPM^F/(MPM^G + MPS^G)$. The Y^F curve, then, shows all combinations of French and German incomes for which the demand for French output equals the supply, and the Y^G curve shows all combinations for which the demand for German output equals the supply. Equilibrium will be given at the intersection, point A, for only here will French and German incomes be mutually consistent.

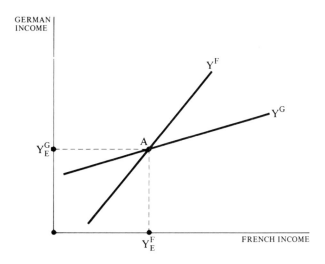

Figure 4.11. General Equilibrium

Suppose now that there is an increase in French investment. Then for each value of German income, French income will increase by an amount equal to the change in investment times the simple French foreign trade multiplier, as discussed in section 4. This is depicted as the shift in the Y^F curve in Figure 4.12, and the "first round" increase in French income is given by the distance AB. This increases French imports from Germany, which then causes German income to increase in the amount BC. This increases German imports from France, thus inducing a "second round" increase in French income of CD, and so on. Final equilibrium is at E. Thus the increase in French investment has caused an increase of AF in French income and an increase of FE in German income.

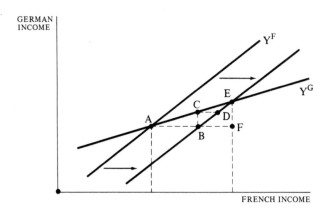

Figure 4.12. EFFECTS OF AN INCREASE IN FRENCH INVESTMENT

One can now calculate more complex multipliers giving the total effect (direct effect plus repercussions) of various disturbances on national incomes. For example there are the four multipliers expressing the effect of a change in investment in each country on income in each country. And multipliers relating to a shift in import demand. The mind boggles at such vast opportunities for algebraic manipulation. But the purpose of this discussion is simply to emphasize the interdependence between income determination in the separate countries. This interdependence has already found expression in the policy problems considered in section 5.

PROBLEMS ———————————————————————————————

4.14 Show how the Y^G curve in Figure 4.11 is derived, and demonstrate that it must have a slope of $MPM^F/(MPM^G + MPS^G)$.

4.15 Using the method of successive rounds, derive the multiplier that relates changes in Y^F to changes in I^F when all repercussions are accounted for.

4.16 Using the method of successive rounds, derive the multiplier that relates changes in Y^F to changes in I^G when all repercussions are accounted for.

4.17 In England consumption equals 100 units plus ¾ of GNP and imports equal 50 units plus ¼ of GNP. England trades with Portugal, where savings are ¼ of GNP and imports are ½ of GNP. Calculate multipliers for each country. What is each country's GNP if English investment equals 200 units and Portuguese investment equals 50 units? Calculate the effects of each of the following:

  a An increase in English I to 300.

  b An increase in Portuguese I to 100.

  c A shift in the English import curve to 40 units plus ⅕ of GNP.

Show how your answers illustrate the use of the formulus you derived in Problems **4.15** and **4.16**.

7. Inflation

Thus far we have assumed that all prices are rigid; this highlights the macroeconomic problems that are the province of Keynesian economics. But inflation is a macroeconomic problem, and inflation, of course, refers to price changes. In this section we consider price changes of the following type: simultaneous movements in the prices of all goods produced by an economy.

THE PHILLIPS CURVE

Such price movements can be due to many causes, most of which would contribute little of interest to the issues already discussed in this chapter. But this is not true of one possible cause: Increases in national output can stimulate inflation. This is illustrated in Figure 4.13 where the rate of inflation is related to the unemployment rate by the curve *AA*, called a Phillips curve, after the Australian economist A. W. Phillips, who advanced both the idea and statistical support. An increase in the unemployment rate is of course associated with a fall in national output. Note that the vertical axis measures not the price *level* but the inflation rate—the rate at which the prices of domestic goods are rising. If the unemployment rate equals that indicated by *B*, the price level will remain constant, a larger national output (lower unemployment rate) will cause prices to steadily rise and more unemployment will cause them to steadily fall.

The authorities presumably wish both the inflation rate and unemployment to be as close to zero as possible. But the Phillips curve indicates that more employment must be "purchased" at the cost of more inflation. The message for policy is simple: there is a trade-off between inflation and unemployment so that policy makers can choose the combination on the curve they most prefer, although they cannot eliminate both.

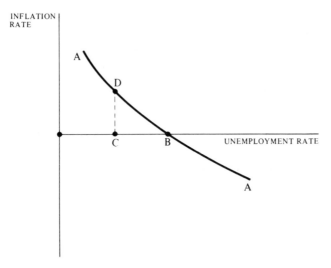

Figure 4.13. THE PHILLIPS CURVE

IS THE PHILLIPS CURVE STABLE?

This policy message is based squarely on the presumption that the Phillips curve exists and is stable, that is, it does not shift around a lot. During the sixties most policy discussion was apparently based on this presumption, but in the seventies many economists questioned its validity (no doubt partly because in the early seventies both inflation and unemployment simultaneously rose in many countries). It is challenged on two grounds.

Sensitivity to exogenous events. Changes in the economy can cause the curve to shift. For example, many economists believe that the recent increase in the labor-force participation of women has shifted the U.S. Phillips curve out, as shown in Figure 4.14. Suppose that this shift occurred as authorities were implementing an anti-inflationary program designed to move the economy from *A* to *B*. Instead it moves from *A* to *C:* both unemployment and inflation rise. Another example could be the oil-price shocks. As firms pass on their increased energy costs in higher prices, and as workers and others try to "catch up," inflation increases, shifting the Phillips curve to the right. When the new relative prices finally become accepted, the inflation ceases, and the curve shifts back. Some hold the view that the curve is so sensitive to such exogenous events that it is useless as a guide to policy.

The natural rate theory. This challenge is more basic. The Phillips curve is said to reflect illusion on the part of economic agents in the follow-

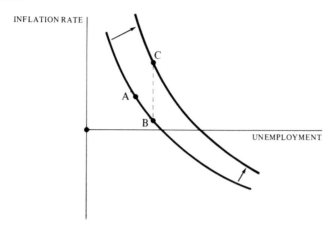

Figure 4.14. A Shift of the Phillips Curve

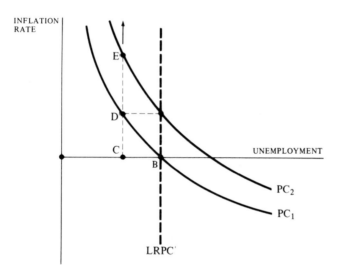

Figure 4.15. Long-Run and Short-Run Phillips Curves

ing way. Suppose the economy is at *B* on the Phillips curve PC_1 in Figure 4.15, so there is no inflation, and no one expects any. All is well. Now suppose the government acts to reduce unemployment to *C*. Then workers (or their unions) realize that labor markets have tightened and they force wages up. Producers raise prices to cover their increased labor costs, workers further force up wages to maintain their purchasing power, and so on. This generates the inflation indicated by *CD*. Now problems arise. The workers will eventually realize that their wage increases are being nullified by price increases and so will escalate their demands, causing escalating price increases. Now that everyone realizes that there will be an inflation of *DC*, this will be "built into" all price decisions, that is, everyone will plan on raising prices by this much more than they would if no inflation were expected. This means that PC_1 shifts up to PC_2. In order to keep the unemployment rate equal to *OC*, inflation must be *EC*, not *DC*. But this is not the end of the story. Once people *expect* inflation to equal *EC*, PC_2 will shift up, and so on and so on. If unemployment stays at *OC*, inflation will increase again and again. Only point *B* (called the *natural rate of unemployment*) is consistent with steady inflation—any reduction in unemployment will cause accelerating inflation. The trade-off illustrated by the Phillips curve PC_1 is transitory at best, according to this view, and the only long-run possibilities are those on the vertical long-run Phillips curve, *LRPC*.

INFLATION IN THE OPEN ECONOMY

Suppose that both the French and German economies have Phillips curves of the type illustrated in Figure 4.13, and suppose for now that they are in fact stable. How does this affect the conclusions of previous sections?

For one thing, the authorities in each country must now choose a combination of output and inflation, as discussed above, so the discussion of policy dilemmas in section 5 must be interpreted in this light. But in addition inflation introduces a new type of interdependence between the two economies.

Suppose that the French inflation rate exceeds the German, either because the French authorities choose a different point on their Phillips curve than do the Germans or because the two curves are themselves different. Then French prices are rising relative to German, and so some relative prices must be changing. To make this clear, suppose that France is specialized to wine production and Germany to machine production. Then the lower German inflation means that the relative price of machines in terms of wine is falling. This will cause French imports to rise and German imports to fall, thereby generating a contractionary force on French income and an expansionary force on German income.

Suppose that Y_6^F is the level of French output consistent with a zero rate of inflation, that is Y_6^F is the output that corresponds to the unemployment rate indicated by *B* in Figure 4.13. Similarly Y_8^G denotes the German output at which German inflation equals zero, so that point *E* in Figure 4.16 indicates the case where there is no inflation in either country. If only French income is increased, as indicated by *A* for example, then French inflation exceeds German, and the relative price of machines in terms of wine is falling. Similarly at *B* the relative price of machines is rising. If both outputs increase in the right proportion, say from *E* to *D* in the figure, both countries will have equal inflation rates so that relative prices do not

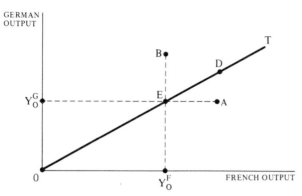

Figure 4.16. INFLATION IN THE OPEN ECONOMY

change. The line OT in Figure 4.16 denotes the combinations of Y^F and Y^G for which German inflation just equals French inflation. Below the line the relative price of machines is falling, and above the line the relative price of machines is rising.

Suppose that the world is initially at E. The relative price of machines is constant. Now suppose that the French wish to increase their output, at the cost of the inflation implied by their Phillips curve; assume that the authorities in both countries adjust their fiscal policies, as discussed in section 4, so that the world moves to A, the new desired position.

Now French inflation exceeds German: the relative price of machines is falling. Thus M^F will be rising and M^G falling, so that French income will tend to fall and German income to rise: the world will be forced back toward the OT line. The authorities can resist this by steadily increasing I^F and decreasing I^G, but unless they are willing to do this continuously, they will eventually be forced back to OT. The presence of inflation thus fundamentally alters the policy problem: incomes in the two countries are intimately linked together (via OT). Also the terms of trade can be influenced by expenditure policy: even if the world returns to OT so that the relative price of machines stops falling, it will have already fallen by a certain amount. The policy conclusion is clear: a country can control its level of income only if it allows the other country to control the terms of trade and that country acquiesces.

THE NATURAL RATE IN THE OPEN ECONOMY

How are these conclusions altered if we accept the natural rate theory outlined above? In this case all points below the OT line in Figure 4.16 correspond to an *accelerating* decline in the relative price of machines, and all points above to an accelerating rise in this price. This clearly strengthens the above argument. Along OT the relative price is constant, but only point

E allows a steady rate of world inflation. Beyond *E*, as at *D,* all prices are rising together at an accelerating rate. Only *E* is consistent with steady inflation in both countries, and both countries will have the same inflation rate.

8. Summary

1. The Keynesian theory of international trade adopts a macroeconomic perspective. It differs from the theory in Chapters 1, 2, and 3 in two basic ways: (a) equilibrium is reached via adjustment in employment rather than in relative prices; and (b) capital moves between countries to accommodate the balance of trade.

2. The multiplier in an open economy is reduced by the propensity of expenditure to leak abroad onto foreign goods. Also variations in exports supply an additional source of autonomous disturbances.

3. The balance of trade is often a policy target in addition to the level of employment. Both targets are unlikely to be reached simultaneously if expenditure policy is the sole available instrument. Trade policy supplies a second instrument that could allow both targets to be reached, but the wisdom of using trade policy in this way is widely questioned.

4. Because of international spillovers, the exercise of expenditure policy in one country affects other countries. Thus such policy will be disruptive of international harmony when countries are out of phase, and mutually reinforcing when they are in phase.

5. Trade policy redistributes expenditures between countries. Thus such policy is disruptive when countries are in phase, and mutually reinforcing when they are out of phase.

6. Inflation rates must be equal between countries in order for relative prices to remain in equilibrium. To the extent that inflation rates are sensitive to employment levels, this requirement establishes a link between income levels in different countries.

SUGGESTED READING

Dixit, A. K. and Norman, V. *Theory of International Trade.* Cambridge: Cambridge University Press, 1980. Chapter 8 discusses contemporary theory.

Dornbusch, R. *Open Economy Macroeconomics.* New York: Basic Books, 1980. See part 2 for a good discussion of employment and the balance of trade.

Machlup, F. *International Trade and the National Income Multiplier.* Philadelphia: Blakiston, 1943. An early but still useful treatment.

Meade, J. E. *The Balance of Payments.* Oxford: Oxford University Press, 1951. See part 2 for a detailed discussion.

Metzler, L. A. "A Multiple-Region Theory of Income and Trade." *Econometrica,* 1950. Extends the theory to a many-country context.

Metzler, L. A. "The Theory of International Trade." In *A Survey of Contemporary Economics.* Edited by H. S. Ellis. Philadelphia: Blakiston Co., 1948. A survey of trade theory stressing the impact of Keynesian ideas.

Metzler, L. A. "The Transfer Problem Reconsidered." In *Readings in the Theory of International Trade.* Edited by H. S. Ellis and L. A. Metzler. Homewood: Irwin, 1949.

Robinson, R. "A Graphical Analysis of the Foreign Trade Multiplier." *Economic Journal* 247, 1952.

Sawyer, John A. *Modelling the International Transmission Mechanism.* Amsterdam: North Holland, 1979. Project LINK.

Further Applications and Extensions of the Pure Theory of International Trade

THE pure theory of international trade studied in Part One is built squarely on the assumption that commodities can be freely traded between countries but factors are completely immobile internationally. Thus commodity markets are international, whereas factor markets are national. This assumption was the ultimate cause of trade in both the classical theory and its neoclassical extensions. Keynesian theory allowed international borrowing and lending. Such *capital movements,* however, were treated as simply passive responses to trade, and labor continued to be completely immobile between countries.

Part Two looks at international economic issues that arise when we depart from this basic assumption.

Recall from the Introduction that international economics is distinguished from general economics not only by its treatment of markets of differing extent, as studied in Part One, but also by the limits of national sovereignty. This second distinguishing feature arises in Chapters 5 and 6, where we discuss the role of national governments in controlling and limiting international trade. Thus we also depart from the assumption that commodities can be freely traded between countries. Chapter 7 then drops the other half of the assumption, that factors are completely immobile internationally, to examine issues involving the movement of productive factors from one country to another. In all three chapters we freely apply the four basic ideas with which Part One has equipped us.

Chapter 5

Tariffs and Trade Theory

"We up in Massachusetts do not want that duty upon molasses, we
trade our fish for molasses, and if you shut out molasses you shut
in fish."
—U.S. CONGRESSIONAL DEBATES (1790)

THE THEORY of international trade makes on balance a strong case for free
trade. Yet governments have always attempted to control trade to at least
some extent, and deliberate free-trade policies have indeed been very rare
historically. In this chapter we examine commercial policy: the attempts of
national governments to influence or control international trade.

Many instruments can be used to exercise commercial policy. Perhaps
the most familiar is a tax on imports, commonly called a *tariff*. Of course
exports might also be taxed, and both imports and exports are sometimes
subsidized (a negative tax). In addition many *nontariff barriers* do not involve taxes or subsidies at all. Quantitative restrictions, for example, limit
the quantities of specific goods that can be imported (or, sometimes, exported). In principle there might be either maximum or minimum quotas
on either exports or imports, but a quota on the maximum quantity of a
good that can be imported in a specific time interval is perhaps the most
familiar form. Sometimes tariffs and quotas are combined. A *tariff-quota*
(or customs quota) does not prohibit imports above the quota amount but
instead subjects them to a higher tariff than that imposed on imports within
the quota.

In addition to taxes and quantitative restrictions, many nontariff barriers occupy a gray area: laws, regulations and procedures which are not
explicitly aimed at international trade but which nonetheless influence it.

Overzealous health inspectors, safety regulations biased toward domestic production methods, and regional development grants and tax privileges to export industries are examples of a host of measures that influence international trade despite altogether different ostensible purposes.

In what follows we shall at first be largely concerned with the economic effects of tariffs. This is because tariffs historically have been the most important form of commercial policy, and because the conclusions we reach with respect to tariffs will easily be adapted to the other forms of protection as well.

1. The Tariff

A tariff is a tax on imports: the price a domestic purchaser pays for an imported good exceeds the amount the foreign exporter receives by the tariff payment. All the economic effects of a tariff follow from this simple fact. But a tariff can take many forms.

SPECIFIC TARIFFS

Perhaps the simplest is a specific tariff: a tax of a certain specified amount on each unit of a specified good that is imported. If P denotes the foreign price of some good and t_s the specific tariff levied upon it, then the domestic price Q is

$$Q = P + t_s. \tag{5.1}$$

AD-VALOREM TARIFFS

Alternatively, tariffs are frequently ad-valorem: a specified percentage of the price paid to the foreign exporter. If P denotes the foreign price of a good subject to an ad-valorem tariff rate t_{AV}, then the domestic price Q is

$$Q = P(1 + t_{AV}). \tag{5.2}$$

The domestic price consists of the payment to the foreigner, P, plus the import tax, Pt_{AV}.

OTHER FORMS

Most actual tariffs are either specific or ad-valorem, but other forms are also encountered. For example, the two types are sometimes *combined*, with the total tariff equal to a specific tariff plus a percentage of the price. Another method is to calculate the tariff as a fixed percentage, not of the foreign price *(P)* but of the price *(Q)*, at which the imported good, or a similar domestic good, is actually sold in the domestic market. The United States for many years used this method, called the American Selling Price

(ASP) system, for a few products and at one time considered adopting the method generally.

Yet another type of tariff is a *variable levy:* the tariff is adjusted to keep the domestic price of imports equal to some target level. Thus if $\overline{Q}$ denotes the target, the variable levy will be equal to $\overline{Q} - P$, so that a fall in the foreign price results in an increase in the levy. Such tariffs have most often been found on agricultural goods, in connection with domestic price support measures. The English Corn Laws of the early nineteenth century were of this type, and such levies are important today because the European Community employs them in connection with its Common Agricultural Policy, as, in effect, do centrally planned economies that isolate their domestic prices from international influences.

SIGNIFICANCE OF THE FORMS

The economic effects of a tariff follow from the fact that it causes the domestic price of a good to exceed the foreign price. Only this difference really matters—not the form of the tariff that brings it about. It is simple arithmetic to calculate the ad-valorem rate equivalent to a specific tariff in a given situation, and vice versa.

Nevertheless it sometimes makes a great deal of difference in practice how tariff legislation is written. A general inflationary rise in all prices will cause tariff charges to rise in the same proportion with ad-volorem rates, but a specific tariff will not change at all and so will become relatively less important. Many actual tariffs are specific, in the United States and elsewhere, and the substantial inflation since the Second World War has greatly reduced their importance.

A second practical difference between the forms arises from the fact that tariff laws necessarily apply to categories of goods, with some products in any category more expensive than others. For example, the U.S. specific tariff of $1.17 per gallon on sparkling wine is proportionally much more significant for an Asti-Spumanti sold for four dollars per gallon by an Italian exporter than for a French Champagne costing thirty dollars a gallon.

We are interested in the economic consequences of tariff protection, regardless of the form it takes. It is simplest to focus on an ad-valorem tariff, even if the protection is actually due to some other form. Also, we shall be mainly concerned with the *overall* effects of protection rather than with the consequences of different tariff rates on different goods (we turn to this later). So suppose that imports face a uniform ad-valorem tariff of t. If P_M equals the price paid to foreigners and Q_M the domestic price,

$$Q_M = P_M(1 + t). \tag{5.3}$$

Suppose that exports are not taxed, so that the price P_X that foreigners pay for our exports equals the price Q_X received by exporters. Let

$q = Q_M/Q_X$, the domestic relative price of imports in terms of exports, and $p = P_M/P_X$, the foreign relative price, or terms of trade. Then, since $Q_X = P_X$,

$$\frac{Q_M}{Q_X} = \frac{P_M}{P_X}(1 + t)$$

or

$$q = p(1 + t). \tag{5.4}$$

Thus the overall economic impact of a tariff is to cause the home relative price of imports in terms of exports to exceed the terms of trade. This can also be emphasized by rewriting (5.4) as

$$t = \frac{q - p}{p}. \tag{5.5}$$

The tariff rate equals the percentage by which q exceeds p.

PROBLEMS

5.1 In the example of the specific tariff on sparkling wine, calculate the equivalent ad-valorem rates on both Asti Spumante and Champagne and compare the two. Suppose instead that sparkling wine is subject to a 10 percent ad-valorem rate. Calculate the equivalent specific tariffs on both products. Suppose that both export prices rise by 50 percent. Calculate the changes in tariff payments in all cases.

5.2 Explicitly derive expression (5.5) from expression (5.4).

5.3 The text discussed some ways in which it would matter in practice whether a tariff is specific or ad-valorem. Try to think of some ways in which an ASP tariff could in practice differ from the other two.

5.4 The United States has always had many specific tariffs and many ad-valorem tariffs. By contrast, European tariffs became largely specific during the 1920s and have become largely ad-valorem since the Second World War. Can you think of any reasons for this change?

2. Comparative Advantage and Tariffs

Suppose that a country taxes all imports at the rate t, producing that gap between q and p indicated in (5.5). What are the economic consequences? To answer this we apply each of the four basic ideas of the pure theory of international trade, starting with comparative advantage.

The very fact that q exceeds p implies that a tariff is inefficient for the world as a whole. Recall from Chapter 1 that if an economy produces both goods, their relative price equals the marginal rate of transformation

(MRT) between them: the amount of one good that must be foregone in order to produce one more unit of the other. Then if both importables and exportables are produced both at home and abroad, the fact that q exceeds p means that MRT_{XM} is greater at home; that is, more exports must be sacrificed to produce one more importable at home than abroad. This means that the world can produce more of either or both goods if the home economy switches resources from importables toward exports, if the rest of the world does the opposite, and if the two countries trade more. This is a straightforward application of the reasoning in Chapter 1, which you should review now if the above argument is not crystal clear.

In similar fashion, q equals the MRS_{XM} of each domestic consumer and p the MRS_{XM} of each foreign consumer. Thus the former exceeds the latter: each domestic consumer is willing to sacrifice more exports to obtain one more import than each foreign consumer would require to supply it. Thus consumers in both countries can be made better off by trading more. This is just a straightforward application of the reasoning in section 8 of Chapter 1.

Thus a literal application of comparative advantage gives the first conclusion about tariffs: *tariffs are inefficient for the world as a whole.*

Comparative advantage also shows that a country that levies a tariff itself suffers in two ways: it pays a *production cost* and a *consumption cost.*

The production cost refers to the fact that a country that levies a tariff produces a mix of goods worth less at international prices than the country is capable of producing. International relative prices equal p, and domestic prices q equal the MRT_{XM}. Since q exceeds p, MRT_{XM} likewise exceeds p. Thus the exports that could be produced by producing one less unit of importables (MRT_{XM}) exceeds the number of exports that are worth the same as one importable (p). The value of national income could be increased by producing fewer importables and more exports.

This is illustrated in Figure 5.1. The international price p is equal to OA/OC, which is the same as OB/OD: the lines AC and BD are drawn parallel. The domestic relative price q equals OH/OG; this exceeds the world price by the amount of the tariff. The domestic production possibility frontier is TT'. Domestic firms will produce where the MRT_{XM} equals q, the relative price they face. This is at E, where the slope of the production possibility frontier (the MRT_{XM}) equals the domestic relative price OH/OG. The line AC shows all combinations of the two goods that are equal in value to combination E at *international* prices. Thus OC shows the international value of domestic output expressed in terms of importables, and OA shows it expressed in terms of exportables.

If the domestic economy were to instead produce at F, where MRT_{XM} equals the international price p, the international value of domestic output would be OD in terms of importables and OB in terms of exportables. Thus because of the tariff, the value of domestic output at international prices is

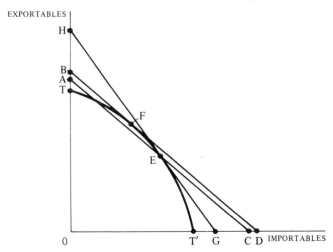

Figure 5.1. THE PRODUCTION COST OF A TARIFF

less than it need be by the amount *CD* in terms of importables, or *AB* in terms of exportables. This loss is the production cost of the tariff. It results from the fact that the tariff causes domestic firms to respond to a distorted price *(q)* rather than to the true international price *(p)*.

The *consumption cost* of a tariff is similarly due to the fact that consumers respond to a distorted price. Since *q* exceeds *p*, consumers purchase fewer imports than they would wish to do if they were free to buy at the international price: the fact that consumers collectively tax themselves by the amount of the tariff causes them to distort their consumption patterns. The loss of welfare resulting from the fact that each consumer purchases a combination of goods less desirable than what he can afford at the international price is called the consumption cost.

This cost can be viewed more formally. The domestic price *q* is equal to the MRS_{XM} of each consumer: the most exports the consumer would willingly sacrifice to obtain one more unit of imports. Since the MRS_{XM} (= *q*) exceeds *p* by the tariff, the consumer is willing to sacrifice more exports to obtain an additional import than he has to pay on the international market (that is, *p*) to do so.

Despite the fact that a country burdens itself with both a production cost and a consumption cost by levying a tariff, we cannot conclude that it is necessarily worse off. This is because a tariff could have additional effects. For example, the tariff could cause the international price to change. If it declines, so that the terms of trade improve, that constitutes a benefit to be weighed against the production and consumption costs. The former could conceivably outweigh the latter. But if a country does benefit from a tariff, it is at the expense of the rest of the world. This is because our first conclusion in this section was that a tariff necessarily harms the world as whole.

PROBLEMS

5.5 Suppose you have the following data for Germany.

P_M/P_W	Ma demand	Ma supply	W demand	W supply
4/3	80	110		30
1	100	100	50	

Suppose the international price of a machine is one wine, and that Germany imports machines with a tariff of ⅓. What is the production cost to Germany in terms of wine? In terms of machines?

5.6 Industries often request tariff protection from foreign competition. But if a tariff *protects* industry, how can it cause a production *cost*?

5.7 The argument in the text concluded that a home tariff harmed the world because the MRT_{XM} and MRS_{XM} at home were larger than abroad. Go through the argument again under the assumption that the home and foreign countries *both* tax their imports.

5.8* As in problem **2.8***, 5 labor units are required to produce a unit of either cloth or wine in England, 100 labor units are available, and the English always consume the two goods in equal quantities. Suppose the world price of wine is ⅓ bolts of cloth, and that England imports wine with a 100 percent tariff. What are the production and consumption costs to England?

3. *Exploring Further: The Geometry of Tariff Costs

This section adds further geometric detail to the previous section. Figure 5.2 illustrates the consumption cost of a tariff. As in Figure 5.1, E represents production in the presence of a tariff. (The rest of the production possibility frontier is not drawn, to reduce clutter.) AC shows the consumption possibilities attainable by trade (OA/OC again equals the terms of trade). The best obtainable consumption is at M, where AC is tangent to a community indifference curve. But the country will not in fact consume here. This is because, at M, the MRS_{XM} (indicated by the slope of the community indifference curve U_0) equals the terms of trade p (reflected in the slope of AC), whereas the tariff causes consumers to equate the MRS_{XM} to the domestic price q, which exceeds p. Thus the economy will consume at that point on the budget line AC where the intersecting community indifference curve has a slope of q. This is illustrated by N, where q, equal to

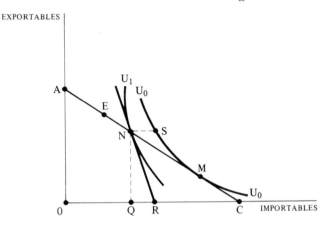

Figure 5.2. The Consumption Cost of a Tariff

NQ/QR, equals the MRS_{XM} (indicated by the slope of the indifference
curve U_1).

The consumption cost of the tariff is reflected in the fact that N is on a
lower indifference curve than M—the tariff causes the community to spend
its actual income in a suboptimal fashion. This cost can be measured in
terms of importables by the horizontal distance NS between the two curves.

Figure 5.3 shows the total effect of the tariff on the domestic economy.
The terms of trade again equal OB/OD (= OA/OC). The highest indifference curve the country can attain at these prices is U_F, reached by producing at F (where $MRT_{XM} = p$) and trading to consume at F^1 (where
$MRS_{XM} = p$). But the tariff distorts the decisions of domestic

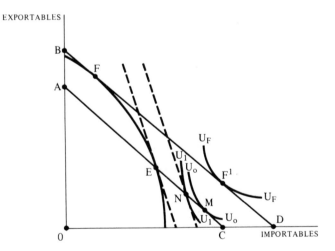

Figure 5.3. General Equilibrium of a Tariff

firms who produce at E instead, where the production cost of CD is incurred, so that the highest attainable indifference curve is now U_0. But even this is not reached, because the tariff also distorts the decisions of domestic consumers, who consume at N rather than M. The dotted lines through E and N are parallel, with the common slope reflecting domestic relative prices.

If the tariff has caused the terms of trade to differ from their free-trade value, Figure 5.3 does not capture the full effect. Figure 5.4 shows a case where the tariff has caused the terms of trade to improve so much that the country is better off than without the tariff, despite the production and consumption costs. Without the tariff, the terms of trade would equal OA^1/OC^1 and U_F is the highest attainable indifference curve, reached by producing at F and consuming at F^1. The tariff has caused the terms of trade to improve to OA/OC, allowing the community to consume at N, which is on a higher indifference curve than is F^1. Thus the country is better off with the tariff, despite the production and consumption costs.

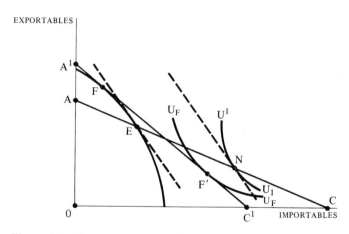

Figure 5.4. PRODUCTION AND CONSUMPTION COSTS OUTWEIGHED BY
A TERMS-OF-TRADE IMPROVEMENT

PROBLEMS

5.9 In Figures 5.3 and 5.4, the dotted line through E is inside the parallel dotted line through N: the combinations of goods equal in value, at domestic prices, to actual production are smaller than the combinations equal in value to actual consumption. Why is this the case? How can you interpret the distance between the two dotted lines?

5.10 Prove that point N in Figures 5.2 and 5.3 must lie northwest of M, that is, the consumption distortion of a tariff reduces trade instead of increasing it. On what does your proof depend?

4. Reciprocal Demand and Tariffs

A country suffers a consumption cost and a production cost from its own tariff, but we are unable to tell whether the country is worse off if we do not know what happens to the terms of trade. The law of reciprocal demand describes how relative prices are determined. We therefore use it to discover the effects of a tariff on both international prices *(p)* and domestic prices *(q)*.

Recall from Chapter 2 that an offer curve shows how much a country is willing to export to obtain each level of imports. The line through points *0, A,* and *B* in Figures 5.5(a) and 5.5(b) shows a country's *free-trade offer curve:* the offer curve if no tariff exists. Suppose now that the country levies a tariff on imports at the rate *t.* What happens to the offer curve?

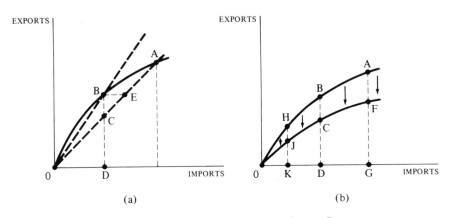

Figure 5.5. THE EFFECT OF A TARIFF ON THE OFFER CURVE

Consider any point, such as *B* in Figure 5.5(a). Since *B* is on the free-trade offer curve, it indicates that in order to obtain the quantity *OD* of imports, citizens of this country are willing to pay *BD* of exports, at a relative price of *BD/OD.* Review section 2 of Chapter 2 if this is not clear. Under free trade, the whole quantity *BD* is what the country is willing to export to the rest of the world in exchange for *OD.* But if there is a tariff, part of the total payment *BD* must be paid to the government for the tariff, and only a portion will be left for the rest of the world. Point *C* in Figure 5.5(a) is drawn so that *BC/CD* equals the tariff rate *t.* Then in order to obtain the quantity *OD* of imports, the citizens of this country are willing to pay the total *BD,* of which *BC* is the tariff payment, so that the country is willing to pay *CD* to the rest of the world in exchange for *OD.* Point *C* thus represents the quantity that would be traded in the tariff-ridden situation; *B* has shifted downward, in the proportion *t,* to *C* as a result of the tariff.

The same is true of every point on the free-trade offer curve: it shifts downward in the proportion *t* as a result of the tariff. In Figure 5.5(b), the curve through *0, J, C,* and *F* is the tariff-ridden offer curve (so that $HJ/JK = BC/CD = AF/FG = t$).

THE TARIFF AND THE TERMS OF TRADE

Now that we know what a tariff does to the offer curve, we can see what it does to relative prices. First, the terms of trade. In Figure 5.6(a), (b), and (c), *OH* represents the free-trade home offer curve, and *OF* the free-trade foreign offer curve. Thus *E* represents the quantities that are exchanged between the two countries without a tariff, and the terms of trade are accordingly *EA/OA*. Now suppose the home country levies a tariff. This produces no effect on the foreign offer curve, because nothing has changed

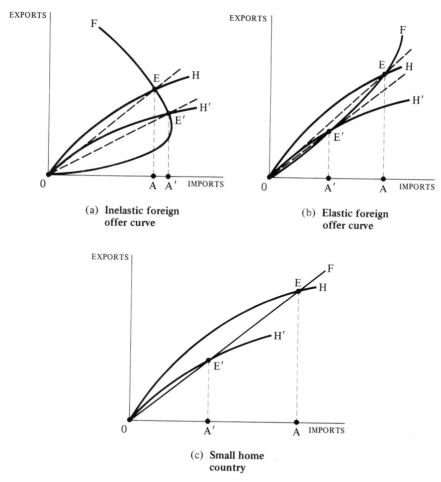

(a) **Inelastic foreign offer curve**

(b) **Elastic foreign offer curve**

(c) **Small home country**

Figure 5.6. THE EFFECT OF A TARIFF ON THE TERMS OF TRADE

in the foreign country. But the home offer curve shifts downward in the proportion of the tariff. The new tariff-ridden home offer curve is illustrated by OH', and E' represents the quantities that are traded. The new terms of trade are $A'E'/OA'$.

The general conclusion is that *a tariff improves the terms of trade of any country sizable enough to influence international prices.* In Figure 5.6(a) the terms of trade after the tariff, $E'A'/OA'$, are much more favorable than before, EA/OA: fewer exports need be paid for each import. Similarly, in Figure 5.6(b) the tariff improves the terms of trade, though not as dramatically as in Figure 5.6(a). In general, by imposing a tariff a country shifts its offer curve down and causes international equilibrium to move along the foreign offer curve toward the origin. This improves the terms of trade of the tariff-levying country. As Figures 5.6(a) and (b) illustrate, the improvment is greater the more *inelastic* is the foreign offer curve.

By levying a tariff, a country induces its citizens to demand fewer imports from abroad, thereby driving down their price. The more inelastic the foreign offer curve, the more the price of imports must fall in order to reduce foreign supply to the lower demand.

If the home country is too small to influence world prices, there can be no improvement in the terms of trade. The tariff simply causes the country to trade less at the same price as before. This is illustrated in Figure 5.6(c), where $E'A'/OA' = EA/OA$.

A tariff produces a terms-of-trade gain, which must be weighed against the consumption cost and the production cost to determine whether the tariff has on balance benefitted the home country. A small country necessarily loses: there is no improvement in the terms of trade.

THE TARIFF AND THE DOMESTIC RELATIVE PRICE OF IMPORTS

How does a tariff influence domestic relative prices? In free trade, the domestic relative price of imports in terms of exports, q_F, equals the international relative price p_F:

$$q_F = p_F. \tag{5.6}$$

With a tariff, the domestic relative price exceeds the international price by the amount of the tariff:

$$q_T = p_T(1+t). \tag{5.7}$$

Thus the tariff, by definition, causes q to increase, *compared to p.* But we have just seen that a tariff also improves the terms of trade, that is, reduces p. Thus it is not clear whether on balance the domestic price rises or falls: whether q_T is greater than or less than q_F. If the international price falls by a smaller percentage than the tariff, the domestic price must rise. For example, if a 10 percent tariff reduces p by 5 percent, then q rises by 5 percent. But if the 10 percent tariff reduces p by 20 percent, q falls 10 percent.

The elasticity of the foreign offer curve influences the behavior of the domestic relative price. This is illustrated in Figure 5.7. Free-trade equilibrium is at *E,* and the tariff-ridden equilibrium is at *E'*. Thus the *free-trade* relative domestic price equals *AE/OA*. To find the *tariff-ridden* domestic price, consider point *G* on the free-trade home offer curve directly above *E'*. In order to buy *OA'* of imports, domestic citizens are paying *A'G* of exports, including the tariff payment. Thus the domestic relative price of imports, q_T, is *GA'/OA'*. The domestic price has increased as a result of the tariff: *GA'/OA'* is greater than *AE/OA*. In this case the foreign offer curve is elastic. But if the foreign curve is instead inelastic, as in Figure 5.7(b), the domestic relative price will actually fall as a result of a tariff. This strange outcome is called the *Metzler Paradox,* after the economist Lloyd Metzler, of Chicago, who showed when it could happen.

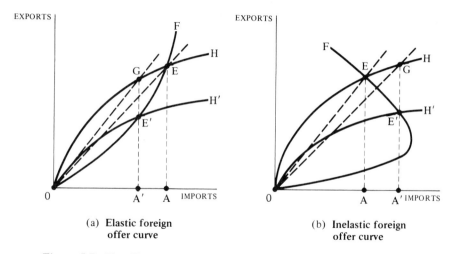

Figure 5.7. THE EFFECT OF A TARIFF ON DOMESTIC RELATIVE PRICES

A tariff reduces the demand for imports from abroad. If the foreign offer curve is elastic, the foreign country can be induced to reduce its supply of exports to us by a smaller reduction in their price: the terms of trade improves by less than the tariff, so *q* rises. But if the foreign offer curve is inelastic, foreigners can be induced to reduce their supply of exports to us only by a larger reduction in their price. The improvement in the terms of trade actually exceeds the amount of the tariff, so that *q* must fall.

PROBLEMS

5.11 If you did Problem **2.7** correctly, you obtained the following offer curve:

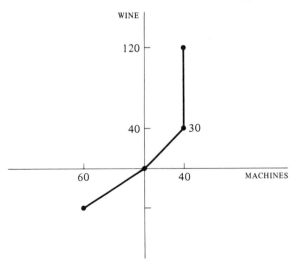

How is it affected by a 50 percent German tariff on wine imports?

5.12 If you did Problem **2.6** correctly, you obtained the following offer curve:

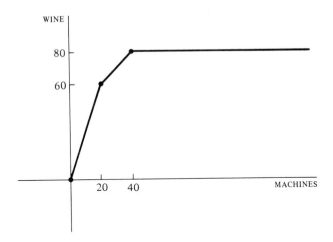

Suppose that France levies no tariff and engages in trade with the Germany of Problem **5.11** above. Show the effect of the German tariff on the trade between the two countries. What is the effect on the terms of trade and on domestic relative prices in both countries?

5.13* The discussion in the text implicitly assumed that the government spends all tariff revenues on exportables. In Figure 5.5(a), for example, domestic citizens pay *DC* to the rest of the world, for the import *OD*, and they pay *BC* to their government as tariff revenue. If some of this revenue, however, is spent on imports, total imports will equal, not *OD*, but *OD* plus the imports that are bought with the tariff revenue. Suppose, contrary to the discussion in the text, that the government always spends *all* tariff revenues on additional *imports*. Show how a tariff affects the home offer curve in this case. Under these circumstances, will a tariff still improve the terms of trade? When will it increase the relative domestic price of imports?

5. Tariffs and the Factor-Endowments Theory

The previous section showed that a tariff raises the domestic price of importables relative to exportables (if the foreign offer curve is not inelastic). Recall from Chapter 3 the *Heckscher-Ohlin theorem:* a country has a comparative advantage in the commodity whose production is relatively intensive in the country's relatively abundant factor.

It follows, then, that a tariff raises the domestic price of the good that uses intensively the country's relatively scarce factor: if France is capital abundant and exports capital-intensive wine, then a French tariff raises the French price of labor-intensive machines relative to wine. The tariff tends to displace resources from wine production to machine production.

A tariff protects that industry which makes intensive use of the country's relatively scarce factor.

The factor-endowments theory also sheds light on how protection influences the domestic distribution of income. Recall the *Stolper-Samuelson theorem:* a rise in the price of any commodity causes the price of the factor used intensively in the production of that commodity to rise in even greater proportion, and the reward of the other factor falls. Since a tariff can be expected to raise the domestic relative price of the good intensive in the country's scarce factor, it follows that the reward of the scarce factor rises relative to both commodities, and the reward of the abundant factor falls reltive to both commodities. The French tariff on machines raises labor's real income and lowers capital's.

A tariff increases the real income of the country's relatively scarce factor and reduces the real income of the relatively abundant factor.

Thus the tariff redistributes income *within* the tariff-levying country, so that some class will favor protection and some class will oppose it. As we have seen, the country as a whole will lose, as long as the terms-of-trade effect of the tariff does not outweigh the consumption and production costs. This means that the abundant factor loses more from a tariff than the scarce factor gains: the former could in principle "bribe" the latter to forgo pro-

tection and still be better off than with a tariff. But in the absence of any
sort of compensation or redistribution, those people whose incomes come
from the earnings of the scarce factor have a definite interest in protection,
even if it is harmful to their country overall.

PROBLEMS

5.14 On the basis of the discussion in this section, which factors of production in the American economy would you expect to favor protection?

5.15 Discuss how commercial policy could help explain the differences in
agricultural yields shown in Table 3.1. How could changes in such policy help
explain the relative wage movements shown in Table 3.2?

5.16 What is the effect of a tariff upon the domestic distribution of income if
the foreign offer curve is inelastic?

5.17* Deduce how the factor-price equalization theorem would be affected
by the presence of a tariff in one or both countries.

6. Tariffs and National Income

We come next to the implications for tariff protection of the Keynesian theory studied in Chapter 4. Recall that this theory looks at the world
from a different point of view than does the classical, and addresses different questions. There are two crucial differences in basic assumptions: (1)
relative prices are rigidly fixed (except for a change in the tariff itself) with
adjustment instead taking place via variations in employment; and (2) international capital movements passively adjust to the balance of trade.

A tariff is an instrument of trade policy, as studied in sections 4 and 5
of Chapter 4. A tariff makes imports more expensive relative to domestic
goods and so induces the population to shift its demand from the former to
the latter: less of a given income will now be spent on imports, and more on
domestic goods. Thus the tariff shifts the import curve down, as shown in
Figure 5.8(a). This in turn stimulates the demand for domestic goods and
increases domestic national income, as illustrated in Figure 5.8(b) and discussed in section 4 of Chapter 4.

> *A tariff stimulates domestic income by switching demand from
> foreign goods to domestic goods.*

Thus in the Keynesian economy, a tariff becomes an instrument for
the control of aggregate demand: increases in the tariff stimulate the economy and tariff reductions dampen it. By switching demand from foreign
goods toward domestic goods a tariff affects the rest of the world in the
opposite direction to its effect on the domestic economy. A tariff increase

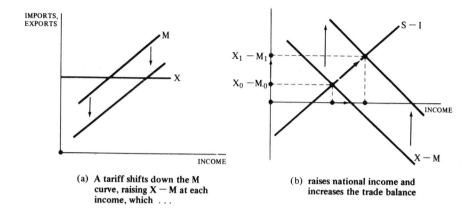

(a) **A tariff shifts down the M curve, raising X — M at each income, which ...**

(b) **raises national income and increases the trade balance**

Figure 5.8. EFFECTS OF A TARIFF IN A KEYNESIAN ECONOMY

tends to lower foreign income as it increases domestic income. This is fine if the rest of the world wishes to reduce aggregate demand, but a source of trouble if it does not. That is, the tariff as an instrument of control over aggregate demand generates international conflict when the domestic economy is in the same stage of the business cycle as the rest of the world; it likewise produces international harmony if the two countries are in opposite phases of the cycle. (Review section 5 of Chapter 4.)

By shifting the import function downward and reducing imports (*M*), a tariff necessarily increases a country's *trade balance:* $X - M$. (By increasing income, a tariff produces a secondary rise in *M*, which cancels out part of the initial fall. But, on balance, *M* must decline or income could not rise in the first place.)

A tariff increases the balance of trade $X - M$.

An increase in the domestic trade balance is the same thing as a decline in the foreign trade balance. As with national incomes, the trade balances of the two countries are influenced in opposite directions by a tariff in one of them.

PROBLEMS

5.18 Would you expect political pressures for protection to be more intense during periods of high unemployment or periods of low unemployment?

5.19 In Figure 5.8, should imports *M* be evaluated at domestic prices or at foreign prices, that is, should *M* include the tariff proceeds or not?

5.20 How does the analysis of this section change if the demand for imports is price inelastic?

5.21 Show geometrically how a domestic tariff influences *foreign* income and the foreign trade balance. Should domestic imports M be evaluated at domestic prices or at foreign prices in this case? How does the analysis change if the domestic demand for imports is price inelastic? Must we revise our conclusions about when trade policy generates international conflict?

7. Nontariff Barriers

The previous four sections developed the theory of tariffs by exploiting each of the four fundamental ideas of international trade theory. The conclusions also apply in large part to nontariff forms of protection. For example, import subsidies operate like tariffs but in the opposite direction—they are in effect negative tariffs. Thus the earlier conclusions need only be reversed to apply to subsidies. In this section we consider several additional forms of protection. Instead of working out a complete theory for each form, we show how tariff theory can be adapted to include these alternatives.

EXPORT TAX

Sometimes exports rather than imports are taxed. To isolate the effects, suppose that a country levies a tax at the ad-valorem rate t on all exports but leaves imports free of tax. The domestic price of importables, Q_M, therefore equals the price paid to foreigners, P_M

$$Q_M = P_M. \tag{5.8}$$

Since exports are taxed, the price at which they are sold to foreigners, P_X, equals the domestic price, Q_X, plus the tax, tQ_X.

$$Q_X(1+t) = P_X. \tag{5.9}$$

To examine relative prices, divide (5.9) into (5.8):

$$\frac{Q_M}{Q_X} \frac{1}{(1+t)} = \frac{P_M}{P_X}$$

or, recalling that q equals the domestic relative price of imports in terms of exports, Q_M/Q_X, and that p equals the international relative price P_M/P_X,

$$q = p(1+t). \tag{5.10}$$

Compare (5.10) with (5.4). They are identical! *A tax on exports is equivalent to an equal tax on imports.* This result is known as Lerner's symmetry theorem, after the economist, Abba Lerner, who elucidated it.

Tariffs and export taxes exert economic effects by influencing relative prices. An export tax differs from a tariff in two ways: (1) it applies to exports rather than imports, and (2) it causes the foreign price of the taxed good to exceed the domestic price (rather than vice versa). These two differences just cancel out, so that, on balance, there is no difference. All the conclusions of the previous four sections concerning tariffs apply equally well to export taxes.

It is important, though, to realize the limitations of the symmetry theorem. It assumes that the only relative price that matters is that of imports in general with respect to exports in general. Thus it says that a uniform tariff on all imports is equivalent to an equal uniform tax on all exports. A tariff of 10 percent on oil is not equivalent to a tax of 10 percent on the export of wheat. The relative price of oil in terms of wheat is not the only relative price; there are many other goods to consider as well.

How important are export taxes in practice? They are certainly far less common than tariffs in the industrial countries. There are in fact *no* American export taxes; they are expressly forbidden by the U.S. Constitution. (This prohibition was inserted in part to mollify the South, the major export region of the country at the time, which feared that the new government might finance itself by taxing Southern exports of cotton and tobacco.) Nevertheless they are important. OPEC's primary instrument of commercial policy is an oil export tax (although it is not often called that). More generally, many LDCs tax the export of primary products, as Brazil does with coffee.

IMPORT QUOTAS

Quantitative restrictions, or quotas, have become increasingly important in recent years. A quota is a blunter instrument than a tariff: instead of taxing imports, it directly limits the quantity that can be brought into the country. Figure 5.9 shows how an import quota works.

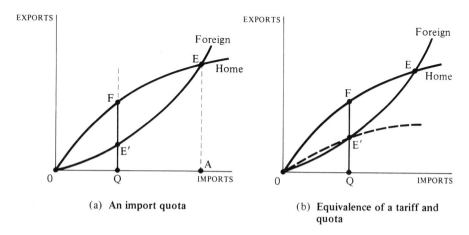

(a) An import quota

(b) Equivalence of a tariff and quota

Figure 5.9. THE ECONOMICS OF AN IMPORT QUOTA

Figure 5.9(a) depicts the free-trade home and foreign offer curves. Equilibrium is at E, so the home country imports OA at terms of trade EA/OA. Now suppose that the home economy imposes an import quota of OQ. This has no effect on the portion of the home offer curve from O to F, because in this region the economy imports less than the quota anyway. But the portion of the offer curve beyond F is now ruled out; in effect the home offer curve becomes $OFE'Q$.

The home economy now imports OQ. In order to supply us with this quantity, the rest of the world must be paid QE' in exports. But domestic citizens are willing to pay the larger quantity QF to obtain the imports. What happens to the difference, FE'? This measures the value of the quota allotment. Since a quota limits the right to import, those individuals who are alloted such rights have something of value. Since the quota amount OQ can be purchased for $E'Q$ and sold for FQ, resulting in a profit FE', this profit is the value of having the right to import OQ.

The disposition of this value depends upon government policy. The government could reserve for itself the right to conduct the country's trade and earn the profit FE', which would thereby enter the coffers of the state. Alternatively, the government could auction off import rights to the highest bidder. In this case the government would be able to sell the rights for the amount FE', which would again be revenue of the government. In either case, E' represents the actual trade between the two countries. The home country imports OQ, for which domestic citizens pay FQ. Of this, $E'Q$ is exported to the rest of the world, and FE' is paid to the domestic government. Thus the international relative price is $E'Q/OQ$, and the domestic relative price is FQ/OQ.

This is exactly the same result that would have been obtained by an appropriate tariff. This is shown in Figure 5.9(b). If the home country had instead levied a tariff at rate $FE'/E'Q$, the home offer curve would have shifted to the dotted curve in Figure 5.9(b). In this case E' would be the quantities exchanged between the two countries, and FE' would have been the government's revenue: exactly the same result as achieved by an import quota OQ. Thus there is a basic equivalence between tariffs and quotas:

> *The results of any quota can be duplicated by an appropriate tariff policy, and the results of any tariff can be duplicated by an appropriate quota policy.*

Because of this equivalence, all our conclusions about the economic effects of tariffs apply equally well to quotas. But just as with the Lerner symmetry theorem, care must be observed in relying upon this result. Jagdish Bhagwati, of Columbia University, and other economists have emphasized that various circumstances might vitiate the equivalence between tariffs and quotas. For example, governments very often do not in fact appropriate the value of quotas. Quota allotments might be distributed in proportion to previous imports, or, especially in the case of intermediate products, they might be distributed in proportion to importers' abilities to process the imports. This method was used with the U.S. quota on petroleum imports that was in effect from 1958 to 1973. In these cases the value FE' goes not to the government but, rather, to those firms or individuals who receive allotments. Alternatively, government officials might pass out the allotments in return for bribes. In this case FE' lines the pockets of corrupt bureaucrats. Under all these circumstances a quota results in a different distribution of domestic income than does a tariff and could confront individuals with different incentives. It could also lead to a different international distribution. The government might not allocate import rights at all, but instead have foreign governments allocate rights to export to us. In this case, FE' is not captured by the domestic economy, but instead accrues to the foreign country. The domestic economy then exports the quantity FQ to import OQ at terms of trade FQ/OQ. This has been the case with some U.S. attempts to limit textile imports. Instead of imposing import quotas on textiles, the U.S. government has persuaded various foreign governments to adopt "voluntary" quotas on exports to the United States. This has ensured that the values of the allotments are captured by foreigners. The equivalence between tariffs and quotas also breaks down in the face of other circumstances, such as imperfect competition and uncertainty about the future, that alter the role of the offer curve.

PROBLEMS

5.22 Show how your answers to Problems **5.11** and **5.12** could be duplicated by an appropriate quota.

5.23 Suppose that a certain country exercises commercial policy solely through an *export* quota. Discuss the economic effects, and draw the analog to Figure 5.9. To what extent are import quotas and export quotas related to each other in the way that the Lerner symmetry theorem relates import taxes and export taxes?

5.24 The Indian government has established import quotas on many goods used as productive inputs by that country's industry. In some cases these quotas have been allocated among importing firms in proportion to the output capacities of the firms. What is the effect of such an allocation system on economic incentives? Discuss the long-run implications and compare them to those of a tariff.

5.25 Suppose that a certain economy uses three goods: imports, exports, and nontraded goods. There are thus two relative commodity prices: the price of imports in terms of exports and the price of nontraded goods in terms of exports. Show how a tariff on imports affects both relative prices (as equations (5.4) and (5.10) do in the text) and do the same for a tax on exports. What do you conclude about the Lerner symmetry theorem?

5.26 Consider a quota and its equivalent tariff, as in Figure 5.9. Show how each form of protection causes equilibrium to respond to

    a An outward shift of the foreign offer curve.

    b An outward shift of the home free-trade offer curve.

8. Case Study: Restrictions on Japanese Automobile Exports to the United States

During 1980 the United States automobile industry lobbied intensively for protection from Japanese imports. The domestic industry was subject to the twin evils of a sluggish U.S. car market—due to both subdued aggregate demand and lessened demand for cars in particular as a result of the second oil-price shock—plus a shift in consumer preferences to smaller, more fuel-efficient cars. The latter benefitted the Japanese, who were able to increase their share of the U.S. market. The domestic industry demanded a "breathing spell" of protection, while changing its product mix, to finance investment in new models and to put unemployed automobile workers back on the job. After an investigation, the U.S. International Trade Commission (about which more will be said in the next chapter) concluded that imports were not the cause of the domestic industry's problems. But public pressure continued, protectionist bills were introduced in Congress, and the new Reagan administration was able to persuade the Japanese government to "voluntarily" restrict exports to the United States. The Japanese announced that they would limit exports to 1.68 million units in the year starting April 1, 1981, would limit the succeeding year's increase in exports to 16.5 percent of the increase in U.S. domestic sales, and would decide later whether to continue limitations for a third year.

The initial year's quota of 1.68 million vehicles is 140,000 less than what Japan had exported to the United States during the previous year, and their sales were expected to grow without the restraint; the effect of the quota is to reduce imports from Japan by perhaps 300,000 units in the first year. But this does not mean a 300,000 unit increase in sales of domestic vehicles: some consumers will purchase non-Japanese imports, and many other consumers will postpone or cancel new-car purchases altogether. Estimates of the first-year increase in sales of U.S. cars due to the quota range from 35,000 to 140,000. For the sake of illustration, let us suppose that the actual figure is 100,000.

Employment. Studies have concluded that each five-unit increase in production boosts employment by one worker. Thus the quota should have made employment in the U.S. automobile industry larger than it would otherwise have been by 20,000—less than 7 percent of the 300,000 automobile workers laid off before the agreement. To find the total effect on U.S.

employment, we should add the increased employment in other U.S. industries to which demand has been switched from Japanese cars, subtract the decreased employment in U.S. export industries that have lost Japanese sales, subtract the employment provided by any jobs the 20,000 workers held while laid off, and account for multiplier effects. The net effect of these secondary considerations is a matter of speculation, but we might as well ignore them because the concern of the quota is in fact employment in the auto industry.

Prices. Figure 5.10 shows the effect of the quota. Estimates put the value of the gap *AB*—the excess U.S. price of small cars—at about $340. Using this figure for illustration, we can regard the restraint as equivalent to a tariff of $340. Had the U.S. government implemented its policy by such a tariff, or by selling import licenses to the Japanese exporters, it would have obtained $571 million (1.68 million × $340) in revenue. But since the U.S. government persuaded the Japanese to themselves reduce exports, the $571 million is instead being paid to Japan.

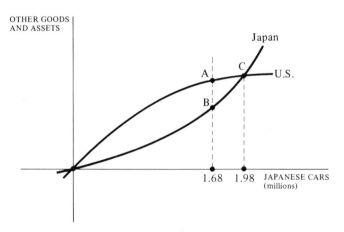

Figure 5.10. THE RESTRAINT ON JAPANESE AUTOMOBILE EXPORTS TO THE UNITED STATES

Two qualifications should be noted. Japanese firms are shifting their export mix to higher grade cars, in an attempt to partly offset the reduction in unit sales by selling more car per unit. To this extent U.S. consumers are receiving something in exchange for part of their $340, even though they would not buy that something if given a free choice. Second, in order to preserve the solvency and good will of their dealer networks, the Japanese firms are allowing their U.S. dealers to keep part of the price rise in higher profit margins. To this extent the consumers are paying part of the $340 to the dealers rather than to the Japanese.

The illustrative price rise of $340 applies not only to Japanese cars but also to other small cars that are directly competitive with the Japanese. Larger U.S. cars are only indirectly competitive; their price has been estimated as $130 higher because of the constraint.

Effect on the U.S. consumer. Table 5.1 adds up the total effect on the U.S. consumer implied by the illustrative figures we are using. The constraint has caused consumers to pay $571 million more for the Japanese cars they are buying, and $160 million more for European cars. If the two qualifications noted above are ignored, this means an increased payment of $731 million to foreigners.

Table 5.1. ILLUSTRATION OF THE EFFECT OF THE RESTRAINT ON U.S. CONSUMERS *(millions of dollars)*

Higher cost of Japanese autos ($340 × 1.68 million)	$ 571		
Higher cost of European autos (340 × .47 million)	160		
Higher cost of foreign cars		731	
Higher cost of small U.S. cars ($340 × 3.00 million)	1020		
Higher cost of larger U.S. cars ($130 × 3.20 million)	416		
Higher cost of U.S. cars		1436	
Total higher direct costs to U.S. consumers			2167
Lower social expenses ($14,700 × 20,000)	294		
Higher taxes for U.S. auto firms	900		
Higher fuel costs	21		
Total indirect savings of U.S. consumers			1173
Net cost to U.S. consumers			994

In addition, U.S. made cars cost $1.436 billion more than they would without the restraint, so that consumers are altogether paying $2.167 billion more for their cars. But consumers are also citizens, so they are indirectly influenced by any effects the restraint has on government spending and tax receipts. Because twenty thousand autoworkers are back on the job, they are paying income taxes and no longer receiving unemployment compensation or other public assistance. This is estimated as equal to $294 million—with any employment effects outside the auto industry not accounted for. Also the increased earnings of the U.S. automobile firms imply higher tax payments, estimated at $900 million. Finally, since the Japanese cars being excluded are among the most fuel efficient, gasoline consumption is higher than it otherwise would be. This is estimated to be responsible for $21 million of the country's oil imports.

Altogether, the restraint on Japanese automobile exports to the United States is calculated to be costing U.S. consumers $.994 billion in the first year. Of this total, $752 million ($731 million for cars plus $21 million for oil) constitutes an added payment to foreigners (subject to the two qualifications noted earlier), and the rest is a redistribution from consumers to the domestic auto industry. Looking at this another way, if the policy is responsible for twenty thousand jobs in the auto industry, each such job is costing consumers $49,700 and is costing the country as a whole $37,600. (These calculations are for illustration: they are based on ball-park figures, and we have had to ignore some considerations completely.)

Other countries. In recent years the Japanese have expanded exports of automobiles to many countries besides the U.S. After the Japanese-U.S. agreement was reached, other countries demanded similar restraints. (Calculations such as the above were noticeably absent from the debates.) The Japanese agreed to restrict 1981 exports to Canada to 174,000 units (about 6 percent below the 1980 level) and to limit the rate of growth of exports to Germany to 10 percent per year. Britain, Italy, and France had already restricted imports from Japan.

PROBLEMS

5.27 Suppose that the United States had in fact limited car imports from Japan by means of a $340 specific tariff. How would this affect the calculations of the costs borne by U.S. consumers, the domestic auto industry, and the nation as a whole?

5.28 Suppose that aggregate U.S. employment is determined by macroeconomic policy, so that any job created in the auto industry by the restraint must be matched by a job lost in some other industry. How are our calculations affected?

5.29 Assuming that without the export restraint, Japan would have sold the United States an additional 300,000 units at an average price of $5,500, calculate the direct effect of the restraint on the U.S. trade balance, on the basis of the figures in this section.

5.30 Recall that because of a 1965 agreement, the United States and Canada basically share a common auto industry. Discuss the effects on Canada of the restraint on Japanese auto exports to the United States. (Do not use specific numbers.)

9. Summary

1. Tariffs and other forms of commercial policy exert real effects by causing the domestic relative price of imports in terms of exports to exceed the terms of trade.

2. Tariffs are inefficient for the world as a whole; they cause the levying country to incur a consumption cost and a production cost, although the country could still conceivably be better off at the expense of the rest of the world.

3. Levying a tariff improves the terms of trade of a country if that country is sizable enough to influence international prices. Otherwise a country just trades less and loses.

4. A tariff protects the industry that makes intensive use of the scarce factor by causing factors to flow into that sector.

5. A tariff increases the real income of the country's relatively scarce factor and reduces the real income of the relatively abundant factor.

6. From a Keynesian perspective, a tariff stimulates domestic income and lowers foreign income by switching demand from foreign to domestic goods.

7. A tariff increases a country's trade balance (X-M), from a Keynesian perspective.

8. A tax on exports and a quota each can be made equivalent to a tariff.

SUGGESTED READING

Dixit, A. K. and Norman, V. *Theory of International Trade.* London: Cambridge University Press, 1980. See chapters 5 and 6 for an advanced treatment of tariff theory.

Jones, R. W. "Tariffs and Trade in General Equilibrium: Comment." *American Economic Review,* June 1969. A neat mathematical statement of basic tariff theory.

Lerner, A. P. "The Symmetry between Import and Export Taxes." *Economica,* August 1936. The Lerner symmetry theorem.

Metzler, L. A. "Tariffs, the Terms of Trade, and the Distribution of National Income." *Journal of Political Economy,* February 1949. The Metzler Paradox.

Michaely, M. *Theory of Commercial Policy.* Chicago: University of Chicago Press, 1977. An extensive survey.

Szenberg, M.; Lombardi, J. W.; and Lee, E. Y. *Welfare Effects of Trade Restrictions.* New York: Academic Press, 1977. An instructive attempt to estimate the welfare effects of restrictions on U.S. footwear imports.

Tower, E. "Commercial Policy under Fixed and Flexible Exchange Rates." *Quarterly Journal of Economics,* August 1973. Tariffs in a Keynesian world.

Chapter 6

Commercial Policy

> "Around the splendid public buildings we are erecting in Phila-
> delphia, there stood till very recently a stiff and angular structure
> of wood. . . . Like that scaffolding is the Tariff around the edifice
> of our national industries. It is not aesthetic. It adds nothing to
> the beauty of the edifice. But we cannot do without it."
> —ROBERT ELLIS THOMPSON (1866)

> "A protective tariff . . . is immoral and dishonest, because its sole
> purpose is to increase prices artificially, . . . thereby enabling one
> citizen to levy unjust tribute from another." —CORDELL HULL

CHAPTER 5 exploited the pure theory of international trade to deduce the economic effects of tariff protection. These effects seem to be largely negative: the world is made worse off by protection, and even the tariff-levying nation suffers a production cost and a consumption cost. Yet extensive protection has been endemic throughout history. In this chapter we examine the reasons for tariffs and look at actual tariff policy.

1. Motives for Protection: International Economic Objectives

Reasons for tariffs can be classified into two groups. In the first are those that address the economic relations of the tariff-levying nation with the rest of the world. These *international* objectives are discussed in this section. The other reasons concern the effects of protection within the tariff-levying country itself, and we discuss these *internal* objectives next. We shall examine eight reasons.

1. THE OPTIMUM TARIFF ARGUMENT

A tariff improves the terms of trade of the levying country, if that country is large enough in world markets. It also reduces the volume of trade, generating production and consumption costs. But a moderate tariff could benefit a large country, that is, the favorable terms-of-trade effect could outweigh the unfavorable consumption and production costs.

This, then, is one possible motive for tariff protection: to increase national welfare by improving the terms of trade. The policy can be pushed just so far; an increase in the tariff increases the production and consumption costs as it improves the terms of trade. Eventually the costs will predominate because, as Chapter 1 showed, free trade is better than no trade, the result of a high enough tariff. The rate that squeezes out as much gain as possible is known as the *optimum tariff*. Figure 6.1 illustrates such an optimum tariff. The figure shows the tariff-ridden home offer curve with equilibrium at E', so that OA imports are paid for with AE' exports, and the terms of trade are AE'/OA. The slope of the foreign offer curve shows the terms on which the volume of trade may be altered: to obtain one more unit of imports, measured off as $E'C$, the home country must sacrifice CD additional exports. *If the home country levies an optimum tariff, the slope of the foreign offer curve must equal the domestic marginal rate of substitution of exports for imports.* If the former (the number of exports that must be paid for an additional import) is less than the latter (the most exports any domestic resident would pay for one more import), the home country should trade more: the tariff is too high. Likewise, if the slope of the foreign offer curve is less than the home MRS_{XM}, the tariff is too small. This is simply one more application of the logic of comparative advantage. (Review Chapter 1 if necessary.)

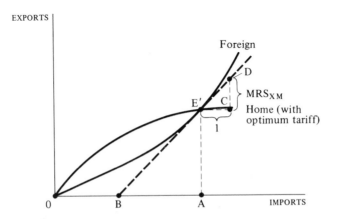

Figure 6.1. THE OPTIMUM TARIFF

■ *The optimum tariff formula.* Figure 6.1 can be used to deduce a formula for the optimum tariff. If the home country does in fact levy such a tariff, the home MRS_{XM} equals $DC/E'C$, or $E'A/BA$, in the figure. Recall that the domestic relative price of imports in terms of exports equals MRS_{XM}. Thus $q = E'A/BA$, and we know that $p = E'A/OA$. Also $t = (q/p) - 1$. Thus

$$t = \frac{q}{p} - 1 = \frac{E'A/BA}{E'A/OA} - 1 = \frac{OA}{BA} - 1 = \frac{OA-BA}{BA} = \frac{OB}{BA} = \frac{1}{BA/OB}$$

Now BA/OB is just the export-supply elasticity of the foreign offer curve, f^* (the asterisk is a reminder that this is the *foreign*, not the domestic, elasticity). The formula for the optimum tariff, then, is

$$t = 1/f^*. \tag{6.1}$$

If the home country is too small to influence world prices, f^* is infinite. Thus (6.1) indicates that t equals zero: the optimum policy for a small country is free trade. But if the home country is not small, the formula calls for a positive tariff. Free trade is not best. ■

Practical relevance of the Optimum Tariff. The essence of the optimum tariff is the exploitation of monopoly power. If a country can influence world prices, the citizens of that country collectively possess monopoly power; by withholding part of their export supply they can force the price up. Equivalently, they have monopsonistic power in the market for their imports, and by restricting demand they can hold price down. The tariff is the instrument by which the country's citizens collectively manipulate the market.

It is important to realize that this argument is strictly a *nationalistic* one. From a global point of view the optimum tariff is zero. With a tariff, the home country imposes a loss on the rest of the world, a loss that exceeds the home country's gain: the country carves a larger slice for itself from a shrinking world pie.

How relevant is all this for actual tariff policy? It does not now seem very relevant for industrial countries. One examines the records of congressional tariff debates in vain for any mention of an optimum-tariff motive for protection. A major reason is that other motives are far more important. Another reason has to do with the feasibility of an optimum tariff strategy. This requires the home country to be able to influence world prices, and the degree of influence must be sizable enough for an optimum tariff to be worth bothering about. But even a large country needs to worry about the possibility of *retaliation.* Our discussion of the optimum tariff took the foreign offer curve as fixed, and therefore assumed a fixed tariff policy on the part of the rest of the world. But if we can use commercial policy to improve our terms of trade, foreigners can presumably do the same to us.

Our tariff could be countered by a foreign tariff and a resultant tariff war. The final outcome could easily leave both countries worse off than in free trade. In any case, the possibility of retaliation greatly reduces the appeal of an optimum tariff policy.

Such a policy is therefore tempting only to a country that is both sizable and reasonably free of the fear of retaliation. The latter requires that the home country be in an asymmetric position vis-à-vis the rest of the world. For example, if a large country trades with many small countries, retaliation is unlikely. Each of the trading partners would be unable to exert significant monopoly power by itself, and, if there are many partners, they would be unlikely to collude. Asymmetry could also be due to the commodity composition of trade. For example, the home country might be the world's only exporter of a certain good, which many other countries import, while importing an assortment of goods also imported by many other countries. Germany, as the predominant exporter of potash, and Chile, as virtually the only exporter of nitrates, were in this position at the turn of the century. Both countries were able to exploit their monopoly positions, until the high prices of their exports induced the development of additional supply sources and of substitutes.

An asymmetry, either of size or of trade pattern, is not currently possessed by any of the industrial countries, with their roughly similar economic structures. The United States was perhaps in such a position at the close of the Second World War, when the other major industrial countries had been devastated. But American policy at the time was oriented toward reducing tariff barriers.

The optimum tariff argument, then, seems to be largely irrelevant to tariff policy in the developed countries. But the argument is by no means irrelevant in the modern world economy, even for the industrial nations. Far from it. OPEC has pursued such a policy. OPEC's policy instruments are not tariffs but, in effect, export taxes and quotas. (This had also been the case with Germany and Chile early in this century.) However these have basically the same economic effects as tariffs. OPEC seems to possess the necessary asymmetry. The manufactured goods and foodstuffs that OPEC imports are probably as vital to them as their oil is to their trading partners. But they can obtain these imports, or close substitutes, from a large and diverse number of countries, and OPEC has accordingly not been seriously threatened with retaliation.

Because of the vital importance of oil in the modern world economy, OPEC alone renders the optimum tariff argument highly significant. Also the earlier examples of Germany and Chile have been cited. The success of OPEC has spawned recent attempts by other primary-product exporters. But, as noted in Chapter 2, most of these have had little success. A possible exception is bauxite, which has in recent years risen sharply in price.

2. THE BALANCE OF TRADE

Concern about a country's trade balance furnishes a second motive for protection. We saw in Chapter 5 that, in a Keynesian context, a tariff could increase exports relative to imports. Why should a country want to do such a thing? Perhaps as part of a general desire to improve the balance of payments, or perhaps from a mercantilist notion that it is inherently desirable that exports exceed imports. Whatever the reason, the desire for a favorable trade balance furnishes another motive for protection.

Economists tend to be skeptical about such a policy. If concerned about the overall balance of payments, we ought to consider the monetary issues discussed in Part Three of this book. Also, a Keynesian context, ignoring as it does the effects of changes in capacity or in relative prices, is generally regarded as of short-run relevance. The tariff is a sluggish policy instrument, often requiring legislative action. Thus a protectionist measure adopted for a short-term objective is likely to be around, inflicting its production and consumption costs, long after the conditions that motivated it have changed. Thus many economists would argue that a concern about the trade balance should be dealt with in other ways.

Despite these reservations, concern about the balance of trade has been a motivating factor behind protectionist measures. In recent years, such concerns have given rise to tariff *surcharges*. These are temporary increases in protection that do not involve changes in a country's basic tariff law. They thus potentially deal with the second objection mentioned above. For example, in August 1971 President Nixon imposed a 10 percent tariff surcharge on American imports. This was done by presidential fiat without congressional approval; the surcharge was terminated several months later when it was judged to have served its purposes. (We shall discuss this episode further in Chapter 11.) Britain, Canada, and Denmark have likewise in recent years imposed tariff surcharges on imports for limited periods of time. In all cases, concern about the balance of trade was a motivating factor. In contrast to these short-term measures, some less developed countries have initiated tariff surcharges that have lingered for years and have therefore become, in effect, permanent increases in protection.

3. TRADE LIMITATION FOR NONECONOMIC REASONS

Sometimes governments wish to limit imports for reasons that are not economic at all. For example, limiting oil imports to 8.2 million barrels per day is an objective of the U.S. government, enunciated by President Carter in 1979. In Figure 6.2 if national policy is to limit imports to OC, a tariff of AB/BC does the trick. The country must pay the production and consumption costs (unless the terms of trade improve enough), but these are the inevitable costs of the national objective. (An attempt by President Carter

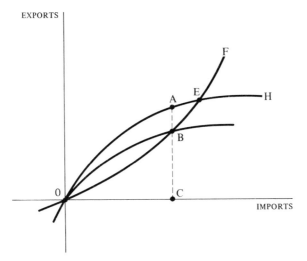

Figure 6.2. IMPORT LIMITATION

to impose a tariff of $4.62 per barrel of oil was overridden by Congress in 1980.)

PROBLEMS

6.1 Some people have urged that the United States use the "wheat weapon" against OPEC, that is, force up the price that OPEC must pay for our agricultural exports just as they have forced up the price of their oil exports. Discuss the feasibility of such a policy.

6.2 We shall see that tariffs are often *second-best* policy tools. That is, they are inferior in some ways to alternative methods of achieving whatever goals the tariffs are being used for. Examine each of the three motives discussed in this section to see if you can think of some other, superior policy.

2. *Exploring Further:* The Geometry of External Objectives

This section adds further geometric detail to our preceding discussion of the motives for protection.

THE OPTIMUM TARIFF ARGUMENT

In Figure 6.3 the foreign offer curve passes through O, E', E, and A, and the curves labeled U_0, U_1 and U_2 are three domestic trade indifference curves. Recall that these curves have a positive slope, and that curves lying to the southeast are preferred to those to the northwest, because increases in

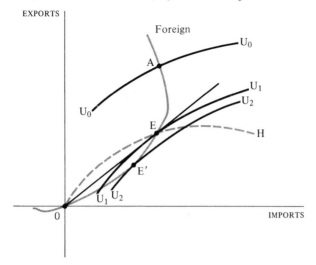

Figure 6.3. TARIFFS AND NATIONAL WELFARE

imports and reductions in exports leave more goods for domestic consumption.

Note, first, that it is never optimal to remain on the foreign offer curve's inelastic portion, which, as illustrated by point *A*, cuts domestic trade indifference curves from above. Thus trade restrictions increase domestic welfare.

Second, free trade is never optimal except for a small country. This is illustrated at *E*, the intersection of the free-trade home offer curve *OEH* with the foreign offer curve. The trade indifference curve through *E*, labeled U_1, must be tangent to the terms-of-trade line *OE*, because trade is free. Thus the foreign offer curve cuts U_1 from above, and the home economy can gain by restricting trade. This fails to be so only if the foreign offer curve coincides with the straight line *OE*, that is, if the home country is small.

TRADE LIMITATION FOR NONECONOMIC REASONS

Figure 6.4 shows the optimal way to implement a trade limitation. *TT′* is the domestic production possibility frontier, and *AD/DC* equals the terms of trade, which we assume the home country cannot influence (since we have already looked at that). With free trade the economy produces at *A*, exports *AJ*, imports *JB*, and consumes at *B*, on the indifference curve U_1. Suppose that, for some reason, the country wishes to import no more than *DC*. This limits trade to the triangle *ADC*. Slide this triangle along *TT′*, keeping *A* on the production possibility frontier. This traces out the curve *TACEH*, which shows the nation's consumption possibilities limited

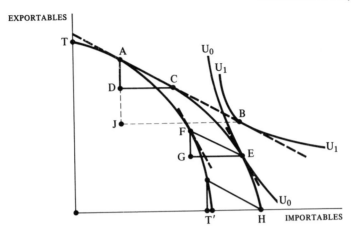

Figure 6.4. THE OPTIMAL WAY TO LIMIT TRADE

by the need to produce on TT' and import no more than DC.. The indifference curve U_1 is no longer attainable: this illustrates that a price must be paid for the noneconomic objective. The best the country can do is to consume at E, where $TACEH$ is tangent to the indifference curve U_0. This happens when production is at F and FG is traded for GE. The common slope of U_0 and $TACEH$ at E equals the slope of TT' at F and reflects the common price that must be faced by domestic producers and consumers in order to attain E. The difference between this price and the terms of trade is the tariff that should be levied to implement optimally the trade limitation. The unavoidable cost of this noneconomic objective is indicated by the distance between U_0 and U_1.

PROBLEMS

6.3 The optimum tariff policy $t = 1/f^*$ would seem to indicate that when on the inelastic part of the foreign offer curve ($f^* < 0$) a *subsidy* to imports ($t < 0$) is best. But we concluded that tariffs should be *increased* in such a case. Reconcile.

6.4 In Figure 6.3, draw community indifference curves for the rest of the world and use them to discuss the effect of an optimum tariff on the foreign country. Is it possible to make *both* countries better off than they are in the tariff-ridden situation? Can this be done simply by changing tariff rates in the two countries?

6.5* Suppose that the home country levies an optimum tariff, and that the foreign country retaliates by levying its own optimum tariff relative to our (tariff-ridden) offer curve. A tariff war ensues. Draw a diagram, such as Figure 6.3 but with indifference curves for both countries, showing a possible outcome of the tariff war in which each country has imposed a tariff that is optimum, *given* the other country's tariff. Can one country be better off than in free trade? Can both? Can both be worse off?

3. Motives for Protection: Internal Economic Objectives

Although the tariff is ostensibly a device for regulating a country's international economic activity, many motives for protection center upon its internal effects. We examine these motives in this and the following sections.

4. REVENUE

The tariff is a tax and it can yield revenue. There is a limit: a higher tariff lowers imports, and a prohibitive tariff yields no revenue at all. But most governments can raise substantial revenues in this way. In order to do so the country must bear the production and consumption costs, so (unless a significant terms-of-trade improvement can be expected) the tariff is inferior to less distortionary taxes.

If the tariff exists to raise revenue, the needs of the government become important in determining the degree of protection. Tariff policy becomes linked politically to how heavily a country wishes to tax itself and to how large a government it wants.

How important in practice is the revenue motive? Not very, as far as the modern industrial economies are concerned. Tariff revenues account for less than 2 percent of the total tax revenue of the U.S. government and are minor sources in other DCs. Public discussions of tariff questions seldom allude to revenue aspects. One must conclude that this is not important in such countries.

But it has not always been so. At one time most nations relied heavily on tariff revenues for government finance. Revenue was the reason Britain maintained some tariffs from the abolition of the Corn Laws in 1846 until the First World War. The American tariff was the principal source of federal revenue throughout the nineteenth century and was not displaced until the income tax was instituted. Even today tariffs are important revenue sources for the governments of most LDCs. For example, in 1976 the government of Chad derived over 52 percent of its revenue from taxes on trade, and Lesotho had similarly raised about 62 percent of its revenues in 1974. The DCs today rely mainly on broad-based taxes (income, sales, and value-added), which are much more effective for raising the enormous revenues required by the governments of modern industrial states. But the efficient administration of such taxes requires a large and reasonably effective government bureaucracy and a reasonably literate population, conditions that were not met in the past and are still not met in large parts of the world. A tariff, by contrast, requires only customs officials stationed (palms upward) in the trading centers and a police force to control smuggling. Seventeenth-century Britain banned tobacco growing because it was easier to tax tobacco imports than to tax a domestic crop.

5. DOMESTIC DISTORTIONS

Because a tariff affects a country's internal price structure and allocation of resources, it can deal with distortions in the domestic economy. Such distortions involve failures of the economy to behave as in Part One of this book and have various causes: monopolies, labor unions, external economies or diseconomies (social benefits or costs not reflected in private prices, such as pollution), government activities or regulations. The basic idea is to use a tariff to cancel partially the effect of such distortions. Suppose, for example, that a brewery, needing pure water for its product, reduces water pollution in its vicinity. The brewer is paid for his beer, but there is no one to reward him in materialistic fashion for purifying the water. Because of this failure to reward brewing fully for its social benefits, the industry will not be as large as socially desirable. A tariff on beer could help to deal with this problem by reallocating resources into the brewery industry.

The fly in the ointment (or in the ale) is the fact that a tariff introduces distortions of its own. These additional distortions must be weighed against the distortions neutralized by the tariff. In the brewery example, a tariff on beer will lead to cleaner water but will also introduce a consumption cost. The inevitable conclusion is that, although protection can be used to deal with domestic distortions, it is better to use more direct methods that do not have the undesirable side effects of tariffs. The best policy with the brewery is a subsidy for purifying water; this would ensure that brewers receive monetary rewards equal to the social benefits they supply, without introducing the distortions of a tariff.

Protection, if carefully employed, can potentially reduce the damage caused by domestic distortions, but tariffs are not as good as measures that directly attack the distortions. Of course direct measures might be ruled out by political or administrative considerations. There is a clear analogy to the use of tariffs to raise government revenue: other methods are more effective in principle, but they are not practical for some countries.

5'. THE INFANT INDUSTRY ARGUMENT

This is a good example of the domestic distortions case for protection. Also, it is important enough in practice to deserve separate mention.

This argument does not dispute that, in the long run, countries are best off with free trade. But, so the argument goes, a country might not be able to realize its true comparative advantage under free trade if other countries are already established in the relevant sectors. For example, a certain LDC might possess all the natural advantages needed to become a successful exporter of steel. But it must compete with existing steel exporters, who possess enormous advantages simply by being in the market to begin with. Our potential entrant must be prepared to suffer huge losses while it establishes the necessary plants, trains the required labor force and managers, and gradually penetrates the international market.

The infant industry argument is that such industries ought to be given tariff protection to help them get off the ground. Then they will gradually develop in the sheltered domestic market until they are ready to compete internationally. At that time tariffs will become unnecessary, and the country will export the products of the no-longer infant industry. The country will be trading according to its long-run comparative advantage, and if the infant industry has been wisely chosen, the gains from this trade will more than compensate for the losses the country had to suffer while the tariffs were effective.

Sometimes the argument is applied at a more general level. Industrialization requires much infrastructure and a sizable labor force with the requisite attitudes, habits, and skills. Thus we have what might be called an "infant country" argument. In any case it is temporary: protection should cease when the long-run pattern of comparative advantage is attained.

The argument has been important in practice. One frequently hears it in reference to LDCs. Alexander Hamilton argued along these lines for the young American republic, and Friedrich List for Germany. John Stuart Mill gave the argument his approval. In the eighteenth century the development of Britain's textile industry, a key element in the industrial revolution, was aided by protection from Asian competition. The growth of American industry in the nineteenth and early twentieth centuries took place behind high tariff walls.

The essential point is that the argument depends upon market distortions. An effective free market would not be hampered by the fact that a new industry must suffer losses before it can compete. Capital markets enable entrepreneurs to borrow to tide themselves over until their projects pay off. If a country has a long-run comparative advantage in steel production, potential steel producers should be able to borrow enough to develop to compete internationally. If they cannot, that fact is an indication that steel production is not really a good bet for the country. In order to justify protection there must be some distortion to be overcome.

For example, it might be unduly difficult to borrow funds for investment in the country because of restrictive legislation, prejudice, or incomplete information on the part of private investors. This would constitute a distorted capital market. Or the infant industry might be one that generates external economies of scale. This means that expansion of the industry reduces costs to all participants, and not simply to the individual firms that expand. In such a case any single firm cannot capture the full social benefit that would result from an expansion of its activities and is, therefore, not likely to expand as much as is socially desirable. In any case, some distortion is necessary to justify protection.

This means that the infant industry argument is subject to the same criticism as above: a tariff causes distortions of its own, which must be weighed against any benefits, so that direct measures are always better. Distortions in capital markets ought to be attacked head on; the best response to external economies of scale is a subsidy on output. This will expand activity and enable the external economies to be realized without the consumption cost of a tariff.

A political objection is also sometimes raised against the infant industry argument. An essential aspect of this argument is that protection be temporary until the industry gets on its legs. Cynics argue that any industry politically powerful enough to obtain protection while an infant would have no trouble retaining special treatment once it had grown even more powerful.

6. NONECONOMIC OBJECTIVES

Closely related to the domestic distortion argument is the view that noneconomic objectives may justify protection. For example, a country might wish to produce its own military hardware, even if similar products are cheaper abroad, to ensure a domestic supply should the country suddenly find itself isolated from foreign sources. Such national defense arguments are heard in Israel, for example. Similarly many countries, including the United States, protect their merchant marines in case another world war should break out. Some argue that the United States should develop domestic energy sources to free itself of the threat of "economic blackmail" by OPEC. The common denominator in all these cases is an assertion of noneconomic reasons to foster some industry. Since the reasons are noneconomic, they are not reflected in prices and so will not be felt in the market place.

Tariffs can be used to realize noneconomic objectives, just as they can attack domestic distortions. The United States can ensure a larger merchant marine by discriminating against foreign shipping; Israel can stimulate its defense industry by discriminating against foreign suppliers; America can stimulate domestic energy production with a tariff on imported oil.

The argument is illustrated in Figure 6.5. With free trade, the relative price of machines in terms of wine is OB/OC, so that the home country produces at A. Suppose consumption is at D, so DE wine is exported in exchange for EA machines. Suppose that this country does not wish to be so dependent on the rest of the world for machinery and wants to produce at F, even though this is more costly than free trade.

The country will produce at F if the domestic price of machines in terms of wine is GF/GH, and the price can be raised to this level by an appropriate tariff.

The tariff imposes, as always, a production cost and a consumption cost. The production cost, measured by LB in Figure 6.5, is unavoidable if

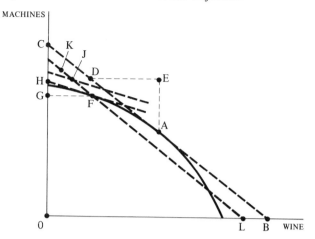

Figure 6.5. NONECONOMIC OBJECTIVES

the country produces at *F* rather than at *A:* this is the price that must be paid for the noneconomic objective. To produce at *F,* the country must consume on the line through *K, J, F,* and *L.* The consumption cost is due to the fact that the tariff prevents the country from consuming at the best spot on this line. For example, *K* might be the best combination of wine and machines to consume, but the tariff causes people to import fewer machines, so that the country consumes at a point such as *J* instead.

Although a tariff can change the country's production pattern from *A* to *F,* other methods can do the same without the consumption cost. For example, the government might pay machine producers a certain sum for each machine that they turn out. This will stimulate machine production and move the economy along its production possibility frontier from *A* toward *F.* A sufficient subsidy will move the economy all the way to *F.* But now consumers can buy at world prices; there is nothing to prevent them from consuming *K.* The production subsidy is superior to the tariff because it aims directly at the noneconomic objective (to increase production), whereas a tariff is indirect and has undesirable side effects.

This conclusion is quite general. Although tariffs can attain noneconomic objectives, they are clumsy instruments. Other methods can attain the same objectives at less cost.

PROBLEMS

6.6 This section showed that a tariff was a second-best way of attaining a noneconomic objective because other methods can do the same without the consumption cost. Does this argument apply to the motive of trade limitation for noneconomic reasons discussed in the previous section? What is the essential difference between the two motives?

6.7 Is the tariff a second-best method of raising government revenue? If so, what methods are better?

4. Motives for Protection: More Internal Economic Objectives

7. INCOME DISTRIBUTION

A tariff increases the real income of a country's relatively scarce factor while reducing that of its relatively abundant factor. A desire to redistribute income in just this fashion could therefore motivate protection. But this suffers from the same shortcoming as many other motives: a tariff involves undesirable side effects, which could be avoided by a more direct method. A tariff harms the abundant factor more than it benefits the scarce factor, so that the country as a whole loses (unless, of course, there is a large enough terms-of-trade improvement—a possibility we already examined with the optimum tariff argument). This loss could be avoided by lump-sum redistributions of income.

Specific factors

The distributional consequences of protection are actually far more subtle than the above argument would suggest. One reason is that factors of production do not move easily between industries, whereas our discussion has so far looked only at long-run situations in which all such movements have taken place.

A country's capital stock is embodied in physical form: factories, equipment, and inventories; the education and training of the work-force; highways, railroads; a judiciary; and so forth. This inhibits mobility: there is no magic wand to transform a cotton gin into a grape press should production shift from cotton cloth to wine. *Specific factors are those that cannot be transferred from one industry to another; they are suitable for a specific use.* The notion is very sensitive to the time perspective one has in mind. Most factors are highly specific over a short time span but can be quite mobile when given sufficient opportunity. The cotton gin must gradually wear out or become obsolescent; its depreciation allowances will eventually be able to finance a grape press. In this sense capital is very mobile between industries, but time is required. The same is true, in varying degrees, of other factors. Most laborers possess specific skills, but even unskilled laborers are often reluctant to switch jobs, especially if the switch involves a change in lifestyle or abode. The "little old winemaker" may very well steadfastly refuse to do anything else. But the old curmudgeon will eventually die and be replaced by a member of a younger generation.

Specific factors and income distribution

The implications of specific factors can be best brought out by an example. Suppose that capital and labor produce wine and machines, with wine relatively capital intensive. Wine is exported and machines imported. The production possibility frontier is illustrated in Figure 6.6. Point *F* shows production under free trade, with an international price of machines in terms of wine equal to *AB/AF*. Now suppose a tariff on machines raises their domestic price to *AC/AF*. New equilibrium production is at *G* (the line through *G* and *H* is parallel to that through *F* and *C*): if capital and labor are freely mobile, production moves from *F* to *G*. But factors are freely mobile only in the long run.

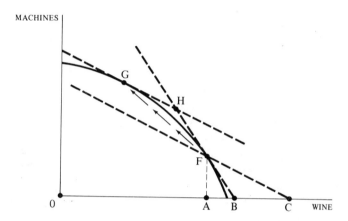

Figure 6.6. SHORT-RUN AND LONG-RUN EFFECTS OF PROTECTION

In the short run the economy remains at *F*. The tariff has raised the price of machines, so factors employed in the machine industry are better off: they receive more for the machines they produce. Factors employed in the wine industry are worse off. In the short run, then, the important consideration is *location;* both capital and labor in the machine industry are better off, and both capital and labor in the wine industry are worse off.

As time goes on, both factors begin to leave the wine industry for the higher rewards available in machine production. The departure might in some cases be involuntary if wine firms shut down; the factors that they had used could face an unemployed spell whose length depends on how specific they are. As resources move from wine to machinery, production gradually shifts from *F* to *G*.

Now relative factor intensities begin to matter. The shrinking wine industry is relatively capital intensive. Thus the wine industry is releasing more capital but less labor than the expanding machine industry, which is labor intensive, wishes to absorb. This causes wages in machine production to rise even more, and rents in machine production to fall. At the same time, wages in the wine industry rise as those wine producers that wish to keep going begin to find that they have a harder time retaining workers than capital.

Eventually the economy reaches point *G*. The two industries now pay equal wages and equal rents, so no factor has an incentive to move. The wage (in both industries) is higher in real terms than before the tariff, and the rent is lower. The important consideration now is the *identity of the factor* and not its location. In the short run, a factor's income is determined entirely by its location, and in the long run, entirely by its identity. During the transition both considerations matter.

The effect of the machine tariff is summarized in Table 6.1. Note that in this example some individuals are affected in the same direction in both the long run and the short run, whereas others are affected in opposite ways. Laborers in the machine industry, for example, are benefited both in the short run (they are located in machinery production) and in the long run (they are relatively intensively used by the protected industry). But capital initially employed in machine production is in an ambiguous position, benefiting in the short run but suffering ultimately. Thus owners of machine capital could either favor or oppose protection for their industry, depending upon their time horizon. This discrepancy helps explain why individuals sometimes adopt positions on tariff issues at odds with their own interests as predicted by the Stolper-Samuelson theorem. For example, the owners of capital invested in labor-intensive industries, such as textiles in the DCs, often plea for protection, even though the Stolper-Samuelson theorem indicates it is contrary to their interests. Emphasis on short-run effects is also strengthened by the fact that factory owners are frequently organized politically on the basis of industrial location. Laborers in the capital-intensive wine industry might be organized in a Federation of Grape Stompers. Because it represents only wine workers, this federation could favor a tariff on wine even though it would harm laborers in general (and its own members in the long run): wine workers who leave the industry also leave the federation.

Table 6.1. Income Effects of a Tariff on Machines (*Labor Intensive*)

	Higher Real Income	*Lower Real Income*
Short Run	Machine Labor Machine Capital	Wine Labor Wine Capital
Long Run	Machine Labor Wine Labor	Machine Capital Wine Capital

Importance of distributional considerations

The distributional motive for protection seems very powerful in reality, if we are to judge by how well individuals' positions on tariff issues accord with their self-interests. But it is hard to tell just how important the motive is. Unless requested by a group generally perceived to have an inequitable income share, an appeal for protection that is not couched in terms of national well-being is unlikely to be persuasive. Thus appeals will be based on noneconomic objectives and on the infant industry and other such arguments (or else on fallacious arguments). Despite this ambiguity, distribution is certainly an important consideration. Thus the tariff, ostensibly aimed at international economic relations, is also a domestic issue: part of the struggle over the distribution of the national income.

8. EMPLOYMENT

Still another motive for tariff protection might be a desire to stimulate domestic income and employment.

In a Keynesian context, a tariff could indeed be successful in this regard. However, as with the other objectives discussed in this section, a tariff is a second-best method because it works only at the cost of additional distortions. Furthermore, many economists would question the wisdom of dealing with cyclical problems such as unemployment by means of tariffs, which have long-run consequences.

In addition, an employment tariff could result in the same sort of foreign retaliation we discussed with respect to the optimum tariff argument. A tariff stimulates domestic employment by shifting demand from foreign goods to domestic goods; thus foreign employment will fall. Foreign countries might well respond in kind. Such a tariff war could result in employment increases for no country but would subject all countries to distortions.

PROBLEMS

6.8 The optimum tariff argument supplies a motive where the tariff is a first-best tool from a *nationalistic* perspective. But from a *cosmopolitan* perspective is it a first-best method for redistributing income between countries? Why? If it is not, what methods are better and why?

6.9* Table 6.1 summarizes the long-run and short-run distributional consequences of protection. Discuss a *medium run* in which one factor (say labor) is completely mobile between industries but the other factor is totally specific. Describe the process of adjustment from short to medium to long run.

5. *Exploring Further:* The Second-Best Nature of the Tariff

Previous sections have shown that tariffs are *second-best* methods of dealing with domestic objectives. This section examines the issues more thoroughly. We consider a domestic distortion in the production of importables, but our analysis applies as well to the other motives discussed in sections 3 and 4.

In Figure 6.7 the terms of trade equal *GH/HA*, so that with free trade and perfect competition the economy would produce at *C*. But the domestic distortion prevents this. The nature of that distortion is not relevant; suppose that all producers of importables are required to belong to a trade association, with a membership fee proportional to output. If that fee equals *FG/HA* in Figure 6.7, the economy will produce at *A*. The quantity *HA* of importables could be sold for *GH* exportables, but *FG* of that goes for the fee, leaving producers with *FH*. Thus producers behave as though the relative price were *FH/HA* rather than *GH/HA*. Consumers are not directly affected by the trade association, so the economy consumes at *B*.

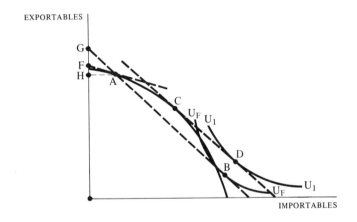

Figure 6.7. A DOMESTIC DISTORTION

If the trade association were broken down, production would shift from *A* to *C*, and the economy would consume the free-trade collection of goods, *D*. This is a *first-best* solution. A subsidy of *FG/HA* per unit on the production of importables would produce the same result, by neutralizing the association's fee.

But suppose a tariff is used instead. The idea would be to protect importables and thereby stimulate their production, to counter the effect of the association in reducing production. Such a tariff cannot possibly be a first-best solution, because it will impose a consumption cost. In fact, the tariff might possibly not improve matters at all.

This is illustrated in Figure 6.8. Again, point *B* on the indifference curve U_F represents initial, free-trade, consumption, and point *D* on the indifference curve U_1 represents consumption if the distortion is removed by a first-best method. With the tariff, production is at *E*, and consumption is at *J* on the indifference curve U_2. By shifting production from *A* to *E*, the

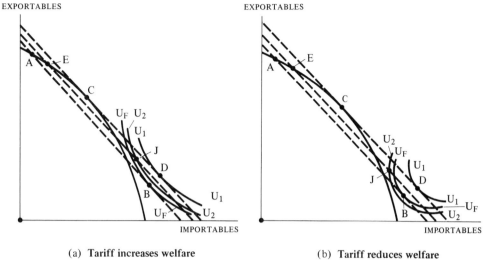

(a) Tariff increases welfare   (b) Tariff reduces welfare

Figure 6.8. A Tariff to Counter a Domestic Distortion

tariff has countered part of the distortion and increased national income. In panel (a) the country has been made better off, since U_2 is above U_F. But the country cannot be as well off as with a first-best policy, that is, U_2 must be below U_1, for two reasons. First, the tariff has not been large enough to completely counter the distortion: production has moved only to E and not all the way to C. Second, the tariff has introduced a new distortion of its own in the consumption cost. U_2 is not tangent to the budget line between E and J; the slope of U_2 at J reflects the domestic (tariff-ridden) relative price. In panel (b) the country is actually worse off than before as a result of the tariff—U_2 is below U_F—and would have been better off doing nothing at all. In this case the harm due to the consumption cost exceeds the benefit from countering the original distortion.

Two further conclusions are demonstrated in Figure 6.9. Panel (a) shows that a *small* tariff will always cause an improvement relative to free trade. With no tariff, the country produces at A and consumes at B, on U_F. A tariff distorts consumers' choices away from importables, causing the consumption point to move from B along the budget line in the direction of the arrow. This will put the economy on a lower indifference curve, thereby imposing the consumption cost. At the same time, the tariff will protect the importables industry, so that production moves away from A, as shown by the arrow. This pushes the budget line outward, illustrating the increase in income from neutralizing the distortion. Suppose now that only a small tariff is imposed. The indifference curve U_F has the same slope at B as does the budget line. Thus a small movement along the latter will not be very different from moving along the former; the movement to a lower indif-

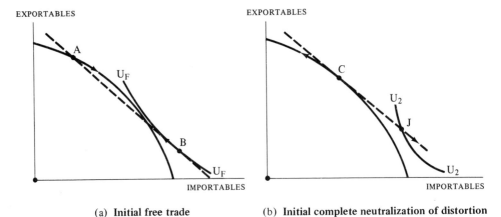

(a) Initial free trade   (b) Initial complete neutralization of distortion

Figure 6.9. THE EFFECTS OF A SMALL CHANGE IN A TARIFF

ference curve will be negligible, and the consumption cost will be insignificant. But the production possibility frontier at *A* cuts the budget line from below, so any movement along the former must push out the latter to a commensurate degree. Thus for a *small* initial tariff, the increase in income due to neutralizing the distortion dominates the consumption cost. This argument applies only to a small tariff; as the tariff is raised, the production point moves to flatter parts of the production possibility frontier, whose slope therefore approaches that of the budget line, and the consumption point moves to steeper parts of the indifference curves.

Panel (b) of Figure 6.9 shows a case where the tariff is just large enough to completely neutralize the domestic distortion. The production point *C* therefore coincides with what production would be with a first-best solution. But there is a consumption cost, illustrated by the fact that the indifference curve U_2 through the consumption point *J* cuts the budget line. The same logic as above now shows that a small tariff *reduction* must benefit this country. Such a reduction will move production in the direction of the arrow from *C* and consumption in the direction of the arrow from *J*. Since the production possibility frontier has the same slope at *C* as does the budget line, the reduction in income will be negligible for a small tariff. But U_2 is steeper at *J* than is the budget line, so that the country must move to a higher indifference curve.

In sum, the following four conclusions apply to the use of a tariff to neutralize domestic distortions.

1. Because it introduces a distortion of its own, a tariff is necessarily second best—that is, inferior to a more direct method.

2. A *small* tariff is always better than free trade.

3. A tariff that completely neutralizes the distortion is too large.

4. A moderate-to-large tariff may be either better or worse than no tariff at all.

PROBLEMS

6.10 This section suggested two possible first-best ways of dealing with the trade association example of a distortion. Are those two ways equivalent? What would determine which should be used?

6.11 Prove each of the four conclusions of this section *without* using community indifference curves.

6.12 Formulate analogs of this section's four conclusions that apply to the use of a tariff to improve the terms of trade.

6. Effective Protection

Thus far we have ignored the fact that countries import many different goods subject to different tariff rates. Such differences become important in some cases, such as when dealing with intermediate goods.

Intermediate goods are used to produce other products, as steel is used to produce automobiles. The price of an automobile covers the cost of the steel embodied in the vehicle as well as the value added in the automobile industry itself. Now, a tariff on automobiles affects its total price, whereas an automobile producer is interested only in the part of the price represented by value added and not in the part that is simply passed on to producers of intermediate goods.

As an illustration, suppose that a firm produces an automobile that, with free trade, sells for $10,000. Suppose further that $5000 of this pays for steel and that the remaining $5000, the value added in the automobile industry, covers wages, rent, profit, and so forth. Suppose that a country imports both automobiles and steel. Consider the effect of a 20 percent tariff on automobiles, with free trade in steel. The domestic price of a car is thus $12,000 (the $10,000 world price plus 20 percent), of which $5000 is still required to pay for the (duty-free) steel. This leaves $7,000 ($12,000 less $5,000) for value added. Thus the 20 percent tariff on cars has enabled the domestic producer to increase value added from $5,000 to $7,000—a *40 percent* rise. It is this latter figure, rather than the 20 percent *nominal* tariff on automobiles, that is of immediate interest to individuals involved in automobile production.

Suppose, next, that trade in automobiles is free, but that steel has a 20 percent tariff. The producer must now sell his car at the world price of $10,000, but the steel that he uses to produce it will cost him $6,000 ($5,000 plus 20 percent), leaving only $4,000 for value added. Thus although the tariff on automobiles is zero, the over-all impact of the tariff policy on the automobile producer is a 20 percent *fall* in value added (a decline from $5,000 to $4,000). Industries are affected not only by tariffs on goods that they produce, but also by the tariffs on all intermediate goods that they purchase.

THE EFFECTIVE RATE FORMULA

The *effective rate of protection* measures the over-all effect of a tariff structure on an individual industry. To see how it is measured, continue with our automobile-steel example, and let P_A and P_S denote the world prices of automobiles and steel, respectively, and suppose that the amount of steel used in the production of a single automobile is denoted by a. Then, at *world* prices, the value added v in a single car is

$$v = P_A - P_S a. \tag{6.2}$$

Suppose that automobile imports are subject to the tariff rate t_A and steel imports to the tariff rate t_S. Then, at *domestic* prices, the value added v' is

$$v' = P_A(1 + t_A) - P_S(1 + t_S)a. \tag{6.3}$$

Now, the *nominal* rate of protection (that is, the tariff) on automobiles is equal to the proportion by which the domestic price exceeds the world price:

$$t_A = \frac{Q_A - P_A}{P_A},$$

where $Q_A = P_A(1 + t_A)$ is the domestic price. The *effective* rate of protection, by analogy, is defined as the proportion by which value added at domestic prices exceeds value added at world prices:

$$e_A = \frac{v' - v}{v}, \tag{6.4}$$

where e_A denotes the effective rate of protection on automobiles. We can obtain a formula with which to measure e_A by substituting (6.3) and (6.2) into (6.4) and rearranging:

$$e_A = \frac{v' - v}{v} = \frac{[P_A(1 + t_A) - P_S(1 + t_S)a] - [P_A - P_S a]}{v}$$

$$= \frac{[P_A - P_S a] + [P_A t_A - P_S t_S a] - [P_A - P_S a]}{v}$$

$$= \frac{P_A t_A - P_S t_S a}{v} = \frac{P_A t_A - P_S a t_A + P_S a t_A - P_S t_S a}{v}$$

$$= \frac{[P_A - P_S a]t_A}{v} + \frac{P_S a[t_A - t_S]}{v},$$

or

$$e_A = t_A + [t_A - t_S]\frac{P_s a}{v}.$$

(6.5)

This formula leads to a number of observations. First, if the automobile industry uses no intermediate goods ($a = 0$), then the effective rate equals the nominal rate ($e_A = t_A$). This is as expected, for in this case the full price of the car goes toward value added. Second, if all goods have the same tariff rate (so that $t_A = t_S$), then the effective rate again equals the nominal rate. Thus effective-rate calculations become interesting when tariff rates differ across commodities. In the above numerical example, if the 20 percent tariff on automobiles and the 20 percent tariff on steel *both* hold, then the domestic price of a car is $12,000 and the cost of steel is $6,000, leaving value added at $6,000, which is just 20 percent above what it would be at world prices ($5,000).

Formula (6.5) implies, third, that if the tariff rate on the final good exceeds that on the intermediate good (so that t_A exceeds t_S), then the effective rate exceeds the nominal rate (e_A is larger than t_A). Finally, the gap between the nominal and effective rates is larger the more important are intermediate goods in the production of the final good (that is, the larger is $P_s a$ relative to v).

USES OF EFFECTIVE RATES

Why use a formula such as (6.5) to calculate effective rates of protection? There are two basic reasons. The effective rates measure the impact of the tariff structure as a whole upon individual *industries,* rather than goods. Suppose one is interested in income distribution in the short run, when factors are specific to the industries in which they are employed. (This was discussed in section 4 of this chapter.) Then the effective rates are the indicators to look at, because value added is what these factors receive. Industry lobbyists care about the effective protection they receive, rather than the nominal protection. Government officials engaged in tariff bargaining with foreign countries use effective-rate calculations to discover the effects of proposed tariff changes on special interests and industry pressure groups.

The second reason has to do with resource allocation. The presumption is that the impact of any tariff structure is to cause resources to flow from industries with low effective rates of protection to industries with high rates, because value added is what resources earn in an industry. Economists therefore look at the set of effective tariff rates of a country if they wish to obtain, for whatever reason, some idea of how that country's tariff structure has influenced its allocation of resources among the various industries.

For some purposes nominal rates are more relevant than effective rates. The relative price of a commodity indicates the opportunity cost of producing more of it, and also the value of more of it to consumers, regardless of how important intermediate goods are in the final stage of that commodity's production. Because of this, nominal tariff rates—which indicate the effects of protection on prices—are relevant to our earlier discussions of such things as the production and consumption costs of protection and the optimum tariff. Effective rates are not necessary for these important topics.

Since the mid-sixties, many economists have made calculations of the effective tariff rates of many countries. One feature that has been given prominence by these studies is the *cascading* nature of the developed countries' tariff structures. These countries typically levy higher nominal tariffs on goods at more advanced levels of processing, so that raw materials have relatively low tariffs and finished goods produced from those materials have relatively high tariffs. Formula (6.5) shows that if the nominal tariff on a good exceeds that on its intermediate input, the effective tariff exceeds the nominal tariff. Thus the cascading nature of the industrial countries' tariffs results in relatively high effective protection of the later stages of production. One study revealed, for example, that although the nominal U.S. tariff on woven wool fabrics was 20.7 percent, the effective rate of protection of the activity of weaving the fabrics was 60.9 percent. Table 6.2 shows overall average nominal and effective rates of protection for the industrial countries as a group. The first column shows how nominal tariffs rise as the stages of production become more advanced, and the second column shows the resulting high effective rates for the more advanced processes. Spokesmen for the LDCs point to such calculations as indications that the DCs' tariff policies constitute a much more serious obstacle to industrialization than the moderate nominal tariff levels would appear to suggest. Industrialization in the LDCs could involve advancing their production to later stages and thereby replacing some of their exports of rudimentary goods with the export of more finished goods. But it is these later stages of production that

Table 6.2.   Average Rates in All Industrial Countries at Various Stages of Production

Stage of Processing	*Nominal Rate (%)*	*Effective Rate (%)*
1	4.6	4.6
2	7.9	22.6
3	16.2	29.7
4	22.2	38.4

SOURCE: *UNCTAD, The Kennedy Round Estimated Effects on Tariff Barriers,* New York: UN, 1968

are highly protected in the developed countries. The tariff structures of the latter thereby tend to lock in the LDCs to the earlier stages.

Another prominent feature is the very high degree of effective protection afforded industrial activities in many LDCs with import substitution policies. A country might wish to develop an automobile industry, for example, and attempt to do this by giving both high protection to finished automobiles and very low protection to many intermediate goods, such as parts. As a result, the share of total cost accounted for by value added is low relative to the share of intermediate goods (because few are produced in the local industry), and the tariff on automobiles substantially exceeds that on inputs. Then, formula (6.5) implies that the effective rate could be very much higher than the nominal rate. Many studies have revealed an extensive tendency for LDCs to shelter industrial activities behind effective tariffs that greatly exceed the (frequently high) nominal tariffs. As a rather extreme example, a study of Turkish policies by the economist Anne Krueger revealed that superphosphate fertilizer, with a nominal tariff of 27 percent, was accorded an effective tariff rate of 925 percent.

PROBLEMS

6.13 Suppose that shoes have a 25 percent nominal tariff rate, leather a 15 percent rate, and two-thirds of the cost of a pair of shoes is due to the leather they contain, and one-third to value added. What is the effective rate of protection of the activity of making shoes from leather?

6.14 Suppose that, in a refinery, a_O barrels of crude oil, a_C tons of coal, and a_M units of materials are combined with value added to yield b_G gallons of gasoline and b_A gallons of aviation fuel. If P_O, P_C, P_M, P_G, and P_A denote the world prices of oil, coal, materials, gasoline, and aviation fuel respectively, if t_O, t_C, t_M, t_G, and t_A denote the corresponding nominal tariff rates, derive a formula, analogous to (6.5), for the effective rate of protection of refining, e_R.

6.15* Consider the example of steel and autos in the text. *Gross* output, denoted X_A and X_S for autos and steel respectively, refers to the total output of an industry. *Net* output (Y_A and Y_S) refers to gross output less that part of output used as an input in other industries (that is, that part of gross output available for consumption or export). Thus, $Y_A = X_A$ and $Y_S = X_S - a X_A$. Chapter 1 showed that relative commodity prices equal the marginal rate of transformation between any two goods that are actually produced. Show that this refers to the *MRT* between *net* outputs. Will the ratio of values added per unit equal the *MRT* between *gross* outputs? Why? What do you conclude about the significance of effective rates of protection?

7. The Political Economy of Tariffs

The various motives for tariffs do not, on the whole, make a very strong case for protection. In nearly all cases, the tariff is second best:

dominated by some other policy tool. The optimum-tariff argument is first best, but only from a narrow nationalistic point of view. In any event, the argument is relevant only to countries that occupy a special place in the world economy. Trade limitation for noneconomic reasons is unambiguously a first-best use of a tariff, but the argument really reduces to protection for its own sake. How, then, do we explain the substantial protection characteristic of both past and present?

FALLACIOUS ARGUMENTS FOR PROTECTION

The most natural way to proceed is first to examine the arguments advanced by protectionists. Our discussion in sections 1, 3, and 4 of various motives noted the times and places when they were so used. But, in addition, one finds many invalid arguments reflecting a misunderstanding of the theory of international trade.

Perhaps the most common is the *cheap foreign labor* argument, the assertion that, because wages in many parts of the world are only a small fraction of wages at home, free trade must result in massive domestic unemployment or massive real wage cuts. The argument is, of course, a fundamental misunderstanding of the principle of comparative advantage. Sometimes factors other than labor occupy center stage, as when attention is directed to modern, efficient foreign plants (cheap foreign capital), and the argument has been carried to its extreme to assert that each product should be accorded protection equal to the excess of the domestic cost of production above the foreign cost, regardless of the source of this difference. This principle, sometimes called that of the "scientific tariff," was actually written into U.S. law in 1922, and the Tariff Commission was given the thankless task of measuring cost differences as a basis for tariff revision (few rates were actually changed in this way).

Another common fallacy is found in the *keep-the-money-at-home* argument: imports should be restricted because the necessity of paying for them results in a loss of the nation's money to foreigners. This reflects an ignorance of reciprocal demand: imports are paid for by the sale of exports and assets to foreigners, to the mutual benefit of both parties.

TARIFFS AND PRESSURE-GROUP POLITICS

Thus far, we have looked at the motives advanced for tariffs. An alternative way to try to explain protection is to examine its structure to see who benefits and who loses, on the presumption that self-interest governs political behavior. We have seen that a tariff always hurts some individuals and benefits others, so that there is always a group with a vested interest in protection. But, except when there is a substantial terms-of-trade improvement, the losses from protection always exceed the gains, so that free trade would attract the majority of "dollar votes" if given the chance. Thus we must examine the political aspect in more detail.

Theories of the economic behavior of representative government have been described by Anthony Downs, Mancur Olson, and Albert Breton. From this perspective, the central relevant fact about protection is that its costs are diffused over many people while the benefits are concentrated on relatively few. Consider, for example, the case of a textile industry in a developed country. If the industry is faced with severe competition from imports, a tariff on textiles could mean the difference between having a job and losing it for textile workers, and between solvency and bankruptcy for textile firms. Thus people in the industry have a vital stake in the tariff question. Protection for textiles would harm many more people, but each person would be affected only slightly. All consumers would have to pay more for textiles, but such purchases account for only a small part of consumers' budgets. Export industries will also be harmed, because factors will be bid away by textile producers and because foreign countries will ultimately have to buy fewer goods from this country if they are forced to reduce their sales to it. But these costs are long term and will be spread over all export industries, so that individual exporters will perceive little effect.

The implication of this asymmetry is that the economic gains from the tariff, though smaller than the economic losses, will translate into a larger political impact. Because the gainers from a tariff have a vital interest in the measure, they have a strong incentive to organize and exert whatever influence they can. Their decision on whether to support elected officials will likely be determined by the officials' positions on the tariff issue. Those who will lose from the tariff are large in number, but since none of them are greatly affected, they have no incentive to organize or even to keep informed about the issue. Their decision on which elected officials to support will be determined by the positions of those officials on other public questions. Moreover, those who gain from a tariff would find it easier to organize than would the losers if the gainers were more likely to come in contact with each other, because they are in the same business, or if they are more geographically concentrated. Such concentration would also make their support more important for politicians from the same region.

Notice that this *pressure-group* argument is related to individuals' time horizons and the degree to which factors are specific to industry, as discussed in section 4 above. If the time horizon is short and factors are highly specific, the gains from a tariff will be concentrated on those actually located in the industry, rather than on the industry's intensive factor wherever located. This strengthens the pressure-group argument.

This connection between politics and economics goes both ways. If tariff protection is in fact important in a country, those industries that most markedly possess the characteristics described above will be the industries most likely to obtain protection and to prosper. Thus the country will tend to develop an industrial structure with these characteristics. Similarly if the ability to benefit members by obtaining tariff protection is important to the appeal of trade associations and labor unions, groups organized on an industry basis and appealing to individuals with a short-term horizon would be the most likely to prosper, because they would appeal most to the people who care most. Thus we would expect to see such pressure groups adopt a short-run, industry-specific view of tariff matters, even if the general population does not.

CHARACTERISTICS OF PROTECTED INDUSTRIES

Do protected industries in fact possess the characteristics that the above discussion suggests would likely lead to protection? Let us look at the limited available evidence.

1. There is evidence that the industrial nations tend to protect most heavily industries that make intensive use of unskilled labor. David Stafford Ball found that the tariff structure of the United States in 1962 tended to give higher effective rates of protection to industries with lower average wage rates. Richard Caves and Ronald Jones, likewise, showed that in the late sixties U.S. tariff rates, both nominal and effective, were higher in industries where wage rates were lower. Similar evidence has been marshaled for Western European countries by M. Constantopoulos and others. All of this is consistent with the pressure-group theory, because unskilled workers typically find it most difficult to find a new job after losing an old one due to import competition; thus their interest in protection should be high. Also, workers are voters. On the other hand, we saw in Chapter 3 that in the industrial countries, wages tend to be lower in import-competing industries, and, more generally, these countries tend to have a comparative disadvantage in goods that intensively use unskilled labor. Since it is the import-competing industries that are protected in any case, one might expect to find a negative correlation between tariffs and wage rates regardless of what actually determines protection. A somewhat different question was addressed by John Cheh. He found that in international tariff negotiations in the mid-sixties, the United States reduced tariff rates the least in those industries with the highest labor-adjustment costs (the costs of moving to a new job), and the extent of unskilled labor was a determinant of those costs. However James Riedel failed to find similar evidence for West Germany.

2. A few studies have related tariffs to the concentration-diffusion characteristics emphasized in the pressure-group theory. A study of the U.S. Tariff Act of 1824 by J. J. Pincus found that high protection tended to go to those industries that were most concentrated, where communication among producers was easiest, and which had a presence in a sizable area. Richard Caves examined the 1963 Canadian tariff structure and compared the ability of alternative theories to explain it: a majority-vote theory predicting

that tariffs would be high when a majority of voters benefit, an industry-size theory predicting that the highest protection would go to the industries that are the largest, actually or potentially, and a pressure-group theory predicting that protection would be highest in those industries where producers were the most concentrated and buyers the least concentrated. The last theory performed the best.

3. Some investigators have looked directly at the tariff-making process rather than the resultant tariffs. The political scientist E. E. Schattschneider wrote a classic account of the passage of the U.S. Tariff Act of 1930. Robert Baldwin has performed a statistical test of congressional voting on the 1974 U. S. Trade Act. He found that protectionist votes were positively related to political party membership (because of party loyalty—the bill was sponsored by a Republican administration), the prominence of protectionist industries in congressional districts, and the receipt of campaign contributions from protectionist unions. The presence in congressional districts of industries opposed to protection seemed to have no effect.

4. The tendency, noted in section 6, of the tariff structures of industrial countries to offer greater protection at more advanced stages of production is clearly consistent with the pressure-group theory. Producers of intermediate goods sell to the industries that use them, so that buyers as well as sellers could be concentrated. Producers of final goods, on the other hand, sell to consumers in general, so that buyers are likely to be far less concentrated than sellers.

PROBLEMS

6.16 List the characteristics likely to be possessed by industries with substantial protection. What specific industries seem to have these characteristics? Find out how protected those industries are.

6.17 On the basis of this section's discussion of what determines relative tariff rates in a country, speculate about what national characteristics should distinguish high-tariff countries from low-tariff ones. How do your speculations stack up against actual policy differences across countries?

8. Case Study: The Tariff History of the United States

A brief overview of U.S. tariff history will illustrate the points made in earlier sections. Table 6.3 shows the average U.S. tariff rate in selected years since 1821.

THE EARLY PERIOD

In colonial times the individual colonies pursued their own commercial policies, and after the Revolution they passed their own tariff laws.

Table 6.3. AVERAGE U.S. TARIFF RATES (TOTAL DUTIES AS A
PERCENTAGE OF TOTAL DUTIABLE IMPORTS)

Year	Average Tariff (%)	Year	Average Tariff (%)
1821	45	1920	16
1830	62	1925	38
1835	40	1932	59
1850	27	1940	36
1861	19	1946	25
1865	48	1950	13
1893	50	1960	12
1900	49	1970	10
1910	42	1975	6

SOURCE: Statistical Abstract of the United States

These were intended to raise government revenue, but the protection of local industries soon became a significant motive as well. Conflicts between the states naturally arose, and attempts at coordination and at using state tariffs as a source of needed national revenue came to naught.

With the adoption of the Constitution, tariff policy became the exclusive responsibility of the new national government, which needed revenue. In April 1789 James Madison introduced a bill in Congress for a moderate tariff. Madison's purpose was simply to raise *revenue*. (He hoped to hit the spring imports, already on the high seas, with a tariff when they arrived!) But protectionist sentiment soon surfaced and influenced the measure that was eventually adopted. Pennsylvania interests obtained protection for their young steel industry, which had been nurtured by local duties before the adoption of the Constitution. Log-rolling soon became evident, as the support of interests harmed by some aspects of the bill were enlisted by the addition of protectionist features for their own benefit. This was indicative of subsequent years. The most common rationale for this protection was the *infant industry argument,* voiced by Alexander Hamilton and others. Nationalist sentiment, especially resentment of the British—important exporters to the United States—also played a role. The level of protection that emerged, little more than 5 percent overall, was nevertheless modest by later standards, as Table 6.3 reveals.

Economic relations with Europe were interrupted by the Napoleonic Wars, by Jefferson's Embargo of trade with France and England (in retaliation for interference by those warring nations with U.S. shipping), and, especially, by the War of 1812, during which the Royal Navy blockaded the coast. This amounted to protection of a very high order indeed! The close of hostilities was followed by new tariffs to protect war-nurtured industries—a pattern consistently followed after later wars. Protection was generally favored by the Northeast, the home of import-competing industries and owners of capital, a relatively scarce factor. Interests in the South and West, where people owned land and produced exports, tended to oppose tariffs. The former were on balance dominant and protection became more intense, culminating in 1828 with an act called the Tariff of Abominations. This produced a dramatic fusion of the tariff issue with that of states' rights when South Carolina vainly tried to nullify the tariff.

THE RESPITE

The coming of Jacksonian democracy reflected a shift in the balance of political power that soon resulted in tariff reductions. This process was also facilitated by a spirit of compromise and by a surplus in the federal budget, for which the tariff was the principal revenue source. Tariffs by and large fell steadily between the 1820s and the Civil War, coinciding with liberal trends in Europe. But the trend was never as strong in the United States and it ended sooner, so that the country continued to be relatively protectionist.

THE AGE OF HIGH PROTECTION

In any event liberalism ended with the Civil War. Secession, of course, shifted political power to Northern interests, who had been protectionists all along. The exporting South, which had enjoyed heavy cotton sales to Britain, had favored free trade. Also, the need to finance the war resulted in increased tariffs, as did the desire to use tariffs to put foreign goods on the same footing as heavily taxed domestic goods.

The end of the war witnessed, in familiar fashion, a continuation of the high-tariff policy. The protectionist era was to continue for over seventy years. Tariff rates fluctuated, a modest downward revision was attempted when Grover Cleveland was president, and there was a real respite in Woodrow Wilson's administration.

Throughout the nineteenth century, the tariff was the major source of federal revenue. This ensured that protection was intimately related to questions of national taxation and the role of the central government, as well as to struggles between economic interests and to debate over the wisdom of industrialization. The tariff was the major political issue of the century, eclipsed only by slavery when that was an open question.

The Wilson administration brought about a large reduction in protection with the Underwood Tariff of 1913, which abolished tariffs on some important products, such as raw wool, iron, and coal. But the liberal respite ended with the usual reaction after the First World War and with the return of the Republicans to power. Tariffs rose during the 1920s, culminating in the Smoot-Hawley Act of 1930.

During the election campaign of 1928, the Democrats had abandoned their traditional opposition to high tariffs and embraced protection in their platform. The original purpose of the tariff bill that the Republicans introduced was to aid agriculture. The important agricultural commodities that were heavily exported could not be helped much by tariffs, and, although many agricultural duties were substantially raised, a proposal for export subsidies for farm products was defeated. But a log-rolling avalanche resulted in a large general rise in tariffs on manufactures. The need for revenue and the infant industry argument, both so prominent in the nineteenth century, were no longer significant motives. The desire to *benefit special interests,* with a generally nationalistic sentiment and the 1929 stock-market crash for background, was the driving force. During the congressional debate, thirty-six foreign countries protested that they would be seriously hurt by the proposed changes, and over one thousand American economists signed a petition against the bill. The petition had little apparent effect, although Senator Smoot complained that opponents of his bill resided "in American schools of economics, and in the cloistered halls of theoretical universities," while Senator Shortbridge described himself as "not overawed or at all disturbed by the proclamation of the college professors who never earned a dollar by the sweat of their brow by honest labor—theorists, dreamers." In any event, the resultant act raised American tariffs to historic highs, comparable to the Tariff of Abominations of a century before.

The result was little short of catastrophic. Within two years, sixty foreign countries had instituted tariff increases of their own. These countries were concerned both to retaliate against the United States and to *stimulate domestic employment* in the face of the deepening world depression. The mutual increases in protection canceled each other out, and the resulting dramatic shrinkage in world trade simply made the Depression worse for all. By 1932 American imports were only 31 percent of their 1929 level, and exports collapsed in even greater proportion.

THE LIBERAL PERIOD

The new Roosevelt administration soon saw the need to revive world trade and hoped to assist American recovery by increasing exports. The result was a landmark in U.S. tariff history—the reciprocal Trade Agreements Act of 1934.

This act authorized the president to enter into bilateral agreements to reduce (or increase) U.S. tariffs by up to 50 percent in exchange for reciprocal foreign concessions. The act (technically an amendment to the Smoot-Hawley tariff, which remains the basic U.S. tariff act to this day) was originally valid for only three years, but it was renewed many times into the sixties.

The Trade Agreements Act was a turning point in two ways. It was, first, intended to break with the old policy of high protection. Second, it transferred tariff-making initiative from the legislative branch, highly subject to the log-rolling of sectoral interests, to the executive branch, with a relatively more national outlook. (Earlier tariff laws had contained provisions for executive flexibility, but, as intended, they had not been widely applied, and not in a liberalizing direction.)

By the Second World War, the United States had reached twenty-one agreements with foreign nations, and the Smoot-Hawley tariff levels were moderately reduced as a result. The liberal period continued after the war, the first major conflict in U.S. history followed by a reduction of protection instead of an increase. We shall examine postwar experience presently. As is clear from Table 6.3, present U.S. tariff rates are far below the basic Smoot-Hawley levels, and quite low in historical perspective.

9. Case Studies: Commercial Policy in Other Lands

In the early nineteenth century, Europe exported manufactures to the United States for primary products. Now let us look at policy from the other side of the ocean.

EUROPEAN TARIFF HISTORY

As Britain emerged from the Industrial Revolution and the Napoleonic Wars, its rising entrepreneurial class challenged the landed aristocracy for both political and economic power. The political struggle culminated in the Reform Bill of 1832, while the economic conflict centered on the Corn Laws, which protected agriculture. These duties were finally repealed in 1846 as Tory Prime Minister Sir Robert Peel executed an historic about-face that shattered his own party. During the next fifteen years Britain repealed the Navigation Acts (known to all students of the American Revolution) and dismantled most of its tariffs. For over eighty-five years the country was to embrace a free trade policy, a policy that was to be a foundation stone of the *Pax Brittanica* and was to be supported by both political parties and challenged by no major public figure until the politician Joseph Chamberlin did so near the turn of the century.

This trend toward free trade was not confined to Britain. Liberalization had taken place in the United States from the 1830s to the Civil War, as we have seen, and was extended to continental Europe by a series of commercial treaties between the major powers. Toward the end of the century a reverse trend set in. The United States was highly protectionist from the Civil War, and Russia had remained so. Rising protectionism on the continent stemmed from the emerging nationalism and imperialism, which embraced commercial policy as a weapon, and from labor migration and reductions in transportation costs, which gave the newly settled temperate zones a comparative advantage over Europe in food, even in continental markets. France and Germany succumbed to the agrarian interest and, in contrast to earlier British behavior, imposed high duties on agricultural imports.

Despite the growing protectionism, tariffs on average remained low, by historical standards, before the First World War. But after that conflict, the trend to protection resumed at an accelerated pace, as war-weary nations turned inward. The Depression and the Smoot-Hawley tariff in the United States gave the process a gigantic boost. Country after country erected barriers in order to separate themselves from the world slump, to export their own unemployment, or to retaliate against new barriers abroad. Britain abandoned free trade in 1932. The form of protection changed, as well as its extent. Before the First World War, commercial policies had relied almost exclusively upon tariffs. Now nontariff barriers became important. France adopted an extensive system of import quotas, and other countries followed; many types of controls, direct and indirect, were instituted.

■ *The Most-Favored-Nation Clause.* The most-favored-nation clause is an agreement between two nations to apply tariffs to each other at rates as low as those applied to any other nation. Thus if a country reduces tariffs on goods from some other country, it also applies these new lower rates to goods from all other countries that have MFN status with it. Thus bilateral agreements have multilateral effects. For example, the United States–United Kingdom trade agreement of 1938 provided for a reduction of U.S. duties on about 47 percent of U.S. imports from the United Kingdom. Because of the MFN clause, duties were also reduced on about 9 percent of U.S. imports from France, 13 percent of those from the Soviet Union, and 14 percent of those from Ireland.

The *MFN* clause has always been prominent during liberal periods. Thus the European commercial treaties of the 1860s relied upon it, and use of the MFN clause was a central part of the U.S. reciprocal trade agreements strategy adopted in 1934. By contrast, during its highly protectionist period, the United States did not employ the MFN clause as described above but, instead, used a much weaker "conditional" version that provided only for negotiations on the extension of tariff reductions granted third countries. When countries with (unconditional) MFN agreements became more protectionist, they often sought to escape by adopting very narrow definitions of commodities in tariff legislation. An example quoted in generations of textbooks was provided by the German tariff law of 1902, which established a separate duty for "brown or dappled cows reared at a level of at least 300 metres above sea level and passing at least one month in every summer at an altitude of at least 800 metres." The purpose was obviously to isolate the duties on Swiss cattle from the MFN clause by defining them to be a distinct commodity.

The United States currently extends MFN status to nearly all countries. A prominent exception is the Soviet Union, Congress having made extension (or reextension) to that nation contingent upon the adoption of a liberal emigration policy. ■

CANADIAN TARIFF HISTORY

Canadian policy is of special interest because the country was for so long caught between the geographical proximity of the large U.S. economy and the political connection with Britain. Table 6.4 shows average Canadian tariff rates in selected years.

Table 6.4. AVERAGE CANADIAN TARIFF RATES (TOTAL DUTIES AS A PERCENTAGE OF TOTAL DUTIABLE IMPORTS)

Year	Average Rate (%)	Year	Average Rate (%)
1850	15.6	1900	27.7
1855	13.7	1913	26.1
1867	19.6	1929	24.4
1870	20.9	1939	24.2
1880	26.1	1946	21.2
1890	31.0	1953	18.6

SOURCE: *Young, J. H.*, Canadian Commercial Policy

Prior to Confederation, in 1867, the separate colonies were allowed to levy their own tariffs—in addition to those set by Britain—even on trade among themselves. In 1791 the former French possessions were split into two parts that were allowed separate tariffs (but not on each other's goods) until 1840. These duties were the most important sources of revenue for the colonial governments and tended to be highest in those colonies with the greatest need for government revenue.

The crucial Canadian exports in those days were wheat and timber, which received preferential treatment in the British market. Trade with Britain exceeded that with the United States. But Canada's position changed after England abolished the Corn Laws in 1846: with goods from all countries admitted free of duty, Canada no longer had a preferential position in the British market. The colonies ended preferences on British goods and began to look south. The Reciprocity Treaty of 1854 established free trade in agricultural products between the United States and the British colonies in North America.

At this time, *revenue* was the primary motive for tariffs, which accounted for about two-thirds of all government revenues. A fall in these revenues as a result of an 1857 recession (and reciprocity with the United States, of course, also reduced revenues) led to rate increases in the Cayley-Galt tariffs of 1858–59. These duties also had a protectionist intent, as sentiment for the protection of Canadian manufacturing began to be significant at this time. Partly in response to these tariffs, but also because of U.S. ill will toward England resulting from the Civil War and because of a general U.S. shift toward protection, that country abrogated the Reciprocity Agreement in 1866.

Confederation in 1867 implied a single national tariff policy. But that policy was at a crossroads. Continued British committment to free trade and the U.S. rejection of reciprocity precluded a preferential Canadian position in either major export market. Sentiment for a protectionist policy continued to grow, but the first choice of the public continued to be for reciprocity with the United States, a policy that both the Liberal and Conservative parties continued to advocate for thirty years. But the United States consistently turned a deaf ear, so Canada chose protection. The country adopted a National Policy of attracting scarce capital and immigrants, building up a manufacturing sector, and giving that sector a domestic market enlarged by westward expansion. A key part of the program was the protectionist National Policy tariff law of 1879. This set the tone of Canadian tariff policy for about sixty years.

At the close of the century Canada granted preferences for British goods, even though Britain refused to abandon free trade to reciprocate. By 1904 preferences of one-third were extended to most of the British Empire. One motive for this policy was to prevent the rapidly growing trade with the United States from dominating Canada's international transactions. The Canadian tariff structure consisted of three parts: a General Tariff, having the highest rates; the Intermediate Tariff, applying to countries with MFN status with Canada; and the Preferential Tariff, applying to the Empire. As the United States and Canada did not grant each other MFN status, tariffs on trade between these countries was quite high by world standards. (These three tariff scales, together with a fourth scale for LDC preferences, characterize Canada's tariff structure to this day.)

In 1911 Canada and the United States concluded a second reciprocity agreement, but the Canadian parliament refused to approve it, even though the country had tried for so many years to obtain just such a pact. The manufacturing sector's desire for a general policy of protection had become too strong.

The Depression struck Canada via a decline in the foreign demand for Canadian exports. Also the U.S. Smoot-Hawley tariff caused much resentment, and the result was more Canadian protection in response. Britain abandoned its policy of free trade, and the Ottawa Conference of 1932 established a new system of Imperial Preferences.

The shift in U.S. policy marked by the Trade Agreements Act of 1934 resulted in a Canadian-U.S. trade agreement in 1935 and again in 1938. These agreements, the first between the two countries since reciprocity in 1854, involved a mutual duty reduction and extension of MFN status.

10. Commerical Policies after the Second World War

As the Second World War drew to a close, the United States and other allied nations grappled with the problem of devising an international order free from the mistakes of the past. The most prominent result was, of course, the United Nations, but also international institutions were created to deal directly with the postwar economy. The guiding principles, reflecting American attitudes, were *liberalism* (minimal restrictions on international transactions) and *symmetry* (all nations should be treated the same). Two of these institutions, the International Bank for Reconstruction and Development (IBRD) and the International Monetary Fund (IMF), will be discussed in subsequent chapters. A conference at Havana in 1948 adopted a complex charter for the third institution, the International Trade Organization (ITO), which was to deal with commercial policy. But the ITO was stillborn, as the charter was never ratified by national governments. Instead an interim arrangement, the General Agreement on Tariffs and Trade (GATT), has by default become the international body dealing with trade matters.

THE GATT

As its name implies, the GATT is technically an agreement rather than an organization (thus participating nations are *contracting parties* rather than member states), but it has acquired a physical form as well, with a small permanent secretariat in Geneva and a Council of Representatives. The GATT is not a treaty; American adhesion was via an executive agreement, and Congress has never passed on the matter.

There are three aspects to GATT. The *first* is the *agreement* itself, establishing standards for the commercial policies of the contracting parties. Two standards are fundamental: quotas are prohibited, and each nation must observe the MFN clause with all contracting parties. There are exceptions to each of these rules; for example, quotas are allowed for dealing with temporary balance of payments problems, and customs unions (which depart from the MFN clause) are permitted.

The *second* aspect of GATT is its role in the *settlement of trade disputes* between nations. GATT has no enforcement machinery, but it does provide an impartial recourse that has been of considerable use in the past, notably during the sixties. Furthermore, GATT procedures help ensure that the interests of third countries are taken into account by the parties directly involved in any dispute.

CASE STUDY: The Great Chicken War

In 1962 EEC nations more than doubled their tariffs on frozen
chickens, of which the United States was the principal exporter,
with the result that U.S. poultry exports to the EEC contracted
by about two-thirds. Accusations and threats flew thick and fast,
and the dispute was brought before a GATT arbitration panel in
1963. The panel ruled that the United States had suffered dam-
ages and could withdraw tariff concessions on up to $26 million
of EEC exports should a settlement not be reached. The parties
were unable to negotiate an end to the chicken war, and in 1965
the United States restored the Smoot-Hawley levels on its tariffs
on brandy, assembled trucks, and a few other imports. Since
some countries outside the EEC also exported some of these
items to the United States, tariffs on some goods especially important to those countries were subsequently lowered as compensation. GATT was unable to resolve the basic poultry
dispute, but by bringing into focus an impartial figure for dam-
ages, it was instrumental in limiting the extent of U.S. retaliation
and in preventing EEC countermeasures, and it did help assure
that the interests of third countries were respected.

The *third* aspect of GATT is its *sponsorship of tariff reductions.* These
reductions have been accomplished in a series of multilateral negotiations,
or rounds.

THE GATT ROUNDS OF MULTILATERAL TARIFF NEGOTIATIONS

There have, thus far, been seven major tariff-cutting rounds. They are
logical extensions of the United States' reciprocal trade agreements in the
sense that each participating country "trades" tariff concessions (that is,
reductions) for concessions from its partners, and the MFN clause applies.
But there is one important difference: the GATT rounds are *multilateral,*
whereas the earlier trade agreements involved *bilateral* negotiation between
the United States and a single foreign nation. Since the MFN clause implies
that a bilateral agreement will have direct multilateral consequences, the
multilateral approach to negotiation is much more efficient.

The first two GATT rounds, held during 1949–51 as the ITO was
dying its slow death, substantially lowered tariffs. This success probably
indicated that special interests were not very sensitive to tariff cuts at that
time: the United States had a very strong position, whereas the weakened
European industries were sheltered by quotas and other direct controls.
However trade was further liberalized when these quotas were eliminated

in the late fifties. The liberalization achieved by GATT is relevant mainly to trade in manufactures between the industrial countries. The more than one hundred nations that either belong to GATT or accept its provisions include many LDCs and a few communist states, in addition to the principal industrial nations. But the LDCs generally continue to follow protectionist policies.

The next three rounds achieved only modest success, as protectionist pressures began to mount. The sixth (1964–67), known as the Kennedy Round because it resulted from an initiative by the Kennedy administration in the United States, was a more ambitious effort designed to prevent the emergence of the European Common Market from dividing the industrial world into exclusive trade blocs. The Kennedy Round differed from earlier efforts in that negotiations covered agriculture and nontariff barriers in addition to tariffs on manufactures. The method of negotiation also changed; whereas the earlier rounds had proceeded on a commodity-by-commodity basis, bargaining in the Kennedy Round was for an *across-the-board* reduction in all tariffs. In the end, little was achieved with respect to either nontariff barriers or agriculture, and the EEC developed a highly protectionist Common Agricultural Policy. But tariffs on manufactures were slashed by an average of one-third, the largest reduction in any single round. As a result, most industrial countries were left with tariffs averaging less than 7 percent on manufactures.

You can get some idea about current tariff rates from Table 6.5. (These figures are not comparable to those in Tables 6.3 and 6.4, which divided revenues by dutiable imports rather than by all imports.) Note in Table 6.5 that the rates are higher for the LDCs than for the DCs. Of course, these figures take no account of nontariff barriers.

The Kennedy Round also witnessed changes in American policy. American participation in the first five GATT rounds had been under the

Table 6.5. Average Tariff Rates of Selected Countries (Receipts from International Trade Taxes ÷ Total Imports)

Country	Rate (%)
Brazil	12.2
Canada	6.0
India	37.3
Korea	11.4
Mexico	22.0
Sweden	2.2
United States	4.0

sources: *IMF*, Government Finance Statistics Yearbook, International Financial Statistics

authorization of extensions of the reciprocal Trade Agreements Act of 1934. This act was not renewed for the Kennedy Round, with Congress instead passing the *Trade Expansion Act of 1962*. This measure gave the president increased negotiating authority and introduced a new feature into American policy: *Trade Adjustment Assistance* (TAA). Since 1934 a basic idea behind American trade liberalization had been that import-competing industries should not suffer. *Escape clauses*, features of U.S. trade agreements since 1947, allowed trade concessions to be terminated should domestic industry suffer from foreign competition as a consequence of those concessions. (Other countries also employ escape clauses, or *safeguard provisions;* they are consistent with the GATT if they are accompanied by equivalent new concessions when invoked.) TAA, which provides for unemployment compensation and retraining assistance for workers and firms injured by import competition, reflects an entirely different philosophy. Instead of resisting the reallocation of resources implied by a movement toward comparative advantage, that reallocation should be accepted and rendered as harmless as possible. From an economic point of view, factors that are specific in the short run, as discussed in section 4, should be compensated for their losses and also rendered less specific. From a political point of view, opposition to trade liberalization should be bought off.

OUTSTANDING TRADE ISSUES

The GATT negotiations have reduced the industrial countries' tariffs on manufactures to relative insignificance by historical standards. Three other issues now seem more pressing.

1. *Trade in agricultural goods.* The central focus here is on the highly protectionist Common Agricultural Policy (CAP) of the EEC, which we will examine in more detail in Chapter 12. This policy, a descendant of the decision in the late nineteenth century by continental countries to protect their agricultural sectors, is currently the most important economic function of the European Community. By contrast, the United States, with its strong comparative advantage in temperate-zone agricultural products, sees the CAP as a unilateral denial to America of a major export market. Thus the issue is a major sore spot in Atlantic relations and promises to remain one for some time to come.

2. *Nontariff barriers.* Tariffs have been the dominant form of protection historically, but in recent decades nontariff barriers have been of steadily increasing importance, and by the 1970s most observers regarded them as at least as significant overall as tariffs. This trend is, of course, due in part simply to the fact that the repeated reductions in tariffs have rendered the latter relatively less important, but two other influences are also at work. First, GATT strictures against the use of tariffs ensure that protectionist pressures find outlets in nontariff barriers. Second, the increased role

of government in the economies of the industrial countries has created new nontariff barriers, made existing ones more significant, and created new opportunities for the employment of such barriers. For example, a preference for domestic firms over foreign rivals in government purchases becomes more significant as the size of the government grows.

3. *The LDCs.* The GATT tariff reductions have centered on the manufactures exchanged among the industrial countries. Those cuts have also applied to LDC exports, because of the MFN clause, but the goods involved have not been of central importance to the LDCs. Increased attention has, accordingly, been given to LDC trade, especially since UNCTAD I in 1964 (discussed in Chapter 2). A new Part IV, for improving LDC trade, was added to the GATT in 1965, and during the seventies the industrial countries adopted systems of tariff preferences for LDC manufactures. But benefits are modest. The retarded state of LDC trade is due in good part to the LDCs themselves, who have adopted protectionist policies and have refrained from aggressive participation in the GATT rounds. Demands for a new international order lose something in credibility when they come from those who are not fully exploiting the existing order. But the DCs have indicated by their deeds that any substantial increase in LDC competition with DC manufacturing industries will meet protectionist resistance. The tariff preferences exclude some sensitive industries, such as textiles, that are in fact the most important for LDC development.

THE TOKYO ROUND

These three outstanding issues were addressed in the seventh and latest GATT negotiating session, the Tokyo Round, concluded in 1979. (When the session was first being organized, in the early seventies, it was known as the Nixon Round; when the former president's name was dropped, in the wake of the Watergate scandals and his resignation, the name of the location of the preliminary ministerial meeting was substituted. Actual negotiations took place in Geneva.) American negotiating authority was established by the *Trade Act of 1974,* which also, among other provisions, established the American system of tariff preferences for LDC manufactures.

The Tokyo Round Agreement will chop a further one-third, on average, off tariffs on manufactures. The negotiations were less successful in dealing with agriculture; although some substantial tariff cuts were agreed upon, the central issue of the CAP was not addressed. Also, the Tokyo Round was not notably more successful than earlier rounds in dealing with LDC trade; indeed, most LDCs angrily boycotted the 1979 signing ceremony. But a major success was achieved in dealing with nontariff barriers. Codes of conduct were agreed upon in various areas: government procurement; customs valuation procedures; technical regulations for safety, health, national security, the environment, and so forth; government sub-sidies; safeguards, or "escape clauses"; dumping. The codes specify, in varying degrees of detail, appropriate government policies and procedures, and each code provides for a GATT committee to help resolve international disputes in its respective area. The codes are not amendments to the GATT itself; they need not be subscribed to by all GATT members, and countries that have not signed the GATT may subscribe to the codes. As the codes are deliberately general, it is too soon to judge how successful they will be in dealing with nontariff barriers: everything depends on how they are imple-mented and what precedents are set.

THE "NEW PROTECTIONISM"

The progressive tariff reductions in the years since the Second World War have, paradoxically, been accompanied by a gradual resurgence of protectionism. Successive extensions of the reciprocal Trade Agreements Act during the fifties were obtained only at the price of concessions to protectionists. The executive branch of the government, to be sure, has retained a relatively liberal outlook on trade, and the Republican party, having captured the White House, is less protectionist than before the war. But Democratic legislators have become steadily less liberal, and the labor movement—important to Democratic politicians—has gradually abandoned its support of free trade. Labor supported extensions of the Trade Agree-ments Act and the Trade Expansion Act of 1962, but in the seventies most major unions had become protectionist. Organized labor supported the abortive Burke-Hartke bill, which would have reversed forty years of American trade policy and restored high protection. The Trade Act of 1974 was a liberal counterattack but was passed with many concessions. Further concessions were required to obtain the enabling legislation necessary for the United States to adhere to the codes negotiated during the Tokyo Round—this legislation, as stipulated in the Trade Act of 1974, was put before Congress on a take-it-or-leave-it basis, with no opportunity for amendment.

One can only speculate about the reasons for the weakening free trade position. Perhaps economic recession in the seventies, together with the decline and redistribution of real incomes implied by the historic rise in oil prices, has strengthened the determination of special-interest groups. A second factor would be the threat that transitional LDCs will capture the world markets for certain sensitive manufactures, such as textiles, shoes, and steel. The great postwar expansion of trade among the DCs, with those countries' economic structures becoming quite similar, has involved an ex-pansion of intra-industry trade rather than industrial specialization. The DCs have, accordingly, largely been spared the disruption involved in reallocating factors of production from one industry to another. A rapid expansion of trade with the transitional LDCs, with their distinctive economic structures, does not promise to be nearly as painless.

The actual protectionist measures adopted in the industrial countries have not, by and large, involved the simple application of new tariffs and quotas in violation of the GATT. Nor have they often utilized GATT-sanctioned measures, such as the escape clause, which would require compensating concessions. There has been, instead, a marked tendency for importing nations to bypass the GATT entirely by negotiating trade-limitation agreements with exporters directly. For example, exports of color television sets to the United States from Korea and Taiwan (and, from 1977 to 1980, Japan) are limited by "orderly marketing agreements" between the respective governments. Exporters enter into such agreements because of the threat that, otherwise, importers would impose even more stringent limitations. Occasional explicit quotas make the threat credible: thus in 1976 the United States imposed quotas on specialty steel imports from the EEC after concluding a bilateral agreement with Japan. Other "voluntary" agreements, quite numerous in the last twenty years, include a multilateral arrangement governing cotton, woolen, and synthetic textiles, a shoe quota, and the restraints on Japanese automobile exports discussed in Chapter 5.

Steady erosion has afflicted the principle, fundamental to both the U.S. trade agreements policy and to GATT, that tariff liberalization should involve reciprocal concessions extended to all nations via the MFN clause. Some of this erosion has been consistent with, or accommodated by, the GATT: customs unions and tariff preferences for LDC exports. Note that the latter violates reciprocity as well as the MFN clause. There have also been outright violations of the GATT, such as the 1965 agreement between the United States and Canada establishing free trade in automobiles and parts by the major manufacturers. Finally, outside the GATT entirely, the "voluntary" export quotas are both nonreciprocal and discriminatory.

After decades of trade liberalization, its future is cloudy. On the one hand, we have the many signs of growing protectionism, and on the other, the new initiative of the Tokyo Round (and the Reagan administration has suggested an eighth round). It remains to be seen which will dominate.

11. Tools of Contemporary Trade Policy

There are four major, explicit trade-policy tools, consistent with the GATT, which the United States may employ, or threaten to employ to obtain a "voluntary" export quota from another nation. Many similar tools are used by other industrial nations.

1. *The escape clause (safeguard provisions).* Since 1947, American trade agreements have included the provision that concessions could be

withdrawn if they produced unforeseen injury to a domestic industry. Other nations use similar clauses, and they are consistent with the GATT and the subject of one of the codes negotiated in the Tokyo Round. Countries injured by such a withdrawal may retaliate if they do not receive mutually acceptable compensating concessions. Under American law, an injured industry may petition for relief to the International Trade Commission (ITC–known as the Tariff Commission until the 1974 Trade Act). The ITC then defines the scope of the industry and determines whether the industry so defined has suffered, or will suffer, serious injury due to increased imports–as a result of the 1974 Trade Act, the increase in imports need not be traced to a tariff concession. If such injury is found, the ITC recommends specific action to the president. This can include adjustment assistance or import protection in the form of higher duties, quotas, or marketing agreements. The president may modify or reject the recommendations, but Congress can then overrule him. The escape clause machinery has been used many times, though it has not usually resulted directly in increased protection. From 1948 to 1953, fifty-one applications to the commission resulted in action in only three minor cases. Since then the law has been tightened and the commission has become more aggressive. In recent years the escape clause has become an important implicit influence leading to orderly marketing agreements–the president has an incentive to negotiate such agreements to placate Congress and the ITC, and foreign countries face implementation of the harsher ITC recommendations if they do not reach agreement with the president.

2. *Anti-dumping duties.* These may be imposed on foreign goods dumped in the American market (sold in America at a price below the price in the country of origin or below the cost of production, or below both). Such duties, to eliminate the price differential, have long been provided for in the laws of many nations and are the subject of one of the new codes negotiated in the Tokyo Round. Under American law, the Commerce Department investigates complaints to determine if goods are being dumped, and simultaneously the International Trade Commission investigates the extent of injury to domestic interests; if dumping is found and the injury is not immaterial, the Commerce Department assesses duties.

Until recently these procedures seldom resulted in actual duties, in other countries as well as the United States. Investigations were protracted, and the authorities often failed to rule that dumping was taking place, even in the face of substantial evidence; firms were accordingly reluctant to file and pursue complaints. But this has changed in recent years. The law has been tightened, and administration has been shifted to the Commerce Department from the Treasury, with the former expected to be more zealous than was the latter. As a result, use of the anti-dumping law has greatly increased, and the statute is likely to become a principal protectionist tool.

CASE STUDY: Polish Golf Carts

Poland has heavy foreign debts and needs to develop whatever export markets she can. In the early 1970s, the country began to successfully market Melex golf carts in the United States—so successfully that in 1974 the American industry charged dumping. The Treasury Department (which at that time administered the law) was thereby faced with a problem to discover whether the carts were actually being sold at less than a fair price. The Treasury could not compare the U.S. price with the Polish price because there was no Polish price: Poland has no golf courses and so no demand for golf carts; all Melexes were sold in the United States. Nor could the U.S. price be compared with the cost of production: Poland is a socialist economy, and the prices of inputs are not market determined. The Treasury was reduced to using as a reference of fair value the costs incurred by a small Canadian manufacturer of golf carts. This cost was about 60 percent above the American Melex price. In 1973 the Treasury ruled that the carts were being dumped, the ITC found injury, and the Treasury imposed stiff anti-dumping duties. Poland protested that its actual costs were lower than those of the small Canadian firm. In 1977 the Treasury agreed that, if Poland would open its books to American customs inspectors so that they could see what actually went into a cart, the cost of these inputs would then be calculated at Spanish prices—Spain was judged to be a market economy with a level of economic development similar to Poland's. Poland agreed to open its books, and the bizarre calculation was performed, yielding a value not much different from the actual price.

   This example is important not merely as an illustration of the difficulties of administering such a law, but also as a precedent applying to developing East-West trade. A later attempt, to use Spanish prices to determine whether Poland was dumping steel in the United States, foundered when the Spanish industry refused to supply data because it feared that it, too, would face anti-dumping action.

But why do countries have anti-dumping laws at all, since the opportunity to buy goods at a low price would seem to be a good thing? No doubt our earlier discussion, of why commercial policies in general are widely used despite the gains from free trade, applies here. But there are also several arguments for singling dumping out for special treatment. Dumping could indicate that a foreign firm has a monopoly over both foreign and domestic markets, because such a monopoly would charge each market the price it would bear. If demand is more elastic in the domestic (importer's) market, the monopolist will charge a lower price here than in the foreign market, as long as the monopolist is able to separate the two markets. There are sound economic reasons for measures to deal with monopoly and to prevent such price discrimination. But simply forcing the monopolist to charge us a *higher* price, as the anti-dumping law attempts to do, makes no sense from a national point of view.

A second argument is that a foreign oligopolist might temporarily dump its products in the domestic market to crush domestic competition or force it to adhere to an international cartel. Prices would be increased once the objective was attained. Anti-dumping laws are thus defended as a way of preventing such tactics. This possibility often figures in public discussions, and in the early part of this century many countries did adopt anti-dumping laws because of fear about the behavior of large American and German firms. But contemporary incidents of this sort are very rare; such an aggressive foreign oligopolist would, after all, be employing a very expensive strategy to attain an advantage it could not realistically hope to keep for long.

A third possibility is that periodic dumping could be the response of foreign firms to recessions, new competition, or other events. These firms might prefer to sell for a time at a price below long-run average cost, rather than closing down completely or even making large lay-offs. The American steel industry accused European firms of doing this in 1979–80. If dumping is used in this way to smooth out production fluctuations, foreign workers enjoy more secure job prospects, and foreign firms presumably need pay a lower wage than they would if they offered less secure jobs. Anti-dumping laws would thus prevent foreign firms from using the domestic market as a buffer in this way.

CASE STUDY: The Steel Reference-Price System

In recent decades many countries have acquired modern steel industries, so that a recession usually produces much surplus steel capacity and strikes especially hard at the older, less efficient industries in the United States and Europe. In 1977 a weak world steel market intensified protectionist pressure in the suffering American industry; U.S. firms filed twenty-three anti-dumping petitions, notably against imports from Europe (where a similar situation prevailed). The administration response was the establishment of the reference-price system in early 1978. Reference prices for steel products were calculated on the basis of production costs in Japan—an efficient producer—and imports sold for less than these prices would automatically trigger an accelerated anti-dumping investigation. The hope was that foreign firms would avoid such investigations by not selling below the reference prices, so that the steel industry would receive protection without actual tariffs or quotas, and protectionist pressures would abate. If foreign steel continued to be imported at low prices, domestic firms would at least be spared the considerable trouble and expense of initiating suits. The steel industry responded to the new system by withdrawing its pending anti-dumping suits.

The system has not been popular. Importers claimed that it was merely another form of protection, raising prices and reducing imports, while the steel industry complained that the reference prices were too low, and that the system was not rigorously enforced—a claim echoed in a 1980 General Accounting Office study. When the government declined in March 1980 to raise the reference prices, U.S. Steel Corporation filed an anti-dumping suit against European steel firms. The administration responded by suspending the reference-price system. It was restored in October 1980 (the midst of a presidential election campaign) at 12 percent higher prices as part of a package of aid for the steel industry. At the same time, U.S. Steel agreed to withdraw its suits. But the industry later filed more.

3. *Countervailing duties.* These may be imposed on imports that have received subsidies from the government of the exporting country, with the duties set so as to cancel out the subsidy. Many countries have such laws, which are the subject of one of the new GATT codes. The American law, like the anti-dumping statute, is administered by the Commerce Department. Government subsidies are ubiquitous these days, so severe application of such laws could conceivably strangle trade. But, again as with anti-dumping laws, countervailing duties were seldom imposed until a few years ago. But usage has greatly increased recently; for example, about 40 percent of U.S. imports from India are subject to countervailing duties.

CASE STUDY: Michelin Tires

In 1973 a countervailing duty of 6.6 percent was imposed by the Treasury Department, which at that time administered the law, on imports of tires produced by France's Michelin Company at a plant in Nova Scotia. Michelin was not paid an export subsidy, but it had been induced to locate its plant in Nova Scotia by the

offer of favorable tax treatment—a frequent practice. The Treasury decided that countervailing duties were, nevertheless, justified because most of the output of the plant was intended for
the American market. This decision set an important precedent
because it was the first time duties had been applied in such a
case, and the decision was taken to court. Michelin has since
continued its attempts to penetrate the U.S. market by opening
plants within the country itself.

4. *Trade Adjustment Assistance.* As we have seen, this was intended as
a liberalizing measure to buy off opposition to free trade and to facilitate
the transfer of resources out of sectors in which the nation has a comparative disadvantage. But the original eligibility requirements of the law were
so stiff that little actual assistance was given until procedures were amended
by the Trade Act of 1974. By then labor had lost faith and turned protectionist. Assistance is now easier to obtain. Indeed in the year ending with
the third quarter of 1981, about $2.7 billion of assistance was given, enough
to make the program unexpectedly expensive and to postpone plans to
extend it. The bulk of this money went to the automobile industry, with
over 300,000 workers eligible for aid. The Reagan administration has significantly cut back the program. Despite the original intention, TAA does
have a protectionist effect. Most of the aid goes, not for retraining and
relocation, but for unemployment compensation and loans to firms. Since
this reduces the pressure to find employment elsewhere, the net effect is to
retard adjustment rather than encourage it. Also, because the program basically provides a type of insurance for the import-competing sector and not
for the rest of the economy, its long-term effect is to subsidize that sector,
thereby reducing trade.

In addition to these four major protectionist tools, various minor provisions are available. The *national security clause,* for example, provides for
increases in protection for threatened industries important to national security; tariffs and quotas may be imposed on *agricultural imports* if necessary to preserve the effectiveness of a domestic agricultural program; the
president may exclude from the country goods that have been marketed
with *unfair import practices,* such as an attempt to monopolize trade in the
United States.

PROBLEM

6.18 Find out about recent U.S. trade policy actions by reading the latest
Annual Report of the Trade Agreements Program and recent reports of the International Trade Commission. Interpret these actions in the light of the discussion in
section 7.

12. Summary

1. Tariffs can be imposed to influence a country's relations with the rest of the world and to influence the domestic economy. International motives include: the optimum tariff argument, improving the trade balance, and limiting trade for noneconomic reasons.

2. Domestic motives include: raising government revenue, countering domestic distortions, the infant industry argument, noneconomic objectives, changing the domestic distribution of income, and increasing employment. The tariff is a second-best tool for these purposes, because it .introduces distortions of its own, which more direct methods would not do.

3. The effective rate of protection measures the excess of actual value added per unit in an industry above what it would be if calculated at international prices. Effective rates differ from nominal rates when intermediate goods and final goods are subject to different tariffs, and the effective rates measure the direct impacts of a tariff structure on factors employed in the various sectors.

4. Tariff structures in industrial countries are often seen as reflections of pressure-group politics within those countries. But evidence linking protection to industry characteristics is ambiguous.

5. Postwar tariff reductions under GATT have reduced to historically low levels tariffs on trade in manufactured goods among the DCs. Nontariff barriers, agricultural trade, and the trade of the LDCs remain serious problems. The Tokyo Round established codes regarding nontariff barriers, but their effectiveness is not yet determined.

6. Major contemporary tools of trade policy include: escape clauses, anti-dumping duties, countervailing duties, and trade adjustment assistance. These tools are employed directly, and the threat to use them often results in orderly marketing arrangements (that is, quotas) between countries.

13. *Exploring Further:* The Specific-Factors Model

The Heckscher-Ohlin-Samuelson (HOS) model treats factors of production as completely mobile between *industries* though not mobile at all between *countries*. The latter feature will be relaxed in Chapter 7. Section 4 of this chapter noted that the validity of the former depends upon the time horizon: factors are often very sector-specific in the short run but a good deal more mobile in the long run. But also the degree of mobility varies across factors: except for the extreme short run or extreme long run, some factors will be quite mobile between sectors, and others will not. This is emphasized in the *specific-factors model:* an analytical structure identical to the HOS model studied in Chapter 3, except that one of the factors—call it capital—is immobile between industries.

Thus suppose two goods—wine and machines—are each produced by labor and capital. The supply of labor is fixed to the country as a whole and perfectly mobile between the wine and machine industries, but each sector employs a fixed amount of specific capital. Since wine capital and machine capital cannot substitute for each other, no mechanism ensures that they are paid equal rents. But the wage will be the same in both industries.

The specific-factors model formalizes much literature antedating the development of the HOS model. Interest in the former has revived in recent years, in part because of the importance of specific factors in determining the effects of tariff changes.

EQUILIBRIUM

Figure 6.10 shows the equilibrium of a single country represented by a specific-factors model. The distance AB measures the total labor supply of the country, with labor in the wine sector measured off to the right from A and labor in the machine sector measured off to the left from B. Thus point C represents an allocation of AC labor to wine production and of CB labor to machine production. Since the amounts of capital in the two sectors cannot be altered, they are not shown in the figure. The WW curve measures, for each level of labor employment in the wine industry, the value of the marginal product of that labor: $P_W MPL_W$. (P_W denotes the price of wine and MPL_W the marginal product of labor in the wine industry, that is, the increase in wine production that would result from the employment of one more laborer.) As more and more labor works with the fixed stock of wine capital, MPL_W falls; thus the WW line slopes down. The MM curve analogously shows the value of the marginal product of labor in the machine industry: $P_M MPL_M$.

Note that the WW curve—and by analogy MM—depends upon three things. First, of course, is the technology for producing wine from capital and labor. If we follow the HOS model this will be the same across countries. The second feature is the price of wine: increases or decreases in P_W shift WW up or down in proportion. Of course P_W will be the same in

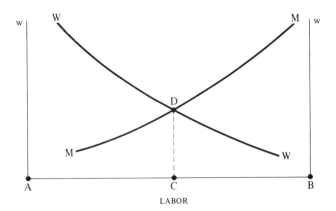

Figure 6.10. EQUILIBRIUM IN THE SPECIFIC-FACTORS MODEL

countries trading freely with each other. The third feature is the stock of wine-specific capital. An additional laborer in the wine industry will raise production more if there is more capital to work with. Thus increases or decreases in the amount of wine-specific capital shift WW up or down. There is no reason to expect different countries to have equal amounts of each specific factor, so this feature will cause WW and MM to differ from country to country.

The value of the marginal product of labor in the wine industry, $P_W MPL_W$, is the amount by which any wine producer can increase his revenue by hiring an additional laborer. As long as that amount exceeds the cost of hiring that worker—the wage w—the firm will do so. Thus the wine industry will continue to hire more labor until $w = P_W MPL_W$. For similar reasons the machine industry will hire labor until $w = P_M MPL_M$. Since the two industries pay the same wage in equilibrium, it must be that $P_W MPL_W = P_M MPL_M$. That is, equilibrium is shown by the intersection point D in Figure 6.10, so that AC is the quantity of labor employed in the wine sector, and CB the amount in the machine sector. The wage rate equals DC.

FACTOR ENDOWMENTS

Now let us consider the effects of changes in the endowments of a country with an equilibrium like that just described. Suppose that the prices of wine and machines do not change. The effects depend upon whether it is the mobile factor or one of the specific factors whose supply alters. Figure 6.11(a) shows the result of an increase in the supply of labor, the mobile factor, in the amount BB' ($= DE = CF$). Point B and the MM curve shift to the right by this amount, so the new equilibrium is given by point D'. The wine industry has increased its employment of labor by CC', and the machine industry its employment by $C'F$. Since each industry has an unchanged quantity of capital, output of both wine and machinery has risen. The wage falls from CD to $C'D'$. (The additional labor must be split between the two sectors so as to keep $P_W MPL_W$ equal to $P_M MPL_M$, and each MPL falls because each worker has less capital to work with.) The rents of both types of capital rise, because each type is worked by a larger quantity of labor and therefore has a greater marginal physical product. Note how an increase in the supply of the mobile factor has consequences in this specific-factors model that are in sharp contrast to the effects, described by the Rybczynski theorem, of an increase in either factor—necessarily mobile—in the HOS model. Review Chapter 3 if necessary.

Panel (b) of Figure 6.11 shows the effects of an increase in the endowment of one of the specific factors, wine capital. Any given quantity of labor in the wine industry now has more capital to work with and thus a larger MPL_W: the effect of the endowment change is to shift WW upward.

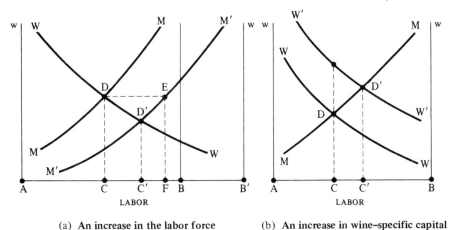

(a) **An increase in the labor force**   (b) **An increase in wine–specific capital**

Figure 6.11. ENDOWMENT CHANGES

Labor must move from the machine industry to the wine industry in order to restore equality between the values of its marginal product in the two sectors. In the figure, CC' labor moves from machine production to wine production. Since the wine industry also has more capital than before whereas the quantity of machine capital has not changed, wine production must rise and machine production fall. Thus changes in supplies of specific factors produce results more similar to those predicted by the Rybczynski theorem in the HOS model than do changes in the supply of the mobile factor. The wage rate rises from CD to $C'D'$, reflecting the fact that labor in each sector now has more capital to work with. The rentals of both types of capital must therefore fall, to keep costs in line with the unchanged commodity prices.

Suppose that two countries engage in free trade, and also suppose, as in the HOS model, that the countries consume wine and machines in identical proportions and share an identical technology. Differences in labor supplies are unlikely to be related in any clear way to the pattern of trade between these countries because, as we have seen, a change in the supply of the mobile factor causes both outputs to change in the same direction. But a change in the supply of a specific factor alters outputs of the two goods in opposite directions, so it is quite likely that each country will export the good using that country's relatively abundant specific factor. Compare this with the Heckscher-Ohlin theorem studied in Chapter 3.

TARIFFS AND PRICE CHANGES

Now that we have examined the structure of the specific-factors model, we are ready to consider the effects of price changes, such as might result from a change of commercial policy. A rise in P_W raises $P_W MPL_W$ in proportion and so shifts the WW curve up. Figure 6.12 shows the effects of an increase in P_W in the proportion ED/DC. Equilibrium moves from D to D'. Thus CC' labor shifts from machine production to wine production. The wage rises, but not by as much as P_W, since D' is lower than E: w rises relative to (the unchanged) P_M but falls relative to P_W. Thus the effect of the price rise on *real* wages is ambiguous and depends on spending patterns; workers who consume mainly machines will be better off and those who consume mainly wine will be worse off. (Technology also counts. A little experimentation will convince you that w might rise nearly as much as P_W or hardly at all, depending on the degrees of steepness of the WW and MM curves.) Contrast this result with the prediction of the Stolper-Samuelson theorem for the HOS model.

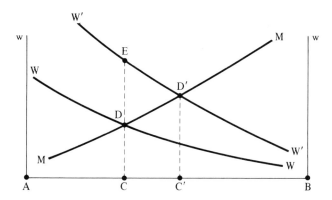

Figure 6.12. AN INCREASE IN THE PRICE OF WINE

The real rewards of the specific-factors, however, do change unambiguously. With more labor to work with, wine capital has a higher marginal product and accordingly receives a higher rental in terms of wine, and therefore in terms of machinery as well. Machine capital has less labor to work with, so its rent falls in terms of machines, and so in terms of wine also.

If a tariff causes a rise in the relative domestic price of imports in terms of exports, the real reward of the factor specific to the import competing sector will increase and the real reward of the factor specific to the export sector will fall. The mobile factor has no clear stake in either protection or free trade. Perhaps, being in the middle, labor will tend to fare about the same as the country as a whole, suffering from protection unless a significant improvement results in the terms of trade. But the direction of change in the welfare of any individual laborer will be sensitive to her pattern of spending.

PROBLEMS _____

6.19 The specific-factors model can be thought of as a picture of the medium run, between the short run and the long run discussed in section 4 of this chapter. Suppose the relative price of wine rises. Describe verbally the process of transition from short run to medium run and from medium run to long run.

6.20 Relate the discussion of skill groups and human capital in section 13 of Chapter 3 to the discussion in this section of the relation between trade patterns and the relative abundance of specific factors. Discuss the usefulness of explaining the pattern of trade in terms of the specific-factors model.

6.21 Show how the effects of an increase in the supply of labor can be described geometrically by a shift of point A and the WW curve in our figure to the left. Compare with Figure 6.11(a).

SUGGESTED READING

Baldwin, R. E. *The Multilateral Trade Negotiations.* Washington: American Enterprise Institute, 1979. The results of the Tokyo Round.

Baldwin, R. E. "The Political Economy of Postwar U.S. Trade Policy." *The Bulletin.* New York University Graduate School of Business Administration, 1976. Mentioned in the text.

Baldwin, R. E.; Mutti, J. H.; and Richardson, J. D. "Welfare Effects on the United States of a Significant Multilateral Tariff Reduction." *Journal of International Economics.* August 1980. An empirical estimate.

Bale, M. D. "Estimates of Trade Displacement Costs for U.S. Workers." *Journal of International Economics,* August 1976. Reports on a sample of such workers.

Ball, D. S. "United States Effective Tariffs and Labor's Share." *Journal of Political Economy,* April 1967. Cited in text.

Bauer, R. A.; Pool, I. D. S.; and Dexter, L. A. *American Business and Public Policy.* 2nd ed. Chicago: Aldine-Atherton, 1973. The political system and the tariff.

Breton, A. *The Economic Theory of Representative Government.* Chicago: Aldine, 1974. Cited in text.

Caves, R. E. "Economic Models of Political Choice: Canada's Tariff Structure." *Canadian Journal of Economics,* May 1976. An empirical investigation of what determines the tariff.

Caves, R. E. and Jones, R. W. *World Trade and Payments.* 3rd ed. Boston: Little, Brown, 1981. See pp. 242–45.

Cheh, J. H. "United States Concessions in the Kennedy Round and Short-Run Labor Adjustment Costs." *Journal of International Economics,* November 1974. Cited in text.

Constantopoulos, M. "Labour Protection in Western Europe." *European Economic Review,* December, 1974. Cited in text.

Corden, W. M. *The Theory of Protection.* Oxford: Oxford Univ. Press, 1971. Effective protection.

Corden, W. M. *Trade Policy and Economic Welfare.* Oxford: Oxford Univ. Press, 1974. The tariff as a policy tool.

Downs, A. *An Economic Theory of Democracy.* New York: Harper and Row, 1957. Cited in the text.

Ethier, W. J. "Dumping," *Journal of Political Economy,* June 1982. Dumping and employment.

Ethier, W. J. "The Theory of Effective Protection in General Equilibrium: Effective-Rate Analogues of Nominal Rates." *Canadian Journal of Economics,* May 1977.

Krueger, A. "Some Economic Costs of Exchange Control: The Turkish Case." *Journal of Political Economy,* October 1966. Cited in the text.

Mayer, W. "Short-Run and Long-Run Equilibrium for a Small Open Economy." *Journal of Political Economy,* September 1974.

Mussa, M. "Tariffs and the Distribution of Income: The Importance of Factor Specificity, Substitutability, and Intensity in the Short and Long Run." *Journal of Political Economy,* November 1974.

Olson, M. *The Logic of Collective Action: Public Goods and the Theory of Groups.* Cambridge: Harvard University Press, 1965. Cited in the text.

Pinchin, H. McA. *The Regional Impact of the Canadian Tariff.* Ottawa: Economic Council of Canada, 1979.

Pincus, J. "Pressure Groups and the Pattern of Tariffs." *Journal of Political Economy,* July 1975. Cited in the text.

Riedel, J. "Tariff Concessions in the Kennedy Round and the Structure of Protection in West Germany: An Econometric Assessment." *Journal of International Economics,* May 1977. Cited in the text.

Schattschneider, E. E. *Politics, Pressures and the Tariff.* Englewood Cliffs: Prentice-Hall, 1935. The classic account of the passage of the Smoot-Hawley tariff.

Stanwood, E. *American Tariff Controversies in the 19th Century.* Boston: Houghton Mifflin, 1903. One of the two basic treatments of U.S. tariff history.

Taussig, F. W. *The Tariff History of the United States.* New York: Augustus M. Kelley, 1967. The other.

Viner, J. *Dumping: A Problem in International Trade.* Chicago: Univ. of Chicago Press, 1923.

Yeats, A. J. *Trade Barriers Facing Developing Countries.* New York: St. Martin's, 1979.

Young, J. H. *Canadian Commercial Policy.* Ottawa: Royal Commission on Canada's Economic Prospects, 1957.

Chapter 7

International Factor Movements

"If the rivalry of first-class powers for the control of foreign markets, whether for the sale of goods or the investment of capital, has proven itself a menace to the peace of the world (and that such is the case, no one will care to deny), the explanation must be sought in the arrested development of political relations rather than in the underdevelopment of industrial conditions. The integration of political control has not kept pace territorially with the expansion of commercial interests."

—HENRY C. ADAMS (1920)

WE HAVE so far concerned ourselves with the international exchange of commodities. International movements of productive factors have been ignored. Indeed, the classical theory and its modern descendants see international factor immobility as the basic cause of international trade. The Keynesian theory, to be sure, does allow international capital movements (borrowing and lending), but these are treated as only passive responses to trade flows.

But international factor movements are prominent in modern economic life. Hundreds of billions of dollars are invested in foreign nations, and our world has been shaped by the great migrations of history. This chapter investigates such factor movements and relates them to international trade.

1. The Basic Theory of International Factor Movements

We can obtain a feel for the role of factor mobility by returning to the simple Ricardian model used to elucidate the first principles of international trade. Table 7.1 reproduces Table 1.1.

Table 7.1.   A SIMPLE RICARDIAN MODEL: LABOR REQUIRED IN
EACH COUNTRY TO PRODUCE ONE UNIT OF EACH GOOD

	Machines	*Wine*
France	6	2
Germany	1	1

Recall that if both countries initially produce both goods, world production will become more efficient if France shifts labor from machine production to wine, if Germany does the reverse, and if France trades wine to Germany for machines. Table 7.2(a) shows that each machine produced in Germany rather than France allows the world to have two additional casks of wine. Table 7.2(b) shows what would, instead, be achieved if labor were to become internationally mobile. If France again produces one less machine, the six workers that then become available now migrate to Germany instead of to the French wine industry. In Germany the six workers can produce the needed machine plus five casks of wine. World production becomes more efficient if factors move from countries where their productivity is low to countries where it is high. Note that factor mobility raises world production more than does trade and specialization: trade is basically a (second-best) substitute for factor mobility.

Table 7.2.   CHANGES IN PRODUCTION

(a) If France Produces One
    Less Machine, Germany
    One More, and the
    Countries Trade.

(b) If France Produces One
    Less Machine, and the
    Labor Moves to Germany.

	Machines	*Wine*		*Machines*	*Wine*
France	−1	+3	France	−1	0
Germany	+1	−1	Germany	+1	+5
World	0	+2	World	0	+5

Beneficial trade is a consequence of *comparative* cost differences—in this case, the fact that 6/2 exceeds 1/1. But beneficial factor movements result from *absolute* productivity differences—6 exceeds 1, and 2 exceeds 1. In this simple example, all production should take place in Germany, where labor is absolutely more productive in both commodities.

FACTOR MOBILITY AND THE FACTOR-ENDOWMENTS THEORY OF TRADE

To proceed further we must leave the simple Ricardian world. The Heckscher-Ohlin-Samuelson model of Chapter 3 is a logical next step since it views trade as due to differences in relative factor endowments.

Figure 7.1—like Figure 3.1—shows the relation between relative commodity costs and relative factor rewards. This relation is purely technological and so common to all countries sharing the technology. In the figure,
machines are relatively labor intensive. Suppose that Germany is relatively
labor abundant, and that France and Germany have similar tastes, so that
in autarky Germany has a lower wage-rental ratio. German relative autarkic prices are *OG* in the figure, and the French are *OF.* Thus German
relative autarkic commodity prices equal *OB,* and the French equal *OA.*

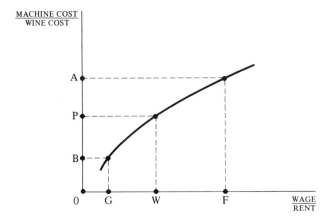

Figure 7.1. RELATIVE FACTOR PRICES AND RELATIVE COMMODITY
COSTS

Now suppose that France and Germany freely trade wine and machines, but that capital and labor remain immobile internationally. Then a
common world price will be established between *A* and *B,* say equal to *OP.*
If both countries continue to produce both goods, they will have equal
factor prices, as indicated by *W.*

But suppose, alternatively, that capital and labor can freely move
between the two countries while wine and machines are not traded. Since
there is now a single world labor market, the wage in France equals that in
Germany, since no one would willingly work for a wage below that available elsewhere. Similarly, capital's rent is the same in both countries. Suppose the common relative factor price is *OW.* Then relative commodity
prices equal *OP* in both countries—even though goods are not traded.

Once again, factor movements and commodity trade are substitutes. If
factor endowments are close enough so that trade leads to factor price
equalization, the two types of international economic intercourse are perfect
substitutes. Otherwise, trade is again a second-best substitute for factor
mobility; if trade incompletely equalizes factor prices, the introduction of

factor mobility would lead each factor to migrate from the country where its (absolute) marginal productivity was lower to where it was higher, to the benefit of world productive efficiency.

The efficiency argument is depicted another way in Figure 7.2. If factors are initially immobile, each country has a given production possibility frontier. Sliding one country's frontier along that of the other traces out the world production possibility frontier, illustrated by TT' in Figure 7.2. This shows the possible combinations of wine and machines available to the entire world if the two countries efficiently specialize and trade, but factors do not move internationally. Between A and B France and Germany both produce both goods, so that factor prices are the same in the two countries. Suppose, again, that wine is capital intensive. Between T and A the capital abundant country, say France, specializes to wine; between B and T', Germany specializes to machines. Thus France has higher wages and lower rents than Germany along TA and BT'. (The more nearly identical France and Germany are, the larger is the segment AB. If both countries have the same endowment of capital per worker, A coincides with T and B with T'. If, on the other hand, France has sufficiently more capital per worker than Germany, the segment AB shrinks to nothing and is replaced by a kink where both countries specialize and factor prices are not equalized.)

In reality, some factors are relatively mobile internationally while others are not. We can represent this by allowing one factor, say capital, to move freely between France and Germany while supposing that labor remains immobile. The segment AB will not be affected by allowing capital to move between countries, because factor prices are already equal there. The two factors are equally productive in both countries. But along TA and BT' it is desirable to shift capital from capital-abundant France, where the

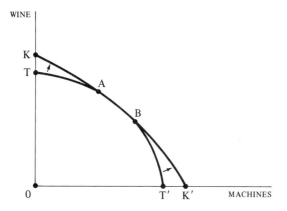

Figure 7.2. WORLD PRODUCTION POSSIBILITY FRONTIERS

factor's marginal productivity is low, to Germany. This will, in fact, happen because capital receives a lower rent in France than in Germany along *TA* and *BT'*. Thus these two portions of the world production possibility frontier shift outward when capital becomes mobile and, consequently, more productive. The new frontier is *KK'*. This shows the menu of possible combinations of wine and machines available to the world if the two countries efficiently specialize and trade goods and capital.

Capital's rent is equalized along the entire frontier *KK'* because there is now a single world capital market. There are two disjoint national labor markets, but in fact the wage must be the same in both countries. If the wages were not equal, the country with the higher wage could not compete in either commodity market, because producers in that country would have to pay just as much for capital and more for labor than would producers in the other country, and technology is the same in both countries. Thus both factor prices are equal everywhere along *KK'*, and the international immobility of labor is of no consequence.

FACTOR MOVEMENTS AND INCOME DISTRIBUTION

Since factor mobility and commodity trade tend to substitute for each other, it should come as no surprise that the two have similar effects on the internal distribution of income. Suppose that France is freely trading with the rest of the world, that both factors are initially immobile internationally, and that trade has not completely equalized factor prices. Now suppose that one factor, say capital, becomes mobile. If France is initially capital abundant, and so has a lower rent than the rest of the world, capital will now flow out of France until the French rental rises to equal that abroad. Thus the income of French capitalists rises. Because capital has left France, labor has become relatively more abundant in that country, and the French wage accordingly falls. Thus capital mobility, like commodity trade, redistributes income from a country's relatively scarce factor to the relatively abundant one.

Factor mobility must make a country as a whole better off because the ability to exchange factors, like that to trade goods, widens opportunities. But a country with monopoly power in world factor markets can potentially make itself even better off, at the expense of the rest of the world, by exercising that power and limiting factor mobility.

THE COMPLEMENTARITY OF FACTOR MOVEMENTS AND INTRA-INDUSTRY TRADE

To the extent that countries trade to economize on scarce factors, trade should substitute for factor mobility. But, as we found in Chapters 1 and 3, countries also trade in order to enlarge the division of labor and to increase product diversity. Suppose, for example, that France and Germany have basically similar endowments, so that both countries produce both goods and, even with no factor mobility, there is only a limited need to trade wine for machines. It could be to the advantage of both countries to have the French wine industry produce, say, red and sparkling wines while Germany concentrates on white wines and sweet wines. If there are *economies of scale,* that is, if a country becomes better at producing a certain type of wine the more it concentrates on it, then both countries could gain by specializing in this way and trading the various types of wine. Otherwise, each country would either have to produce all types of wine itself, and lose the benefit of economies of scale, or else produce and consume only one or two wine types and lose the benefits of product diversity. Also, the world machine industry could be made more productive if, instead of having each country produce entire machines from scratch, they enlarge the division of labor by having each country specialize to different parts of the machine and then trade those parts.

This *intra-industry trade* (the exchange of machine parts, or of white wine for red wine, and so forth) is related to factor mobility in a quite different way than is *inter-industry trade* (the exchange of wine for machines). Suppose that endowments in the two countries differ greatly and that France specializes to wine and Germany to machines. Then intra-industry trade cannot take place; all trade is inter-industry. Now suppose factors become internationally mobile and inter-industry trade declines as factor movements substitute for it. Both countries will eventually begin to produce both goods, and then intra-industry trade will become possible. Thus, while factor mobility is a substitute for inter-industry trade, it is *complementary* to intra-industry trade.

PROBLEMS

7.1 In the simple Ricardian example of Table 7.1 and Table 7.2, is it meaningful to talk of the French and German production possibility frontiers once labor becomes internationally mobile? What about the world frontier? Draw such a curve, if you can, and compare it with Figure 1.2(a). (Assume, as in Chapter 1, that, initially, France has 600 workers and Germany 500.)

7.2 Our discussion of the simple Ricardian model tacitly assumed that French and German laborers were identical and that the productivity differences in Table 7.1 reflected differences in climate. Suppose, instead, that Table 7.1 shows each country's labor productivity *at home,* but that three French laborers are always required to do the same work that could be done in the same country by one German worker (thus two German workers can produce a machine in France, and so forth). Derive the world production possibility frontier in this case. Describe who produces what, where, at various points along this curve.

7.3 In Problem **7.2**, suppose that everyone in the world always consumes equal amounts of wine and machines. Fully describe international equilibrium.

7.4* How is our discussion of international factor mobility and the Heckscher-Ohlin-Samuelson model affected if, before either factor is internationally mobile, the two countries are separated by a factor-intensity reversal?

7.5* Discuss how our treatment of factor mobility and the Heckscher-Ohlin-Samuelson model changes if technology is different in the two countries.

7.6* Figure 3.6 used the Rybczynski theorem to show the effect of economic growth on international trade. In similar fashion, depict the effects of international factor movements on international trade.

7.7* Suppose two countries, each resembling the specific-factors model described in section 13* of Chapter 6, engage in free trade. Discuss the results, for factor-price equalization and other possible properties, if the *intersectorally* mobile factor, labor, also becomes *internationally* mobile. What happens if, instead, one of the sector-specific factors becomes internationally mobile (but remains intersectorally immobile)? Discuss how international factor mobility can substitute for intersectoral factor mobility.

2. Labor Migration

Thus far we have looked at factor mobility in general terms. The remainder of this chapter focuses on problems peculiar to individual factors. We start with labor.

The massive eighteenth- and nineteenth-century migrations from Europe to the Western Hemisphere and Australia certainly constituted a significant international factor movement, to which the theory of section 1 applies. For example, when settlement in the new temperate zone regions and a fall in transport costs caused Western Europe to develop a comparative disadvantage in grain, the imports of the latter drove much of the rural continental population first into the cities and then to overseas emigration. The relation between trade and factor mobility was also illustrated by the late-nineteenth-century response of many continental countries: tariffs on agricultural imports to reduce rural depopulation.

But what unique considerations attach to labor? Most obviously, the role of productive factor is but one facet of human existence. Thus the decision to migrate hinges on an overall comparison of the quality of life in the prospective destination with that at home, and not merely on a comparison of wage rates. Labor might therefore not respond to wage differentials, and migration could be a result of political or social upheavals not related to wage rates. Perhaps all this is partial justification for the classical theory's assumption that labor is simply immobile internationally. Still, the purely economic motive, in the form of wage differentials, is certainly an important determinant of migration.

The consequences of migration also reflect labor's unique character. The distributional and efficiency implications discussed in section 1 are important, but so are the social and cultural implications. Opposition to immigration is often, in part, a response to the latter's effect on the real wage, but it usually also reflects fears about the disruptive effects of a large influx of foreigners. Let us now look in detail at contemporary issues involving labor mobility.

THE BRAIN DRAIN

Labor is not homogeneous: individual skills and occupations define separate labor markets, which are only imperfectly related. The degree of international mobility also varies from occupation to occupation, so that some skills determine what are relatively close to world markets while other skills are characterized by almost complete international immobility. The former category includes a number of professions requiring intensive education: scientists, engineers, medical doctors, and so forth. These fields, accordingly, feature significant migration from countries where the professions command relatively low rewards to those with higher remunerations: a process known as "the brain drain." The emigration of British professionals to all corners of the English-speaking world, LDC students in DC universities who never return home, English rock stars living anywhere but Britain, and Bjorn Borg relocated to southern Europe (evidently "brain" can be broadly defined), all furnish examples.

Such trained migrants generally assimilate easily into the countries to which they move, and social and cultural problems are minimal. Most countries have relatively lenient immigration laws for such individuals. Concern about the phenomenon relates mostly to the nations from which these people come. A large part of this concern is probably unfounded: when a trained professional leaves, the loss of a productive contributor to society is noted, but the implied removal of someone with a large claim on society is often overlooked. But still there are real problems.

One policy issue stems from the fact that the high mobility of such persons limits the ability of individual countries to conduct independent tax and social policies. Nations with national health systems must deal with doctors moving abroad in search of higher incomes or more congenial working conditions. The adoption of unusually progressive income tax schemes induces the emigration of individuals with unusually high incomes.

These problems stem from the high mobility of the persons involved. Other problems reflect a second characteristic of the brain drain: the individuals are highly trained, so that their emigration is simultaneously a movement of labor and a movement of human capital. LDCs are especially concerned about this aspect of the phenomenon, for two reasons.

First, if the training or education was collectively financed (or paid for by an aid source), the country loses its investment when the human capital is deported via emigration. With capital in all forms scarce, this could be a serious loss for the LDC, even if the move transfers the capital to a location where its productivity rises, thereby contributing to global efficiency.

Second, the presence of professionals may confer external benefits (that is, benefits not reflected in salaries). The interaction of trained people is professionally valuable, their presence motivates positive social attitudes toward skills, learning, and research, and such people themselves find life more enjoyable when they can associate with their own kind in a society that honors their own values. The brain drain probably does not contribute much in the way of such externalities to the destination DCs, where professionals are abundant to begin with, but their departure can inflict a serious loss of externalities on LDCs with precious little human capital. Also, by causing a net loss of externalities to the world as a whole, the brain drain could conceivably be globally inefficient even when it involves the movement of professionals to countries where their direct productivity is enhanced.

GUEST WORKERS

In many parts of the world, the *temporary* migration of largely un-skilled workers is an important phenomenon. Prominent examples include the employment of migrant Latin American labor in United States agriculture and light industry, large numbers of south European and North African workers in the labor-intensive industries of northern Europe, and the extensive reliance of oil-rich Middle Eastern countries on labor from elsewhere in the Middle East and from southern Asia. At times migrants have constituted over one-quarter of the Swiss labor force, for example.

These migrations are subject to diverse legal arrangements. The European Economic Community provides for *unrestricted factor mobility* among members, so that Italians are free to take jobs in Germany. The accession of Greece to the EEC, and the possible accessions of Spain and Portugal, promise to significantly increase this unfettered mobility.

Migrant labor movements into northern Europe, aside from this intra-EEC mobility, are generally subject to *guest-worker* systems: the host country government issues temporary permits to foreign workers to enter the country and take jobs. By controlling the number of permits, the host country can adjust the flow of migrant workers in response to changing economic and social conditions. Such systems govern the extensive employment of Yugoslavs, Turks, and North Africans in France, Switzerland, and Germany (and of Italians in Switzerland, not a member of the EEC).

The United States has also sometimes used such a system on a limited scale for Mexican migrant farm workers, and the Reagan administration has an experimental guest-worker system under consideration. But, in general, American law has made no provision for the temporary entry of foreign unskilled labor. Partly as a result, the strong pull of high U.S. wages on abundant labor pools south of the border causes considerable *illegal immigration.* In recent years this has been of the same order of magnitude as legal immigration.

Migrant labor has two basic effects on host countries. The workers are unskilled and are willing to accept wages that are low by the host country's standards and jobs that native workers would not want at viable wage levels. Travelers to northern European cities such as London immediately notice how many chambermaids, transit conductors, and so forth are foreign. Labor-intensive industries that would not be able to compete on world markets if they had to pay native wages can survive by hiring cheaper migrant workers. Since these industries also employ some domestic factors, painful adjustments are avoided. Thus the Florida vegetable growers who complain about the competition of cheap Mexican tomatoes themselves hire migrant Mexican workers. This is, of course, another case of factor mobility substituting for international trade. Instead of exporting textiles to Europe, North Africa sends guest workers who keep the European textile industry viable. Since such workers typically send part of their pay to relatives back home, North Africa receives an income for the labor it "exports." If Europe increases the tariff on textiles, North African firms become less able to compete in Europe, but guest workers in the European textile industry benefit, and North African remittances from emigrants rise.

Guest workers also increase the ability of the host country to deal with macroeconomic disturbances. The country can keep average aggregate demand high and use the guest workers as a buffer against fluctuations. This is illustrated in Figure 7.3. Suppose that autonomous expenditure I fluctuates, with I_H illustrating a case of high demand and I_L one of low demand. ON shows the output that can be produced by the native labor force, OL is aggregate demand in the low case, and OH equilibrium aggregate demand in the high case. Without guest workers, as panel (a) shows, OH cannot be produced, leading to what elementary textbooks call an "inflationary gap" equal to AB. In the low demand case, the workers that would produce LN lose their jobs, and the country is in a recession.

With a guest worker system, the country can have the fluctuations take place around a high average level of aggregate demand. When equilibrium demand equals OH, the authorities issue permits to enough foreign workers to produce NH, and the inflationary gap never emerges. When demand falls, the guest workers that could produce LH are sent packing, and native workers suffer no unemployment. The home country essentially "exports" the business cycle to foreign workers. During the boom years of the sixties, northern Europe attracted record numbers of guest workers, many of whom were sent home during the recessions of the seventies.

Arrangements like these can potentially be of benefit to all concerned. Workers in the prosperous host country obtain the security of insulation from the effects of business fluctuations by "trading" them to foreign guest workers, who in return receive higher average wages than they could earn at home.

Migrant workers also cause problems for host countries. Although these workers typically take jobs that most native workers do not want,

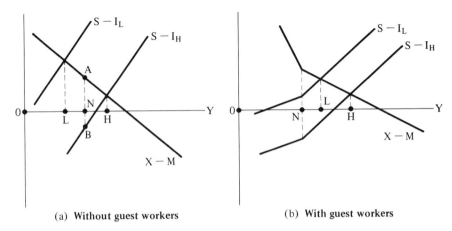

(a) **Without guest workers**   (b) **With guest workers**

Figure 7.3. A GUEST WORKER SYSTEM

there are inevitably some groups of host-country unskilled workers that do compete with the foreign laborers and who therefore suffer because of such migration. The United Farm Workers in California oppose the admission into the country of migrant workers from Mexico. Also the presence of such workers in significant numbers or for extended periods, or both conditions, can produce serious social tensions: continued reliance on foreign workers has, for this reason, been a prominent political issue in Switzerland.

The countries from which the migrants come likewise receive both benefits and costs. On the plus side, part of the population (the migrants themselves) receive employment offers better than they can apparently find at home, and the remittances of these workers benefit the rest of the source country. For some LDCs, these remittances are quite significant. For example, in 1979 Pakistan's remittances from its workers abroad were fully 77 percent as high as the country's earnings from commodity exports. Furthermore, the export of workers into the DC labor-intensive industries is an indirect way to penetrate markets from which the LDCs are significantly excluded by DC protection. Labor emigration can also be an important safety valve to release tensions in an LDC with a large supply of unemployed labor. It is partly for this reason that Mexico has urged the United States to admit more migrant workers.

On the negative side, source countries may find themselves faced with more severe business fluctuations. A recession in the DC host country will send unemployed guest workers returning home at the same time that domestic export industries find demand drying up in their DC markets. When these workers do return, they often bring with them alien tastes and habits acquired abroad. Sometimes they even refuse to accept at home the kind of jobs they held abroad. Also the migrant workers are sometimes relatively highly skilled by LDC standards, so that what looks like an influx of unskilled migrant workers to a host DC could appear to be a brain drain to the source LDC. Finally, concern about the treatment that guest workers receive can sometimes involve the host and source countries in conflict.

PROBLEMS

7.8 In Figure 7.3(b), the various schedules are drawn so that each changes its slope when Y equals N. Can you think of any reasons why this should be so?

7.9 In Chapter 6 we saw that a small tariff would improve the welfare of any country large enough to influence its terms of trade. How is this argument affected if the importable sector is relatively intensive in the use of unskilled (migrant) labor, and if the incomes of such migrants are not counted as part of national welfare?

3. International Capital Movements

Important as the international migration of labor is, it receives much less attention than cross-country investment. Accordingly, we next consider the international movement of capital.

WHAT ARE INTERNATIONAL CAPITAL MOVEMENTS?

By an international capital movement we do *not* mean the sale by one nation to another of capital equipment such as tools, machines, or building supplies. This is international *trade*. International capital movements refer to borrowing and lending between countries. An example would be a French sale of bonds in Germany. The French can use the proceeds of the bond sale to purchase equipment and thereby increase their stock of capital; by purchasing French bonds, German savers reduce the volume of savings that can be used for investment in Germany. Thus the French capital stock increases and the German falls, relative to what would have happened without the bond sale, producing the international reallocation of real capital studied in section 1. Alternatively, the French might simply spend the proceeds on high living, that is, borrow in order to enjoy today at the expense of tomorrow.

Such a transaction is variously described as a French *capital inflow*, an *international sale of assets* (the bonds), or *international borrowing*. The opposite side of the transaction (that is, the German point of view) is, likewise, described by the synonyms: capital outflow, purchase of foreign assets, foreign lending.

WALRAS'S LAW

If it cannot borrow, a nation must pay for its imports with exports: $pM \equiv X$. This was assumed in the first three chapters of this book. International capital mobility allows a country to pay for imports by selling either goods (exporting) or assets (borrowing). Furthermore, if the country owns foreign assets, such as bonds, it will be receiving interest payments from abroad, and this interest can also be used to pay for imports. Thus

$$pM \equiv X + C + E. \tag{7.1}$$

Here C denotes the net international sale of assets (total assets sold to foreigners minus total assets bought from foreigners), expressed in units of exportables, and E denotes net interest payments from abroad (interest received from foreigners minus interest paid to foreigners), also expressed in units of exportables. C and E are not directly related, because the former describes *present* asset exchanges, whereas the latter is determined by *past* borrowing and lending. But the two are related over time: if C rises now, we are selling more assets on which we must subsequently pay interest, so E will be reduced in the future.

Rearranging Walras's Law (7.1) allows us to display, in Figure 7.4, the classification of a nation's international transactions. The *trade balance,* or excess of the value of exports over imports, is added to net receipts of foreign investment income to obtain the *current balance. E* can be interpreted as the sale of capital services: if we receive interest from abroad because we have purchased a bond, that interest is, in effect, the fee that foreigners are paying to us for the use of the principal value of the bond. Thus the current balance can be regarded as the net sale of goods and services to the rest of the world. The capital balance is likewise the net sale of assets to the rest of the world. These two balances are really two ways of describing the same thing, because by Walras's Law one always equals minus the other.

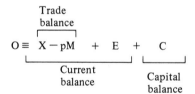

Figure 7.4. INTERNATIONAL TRANSACTIONS BALANCES

CAPITAL MOVEMENTS IN PERSPECTIVE

In the latter part of the nineteenth century, Great Britain was by far the world's most significant capital exporter, with British loans financing the construction of railroads the world over. Just before the First World War, about one-quarter of British national wealth consisted of foreign assets, and the interest from these assets accounted for about one-tenth of British national income. Because of this, the country was simultaneously able to import more than it exported and still acquire additional net foreign assets; in Figure 7.4, E was sufficiently large and positive so the $X - pM$ and C could both be significantly negative at the same time.

CASE STUDY: Piracy and the Wealth of Nations

Elizabeth I invested a portion of her share of the swag from Francis Drake's voyage of discovery in the *Golden Hind* in a company that formed the basis of England's foreign investment. Keynes was fond of pointing out that, if one assumed a reasonable rate of return on this investment and also assumed that about half of the investment income was reinvested abroad (as was actual British performance about the turn of this century), a compound interest calculation would show a time path of accumulation of Elizabeth's original investment roughly similar to the actual course of British foreign investment holdings.

The United States was a net debtor throughout the nineteenth century: the great transcontinental railroads were financed with foreign capital and built by migrant labor. By the end of the century, the country was on balance acquiring assets from the rest of the world, and about the time of the First World War became a net creditor. Europe sold off the bulk of her foreign assets to finance two world wars. The United States is now the most important creditor nation. Table 7.3 shows the American position. Panel (a) summarizes the international transactions in 1980, while panel (b) shows the international investment position as of the end of that year. The numbers in panel (a) are *flows,* the transactions taking place during the year, whereas panel (b) shows *stocks,* the accumulated total of all past transactions at a particular time (the end of 1980).

Table 7.3. AMERICAN CAPITAL MOVEMENTS AND POSITION
(*billions of dollars*)

(a) International Transactions, 1980		*(b) International Investment Position, end of 1980*	
Current Balance	.1	U.S. Ownership of	
(Of which: Net		Foreign Assets	592.5
Investment Income)	(32.5)	Foreign Ownership of	
Capital Balance	−.1	U.S. Assets	480.9
		Net U.S. International	
		Investment	111.6

SOURCE: Survey of Current Business

The net American investment position is large and, accordingly, yields a substantial yearly income. Nevertheless, this income was but 1.2 percent of the 1980 GNP of $2.6 trillion. For U.S. net foreign investment income to be proportionally as significant to our economy as in Britain before the First World War, our net investment position would have to be over eight times as large!

CASE STUDY: The OPEC Surplus

The oil price shocks greatly increased OPEC's oil revenues, and only part of this increase was offset by increased imports. As a result, these countries have accumulated a large stock of foreign assets, as shown in Table 7.4. From 1974 to 1981, OPEC ran a total current account surplus of $384 billion, which purchased external assets, increasing their total net holdings from $5 billion to $389 billion and making OPEC a major creditor in the modern world economy. These assets are not, of course, evenly spread among the OPEC nations, since some spent nearly all their oil revenues on goods and services as they were earned.

Table 7.4. CUMULATIVE OPEC INTERNATIONAL TRANSACTIONS, 1974–81 *(billions of dollars)*

Net Stock of External Assets, 1974	*$ 5*
OPEC International Transactions 1974–81	
Cumulative Net Investment Income	56
Cumulative Oil Sales	1323
Cumulative Net Export of Other Goods and Services	− 945
Cumulative Net Official Transfers	− 50
Cumulative Current Account	$384
Net Stock of External Assets, end of 1981	$389

SOURCE: *Morgan Guaranty Trust Co.,* World Financial Markets

Over 40 percent of these assets are owned by one country: Saudi Arabia. The interest income earned by these assets should soon become an important source of national income. Finally, note that the $384 billion figure represents the *foreign* assets acquired by oil sales and not the total assets. This is because the OPEC countries used part of their revenues to import equipment, construction services, and so forth, thereby acquiring *domestic* assets.

TYPES OF CAPITAL MOVEMENTS

Capital transactions differ in three ways, summarized in Table 7.5. The first basis is the identities of the individuals exchanging assets. *Official* capital movements are those undertaken by a country's official monetary authority, such as a central bank. Such movements are a result of the authority's management of the nation's money, and we shall study them when we turn to international monetary economics. In this chapter, we confine our attention to nonofficial movements. The latter are, in turn, classified by time to maturity. An international capital movement is an exchange of assets, and an asset is a promise to pay interest and at some date to mature—that is, to be redeemed for money. *Short-term* capital movements are those involving assets whose original time to maturity was less than a year, and other capital movements are *long term*. Short-term assets include demand deposits and cash (which are already matured), as well as treasury bills, commercial paper, and so forth. Long-term assets include equity and real estate (which never mature), and bonds, notes, mortgages, and so forth.

Table 7.5. TYPES OF INTERNATIONAL CAPITAL MOVEMENTS

Nonofficial
  Long term
    Portfolio
    Direct
  Short term
Official

Short-term and long-term transactions are separated to distinguish capital movements that finance international trade or involve speculative flyers from those that accommodate the international transfer of means of production, as treated in section 1. This chapter is predominantly concerned with the latter. Of course this attempt at separation is imperfect, because there is nothing to prevent someone from turning a treasury bill over and over as it matures, or from selling a share of common stock the day after it is purchased, or from buying a twenty-year bond in the secondary market one week before its date of maturity.

Long-term capital movements are themselves further classified according to whether the purchaser of the asset has operating control over the issuer of the asset. If so, the movements are termed *direct,* and if not, they are *portfolio* investments. If you buy shares of common stock in a corporation, you become part owner and can vote at annual meetings. Buy enough shares and you can acquire control. But if you instead purchase bonds issued by that corporation, you have no share of ownership and no right to help make decisions, no matter how many bonds you own. This is essentially the distinction between direct and portfolio investment. Of course, the ownership of a single share of common stock gives no real control. Thus, to be classified as a direct investment, a single individual or entity must own a minimum share of the foreign firm. Sometimes this minimum is 25 percent; for U.S. statistics it is, in practice, 10 percent. Direct investment generally consists of national corporations setting up foreign subsidiaries or buying substantial shares in foreign firms.

British foreign investments before the First World War were largely portfolio, but American investments are significantly direct. Table 7.6 gives a detailed breakdown of the foreign investment position summarized in Table 7.3(b).

Table 7.6.   THE U.S. FOREIGN INVESTMENT POSITION, END OF 1980

	U.S. Foreign Assets	Foreign U.S. Assets	Net U.S. Position
Private Long Term	275.6	139.5	136.1
Direct	213.5	65.5	148.0
Portfolio	62.1	74.0	−11.9
Other	316.9	391.4	−74.5
Total	592.5	480.9	111.6

SOURCE: *Survey of Current Business*

The theory presented in section 1 describes in general terms the real effects of international capital movements. Succeeding sections will address two further issues especially characteristic of capital. In section 4 we investigate the *immediate* effects on international equilibrium of an international sale of assets, before the real change in factor endowments, discussed in section 1, comes about. Subsequently, we examine direct investment in detail, so as to find out whether it matters in what form the capital movement takes place.

PROBLEMS _____

7.10 For each of the following transactions, tell, from the point of view of each country, whether the transaction contributes to the current balance or the capital balance and, if the latter is the case, what type of capital movement it is.

   a New Yorkers use checks drawn on a New York bank to buy bonds from a Canadian corporation.

b The Soviet Union sends oil to Germany in exchange for oil-drilling equipment.

c The Soviet Union, in exchange for oil-drilling equipment, promises to send Japan 100 million barrels of oil from the new well in five years.

d An American firm issues six-month commercial paper in London to finance the purchase of a British department store.

e You use a check drawn on a Philadelphia bank to buy a vacation home on the Mediterranean.

7.11 In section 2 we saw that remittances from natives working abroad are important sources of income for some countries. How do you think that such payments fit into the scheme of Figure 7.4?

4. The Transfer Problem

This section examines the immediate effects on international equilibrium of an international sale of assets. Suppose that domestic residents pay the amount T, expressed in home exportables, to foreigners in exchange for foreign bonds. Then the home economy has T less to spend and the foreign economy has T more. Such a simultaneous fall in one country's spending and rise in that of another is called an international *transfer*. Such transfers need not result solely from the purchases of foreign assets. The transfer might be foreign aid or reparations; in this case, the home government taxes its citizens the amount T and remits that sum to the foreign government, which then reduces its taxes accordingly.

The *transfer problem* concerns only the direct effects of this. Ignored are any changes in real productive resources thereby made possible—these were examined in section 1. Also ignored are the reverse transfers—interest payments and repayments of principal—that will eventually take place if the initial transfer is due to a loan.

There are two aspects to the transfer problem. The first is the question of whether the *financial* transfer described above will easily produce a corresponding *real* transfer, that is, an excess of domestic exports over imports. Before the transfer,

$$pM - X \equiv C + E, \tag{7.2}$$

where C denotes the net sale of assets to foreigners (international borrowing), and E the net income from outstanding foreign investments. Suppose that initially there is no international borrowing and lending, so that C and E are zero, and $pM = X$. Now, the home country makes the transfer payment T. Total payments due foreigners are now T and pM, and these payments can be settled either by selling goods (X) or other assets (C') to foreigners. Thus,

$$T + pM \equiv X + C'. \tag{7.3}$$

(Note that (7.3) is consistent with (7.2) because $E = 0$ and $C = C' - T$.) If, in fact, $C' = 0$, so that $T = X - pM$, we say that the transfer has been *effected:* the financial transfer has generated an equal trade surplus, thereby making the transfer in real terms. If $C' > 0$, so that $T > X - pM$, the transfer has been *undereffected:* the trade surplus is less than the financial transfer, part of which is settled by a sale of assets, or foreign borrowing, C'. Thus, in real terms, only part of the transfer has been made, with part postponed into the future, when the borrowing must be repaid. If, on the other hand, $C' < 0$, or $T < X - pM$, we say that the transfer has been *overeffected.*

The second aspect of the transfer problem involves the effect of the transfer upon international trade. Will the terms of trade of the paying country deteriorate, improve, or be unchanged? If they deteriorate, we say that the paying country has suffered a *secondary burden:* in addition to the transfer itself (the "primary" burden), the country must also pay more than before for imports. If, on the other hand, the terms of trade of the paying country improve, it has received a secondary benefit, with part of the burden of the transfer offset by cheaper imports.

What determines if a transfer will be undereffected or overeffected, or if the paying country will suffer a secondary burden? To see this, consider what happens, at the *initial terms of trade,* when the home country makes a transfer payment T. Home incomes fall in the amount T when this is remitted abroad. Then domestic imports must *fall* in the amount mT, where m denotes the home marginal propensity to import. When the foreign country receives the payment T, their income increases by this amount, and they accordingly *increase* their imports in the amount m^*T, where m^* denotes the foreign marginal propensity to import. Foreign imports are domestic exports, so, at the initial terms of trade, the transfer T increases the domestic balance of trade $X - pM$ by $m^*T + mT$ (because X increases by m^*T and pM falls by mT). The transfer is, accordingly, undereffected if $T > m^*T + mT$ (that is, if $1 > m + m^*$) and overeffected if $T < m^*T + mT$ (that is, if $1 < m + m^*$).

Consider next the effect of the transfer on the market for imports. Before the transfer payment, this market is in equilibrium: world demand equals world supply. The transfer reduces domestic demand, as we have seen, by mT, at the initial terms of trade. What about foreign supply? Since m^* denotes how much of an additional dollar's worth of income foreigners will spend on imports, $1 - m^*$ must equal how much of an additional dollar they will spend on exportables. Now when foreigners consume more of their own exportables, they have fewer left over to export to the home country. Thus the transfer T causes the foreign country to *reduce* its supply of home-country importables by $(1 - m^*)T$. Therefore, demand declines by mT and supply by $(1 - m^*)T$.

If $mT < (1 - m^*)T$ [that is, if $m + m^* < 1$], the transfer causes the demand for home imports to exceed their supply. Thus, their price will be forced up: the terms of trade of the paying country will deteriorate. If, on the other hand, $mT > (1 - m^*)T$ [that is, if $m + m^* > 1$], the terms of trade of the paying country improve.

To summarize, if it happens that $m + m^*$ just equals unity, international markets easily accommodate transfers. Such payments are fully effected at once, and there is no tendency for the terms of trade to change. But otherwise life is not so simple. The transfer is initially undereffected, and the terms of trade of the paying country will deteriorate if $m + m^* < 1$ (this condition is sometimes called the *classical presumption* because many classical authors confined themselves to this outcome); $m + m^* > 1$ produces an initially overeffected transfer and a deterioration in the receiving country's terms of trade.

If $m + m^* \neq 1$, terms-of-trade changes are necessary for the world economy to accommodate a transfer. This means that elasticity optimism and pessimism once again come to the fore. If price elasticities are high enough, transfers can be effected and commodity markets cleared by only modest changes in the terms of trade; low elasticities spell trouble. In general, then, the international economy can more easily accommodate transfer payments the closer is $m + m^*$ to unity and the higher are the price elasticities.

PROBLEMS

7.12 Suppose that the French marginal propensity to import is one-fifth and the German is three-tenths. France makes a transfer payment of $10 billion to Germany.

   a Will the transfer be over- or undereffected, and what will happen to the terms of trade?

   b Calculate the exact amount by which, at the initial terms of trade, the transfer is not effected. What is the induced capital movement (C')?

   c Calculate the value of the excess demand for French importables produced by the transfer at the original terms of trade. What is the excess demand for French exportables?

7.13 The Heckscher-Ohlin-Samuelson model studied in Chapter 3 assumed that both countries had identical tastes. How are our conclusions about the transfer problem affected if this assumption is accurate? What do you conclude about the influence of international taste similarities on the ability of the world economy to accommodate transfers?

7.14* The discussion in the text assumed just two countries, the payer and the receiver. Suppose that there is a third country, the rest of the world, which does not participate in the transfer payment but with which both the paying and receiving countries trade. How are our conclusions affected?

7.15* Discuss how our analysis of the transfer problem should be amended if, in both the paying and receiving countries, there is, in addition to importables and exportables, a class of nontradable goods.

5. Case Study: German Reparations and the Transfer Problem

Economists' attention was drawn to the transfer problem by reparations levied on France after the Franco-Prussian War and, especially, on Germany after the First World War. The victorious allies required Germany to pay them large reparations, and the United States demanded that the other allies repay large debts contracted during the war. At the same time, the various creditor nations were reluctant to run the trade deficits through which transfers could be effected. These transfer obligations constituted a major source of international controversy throughout the twenties. Keynes, who had participated in the Versailles Conference, vehemently attacked the peace settlement in a highly influential book entitled *The Economic Consequences of the Peace.* An academic controversy over the theory of the transfer problem then developed between Keynes and Ohlin. Keynes's position was based on classical arguments, and he followed some (but not all) earlier writers in ignoring the direct effects of a transfer through marginal propensities to import. This basically amounted to assuming that $m + m^*$ was close to zero. Add to this the belief that price elasticities were not extremely high, and the conclusion that sizable reparations spell much trouble follows at once. Ohlin, on the other hand, recognized the role of marginal import propensities, and he tacitly assumed that $m + m^*$ was nearer unity. This gave a conclusion quite different from Keynes's. In any event, the bulk of the reparations were never made.

6. Direct Investment and the Multinational Corporation

The theory of section 1 applies to both direct and portfolio capital movements. This section and the following discuss the distinctive questions associated with direct investment. Direct investment consists of the acquisition by domestic firms of foreign subsidiaries and (wholly or partially owned) affiliates. Such investment has grown very rapidly since 1945, and this has thrust into prominence the multinational corporation—a giant enterprise spanning many countries, arranging its operations on a global scale. This phenomenon has been the subject of an enormous literature, both popular and academic. Some see such firms as harbingers of a new dawn, diffusing modern technology and capital into dark corners of the globe; others see our future dominated by faceless corporate bureaucracies with loyalties only unto themselves.

This section examines multinational firms and the reasons for their existence and rapid recent growth. The next section addresses policy issues.

Multinational firms operate production facilities in a number of different countries; the term does not apply to companies that merely export from a single country, no matter how large the exports. The precise definition of a multinational enterprise (MNE) differs from writer to writer. Depending upon the definition, there are 250–750 of these firms, about half of them based in the United States; a few of the others are state-owned. The 50 largest multinationals are, together, at least as sizable as all others combined. Over a fifth of the total GNP of the noncommunist world is produced by MNEs, with the fraction exceeding a third for some individual countries. About a fourth of world trade now consists of trade between subsidiaries and branches *within* MNEs.

CASE STUDY: The Giants

The ten largest corporations are all in either petroleum or motor vehicles, when ranked by dollar value of sales; the rise in oil prices obviously boosted petroleum companies in this method of ranking. For perspective, these sales figures are sometimes compared to national GNPs. In 1976 the GNP of the United Kingdom was $220 billion; of Switzerland, $59 billion; and of Greece, $23 billion. That of Ireland, $8 billion, was less than the total sales of each of the twenty-five largest corporations. These common comparisons are misleading because GNP is a *value added* measure (output minus intermediate inputs), whereas total sales is not. But, nevertheless, these corporations are gigantic.

Table 7.7. MULTINATIONAL CORPORATIONS, 1976

Name	Rank by Sales	Home	Industry	Sales ($ billion)	Foreign Sales as % of Total	Foreign Assets as % of Total
Exxon	1	US	Petroleum	48.6	72	54
GM	2	US	Motor Veh.	47.2	24	12
Royal Dutch/Shell	3	Neth/UK	Petroleum	36.1	62	50
Ford	4	US	Motor Veh.	28.8	31	40
IBM	11	US	Office Equip.	16.3	50	36
Unilever	12	UK/Neth	Food	15.8	48	36
G.E.	13	US	Electrical	15.7	38	27
Hoechst	21	Germany	Chemicals	9.3	67	—

SOURCE: *UN Economic and Social Council*

PATTERNS OF DIRECT INVESTMENT

About half of all MNEs, and eleven of the largest fifteen, are based in the United States. Indeed nearly half of all direct investment has come from the United States, as Table 7.8 shows. The table also shows that the capi-

Table 7.8. SOURCES OF ACCUMULATED STOCK OF DIRECT
INVESTMENT, 1976

Source Country	Stock ($ billion)	World Total (% of)
U.S.	137	48
U.K.	32	11
Germany	20	7
Japan	19	7
Switzerland	19	7
Canada	11	4
World Total	287	100

SOURCE: *UN Economic and Social Council*

tal-abundant part of the world is, in fact, the dominant source of direct
investment.

The ownership patterns are, however, becoming more diversified.
Foreign MNEs have been growing faster than American, so that the American share of world direct investment has declined. Foreign direct investment in the United States has, in recent years, grown at a significantly faster
pace than American direct investment abroad (23 percent versus 15 percent
in 1979), although the latter is still nearly four times as large as the former,
as Table 7.5 shows. Transitional LDCs, such as Brazil, Hong Kong, and
Mexico, are now acquiring significant direct investments, and communist
countries also are establishing foreign operations.

Table 7.9 shows where direct investments have been made. Two features stand out. Most direct investment is located in the relatively capital-
abundant part of the world, so that direct investment flows have not,
typically, been from capital-abundant to capital-scarce countries, even
though, on balance, the DCs are heavy creditors of the LDCs in such investment. Note the analogy with trade patterns involving these country
groups, studied in Chapter 1. Second, direct investment is, by and large,
heaviest between those areas that trade the most with each other (that is,
between the DCs). This is also apparent in the location of U.S. foreign
direct investments: nearly a quarter are in Canada, over a third are in
Western Europe, and Latin America is the most important LDC area. Thus
trade and direct investments are broadly *complementary*. This contrasts
sharply with the analysis of section 1, concluding that trade and factor
movements are *substitutes*.

While thinking about these patterns, it is important to realize that
direct investment need not imply an actual movement of capital. Suppose
that an American firm purchases a subsidiary in the United Kingdom with
funds raised in the United States. This act of direct investment does constitute a movement of capital, because the United States has on balance ac-

Table 7.9. LOCATION OF OUTSTANDING DIRECT INVESTMENT, 1975

Host Area	World Direct Investment, % of
DCs	74
OPEC	6
Other LDCs	20

SOURCE: *UN Economic and Social Council*

quired foreign assets (the subsidiary). But suppose that instead the subsidiary had been purchased with funds the American firm acquired by selling bonds in London. In this case there has been no capital movement—the United States and the United Kingdom simply traded assets (the subsidiary for bonds). A direct investment outflow from the United States has been offset by a portfolio investment inflow. This sort of thing is, in fact, important because MNEs do raise a significant amount of capital locally in host countries. The phenomenon is apparent in Table 7.6, which shows that the United States is a heavy creditor in terms of direct investment but a debtor with regard to other types of capital flows. In effect, about 40 percent of the net foreign direct investment is canceled by other types of foreign borrowing, so that only 60 percent reflects a net movement of capital.

LONG-TERM PERSPECTIVE

International capital movements have been prominent for a long time, but MNEs have become so only since the Second World War. Why this rapid recent growth? One immediately thinks of modern advances in communications and information processing. Efficient global management obviously requires efficient global communications. The first American plant in Europe—a Singer sewing machine factory in Scotland—was opened in the 1860s, soon after the first transatlantic cable was laid.

But it is also true that a little historical perspective makes the MNE seem like less of a distinctly modern animal than contemporary discussions imply. American foreign investment has always been predominantly direct, while European foreign investments have tended more to portfolio. Thus the emergence of the United States as the major source of capital would, by itself, greatly increase the role of direct investment in the world. As Table 7.10 shows, American foreign investment in 1914 was largely direct, just as in 1980. The difference is that in 1914 the country was a net debtor to the rest of the world. But even then, the United States had a net creditor position with respect to direct investment alone! British popular publications in the early years of this century, with a strangely modern flavor, decried the

Table 7.10. THE U.S. FOREIGN INVESTMENT POSITION, 1914

	U.S. Assets Abroad	Foreign Assets in U.S.	Net U.S. Position
Private Long Term	3.5	6.7	−3.2
Direct	2.6	1.3	1.3
Portfolio	.9	5.4	−4.5
Other	—	.5	− .5
Total	3.5	7.2	−3.7

SOURCE: Statistical Abstract of the United States

takeover of local businesses by American firms—even as Great Britain was by far the world's dominant capital exporter!

An additional perspective on the postwar surge of direct investment is afforded by recognition of the role of the Depression, which caused foreign investment to dry up. The Second World War followed, so that direct investment did not resume until after 1945, when it had a lot of catching up to do. From this point of view, the heavy postwar direct investment is not a new phenomenon so much as a return to the long-term trend. The stock of U.S. foreign direct investment in 1980 bears about the same relationship to U.S. GNP (8 percent) as it did in 1914.

Although an historical perspective erodes the popular impression of MNEs as distinctly recent phenomena, significant changes have occurred. The diffusion of direct investment sources has already been noted. The character of MNEs also has evolved. Before the Depression, the majority of American-based MNEs dealt with natural resources: *mining, agriculture, and petroleum.* The expansion since the war has been concentrated in *manufacturing.* Thus while in 1914 less than 20 percent of U.S. foreign direct investment was in manufacturing, over 40 percent is now. Likewise, about 40 percent of foreign direct investments in the United States involve manufacturing. There has also been a shift in industrial organization. Formerly, most MNEs were *vertically integrated:* the divisions of the firm form a succession of stages along which products pass for further processing. Such an organization is most likely for firms dealing with natural resources and has characterized the large oil companies for many years. But now *horizontal integration,* where similar products are simultaneously produced in different countries, has become more important (for example, Heinz and other food-processing firms).

REASONS FOR MNES

Why do MNEs exist? The answer is not obvious, because neither international trade nor international capital movements require that firms be international also. Some firms choose to go multinational and some do not. Those that do generally possess some distinctive attributes that they wish to exploit: trademarks, patents, reputation, managerial ability, the knowledge of how to exploit markets for particular product groups, and so forth. Firms set up foreign operations in order to apply these *firm-specific advantages* and capture their full value, that is, in order to earn world-wide monopoly rents on attributes that are shared with no other firm. This implies that MNEs are imperfectly competitive by their very nature. This theory applies most naturally to horizontally integrated MNEs, but often it seems to apply in a reverse sense to vertically integrated firms as well. These firms frequently go multinational by integrating backward to obtain control of sources of raw materials. This is often done for defensive reasons to ensure that the firm will not be cut off from such supplies, that is, so that the raw materials do not become the unique attributes of competitors.

The firm-specific attribute theory has casual support in that industries where such characteristics seem most natural have many MNEs while firms in other industries, such as steel and textiles, rarely go multinational. Furthermore, empirical research in the last dozen years has conclusively shown that MNEs tend to be larger than other firms and tend to devote proportionally more resources to research and development. Both traits are consistent with the theory. But such evidence cannot be conclusive: for example, are firms multinational because they are large, large because they are multinational, or both large and multinational because of some other reason?

If we do, in fact, accept the hypothesis that companies go multinational in order to earn monopoly rents on firm-specific attributes, we then face the question of why they do not earn these rents in some other way. Consider a firm that owns, say, a valuable patent and wishes to obtain the monopoly rent that the patent could earn in a certain foreign market. There are three basic ways of doing this.

1. The firm could produce the patented product at home and export it to the foreign market.
2. The firm could license a foreign firm to produce the patented product in the foreign market.
3. The firm could acquire a subsidiary in the foreign market to produce the patented product.

These methods are sometimes combined. For example, a foreign subsidiary is often set up to assemble parts manufactured in the home country; this is a combination of methods 1 and 3. Or the home firm might attempt to enter the foreign market by combining with firms from other countries; such a *joint venture* is essentially a combination of methods 2 and 3.

Any of these methods can capture the full monopoly rent of the patent. Method 2 does this directly by charging a monopoly fee for use of the patent, while the other methods do it indirectly by selling the patented product at a monopoly price. Why, then, should the firm go multinational, that is, choose method 3? Note that this is the same problem that arose in section 14 of Chapter 3, which discussed the possibility of exporting a patented product, method 1, to exploit a comparative advantage in R&D.

Sometimes *locational* considerations can narrow the choices. Perhaps method 1 is ruled out because production costs for the patented product are lower in the foreign market, or because transportation costs, tariffs, or foreign tax breaks make foreign production more attractive. But these considerations give no basis for choosing between methods 2 and 3. Also we have seen that direct investment is heaviest between the industrial countries, where cost conditions are relatively similar, and trade barriers relatively low.

The choice between licensing and establishing a foreign subsidiary involves a choice of how much reliance to place on market transactions and the price system as opposed to administrative decisions within the firm. If the patent is licensed to a foreign producer, the technology is transferred between countries via a market at a market price (the licensing fee). But if, instead, a foreign subsidiary is acquired, the technology transfer is *internalized* within the firm, and no market mechanism is used. Market transactions and internal administration are both costly. The choice between these two methods will presumably hinge upon which costs less. Such an explanation of firm size was advanced many years ago by Ronald Coase.

To summarize, our theory concludes that MNEs will tend to develop in industries with three characteristics. First, the firms in the industry must possess *unique attributes* that can be exploited in different countries. *Locational characteristics* must be such that, second, efficient exploitation of these characteristics entails production of goods or services in a number of different countries. Finally, it must be *cheaper to internalize* the transfer of these attributes between countries that to do so through markets.

■ *Why Are There Universities?* The distinction between internal administration and market transactions is nicely illustrated by the university. Universities exist to conduct research and disseminate its results through teaching. But individual faculty members independently undertake research projects and design and teach courses. Thus there could, in principle, be much more extensive use of market transactions. For example, individual professors could set and charge tuition fees for their courses and issue individual "diplomas." A student would then acquire a college education by dealing directly with professors and earning a few dozen diplomas. Instead, all this is internalized within the university to which the student pays a lump sum fee. What do you think are the "costs" of the decentralized system that results in there being universities instead? What advantages would the decentralized system have? ■

PROBLEMS

7.16 Give an example of a vertically integrated MNE in a natural-resource industry. Why is it "natural" for firms in such industries to integrate vertically? Can you explain this in terms of our general theory of why firms go multinational?

7.17 Suppose that you are an executive in a firm with a valuable patent to be exploited in a foreign market. You must choose whether to do so by setting up a foreign subsidiary or by licensing the patent to a foreign firm. What concrete factors would you consider?

7.18 IBM decided to close down its operations in India rather than to comply with a law requiring substantial local ownership. Can you think of any reasons why IBM would prefer doing no business at all to participating in a joint venture?

7. Public Policy toward the Multinational Enterprise

This section inquires how the governments of source and host countries view the MNE and the policies they employ.

THE MNE AND NATIONAL SOVEREIGNTY

Perhaps the most serious issues involving MNEs stem from the fact that they constitute a degree of integration of business enterprise not matched by political integration. This generates three sorts of problems involving political-economic interaction.

1. An MNE spans several countries, which might each wish to influence the firm's behavior in contradictory ways. With the source country pressuring the parent in one direction and the host country pressuring the subsidiary in another, the firm is caught in the middle. For example, on several occasions American pressure through the parents has prevented French subsidiaries of American firms from selling advanced products and technology to the French government and French firms. Again, the United States government has sometimes succeeded in preventing foreign subsidiaries of American MNEs from trading with communist nations, even though the host countries wished to encourage such trade. These examples involve the source country influencing the subsidiary via the parent. Sometimes, though less often, the host country attempts to influence the parent via the subsidiary, as some Arab governments have tried to do to limit trade with Israel.

2. MNEs can also influence governments in both host and source countries. Thus the firm might try to shape relations between the two. For example, in the early seventies, the International Telephone and Telegraph Company, whose Chilean subsidiaries were having trouble with the government of leftist President Allende, tried to induce the U.S. government to pursue a strong anti-Allende policy.

3. To the extent that MNEs can shift operations between subsidiaries in different countries, national governments lose influence over firms within their borders. Both direct controls and "moral suasion" become less compelling when the firm to which they apply can simply pack up and leave.

CASE STUDY: The Transfer Price Issue

This is an especially prominent example of how MNEs can cause trouble for national policy. *Transfer prices* are those that the various divisions of an MNE charge each other; for example, the price that Ford pays to its Italian subsidiary for cylinder heads imported into America by the parent to use in Escorts produced in New Jersey. From a global viewpoint, transfer prices are simply what the MNE charges itself. The firm has an incentive to artificially set these prices so as to minimize its global tax bill. For example, if corporate profits are taxed less in Italy than in America, Ford can lower its total tax bill by increasing the transfer price of the cylinder heads, thereby reducing the profits of the parent and increasing those of the Italian subsidiary in equal amounts. Such behavior can potentially undermine the ability of governments to fashion their own tax systems. Governments, therefore, frown on the use of artificial transfer prices, so it would be risky for Ford to charge itself a price dramatically different from what it charges outside customers for the cylinder heads. But what if there are no outside customers, or what if the transfer price is, say, a licensing fee for a patent whose true "value" we can only guess about? After all, the theory in Section 6 suggested that an important reason MNEs exist in the first place is to internalize transactions not easily priced. But there is an incentive for firms to refrain from deliberately setting false transfer prices: the need for efficient global management. Using "wrong" prices can cause managers to make "wrong" decisions, and artificially shifting profits around makes it very difficult to judge executive performance.

In summary, the commercial integration represented by MNEs has outstripped political integration and thereby eroded national sovereignty and furnished new channels for a government of one country to influence events in another: a recipe for political conflict. In principle, these effects are symmetrical between source and host countries, but, in practice, the latter seem to lose the most sovereignty. Thus this question of the erosion of national sovereignty is a much more serious issue in host countries.

SOURCE-COUNTRY ISSUES

Two issues figure prominently in discussions within source countries.

1. *Taxation.* Two provisions of current tax laws have caused intense debate in the United States. American MNEs must pay corporate income taxes on their global profits, but they may deduct from their U.S. taxes any taxes paid to foreign governments. The reason for this is to avoid double taxation of foreign subsidiaries, and it is done in such a way as to give the host country first crack at taxing them. This is common international practice, but it works to the disadvantage of source countries. The parent MNE cares only about after-tax earnings, but to the source country as a whole tax revenues also matter. Thus the effect of this provision is to redistribute part of MNE gross earnings from source to host countries. In 1977 foreign tax credits of $26 billion reduced total U.S. corporate taxes by almost one-third. The provision also invites abuse. Some Arab countries have called the payments that they exact from oil companies "taxes," rather than royalty fees for drilling or sale prices for oil. As taxes, the total payments can be deducted from the companies' U.S. tax liabilities; as fees or prices they could only be used to reduce taxable earnings. In 1977 oil companies claimed about 70 percent of the $26 billion in foreign tax credits. IRS regulations were tightened in 1980 in an attempt to end this behavior.

A second controversial provision is that U.S. taxes on the profits of foreign subsidiaries need not be paid until those profits are actually repatriated to the U.S. Thus by reinvesting the earnings in the subsidiary, the MNE can defer taxation and in effect put the taxes to work for itself; continual reinvestment allows indefinite deferral. In 1979 total U.S. earnings on foreign direct investment were almost $38 billion, of which over $18 billion was reinvested abroad by corporations. Of course the subsidiaries cannot defer host country taxes, unless specifically allowed to, so that this provision makes no difference if the host country tax rate is at least as high as the U.S. tax rate: there would be no U.S. tax liability in any case. But when the host-country rate is lower, this regulation increases the return to foreign investment relative to home investment and gives the MNE an incentive to reinvest its foreign earnings abroad.

■ MNE *Taxation Example.* Suppose a home-based MNE is considering an investment of $5 million, which it can make either at home or abroad. The investment would be equally productive in each place, yielding a pre-tax annual return of $1 million. The home tax rate is 50 percent, and the foreign rate is 25 percent. The U.S. tax liability on the firm's earnings will be $500,000. If the MNE invests abroad, it will incur a foreign tax of $250,000. But this can be deducted from its U.S. taxes, so that after-tax earnings will be $500,000 regardless of where the investment is made. The absence of double taxation is globally efficient: the MNE perceives the

Table 7.11. COMPARISON OF HOME AND FOREIGN INVESTMENTS

	Abroad	At Home
Pre-tax earnings	$1 million	$1 million
Foreign tax liability	$250,000	—
Home tax liability	$250,000	$500,000
After-tax earnings of MNE	$500,000	$500,000
Total home country earnings	$750,000	$1 million
After-tax earnings of the MNE if not repatriated	$750,000	$500,000

alternatives as equivalent and they are equally productive ($1 million) to the world as a whole. But they are not equally advantageous to the home economy, because total domestic earnings (domestic tax revenues plus MNE after-tax earnings) would be $1 million if the investment is made at home and only $750,000 if made abroad. Now suppose that the MNE plans to reinvest all earnings indefinitely wherever the investment is made. In this case, U.S. taxes can be deferred indefinitely if the investment is abroad. This does not alter total home-country earnings of the two alternatives, but the MNE's after-tax earnings of the foreign alternative rise to $750,000. Thus the MNE perceives the foreign investment as superior, even though it remains equivalent to the domestic alternative from a global point of view and inferior from a domestic point of view. ■

2. *Labor.* Organized labor in the United States generally opposes foreign direct investment by American firms and has supported proposals to limit it, such as repeal of the above tax provisions. Labor's argument is that American jobs are "exported" when MNEs set up foreign subsidiaries instead of expanding at home. Defenders of MNEs retort that direct investment generates more American jobs than it eliminates, in part because the alternative to foreign subsidiaries, which themselves import from America, is a loss of markets to foreign firms. Who is right?

Note, first, that the total number of jobs available in America depends primarily on macroeconomic conditions and policies rather than on the allocation of capital. But there are still two senses in which labor may have a case. Section 1 showed that an outward movement of capital could redistribute domestic income from labor to capital. The country as a whole would gain (except possibly if the capital flow is in response to artificial distortions, such as the tax laws), though this need not be much consolation to labor. But recall that direct investment need not coincide with real capital movements, and, as MNE defenders point out, foreign direct investment does seem, on the whole, to be complementary to domestic exports. A second point is that organized labor's bargaining position is weakened when a corporation can threaten to shift operations abroad. Unions could in principle go multinational themselves and bargain on a global scale. But this has not in fact happened, although there has been some increase in international labor communication. One potential problem is that a multi-national union would absorb within itself the inherent conflicts of interest between its national branches. An MNE, concerned itself only with global profits, might still be able to play one branch off against another. In any event, MNEs have in the past refused to bargain with international labor federations.

HOST-COUNTRY ISSUES

Host countries have displayed ambivalent attitudes toward direct investment. Sometimes they entice MNEs with tax breaks and other inducements; at other times they subject these firms to hostile propaganda, severe restrictions, and even outright nationalization of subsidiaries. This ambivalence reflects the fact that these countries perceive both benefits and costs. On the plus side, MNEs are seen as sources of outside capital, advanced technology, modern business methods, and jobs—the latter the flip side to American labor's attitude. How important are these advantages? In general, they can be realized without the MNE, as we saw in the preceding section: capital movements need not take the form of direct investment, new technology can be embodied in imports or licensed directly, and even managerial ability can be hired. But the MNE may help. Tax laws may cause capital to flow more readily through the firm, and firm-specific attributes such as patents may be transferred exclusively, or at least more cheaply, within the MNE. LDCs in particular often find direct access to capital and technology difficult to come by.

Host-country complaints are that MNEs are too restrained in conferring these benefits, that they lead to a loss of national sovereignty as discussed above, and that they exploit the host country. Let us look at these in detail.

1. *Exploitation.* Host countries often charge that the subsidiaries of MNEs earn excessive profits, and these subsidiaries are indeed frequently more profitable than their parents. If the profits reflect high seller concentration within the host country, then the problem is to reduce this concentration, whether it is in domestic or foreign hands, and *not* simply to transfer it from the latter to the former by restricting direct investment. If, on the other hand, the MNE is exacting a monopoly price for a unique attribute that it is bringing to the host country, then the latter can obtain for itself some of this monopoly rent by bargaining with the MNE over terms of entry. LDCs often charge that oil and mineral extraction operations are much too profitable to MNEs. Exploration rights naturally fetch a modest price when no one knows what, if anything, will be found; charges of exploitation are sometimes the result of looking only at the high returns to

those projects that pay off while ignoring the counterbalancing losses from those that fail. Other times the charge is that a corrupt (previous) regime, for personal gain, disposed of the nation's birthright at too low a price. This involves the MNE in domestic politics.

2. *Inadequate Transfer of Capital and Technology.* The complaint here is that MNEs do not bring enough new capital into host countries, and that they tend to make the host country technologically dependent upon the firm. It is true that MNEs raise much capital locally, and that they typically concentrate R&D in the source country. But the basic problem is not so much that MNEs retard these transfers as that host countries want more. Another charge is that technology is often not transferred in an efficient way. Techniques are not sufficiently adapted to distinctly local conditions, or are made unnecessarily obscure (so that the MNE would continue to be indispensable). The evidence is mixed on such charges. One of the demands in the proposal for a New International Economic Order is that capital and technology be transferred from DCs to LDCs independently of MNEs.

HOST-COUNTRY POLICIES TOWARD DIRECT INVESTMENT

The combination of a generally hostile attitude toward MNEs and a consciousness of the benefits they can bring ensures ambivalent and variable host-country policies. Communist countries prohibit foreign investment, as they do large private investment in general, but many highly visible joint ventures with foreign firms have been undertaken. LDC attitudes vary greatly from country to country and from regime to regime, although foreign direct investment is almost always restricted in some ways. Some countries, such as Mexico, prohibit foreign majority control. The industrial nations have generally been more liberal, but all restrict direct investment in some way. Except for the United States and Germany, all have applied formal screening procedures to new investments, with the screening ranging from pro forma in Italy's case to quite stringent in Japan's.

8. Case Study: Canadian Policy toward Foreign Direct Investment

Canadian policy is of special interest because of the dominant position of foreign direct investment in Canada's industry, and because more United States direct investment has been directed to Canada than to any other single country.

Like the United States, Canada was a heavy borrower in the nineteenth century. Britain was the primary source: by 1900 Britain held about 85 percent of outstanding Canadian international debt. Most of the rest was held by the United States, which, though still a net debtor overall, had begun to acquire substantial foreign assets.

Relative to GNP, and also in per capita terms, foreign investment in Canada peaked during 1900–1914, when prairie settlement generated a boom and a large demand for capital, about a third of which was satisfied from abroad. Since 1914 Britain's importance has declined and that of the United States has increased, with the latter overtaking the former in the twenties as the largest creditor. Today the United States accounts for more than 80 percent of outstanding foreign investment in Canada, with the rest about evenly divided between the United Kingdom, on the one hand, and all other countries on the other.

Significant direct investment in Canada goes back to Confederation in 1867, but portfolio investment was the overwhelmingly dominant form before the First World War. After the war, the relative importance of direct investment rose, and in the fifties the total stock of outstanding foreign direct investment in Canada overtook that of portfolio investment.

As the economy grew and became more capital abundant, Canada relied less and less upon foreign investment for new capital, and even began to acquire substantial foreign investments of her own. But, unlike the United States, Canada did not cease to be a net borrower. Table 7.12 summarizes Canadian international transactions in 1980, showing the net international sales of various assets. On balance the country sold $1.6 billion of assets to the rest of the world. In recent years Canadian direct investments in the United States have increased, making Canada the third-largest foreign direct investor in that country. Indeed Canadian per capita holdings in the United States exceed U.S. per capita holdings in Canada, but in view of the size disparity, Canada is a heavy net debtor vis-à-vis its southern neighbor. Note from Table 7.12 that Canada, like the United States, is actually *acquiring* direct investments in the rest of the world, essentially financing the purchases by selling other assets. Since 1975 new Canadian direct investments abroad have exceeded new foreign direct investments in Canada (however, Canadian figures ignore reinvested earn-

Table 7.12. CANADIAN INTERNATIONAL CAPITAL TRANSACTIONS, 1980 *(billions of Canadian dollars)*

Current Balance		−1.6
Capital Balance		1.6
Direct Investment	−2.6	
In Canada:	.6	
Abroad:	−3.2	
Portfolio		5.4
Other Private		−1.7
Official		.5

SOURCE: *IMF,* Balance of Payments Statistics

ings). But the country's situation differs from that of the United States in two ways: in terms of total *stocks* of outstanding direct investment Canada remains a debtor, and the recent increase in net new direct investment abroad is in part a response to Canadian public policy.

Canada displays the host-county ambivalence toward direct investment that we discussed in section 7. The country has encouraged capital inflows, including direct investment, to spur development. The National Policy tariff of 1879, for example, induced direct investment in Canada by foreign firms who could no longer export competitively to the Canadian market in the face of higher protection. Also protection tended to raise the reward of relatively scarce Canadian capital and so to attract foreign investment. But during the twenties Canadians began to have substantial doubts about direct investment as the country became aware of the prominence foreign firms were acquiring in Canadian industry. These doubts grew with the rapid expansion of foreign investment in Canada following the Second World War. The Gordon Report of 1958 and the Gray Report of 1972 emphasized the costs of such a situation, and restrictive policy measures followed. At the same time, some foreign investments continue to be encouraged—recall the Michelin example in Chapter 6.

The importance of direct investment in Canada is revealed in Table 7.13. Almost three-fifths of Canadian industry is foreign controlled (over 80 percent of foreign direct investment in Canada is from the United States). Three major policy measures limit foreign investment. First, the Foreign Investment Review Act of 1973 requires that all new foreign direct investments in Canadian industry be reviewed in order to obtain government approval. The review agency has in fact approved most applications, but it has tended to become more exacting over time, and its powers are being broadened. Second, the Canada Development Corporation makes investments in important sectors of the economy thought likely otherwise to attract foreign capital. Third, the National Energy Program, announced in

Table 7.13. PERCENTAGE OF TOTAL CANADIAN SALES ACCOUNTED
FOR BY FOREIGN-CONTROLLED FIRMS, 1976

All Nonfinancial Corporations		35%
Industry		58
Food	36	
Chemicals	82	
Transportation Equipment	87	
Petroleum and Coal Processing	96	
Mining and Smelting	66	
Distribution		21

SOURCE: *Statistics Canada*, Corporations and Labour Unions Returns Act Report

a corporation can threaten to shift operations abroad. Unions could in October 1980, has as one of its goals the "Canadianization" (at least 50 percent Canadian ownership) of the oil and natural gas industry. Proposed elements of this program include the scaling of government grants for exploration and development to the degree of Canadian ownership, and the exclusion of foreign controlled companies from exploitation in the federal Canada Lands. Direct investment is also limited by a number of minor measures, such as laws that do not allow Canadian companies tax deductions for advertising in Canadian editions of foreign owned publications or in foreign television stations with a Canadian audience. These measures have caused resentment in the United States, with the result that proposals have been made to retaliate against the growing direct investment from Canada.

PROBLEM

7.19 In view of the discussion in sections 6 and 7, what do you think are the pros and cons of foreign direct investment for a country such as Canada? Are the Canadian policies wise?

9. Summary

1. In Ricardian theory, factor mobility raises world production more than does trade and specialization. Beneficial trade is a consequence of comparative cost differences, whereas beneficial factor movements are a consequence of absolute productivity differences.

2. In factor-endowments theory, factor movements are perfectly substituted for by commodity trade if trade leads to factor price equalization. With incomplete factor price equalization, factor mobility will lead to migrations from low marginal product areas to high marginal product areas.

3. Factor mobility, like commodity trade, redistributes income from a country's relatively scarce factor to the relatively abundant factor.

4. Intra-industry trade and factor mobility are complementary, whereas factor mobility and inter-industry trade are substitutes.

5. The Brain Drain is an outflow of both labor and human capital and limits the ability of individual countries to conduct independent tax and social policies.

6. Guest workers accept low wages in host countries and increase the ability of the host country to deal with macro-disturbances. The host country exports business cycles to foreigners.

7. International capital movements (borrowing and lending between countries) allow countries to pay for imports by selling either goods or assets.

8. There are three types of capital movements: official, nonofficial short term, and nonofficial long term. The latter are divided between direct and portfolio (long-term) investments.

9. The transfer problem deals with the direct effects of a simultaneous fall in one country's spending and rise in that of another.

10. If $m + m^*$ exceeds (falls short of) unity, the transfer is over (under) effected and the paying country's terms of trade improve (deteriorate).

11. MNEs exist when (1) there are firm-specific attributes that can earn monopoly rents in a number of countries; (2) locational considerations indicate costs can be lowered by producing in different countries; and (3) the internalization of some international transactions within firms is cheaper than the use of markets.

12. Host countries have ambivalent attitudes toward foreign direct investment.

SUGGESTED READING

Barnet, R. J. and Muller, R. E. *Global Reach, The Power of the Multinational Corporations.* New York: Simon and Schuster, 1974. A detailed but popular critical discussion.

Behrman, J. N. *National Interests and the Multinational Enterprise.* Englewood Cliffs: Prentice Hall, 1970. The sovereignty problem.

Caves, R. E. "International Corporations: the Industrial Economics of Foreign Investment." *Economica,* Feb., 1971. Imperfect competition and the *MNE*.

Coase, R. H. "The Nature of the Firm." In *Readings in Price Theory.* Edited by G. J. Stigler and K. E. Boulding. Homewood: Irwin, 1952. Coase's theory of the firm, cited in the text.

Christelow, D. B. "National Policies Toward Foreign Direct Investment." Federal Reserve Bank of New York, *Quarterly Review,* Winter 1979–80. A survey of such policies.

Ellis, H. S. and Metzler, L. A. *Readings in the Theory of International Trade.* Homewood: Irwin, 1950. Chapters 6 and 7 form the Keynes-Ohlin exchange on the transfer problem, and Metzler discusses employment aspects of the problem in chapter 8.

Feis, H. *Europe: The World's Banker, 1870–1913.* New York: Norton, 1966. An historical account of capital movements before the First World War.

Foreign Direct Investment in Canada. Ottawa: Government of Canada, 1972. A policy-aimed discussion: the Gray Report.

Hood, N. and Young, S. *The Economics of Multinational Enterprise.* London: Longman, 1979. An extensive survey of the literature.

MacDougall, G. D. A. "The Benefits and Costs of Private Investment from Abroad: A Theoretical Approach. " *Economic Record,* March, 1960.

Mundell, R. A. "International Trade and Factor Mobility." *American Economic Review,* June, 1957. A basic theoretical treatment.

Ohlin, B. *Interregional and International Trade.* Rev. ed. Cambridge: Harvard University Press, 1967. Stresses the relation between trade and factor mobility.

Piore, M. J. *Birds of Passage.* Cambridge: Cambridge University Press, 1979. Migrant labor in the modern world economy.

Samuelson, P. A. "The Transfer Problem and Transport Costs." *Economic Journal,* June 1952 and June 1954. Standard statement of the theory.

Servan-Schreiber, J. J. *The American Challenge.* New York: Atheneum, 1968. An influential polemic.

Singer, H. "The Distribution of Gains between Investing and Borrowing Countries." In *Readings in International Economics.* Edited by R. E. Caves, and H. G. Johnson. Homewood: Irwin, 1968. A discussion of foreign investment in LDCs.

Thomas, B. *Migration and Economic Growth.* Rev. ed. Cambridge: Cambridge University Press, 1972. The great migrations to the Western Hemisphere.

Part Three

International Monetary Theory and Applications

NATIONAL sovereignty gives international economics much of its distinctive character. A notable example is the fact that different countries have different monetary systems, with international transactions complicated accordingly. When you travel across the United States you see prices quoted in the same dollars that you carry in your wallet, that you make other payments with, and in which your paycheck is denominated. But when you visit Germany you find prices quoted in marks and face the problem of making sense of, say, a price of DM10 for a haircut. At the same time, a German brewery exporting beer to the United States is concerned with how many marks it will get for the $100,000 it is being paid for the beer—a consideration absent from German sales. Questions like these are answered by the *exchange rate:* the price of one country's money in terms of that of another. For example, if the U.S.-German exchange rate is DM2 per dollar, that haircut will set you back $5 and the brewery will receive DM200,000 for its beer.

Now if we could be sure that the exchange rate would always be DM2/$1, the difference in monies would be no more than a nuisance, just as the fact that in the United States length is measured in feet and inches whereas Europeans use meters and centimeters. But exchange rates are neither units of measurement nor laws of nature. They are prices and as such are subject to change. The table shows how much of various currencies could be purchased for 1 U.S. dollar at the end of certain time periods. For example, at the end of 1981, 1 U.S. dollar would have bought 219.90 Japanese yen (1 yen would have bought .0045 [= 1 ÷ 219.9] dollars); at the end of 1980 the French-German exchange rate was 2.305 (= 4.516 ÷ 1.959) francs per mark. The two bottom currencies illustrate the great diversity of behavior: while the Liberian-U.S. exchange rate remained fixed at unity, the Argentine-U.S. rate changed enormously.

SELECTED EXCHANGE RATES
(NATIONAL CURRENCY PER U.S. DOLLAR, END OF PERIOD)

Currency	1970	1975	1979	1980	1981
U.S. dollar	1.0000	1.0000	1.0000	1.0000	1.0000
Canadian dollar	1.0112	1.0164	1.1681	1.1947	1.1859
Japanese yen	357.65	305.15	239.70	203.00	219.90
French franc	5.5200	4.4855	4.0200	4.5160	5.7480
Deutsche mark	3.6480	2.6223	1.7315	1.9590	2.2548
Pound sterling	.41776	.49419	.44964	.41929	.5241
Argentine peso	4.0	60.9	1618.5	1992.5	10,575.0
Liberian dollar	1.0000	1.0000	1.0000	1.0000	1.0000

SOURCE: *International Financial Statistics*

Exchange rates are facts of life to international travelers and businessmen. *Balance of payments* surpluses and deficits, by contrast, do not touch most people directly, although they do sometimes grab headlines. There are different concepts of payments imbalances, and we shall examine them in due course, but for now we can introduce the idea with the aid of Walras's Law, expressed in equation (1).

$$(P_M M - P_X X - E) - C \equiv O \tag{1}$$

This law, you will recall, says that the total value of excess demands in all markets always equals zero, or, when arranged as in (1), that the sum of the current account balance and the capital account balance is likewise zero. Since we are now introducing money, equation (1) is expressed in (domestic) money terms: P_M and P_X denote the money prices of imports and exports, C is the money value of the net supply of assets, and E is net interest income from abroad in terms of money. Since money is itself an asset, one natural way to add the excess demand for money to (1) would be to include it in C. But since we shall want to focus on money in this part of the book, we instead treat it separately, using C to stand for the money value of the excess supply of all non-monetary assets and introducing a new symbol, B, for the net home country demand for money, both domestic and foreign. Then (1) must be rewritten

$$(P_M M - P_X X - E) - C + B \equiv O \tag{2}$$

or, rearranging,

$$B \equiv (P_X X - P_M M + E) + C. \tag{3}$$

In this form the equation defines the *balance of payments surplus* B as the sum of the current account surplus $(P_X X - P_M M + E)$ and the capital account surplus C. This sum equals the excess of all payments received from foreigners for exports, interest, and the sale of assets over all payments made to foreigners for imports, interest and the purchase of assets; thus B equals the net receipt of money from abroad.

What determines exchange rates and payments imbalances? What difference does it make what happens to either? This is the first set of questions addressed by international monetary theory. A second set was suggested in Chapter 4, which introduced open economy macroeconomics and gave us just enough equipment for the policy discussions of Part Two. How does macroeconomic policy work in an open economy? What is the relation between internal economic objectives and external ones? Between macroeconomic policy in one country and performance in another? Such questions, first raised in Chapter 4, can now be treated in depth.

Chapters 8 and 9 give answers to these two sets of questions. In Chapter 8 we focus on payments imbalances while ignoring exchange rate changes. This amounts to treating different national monies as merely different ways of measuring the same thing, so as to focus efficiently on the implications of the fact that the international economy is a monetary one. Chapter 9 then examines the role of exchange rates, thus focusing on the fact that different nations do indeed have different monies.

Together with Part One, these chapters comprise the six core theoretical chapters of this book. Part One is pure, and Part Three is monetary; alternatively Chapters 1, 2, and 3 present international microeconomics, while 4, 8, and 9 deal with international macroeconomics.

Chapter 8

The Automatic Adjustment Process

> "Suppose four-fifths of all the money in Great Britain to be annihilated in one night, ... what would be the consequence? Must not the price of all labour and commodities sink in proportion ...? What nation could then dispute with us in any foreign market ...? In how little time, therefore, must this bring back the money which we had lost, and raise us to the level of all the neighboring nations? Where, after we have arrived, we immediately lose the advantage of the cheapness of labour and commodities; and the farther flowing in of money is stopped by our fulness and repletion. ...
>
> "Now, it is evident, that the same causes ... must for ever, in all neighboring nations, preserve money nearly proportionable to the art and industry of each nation." —DAVID HUME

THIS CHAPTER investigates those problems that arise simply from the existence of money. In the next chapter we focus on the implications of the fact that different economies have distinct monies. The key idea in this chapter is that of the automatic adjustment process of the balance of payments, the exposition of which is generally credited to David Hume and, sometimes, to Richard Cantillon.

Comparative advantage and reciprocal demand constitute the essence of the classical theory of international trade. The automatic adjustment process is the heart of the classical monetary contribution, so the three ideas together can be thought of as the classical theory of international economics.

DAVID HUME (1711-1776)

One of the pre-eminent eighteenth-century thinkers, Hume, like his close friend and fellow Scot Adam Smith (and like John Stuart Mill but unlike Cantillon and Ricardo), was a philosopher who also made important contributions to economics—and to history, politics, aesthetics, sociology, and psychology. For Hume all these concerns were aspects of a single system of philosophy. His economic thought focused on the underlying causes of industrial progress and was one of the principal predecessors of the work of Adam Smith, whose *Wealth of Nations* was published the year that Hume died.

E S S A I

SUR LA NATURE

D U

COMMERCE

EN GÉNÉRAL.

TRADUIT DE L'ANGLOIS.

A LONDRES,

Chez FLETCHER GYLES,
dans Holborn

M. DCC. LV.

Cantillon's famous essay

RICHARD CANTILLON (1680-1734)

Like Ricardo and Keynes, Cantillon was an economist who accumulated a fortune through financial dealing. He was from an Irish family of sympathizers of the Stuart pretenders to the English throne, and for years lived in Paris, where many Stuart sympathizers took refuge. While there he understood the defects in a financial scheme being masterminded by John Law. This earned him the hostility of Law and his friends, but when the scheme collapsed Cantillon had his fortune. A mistake in labor relations, however, was to cost him his life. While living in London he fired his cook, who then set fire to the house, taking care that Cantillon was in it at the time.

1. International Monetary Equilibrium

As we explore the monetary complement to trade theory, we shall follow the same strategy as in Chapter 1: first the basic ideas in a very simple framework, and then various extensions and applications. As before, imagine that the world consists of two countries, France and Germany, and two goods, wine and machines. Comparative advantage will determine the direction of trade, and reciprocal demand the terms of trade. Suppose that France exports wine.

MONEY SUPPLIES AND MONEY PRICES

For starters, assume that money consists of gold coins and nothing else. There is a fixed number L of such coins, so that if L^F is the money supply in France and L^G that in Germany, $L = L^F + L^G$. The LL' line in Figure 8.1 shows the various ways that the total world money supply can be distributed between the two countries. The length of OL $(= OL')$ measures the total number of gold coins; at point E, for example, the German money supply is equal to OA and the French to OB.

P_W is the world money price of wine (the number of gold coins needed to buy one unit of wine), and P_M is the money price of machines. The relative price of machines in terms of wine, $p = P_M/P_W$, is determined by the two offer curves, as discussed in Chapter 2. But the pure theory cannot determine the two *money* prices.

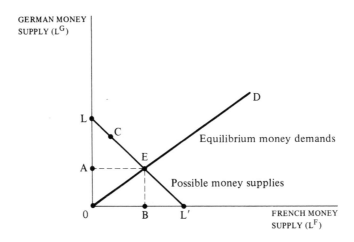

Figure 8.1. INTERNATIONAL MONETARY EQUILIBRIUM

THE QUANTITY THEORY OF MONEY

Money is required for making transactions, and the number of transactions is determined by national income. Suppose that the coins required for the transactions associated with a unit of annual national income is institutionally determined—call it k. Then the French demand for money is $kP_W y^F$, where y^F denotes total French output measured in units of wine. The demand for money in France will accordingly equal the supply when

$$L^F = kP_W y^F. \tag{8.1}$$

This equation expresses a rudimentary version of what is called the "quantity theory of money." Similarly, the demand for money in Germany will equal the supply when

$$L^G = kP_M y^G \tag{8.2}$$

where y^G denotes total German output measured in terms of machines. (Assume for simplicity that k is the same in Germany as in France.) The quantity theory can be used to determine two things: the equilibrium distribution of the world money supply between France and Germany, and absolute money prices.

KEY CONCEPT

The *quantity theory of money* asserts that the demand for money is proportional to national income. In its most *crude* form, the theory asserts that k in equation (8.1) is a constant of nature and that output y^F is determined by non-monetary considerations, so that the demand for money is always proportional to the price level. This gives a simple theory of inflation: the inflation rate is always determined by and equal to the rate of change of the money supply. A more *sophisticated* quantity theory realizes that both the price level and real output are sensitive to monetary factors and allows k to respond to economic considerations— though presumably in a predictable fashion. The most wishy-washy use of equation (8.1) would be simply to define k. This would be no theory at all.

EQUILIBRIUM DISTRIBUTION OF THE WORLD'S MONEY

For the world to be in equilibrium, the demand for money in each country must equal the supply, that is, (8.1) and (8.2) must hold. Dividing (8.1) into (8.2)

$$\frac{L^G}{L^F} = \frac{k\,P_M y^G}{k\,P_W y^F} = py^G/y^F. \tag{8.3}$$

The right-hand side of (8.3) depends upon the terms of trade p, determined by the intersection of the offer curves. Thus (8.3) tells us what the ratio of the two money supplies must be in equilibrium. This is depicted in Figure 8.1 by the line OD, whose slope (EB/OB) equals $p\,y^G/y^F$.

The world must be on the LL' line in Figure 8.1 for the money supplies in the two countries to total the world stock of gold coins, and it must be on the line OD for equilibrium. Thus the intersection E depicts the equilibrium money supplies in the two countries: L^F should equal OB, and L^G should equal OA.

MONEY PRICES

The intersection of the offer curves determines the terms of trade p, the ratio of P_M to P_W, but not the absolute values of P_M and P_W. This is a task for the quantity theory. Adding together (8.1) and (8.2), the quantity equations for the two countries, gives a world quantity equation that equates the total world supply of money to the total world demand:

$$L^F + L^G = L = k[P_W y^F] + k[P_M y^G] = P_W k[y^F + p y^G]. \qquad \textbf{(8.4)}$$

Everything on the extreme right-hand side of (8.4) except P_W is determined; thus (8.4) says that P_W is proportional to L. The world stock of money determines the absolute price of wine, and thus the absolute price of machines as well, since $P_M = p P_W$.

Figure 8.1 and Figure 2.2 (showing the intersection of two offer curves) jointly depict full classical equilibrium. The latter diagram illustrates the real aspect of the problem, with the intersection of the offer curves yielding the relative price that causes demand to equal supply in both commodity markets. Figure 8.1 illustrates the monetary aspect, with the intersection yielding the distribution of world money that causes the demand for money to equal the supply in each country. Note that the real aspect can be analyzed independently of the monetary, as in Part One; monetary factors do not influence the equilibrium terms of trade or other real variables, but only monetary ones. This aspect of the classical viewpoint is often summarized in the claim that "money is a veil."

PROBLEMS

8.1 Suppose that America and Europe trade, America specializing to and exporting wheat and Europe specializing to and exporting cloth. American wheat production equals 1,000, and European cloth production 600. In equilibrium 5 wheat exchange for 1 cloth. The world money supply consists of 2,000 gold coins, and k equals $\frac{1}{2}$. Describe international monetary equilibrium and illustrate with a diagram analogous to Figure 8.1. Suppose the world money supply increases to 4,000 gold coins; calculate the effect on your answer and illustrate the change in your diagram. Do the same if instead the terms of trade were to alter so that 5 wheat exchange for 3 cloth.

8.2 The discussion in the text supposed that k had the same value in both countries. Show in detail how the argument would change if k were different in Germany than in France. How would your answer to the first part of the above problem change if k were to fall to $\frac{1}{4}$ in America but remain at $\frac{1}{2}$ in Europe?

8.3 In your answer to Problem **2.14**, assume that in equilibrium the German supply of machines is 111 and supply of wine is 21. Suppose that the world money supply consists of 1,520 gold coins and that k equals 2. Find the equilibrium money supplies in the two countries and the equilibrium money prices of the two goods.

8.4* As in Problem **2.15***, England has 100 labor units, of which 5 are required to produce either a cask of wine or a bolt of cloth. The English always consume equal quantities of the two goods. Portugal has 100 labor units with 1 required to produce a cask of wine and 4 to produce a bolt of cloth; the Portuguese always consume equal-valued quantities of wine and cloth. The world money supply consists of 150 gold coins, and k equals 1. Describe and illustrate international monetary equilibrium. Show what happens if England's labor force increases to 1000.

8.5* Show how the discussion of this section changes if, instead of remaining fixed, L constantly *increases* at the rate of 10 percent per year.

2. The Automatic Adjustment Process

The previous section described the international monetary equilibrium that is the counterpart to the real equilibrium studied in Part One. But one point has been left dangling: the existing supply of gold coins requires the world to be somewhere on the line LL' in Figure 8.1, but is there any reason to think that it will be at point E? This is the subject of the automatic adjustment process, the key idea of this chapter.

THE BALANCE OF PAYMENTS

If the citizens of a country, say France, wish to import the quantity M of machines, they must pay $P_M M$ in money (gold coins) to do so; similarly their exports X of wine will yield them $P_W X$ in return. Thus the French *trade balance* $P_W X - P_M M = B$, or *balance of payments surplus*, equals the net amount of money the French are receiving from abroad. Alternatively, if the French wish to increase their money holdings, and if the total number of gold coins in existence does not change, the only way they can do so is by exporting a larger value of goods to Germany relative to their imports. (Note that this is an application of Walras's Law to a world with three markets: wine, machines, and gold coins. Because there are no assets other than money, the terms C and E in equation (3) on p. 287 have dropped out.) If the world is in equilibrium the wine and machine markets are in equilibrium—and each country's exports are equal in value to its imports, so that their balances of payments are zero. This is reflected on the monetary side by the fact that at point E in Figure 8.1 each country's demand for money is equal to its supply.

OVERVIEW OF THE ADJUSTMENT PROCESS

What if the world's money is not distributed in the equilibrium fashion? Suppose, for example, that we are at point C in Figure 8.1 rather than at E. Then the German money supply exceeds its equilibrium level while the French supply falls short. We shall soon examine in detail four mechanisms that induce the Germans to use their excess money to purchase more wine from France, and to consume more of their own machines, thereby exporting fewer. Thus German imports exceed exports in value; Germany runs a balance of payments deficit. The French money supply, on the other hand, is deficient, so that the mechanisms we shall examine induce the French to decrease their purchases of German machines (cutting imports) and of French wine (freeing more for export); France runs a balance of payments surplus. The German deficit and corresponding French surplus mean that on balance Germany is selling gold to France for goods. The French money supply is increasing and the German money supply is falling. In Figure 8.1 the world is moving along the LL' line from C toward E. This continues until the supply of money in each country equals the demand, that is, until E is reached.

This is the essence of the automatic adjustment process. Note that it contains three basic ingredients. (1) The quantity theory of money determines the equilibrium allocation of the world's money supply between countries. (2) A nonequilibrium distribution of the world's money causes balance of payments deficits and surpluses. (3) These deficits and surpluses redistribute money between countries. The first ingredient was studied in section 1. The explicit mechanics behind (2) will be examined in detail in the following sections. The essential requirement of (3) is that a country with a balance of payments deficit should have a contracting money supply and a country with a payments surplus an expanding money supply, a requirement sometimes called the "Rules of the Game." This is trivial in the present context, where a payments surplus and an increase in the money supply are really just two different names for the same thing. But this is not true with the more elaborate financial arrangements that actually exist in the world, so we shall return to the Rules of the Game in section 12 of this chapter.

KEY CONCEPT

The Rules of the Game: A balance of payments deficit should be fully reflected in a reduction in the supply of money, and a surplus should be fully reflected in an increased money supply.

IMPLICATIONS OF THE AUTOMATIC ADJUSTMENT PROCESS

The classical automatic adjustment process has two broad implications. *First,* balance of payments deficits or surpluses are both the symptoms of an international misallocation of money and the means by which such misallocations are corrected. Thus payments imbalances are transitory and beneficial and no cause for alarm.

Second, the adjustment process ensures that the world has a single international monetary system in which individual countries cannot pursue independent monetary policies (except transitorily). This is illustrated in Figure 8.2. Suppose the French create sufficient money to double their money supply, so that the world moves from E to H and the LL' line shifts to L_1L_1', the length EH measuring the French money creation. (Perhaps the French find this much gold in a cave, or they discover the philosopher's stone and turn this much base metal into gold, or better yet, they print this much paper money and are able to convince everyone that it's just as good as gold.) The equilibrium is at E_1. With the world at H, France develops a payments deficit, and Germany a surplus; this continues until the French money supply has shrunk and the German expanded sufficiently to reach E_1. Despite the creation of EH of new money the French have managed to increase their money supply only by EJ, and they have been able to do this only by increasing Germany's money supply in the same proportion. Thus the automatic adjustment process ensures that a country can have nontransitory control over its money supply only by controlling that of the entire world. This point has even more force when we realize that a single country, even a relatively large one, will be small compared to the rest of the world. Suppose, for example, that France is one-twentieth of the world, in the sense that in equilibrium the French money supply will equal 5 percent of world money. Then in order to increase their money supply any specified amount, the French would have to create 20 times that amount of new money; nineteen-twentieths of any money created will flow out of the country in balance of payments deficits. This is illustrated in panel (b). Even if the French are undaunted by this and try to wag the tail by swinging the dog, other countries are unlikely to remain passive and allow France to determine their monetary policies. Thus the classical automatic adjustment

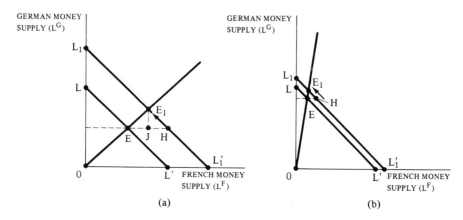

Figure 8.2. FRENCH MONEY CREATION

process effectively implies that individual countries lack control over their money supplies, except transitorily. Or, equivalently, independent national monetary policies require that the automatic adjustment process be aborted.

PROBLEMS

8.6 As in Problem **8.1,** America produces 1,000 wheat, Europe 600 cloth and in equilibrium 5 wheat exchange for 1 cloth. Initially, the world money supply consists of 2,000 gold coins, and $k = \frac{1}{2}$. Now suppose that the world money supply increases to 4,000 coins, with the increase taking place in America. Calculate the cumulative payments imbalances necessary to restore equilibrium.

8.7 In Problem **8.6,** suppose that the American money supply remains equal to 2,000 gold coins, but that economic growth in America raises wheat production to 2,000 units. Calculate the cumulative payments imbalance necessary to restore equilibrium.

8.8 Suppose that, in Problem **8.4*,** Portuguese tastes permanently change so that each Portuguese now always spends one-fourth of her income on cloth and three-fourths on wine. Find the new monetary equilibrium and calculate the cumulative payments imbalances that are necessary in order to reach this new equilibrium from the old one.

8.9* Show how the discussion of this section changes if the French, instead of doubling their money supply just once, double it every year forever.

3. Hoarding and Dishoarding: The Monetary Approach

A crucial component of the automatic adjustment process is the proposition that misallocations of world money generate payments imbalances. There are four principal channels through which this can happen. In this section we discuss the first channel, in which the world price level plays a key role. Relative prices, by contrast, play no role at all, so we assume that p, the relative price of machines in terms of wine, is constant.

Suppose that the French money supply is doubled, as with the movement from E to H in Figure 8.2. What will the French do with their extra money? They will spend it, or *dishoard:* spend more on goods than their income from selling goods. This dishoarding will continue until the French have reduced their money balances to the level that they want, that is, until the supply of money in France equals the demand. Figure 8.3(a) shows how the French would respond to a divergence between the money they have and the money they want by hoarding or dishoarding. At the origin the excess demand for money is zero—the French have just the quantity they want—so hoarding is zero also. The curve HH illustrates how much the French would hoard in response to each excess demand or dishoard in response to each excess supply. If supply exceeds demand by OA, the French dishoard AB.

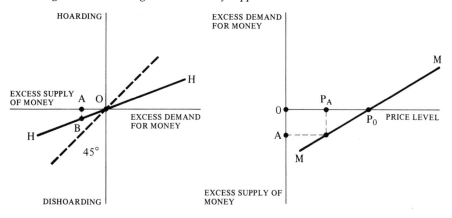

(a) **Hoarding depends upon the excess demand for money, which . . .**

(b) **is determined by the price level, given the money supply, so . . .**

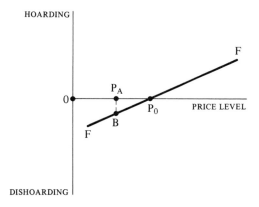

(c) **hoarding is determined by the price level, given the money supply.**

Figure 8.3. HOARDING AND DISHOARDING

KEY CONCEPTS

A nation spends less than its income in order to *hoard,* or accumulate money. If money holdings exceed demand the nation *dishoards,* or spends more than its income. Hoarding or dishoarding continues until money demands and supplies come into balance, with the time taken for this determined by the *propensity to hoard.*

The response of hoarding to an excess demand, which we call the "propensity to hoard," depends upon how impatient the French are to adjust their money holdings. If they are very impatient, and therefore are willing to temporarily decrease or increase spending in a great amount to hoard or dishoard, the *HH* line will be steep. If this line coincides with the 45-degree line, any excess money supply will be fully dishoarded at once so that adjustment is immediate. A flatter line indicates slower adjustment.

Panel (b) of Figure 8.3 shows how the demand for money depends upon the price level—the *MM* line graphs the French excess demand, $kP_W y^F - L^F$, against the French price level P_W. Point P_o shows the price that causes the demand for money to just equal the existing supply. Higher prices raise demand above this supply and lower prices reduce demand below it, so the curve has a positive slope. An increase in the French money supply would shift the curve downward by the amount of the increase.

The *HH* line shows how hoarding depends upon the excess demand for money, which *MM* in turn relates to the price level. Thus the two together have the price level determining hoarding, as shown by the *FF* schedule in panel (c). For example, the price P_A generates an excess supply of *OA*, from *MM*, and this excess supply causes hoarding of $-AB$ in panel (a). Thus *FF* shows the price P_A producing this much hoarding.

It is now time to bring Germany back into the discussion. If the French do succeed in dishoarding, that is, in buying goods with some of their extra money, it is necessary that Germany sell the goods for the money—or hoard. One country's hoarding must always be matched by dishoarding in the other country. Thus when we derive Germany's analog to the *FF* schedule, we reverse ourselves by measuring German *dishoarding* in an upward direction on the vertical axis. (Remember how the two countries were assigned opposite roles in Chapter 2, when we drew their offer curves, because we knew what one country would import the other would export. The situation is the same now.) In panel (a) of Figure 8.4, *FF* represents the French hoarding schedule, as in Figure 8.3, and *GG* represents the German. This panel corresponds to full international equilibrium, depicted earlier at point *E* in Figure 8.2. French dishoarding just matches German hoarding at the intersection of the *FF* and *GG* lines. This intersection is at *A*, on the horizontal axis, so each country's hoarding is zero: money supply equals demand in both countries. The price level, measured as *OA* in the figure, gives the value of P_W that satisfies equation (8.4).

Now suppose that the French money supply increases. This shifts *FF* downward to *F'F'* as shown in Figure 8.4 (a). Since Germany's money supply is unchanged, *GG* stays put. At the initial price level *OA* the French now want to dishoard the amount *AB*, that is, to buy additional goods worth this much from Germany. But the Germans, at *A*, do not wish to hoard. Thus the world now has an excess demand for goods (excess supply of money), so that prices must rise. Since the mechanism we are about to

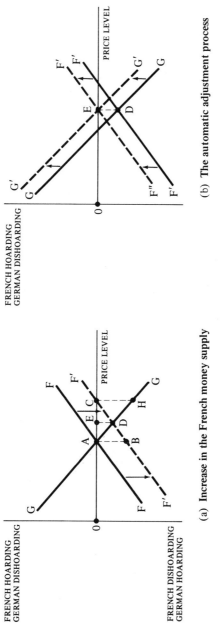

(a) Increase in the French money supply

(b) The automatic adjustment process

Figure 8.4. RESPONSE TO AN INCREASE IN THE FRENCH MONEY SUPPLY

investigate works through the world price level and not through relative price changes, we might as well suppose that the terms of trade p remains unchanged at its equilibrium value: P_W and P_M change in equal proportions.

If prices rise in the same proportion as the French money supply, so will the French demand for money. For example, if France's money supply doubles, a price rise from OA in Figure 8.4(a) to OC, where $OA = AC$, would leave the country in equilibrium with a desire to neither hoard nor dishoard. But now Germany would be out of balance; the price rise would increase the German demand for money above its unchanged supply, causing the country to want to hoard in the amount CH. This would constitute an excess supply of goods (demand for money) and would force prices back down. In fact, the price level must rise to OE, where French dishoarding of ED just matches German hoarding. Thus the increase in *France's* money supply causes temporary inflation in *both* countries and gives France a balance of payments deficit and Germany a surplus equal to ED.

Note the subtle role of price changes. An increase in one country's money supply generates world-wide inflation, but at a rate less than that of the country's monetary expansion. Thus we get an excess supply of money in one country and an excess demand in the other. This brings about the payments imbalances that set the automatic adjustment process in motion. The French deficit of ED in Figure 8.4 reduces the French money supply and increases the German money supply in the same amount. These money supply changes shift the $F'F'$ and GG schedules upward, as shown in panel (b). This shift reduces the payments imbalance and eventually eliminates it completely when the curves have moved to $F''F''$ and $G'G'$, which intersect on the horizontal axis at point E. The demand for money once again equals the supply in each country, and full equilibrium has been restored. The price level now remains constant at this new level, OE.

A key parameter is the propensity to hoard. If this is large, the initial payments imbalances are large but the world moves to the new equilibrium with great dispatch. A small propensity implies a modest but long-lived payments imbalance.

PROBLEMS

8.10 Write out Walras's Law for France, Germany, and the world. What is the sign of each term if the world is at point D in Figure 8.4(a)?

8.11 Suppose that Italy's income is equal in value to 10,000 olives and that Spain's equals 4,000 goats. In equilibrium 2 olives exchange for 1 goat. If the world money supply consists of 180,000 ounces of gold, and if $k = 2$, what are the equilibrium money supplies and money prices? If a Spanish peseta equals 2 ounces of gold and the Italian lira equals $\frac{1}{2}$ ounce of gold, what are the money supplies and money prices in terms of pesetas? In terms of lire?

8.12 Suppose, in the previous problem, that Spain obtained 72,000 ounces of additional gold from the New World. How must the money prices of goats and olives change if the Spanish excess supply of money is to just equal the Italian excess demand? Suppose that the propensity to hoard of each individual is such that everyone wants to take exactly ten years to adjust money supply to demand, performing one tenth of the adjustment in each year. What are the Spanish and Italian imbalances in the first year after the Spanish obtain the new gold? What are the new money supplies after one year, and the payments imbalances in the second year? Continue to give answers for succeeding years until the new equilibrium is reached.

8.13 Suppose that everything is as in Problem **8.12**, except that the propensity to hoard is different: each individual always wants to eliminate one-half of any discrepancy between money demand and supply in one year. Answer the questions of Problem **8.12**, for the first three years after the new gold is obtained.

8.14 Suppose in Problem **8.13**, that the Italians always wish to completely adjust their money balance to desired levels in one year, whereas the Spaniards always wish to make $\frac{7}{10}$ of the adjustment in one year. Answer the questions of Problem **8.12**.

8.15 The text described the response to a *monetary* disturbance: an increase in the French money supply. Suppose instead that the disturbance is *real*, say economic growth in Germany in the form of an increase in y^G. Analyze the response using diagrams such as Figure 8.4.

8.16 Suppose that France discovers credit cards, so that k falls in France, but not Germany. Analyze the response using a diagram such as Figure 8.4.

8.17* How do your answers to Problems **8.11** and **8.12** change if the Spanish obtain an additional 72,000 ounces of gold not just once, but each and every year?

4. Relative Price Changes: The Price-Specie Flow Mechanism

Section 3 looked at the adjustment process when all prices move together, so that relative prices are constant. When the latter in fact vary, a second aspect of the adjustment process becomes relevant. This second aspect is the one on which Hume and Cantillon themselves concentrated and is known as the price-specie flow mechanism. (Specie means precious metal, such as gold.) The terms of trade is the only relative price in our rudimentary model, so suppose that it is completely free to adjust. The discussion will be simplified if each country is completely specialized to its export good. Then y^F equals the wine produced in France when all resources are allocated to that sector, and y^G is the constant level of machine output in the specialized German economy.

Suppose again that the French double their money supply. With the terms of trade variable, the French price P_W is free to double in response, as implied by (8.1). The German money supply has not changed, so P_M remains unaltered—nothing has changed in expression (8.2). Thus the misallocation of the world's money has caused a change in relative commodity prices: the relative price p of machines in terms of wine has fallen. As a result, people shift their consumption away from wine and toward machinery. French wine exports fall and machine imports rise; France develops a payments deficit. Germany develops a corresponding surplus, as the Germans import less wine and export more machinery. As the French money supply falls and the German rises, P_W likewise falls and P_M rises, so that p rises and the payments imbalance diminishes, until the world reaches equilibrium, where p has returned to its original value and the payments imbalance has disappeared. P_W and P_M will have both increased by the same proportion as the world money supply.

The key parameters now are the trade *price elasticities*. If they are large, the change in the terms of trade induced by the monetary misallocation will produce a large change in the volume of imports and exports and thus a large payments imbalance. The movement to the new equilibrium will be rapid and the payments imbalances will be large but short-lived. Low elasticities, on the other hand, imply small, or nonexistent, payments imbalances but also preclude prompt adjustment in response to monetary misallocations.

The price-specie flow channel is illustrated in Figure 8.5. Originally, the world is at A, the intersection of the two offer curves, and the terms of trade p equals DO/DA. Suppose that the French money supply increases, thereby raising P_W and reducing p to BJ/OJ. France is at B, and Germany at C. The French wish to import OJ machines and pay BJ for them. The Germans, however, buy only CK ($=HJ$) wine from France, so the French must pay the difference BH in gold, that is, BH measures the French balance of payments deficit (measured in wine). In panel (a) the price elasticities are large and the payments imbalance is sizable, so the world will soon

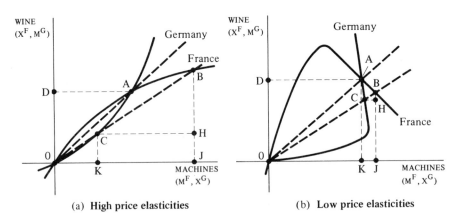

(a) High price elasticities   (b) Low price elasticities

Figure 8.5. The Price-Specie Flow Mechanism

return to *A*. Panel (b) shows that if price elasticities are low, the payments deficit *BH* will be small.

The relation with section 3 should be apparent. The key to hoarding and dishoarding is adjustment of the world price level: all prices change simultaneously. If these changes are not equiproportional, the price-specie flow mechanism also becomes relevant. In this section we have looked at the terms of trade because that is the only relative commodity price in our simple model. But in reality the price-specie flow mechanism can involve other relative prices as well. For example, all nations produce some goods and services that do not enter into international trade at all. The prices of such *nontraded goods* are more exclusively sensitive to domestic conditions, including domestic monetary conditions, than are the prices of traded goods, which compete in world markets. Thus changes in monetary conditions could induce changes in the prices of nontraded goods relative to traded goods. For example, an increase in the French money supply would cause the prices of French nontraded goods to rise relative to the prices of internationally traded goods. Then the elasticity corresponding to this relative price becomes a key parameter of the adjustment process.

Still another possibility arises from the fact that costs of shipping goods between markets and various types of *product differentiation* allow even highly similar products from different countries to sell for different prices over substantial lengths of time. Thus if both countries are producing both goods, monetary expansion in France could cause the prices of French wine and machinery to rise above the prices of German wine and machinery, respectively. The distinguishing feature of the price-specie flow mechanism is that it involves changes in *some* relative price(s). The key parameters of this channel are the price elasticities corresponding to the relevant relative price(s).

PROBLEMS

8.18 When the California Gold Rush began, the prices of ordinary consumer goods and services were driven to very high levels in the mining regions. After a while these prices fell to more normal levels. Discuss in terms of the automatic adjustment process, including reference to the channels examined in this and the preceding sections.

8.19 As in Problem **8.11,** Italy's income is 10,000 olives, Spain's is 4,000 goats, the equilibrium terms of trade equal 2 olives per goat, and $k = 2$. Initially Spain's money supply is 80,000 gold coins, and Italy's is 100,000 gold coins. Whenever the relative price of goats in terms of olives increases by one olive, the Spanish respond by increasing their imports from Italy by 1,800 olives and the Italians purchase 900 fewer goats from Spain. Suppose the Spanish money supply increases by 72,000 gold coins. Describe in detail the resulting adjustment.

8.20 The text's discussion of the price-specie flow mechanism assumed, as in equations (8.1) and (8.2), that the demand for money in each country is proportional to that country's *production* of goods. Sometimes it is argued instead that money demand is proportional to *demand* for a country's goods. Can you think of any reason for one to be the case rather than the other? To see what difference it makes, suppose that each country consumes only the other country's products, that is, the French consume only machines, and the Germans only wine. Then French demand for money will be proportional to (py^G) rather than to y^F, and German money demand will be proportional to (y^F/p) instead of to y^G. What difference does this make to this section's discussion of the automatic adjustment process?

8.21* In section 4 of Chapter 7 we examined the *transfer problem:* the effect of an international transfer upon the terms of trade. The price-specie flow mechanism is really just the transfer problem in reverse: a change in the terms of trade (due to an international misallocation of money) causes a transfer (that is, a payments imbalance). In view of this, what condition must the marginal propensities to import of France and Germany satisfy in order for the price-specie flow mechanism to operate as discussed in this section? How would our discussion have to be changed if this condition were violated?

8.22* Discuss the role of the Marshall-Lerner condition in the price-specie flow channel of the automatic adjustment process.

5. **Exploring Further:* Nontraded Goods

This section looks in more detail at the role of nontraded goods. Figure 8.6 shows a case where the terms of trade remain fixed, but both traded goods prices change relative to the price of nontraded goods. With the price of machines in terms of wine invariant, we can use this price to compare the two products and then measure their total, expressed in units of wine, on the vertical axis. The nontraded good is measured on the horizontal axis, and TT' denotes the country's production possibility frontier.

In initial equilibrium, the country produces at E, where TT' is tangent to the community indifference curve U_E. Thus OA nontraded goods are produced and, since they are nontraded, OA must be the quantity consumed as well. The country is producing AE traded goods, valued in terms of wine, and since the balance of payments is in equilibrium, AE must also equal the value of traded goods consumed, so that point E represents consumption as well as production. (Since the diagram adds all traded goods together, it cannot show the exchange of wine for machines.) Now suppose the money supply increases. Panel (a) shows what happens if all prices rise in the same proportion, so that the only reaction is the hoarding discussed in section 3. With relative prices unchanged, production remains at E, so that the dashed line through E still reflects national income. But the larger money supply causes the country to dishoard or spend more than its income: the dashed line through B now reflects national spending. Since OA nontraded goods are still produced, OA must be consumed. The country produces AE traded goods and consumes BA. The difference BE shows total dishoarding and equals the balance of payments deficit.

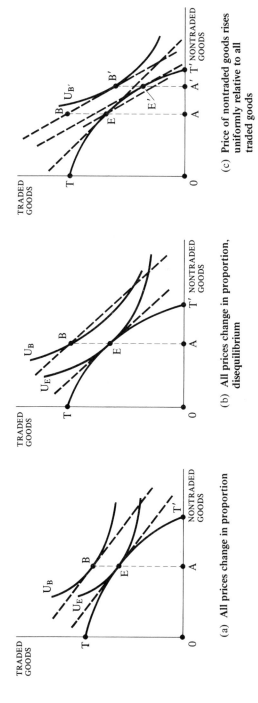

Figure 8.6. Nontraded Goods and the Adjustment Process

But probably relative prices will change. The indifference curve through *B* may not be tangent to the spending line—this is shown in panel (b).

Panel (c) shows how things change when domestic monetary expansion raises nontraded goods prices relative to those of traded goods (but with the terms of trade unchanged). Domestic prices are now reflected in the steeper spending line through *B* and *B'*. The higher nontraded goods prices cause production to shift from *E* to *E'*. Consumption of nontraded goods must equal their production, *OA'*, so dishoarding and the balance of payments deficit now equal *B'E'*. Price elasticities now become important because they determine the movements from *E* to *E'* and from *B* to *B'*.

PROBLEM

8.23 The presence of nontraded goods increases the likelihood that relative price effects will influence the adjustment process, but are they likely to increase or to decrease the speed of that adjustment and the size of payments imbalances? Why?

6. Income Adjustment

We come next to the role in the adjustment process of the Keynesian theory studied in Chapter 4. Since this channel works through income changes rather than either absolute or relative prices, assume that both P_W and P_M remain fixed so that we not worry about what we have just studied.

Figure 8.7 shows our initial full equilibrium. Income equals *OE* and $X - M = O$ so that there is no payments imbalance. (Review Chapter 4 if necessary.) Now consider again a doubling of the money supply. The easier monetary conditions decrease *S-I*. This could happen for either or both of two reasons. First, individuals with larger money balances might now dis-

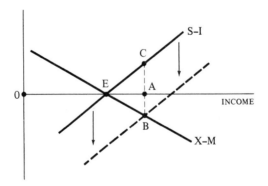

Figure 8.7.   INCREASE IN INVESTMENT

hoard, as discussed in section 3. This would be reflected in a reduction of saving, S. Second, the easier monetary conditions could stimulate investment, I. In Figure 8.7 the S-I curve shifts down by the amount CB, producing a multiplied increase in income from E to A. As income increases, imports do likewise. There has been no increase in the foreign money supply and accordingly no stimulus to foreign S-I, so that domestic exports do not change. Thus we develop a balance of payments deficit of AB. Once again the automatic adjustment process is off and running.

Note that the S-I curve plays the same role here as the hoarding schedule in section 3: S-I equals domestic hoarding. The only difference is that in section 3 hoarding depended on the price level; now it depends on income, reflecting our shift in interest.

As the deficit continues, the consequent flow of money abroad tightens monetary conditions at home and loosens them abroad. This erodes the initial stimulus to domestic income and begins to stimulate income abroad, reducing the payments imbalance. The payments imbalances cease when the world reaches the new equilibrium. Both home and foreign incomes have now increased in the same proportion as the world's money supply. How would this process affect equations (8.1), (8.2), (8.3), and (8.4) if it were in response to an initial increase in the French money supply?

If both countries initially were experiencing no unemployment these higher levels cannot be sustained. Both countries have moved along their Phillips curves, as discussed in section 7 of Chapter 4. World inflation will ensue until both incomes fall back to their initial levels and both price levels rise in the same proportion as the stock of world money, that is, until after a period of stagflation.

Key parameters for the income channel of the automatic adjustment process are the *marginal propensities to import*. If these propensities are high, the income adjustments caused by monetary misallocations will induce large payments imbalances, and thus rapid adjustment.

PROBLEMS

8.24 How does the discussion in the text change if the home country is so small that the flow of money abroad brought about by the home balance of payments deficit has no significant effect on the rest of the world? Show the final equilibrium in Figure 8.7.

8.25 Suppose that domestic residents suddenly decide to save more than before at each level of income. Discuss the consequences. Do the same if instead domestic goods become more attractive to foreigners, so that exports rise.

7. International Capital Mobility

So far we have considered nothing beyond imports and exports other than the means of payment (gold coins, or money). Thus the balance of trade surplus (value of exports minus that of imports) has coincided with the balance of payments (total payments received from foreigners minus total payments made to foreigners, or the net acquisition of money from abroad).

The fact that countries also borrow from and lend to each other furnishes a fourth channel of adjustment. A sale of assets (other than money) to foreigners—denoted by C—and the interest income from assets previously purchased from foreigners—denoted by E—can both be used, like the sale of exports, to finance the purchase of imports. The excess of the three former items over the latter equals the net receipt of money from abroad, or balance of payments surplus, denoted B.

$$(P_W X - P_M M) + E + C \equiv B. \tag{8.5}$$

Individuals in both France and Germany can hold their wealth either in the form of money or in non-monetary form. Presumably they choose the most desirable proportions, weighing the fact that money is highly liquid against the fact that other assets yield a return (interest). Suppose now that, as before, the French money supply doubles. This sets in motion the adjustments described in previous sections. But in addition the French have greatly increased their holdings of monetary assets vis-à-vis non-monetary assets. In order to redress the balance they will wish to exchange a good part of their additional money for other assets; that is, to run a capital account deficit and accompanying balance-of-payments deficit. The prices of non-monetary assets will be bid up sufficiently to induce the Germans to supply them in exchange for money in quantities equal to the French demand for the former and supply of the latter. The result is that the capital account *(C)* and the balance of payments *(B)* both become negative and the world quickly adjusts, whereupon the payments imbalances quickly cease. Thus international capital movements allow an international monetary misallocation to be substantially corrected by a prompt reshuffling of assets between countries, avoiding to that extent the more or less prolonged trade deficits required by the other three channels of adjustment.

The key parameter is the *degree of international capital mobility.* To the extent that the international exchange of assets is limited, whether by regulation, by the lack of international financial markets, or by an unwillingness on the part of citizens of one country to acquire the assets of another, adjustment must take place through the other channels via the balance of trade. In practice capital mobility varies widely. Bonds issued by multinational corporations and the governments of industrial states have international markets, whereas the obligations of smaller entities tend to be traded only locally. Some governments severely restrict the freedom of their residents to trade assets with foreigners, while other countries are viewed as so risky that they can sell few if any of their assets. Canadian firms and governing bodies regularly float bond issues in New York, but many LDCs can sell few bonds and must borrow largely from banks.

Figure 8.8 illustrates adjustment via international capital movements and shows the role of the degree of capital mobility. *FF* depicts the French excess demand for bonds (or for non-monetary assets in general). The position of this curve depends upon the size of the French money supply and the French supply of bonds. The line has a positive slope because an increase in the interest rate paid by bonds makes them more attractive compared to money, which pays no interest, and so increases the demand for bonds. Similarly, an increase in the interest rate raises the German demand for bonds; thus *GG*, which shows the excess *supply* of bonds in Germany, slopes down.

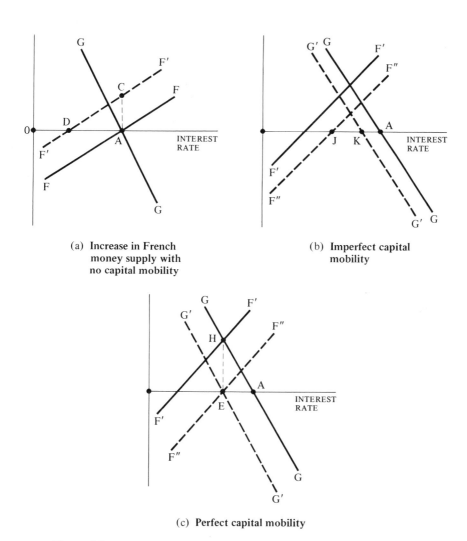

(a) **Increase in French money supply with no capital mobility**

(b) **Imperfect capital mobility**

(c) **Perfect capital mobility**

Figure 8.8. INTERNATIONAL CAPITAL MOVEMENTS

> **KEY CONCEPTS**
>
> *Perfect international capital mobility* means that domestic and foreign bonds are regarded as equivalent by the market, so they must yield the same interest. With *no international capital mobility* national bonds cannot be traded between countries, so there is no direct pressure to equalize interest rates. The intermediate possibility of *imperfect international capital mobility* encompasses all cases where national bonds can be traded internationally but are not fully equivalent: a reduction in the domestic interest rate relative to the foreign rate will make domestic bonds less attractive but will not cause everyone to refuse to hold any of them.

Suppose that initially the world is in equilibrium at *A*. The demand for bonds equals the supply in both countries, which share a common interest rate equal to *OA*. Now suppose the French money supply increases. Since the French intitally owned money and bonds in the proportions they desired, they now have relatively too much money and too few bonds, that is, the excess demand for bonds has risen. *FF* shifts up to *F'F'* in Figure 8.8(a).

What happens next depends upon the degree of international capital mobility. Panel (a) shows the case of absolutely no mobility. Nothing has happened in Germany: the German interest rate remains equal to *OA* and the demand for bonds continues to equal the supply. But in France there is now an excess demand for bonds of *AC* at the initial interest rate *OA*. The French cannot buy the bonds they want from the Germans, so they try to buy them from each other. As French bond sellers realize how easy it has become to sell bonds, they reduce the interest they pay. The French interest rate then falls to *OD*, where the demand for bonds again equals the supply. The capital account balance necessarily remains equal to zero, and the balance of payments can be influenced only by the three channels discussed in earlier sections. For example the increased money supply could also raise prices, and the reduction in interest rates from *OA* to *OD* should spur investment.

Panel (c) shows the opposite extreme of perfect capital mobility: there are no barriers to international asset sales, and everyone views French and German bonds as equivalent. Then the two must pay the same interest, because no one would ever buy the bond with a lower interest rate. In this case the international bond market comes into equilibrium at point *H*, where the French excess demand for bonds just equals the German excess supply, at a common interest rate *OE*. Germany sells the quantity *HE* of bonds to France, so that France runs a capital account deficit of that magnitude and Germany a corresponding surplus. When the transaction is completed, the French curve $F'F'$ shifts down, because the French have more bonds and less money than before. Similarly GG shifts down because Germany has fewer bonds and more money. The two curves shift respectively to $F''F''$ and $G'G'$, which intersect at the new equilibrium, E. Each country's capital account balance is now zero: the international asset adjustment has been accomplished.

The intermediate case of imperfect capital mobility is shown in Figure 8.8(b). French and German bonds are traded but they need not pay the same interest rate because they are not perfect substitutes for each other. The French interest rate falls to OJ and the German to OK. The French interest rate falls more than it would with perfect mobility but less than with no mobility, whereas the German rate does just the opposite. The French purchase German bonds, experiencing a capital account deficit. When the sale is completed, the deficit disappears and $F'F'$ and GG shift to $F''F''$ and $G'G'$ respectively. Further adjustment takes place through the channels discussed in earlier sections and affects the trade balance. The French interest rate OJ remains less than the German rate OK even though the capital account now remains in balance. But the difference in national interest rates is not as large as it would be with no capital mobility, as shown in panel (a).

PROBLEMS

8.26 A minor qualification is necessary to the above discussion. The initial increase in France's money supply implies that world wealth has been reallocated from Germany to France, although by a much smaller proportion than the rise in French money since money is only one part of wealth. Thus the French might desire to dishoard *wealth,* and the Germans hoard it until the original proportions are restored. This means that the intial international capital movement will not move the world quite all the way to its new equilibrium. In this case, how would the rest of the adjustment be accomplished, if at all?

8.27 This section showed how an increase in the French money supply would cause a permanent fall in the French interest rate and, unless capital is completely mobile internationally, a temporary capital account deficit. But nothing was said about net interest income, represented by E in equation (8.5). Discuss the behavior of E in both the short run and the long run. How does this behavior fit into the automatic adjustment process?

8.28* How is the discussion of this section changed if the French increase in money is repeated year after year indefinitely?

8.29* How is the discussion of this section changed if the intial disturbance is not an increase in the French money supply but rather an increase in real output y^F? If y^F continues to increase at the same rate year after year indefinitely?

8. Overview: The Channels of Adjustment

We have now examined four distinct channels through which monetary misallocations induce payments deficits: hoarding, relative price changes, variations in aggregate demand, and international capital movements. Thus we would expect that an increase in the French money supply would be partially offset by a prompt and large but fleeting capital-account deficit, would raise world prices and thus stimulate hoarding in Germany and dishoarding in France, would raise French prices relative to foreign ones and so make French goods less competitive in world markets, and would also stimulate French aggregate demand. The relative importance of these four channels would be sensitive to the magnitudes of the key parameters discussed above and constitutes a difficult empirical problem.

But it is also true that the four channels reflect quite different views of how the world economy operates. The hoarding mechanism is basically an extension of the classical view of money as a "veil"; adjustment is completely independent of relative prices and employment. For this reason analysis emphasizing this channel is sometimes referred to as the "monetary approach to the balance of payments," a usage that could be a bit confusing in that the automatic adjustment process is itself a monetary phenomenon, regardless of the channel through which it works. Adjustment through international capital movements reduces the process to one of rearranging financial portfolios and so is likewise in itself independent of the real side of the economy. Those who see the automatic adjustment process as working mainly through these two channels would be unlikely to see much scope for independent national monetary policies.

The heart of the price-specie flow mechanism, on the other hand, is an essential interaction between the real and monetary sides of the economy via the price system. Thus elasticity optimism and elasticity pessimism, discussed in Chapter 2, once again come to the fore. For example, an elasticity pessimist who viewed the price-specie flow mechanism as the chief channel of adjustment would expect payments imbalances to correct themselves very slowly, if at all, so that individual countries would possess considerable scope for independent monetary policies, though such independence would be expected to be quite disruptive if exercised.

Income adjustment, simply because it makes employment endogenous to the adjustment process, necessarily implies greater concern with the adjustment relative to the final result. In addition those who regard this channel as the basic one also tend both to regard that process as slow and uncertain and to be much more concerned with short-run to medium-run problems. Thus they would give little if any weight to the self-corrective aspects of the theory and instead emphasize measures to deal with the transitional employment problems. The automatic adjustment process is seen as a constraint rather than a blessing, and so the policy view is that it ought to be aborted whenever convenient to do so. This gives rise to a conflict between internal balance (aggregate demand) and external balance (the balance of payments) analogous to that discussed in Chapter 4. We shall return to this later.

We examined the various channels of adjustment by discussing the consequences of a purely *monetary* disturbance—an increase in the French money supply. The process can be further illuminated by examining the consequences of a *real* shock. Suppose, for example, that people's tastes change from French goods toward German goods, or from wine toward machinery, so that the equilibrium relative price p of machines in terms of wine rises (in terms of the discussion of Chapter 2, the German offer curve shifts in and the French offer curve shifts out). In Figure 8.9 the line OH shifts to OH', so that E_1 is the new equilibrium. (The amount of this shift, and the distance between E and E_1, will be smaller the larger the price elasticities happen to be, since large elasticities mean that only small price changes are necessary to effect large quantity changes.)

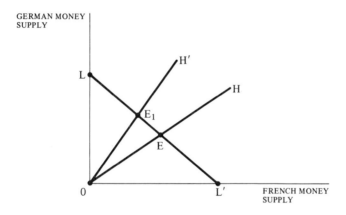

Figure 8.9. A REAL DISTURBANCE

If the increased demand for German goods and reduced demand for French goods cause relative prices quickly to adjust to clear the commodity markets, the necessary monetary adjustment from E to E_1 can be achieved by international capital movements and/or hoarding and dishoarding. The Germans acquire the additional money they need by selling goods and bonds to the French. But to the extent that prices are sluggish, the other two channels will be utilized. The increase in machine demand and reduction in wine demand will increase French imports and reduce exports, causing a recession in France and a boom in Germany. The payments deficit will move the world from E toward E_1, with the monetary contraction in France tending to push down prices (as well as income and employment) and the reverse in Germany, eventually bringing about the required relative price adjustment.

9. Monetary Systems

So far we have assumed a very rudimentary monetary system. It is time to consider more complex and realistic systems.

The Gold Standard. The monetary units (francs, marks, lire, dollars, and so on) of the countries adhering to a gold standard are all defined in terms of gold. So far in this chapter we have assumed that money consists solely of gold coins, so that the only difference between French and German money is the symbol appearing on the coins. This is a special example of the gold standard, called the *gold-coin standard.* Such a system has never really existed in pure form, perhaps the closest recent example being Egypt in the days of the British Empire, where British gold sovereigns formed the main medium of exchange.

A more realistic description would be as follows. Money consists of both gold coins and paper notes (and perhaps also of demand deposits). The government mint will accept gold to be struck into coins or vice versa, as under a gold-coin standard. The central bank would also be prepared to redeem paper money for gold on demand. Thus all of the country's money would be valued in terms of gold, although gold need not form a large part of the actual circulating medium.

Indeed gold coins might be dispensed with entirely. Ricardo advocated a *gold-bullion standard* in which gold would not be minted into coins, so that money would consist only of paper notes (and deposits), which the central bank would exchange on demand for gold bars.

The central feature of the gold standard is the direct fixing of the *value* of a country's money in terms of gold. Thus the monies of any pair of countries on a gold standard are fixed in value relative to each other, regardless of whether they consist of identical physical objects, as under a gold-coin standard. In the latter case a government has little monetary responsibility beyond the operation of a mint to strike coins as required. In the other forms of the gold standard the central bank must hold *reserves,* a stock of gold that can be used to redeem paper money. It is the willingness of the central bank to sell from its reserves in exchange for paper money, or to add gold to its reserves by buying it with newly created paper money, which maintains the value of the nation's money in terms of gold.

Gold-Exchange Standard. A country can tie the value of its money to gold not only directly, by standing ready to exchange its money for gold, but also indirectly by standing ready to exchange its money for that of some other country which is on a gold standard. This is called a *gold-exchange standard.* The central bank of a country on such a standard would hold its reserves not in gold (though it might still own some) but in the money of some gold-standard country or else in bonds or bills denominated in that money. For example, in the years before the First World War India held its reserves in the form of assets denominated in British sterling and maintained the value of the rupee in terms of the pound. Since Britain was on the gold standard this served to indirectly maintain the value of the rupee in terms of gold.

Other Metallic Standards. Other metals might play the role of gold in the above discussion. Copper has been used for money and silver long served as a medium of exchange along with, or instead of, gold. Thus we can think of various types of silver standard analogous to the versions of the gold standard. The *bimetallic standard* fixes the value of money in terms of both gold and silver, and thus also fixes the relative price of the two precious metals.

Convertible Paper. A country might also tie the value of its money to that of another country which is not on the gold standard; the first country would then hold its international reserves in the form of assets denominated in the currency of the latter country. The monies of a group of countries tied together in such a way would be fixed in value relative to each other.

Inconvertible Paper (Flexible Exchange Rates). The above monetary standards all share one crucial property: the relative values of the monies of all countries on a standard are fixed. That is, they imply *fixed exchange rates* (an exchange rate, you will recall, is the relative price of one money in terms of another). It is also possible that central banks might just issue fiat money and *not* stand ready to redeem it at a fixed price for some commodity (such as gold) or some foreign money. In this case exchange rates would not be fixed but would be determined by market conditions, as are the prices of other assets and goods. International adjustment through the balance of payments, the topic of this chapter, would be replaced or supported by adjustment through exchange-rate variations. Such adjustment is the topic of the next chapter.

THE AUTOMATIC ADJUSTMENT PROCESS UNDER VARIOUS STANDARDS

The discussion of the automatic adjustment process was conducted on the assumption of a gold-coin standard. It applies, however, to all the systems described in this section, except for flexible exchange rates. The automatic adjustment process consists of three basic ingredients, of which the first two, the equilibrium allocation of world money and the payments imbalances generated by a misallocation, depend crucially upon fixed exchange rates. These are common to all the standards. Let us consider, therefore, the third ingredient, the Rules of the Game.

Suppose that France is experiencing a balance of payments deficit and Germany a surplus. Then the Germans are selling more goods and non-monetary assets to France than they are buying, and are therefore acquiring French money. Under a gold-coin standard the Germans acquire French gold coins. These can be circulated in Germany, or they can be melted down and struck into German coins by the German mint. The institutional arrangement inevitably implies that the French money supply decreases and the German increases by the amount of the payments imbalance.

Suppose then that one of the other standards (except for flexible exchange rates) holds, and that the Germans acquire French notes rather than gold coin. The Germans require German money rather than French money. Therefore they redeem their French notes with the French central bank for gold (gold standard) or for some other money (gold-exchange standard or convertible paper), which they then sell to the German central bank for marks. The French central bank sells international reserves and buys francs in an amount equal to the payments deficit, and the German central bank acquires reserves and sells marks in a like amount. Thus the payments imbalance reduces the French money supply and increases the German, just as under a gold-coin standard. Indeed it might even have a greater effect now, if the loss of reserves by the French central bank causes it to contract the note issue, or if the monetary assets purchased by the French central bank served as the base for a private banking system.

Monetary Standards in Practice. Gold and silver served as the basis for most monies until well into the nineteenth century. During that century gold gradually displaced silver until, during the quarter century or so before the First World War, the major nations were joined in a gold standard. India and Austria-Hungary participated via gold-exchange standards. The war brought about the collapse of this system, but afterwards there was an attempt to restore the gold standard. But because of wartime inflation, and because the United States had acquired many assets, including gold, during the war, people feared that there was a shortage of gold elsewhere. Thus when the gold standard was restored, Britain adopted the gold bullion form (dispensing with the need for gold for coinage) and some other countries adopted a gold-exchange standard (dispensing with the need for gold reserves). The British return to the gold standard in 1926 was criticized by Keynes (notably in a pamphlet entitled "The Economic Consequences of Mr. Churchill"—Winston Churchill was chancellor of the Exchequer at the time) on the grounds that it would necessitate unemployment. At any rate the British economy stagnated. The Depression occasioned a widespread abandonment of the gold standard and cases of both convertible and inconvertible paper. After the Second World War a gold exchange standard was established in which the United States assumed the responsibility of fixing the value of the dollar in terms of gold, and other countries undertook to fix their currencies in terms of dollars. During the sixties the U.S. responsibility gradually eroded so that the system came to more closely resemble a paper (dollar) standard. In the seventies the major industrial countries have ceased to commit themselves to maintain the values of their currencies relative to any common standard, so that the system of fixed exchange rates has ended. However most LDCs continue to fix the values of their currencies in terms of some major currency or composite of currencies (so there is a group of countries on a dollar standard, and so on), and a varying group (the "snake") of European countries have undertaken to maintain the values of their currencies relative to each other. Also the major industrial countries have continued to buy and sell reserves even though they no longer accept obligations to maintain fixed exchange rates.

10. Case Study: The Gold Standard of 1880–1914

Several features of the period of the gold standard are noteworthy. *First,* this was a time of relatively free trade and substantial international capital mobility, although some countries were quite protectionist and nationalism became increasingly prominent. *Second,* the major countries remained on the system without major difficulty, that is, the gold standard worked. *Third,* Britain played a central role. London was the major internaional financial center, and Britain, as we saw in Chapter 7, was a large-scale lender of long-term and short-term capital. *Fourth,* because of London's role as a financial center, the Bank of England was able to influence substantially short-term capital flows by changes in interest rates, and was thereby able to manage with relatively small gold reserves. Other countries maintained larger reserves and experienced swings in them. *Fifth,* the major countries experienced boom and bust together, and there appear to have been no large adjustments of relative prices. *Sixth,* there were large current account deficits and surpluses financed by large-scale long-term capital movements, with Britain, France and Germany the main lenders.

Economic historians have often noted that price movements apparently did not take place to bring about international adjustment, as required by the price-specie flow mechanism. It is natural to try to explain this in terms of the other three channels of adjustment. We noted above that capital movements played a role. Adjustment through variations in incomes and employment and through hoarding have also been offered as explanations. Further, the absence of sizable price movements does not imply that the price-specie flow mechanism was not relevant. If price elasticities are large—the circumstance most conducive to the mechanism—only small or incipient price changes are necessary to induce adjustment.

The simplest explanation is pure luck: perhaps things just happened to work out in those years so that adjustment was not necessary. A more sophisticated version of this explanation would note that the collection of countries participating in the gold standard was not determined at random: individual countries elected to adopt the standard when they viewed participation as feasible and advantageous. This self-selection process would imply that adjustment problems would be much more likely to arise between countries on the standard and those off of it, rather than among the countries adhering to the gold standard.

Although the gold standard worked, the countries on it experienced much boom and bust together. Also the disastrous attempt to restore the standard after the First World War gave it a bad name for many years. But some of President Reagan's advisers would like to bring it back, and a commission was appointed to study the issue as part of an investigation into the role of gold.

11. The Balance of Payments and the Domestic Banking System

A hypothetical example profitably illustrates the mechanics of payments imbalances with actual modern banking systems. Suppose that the French and German central banks hold international reserves in the form of U.S. dollars ($). The French central bank will buy or sell reserves for francs (fr) at the rate of fr4 per dollar. The German central bank likewise maintains the value of the Deutsche mark (DM) at two per dollar. Thus fr2 will always exchange for DM1. Table 8.1 shows hypothetical balance sheets for all parties. A balance sheet lists all the assets and liabilities of a party at a particular time. Since net worth is defined as the excess of assets over liabilities, the total value of all assets must always exactly equal the total value of all liabilities plus net worth.

In this example, the assets of the French public consist of fr2500 in demand deposits in French commercial banks plus fr1000 of other assets; the sole liabilities of the public are fr2000 in loans borrowed from the commercial banks. Thus the net worth of the French public is fr1500, the excess of total assets over liabilities.

The demand deposits of the public constitute the liabilities of the commercial banks, since a deposit is an obligation to pay the depositor. Suppose that the commercial banks are required to keep reserves at the central bank, equal to one-fifth of total deposits, and suppose that the commercial banks hold only this minimum requirement. Then the assets of the commercial banks consist of the required reserves (fr500) plus the loans they have made to the public. The liabilities of the French central bank are the fr500 of reserves deposited there by the commercial banks. Assets consist of French government bonds owned by the central bank plus its stock of

Table 8.1. Hypothetical Initial Situation

(a) The French Public

Assets	Liabilities, Net Worth
Demand Deposits: fr2500	Loans: fr2000
Other Assets: fr1000	Net Worth: fr1500

(b) French Commercial Banks

Assets	Liabilities
Reserves: fr500	Demand Deposits: fr2500
Loans: fr2000	

(c) The French Central Bank

Assets	Liabilities
Government Bonds: fr300	Commercial Bank Reserves: fr500
International Reserves: fr200 [$50]	

(d) The German Public

Assets	Liabilities, Net Worth
Demand Deposits: DM1500	Loans: DM1200
Other Assets: DM500	Net Worth: DM800

(e) German Commercial Banks

Assets	Liabilities
Reserves: DM300	Demand Deposits: DM1500
Loans: DM1200	

(f) The German Central Bank

Assets	Liabilities
Government Bonds: DM200	Commercial Bank Reserves: DM300
International Reserves: DM100 ($50)	

international reserves. Suppose that the latter consists of $50, valued therefore at fr200.

Panels (d), (e), and (f) of Table 8.1 show the analogous information for Germany. The example supposes that German commercial banks are also required to hold reserves equal to one-fifth of total deposits, and that the German central bank owns $50 of international reserves.

Now suppose that France runs a balance of payments deficit of fr100 (= DM50) with Germany by buying that value of goods more from Germany than it sells. Table 8.2 shows all the changes in balance sheets resulting from the deficit. The French pay for the extra fr100 worth of goods by means of a check drawn on their account with a French commercial bank. Thus the immediate impact of the deficit, labeled (1), is that the French public's demand deposits decline by fr100, and this also constitutes a decline in net worth. The German public receives the check, so its net worth increases by DM50 (= fr100) and its assets are augmented by a demand deposit of fr100. The German public, however, wants its money in the form of marks, not francs, so in the second stage, denoted (2), the German public sells to the French central bank (either directly or through intermediaries) the fr100 check in exchange for $25 of international reserves. The German public then sells the $25 to the German central bank for DM50, which it deposits in its accounts with the German commercial banks, whose reserves thereby increase by DM50. When the French central bank clears the fr100 check with the French commercial bank on which it is drawn, the latter must pay from its reserves, which therefore fall by fr100. The final stage, labeled (3) in the table, occurs when the commercial banks adjust to their new reserve positions. The French commercial banks have lost fr100 of reserves; with a reserve requirement of one-fifth, this requires a fr500 contraction of deposits. Deposits have in fact fallen by only fr100, so the banks must call in loans and allow deposits to fall by another fr400. The German commercial banks are in just the opposite position.

The final situation is shown in Table 8.3. Note, first, that the payment imbalance of fr100 (= DM50 = $25) has resulted in a flow of $25 of international reserves from the French central bank to the German central bank, and a corresponding decline in French net worth and rise in German net worth. This is the analog to the flow of gold coins discussed earlier in this chapter. The reserve flow does not itself constitute changes in money supplies, as it does under the simple gold-coin standard. But it does act directly to reduce commercial bank reserves in the deficit country and increase them in the surplus country. This in turn causes a contraction of the money supply in the former and an expansion in the latter, to a degree determined by reserve requirements. With a requirement of one-fifth, the French money supply has contracted by fr500 and the German has expanded by DM250.

Table 8.2. Mechanics of a fr100 French Payments Deficit (DM50 German Payments Surplus)

(a) The French Public

Assets	Liabilities, Net Worth
Demand Deposits: (1) − fr100 (3) − fr400	Loans: (3) − fr400
	Net Worth: (1) − fr100

(b) French Commercial Banks

Assets	Liabilities
Reserves: (2) − fr100	Demand Deposits: (2) − fr100 (3) − fr400
Loans: (3) − fr400	

(c) The French Central Bank

Assets	Liabilities
International Reserves: (2) − fr100	Commercial Bank Reserves: (2) − fr100

(d) The German Public

Assets	Liabilities, Net Worth
Demand Deposits: (1) + fr100 (2) − fr100 (2) + DM50 (3) + DM200	Loans: (3) + DM200
	Net Worth: (1) + DM50

(e) German Commercial Banks

Assets	Liabilities
Reserves: (2) + DM50	Demand Deposits: (2) + DM50 (3) + DM200
Loans: (3) + DM200	

(f) The German Central Bank

Assets	Liabilities
International Reserves: (2) + DM50	Commercial Bank Reserves: (2) + DM50

Table 8.3. Situation After the Fr100 Payments Imbalance

(a) The French Public

Assets	Liabilities, Net Worth
Demand Deposits: fr2000	Loans: fr1600
Other Assets: fr1000	Net Worth: fr1400

(b) French Commercial Banks

Assets	Liabilities
Reserves: fr400	Demand Deposits: fr2000
Loans: fr1600	

(c) The French Central Bank

Assets	Liabilities
Government Bonds: fr300	Commercial Bank Reserves: fr400
International Reserves: fr100 ($25)	

(d) The German Public

Assets	Liabilities, Net Worth
Demand Deposits: DM1750	Loans: DM1400
Other Assets: DM500	Net Worth: DM850

(e) German Commercial Banks

Assets	Liabilities
Reserves: DM350	Demand Deposits: DM1750
Loans: DM1400	

(f) The German Central Bank

Assets	Liabilities
Government Bonds: DM200	Commercial Bank Reserves: DM350
International Reserves: DM150 ($75)	

PROBLEMS

8.30 Work through the example in the text if the French reserve requirement is one-tenth rather than one-fifth (keep the German equal to one-fifth).

8.31 Suppose that in Italy the money supply is 300,000 lire while the Spanish money supply equals 60,000 pesetas. In each country money is in the form of paper notes, but the central bank will exchange its money on demand for gold. In Spain the central bank will buy or sell pesetas for 2 ounces of gold each, and the Italian central bank will exchange a half-ounce of gold for each lira. Each central bank has 50,000 ounces of gold in its international reserves. Suppose that Italy experiences a balance of payments deficit of 40,000 lire, and Spain accordingly has a surplus of 10,000 pesetas. Describe what happens, and calculate the money supplies and international reserve stocks in the two countries after the payments imbalance takes place.

8.32 In Problem **8.31,** suppose that Italian law or custom guarantees that at all times the size of the Italian money supply equals exactly 6 lire for each ounce of gold contained in the international reserves of the Italian central bank. How does your answer to Problem **8.31** change?

8.33 Suppose, in Problems **8.31** and **8.32,** that each central bank initially has a stock of reserves equal to 50,000 dollars, that the Italian central bank will exchange 2 lire for a dollar, and that the Spanish central bank will exchange a peseta for 2 dollars. How do your answers change?

12. The Rules of the Game and Monetary Policy

The third ingredient of the automatic adjustment process, the Rules of the Game, is that payments deficits should reduce a nation's money supply and that surpluses should increase it. This is inevitable under a gold-coin standard but not with more realistic monetary systems.

STERILIZATION

Suppose that France is running a balance of payments deficit, with the French central bank selling reserves for (paper) francs and the German central bank correspondingly selling marks for reserves. Then the French money supply is falling and the German is rising. If this is the whole story (and under the gold-coin standard it must be, unless the world gold stock changes), then the payments imbalance is in fact redistributing world money as required for the automatic adjustment process. But this need not be the whole story. For example, the French central bank could further reduce the French money supply by selling bonds for francs, thereby taking the latter out of circulation. In this case the policy *reinforces* the monetary contraction produced by the payments deficit: the Rules of the Game are being followed. But, on the other hand, the French central bank might put new francs into circulation (by buying bonds from the public with newly printed francs). This policy tends to *sterilize* the monetary contraction produced by the payments deficit; the Rules of the Game are being violated. If the French central bank creates money at a rate equal to the payments deficit the latter is completely sterilized by the former and the French money supply remains constant. Analogously the German central bank could withdraw marks from circulation (by selling bonds to the public) so as to prevent the German money supply from rising. In such a case the payments imbalance is redistributing international *reserves* from France to Germany but it is not redistributing *money;* the automatic adjustment process is being aborted.

KEY CONCEPT

A central bank *sterilizes* a payments imbalance (violates the Rules of the Game) if it wholly or partially prevents that imbalance from changing the size of the domestic money supply.

Table 8.4 shows the changes in the balance sheet of the French central bank if it sterilizes the fr100 deposit shown in Tables 8.2 and 8.3. The entries in *italics* are the same as in Table 8.2 and show the direct effect of the payments deficit: a reduction in international reserves and in the reserves of the commercial banks, the latter leading to a decrease of the money supply. The other two entries show the sterilization operation: an increase in the holdings of government bonds and in commercial bank reserves. (Sterilization is just like any other open market operation. The central bank buys bonds from the public with a check drawn on itself; the public deposits the check in a commercial bank, which in turn adds the check to its reserves with the central bank.) On balance, the liabilities of the central bank do not change at all, so that, as desired, the money supply is not affected. The only effect of the sterilized deficit is to alter the composition of central-bank assets: government bond holdings increase and international reserves fall by equal amounts.

In Figure 8.10 point *H* represents an international monetary misallocation at which France is running a payments deficit and the rest of the world is running a surplus. France is depicted as small relative to the rest of the world, realistic for a single country. If both central banks refrain from

Table 8.4. ATTEMPTED STERILIZATION OF A FR100 DEFICIT

Assets	*Liabilities*
Government Bonds: +fr100	Commercial Bank Reserves:
International Reserves: *−fr100*	*−fr100;* +fr100

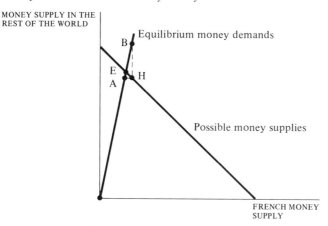

Figure 8.10. Sterilization

interfering with the monetary consequences of the payments imbalances, the world gradually moves from *H* to equilibrium at *E*. Central-bank reinforcement of these payments consequences speeds up the movement, and partial sterilization slows it down. If both central banks completely sterilize, the world stays put at *H* and the payments imbalances continue unchecked.

Why might a central bank wish to do this? To prevent the internal economic adjustments associated with the correction of the payments imbalance. Consider income adjustment for example. To the extent that this channel is relevant, the reduction of the French payments deficit requires a reduction in French aggregate demand and perhaps an increase in unemployment; correction of the foreign surplus requires an increase in aggregate demand abroad. A country might well prefer to leave payments imbalances uncorrected rather than experience such internal adjustments. For example, the disequilibrium in Figure 8.10 might be due to a shift in tastes away from French goods, which the authorities expect to be reversed in the future. Then they might want to sit out the deficit rather than adjusting from *H* to *E* and then back again when tastes change. Also there is the chance that through sterilization a country might force the burden of adjustment onto the rest of the world. Suppose, for example, that France completely sterilizes its deficit but that the rest of the world does not sterilize its surplus, at least not completely. Then the French money supply remains constant and the foreign money supply gradually increases. In Figure 8.10 the world moves from *H* to *B*, where equilibrium is restored (this is apt to take quite a while since the cumulative French deficit must increase the money supply in the entire rest of the world in proportion to the original excess French money supply). If, on the other hand, the rest of the world completely sterilizes its surplus but France does not sterilize its deficit, the world moves from *H* to equilibrium at *A*.

LIMITS TO STERILIZATION

Sterilization is impossible in a pure gold-coin standard, but even in more realistic monetary systems there are two significant factors which limit, in varying degrees, the ability of a central bank to sterilize payments imbalances.

1. *Central-bank assets.* Suppose France is running a payments deficit that she completely sterilizes. Then the French central bank is simultaneously selling international reserves for francs and selling francs for domestic bonds. Thus on balance the central bank is exchanging international reserves for domestic bonds. This is clear in Table 8.4. Obviously this process can continue only as long as the central bank possesses international reserves to sell. If nothing is done to correct the payments deficit, sooner or later the central bank will begin to run out of reserves. Then unless the central bank can somehow borrow additional reserves from abroad, the French must choose between two alternatives. They can cease sterilization (that is, stop trying to control their own money supply) and allow the automatic adjustment process to correct the deficit. Or they can cease maintaining the value of the franc and stop selling international reserves (that is, abandon fixed exchange rates). If the French completely run out of reserves only the second alternative is available. A stock of reserves is required to allow the automatic adjustment process to work because the payments deficit will be corrected only gradually; sterilization requires even larger reserves whereas a policy of reinforcing the monetary consequences of payments imbalances reduces the need for reserves.

2. *International capital movements.* Suppose again that the French have a payments deficit that the central bank attempts to sterilize. Then the French central bank is buying domestic bonds from the public in exchange for francs at the same rate that the public is selling francs to the rest of the world through the payments deficit. Then on balance the French public is retaining a constant money supply but losing bonds at a rate equal to the payments deficit, that is, the public's holdings of bonds relative to money is falling. To redress the balance the public will buy bonds from the rest of the world in exchange for money. This increases the balance of payments deficit above what it would have been otherwise, and this increase *offsets* the sterilization operation. The degree of offset depends upon the degree of international capital mobility. If capital is completely immobile, the French public buys no foreign bonds, there is no offset, and the only constraint on the central bank is the size of its stock of international reserves, as discussed above.

If, at the other extreme, capital is perfectly mobile internationally, the French public will simply buy from abroad bonds to completely replace those sold to the central bank; the bank's attempt to sterilize will be totally offset by an equal capital account deficit. The only effect of such a sterilization operation will be to increase the size of the payments deficit and thus the rate at which the bank's stock of international reserves is depleted; the automatic adjustment process will not be at all affected.

If capital mobility is of an intermediate degree, an attempt at sterilization will be partially offset: a portion of the sterilization effort will be nullified by a consequent capital account deficit, and the remaining portion will add to the French money supply. The degree of offset depends upon the degree of capital mobility. With imperfect capital mobility (and so partial offset) the authorities can still hold the money supply constant and abort the automatic adjustment process, but in order to do so they must conduct sterilization operations on a larger scale than what the payments imbalance would otherwise be, because they must also sterilize the monetary consequences of the capital account deficit induced by the sterilization operation itself. Thus the balance of payments deficit, and the consequent rate of depletion of international reserves, will be increased by sterilization, to an extent dependent upon the degree of capital mobility.

Table 8.5 shows the balance sheet entries for the French central bank if capital flows offset its attempt to sterilize the fr100 deficit in our earlier illustration. Panels (a) and (b) show the same four entries as does Table 8.4 for the direct effects of the payments deficit and for the sterilization operation. The additional entries shown in bold-faced type result from offsetting capital flows. If capital mobility is perfect, as in panel (a), the public purchases from abroad all the fr100 of bonds that have been sold to the central bank, resulting in another fr100 deficit. The net effect on commercial bank reserves, and thus on the French money supply, is the same as if no sterilization had been attempted. The only effect has been to double the size of the payments deficit and of the resulting loss of international reserves.

If, on the other hand, there is no capital mobility at all, that is, if domestic residents are completely unwilling or unable to sell bonds to foreigners or to buy bonds from them, there will be no offset to sterilization. Table 8.4 still applies.

Panel (b) of Table 8.5 shows the offset in an intermediate case where international capital mobility exists but is not perfect. This illustration assumes that French citizens purchase enough foreign bonds to replace three-fourths of the domestic bonds sold to the central bank. In this case the sterilization operation succeeds in limiting the decline in commercial bank reserves to fr75, rather than fr100, but at the cost of a balance of payments deficit and international reserve loss of fr175 rather than fr100. Panel (c) makes the same assumption about international capital mobility and shows what happens if the central bank perseveres and conducts open market operations on a scale sufficient to prevent the money supply from falling. This requires a payments deficit and international reserve loss fully four times as great as that which would occur with no attempt at sterilization.

In general, then, the ability of a country to sterilize the monetary

Table 8.5. Sterilization and Offsetting Capital Flows

(a) Perfect Capital Mobility

Assets	Liabilities
Government Bonds: +fr100 International Reserves: −*fr100* **−fr100**	Commercial Bank Reserves: −*fr100* +fr100 **−fr100**

(b) Imperfect Capital Mobility and Partial Sterilization

Assets	Liabilities
Government Bonds: +fr100 International Reserves: −*fr100* **−fr75**	Commercial Bank Reserves: −*fr100* +fr100 **−fr75**

(c) Imperfect Capital Mobility and Complete Sterilization

Assets	Liabilities
Government Bonds: +fr400 International Reserves: −*fr100* **−fr300**	Commercial Bank Reserves: −*fr100* +fr400 **−fr300**

effects of a payments imbalance depends both upon the size of its stock of international reserves and other assets and upon the degree of international capital mobility. In addition, some central banks simply do not have the ability to make extensive sterilization attempts. For example, the facilities for large-scale open market operations are often lacking. One would expect differing views about the relative importance of the channels through which the adjustment process works to be associated with different views of the possibility of sterilization. Those who see international adjustment as taking place mainly through international capital movements and hoarding-dishoarding tend also to see little scope for sterilization. Thus, in their view, individual countries must choose between maintaining fixed exchange rates and forsaking an independent monetary policy, on the one hand, or pursuing an independent policy and forsaking fixed exchange rates, on the other. At the other extreme, those who see adjustment as working largely through income changes are likely to view sterilization as possible for substantial periods of time and as desirable, since they would attach priority to internal adjustment.

STERILIZATION IN PRACTICE

Since the Second World War, governments and central banks have accepted a responsibility for maintaining desirable internal aggregate economic conditions. Before the First World War, by contrast, central banks interpreted their basic responsibility to be the maintenance of the external value of the national currency. Thus one would expect sterilization to be more prominent in the more recent period.

Studies by Arthur Bloomfield and by Ragnar Nurkse have nevertheless revealed that in the period before the First World War—the heyday of the gold standard—and also in the inter-war period, central bank transactions in domestic assets violated the Rules of the Game more often than not. Since the Second World War, sterilization has been common. A number of important industrial countries have routinely sterilized the monetary effects of all payments imbalances so as to allow the discretionary component of monetary policy to be aimed unambiguously at internal objectives.

Throughout the last quarter-century or so the principal industrial economies have become more integrated, and, as an inevitable consequence, the degree of capital mobility between them has increased. One would expect therefore that sterilization has steadily become more difficult. Recent decades have seen numerous instances where central banks have abandoned fixed exchange rates to maintain control over their money supplies.

PROBLEMS

8.34 In Problem **8.31,** suppose that the Italian central bank sterilizes completely the Italian deficit, and that there is no offset. How do your answers change? What are the changes in the bond holdings of the Italian public? The Italian central bank? How do your answers change if the Spanish authorities also fully sterilize the Spanish surplus?

8.35 Suppose, in Problem **8.34,** that the Italian authorities completely sterilize and the Spanish do not sterilize at all. Suppose also that one-half of any Italian sterilization is offset by a purchase of foreign bonds: whenever the Italian central bank buys two lire worth of bonds from the Italian public, the public then buys one lira's worth of bonds from abroad. How do your answers to Problem **8.33** change? How do they change if, instead, three-fourths of any sterilization is offset?

8.36 In Problem **8.12,** suppose that the Spanish authorities "create" enough additional gold to always sterilize completely any payments deficits, and there is no offset. How do your answers change? How do they change if, instead, only one half of any deficit is sterilized?

8.37 Sterilization is simply monetary control motivated by the balance of payments, so any method of monetary control can be used for sterilization. The text discussed open market operations; alternative methods are changes in reserve requirements and in discount rates. How would the latter two be used to sterilize the effects of a deficit? Rework the example of Tables 8.4 and 8.5 if the French authorities try to sterilize by changing reserve requirements rather than by open market operations.

13. Case Study: West Germany in the Sixties

The problems that the automatic adjustment process poses for national monetary policy are well illustrated by the experience of Germany in the 1960s. Richard Herring and Richard Marston, of the University of Pennsylvania, have made a study of international financial markets in the period that included the estimation of an empirical model of the monetary sector of the German economy. They used their estimated model to simulate the effects of various hypothetical policy measures and events. Table 8.6 shows the simulated effects of a hypothetical attempt by German authorities, in the first quarter of 1964, to increase the German money supply by purchasing DM250 million worth of bonds from the public (there are other ways of influencing the money supply, but for convenience we describe them all as purchases and sales of bonds).

As discussed in the previous section, this attempt would induce the public to purchase bonds from abroad and so generate a capital account deficit. This would require the central bank to purchase marks and sell international reserves, thereby offsetting the initial attempt to increase the money supply, and also depleting the central bank's stock of international reserves. The bank could attempt to sterilize this offsetting effect of the deficit by purchasing more bonds from the public. This would further increase the offsetting capital account deficit and require further sterilization, and so on. The table shows the total simulated outcome. The first row of the table shows the effects that are simulated to occur in the quarter in which the initial purchase is made; the second row includes two years of sub-

Table 8.6. SIMULATED EFFECTS OF A HYPOTHETICAL PURCHASE OF DM250 MILLION WORTH OF BONDS FROM THE PUBLIC BY THE GERMAN AUTHORITIES IN THE FIRST QUARTER OF 1964 *(millions of DM)*

	(1) Total Reduction of International Reserves	(2) Sterilization	(3) Total Purchase of Bonds from Public [(2) + 250]	(4) Net Effect [(3) − (1)]
Current Quarter	603	553	803	200
After Two Years	784	720	970	186

SOURCE: *Herring and Marston,* National Monetary Policies and International Financial Markets

sequent repercussions. The third column shows that the total purchase of bonds (the initial DM250 million plus all the sterilization operations) is DM803 million in the initial quarter. The first column shows that DM603 million of this—fully 75 percent—would have been offset by an induced capital account deficit, thereby reducing international reserves by that amount. The authorities would then typically have sterilized the effects on the money supply of this sale of international reserves to the extent of DM553—or 92 percent. The remaining DM50 million would be unsterilized so that the net effect on the public—the total purchase of bonds from the public minus the total sale of international reserves to the public—was DM200 million, or 80 percent of the original DM250 million.

This is a picture of determined sterilization overcoming a high degree of international capital mobility to maintain substantial control of the money supply. By sterilizing 92 percent of offsetting capital flows, 80 percent of the intitial operation is made to stick in the current quarter. But to do this the central bank is forced to accept a loss of international reserves more than three times the size of the net effect on the public.

When two years of repercussions are added in, the effects are even more pronounced. The fraction of bond sales to the public that are offset by international capital movements rises from 75 percent to 81 percent. With the authorities still typically sterilizing 92 percent of these offsetting movements, the net effect on the public falls to DM186 million, or 74 percent of the initial operation. And the total loss of international reserves (DM784 million) is now more than four times the size of the net effect on the public.

14. Reserve Currencies

The key institutional feature behind the automatic adjustment process is fixed exchange rates, which ensure that the monies of different countries are substitutes for each other. As we saw in section 9, many possible monetary arrangements incorporate this feature. In several of these arrangements, such as a gold-exchange standard or convertible paper, some countries might hold their international reserves in whole or in part in assets denominated in the currency of some other country. In this case the latter country is in a unique position. This can be seen by comparing two examples.

Suppose that international reserves consist of gold and of dollars. In the first example, France is running a balance of payments deficit with Germany, and the two countries have neither deficit nor surplus with the rest of the world. France must be losing international reserves—gold and/or dollars—in an amount equal to its deficit, and Germany must be acquiring them in an amount equal to its surplus. If neither country sterilizes, the French money supply is falling and the German money supply is rising.

Now suppose that the United States is running a deficit and Germany (or the rest of the world) a surplus. Since the dollar is the American currency, U.S. international reserves consist only of gold. The German central bank is selling marks and acquiring dollars. If the Germans simply add the dollars to their reserves, German international reserves have increased by the amount of the German payments surplus, just as in the first example, but the American reserves have not fallen at all! Instead the American authorities have increased their liabilities to the German authorities (because dollars are a liability of the U.S. central bank). Only if the German central bank sells some or all of the dollars it has bought to the American authorities for gold, or if the Americans sell gold directly to the public, will the U.S. stock of international reserves be depleted by the deficit. Similarly, an American balance of payments surplus would not increase the U.S. stock of international reserves to the extent that the rest of the world financed its deficit by selling dollar reserves to the public. The conclusion is that a country with a reserve currency need not be restrained by the size of its international reserves.

All this is illustrated by Table 8.7. The top entry shows the cumulative U.S. balance of payments deficit for the fifteen years 1963–1977. The United States was in deficit during most of this time, and the cumulative total is large. But only a small part of this deficit was financed by a sale of U.S. reserve assets; most of it took the form of increased U.S. liabilities to foreign authorities, that is, of increased holdings of dollar reserves by foreign officials.

The bottom three entries of Table 8.7 illustrate a second implication of a reserve currency. In our example, when the German central bank accumulated reserves by adding to its stock of dollars, it also increased the world total of reserves: German reserves rose but U.S. reserves did not fall. That is, the deficits or surpluses of a country with a reserve currency change the total supply of reserves in the world. Most of the large increase in world

Table 8.7. Cumulative Totals of U.S. Deficits and World
Reserves, 1963–77 *(billions of dollars)*

U.S. Balance of Payments Deficit	118	
Sale of U.S. Reserve Assets		6
Increased U.S. Liabilities to Foreign Official		
Institutions		112
Increase in World Reserves	256	
Increase in Foreign Exchange Reserves		224
Increase in Other Reserve Assets		32

source: *International Financial Statistics*

reserves that occurred between 1963 and 1977 was accounted for by increases in foreign-exchange reserves (reserves in the form of reserve currencies—the dollar and a few others).

There is a third way in which countries with a reserve currency may differ from others. In the above example, suppose that Germany does add the dollars acquired from its payments deficit to its reserves. It would be foolish for the Germans to hold these dollars in the form of money, which earns no interest. Instead, they will hold the dollars in the form of dollar-denominated interest-bearing assets, such as Treasury bills or bonds. Thus, when the German authorities purchase dollars for marks as a result of their payments surplus, they then sell the dollars for dollar-denominated assets: the U.S. deficit is sterilized. The combined effect of the two German operations is to sell marks to the public in exchange for dollar-denominated assets, so that the public's holdings of dollars do not change. The U.S. payments deficit is automatically sterilized by the German central bank without the need for any U.S. action.

In sum, a country with a reserve currency differs from other countries in three ways, *if* the other countries respond to surpluses or deficits by adding to or subtracting from their official holdings of the reserve currency. To the extent that the latter takes place, payments imbalances of the reserve-currency country: (1) do not change that country's stock of international reserves; (2) do change the total world stock of international reserves; (3) are automatically sterilized.

The U.S. dollar is now the most important reserve currency, and these three features have applied to American payments imbalances. Several other currencies have a limited reserve role, and the three features have a limited relevance to them. The British pound, formerly an important reserve currency, still has a little significance; the French franc is a reserve currency for some former French colonies; and several other currencies have gained a reserve role in recent years.

PROBLEMS

8.38 In the text we showed that imbalances of a reserve-currency country could be automatically sterilized. But sterilization will be offset, to some degree, if capital is internationally mobile. Suppose that foreign central banks hold reserves only in the form of U.S. dollars. What does this imply about a U.S. balance of payments deficit if there is partial mobility of capital between the U.S. and the rest of the world? If capital is perfectly mobile? How do your answers change if foreign central banks always hold half of their international reserves in the form of dollars and half in the form of gold?

8.39 In Figure 8.10, suppose that France supplies a reserve currency for the rest of the world. Show what happens if the French increase their money supply and the rest of the world sterilizes its own imbalances; if the rest of the world does not sterilize; if the rest of the world tries to increase its money supply.

15. Internal and External Balance under Fixed Exchange Rates

We saw in Chapter 4 how a country could face a dilemma between goals for internal balance (aggregate demand) and for external balance (the balance of payments) if the only available policy instrument was expenditure policy. Now that we have begun to consider monetary factors, we have two ways of controlling expenditure: fiscal policy and monetary policy. If these two tools are not identical in their effects, they might supply a road of escape from our dilemma.

In Figure 8.11 the vertical axis measures the interest rate, determined by monetary policy. Suppose that the authorities are able and willing to sterilize payments imbalances so as to exercise independent monetary policy for a prolonged period. The horizontal axis measures the government's budget deficit, a reflection of fiscal policy. Suppose that at *A* aggregate demand is as desired by the authorities. If government spending rose and increased the budget by *AB*, national income would be stimulated and aggregate demand would exceed the desired level. An increase in the interest rate would reduce private investment and thereby depress aggregate demand back down. Suppose that an increase from *B* to *C* would just do the trick. Then *C*, like *A*, indicates a policy combination corresponding to internal balance: aggregate demand equals the target of the authorities. The *IB* line in Figure 8.11 indicates all such policy combinations. We have just shown that it has a positive slope.

Now consider external balance. Suppose that foreign interest rates, prices, and incomes are not appreciably affected by what happens at home. An increase in the government deficit, by stimulating income and therefore

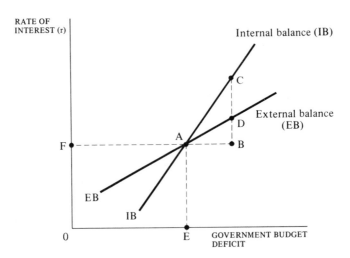

Figure 8.11. INTERNAL AND EXTERNAL BALANCE

imports, will increase the balance of payments deficit. An increase in the interest rate will decrease the payments deficit for two reasons. By reducing national income, it reduces imports and so decreases the balance of trade deficit; a higher interest rate also makes domestic assets more attractive relative to foreign assets and so generates a capital-account surplus, provided that capital is internationally mobile.

Suppose that the policy combination indicated by A results in external balance (a balance of payments deficit equal to zero, or to whatever the authorities wish). If the government deficit increases by AB, the trade account will increase its deficit. To restore external balance the interest rate must rise. If it rises by BC, national income will fall back to what it was at A, and therefore imports and the trade balance will do likewise. If capital is immobile internationally, the balance of trade coincides with the balance of payments and C, like A, indicates a policy combination corresponding to external balance. But if capital is internationally mobile, the increase in the interest rate from B to C will induce a capital account surplus. Since the balance of trade is the same at C as at A and the capital account surplus is greater, the balance of payments must have a larger surplus at C than at A. To restore external balance, the payments surplus must fall, that is, the interest rate must decline to somewhere between C and B. Suppose that the movement from C to D will accomplish this. Then D, like A, indicates a policy combination corresponding to external balance. The EB line shows all such combinations. We have shown that this line slopes upward, and also that it is less steep than the IB line, provided that capital is not completely immobile internationally.

Since the IB and EB lines have different slopes, they must intersect. The intersection is illustrated by A in Figure 8.11. This corresponds to the single policy combination giving both internal balance and external balance. By setting the budget deficit equal to OE and the interest rate equal to OF the authorities can simultaneously hit their targets for the balance of payments and for aggregate demand: there is no conflict between internal balance and external balance. The two *targets* can both be met by the proper use of the two *instruments*.

This happy escape from our policy dilemma is due to international capital mobility, which causes the two instruments to have differential effects. If capital is immobile internationally, monetary and fiscal policy are simply two different ways of manipulating a single instrument: expenditure policy. To see this, note that if capital were not mobile points C and D in Figure 8.11 would coincide, that is, the IB and EB lines would have the same slope. We would then be in exactly the same situation as in Chapter 4. If the target for national income happened to be the level that caused imports to equal exports, all would be well. The IB and EB lines would coincide, and any combination of the interest rate and budget deficit on this common line would do. But if targeted income caused imports to not equal exports, the *IB* and *EB* lines would be distinct and parallel: they would never intersect. The authorities could attain one target or the other but not both (unless they come up with yet another policy instrument).

As capital becomes mobile the *EB* line becomes flatter than the *IB* line, and the two intersect. If capital is perfectly mobile the domestic interest rate must always equal the foreign interest rate, so that the *EB* line becomes horizontal. That is, it coincides with the line *FAB* in Figure 8.11. In this case monetary policy is useless to attain internal balance, because nothing the authorities can do will influence the interest rate and thereby affect expenditure. Any attempt to alter the money supply will be quickly neutralized by payments imbalances; the automatic adjustment process prevents the country from pursuing an independent monetary policy. Fiscal policy is, however, an effective way to control internal balance. With external balance taken care of by the automatic adjustment process, economic policy reduces to simply setting the budget deficit equal to the level at which the *IB* line intersects the horizontal *EB* line.

Our policy conclusions depend crucially on the ability of the interest rate to influence the balance of payments *independently* of its influence through aggregate expenditure, and this independence follows from the fact that an increase in the interest rate generates a capital account surplus. But section 7 showed that a permanent change in the interest rate had only a temporary effect on the capital account. Thus our conclusions are strictly short run. This means that we have found only a temporary escape from the internal balance–external balance dilemma, unless the authorities are prepared to progressively intensify their policies again and again in order to obtain a succession of short-run effects. In addition, policy changes could be quite hard to implement because it often requires a lot of time to change fiscal policy: spending changes must be planned and often laws must be altered. Thus if the authorities change both fiscal and monetary policy at the same time, the short-run effect on the capital account could be over before fiscal policy even begins to do its thing.

In addition to this short-run effect on the capital account, two other consequences of a change in interest rates could be important. If the economy is growing, in the sense that residents are steadily saving and accumulating new assets, they will continually be putting some of their new savings into foreign assets, and the proportion devoted to foreign assets will be sensitive to interest rates. If the domestic interest rate falls, residents will increase their purchases of foreign bonds as they continue to save. Thus monetary policy could have some permanent effect on the capital account after all. However, in the long run interest rates will also influence the *current* account (in addition to its effect on the trade balance through expenditure), and this must be considered once we go beyond a short-run horizon. An increase in domestic interest rates *reduces E*, net interest income received from abroad, both because we must now pay more interest on our bonds held by foreigners and because foreigners own more of our bonds as a result of our temporary capital account surplus.

PROBLEMS

8.40 The *IB* and *EB* lines in Figure 8.11 divide the plane into four zones. What is the interpretation of each of these zones in terms of policy goals?

8.41 Suppose that savings are small so that the increase in the capital account surplus caused by a rise in the domestic interest rate almost entirely disappears after the short run. Show what the relative positions of the *IB* and *EB* schedules in Figure 8.11 look like in both the short run and the long run. What do you conclude about policy?

8.42 Suppose that the economy is initially in external balance at point *D* in Figure 8.11, and, in order to also attain internal balance the interest rate is reduced by *BD* and the budget deficit by *AB*. Show in the diagram what happens after the short-run change in the capital account disappears, assuming that both the continuing effect on the capital account and the long-run effect on net interest income are small enough to be ignored. Show what additional policy measures the authorities must take in order to preserve internal and external balance.

8.43* The intersection of the *IB* and *EB* lines in Figure 8.11 gives a specific policy prescription (point *A*). But in actual situations we will have at best only a very hazy idea of the shape and position of these curves, and so will not know where *A* is. It is therefore useful to have simple rules for adjusting the targets so as to "grope" toward *A*. One simple rule would be to assign each instrument to one target. For example, if the interest rate were assigned to internal balance and the budget deficit to external balance, one would reduce the interest rate whenever the economy was in a recession and reduce the budget deficit whenever there was a balance of payments deficit. An alternative assignment would be monetary policy to external balance and fiscal policy to internal balance. Discuss the relative merits of these two assignments as means to attain point *A*.

16. Summary

1. The automatic adjustment process of the balance of payments is the heart of the classical international monetary contribution.

2. The process has three central ingredients: the quantity theory of money determines the equilibrium allocation of the world's money among countries; nonequilibrium allocations cause payments imbalances; the Rules of the Game assure that the payments imbalances redistribute money so as to attain the equilibrium allocation.

3. The two basic implications of the process are that payments imbalances are temporary and that individual countries cannot control their own money supplies.

4. Nonequilibrium allocations of money cause payments imbalances in four ways. (1) Hoarding and dishoarding are associated with uniform changes in world

prices, with propensities to hoard as key parameters. (2) Relative price changes also influence payments imbalances (the price-specie flow mechanism), with price elasticities key parameters. (3) Sticky prices give a role to changes in aggregate demands so that marginal propensities to save and import become important. (4) International capital movements depend upon the degree of international capital mobility.

5. The key requirement for the automatic adjustment process is fixed exchange rates. The process is relevant to any monetary system once this requirement is met.

6. Those who believe that the automatic adjustment process takes a long time to work are more concerned with what happens as the process occurs and give less emphasis to the self-correcting nature of payments imbalances or the ultimate lack of national monetary control.

7. Countries sometimes attempt to retain control over domestic monetary policy by sterilizing payments imbalances. Their ability to do so is limited by their holdings of international reserves and by the degree of international capital mobility.

8. A country with a reserve currency differs from other countries in three ways if other countries change their holdings of the reserve currency in response to surpluses and deficits. Payments imbalances of the reserve currency country: (1) do not change that country's stock of international reserves; (2) do change the total world stock of international reserves; (3) are automatically sterilized.

9. International capital mobility causes fiscal and monetary policies to have differential relative effects on internal and external balance in the short run. This means that an appropriate mixture of the two policies can resolve the dilemma between internal and external balance. But the long-run situation is ambiguous.

17. *Exploring Further: IS-LM* Analysis in an Open Economy

Many readers will have learned about *IS* and *LM* curves while studying macroeconomics. The same tools can be used to analyze the automatic adjustment process.

To make things simple, we focus on a country that is relatively small in the sense that its behavior has only a negligible effect on foreign prices, interest rates, and incomes, which we take as fixed. For the home country to be in complete equilibrium three conditions must be met: the demand for the country's output must equal its supply, the country's demand for money must equal the supply, and the balance of payments must be in neither deficit nor surplus. Each condition is described by a separate curve, which we examine one at a time.

THE *IS* CURVE

This curve shows the combinations of output (y) and the rate of interest (r) for which the demand and supply of the country's output are equal.

The curve corresponds to a given price level in the country. As we studied in Chapter 4, the demand for national output will equal the supply when $X - M = S - I$; this is illustrated in Figure 8.12(a). Now exports X are just foreign imports, and these are determined by prices and foreign incomes, which are fixed; thus X is fixed. But investment I depends upon the rate of interest r: low values of r will cause firms to invest more because the cost of borrowing to finance investment is low. Suppose that r is equal to the distance OA in Figure 8.12(b). This determines the level of investment, call it I_A, and therefore the position of the $S\text{-}I_A$ curve, which is drawn in panel (a). Thus y will equal OF, marked off in each panel, and point C in panel (b) is a combination of r and y for which the demand and supply of home output are equal. Suppose that the interest rate were to fall, say to OB. This would cause domestic investment to rise, say by the amount DE in panel (a). Thus y rises by the amount FH, indicated in both panels. Point D in the latter is accordingly another combination of r and y for which the demand and supply of output are equal. The IS curve is the collection of all points, such as C and D, for which this is true. We have just demonstrated that this curve has a negative slope.

The IS curve is drawn for a specific domestic price level. Thus a change in domestic prices will *shift* the curve. Suppose domestic prices fall. This makes domestic goods more competitive relative to foreign goods and so increases the demand for domestic output: $X\text{-}M$ shifts up in Figure 8.12(a). Thus for any level of investment I (that is, for any value of r), the equilibrium y increases: the IS curve shifts to the right. Analogously, a rise in domestic prices shifts the IS curve to the left.

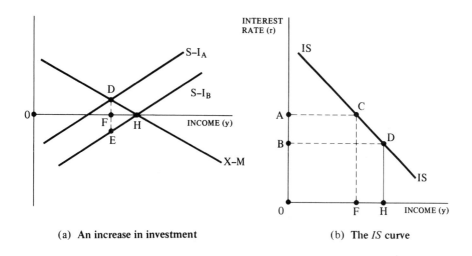

(a) An increase in investment   (b) The *IS* curve

Figure 8.12. DERIVATION OF THE *IS* CURVE

THE *LM* CURVE

This curve shows the combinations of output (y) and the rate of interest (r) for which the country's demand for money equals the supply. The curve corresponds to a given level of the country's money supply as well as a given level of the country's prices. Higher levels of income require more money for transactions. Thus an increase in y increases the demand for money, which was reflected in equation (8.1). If r goes up, people would sacrifice more interest income by holding their wealth in the form of money, which earns no interest, rather than in the form of assets that do earn interest. Thus they would be more tempted to economize on money holdings: an increase in r reduces the demand for money (in equation (8.1), an increase in r would lower the value of k). Suppose that at point C in Figure 8.13 the demand for money is equal to the supply. If y increases but r remains unchanged, as in a move from C to E, the demand for money will rise and therefore exceed the fixed supply. To make demand once again equal to supply, and to thereby get back on the *LM* curve, the rate of interest must rise. This is illustrated by the movement from E to G. The *LM* curve consists of all points, such as C and G, for which the demand for money equals the given supply; as we have just demonstrated, the curve has a positive slope.

The *LM* curve is drawn for a specific domestic money supply and a specific domestic price level. A change in either will shift the curve. Suppose, for example, that the domestic money supply increases. Then the demand for money must rise in order to once again equal the supply. Since

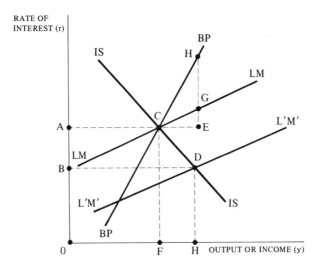

Figure 8.13. *IS-LM-BP* ANALYSIS

a rise in y and/or a fall in r will increase the demand for money, the LM curve must shift downward and to the right.

THE BP CURVE

This curve shows the combinations of y and r for which the balance of payments is in neither surplus nor deficit. The curve corresponds to a given level of foreign indebtedness as well as a given level of the country's prices. An increase in y will increase imports and increase the balance of payments deficit by increasing the current account deficit. An increase in r, on the other hand, will make domestic assets more attractive relative to foreign assets. The capital account surplus will accordingly increase, and therefore the balance of payments surplus as well.

Suppose that at point C in Figure 8.13 the balance of payments is in neither surplus nor deficit. An increase in y at unchanged r (represented by a movement from C to E) would produce a balance of payments deficit by stimulating imports. To eliminate this deficit the interest rate r must rise so as to generate a capital account surplus (the rise in r is represented by a movement from E to H). Thus point H, like C, represents a combination of y and r for which the balance of payments is in neither surplus nor deficit. The BP curve consists of all such points; as we have just seen, this curve must have a positive slope.

The slope of the BP curve will be sensitive to the degree of international capital mobility. If capital is perfectly mobile internationally the domestic interest rate must equal the rate of interest in the rest of the world: otherwise there would be no demand at all for the assets of the country paying the lower rate of interest. Thus the BP curve is a horizontal line with a height equal to the rate of interest in the rest of the world. If, on the other hand, capital is completely immobile, the balance of payments will coincide with the balance of trade. The BP curve will therefore be a vertical line with a distance from the r-axis equal to that level of y which will cause imports to exactly equal the given level of exports. In general, the greater the degree of international capital mobility, the flatter the BP curve.

The BP curve is drawn for a specific level of foreign indebtedness and a specific domestic price level. A change in either will shift the curve. Suppose, for example, that domestic citizens lose some foreign assets (an increase in foreign indebtedness). At the initial rate of interest, domestic residents were previously buying or selling foreign assets at the rate they wished. Since they now suddenly find themselves with fewer of these assets, they will wish to buy them at a faster rate: the capital account deficit will rise, and therefore the balance of payment deficit as well. This deficit can be eliminated by a rise in r (making domestic assets more attractive relative to foreign) and/or by a fall in y (reducing imports and thereby increasing the trade account surplus). Thus an increase in foreign indebtedness shifts the

BP curve upward and to the left. Analogously, a reduction in foreign indebtedness will shift the curve downward and to the right.

EQUILIBRIUM

For the economy to be in complete equilibrium, *r* and *y* must equal the values at a common intersection of all three curves, such as point *C* in Figure 8.13. To see *IS-LM-BP* analysis in action, suppose the domestic money supply is suddenly increased. This will shift the *LM* curve downward and to the right, say to the curve *L'M'*. The new equilibrium is at *D*. Since *D* is below the *BP* curve there is a balance of payments deficit; the reduction in *r* (from *OA* to *OB*) will tend to generate a capital account deficit, and the increase in *y* (from *OF* to *OH*) will tend to generate a balance of trade deficit. Thus the diagram illustrates in comprehensive fashion the effects of the monetary disturbance.

However *D* does not represent a permanent equilibrium. The balance of payments deficit will cause the domestic money supply to fall (the Rules of the Game), and therefore gradually shift the *LM* curve back up and to the left, so that *D* will begin to move up along the *IS* curve. Also, the capital account deficit will increase the ownership of foreign assets and therefore cause the *BP* curve to shift down and to the right, while the increase in *y* from *OF* to *OH* will stimulate domestic inflation. The resulting rise in the domestic price level will shift the *IS* curve to the left. These shifts will continue until the three curves once again have a common intersection, when the home economy will again be in complete equilibrium.

PROBLEMS

8.44 How does a rise in the domestic price level affect the *LM* curve? The *BP* curve?

8.45 How is each of the curves affected by a rise in the foreign price level?

8.46 Draw the *IS-LM-BP* diagram in the classical case where real income *y* is always at the full employment level. Analyze in detail the effects of an increase in the domestic money supply.

8.47 Analyze the effects of a permanent improvement in the terms of trade (due, say, to a shift in tastes from foreign goods toward domestic goods).

8.48 Analyze the effects of a more expansionary fiscal policy.

8.49 Use *IS-LM-BP* analysis to restate the discussion in section 15 of internal and external balance.

8.50 Use *IS-LM-BP* analysis to discuss the effects of an increase in the money supply with complete sterilization of all payments imbalances.

SUGGESTED READING

Bloomfield, A. *Monetary Policy under the International Gold Standard.* New York: Federal Reserve Bank of New York, 1959.

Dornbusch, R. *Open Economy Macroeconomics*. New York: Basic Books, 1980. See chapters 7 and 10.

Dornbusch, R. and Fisher, S. *Macroeconomics*. New York: McGraw-Hill, 1978. Chapter 18 contains a discussion along *IS-LM* lines.

Emminger, O. "The D-Mark in Conflict between Internal and External Equilibrium." Princeton, *Essays in International Finance*, No. 122, 1977. An account of German experience by the former head of the central bank.

Frenkel, J. and Johnson, H. G., eds. *The Monetary Approach to the Balance of Payments*. Toronto: Toronto University Press, 1976. A collection of basic papers.

Herring, R. and Marston, R. *National Monetary Policies and International Financial Markets*. Amsterdam: North Holland, 1977.

Hume, D. "Of the Balance of Trade." In *Essays, Moral, Political and Literary*. London: Longmans Green, 1898. The classic reference.

International Monetary Fund. *The Monetary Approach to the Balance of Payments*. Washington: IMF, 1977. A collection of papers by IMF staff members.

Mundell, R. A. *International Economics*. New York: Macmillian, 1968. Chapters 8, 14, 15, and 16 are especially relevant to this chapter.

Neary, P. "Non-Traded Goods and the Balance of Trade in a Neo-Keynesian Temporary Equilibrium." *Quarterly Journal of Economics 3*, 1980. An advanced treatment.

Nurske, R. *International Currency Experience*. Geneva: League of Nations, 1944.

Samuelson, P. "A Corrected Version of Hume's Equilibrating Mechanisms for International Trade." In *Flexible Exchange Rates and the Balance of Payments*. Edited by J. S. Chipman and C. P. Kindleberger. Amsterdam: North Holland, 1980. A recent statement of the classical process.

Swan, T. "Longer-Run Problems of the Balance of Payments." In *Readings in International Economics*. Edited by R. E. Caves and H. G. Johnson. Homewood: Irwin, 1968. Internal and External Balance.

Viner, J. *Studies in the Theory of International Trade*. New York: Harper and Brothers, 1937. Excellent discussion of the development of classical thought.

Yeager, L. *International Monetary Relations: Theory, History, and Policy*. 2nd ed. New York: Harper and Row, 1976. Discusses the history of different international monetary systems.

Chapter 9

The Exchange Rate

"What, then, has determined and will determine the value of the franc? First, the quantity, present and prospective, of the francs in circulation. Second, the amount of purchasing power which it suits the public to hold in that shape." —J. M. KEYNES

"Well, I don't give a [expletive deleted] about the lira."

—R. M. NIXON

THE PREVIOUS chapter studied the role of money in the international economy with *fixed exchange rates*—one country's money could always be exchanged for that of another at a fixed price. Because of this there was no need to distinguish national monies from each other, and we could speak unambiguously of *the* world money supply. But control of the medium of exchange is one aspect of national sovereignty, and exchange rates need not be fixed unless institutional arrangements mandate that they be. As the table on page 286 reveals, exchange rates do in fact often change. The modified gold-exchange standard instituted after the Second World War collapsed in 1973, and since then exchange rate changes have been central to international economic relations among the DCs.

   In this chapter we study the second facet of money in the international economy: the fact that the monies of different countries are not perfect substitutes for each other. We focus on exchange rates: how they are determined and what happens if they change. The basic idea of exchange-rate adjustment as a key part of the attainment of international monetary equilibrium has been shared by many economists in many lands and at many times. But it is appropriate to associate it with the American economist Frank Taussig, who early in this century developed a basic analysis that his students then used in empirical studies.

FRANK W. TAUSSIG (1859-1940)

Frank Taussig's father migrated from Prague to the U.S. Midwest and became a merchant, medical practitioner, mayor, judge, tax collector, banker, bridge builder, and railroad president. Taussig was only an economist. He spent his career on the Harvard faculty and lived in Cambridge, Massachusetts, for over sixty years. Taussig became the foremost American applied economic theorist, his *Principles of Economics* was for many years the leading text, and he was for forty years the editor of the *Quarterly Journal of Economics,* a leading professional journal. The increasing specialization of the field is indicated by the fact that Taussig was the first leading economist to specialize in the subfield of international trade. In 1917 Taussig became the first chairman of the Tariff Commission (now called the International Trade Commission, discussed in Chapter 6), and as economic adviser to President Woodrow Wilson he, like Keynes, attended the Versailles peace conference after the First World War.

---

1. International Monetary Equilibrium

We start by examining a very simple arrangement, one identical in most respects to that discussed in section 1 of Chapter 8. We have two countries, France and Germany, in the same framework of international trade. But monetary arrangements are different. Now the French money supply consists of a fixed quantity L^F of francs, and the German money supply consists of a fixed quantity L^G of marks. Francs and marks are distinct; they are no longer merely different names for the same thing. The authorities in each country control the size of their country's money supply. The French exchange rate, R, is the price of a mark in terms of francs.

MONEY PRICES AND THE EXCHANGE RATE

P_W is the world money price of wine; since France exports wine, measure this price in francs, so that P_W is the number of francs required to purchase a unit of wine. Similarly, P_M, the money price of machines, is measured in marks. For these two prices to be comparable they must be expressed in a common currency, and the exchange rate is used for this. For example, the price of machines in terms of francs is RP_M. (What is the price of wine in terms of marks?) The relative price of machines in terms of wine is $p = RP_M/P_W$. As discussed in Chapter 2, the equilibrium value of p is determined by the intersection of the two offer curves.

THE QUANTITY THEORY OF MONEY

As before, we start with a rudimentary version of the quantity theory of money. If L^F denotes the French money supply (francs), the demand for francs will equal the supply when

$$L^F = kP_W y^F, \tag{9.1}$$

where y^F stands for French national income measured in units of wine and k denotes the number of francs that the French wish to hold for each franc of income. Similarly, the demand for money in Germany will equal the supply L^G of marks when

$$L^G = kP_M y^G, \tag{9.2}$$

where y^G denotes German income in terms of machines. If we multiply both sides of this equation by R, we can express it in terms of francs and so make it comparable to (9.1):

$$RL^G = k(RP_M)y^G. \tag{9.3}$$

THE EQUILIBRIUM EXCHANGE RATE

For the world to be in equilibrium the demand for each type of money must equal the supply, that is, (9.1) and (9.3) must hold. Dividing (9.1) into (9.3),

$$R\frac{L^G}{L^F} = \frac{k(RP_M)y^G}{kP_W y^F} = p\frac{y^G}{y^F}. \tag{9.4}$$

The expression on the right is determined by the terms of trade p, given by the intersection of the offer curves. Thus (9.4) says that the product of the exchange rate, R, and the relative money supplies, L^G/L^F, must be constant for the world to be in equilibrium. This is illustrated in Figure 9.1 by the curve DD'. This curve (an example of what is called a "rectangular hyperbola") shows for each value of the exchange rate R the ratio L^G/L^F that would be demanded in equilibrium. The area $OBES$ in the figure equals the magnitude (py^G/y^F), and this is true of any rectangle formed by taking as a corner any point, such as E, on the curve DD'. If OS measures the actual relative supply of the two monies, the world must be somewhere on the line SS', so that equilibrium is at E, the intersection of the demand and supply curves. Thus OB measures the equilibrium exchange rate.

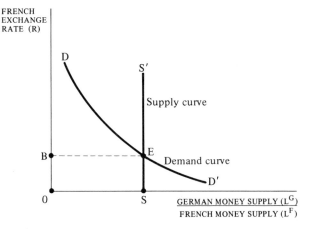

Figure 9.1. INTERNATIONAL MONETARY EQUILIBRIUM

Figure 9.1 depicts international monetary equilibrium in a different way from Figure 8.1 and reflects a different institutional arrangement. In the previous chapter we took the exchange rate as fixed, and Figure 8.1 showed how money had to be distributed between the two countries. Now we take money supplies as fixed, and Figure 9.1 shows what the exchange rate must be. Thus the diagrams are really two sides of the same coin.

PROBLEMS

9.1 Suppose that the United States produces 1,000 bushels of wheat, Europe produces 600 bolts of cloth, 5 wheat exchange for 1 cloth in equilibrium, k equals $\frac{1}{2}$, the U.S. money supply consists of 2,000 dollars and the European money supply consists of 3,000 pounds. Describe international monetary equilibrium and illustrate with a diagram analogous to Figure 9.1. Suppose the U.S. money supply were to rise to 4,000 dollars; calculate the effect on your answer and illustrate the change in your diagram. Do the same if instead the terms of trade were to alter so that five wheat exchange for three cloth.

9.2 In the discussion in the text, how will the equilibrium French exchange rate be affected by:

a an improvement in the French terms of trade; or
b a growth of German income relative to French?

9.3 Suppose that the franc becomes worth fewer marks (so R rises). What will be the direct impact of this on French and German firms if they pursue the following alternative pricing policies:

a each firm holds the domestic currency price of its product fixed and adjusts the foreign currency price;
b each firm holds constant in foreign currency the price of its product and adjusts the domestic currency price; or
c each firm holds constant *both* the domestic currency price at which it sells

in domestic markets and also the foreign currency price at which it sells in foreign markets.
What consequences would likely develop in each case for the respective firms? Can you think of any reason why firms might respond in one way rather than in others?

9.4 Show the effects of an increase in the French money supply in Figure 9.1. What happens to the equilibrium exchange rate if the French increase their money supply by 25 percent each and every year? What happens to the money prices of both goods?

2. Exchange-Rate Adjustment

Suppose that, in Figure 9.2, equilibrium is at *E* but the actual exchange rate is *OC*, so that the world is at *E'*. The origin of such a disequilibrium need not concern us. We ask what will be its consequences.

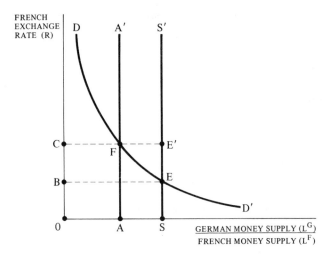

Figure 9.2. A Disequilibrium Exchange Rate

PREVIEW OF EXCHANGE-RATE ADJUSTMENT

With the actual exchange rate at *OC*, the demands and supplies of the two monies do not match. The relative demands corresponding to the exchange rate *OC* are indicated by *F*: demand *OA* is less than the actual supply *OS*. The exchange rate corresponding to the relative supply *OS* is indicated by *E*, and *SE* falls short of *SE'*.

Thus the French exchange rate (the price of marks) is too high, and/ or the supply of German money (marks) is too high. One could equivalently say that the German exchange rate (the price of francs) and/or the supply of French money (francs) are too small. The monetary authorities in France and Germany could react in two distinct ways.

They could, first, maintain the value of their currencies by freely exchanging them for international reserves. This is shown in Figure 9.3(a). In this case the exchange rate is held fixed at *OC*, and, as we saw in Chapter 8, a French balance of payments surplus and German deficit will emerge. French authorities would buy international reserves with francs, and the German authorities would sell international reserves for marks. With the French money supply rising and the German falling, the world moves from

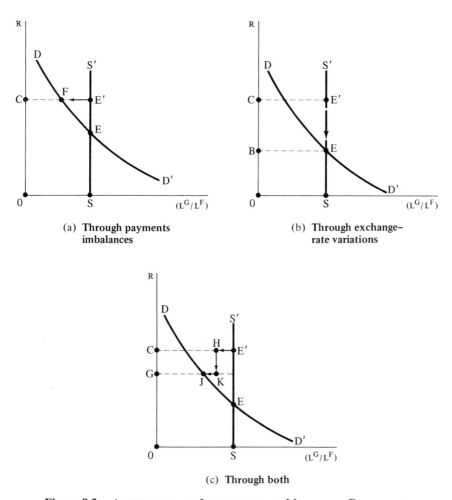

(a) **Through payments imbalances**

(b) **Through exchange-rate variations**

(c) **Through both**

Figure 9.3. ADJUSTMENT TO INTERNATIONAL MONETARY EQUILIBRIUM

E' toward equilibrium at *F.* The authorities might sterilize, in whole or in part, the monetary consequences of the payments imbalances. If so, the movement from *E'* to *F* will be slowed down or halted, with a magnification of the payments imbalances and changes in central-bank reserves. (We ignore, for now, the effects of any changes in incomes or relative prices.)

On the other hand the authorities could refrain from buying and selling the two currencies, and thus keep the respective money supplies fixed but alter exchange rates instead. In this case L^G/L^F remains equal to *OS.* If the exchange rate falls from *OC* to *OB* in Figure 9.3(b) the world will move from *E'* to *E* and reach equilibrium; people are just willing to hold the existing supplies of the two currencies, and payments imbalances will not arise. Thus there is an alternative method of adjustment: variations in exchange rates.

These two distinct methods of international adjustment might in practice be combined in various ways. For example, the authorities might at first hold the exchange rate fixed and sterilize the payments imbalances, thereby remaining at *E'*, until the deficit country begins to run out of reserves, and only then alter the exchange rate to *OB.* Figure 9.3(c) shows another possibility. The authorities could initially fix the exchange rate and not sterilize completely, thereby moving from *E'* to *H.* They then alter the exchange rate from *OC* to *OG.* This eliminates much of the disequilibrium but not all of it; the payments imbalances continue until the world moves from *K* to *J.* The new equilibrium at *J* differs from that at *E'* in both relative money suplies and the exchange rate.

There are four basic channels through which exchange-rate variations influence international adjustment, and we shall examine these channels one at a time in succeeding sections. As you might expect, these four channels are closely analogous to the four channels through which the automatic adjustment process works.

IMPLICATIONS OF EXCHANGE-RATE ADJUSTMENT

There are two broad implications of exchange-rate adjustment. *First,* balance of payments deficits and surpluses can be corrected or prevented by variations in exchange rates. This would reduce or eliminate the need for central banks to buy or sell international reserves.

Second, exchange-rate variations allow individual countries to control their own money supplies. Suppose the French and German monetary authorities desire money supplies in the ratio *OS* in Figure 9.3. If the exchange rate is fixed at *OC,* the automatic adjustment process will tend to move the world from *E'* to *F,* so that relative money supplies tend to move away from the desired ratio *OS* toward *CF.* But if the exchange rate is altered to *OB,* the world will move to *E* and the authorities will be able to maintain the desired ratio.

DEPRECIATION AND APPRECIATION; DEVALUATION AND REVALUATION

A currency is said to *depreciate* if it becomes worth less in terms of foreign currencies, that is, if more domestic currency is required to buy a unit of foreign currency. Similarly an *appreciation* is an increase in the value of domestic currency in terms of foreign currency: less home money is needed to buy a unit of foreign money. In Figure 9.3(b) a change in the exchange rate from *OC* to *OB* constitutes an appreciation of the franc and a depreciation of the mark.

A *devaluation* is a reduction in the value of a currency relative to its monetary standard. Thus if a country is on a gold standard, a devaluation means that the country's money is worth less in terms of gold, or that more of the currency is required to buy an ounce of gold. Similarly, an increase in the value of a currency relative to its standard is called a *revaluation.*

Suppose that a group of countries are on a gold standard and that one of them, say France, reduces the value of its currency (the franc) in terms of gold, but that all other countries maintain the values of their currencies. Then the franc has been devalued. Since the franc is worth less in terms of gold and all other currencies are worth the same as before in terms of gold, the franc must be worth less in terms of all other currencies. Thus the franc has depreciated relative to each other currency on the standard. Similarly, each of these other currencies has appreciated relative to the franc, but not relative to each other. Also the other currencies have been neither revalued nor devalued.

PROBLEMS

9.5 In Problem **9.1,** what cumulative payments imbalance would result if the exchange rate were held fixed after the increase in the U.S. money supply? What exchange-rate adjustment would instead be required if the U.S. money supply were maintained at 4,000 dollars? What would happen if, after the initial increase in the U.S. money supply to 4,000 dollars, the authorities decided not to let it subsequently fall below 3,000 dollars?

9.6 Suppose that England is on a gold standard, China on a silver standard, and France on a bimetallic standard. France increases the franc price of silver but does not change the price of gold. Which currencies have devalued, revalued, depreciated, or appreciated, and relative to what?

9.7 Suppose that German real income y^G grows by 10 percent each year, but that French real income y^F remains constant. What happens to international equilibrium if the French increase the supply of francs by 5 percent a year and Germany increases the supply of marks by 10 percent per year?

9.8 In the last two columns of the table on page 286, Selected Exchange Rates, which currencies are shown to have appreciated and which to have depreciated relative to the U.S. dollar? Relative to the franc?

3. Exchange-Rate Regimes

An exchange-rate regime is the arrangement used by a group of countries to settle payments among themselves and to determine their exchange rates. There are basically five distinct regimes. Chapter 8 and the present chapter describe two different methods of international adjustment. Exclusive reliance on one or the other of these methods gives us two possible exchange regimes. There are also two hybrid regimes that combine the two methods in different ways. The fifth regime involves dispensing with both methods in favor of direct government controls over international monetary transactions. Let us briefly describe each regime.

1. *Fixed Exchange Rates.* The authorities in each country freely buy and sell the national currency for international reserves at a permanently fixed price. Chapter 8 describes this regime. In terms of Figure 9.3, disturbances to demand and supply result in horizontal adjustments, as shown in panel (a).

2. *Floating Exchange Rates.* The authorities never exchange national money for international reserves, so each country's overall balance of payments is never in deficit or surplus. Exchange rates freely adjust in private markets to equilibrate demands and supplies of the national monies. In terms of Figure 9.3, disturbances to demand and supply conditions result in vertical adjustments, as in panel (b).

3. *Adjustable Peg.* In this, the first hybrid regime, authorities buy and sell the national currency for international reserves at a fixed price (the peg), but that price can be adjusted from time to time if payments imbalances are large.

4. *Managed Floating.* In this regime, as with floating exchange rates, the authorities do not fix a price for the national currency, but they may nevertheless buy and sell it to influence the exchange rate.

5. *Exchange Control.* This regime differs from all others in that the authorities directly administer exchanges of national monies. For example, citizens who acquire foreign currency by selling goods, services, or assets to foreigners may be required to sell that currency to the authorities for domestic money, and citizens who wish to buy goods, services, and assets from abroad may need to apply to the authorities for the foreign currency they require. If the authorities simply bought and sold foreign exchange on demand at a price that kept receipts equal to sales, this regime would be identical to floating exchange rates, except for the authorities serving as a clearinghouse. But they do not do this. Instead, their willingness to deal with domestic citizens, and the terms on which they deal, varies according to the identity of the citizen, the nature of the commodity the citizen wants to buy or sell, and the foreign country he wants to deal with. For example, the authorities might be willing to sell foreign exchange to citizens to import goods from country *A,* but not to import the same goods from country *B.* Or

a food importer might be able to obtain foreign exchange from the authorities at a low price, whereas a bicycle importer has to pay a higher price for a limited amount of foreign exchange, and a would-be automobile importer is denied foreign currency altogether. In this way exchange control is used to manipulate international trade and investment, as well as to adjust the balance of payments and exchange rates.

PROBLEMS

9.9 Section 2 of Chapter 8 mentioned two basic implications of the automatic adjustment process, and two implications of exchange-rate adjustment were indicated in section 2 of this chapter. Discuss how these four implications apply to each of the five basic regimes discussed in this section.

9.10 Discuss reasons why a country might prefer one regime over another.

9.11 Using the source material described in Appendix II, find examples of countries employing each of the five regimes discussed in this section. Describe in detail the specific arrangements of each country. Do they illustrate the possible reasons you gave in your answer to Problem **9.10**?

4. What Exchange Depreciation Does: Inflation

We now examine the first of the channels through which an exchange-rate variation works. This is analogous to hoarding and dishoarding, the first channel of the automatic adjustment process, studied in section 3 of Chapter 8, and relative price changes play no role in the argument.

Suppose that the franc depreciates, or R increases. Since the mark is more expensive, German goods cost more francs to buy (an increase in R raises RP_M). If relative prices are not to change, the franc price of French goods will rise also. Thus depreciation of the franc increases inflation in France. Similarly, appreciation of the mark reduces inflation in Germany.

■ *The Law of One Price.* If the exchange rate is initially two francs per mark, and if German firms sell machines for DM100 each, the machines sell for fr200 in France and thereby compete on equal terms with machines sold by French producers for fr200. If the franc depreciates by 50 percent, so that three are now required to buy a mark, the German machines will sell for fr300 in France. There is no reason why anyone should buy a German machine at this price when an identical French machine can be had for fr200. Thus French firms can raise their prices and German firms must lower theirs. A reduction in German prices to DM75 and an increase in French prices to fr225 would restore equality. This is an example of the *Law of One Price:* within a single market identical goods must sell at identical prices.

A related but more demanding proposition is that the relative price of *different* goods (for example, the terms of trade) is determined by real considerations independently of the exchange rate. In the above example, suppose that France also produces wine that is sold in the French market for fr400 per cask. Thus two machines initially sell at the same price as one cask of wine. Now suppose, as above, that the franc depreciates and that the price of a machine rises to fr225. Thus wine has become cheaper relative to machines so that buyers will tend to shift their purchases from machinery toward wine and firms will tend to do the opposite with their production. This puts upward pressure on wine prices and downward pressure on the prices of (both French and German) machines. If the price of wine rises to fr450, the pre-depreciation relative prices will be restored. ∎

Algebraically, if the terms of trade p is fixed by the intersection of the offer curves, then, since $p = RP_M/P_W$, P_M/P_W must fall in the same proportion that R rises. For example, if R rises by 50 percent then a 25 percent fall in P_M combined with a 25 percent rise in P_W will suffice to leave p unchanged. In this case the right-hand side of (9.1) increases by 25 percent and the left-hand side is unchanged, so that the demand for money in France rises relative to the supply. At the same time, the 25 percent fall in P_M reduces the right-hand side of (9.2) by 25 percent without affecting the left-hand side, so that the demand for money in Germany falls relative to the supply. The French try to satisfy their increased demand for money by consuming fewer goods and instead selling more goods to Germany for money. The Germans respond to their lower demand for money by using some of their extra money to buy more goods from France. Thus the depreciation of the franc tends to increase the French trade balance (and the appreciation of the mark tends to reduce the German trade balance).

The key step in this chain of reasoning is the idea that relative prices are fixed (by non-monetary considerations), so that the depreciation of the franc (rise in R) equals the difference between the fall in the German price level and the rise in the French price level. The proposition that the depreciation of a nation's currency is equal to the difference between the rise in that nation's price level and the rise in foreign prices is known as *purchasing power parity* (*PPP*).

KEY CONCEPT

A currency maintains its *purchasing power parity* if it depreciates by an amount equal to the excess of domestic inflation over foreign inflation:

(PPP) (depreciation) = (domestic inflation) − (foreign inflation).

If this holds, the purchasing power of domestic currency remains constant relative to the purchasing power of foreign currency; hence the term purchasing power parity.

It is important to realize that *PPP* relates exchange rates and price levels without saying anything about cause and effect. The inflation rate in a large country like the United States is probably due mainly (but certainly not entirely) to internal considerations, so that on balance changes in U.S. inflation tend to influence depreciation of the dollar rather than vice versa. For small countries the reverse is much more true. In general, inflation and depreciation are interdependent and jointly determined.

If purchasing power parity holds, at least to some extent, then the degree of improvement in the trade balance of the depreciating country depends upon the *propensity to hoard:* the speed with which individuals wish to adjust money supplies to money demands by varying expenditure. The analog with section 3 of Chapter 8 is exact: if the propensity to hoard is large, depreciation will increase the trade surplus by a large amount. Low propensities imply a small impact of exchange-rate variations on trade balances.

We can illustrate this with some geometry similar to that of Chapter 8. Figure 9.4 (like Figure 8.4) shows how the French will hoard and the Germans will dishoard at each price level. Both axes are measured in terms of francs.

Recall that the French hoarding schedule, *FF*, depends upon the size of the French money supply. The German schedule *GG* likewise depends on the German money supply, but it also depends on the exchange rate because the Germans hoard marks and measure prices in marks, whereas the axes of Figure 9.4 are measured in francs. (The *GG* schedule is the graph of $RL^G - kP_w p y^G$.) A 50 percent depreciation of the franc, for example, would shift the *GG* curve away from the origin—upward and to

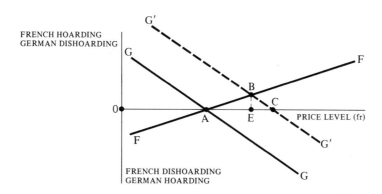

Figure 9.4. A DEPRECIATION OF THE FRANC

the right—by 50 percent since any mark price and any hoarding of marks would now be 50 percent larger when measured in terms of francs.

Suppose that initially the world is in equilibrium at point *A*. If the franc is depreciated in the proportion *AC/OA*, the *GG* line shifts to *G′G′* in Figure 9.4. The equilibrium is at *B*, where France will develop a payments surplus of *BE* and Germany an equal deficit. The French price level has risen by *AE* in francs, and the German price level has fallen by the mark equivalent of *EC*. Thus the diagram shows how exchange depreciation both improves the payments balance and increases inflation. If the new exchange rate is not altered, the payments imbalances continue until the French money supply rises and the German falls enough so that *FF* and *G′G′* both shift downward to intersect on the price level axis.

The diagram also illustrates how the automatic adjustment process and exchange-rate variations offer alternative means of adjustment. For if the world is initially at *B*, in disequilibrium, an alternative to the payments imbalances just described would be an appreciation of the franc that shifts *G′G′* to *GG*. Thus the world would immediately move from *B* to *A* and attain equilibrium, with no changes in national money supplies.

This analysis hinges on purchasing power parity. How important is *PPP* in reality? Table 9.1 summarizes the recent experience of several countries.

The 1st column of the table shows the total percentage change in each country's price level between 1975 and 1980, minus the change in the U.S. price level. Thus Canadian prices rose 11 percent more than did U.S. prices in this period, and German prices rose 20 percent less. The 2nd column shows the total depreciation of each country's currency relative to the U.S.

Table 9.1. Relative Inflation Rates and Depreciation, 1975–1980 (Price levels are GNP and GDP deflators.)

Country	National Inflation Less U.S. Inflation	Depreciation Relative to U.S. Dollar
Australia	20	6
Canada	11	18
France	20	1
Germany	−20	−25
Italy	82	36
Japan	−17	−33
Korea	109	36
Malawi	30	8
U.K.	56	−18

source: *International Financial Statistics*

dollar. If *PPP* held exactly, the two columns would be identical. This is certainly not the case, but there are significant tendencies in this direction. Each country with a higher inflation rate than that of the United States had a depreciating currency, with the notable exception of the United Kingdom, and each currency with a lower inflation rate experienced appreciation. The biggest inflators, Italy and Korea, also experienced the sharpest depreciations, and the absolute size of the inflation differential is always smaller after correction for depreciation—except for the United Kingdom. But, on the other hand, there are substantial differences between depreciations and inflation differentials for all the countries. Overall there are ample indications of both *PPP* and departures from *PPP*. The table shows that these indications differ from country to country, and further examples would show that they also differ substantially from year to year. Tendencies toward *PPP* are often more pronounced over longer time intervals, when price levels and exchange rates have greater opportunities to adjust to each other. The possiblity of year-by-year variability is brought out in Table 9.2, which examines the U.K. experience in greater detail. From 1975 to 1978, *PPP* held almost exactly, but in 1979–1980 the pound appreciated sharply relative to the dollar, despite substantially larger U.K. inflation. (This was widely attributed to be due to expectations of a favorable effect of Britain's North Sea oil on her balance of payments.) In the first half of 1981 this appreciation was partly reversed by a sharp fall against the dollar.

Table 9.2. RELATIVE U.K.-U.S. INFLATION AND EXCHANGE DEPRECIATION

	1975–78	1979–80	Jan. 1981– June 1981
U.K. Inflation Less U.S. Inflation	23	33	8
Depreciation of Pound Relative to Dollar	22	−40	19

SOURCE: *International Financial Statistics*

The substantial deviations from *PPP* require that we examine further aspects of exchange-rate adjustment. Three additional channels are treated in succeeding sections.

PROBLEMS

9.12 Suppose that Italy's income equals 10,000 olives, Spain's equals 4,000 goats, and that two olives exchange for one goat. Italy's money supply equals 100,000 lire, Spain's 80,000 pesetas, and $k=2$. What is the equilibrium exchange rate and prices of the two goods in the two currencies?

9.13 Suppose, in Problem **9.12** above, that the peseta depreciates relative to the lire, by one-half of its equilibrium value. If *PPP* holds, what must happen to the money prices of the two goods in the two currencies if the excess demand for lire is to equal in value the excess supply of pesetas?

9.14 The discussion in the text showed that exchange depreciation tends to increase domestic inflation relative to foreign inflation. Suppose that some exogenous event causes the domestic inflation rate to rise but does not influence foreign inflation. What will be the likely effect on the exchange rate, if the latter is free to adjust? What, in turn, will be the consequences of this adjustment? Compare with the effects of increased domestic inflation when exchange rates are fixed.

9.15 Show how Figure 9.4 can be used to analyze a depreciation of the franc if both axes are measured in *marks*.

9.16 In the text's example of the Law of One Price and exchange depreciation, discuss what happens in *German* markets.

9.17 Can you think of any reasons, in terms of the discussion of this section, why prospects of large-scale exports of North Sea oil should cause the pound to appreciate, as some have suggested?

5. What Exchange Depreciation Does: Relative Price Changes

Purchasing power parity assumes that the terms of trade are fixed so that exchange-rate variations are accompanied by offsetting changes in price levels. To the extent that this is not true there will be changes in relative prices such as the terms of trade. This brings us to the second channel, analogous to the price-specie flow mechanism of the previous chapter. In order to focus clearly on this channel, suppose that the terms of trade p is free to adjust but that the national price levels—P_M and P_W—are fixed.

EXCHANGE RATES AND THE TERMS OF TRADE

Suppose again that the franc depreciates, that is, that R rises. Since $p = RP_M/P_W$ and both P_M and P_W are fixed, the rise in R implies an equiproportional rise in p: German exports become expensive relative to French exports. Individuals will therefore be led to purchase fewer German goods and more French goods. The French balance of trade will increase and the German balance of trade will decline.

The explantion for this is straightforward. Depreciation means that foreign money costs more in terms of domestic money. Since foreign money is needed to purchase foreign goods, foreign goods also cost more in terms of domestic money. Depreciation equivalently means that domestic money is cheaper in terms of foreign money, so that domestic goods are also cheaper for foreigners to buy.

The key parameters are now the *price elasticities*. If these elasticities are large, the change in the terms of trade produced by the depreciation of the franc will bring about a large increase in the French trade balance. Low elasticities imply little or no improvement in the French balance of trade.

This is illustrated in Figure 9.5. In each panel, the initial terms of trade are BJ/OJ. At these terms, France would develop a trade deficit equal to BH, expressed in wine. Suppose that the franc depreciates so that the terms of trade change to $B'J'/OJ'$ in each panel. Then the corresponding trade deficit drops from BH to $B'H'$. In panel (a), where elasticities are high, this improvement is considerable, but in panel (b), with low elasticities, the improvement is slight.

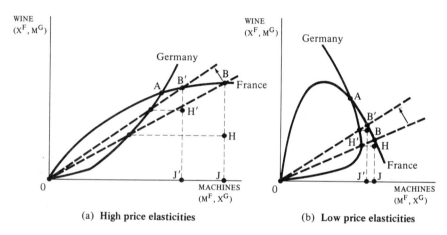

(a) High price elasticities   (b) Low price elasticities

Figure 9.5.   DEPRECIATION AND THE TERMS OF TRADE

EXCHANGE RATES AND RELATIVE PRICES

We now have two alternative ways in which exchange rates relate to relative prices. To the extent that purchasing power parity holds, differences in inflation rates cancel out changes in exchange rates, so that domestic goods do not become cheaper or more expensive relative to foreign goods: depreciation makes itself felt through changing demands for money. But to the extent that *PPP* does not hold, exchange-rate changes will change relative prices, and depreciation will make itself felt in commodity markets. Some prices are more sensitive to the exchange rate than are others. It is useful to classify goods into three categories for this purpose.

1. *Standardized, internationally traded goods.* This category includes goods that enter into international trade and for which one firm's product is virtually indistinguishable from that of another firm: raw materials, intermediate goods such as steel and chemicals, and so forth. The tendency toward *PPP* is strongest for these goods, with the Law of One Price most

compelling. If a certain chemical produced by a U.S. firm is identical to the same chemical produced by a British firm, why should any customer buy from a more expensive source? A depreciation of the pound relative to the dollar will result in great pressure on the U.S. firm to lower its dollar price so as not to lose all its customers to the British rival. If the latter is initially operating at full capacity and thus unable to accept more customers, it will be sorely tempted to raise its pound price and expand profits.

2. *Differentiated, internationally traded goods.* In some cases, such as many consumer goods, the products of competing firms are viewed as distinct by purchasers. An increase in the price of a German Audi automobile relative to a French Peugeot, for example, will cause the former to lose some customers to the latter, but certainly not all potential Audi buyers will switch. Many will be content to pay a higher price for the characteristics unique to the now more expensive product. A depreciation of the franc relative to the mark, then, while putting some pressure on Peugeot to raise prices and on Audi to lower them, would be unlikely to result in the same strong tendency toward *PPP* as with standardized traded goods.

3. *Nontraded goods and services.* Many goods, and especially services, do not compete in international markets at all and therefore need display no direct tendency toward *PPP*. A barber in Brockton, Massachusetts, will not be unduly concerned to learn that a depreciation of the pound has made haircuts in Bristol, England, relatively cheaper.

The distinct responses to exchange-rate variations of these three types of commodity prices result in a mixture of distinct effects on the balance of trade. Exchange depreciation will induce an inflation of domestic prices relative to foreign prices because of the first two categories (especially the first). To this extent propensities to hoard become crucial, as discussed in the previous section. But there will also be a change in the terms of trade as domestic differentiated traded goods become more competitive relative to their foreign counterparts; thus the price elasticities of imports and exports matter. Finally, the prices of both types of traded goods will tend to rise relative to those of nontraded goods. This will cause firms to switch production from the latter to the former, thereby supplying more traded goods for export, and it will also cause consumers to switch their purchases from the former to the latter, thereby reducing imports. The extent to which the trade balance will be improved in this way will depend upon the price elasticities of traded and nontraded goods.

In the long run, the tendency toward *PPP* should become stronger for all three types of goods, including the latter two. The real relative price of Audis and Peugeots should ultimately be determined by underlying considerations of demand and supply and not by exchange rates. If depreciation increases the price of traded goods, this should have an upward effect on the prices of competing nontraded goods. Also the inflation should force up wages, which would in turn raise the prices of nontraded goods: if depreciation of the pound increases inflation in the United Kingdom, wages will rise and therefore the price of haircuts in Bristol, England, will eventually go up, even though they do not compete at all with haircuts in Brockton, Massachusetts.

RECENT EXPERIENCE

Table 9.3 looks in some detail at recent U.S.-Japanese and U.S.-German experience. The first row shows the dollar price of the yen, with 1975 taken as a base year and set equal to 100. Thus in 1977, $141 were required to buy the same quantity of yen that could be purchased for $100 in 1975, that is, the dollar depreciated by 41 percent. The second row shows Japanese wholesale prices converted to dollars and divided by U.S. wholesale prices, with 1975 again set equal to 100. The third row does the same for consumer prices. If *PPP* held exactly, Japanese prices would not change relative to U.S. prices when expressed in the *same* currency, so the bottom two rows would consist only of 100s. If *PPP* did not hold at all, Japanese prices would not change relative to U.S. prices when expressed in *their own* currencies, so that the bottom two rows would both be identical to the top row. The German part of the table is interpreted analogously. The table shows a tendency toward *PPP*, but only a partial one. Furthermore, *PPP* is reflected more strongly in the second row than in the third, in each part of the table. Consumer price indices include more services and relatively more final differentiated goods than do wholesale price indices, and give relatively more weight to nontraded goods.

As part of the International Comparison Project, an extensive effort to render key economic variables comparable across countries, Irving Kravis, of the University of Pennsylvania, and Robert Lipsey, of Queens College,

Table 9.3. INDICES OF U.S. EXCHANGE RATES AND RELATIVE PRICES

		1975	1977	1980	June 1981
Japan:	Exchange Rate ($/Y)	100	141	131	135
	Japan. Wholesale Prices ($) / U.S. Wholesale Prices	100	133	108	103
	Japan. Consumer Prices ($) / U.S. Consumer Prices	100	148	117	105
Germany:	Exchange Rate ($/DM)	100	106	135	104
	Germ. Wholesale Prices ($) / U.S. Wholesale Prices	100	99	102	76
	Germ. Consumer Prices ($) / U.S. Consumer Prices	100	102	108	80

SOURCE: *International Financial Statistics*

made detailed investigations of price behavior. They found departures from *PPP* to be more marked for nontraded goods than for traded goods, but violations of the Law of One Price were extensive and remained significant even when great care was taken to try to compare actual prices of goods as identical as possible. This suggests a wide relevance for our discussion of differentiated, internationally traded goods. Kravis and Lipsey also found evidence that exchange depreciation tends to lower the prices of nontraded goods relative to traded goods and to lower the prices of domestically produced goods relative to foreign goods.

PROBLEMS

9.18 Suppose again that Italy produces 10,000 olives, Spain 4,000 goats, 2 olives exchange for 1 goat in equilibrium, $k=2$, and that Spain's money supply consists of 80,000 pesetas and Italy's of 100,000 lire. Suppose the peseta depreciates by one-half of its equilibrium value, and that the lire price of olives and the peseta price of goats are unchanged. What happens?

9.19 Table 9.3 summarizes U.S.-Japanese and U.S.-German experience. Calculate the analogous table for German-Japanese experience, and discuss it.

9.20* Draw Figure 9.5 so as to display a violation of the Marshall-Lerner condition. Show a disequilibrium terms of trade near an equilibrium where the condition is violated, and show the effects of a depreciation of the currency of the deficit country. What do you conclude?

6. Income Consequences of Depreciation

If depreciation improves the trade balance via relative commodity prices, part of that improvement could be nullified by the third channel: income adjustment. Suppose, for example, that the franc depreciates and that this depreciation increases the relative price of German goods in terms of French goods. Then French imports from Germany decline and German imports from France rise, in amounts determined by price elasticities, so that the French trade balance rises and the German trade balance falls.

French employment and income rise as the French produce the additional goods needed for the increased exports to Germany. At the same time German employment and income fall because the Germans are reducing their production of goods destined for France. The rise in French income then brings about a rise in French imports, as part of the additional income is spent on foreign goods, and the decline in German income likewise produces a decline in German imports. Thus part of the initial improvement in the French balance of trade is nullified by the income changes induced by that improvement itself.

The crucial parameters now are the usual Keynesian parameters—the marginal propensities to save and the marginal propensities to import.

Small values of the *MPS* and large values of the *MPM* imply that a large part of the initial improvement in the trade balance will be offset by induced income changes. A small *MPS* implies a large value of the multiplier, so that the initial trade balance improvement induces a large increase in income. A high *MPM* then implies that a large part of this increased income is spent on foreign goods.

In addition, the initial level of employment is itself important for the success of depreciation in generating a trade surplus. If resources are initially fully employed, there is no way for the economy to produce the additional exports made possible by the rise in *R*. The following point of view is instructive.

The balance of trade surplus *B* is by definition the excess of exports over imports:

$$B = \text{exports} - \text{imports}. \tag{9.5}$$

In addition to exports the economy also produces goods that it does not export but instead uses itself. Since the quantity of such goods that is produced coincides with the quantity that is used, we can rewrite (9.5) as

$$B = (\text{exports} + \text{production of goods not exported}) - (\text{imports} + \text{use of goods not imported}). \tag{9.6}$$

The first term on the right, exports + production of goods not exported, necessarily equals the total production of goods, or income, denoted *Y*. The second term, imports + use of goods not imported, is the total quantity of goods used by the economy. This total is often called *absorption* and denoted *A*. Then (9.6) can also be written

$$B = Y - A . \tag{9.7}$$

This identity is just another way of writing (9.5), but it is useful because it looks in another way at the balance of trade, which it describes in macroeconomic terms. Expression (9.7) makes quite clear the basic point that the trade balance *B* can be increased only by increasing *Y* or reducing absorption *A*. If the economy is at full employment to begin with, so that *Y* cannot be further increased, then it is necessary to reduce *A* in order to increase *B*. A rise in *p* that merely *switches* expenditure from foreign goods toward domestic goods will be ineffective because a *reduction* in expenditure, or absorption, is what is called for.

This reduction in absorption could be brought about in other ways, such as restrictive monetary and fiscal policies. Or the depreciation could itself reduce *A* by working through another channel. For example, the increase in *R* could raise *p* and so switch expenditure toward domestic goods. With the home economy already at full employment it would be impossible to supply the additional demand for domestic goods. This could force their price up, that is, generate domestic inflation. This inflation would increase the demand for money above the supply, as indicated by (9.1), and thereby cause domestic residents to accumulate additional money by cutting back expenditure, that is, by lowering A. As (9.7) reveals, this will improve the balance of trade. This chain of events is simply the channel discussed already in section 4 above.

Figure 9.6 shows the role of income. In this simple context, S-I equals Y-A, because income Y consists of saving S and consumption C while absorption A is composed of investment I plus consumption (thus $Y - A = [S + C] - [I + C] = S$-$I$). Depreciation makes domestic goods cheaper relative to foreign goods and thereby shifts the X-M curve up; this is shown by the shift to X'-M' in the figure. At unchanged income, the depreciation is just sufficient to eliminate the initial trade deficit, AE. But income increases by AH and consequently the trade deficit is merely reduced, from AE to HD. But even this need not happen if unemployed resources are not readily available. Suppose, for example, the economy was initially fully employed at A. Then income cannot be raised by AH, and the upward shift in X-M therefore produces an excess demand for domestic goods in the amount AE. This forces domestic prices up, making domestic goods more expensive relative to foreign goods and shifting the X-M schedule back down. This continues until the X-M line returns to its original position: depreciation has had no effect on the trade balance and has only raised prices. Elimination of the trade deficit requires that Y-A also shift up. If both schedules shift as indicated in Figure 9.6, their new intersection is at A, where the deficit has been eliminated and income is unchanged.

Although the income effects of depreciation are likely to be troublesome when the economy is at or near full employment, they will not be so otherwise. With substantial unemployment, the income effects will neutralize only a portion of the depreciation-induced increase in the balance of

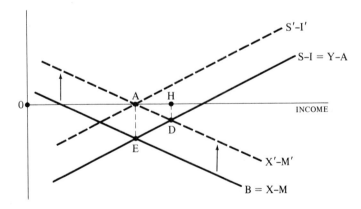

Figure 9.6. DEPRECIATION AND NATIONAL INCOME

trade. But, more importantly, in these circumstances the stimulating effect of depreciation on income and employment would be most welcome. Many devaluations that took place in the 1930s were motivated, at least in part, by a desire to combat the Depression.

PROBLEMS

9.21 Suppose the French suddenly acquire an enhanced taste for German goods. Analyze how the exchange rate must adjust to maintain balance of payments equilibrium.

9.22 Suppose that a country is initially at full employment and levies a tariff. Discuss the effects on the balance of trade and on aggregate demand, at the initial exchange rate. How must the exchange rate be altered to keep the balance of trade unchanged?

9.23 Does it matter whether the axes in Figure 9.6 are measured in terms of domestic currency or of foreign currency? Why?

9.24* Must the discussion of Figure 9.6 be altered if the demand for imports is price inelastic?

7. Interest Parity

Preceding sections examined three channels through which exchange depreciation exerts its effect on the balance of payments. All of these involved the balance of trade. But depreciation also influences international capital movements.

Individuals in France will hold their wealth partly in the form of money (francs), partly in the form of bonds denominated in francs, partly in the form of assets denominated in foreign currency (marks), and partly in the form of assets denominated in no currency at all (stocks, real estate, and so on). Wealth will be divided among these various forms in whatever proportions best suit its owner. Now suppose the franc depreciates. The response of French wealth owners to this depreciation will depend upon how they expect the franc to behave in the future.

Suppose, first, that people view the depreciation of the franc as *permanent*, that is, they expect it to remain at its new level. The value of assets denominated in marks has risen in terms of francs. If the French were initially holding the various forms of wealth in the desired proportions, they cannot be doing so now. They will respond by selling mark assets to buy more of the other assets. This tends to increase the French capital account surplus. This increase will be maintained only as long as it takes for people to restore their desired proportions of the various assets relative to each other.

■ *Portfolio Valuation Example.* Pierre wishes to hold three-fourths of his wealth in franc assets and one-fourth in mark assets. He owns fr30,000 of franc bonds and DM10,000 of mark bonds. If the exchange rate is initially one franc per mark, the mark bonds are worth fr10,000 and Pierre has his desired portfolio. Now suppose the franc depreciates so that two francs buy a single mark. If Pierre expects this change to be permanent he will now feel that his portfolio has too many mark bonds, since the DM10,000 of the latter are now worth fr20,000, or two-fifths of the entire portfolio. He will then sell the extra mark bonds (how many?), contributing to an increased French capital-account surplus. This influence is not permanent and ends when Pierre, and others like him, have their desired portfolios. ■

Suppose, next, that people view the depreciation of the franc as *temporary*, that is, they expect it to appreciate back in the future, or they expect the mark to depreciate. Such expectations influence the relative attractiveness of franc bonds and mark bonds. Suppose, for example, that people expect the mark to depreciate by d percent. Consider a French broker, Marie, wondering how to invest her clients' wealth. If she invests in French bonds, she earns the French rate of interest, call it i_F. If she instead invests in German bonds, she will earn the German rate of interest i_G. But in the latter case her investments will be in the form of marks, and the mark is expected to decrease in value by d percent relative to the franc. Thus the net return to Marie's clients for investing in German bonds is $i_G - d$. In deciding where to put her entrusted wealth, Marie will compare i_F to $i_G - d$. If Marie now comes to expect that the mark will depreciate by more than she had previously thought, that is, if d rises, then German bonds become less attractive relative to French bonds, and she will be led to buy the former and to sell the latter.

If, then, a depreciation of the home currency is regarded as temporary, people will expect it to appreciate back, and domestic bonds become more attractive relative to foreign bonds, so that the capital account surplus will tend to rise. Again, this tendency is temporary and ceases once people acquire the portfolios they desire. What happens next depends upon the future behavior of interest rates and exchange-rate expectations.

The extent of adjustment through the capital account depends upon the degree of international capital mobility. If citizens of each country are completely unwilling or unable to own the bonds of other countries, the present channel of exchange-rate effects will be totally absent. At the other extreme is *perfect international capital mobility:* residents of each country treat the bonds of all countries as perfect substitutes and so always buy the one with the highest yield. In this case, i_F and $i_G - d$ must be equal, because no one would be willing to hold any of the bond with the lower return (thus forcing up its interest rate). Thus $d = i_G - i_F$.

> **KEY CONCEPT**
>
> If capital mobility is perfect, expected exchange rate changes are related to differences in interest rate levels by *interest parity:*
>
> *(IP)* (expected depreciation) = (domestic interest rate) − (foreign interest rate).

This relationship expresses the idea that the expected rate of depreciation of a nation's currency cancels out international differences in interest rates. Interest parity is a characteristic of perfect capital mobility; the more nearly perfect are international capital markets, the stronger is the tendency toward *IP.*

ILLUSTRATION OF INTEREST PARITY

The degree to which interest parity holds can be interpreted as a measure of the degree of international capital mobility. But unfortunately we cannot look within the hearts and minds of individuals to discern their expectations about the future. For example, the 1st column of Table 9.4 shows the amount by which prime interest rates in various countries exceeded that in the United States in January of 1981. The 2nd column shows the *actual* depreciations (at annual rates) of the respective currencies over the next three months. The columns would coincide if interest parity were exact. There is in fact little indication of interest parity; only Canada comes close, and in four cases the two entries do not even have the same sign. But there is a basic reason why this can indicate nothing about the degree of capital mobility: we have no idea of how successful people had been in forecasting the actual depreciations before they took place. We would expect that, over

Table 9.4. INTEREST DIFFERENTIALS AND DEPRECIATION, JANUARY 1981

Country	*Excess of Prime Rate above U.S. Rate*	*Actual Subsequent Depreciation Relative to Dollar*
Canada	.28	.00
France	−5.42	8.00
Germany	−7.22	5.00
Italy	.70	10.00
Japan	−8.35	5.00
U.K.	−3.48	11.00

time, errors in one direction would tend to cancel out errors in the other direction, so that interest differentials and exchange depreciations would more nearly match on the average over the long run. Table 9.5 shows average interest differentials over 1979 as a whole and average subsequent depreciations relative to the dollar. The correspondence between the two is much closer than that in Table 9.4. Nevertheless, quantification of the importance of interest parity is basically prevented by the fact that people's expectations are not observable.

Table 9.5. AVERAGE INTEREST DIFFERENTIALS AND DEPRECIATIONS, 1979

Country	Average Interest Differential* Over U.S.	Average Subsequent Depreciation Relative to Dollar
Canada	1.6	2.7
France	−3.2	−6.1
Germany	−5.3	−6.4
Italy	.7	−1.2
Japan	−5.6	−6.1
U.K.	3	5.3

* Call money rates for France, Germany, Italy, and Japan; treasury bill rates for Canada and U.K.

SOURCE: *International Financial Statistics*

When the expected rate of depreciation is in fact the actual rate of depreciation, interest parity (*IP*) and purchasing power parity (*PPP*) together imply that

(domestic inflation) − (foreign inflation) = (domestic interest rate) − (foreign interest rate).

International differences in interest rates match international differences in inflation rates.

PROBLEMS

9.25 What would have happened, in the discussion in the text, if people had regarded the depreciation of the franc as temporary, but as merely the first in a series of depreciations, rather than as a change to be reversed?

9.26 Discuss the effects of a French decision to depreciate the franc relative to the mark by 10 percent each year indefinitely.

9.27 The French increase their money supply by 50 percent and decide to adjust the exchange rate so as to keep the balance of payments equal to zero. Describe what could happen.

9.28 Describe the effects of a shift in the preferences of French wealth holders toward German bonds and away from all other assets.

8. Overview of Exchange-Rate Adjustment

The four aspects of exchange-rate adjustment identify different key parameters. The relative importance of the various channels then determines the relative importance of the different parameters, but it is also true that the sizes of the parameters help determine which aspects are more important. Another key consideration is the degree of *price flexibility:* if prices are flexible enough to respond promptly to exchange-rate changes, the latter will not cause significant changes in relative prices. Thus purchasing power parity and international capital movements must be the important aspects. Different views of which aspect is important result in different views of the role of the exchange rate: the latter is likely to be regarded as an important policy variable by someone who thinks income adjustment is dominant.

COMMODITY FLOW AND ASSET MARKET THEORIES OF THE EXCHANGE RATE

Price flexibility is closely related to yet another pair of divergent interpretations of the role of the exchange rate. Inflexibility implies that relative price changes and income adjustments are important: the exchange rate is linked to *commodity* markets and *flows* of demands and supplies of goods. In this view the symptom of an equilibrium exchange rate is its ability to reconcile these demands and supplies and to produce an equilibrium balance of trade. It will do this because it directly influences relative commodity prices.

A high degree of price flexibility, on the other hand, gives prominence to the hoarding and dishoarding of monies and to the international exchange of assets denominated in various currencies. The exchange rate is linked to *asset* markets. In this view the symptom of an equilibrium exchange rate is its ability to equilibrate the demands and supplies of *stocks* of various assets. It can do this because it is the relative price of two assets: home and foreign money.

AN ECLECTIC VIEW

Since prices are neither completely flexible nor totally inflexible, both of these very divergent views of the exchange rate are valid. One might wonder how a single exchange rate can adjust both to equilibrate commodity markets and simultaneously to clear asset markets. The reason is that the exchange rate does not have to do either job by itself; partial flexibility of commodity prices help in the flow markets, and interest rates adjust stock demands and supplies. But while an eclectic view is certainly called for, there is much disagreement over the relative importance of the various aspects of adjustment, and also uncertainty about how the different views fit together.

One prominent description of how the commodity flow and asset market roles of the exchange rate come together asserts that in the short run asset markets primarily determine the exchange rate. The reason is that asset markets seem to adjust very quickly. The value of the exchange rate determined in the asset markets then influences commodity markets, where prices adjust slowly. This influence affects the balance of trade, the level of national income, and rates of price changes. All this then feeds back into the asset markets. For example, money supplies may change in response to the trade balance if the authorities intervene to prevent a pure float of the exchange rate. Demands for money and assets will be influenced by changing prices, the trade balance, and the level of employment, as well as by how the markets expect the authorities to react to all these. The changed asset market conditions then alter the exchange rate, and so on.

PROBLEM

9.29 Suppose everyone becomes aware that in one year increased exports of North Sea oil will improve Britain's trade balance. Describe the effect on a floating exchange rate according to:

    a A pure commodity flow theory of the exchange rate.

    b A pure asset market theory.

9. Case Study: Exchange-Rate Volatility

One attractive feature of the previous section's description of the relation between the two views of the exchange rate is that the latter is hypothesized to behave in the short run like an asset price. That is, it should fluctuate a lot in response to new information, just as stock prices on Wall Street react dramatically to news reports. The reason this is attractive is that in recent years exchange rates have in fact fluctuated much more than would be necessary to respond to changes in prices or likely changes in underlying equilibrium conditions. Whether these fluctuations indicate that foreign exchange markets are working badly or not is a question we shall confront in Chapter 10, when we study those markets.

Jacob Frenkel, of the University of Chicago, has compared exchange rate volatility with that of price indices. The first column of Table 9.6 shows, in percentages, the mean month-to-month change in the consumer price indices of four countries, and the second column does the same for each

Table 9.6. MEAN MONTH-TO-MONTH ABSOLUTE PERCENTAGE
CHANGES, JUNE 1973–JULY 1979

Consumer Prices

Country	National	National Relative to U.S.	Exchange Rate Relative to $U.S.	Stock Market
U.S.	.7	—	—	3.7
U.K.	1.2	.7	2.1	6.6
France	.9	.3	2.0	5.4
Germany	.4	.4	2.4	3.0

SOURCE: *J. Frenkel, "Flexible Exchange Rates, Prices, and the Role of 'News': Lessons from the 1970s,"* Journal of Political Economy, *August 1981*

country's index relative to that of the United States. Thus the French consumer price index on average changed by three-tenths of 1 percent relative to the United States' consumer price index each month during the period. The third column shows that exchange rates varied much more. This large variability is to be expected of a stock market, as indicated by the last column. The fact that exchange rates varied less than stock prices could indicate the presence of some commodity flow role for the former, or it could indicate the presence of intervention, that is, less than free floating. Frenkel presented evidence that the variations in exchange rates were linked to receipt of new information (reflected in unexpected interest rate changes).

10. *Exploring Further:* Floating Exchange Rates

We can further investigate the relation between the different views of the exchange rate by focusing on a floating rate: the authorities in each country control their own money supply and make no attempt to influence the exchange rate.

Figure 9.7(a)—a reproduction of Figure 9.1—shows the equilibrium exchange rate determined by the intersection of the demand and supply curves. The ray through the origin in Figure 9.7(b) shows what the equilibrium exchange rate must be for each value of the ratio of the French price level to the German price level.

We know that $p = RP_M/P_W$, or $R = p (P_W/P_M)$ where the equilibrium terms of trade p is determined by real considerations. Thus R is related

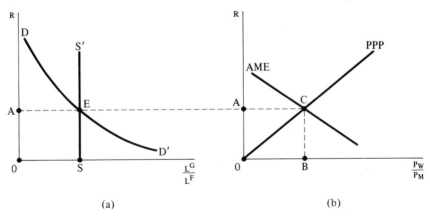

Figure 9.7. Long-Run and Short-Run Equilibrium

to P_W/P_M by a straight line with slope equal to p. The world must be somewhere on this line in equilibrium; the money supplies determine exactly where. With the German money supply relative to the French equal to OS in Figure 9.7(a), equilibrium is at C in Figure 9.7(b). If R and P_W/P_M move together on this line, the relation between them will not change: purchasing power parity will be exactly preserved. Thus the line is labeled *PPP*.

The world must be on the *PPP* line for long-run equilibrium. In the short run asset markets determine the exchange rate. The *AME* (asset market equilibrium) line shows what the exchange rate will be for any ratio of the French and German price levels. Since C is an equilibrium, *AME* must intersect *PPP* at that point. If the world will eventually get to long-run equilibrium, and if people have at least a rough idea of how the exchange rate will change, *AME* must have a negative slope. For suppose the actual exchange rate is above its long-run equilibrium value of OA in Figure 9.7(b). Then people expect that R will fall, that is, that the franc will appreciate. This makes franc-denominated assets more attractive than mark-denominated assets, so the French interest rate must be relatively low to compensate. But low French interest rates would cause the French demand for money to exceed the fixed supply of francs. This can only be prevented if the French price level is also relatively low, implying a lower demand for money. Thus if R is above its long-run equilibrium value, P_W/P_M must be below: *AME* has a negative slope.

Now suppose that the French authorities increase their money supply. This lowers the ratio L^G/L^F, shifting the supply curve SS' to the left, as indicated in Figure 9.8(a), so that the new long-run equilibrium is at E', corresponding to C' in panel (b). *AME* shifts to $A'M'E'$, through C'.

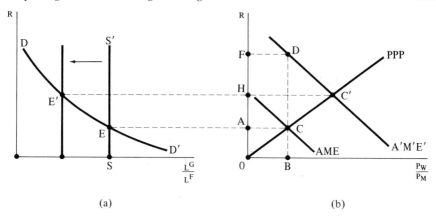

Figure 9.8. ADJUSTMENT TO A MONETARY SHOCK

Somehow the world economy must move from C to C'. One possibility would be for R and P_W/P_M to rise together, so that the movement is along the PPP line. In this case purchasing power parity would always hold exactly, there would be no relative price changes and no real effects, and we would have a purely monetary theory of the exchange rate. But we have seen that purchasing power parity does not in fact work in this relentless way. So suppose instead that commodity prices react slowly; initially P_W/P_M does not rise but remains equal to OB. Since the world must be on $A'M'E'$ for asset market equilibrium, the exchange rate must rise by DC, giving a new short-run equilibrium at D. Thus the increase in the French money supply produces a large depreciation of the franc. This also involves a departure from purchasing power parity, with French goods now cheaper relative to German. The French develop a trade surplus—and corresponding capital account deficit—and French aggregate demand is stimulated. The reverse takes place in Germany.

Eventually the higher demand for French goods and lower demand for German goods must cause P_W/P_M to begin rising. The world moves along $A'M'E'$ from D toward C'. This movement violates purchasing power parity, but that is necessary to compensate for the opposite violation in the movement from C to D. When the world arrives at the new long-run equilibrium at C', purchasing power parity will have been verified in the long-run sense of a comparison of C and C', although the movement from one to the other involved sharp departures from PPP in opposite directions. Also the adjustment process will have involved much volatility of the exchange rate: first it increased from OA to OF—overshooting its long-run equilibrium value of OH—and then gradually fell part way back.

We have looked at the consequences of a monetary disturbance, so let us now consider a real one. Suppose that consumers shift their tastes from

German goods (machines) toward French goods (wine). This means that
the equilibrium value of *p*—the relative price of machines in terms of
wine—must fall. This is indicated by the shift of the *PPP* line to *PPP'* in
Figure 9.9. The new long run equilibrium is at *C'*, and the world must get
there from *C*. How is this to happen?

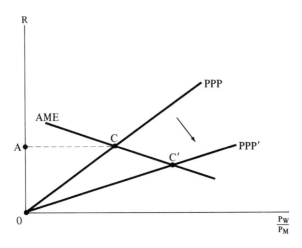

Figure 9.9.   ADJUSTMENT TO A REAL DISTURBANCE

At the initial prices and exchange rate, the shift in tastes toward
French goods produces a French trade surplus (and thus a corresponding
capital account deficit). This tends to stimulate French income. Also people
know that, with the world at *C* but long-run equilibrium at *C'*, the franc
must appreciate. This makes franc denominated assets more attractive, so
asset market equilibrium requires that the French interest rate fall to compensate. This further stimulates aggregate demand in France. Germany
experiences the reverse of all this.

Eventually the higher demand for French goods and lower demand
for German goods starts to force P_W/P_M up. Then *R* must fall to preserve
asset market equilibrium: the world moves from *C* to *C'* along *AME*.

This adjustment in response to a real shock has differed in two ways
from the earlier adjustment to a monetary shock. First, *PPP* has been violated not only during the transition, but also in terms of the long-run
comparison of *C* and *C'*. This must be so because a real shock changes
equilibrium relative prices. Second, the adjustment from *C* to *C'* involved
no more volatililty of the exchange rate than of commodity prices: even
though we still assumed that the latter must adjust slowly, the exchange rate
did not overshoot. Instead interest rates were volatile: the French interest
rate initially dropped abruptly relative to the German and then gradually

moved back into alignment. The prices of securities—linked to the interest they pay—were the volatile elements. With a real shock the exchange rate behaved like commodity prices and not like asset prices, whereas the opposite was the case with a monetary shock.

PROBLEMS

9.30 Can the different responses of the exchange rate to monetary and real shocks help explain why in Table 9.6 exchange rates were more volatile than commodity prices but less so than asset prices?

9.31 The monetary shock analyzed in this section was an unanticipated increase in the French money supply. Suppose instead that the French authorities announce that in one year they will increase the money supply by a certain amount, that eveyone believes them, and that they then do so. Discuss the likely consequences.

9.32* The discussion of the slope of the *AME* line assumed that people expected the exchange rate to move toward its long-run equilibrium value. Suppose instead that they expect any departure from that value to be accentuated, at least for a while. How might this affect the slope of the *AME* line and the subsequent analysis?

11. Exchange Regimes in Practice

Section 9 of Chapter 8 briefly described present exchange-rate arrangements. The current situation can be described only as complex. It is complex, first, because different countries have different regimes. The European Economic Community nations (except for Greece) have formed the European Monetary System (EMS) and (except for Britain) maintain adjustable pegs vis-à-vis each other. Other industrial countries, by and large, have managed floats. Thus the French franc is pegged to the German mark and Italian lira but floats, with management, relative to the U.S. dollar and the Japanese yen. The EMS arrangement is called the "snake" because the participants' currencies jointly meander relative to the currencies of outsiders. Figure 9.10 shows the recent behavior of EMS exchange rates relative to the dollar.

Many LDCs maintain adjustable pegs relative to the U.S. dollar, and some peg to the French franc, U.K. pound, Spanish peseta or South African rand. A few of these pegs are unadjustable, that is, fixed. The relation of these currencies with each other is determined by the relations between the currencies to which they are pegged. For example, the Panamanian balboa is fixed in terms of the dollar, Botswana pegs its pula to the dollar, and the Gambia pegs its currency, the dalasi, to the U.K. pound. Thus, indirectly, the balboa and the pula are pegged to each other and in a managed float against the dalasi. Still other countries peg to a basket of currencies rather

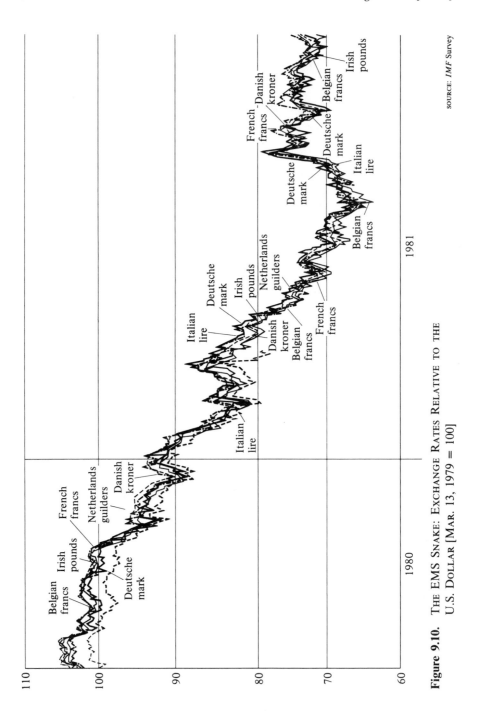

Figure 9.10. THE EMS SNAKE: EXCHANGE RATES RELATIVE TO THE
U.S. DOLLAR [MAR. 13, 1979 = 100]

SOURCE: *IMF* Survey

than a single one. Thus Saudi Arabia pegs the riyal to a basket consisting of specified amounts of dollars, marks, and so on. The riyal might appreciate against the dollar, say, if that appreciation is offset by a depreciation relative to other currencies in the basket. Finally, exchange control is widespread. Most European countries had extensive controls until 1958 and still sometimes impose limits on their citizens' freedom to exchange assets with foreigners. The United States had controls on capital movements in the late sixties and early seventies, and Britain retained various restrictions until the late seventies. But, by and large, exchange controls in the DCs are isolated measures aimed at specific limited purposes and not representative of the basic character of the exchange regimes. This is not true of the LDCs and the communist states, where exchange control is pervasive.

A second reason for the complexity of contemporary practice is that individual countries typically rely on combinations of regimes. The isolated use of exchange controls by DCs has already been cited. Countries that peg their currencies seldom do so completely. Instead they typically establish a band around the peg in which the exchange rate floats (with or without management), and pegging consists of preventing the exchange rate from leaving the band. For example, when the EMS officially began in March 1979 the French franc was pegged to the German mark at fr2.31/DM. On September 24, 1979, the peg was adjusted by 2 percent to fr2.356/DM. But the upper and lower limits of intervention are 2.25 percent on each side of the peg, that is, the authorities are in fact obligated to keep the exchange rate within a 4.5 percent band, centered on the peg. Figure 9.11 illustrates the situation.

Pegging involves keeping the market rate in the band, within which it floats, perhaps with management. Thus countries with an adjustable peg also typically float to some extent. Still another combination is a *duel exchange market,* utilized by Belgium, Italy, and some other countries. In Belgium, for example, citizens who require foreign currency to purchase

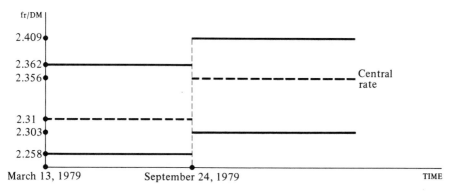

Figure 9.11. THE FRANC/MARK EXCHANGE RATE IN THE EMS

foreign goods must buy the currency at the *commercial* foreign exchange rate, while citizens who wish to buy and sell financial assets must use the *financial* rate. The commercial rate is pegged (Belgium is in the EMS), and the financial rate floats. The system is thus a combination of three regimes: exchange control, adjustable peg, and floating. A dual exchange market is a special case of *multiple exchange markets,* used by many LDCs. Foreign exchange dealings are segmented into a number of separate markets, and a citizen must use a specific market depending upon the reason she wants to buy or sell foreign currency. Arrangements often differ between markets, with a pegged rate in one market, a floating rate in another, and complete reliance on administrative controls in yet another market.

Still another source of complexity is the fact that different countries often use a single regime in markedly different ways. Methods of exchange control differ enormously from country to country. The degree of management of a managed float can vary. American authorities, for example, have typically practiced light management whereas the Japanese have often intervened on a large scale, sometimes to the extent of, in effect, pegging the yen. The adjustability of an adjustable peg can vary from country to country. A number of Latin American countries routinely adjust their pegs each month. By contrast, throughout the fifties and sixties the DCs were very reluctant to ever adjust their pegs, even in the face of large payments imbalances. Malaysia pegs its Ringgit to a basket, but the composition of the basket is a secret.

Complexity also arises from the fact that countries often alter their exchange regimes or their ways of administering regimes. Methods of exchange control are often varied; many countries have stopped pegging to the dollar and begun pegging to currency baskets. Some countries have switched from an adjustable peg to a managed float or vice versa, the extent of management of a float has varied from year to year or from month to month, and so on. For example, after following a basically passive policy, U.S. authorities announced in late 1978 that they would actively attempt to limit depreciation of the dollar. But then in early 1981 authorities announced that the United States would not intervene at all (that is, shift from managed floating to free floating), except under extraordinary circumstances, such as the immediate aftermath of an attempted assassination of President Reagan. As another example, the European snake was in existence for five years before the start of the EMS in 1979, and during those years participation in the scheme varied greatly.

ADVANTAGES AND DISADVANTAGES OF THE VARIOUS REGIMES

Exchange control is a method of influencing international trade and investment, as well as the payments mechanism. Thus it possesses the advantages and disadvantages of other means of protection, discussed in detail in Chapters 5 and 6. The regime is attractive to governments that want to pursue economic or political goals at odds with free-market behavior, and therefore exchange control is most likely to appeal to those nations that generally try to manipulate the economy. This is why the regime is common in LDCs and communist countries. The disadvantages are those that pertain to economic controls generally: distortions, inequities and inefficiencies, and a tendency for black markets and other evasive practices to develop and for bureaucratic control to grow in response.

CASE STUDY: Financial Wizardry in the Third Reich

During the Depression many governments resorted in desperation to exchange controls, the practice attaining a perfection of sorts in Hitler's Germany with an elaborate system devised by economics minister Hjalmar Horace Greely Schacht (his father had lived for a time in America and acquired an admiration for the famous journalist). Experience with the system was described by Douglas Miller in a book review in the *American Economic Review* (December 1943, pp. 923–25).

> . . . New decrees were published so rapidly that American government representatives could not keep pace in translating and dispatching them to Washington. . . .
>
> When the text of new laws and decrees was published, printed copies were piled on the floor beside the desk of the unhappy translator, higher than the top of his desk. In ordinary trade practice there is a normal lapse of several weeks or months between the placing of an order for foreign goods and the final shipment to the customer. During this period so many changes in regulations could and did take place that business men became discouraged and were unwilling to make new contracts. . . .
>
> Dr. Schacht's cynicism about Germany's financial integrity went so far that he even seemed to take pleasure in the distress of foreign creditors, and he enjoyed the sensation of confusing and bewildering them. . . .
>
> . . . It became well known in Berlin that successful applications for exchange permits should be accompanied by tangible rewards. Sometime these ran into high figures. Curiously enough, in many cases small gifts of rare articles were very successful in obtaining needed official documents. It was reliably reported that the standard bribe of two cartons of American cigarettes would usually insure the granting of exchange permits in doubtful cases, when there was no sub-

stantial objection. Some of the German officials had acquired
the un-German habit of smoking American cigarettes with
their characteristic flavor and could no longer be satisfied by
the domestic brands. The exchange and tariff regulations
brought the cost of an ordinary 15-cent packet to the price of
6 marks in tobacco stores and 9 marks plus 10 per cent tax in
hotels and night clubs. This price raised them to the status of
real luxuries, presents fit for a Nazi bigshot.

The great advantage of fixed exchange rates is that each nation's
currency becomes more useful as money. The basic economic roles of
money are store of value, medium of exchange, and unit of account. When
foreign currency has a fixed value in terms of domestic currency, it becomes
a simple matter to make sense of foreign-currency prices of foreign goods;
travelers are likely to find foreigners willing to accept the travelers' money
as payment; and no one need worry about which currency is the safer form
of holding liquid balances. Both domestic and foreign currencies are more
useful as money than either would be if the exchange rate were liable to
fluctuate. You can easily appreciate this point if you imagine for a moment
that New York and New Jersey each had its own money, with a flexible
exchange rate between the two. Consider the plight of a New Jersey com-
muter working in New York. She would be paid in N.Y. dollars but would
have large obligations, such as a mortgage, in terms of N.J. dollars and so
would be unsure about how much of her salary would be required for these
obligations. But in addition to her N.J. bills she would have to make some
N.Y. purchases (for example, lunches) and so would always have to keep
some of each currency on hand. Many consumer items could be bought in
either New York or New Jersey, so she would be constantly trying to compare prices expressed in terms of the two currencies. Finally the consumer
would need to worry about whether it would be safer to keep her savings
account, bonds, and so forth in terms of N.Y. dollars or N.J. dollars.

As this example makes clear, the basic advantage of fixed exchange
rates is also the basic disadvantage of floating rates. The converse is also
true. The great advantage of floating exchange rates is that they allow
individual countries to control their own money supplies, whereas with
fixed rates national monetary policies are inextricably linked.

Chapter 11 will look in detail at the efforts of the countries of the
world to fashion an efficient international monetary system. These efforts
involve much debate about the alleged advantages and disadvantages of
the various exchange regimes. Such debate really consists only of elabora-
tion of the basic points just discussed, and applications of the basic theory
contained in Chapters 8 and 9.

PROBLEMS

9.33 This section gave reasons why a country might wish to peg its currency rather than to float. But why might it want to peg to a currency basket rather than to some individual currency? What considerations might influence the decision of which currency or currency basket to peg to? Does it matter whether the authorities hold a commodity flow or an asset market view of the exchange rate?

9.34 With a pegged exchange rate the authorities usually establish a band around the peg within which the exchange rate is allowed to float, perhaps freely, perhaps not. Under the gold standard a similar band was common, not because of policy, but because of the cost (shipping, insurance, and foregone interest) of transporting gold from one country to another. Suppose that in Paris the French authorities freely exchanged gold and francs at the rate of fr100/ounce while in Berlin the German authorities bought and sold gold for DM50/ounce. Suppose it cost the equivalent of one-tenth of an ounce of gold to transport each ounce between Paris and Berlin. Calculate the band within which the franc price of a mark must fall.

12. Aggregate Demand Management with Floating Exchange Rates

We now consider how monetary and fiscal policy operate in an open economy with a floating exchange rate. Since the major advantage of such an exchange-rate regime is that it gives an individual country control over its monetary policy, let us consider that first.

MONETARY POLICY

Suppose that the authorities expand the domestic money supply through open market operations (buying bonds from the public). The easier monetary conditions will force down the domestic interest rate and stimulate aggregate demand. Lower interest rates make domestic assets less attractive relative to foreign assets, and therefore, at the original exchange rate, a capital-account deficit would emerge. Also the expansion of aggregate demand would involve an increased demand for imports so that a trade-account deficit would also develop. Now, with floating exchange rates the authorities do not sell international reserves, so the exchange rate must adjust to prevent these deficits from emerging and to keep the overall balance of payments equal to zero. Thus, *an expansionary monetary policy causes the exchange rate to depreciate.* This depreciation will make domestic goods more attractive to consumers, relative to foreign goods, and thereby increase aggregate demand still more. *With a floating exchange rate, expansionary monetary policy stimulates aggregate demand.* Note also that inflationary pressures rise: the increase in aggregate demand of course tends to stimulate inflation, but in addition exchange depreciation is itself infla-

tionary, as we saw in section 3. Recall from Chapter 8 that with fixed
exchange rates a country has only transitory control over its money supply;
indeed section 15 of Chapter 8 showed that, if capital is perfectly mobile,
monetary policy has no effect at all on aggregate demand. Thus monetary
policy is more effective under floating rates than under fixed rates.

The role of capital mobility.
 The above conclusions do not depend upon the degree of international capital mobility. But that degree is still very important. This can be
seen most clearly by contrasting the cases of no mobility and perfect mobility. This is done in Figure 9.12. With no capital mobility, the increased
money supply is free to force down the domestic interest rate without causing a capital-account deficit; this stimulates investment and so shifts the
curve *S-I* downward to *S'-I'* in Figure 9.12(a). At the initial exchange rate
this would shift equilibrium from point *A* to *C*, so that aggregate demand *y*
would rise from *OA* to *OB*. But this would cause a trade deficit, and therefore balance of payments deficit, equal to *BC*. To prevent this, the exchange
rate depreciates, shifting the *X-M* line up to *X'-M'*. The equilibrium is at *D*,
where aggregate demand has increased from *OA* to *OD*, and where trade is
balanced. In fact monetary policy has been just as potent as it would have
been in a closed economy.
 If, in contrast, international capital mobility is perfect, domestic interest rates cannot diverge from foreign interest rates, so monetary policy
cannot produce a shift of the *S-I* line in Figure 9.12(b): the bonds purchased from the public are replaced by new purchases abroad. But this

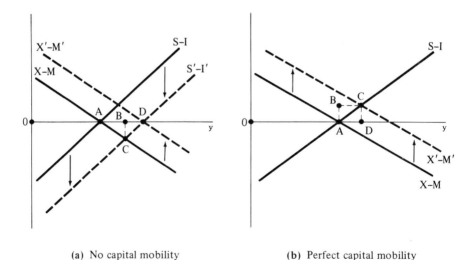

(a) No capital mobility   (b) Perfect capital mobility

Figure 9.12. EXPANSIONARY MONETARY POLICY

means that a capital-account deficit is generated. Suppose this deficit equals the distance AB in the figure. Since the overall balance of payments cannot be in deficit, the exchange rate must depreciate enough to generate a trade surplus just equal to AB. This will be accomplished by a depreciation that shifts the X-M line up to X'-M'. New equilibrium is at C so that aggregate demand has increased from OA to OD.

In both cases monetary policy succeeds in raising aggregate demand, but it does so in quite different ways and accordingly has different results. In panel (a) the new equilibrium involves balanced trade and no net capital flows, but with perfect capital mobility the new equilibrium in panel (b) features a trade surplus and a capital-account deficit. This means that the new equilibrium is only *temporary:* once domestic citizens have bought enough bonds from abroad to replace those sold to the authorities the capital account deficit will cease and the economy will revert back to point A. In order to permanently maintain the higher level of aggregate demand the authorities must continue their expansionary monetary operations and not merely conduct them once, as would be sufficient with no capital mobility. Thus, *the greater is the degree of international capital mobility, the more temporary will be the stimulative effects of a monetary expansion.*

Even more important is the difference in international repercussions. In panel (a) the foreign economy is not affected through the capital account by domestic monetary policy, because there is no capital mobility by assumption. There are no effects through the trade account either, because trade is balanced in both the new equilibrium and the old. Thus domestic monetary policy has no macroeconomic effect abroad. (It may have microeconomic effects, however, if the exchange depreciation alters relative prices abroad. Thus it is not correct, even with no capital mobility, to say that domestic monetary policy has no foreign repercussions in a floating-rate regime.) But with perfect capital mobility the new equilibrium features a balance of trade surplus, so that the foreign country has a trade deficit and therefore a lower level of aggregate demand. That is, monetary policy stimulates the domestic economy by depressing the rest of the world. (If the home economy is large enough, domestic monetary policy might change both domestic and foreign interest rates together and thereby also influence the foreign economy in that way.) Thus, *the greater the degree of international capital mobility, the greater are the perverse foreign repercussions of domestic monetary policy.*

FISCAL POLICY

Recall that fiscal policy can be used under fixed exchange rates to control aggregate demand, even if capital is perfectly mobile. The easiest way to evaluate the effectiveness of fiscal policy with floating rates is to separately consider the two extreme cases of no capital mobility and perfect mobility. This is done in Figure 9.13.

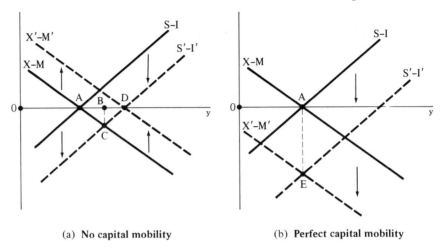

(a) **No capital mobility**   (b) **Perfect capital mobility**

Figure 9.13. EXPANSIONARY FISCAL POLICY

Suppose first that capital is completely immobile and that the authorities increase government spending, that is, they raise autonomous expenditure *I*. This would shift the *S-I* curve downward and stimulate aggregate
demand. Now as aggregate demand rises, citizens require more money because of the higher number of transactions. But the money supply is unchanged, because monetary policy is not being used. Thus the domestic
interest rate is forced up (remember, there is no international capital mobility). This rise in the interest rate reduces private investment so that *I*
actually rises by less than the increase in government spending—the latter
partially "crowds out" private spending. The net effect is to shift *S-I* down
to *S'-I'* in Figure 9.13(a). (Of course *S-I* would shift even more if the
authorities were to supply the needed additional money and prevent the
interest rate from rising—monetary and fiscal policy together would be more
potent than fiscal policy alone.) This implies a trade deficit (equal to *BC*) at
the initial exchange rate, so the latter depreciates enough to shift *X-M*
upward to *X'-M'*. New equilibrium is at *D*, and fiscal policy successfully
increases aggregate demand from *OA* to *OD*. Again there are no macroeconomic effects on the rest of the world. (Note that Figure 9.13(a) is just like
Figure 9.12(a).)

Now suppose that capital mobility is perfect. Expansionary fiscal policy again shifts *S-I* downward, but in this case the domestic interest rate
cannot rise above the foreign interest rate, so that *S-I* shifts down by the full
amount of the increase in government spending. Thus this increase equals
AE in Figure 9.13(b). Now as aggregate demand begins to rise, citizens
again demand more money. But with perfect capital mobility, any tendency
for the domestic interest rate to rise attracts enough foreign capital to prevent the rise. This capital-account surplus must be matched by a trade-ac-

count deficit, so the exchange rate appreciates. How far must the exchange rate appreciate? Far enough so that the trade account deficit exactly equals the increase in government spending. For in that case there is no net effect on aggregate demand so that citizens still demand the unchanged supply of money. This is illustrated by the shift of *X-M* to *X'-M'* in Figure 9.13(b). Fiscal policy is totally ineffective—any increase in government spending simply flows abroad through the balance of trade. (All this can be described in another way. To finance its increased spending, the government must sell bonds to the public. With perfect capital mobility these bonds are all sold to foreigners and, in order to prevent the balance of payments from going into surplus, the exchange rate must appreciate enough to generate a trade deficit equal to this bond sale, that is, equal to the increase in government spending.) Although fiscal policy, unlike monetary policy, is powerless to influence aggregate demand, with floating rates and perfect capital mobility, it nonetheless also has foreign repercussions. But there is a difference: whereas expansionary domestic monetary policy depresses the rest of the world, expansionary fiscal policy stimulates the foreign economy. In effect, fiscal policy can influence the domestic economy only to the extent that the policy is huge enough to influence the entire international economy. In summary, *with flexible exchange rates, the greater the degree of international capital mobility the less effective is fiscal policy over domestic activity and the greater are the international repercussions of that policy.*

As we have seen, the principal advantage of floating exchange rates is that they allow individual countries to control their own monetary policies. But they do not prevent international repercussions to domestic economic events, and the repercussions of policy can become large with a high degree of international capital mobility. Floating exchange rates do not eliminate international economic interdependence. When the DCs were on an adjustable peg system there were constant debates about the relative advantages of fixed and floating exchange rates. Most of these debates were based

Table 9.7. EFFECTS OF ALTERNATIVE POLICIES UNDER ALTERNATIVE EXCHANGE-RATE REGIMES

Exchange Regime	Policy	low capital mobility		high capital mobility	
		Domestic Effect	Foreign Repercussion	Domestic Effect	Foreign Repercussion
fixed rates	Monetary	substantial (temporary)	substantial	slight	substantial
	Fiscal	substantial	substantial	substantial	substantial
floating rates	Monetary	substantial	slight	substantial (temporary)	substantial (temporary)
	Fiscal	substantial	slight	slight	substantial

on positions developed in the fifties and early sixties, when the degree of international capital mobility was fairly low. But when adjustable pegs were abandoned, in the early seventies, the degree of mobility had greatly increased. Many people were accordingly surprised by the amount of policy interdependence that still remained.

PROBLEMS _____

9.35 Suppose that France and Germany have a floating exchange rate, and suppose that there is an exogenous increase in the German desire to consume French goods. What will be the results? How does your answer depend upon the degree of capital mobility? Contrast your answer with what would happen under fixed rates.

9.36 Suppose that France and Germany have a floating exchange rate and that there is an exogenous increase in the German desire to own French bonds. What will happen? How does your answer depend upon the degree of capital mobility? Contrast your answer with what would happen with fixed rates.

9.37 The text showed that, with floating exchange rates and perfect capital mobility, monetary policy could influence domestic aggregate demand, but the influence would be temporary. Fiscal policy would have no influence. Is this lack of influence of fiscal policy also temporary? Explain.

9.38* How are our conclusions about the temporary effect of monetary policy in the presence of capital mobility altered when account is taken of: (a) the fact that there will be continuing capital flows in a growing world with positive net saving, and (b) international payments of interest income?

13. Policy Dilemmas

INTERNAL AND EXTERNAL BALANCE

Chapter 4 described the dilemma facing national authorities who are concerned simultaneously with aggregate demand (internal balance) and the balance of trade (external balance): adjusting expenditure policy to influence one of the targets will influence the other also. Escape from the dilemma requires a second policy tool, or instrument. Recall that Chapter 4 made two basic assumptions: relative prices were fixed (consistent with fixed exchange rates), and there was no active capital account (that is, international lending passively adjusted to balance out the trade account). Section 14 of Chapter 8 showed that, when this latter assumption was abandoned and notice was made of active capital movements in response to interest rate differentials, monetary and fiscal policy no longer had identical relative effects on internal and external targets. Thus the two policies became distinct tools and could, in principle, be used together to attain simultaneous internal and external balance. The disadvantage of this escape from the dilemma was its temporary character.

A second possible escape from the dilemma arises if we forgo fixed exchange rates. A floating exchange rate would automatically attain external balance, in the sense that the overall balance of payments would always be zero, so that monetary and fiscal policies could be concentrated on internal balance. The previous section showed that such policies could in fact control aggregate demand with a floating exchange rate. Managed floating and a (truly) adjustable peg could also work: once the exchange rate is treated as a second instrument and adjusts (or is adjusted) to take care of external balance, the dilemma disappears. (Recall the discussion of trade policy in Chapter 4; the exchange rate could be the means of implementing such policy.)

INTERNATIONAL POLICY INTERDEPENDENCE

Will the use of the exchange rate as a policy tool eliminate policy conflicts between countries? One might think so, because a floating exchange rate eliminates trade imbalances, and the prime cause of the policy conflicts studied in Chapter 4 was the international transmission of policy effects through the balance of payments. But the answer is not that simple: the previous section showed that domestic policy had foreign repercussions even with floating exchange rates. Figure 9.14 (identical to Figure 4.9) shows the possible situations a pair of countries could conceivably face. The levels of aggregate demand desired by the French and German authorities are y_D^F and y_D^G respectively, so that point D represents the joint target and divides all possibilities into four zones. If the world were in zone *I*, for example, authorities in both countries would wish to reduce aggregate demand; in zones *II* and *IV* the two countries have opposite desires.

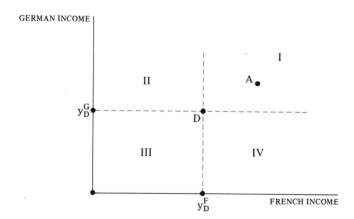

Figure 9.14. Possible Policy Conflicts

Suppose that France and Germany have a floating exchange rate, and that they do find themselves in zone *I,* say at point *A.* Then both countries will adopt contractionary monetary and fiscal policies. With the two countries acting in tandem, there would on balance be little effect on the exchange rate and no tendency toward policy conflict. But it is important to note that this conclusion requires both countries to use expenditure policy for internal balance and to leave the exchange rate to take care of external balance. If instead the exchange rate were manipulated for internal purposes, conflict would immediately erupt. Both countries would wish to appreciate to reduce aggregate demand, but there is only one exchange rate between them. One argument for fixed exchange rates is that they would prevent such conflict by preventing the use of the exchange rate as a policy instrument for internal balance.

Suppose next that the world is in zone *II,* so that the French adopt expansionary policies and the Germans contractionary ones. The degree of international capital mobility once again becomes important, so let us start by assuming that there is none. The expansionary monetary and fiscal policy will increase aggregate demand in France, and the reverse in Germany. The franc will depreciate relative to the mark; this will serve to prevent a trade imbalance from developing. The situation is clearly better than it would be with fixed exchange rates. In the latter case, trade imbalances would cause each country's policy efforts to frustrate the other country's efforts. By preventing these imbalances, a floating rate "bottles up" each country's policy at home and thereby eliminates international conflict and renders policy more locally potent.

Now suppose that capital is highly mobile internationally. The previous section leads us to expect that monetary and fiscal policy will have quite different effects, so we shall consider them separately. Look at monetary policy first: suppose the French authorities increase the money supply by buying bonds from the public, and the German authorities contract the German money supply by selling bonds. Then the French public buys bonds from the German public. France has a capital account deficit; the franc depreciates; and a trade surplus emerges. At the same time, Germany experiences a capital account surplus, an appreciated mark, and a trade-account deficit. Thus there are international repercussions to the national policies. But these repercussions are not indicative of conflict; indeed they are the means by which each country's policy works. The French trade surplus stimulates the French economy while the German trade deficit depresses Germany, just as desired. If, by contrast, there were a fixed exchange rate, each country's policy would have been frustrated: the French capital-account deficit and German surplus would have been matched, not by trade imbalances with their consequent desirable effects, but by a movement of international reserves from the French central bank to the German central bank. Again, floating exchange rates are more conducive than fixed to both international harmony and national policy effectiveness. Note also that if the authorities tried instead to manipulate the exchange rate to attain internal targets, this would not now be a source of conflict. Each country would desire a depreciated franc and an appreciated mark.

Now suppose that fiscal policy is used: the French increase government spending and the Germans reduce it. Then the French develop a capital-account surplus; the franc appreciates; and their trade balance goes into deficit. The opposite takes place in Germany. This is a very disruptive situation: the trade imbalance nullifies each country's policy effort. This situation now is worse than it would be with fixed exchange rates. In the latter case part of each country's change in government spending leaks abroad and frustrates the efforts of the other government; the exchange-rate change that now occurs *increases* that leakage.

In sum, a floating exchange rate can cause more international conflict than fixed rates when exchange-rate manipulation is likely to be used for internal objectives by governments whose objectives are similar, or when fiscal policy is used to attain internal balance and capital is highly mobile. Otherwise floating rates increase national autonomy and reduce international conflict.

MONETARY AND FISCAL POLICY FOR INTERNAL AND EXTERNAL BALANCE

If the exchange rate is available as an instrument of policy, a government can attain both internal and external balance by using expenditure policy for the former and the exchange rate for the latter. But governments are often reluctant to use the exchange rate as an instrument. Instead they frequently treat it as a policy objective in its own right. There are two reasons for this. First, we have seen that even with floating exchange rates policy has international repercussions: an exchange-rate change affects other countries. This ensures that the level of the exchange rate has international political implications and thereby makes it an element in the government's calculations of international relations. Second, the exchange rate has distinct domestic implications. Section 3 showed that depreciation increases inflation directly, and not only through its effect on aggregate demand, and section 4 showed that depreciation influences domestic relative prices, and therefore the domestic distribution of income.

For all these reasons, governments may regard the exchange rate as a target, like aggregate demand, rather than as an instrument, like monetary and fiscal policy. If so, this brings us right back to the discussion of section 15 of Chapter 8. With capital internationally mobile, monetary and fiscal policies have differential effects on internal and external balance. Only now "external balance" means the attainment of a targeted exchange rate, rather than a targeted balance of payments deficit.

PROBLEM _____

9.39 Suppose that inflation in each country is related to aggregate demand as discussed in section 7 of Chapter 4. How does this modify the discussion in this section?

14. Summary

1. The equilibrium exchange rate is determined by the condition that the relative demands for home and foreign monies equal the relative supplies.

2. A disequilibrium exchange rate can be corrected in four basic ways: (1) by allowing payments imbalances to alter relative money supplies until the actual exchange rate becomes an equilibrium one (automatic adjustment process); (2) by altering the exchange rate to its equilibrium value; (3) by some combination of the first two methods; and (4) by direct controls.

3. Exchange rate adjustments have two basic implications: they can eliminate payments imbalances, and they allow individual countries control of their own money supplies.

4. Variations in exchange rates can influence international adjustment in four ways. (1) If purchasing power parity holds, depreciation induces domestic inflation relative to the rest of the world, thereby increasing the relative demand for domestic money and so stimulating domestic hoarding and the reverse abroad. (2) With sticky prices depreciation makes domestic goods more expensive relative to foreign goods and thereby increases the domestic balance of trade. (3) The stimulating effect of depreciation on domestic income reduces the trade balance. (4) Depreciation and the expectation of future depreciation influence people's desired portfolios of assets denominated in home and foreign money, thereby stimulating activity on the capital account.

5. Fixed exchange rates make national monies more useful as money. Flexible rates give individual countries control over their own money supplies but do not eliminate international economic interdependence.

6. The greater the degree of international capital mobility, the more temporary will be the stimulating effects of monetary expansion and the greater the perverse foreign repercussions of domestic monetary policy.

7. With flexible rates, the higher the degree of international capital mobility the less effective is fiscal policy over domestic activity and the greater are the international repercussions.

8. Floating exchange rates can cause more international conflict than fixed rates can cause—when exchange-rate manipulation is likely to be used for internal objectives by governments whose objectives are similar, or when fiscal policy is used to attain internal balance and capital is highly mobile. Otherwise floating rates increase national autonomy and reduce international conflict.

15. *Exploring Further:* Exchange-Rate Variations and *IS-LM* Analysis

Section 17* of Chapter 8 showed how *IS-LM* analysis could be extended to an open economy with fixed exchange rates. We now inquire how exchange-rate variations can be accommodated. As before, we focus on a relatively small economy whose behavior has a negligible effect on foreign prices, interest rates, and incomes. Figure 9.15 shows the equilibrium (at point *A*) of such a country for a given exchange rate, price level, money supply, and foreign indebtedness.

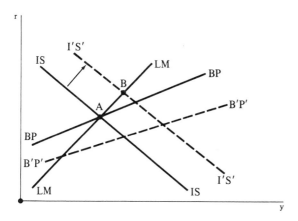

Figure 9.15.   EXCHANGE DEPRECIATION

Recall from the earlier discussion that the *IS* curve shows the combinations of the interest rate *r* and the income *y* for which the demand for the country's national output equals the supply ($I + X = S + M$). The position of the curve depends upon prices: an increase in the price level shifts the *IS* curve to the left. The exchange rate also matters. A depreciation of domestic currency will tend to make domestic goods cheaper relative to foreign goods. This will cause the demand for domestic output to exceed the supply, so that, at constant *r*, *y* must increase to restore balance. That is, depreciation shifts the *IS* curve to the right.

The *LM* curve shows the combinations of *r* and *y* for which the demand for domestic money equals the supply. The position of this curve depends on the price level and on the money supply: either a fall in the price level or a rise in the money supply will shift the curve downward and to the right.

Finally, the *BP* curve depicts combinations of *r* and *y* for which the balance of payments is in neither deficit nor surplus. Recall that the slope of this curve reflects the degree of international capital mobility: it is horizontal with perfect mobility and vertical with no mobility at all. Points above the curve correspond to a payments surplus and points below to a deficit. The position of the curve depends upon the price level and the amount of foreign debt: an increase in either shifts the *BP* curve upward and to the left. Now the exchange rate also matters. A depreciation will cause a balance of payments surplus at the original *r* and *y*, which accordingly find themselves above the new *BP* curve. That is, depreciation shifts the curve down and to the right.

Suppose that the economy is initially at point *A* in Figure 9.15, and suppose also that the trade balance and capital account balance each equal zero. Consider the effects of a once and for all depreciation of the domestic currency. This shifts the *IS* curve to the right, to *I'S'* in the figure, so that equilibrium moves from *A* to *B*. Depreciation thus increases both national income and the interest rate. The trade and capital accounts are also in surplus, with point *B* above *B'P'*, the new external balance line. The increase in *y* tends to limit the improvement in the trade balance, as discussed in section 6 above, but it does not reverse it. The rise in *r*, on the other hand, makes domestic assets more attractive and so reinforces the effects on the capital account discussed in section 7 above.

Point *B* does not represent a permanent equilibrium, however. Once domestic residents sell to foreigners the quantity of assets they wish, the capital account surplus will come to an end and the *BP* curve will shift upward. Furthermore, the depreciation will generate domestic inflation, as discussed in section 4 above, and this will be intensified by the increase in *y* involved in the movement from *A* to *B*. This rise in the domestic price level causes the *BP* and *LM* curves to shift upward, and *I'S'* to shift to the left. These shifts will eventually come to an end when the three curves once again intersect in a new long-run equilibrium, at some point directly above *A*.

PROBLEMS

9.40 Analyze in detail the effects of an increase in the domestic money supply if the authorities adjust the exchange rate to prevent a balance of payments deficit.

9.41 Analyze in detail the effects of expansionary fiscal policy, if the authorities adjust the exchange rate to prevent a balance of payments deficit.

9.42 Use *IS-LM-BP* analysis to discuss the influence of the degree of international capital mobility on the effectiveness of monetary and fiscal policy.

9.43 The discussion in the text on the long-run consequences of depreciation assumed that the money supply remained constant, that is, that all payments imbalances were completely sterilized. How must the discussion change if instead there is no sterilization at all?

SUGGESTED READING

Alexander, S. "Effects of a Devaluation on a Trade Balance." In *Readings in International Economics.* Edited by R. E. Caves and H. G. Johnson. Homewood: Irwin, 1968. The absorption, or income, approach.

Cooper, R. N. "Monetary Theory and Policy in an Open Economy." *The Scandinavian Journal of Economics* 78 (1976): 146–68. This issue contains other papers with an asset-market view of the exchange rate.

Dornbusch, R. "Devaluation, Money, and Nontraded Goods." *American Economic Review* 63 (1973): 871–80. The monetary approach

Dornbusch, R. "Exchange Rate Economics: Where Do We Stand?" *Brookings Papers on Economic Activity* (1980): 143–206. A useful statement and discussion.

Dornbusch, R. *Open Economy Macroeconomics.* New York: Basic Books, 1980. See in particular chapters 9, and 11–14.

Dornbusch, R. and Fisher, S. *Macroeconomics.* New York: McGraw-Hill, 1978. Chapter 19 contains a treatment in *IS-LM* terms.

Frenkel, J. "Flexible Exchange Rates, Prices, and the Role of 'News': Lessons from the 1970s." *Journal of Political Economy* 89 (1981): 665–705.

Frenkel, J. and Johnson, H., eds. *The Economics of Exchange Rates.* Reading: Addison-Wesley, 1978. A collection of papers taking the asset-market view.

Kravis, I. and Lipsey, R. "Price Behavior in the Light of Balance of Payments Theories." *Journal of International Economics* 8 (1978): 193–246. This issue contains additional papers dealing with purchasing power parity.

Mundell, R. A. *International Economics.* New York: Macmillan, 1968. Chapters 11, 12, 16, 17, and 18 are especially relevant.

Mundell, R. A. *Monetary Theory.* Pacific Palisades: Goodyear, 1971. See chapters 9–11, and 15.

Mussa, M. "Macroeconomic Interdependence and the Exchange Rate Regime." In *International Economic Policy.* Edited by R. Dornbusch and J. A. Frenkel. Baltimore: Johns Hopkins, 1979. An excellent survey.

Robinson, J. "The Foreign Exchanges." In *Readings in the Theory of International Trade.* Edited by H. S. Ellis and L. A. Metzler. Homewood: Irwin, 1950. The elasticities, or relative price, approach.

Taussig, F. W. *International Trade.* New York: Macmillan, 1927. Part 3 contains Taussig's treatment of the causes and effects of exchange-rate changes.

Tobin, J. and de Macedo, J. B. "The Short-Run Macroeconomics of Floating Exchange Rates: an Exposition." In *Flexible Exchange Rates and the Balance of Payments.* Edited by J. S. Chipman and C. P. Kindleberger. Amsterdam: North Holland, 1980. Useful.

Tsiang, S. C. "The Role of Money in Trade-Balance Stability: Synthesis of the Elasticity and Absorption Approaches." *American Economic Review* 51 (1961): 912–36. An algebraic treatment of aspects of the commodity-flow view.

Whitman, M. "Policies for Internal and External Balance." Princeton University, *Special Papers in International Economics* 9 (1970). A survey of the literature of the sixties.

Part Four

Further Applications of International Monetary Theory

THIS part of the book puts to work the two basic ideas of international monetary theory: automatic adjustment process of the balance of payments and exchange-rate adjustment. Chapter 10 looks in detail at the markets in which international monetary transactions actually take place. Chapter 11 then examines efforts to establish a workable international monetary system.

Chapter 10

International Financial Markets

> "How much have these speculators thrown away? . . . Nothing
> like it has been known in the history of speculation—so large
> and so widespread. Bankers and servant girls have been
> equally involved. . . . The argument on which bankers bought
> was the same as the argument on which servant girls bought
> . . . so little do bankers and servant girls understand of history
> and economics."
> —J. M. KEYNES

> "For every problem, economists have an answer. Simple, neat
> and wrong."
> —H. L. MENCKEN

VARIOUS financial markets exist so that international transactions may take
place. These include foreign exchange markets, where national currencies
are traded, and credit markets in which countries borrow and lend to each
other. Also included are the Euromarkets—new and rapidly growing institutions that testify to the degree of economic integration that has occurred
in the international economy since the Second World War.

This chapter describes these various markets and discusses them in the
light of the international monetary theory of Part Three.

1. The Foreign Exchange Market

The currencies of different countries are exchanged for each other
on the foreign exchange market. *Foreign exchange* is simply the money of a
foreign country: thus French francs are foreign exchange to an American
but not to a Frenchman. The basic purpose of this market is to facilitate
international trade and investment.

There are two aspects to the foreign exchange market. The *retail* portion of the market is where firms and individuals who require foreign currency can buy it, or where they can dispose of any foreign money they may have acquired. Typical transactions include a firm buying foreign exchange from its bank in order to purchase foreign goods, or a tourist exchanging her own money for foreign money at an airport bureau of exchange.

Suppose, for example, that an American firm, Acme Spirits, wishes to purchase 200 cases of whiskey from a distillery in Scotland. The distillery charges £10,000 for the whiskey; that comes to $20,000 at an exchange rate of $2.00/£. Acme Spirits wishes to pay in dollars, whereas the distillery wants to be paid in pounds: this is where the foreign exchange market comes in. If the contract between the two firms calls for payment in pounds, Acme Spirits will have to buy £10,000 from its bank; if, on the other hand, the contract calls for payment in dollars, the U.K. distillery will sell $20,000 to its bank. In either case, the British sale of whiskey to the United States requires that some firm buy pounds for dollars from the banking system.

Suppose the contract is in pounds. Then when it comes time to pay for the whiskey, Acme Spirits will go to the foreign exchange department of its bank, say Bank *A* in New York, to buy the necessary pounds. Acme Spirits will pay Bank *A* $20,000 and receive in exchange a check for £10,000 drawn against some British bank, say Bank *B* in London. The firm then pays for its whiskey by sending the check to the distillery in Scotland. Figure 10.1 schematically depicts Acme Spirits's transactions.

Where did Bank *A* get the £10,000 it sold to Acme Spirits? This brings us to the second part of the foreign exchange market, the *interbank market*. It might conceivably be the case that Bank *A* numbers among its customers firms exporting to Britain who acquire pounds that they sell to the bank. If so, the bank could then sell these pounds to Acme Spirits. But it is very unlikely that things will exactly balance out in this way. So suppose that the pounds that Acme Spirits, and other firms, wish to buy from Bank *A* exceeds the pounds that are offered to Bank *A* for sale. Then, in order to meet its customers' needs, the bank must acquire additional pounds. It gets them

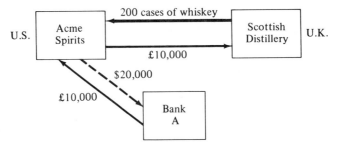

Figure 10.1. TRANSACTIONS INVOLVED IN U.S. IMPORTING

from other banks. It might be able to buy them from another New York bank that finds itself with more pounds than necessary for business. Or Bank *A* could buy the pounds from a British bank, say Bank *B* in London.

Why should Bank *B* sell pounds, that is, buy dollars? To service the needs of its own British customers who require dollars in order to purchase goods, services, or assets from the United States. Perhaps a British firm, Coagulated Mush, Ltd., has agreed to pay $20,000 to an American exporter for 4,000 bushels of soybeans. Then Coagulated Mush will wish to buy $20,000 from its bank, say Bank *B*. Figure 10.2 shows schematically the related transactions in commodity and foreign exchange markets. In real terms, the United States is trading soybeans to the United Kingdom for whiskey. The foreign exchange market allows this trade to take place between two monetary economies using different monies. Note that, after all transactions have been made, each country's money is still circulating within the country. The £10,000, for example, were paid by Coagulated Mush and received by the distillery, which perhaps keeps them on deposit in Bank *B*. The $20,000 were paid by Acme Spirits and received by the agricultural exporter, who perhaps keeps them on deposit in Bank *A*.

THE INTERBANK MARKET

Participants in the interbank foreign exchange market are the international departments of large commercial banks in the major financial

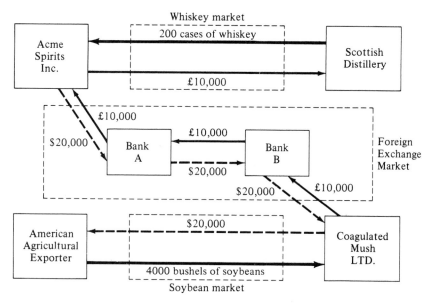

Figure 10.2. INTERNATIONAL TRADE AND THE FOREIGN EXCHANGE MARKET

centers of the world: London, New York, Zurich, Frankfurt, Paris, Tokyo, Singapore, Toronto, and so forth. There is some activity in secondary centers, such as Osaka and San Francisco, and large banks outside these centers often participate via affiliates; small regional banks do not participate, but instead meet their customers' foreign exchange needs by dealing with correspondent banks that are in the market (thus Acme Spirits, even if located in Lexington, Kentucky, need not go to New York to obtain its £10,000). Because of its world-wide dispersion, the foreign exchange market is active twenty-four hours a day, although individual banks by and large observe normal working hours.

A participating bank typically maintains a trading room equipped with telephones and telex machines over which dealers make and receive price quotations and agree to transactions. The bank will likely communicate directly with the trading rooms of banks in foreign centers but will go through a broker when dealing with other banks in the same center. There are eight such brokers in New York. The trading room of a major New York bank will then be connected, by direct telephone and telex lines, to brokerage offices and to trading rooms in other countries. A bank will make transactions in response to the collective needs of its commercial customers, but, in addition, many major banks will "make a market" in one or more currencies, that is, they will be continuously prepared to deal.

The foreign exchange market is made into a unified, world-wide whole by what is known as *arbitrage* (buying cheap and selling dear). Suppose, for example, that a dealer were to discover that a bank in New York was dealing in Swiss francs at the rate of $.6140/Sfr, whereas a bank in Zurich was doing so at $.6145/Sfr. The dealer could then buy Swiss francs from the New York bank and sell them to the Swiss bank, earning a profit of $.0005 per franc. This may not seem like anything to get excited about, but it becomes significant when you realize that even a "small" deal on the interbank market involves multiples of $100,000, and that the transaction would tie up funds for only minutes or seconds. Such arbitrage would quickly drive up the price of Swiss francs in New York, where they are being bought, and drive down the price in Zurich, so that a single world price would be established. In the same way, exchange rates in various centers are made mutually consistent, a process known as *triangular arbitrage*. Arbitrage is part of any market, but it is especially relentless with foreign exchange because of the great communication between participants and the homogeneity and storeability of the product (money). Indeed such arbitrage operations rarely need actually occur anymore: exchange rates seldom get out of line in the first place because everyone knows that massive arbitrage would take place if they did.

■ *Triangular Arbitrage Example.* Suppose that London banks are dealing in dollars at $2.30/£ and in Swiss francs at Sfr3.83/£, whereas in Zurich

Swiss francs cost $.6010 each. Then by using dollars to buy pounds in London and using these pounds to in turn buy Swiss francs, a bank could obtain Swiss francs in London for $.6005 [= 2.30/3.83] and then sell them in Zurich for $.6010. Such arbitrage would soon make the rates consistent. ∎

The supplies and demands of various currencies by the participating banks are the proximate determinants of exchange rates, which are liable to fluctuate throughout the day. These rates then determine the prices individual banks charge corporate customers. Representative rates are published daily in the financial press; Table 10.1 reproduces some typical quotations in New York.

Table 10.1. FOREIGN EXCHANGE RATES (NEW YORK, THURSDAY, OCTOBER 8, 1981)

	$ Value per Unit of Foreign Currency		Units of Currency per Dollar	
	Thurs.	Wed.	Thurs.	Wed.
Argent (Peso-convert.)	.000176	.000200	5687.00	5653.00
Argent (Peso-financial)	.000126	.000100	7925.00	7425.00
Australia (Dollar)	1.1540	1.1545	.8666	.8662
Austria (Schilling)	.0642	.0645	15.58	15.51
Belgium (Franc)	.0270	.0270	36.98	37.07
Bolivia (Peso)	.0404	.0404	24.75	24.75
Brazil (Cruzeiro)	.0091	.0092	110.12	108.40
Britain (Pound)	1.8950	1.8800	.5277	.5319
30-day fut	1.8947	1.8790	.5278	.5322
60-day fut	1.8956	1.8800	.5275	.5319
90-day fut	1.8965	1.8825	.5273	.5312
Canada (Dollar)	.8338	.8338	1.1993	1.1993
30-day fut	.8303	.8309	1.2044	1.2035
60-day fut	.8289	.8294	1.2064	1.2056
90-day fut	.8275	.8280	1.2085	1.2078
Chile (Peso)	.0256	.0256	39.00	39.00
Columbia (Peso)	.0177	.0177	56.49	56.49
Denmark (Krone)	.1403	.1403	7.1275	7.1300
Egypt (Pound)	1.45	1.45	.6900	.6900
Ecuador (Sucre)	.0352	.0352	28.42	28.42
Finland (Mark)	.2285	.2280	4.3770	4.3710
France (Franc)	.1805	.1795	5.5400	5.5700
Greece (Drachma)	.0179	.0178	55.80	56.20
Holland (Guilder)	.4077	.4069	2.4530	2.4675
Hong Kong (Dollar)	.1660	.1658	6.0250	6.0300

SOURCE: New York Times

Among the participants of the foreign exchange market are the various central banks. They participate for two reasons. First, they service the foreign exchange needs of their respective governments, agencies, and government-owned firms, just as commercial banks enter the market in order to serve their customers. But central banks also participate in order to administer a fixed or pegged exchange-rate regime, or to manage a float. That is, they intervene in the market to influence exchange rates by altering demand and supply conditions. In the United States such official dealings are performed in the New York market by the Federal Reserve Bank of New York.

CASE STUDY: The Foreign Exchange Market and the Electronic Age

The interbank transactions arranged by foreign exchange dealers are actually settled by cable transfers of funds. Suppose Bank A in New York agrees to buy £1 million from Bank B in London for $2.0 million. At settlement time, Bank A credits Bank B's account in Bank A with a deposit of $2.0 million, or else it deposits by cable that amount in Bank B's account in some other American bank. Similarly Bank A has its London account credited with £1 million.

The interbank market depends upon modern means of communication. When these methods were more primitive, substantial efforts went into arbitrage, "foreign exchange" consisted of bills and acceptances rather than bank deposits, and exchange rates in different centers could remain apart for some time. In the years between the two world wars, a precautionary payment to a telephone operator was a not-unwise way to try to ensure that a dealer's call to a foreign bank would quickly get through should lines become jammed in a time of crisis. The technology and business methods continue to evolve. Some banks are replacing or supplementing verbal quotations with the simultaneous electronic display of current dealing prices, brokers are expanding their activities across national borders, and automated electronic payments systems promise to replace cable transfers.

SPECIAL ROLE OF THE DOLLAR

The U.S. Dollar is the most important single currency and has a qualitatively distinct role in several respects. The dollar is, first of all, a *vehicle* currency, or medium of exchange in the foreign exchange market. That is, exchanges between third currencies often take place through dollars rather than directly. If a bank in Norway required Swiss francs, for example, instead of trying to buy the francs directly for Norwegian kroner, the bank would likely buy dollars for kroner in Oslo and then use the dollars to buy francs in Zurich. Because of this, the dollar market is the largest part of the market in foreign centers. Each country is the ultimate source of its own currency. Thus the dollar-pound market is the largest part of the London foreign exchange market, and London is also the most important center for dollar-pound transactions. The second most important center is New York. Similarly, dollar–Swiss franc exchanges are the largest activity in Zurich, Zurich is the most important center for such activity, and New York is second. Because it is second in so many individual markets, New York is overall the largest foreign exchange center in the world.

CASE STUDY: Foreign Exchange Dealings in New York

In April 1977 the Federal Reserve Bank of New York surveyed forty-four U.S. banks about their foreign exchange operations, and in March 1980 another survey (of ninety banks) was conducted. Average daily turnover in each month is summarized in Table 10.2.

Table 10.2. Average Daily Turnover in the New York Foreign Exchange Market

Currency	*Percentage of Total Turnover*	
	April 1977	*March 1980*
German Mark	27	32
Pound sterling	17	23
Canadian dollar	19	12
Japanese yen	5	10
Swiss franc	14	10
Other	18	13
Average Total Dealings	$5.3 billion/day	$23.4 billion/day

Foreign central banks also use the dollar as a vehicle, or *intervention currency*. That is, the Bank of England manages the float of the pound by exchanging pounds and dollars in the London foreign exchange market so as to influence the pound-dollar rate, the Bank of Japan exchanges dollars and yen in Tokyo, and so forth. Partly because of this, a large portion of official international reserves are held in the form of dollars (and dollar-denominated assets), as we saw in Chapter 8.

Finally, commercial contracts are sometimes denominated in dollars, and payment is sometimes made in dollars, even when neither party to the contract is American. For example, European countries use dollars to pay for Middle East oil. This practice is most common in raw material and commodity markets, which are unified globally and deal in standardized contracts. The extensive Japanese imports of raw materials from Southeast Asia and Australia are largely denominated in dollars. Thus the dollar is in some degree an international money, conferring upon a part of the international economy those advantages, discussed in section 11 of Chapter 9, that come from having a single medium of exchange.

PROBLEMS

10.1 Figures 10.1 and 10.2 assumed that contracts were in terms of the currency of the exporter. How are the figures changed if contracts are in the importer's currency? If all contracts are in dollars?

10.2 In Figure 10.2, trade between the United States and the United Kingdom was assumed to be in balance. Suppose instead that, at the same prices, Acme Spirits imports 400 cases of whiskey, soybean exports remaining equal to 4,000 bushels. How is the figure changed? Discuss various possible consequences, using the theory of Chapters 8 and 9.

10.3 Table 10.2 reveals significant dealings in Swiss francs despite the fact that Switzerland and its economy are quite small relative to many countries not mentioned in the table (and therefore included in the "other" category). Can you think of any possible reasons for this? Answer the same question with regard to the Canadian dollar. Would you expect these currencies to be equally important in a table summarizing turnover in London?

10.4 The foreign exchange market described in this section involves bank deposits. But exchanges of *currencies* also take place, though on a very much smaller scale. For example, a tourist might buy a few pound notes from her New York bank before leaving for London, and she might sell a few pound notes to that bank when she returns. Describe the influence of arbitrage on the relation between the dollar price of pound notes in New York and the pound price of dollars in London. How do you think this influence compares with that of arbitrage in the foreign exchange market as discussed in the text?

2. The Forward Market

When two banks agree on a foreign exchange transaction, they also agree on when that transaction shall actually take place. Most common is a *spot transaction,* which calls for settlement two business days (sometimes one day) after the deal is made. But sometimes the banks agree to make the transaction further in the future, say in 30, 60, or 90 days. These are called (30-, 60-, or 90-day) *forward* contracts. Table 10.1 included rates for forward contracts in a couple of currencies. An agreement to exchange two currencies in two months is not the same as an agreement to exchange them in two days, so the agreements can be expected to involve different prices. This is reflected in the table. The demand and supply for spot foreign exchange will determine the spot exchange rate, the demand and supply for 30-day forward foreign exchange will determine the 30-day forward rate, and so forth.

Why do forward markets exist? Return to the example of Acme Spirits. Suppose the company agrees to buy 200 cases from the Scottish distillery for £10,000. The contract between the two firms will call for the whiskey to be delivered by a certain date and for the pounds to be paid by a certain date. Suppose the latter is in 90 days. By contracting to purchase the whiskey, Acme Spirits has obligated itself to pay £10,000 in 90 days. The firm can easily find out what a pound costs now, by opening a newspaper or calling a bank, but it has no way of knowing how many dollars will be required to buy £10,000 in 90 days, when the times comes to pay. If the pound should appreciate in the interval, Acme Spirits could sustain a serious loss. Of course there are all sorts of other risks also involved in doing business, but this *exchange risk* is unique to foreign trade; it does not arise when Acme Spirits purchases sour mash whiskey from a Kentucky distillery.

Acme Spirits can escape from this risk by means of forward exchange. When the firm agrees to buy the whiskey and pay for it in 90 days, it can also purchase £10,000 90 days forward from its bank (Bank *A*). If the 90-day forward exchange rate is $2.00/£, Acme Spirits would be obligating itself to pay the bank $20,000 in 90 days and to then receive £10,000 in return, which it would pay to the Scottish distillery. In this way Acme Spirits escapes all exchange risk—its future obligation is now in terms of dollars, and the firm need not worry about what happens to the spot exchange rate in the future.

This transaction does not actually eliminate the exchange risk: it simply transfers it from the company, whose business is liquor, to the bank, whose business is foreign exchange. Bank *A* is now obligated to come up with £10,000 in 90 days. As all good bankers abhor risk, Bank *A* will seek to escape it. How? By buying pounds forward from another bank, say Bank *B*, which has sold dollars forward to customers who have contracted to make dollar payments in 90 days. The forward transactions are exactly the same as the foreign exchange market transactions illustrated in Figure 10.2. These transactions are agreements to make the indicated payments in 90 days. No market participant is left with any exchange risk. This is a major economic function of the forward exchange market: to allow international trade to proceed unimpeded by exchange risk.

Forward contracts can be readily obtained for the currencies of the major industrial countries for periods of up to a year. Forward markets do not exist for most LDC currencies, and forward coverage in any currency is difficult to obtain for more than a year ahead. This hampers LDC trade and long-term trade agreements.

CASE STUDY: The Forward Market

The Federal Reserve survey of New York foreign exchange activity, alluded to in section 1, also revealed the following percentage composition of various types of transactions:

Type (%)	April 1977	March 1980
Spot	55	64
Swap*	40	30
Outright forward	5	6

*(A *swap* is a contract to buy a currency at one date and sell it back at a later date.)

INTEREST ARBITRAGE

The spot and forward markets for any pair of currencies all have their own exchange rates, but these rates are not independent. To see how they are related, consider the position of a trader who has some funds that he will not need for 30 days. Presumably he wishes to invest the money in the interim. A safe way to do so would be to buy U.S. Treasury bills. If i_{US} denotes the interest rate earned in 30 days, than each dollar invested in the Treasury bills will be worth $1 + i_{US}$ dollars when the bills mature 30 days hence. But foreign governments also issue treasury bills of their own, so our trader could also buy, say, U.K. Treasury bills. Suppose the latter earn the rate i_{UK}. The dealer could then compare i_{US} and i_{UK} to see which bill pays more. But such a comparison ignores *exchange risk:* if the dealer buys U.S. Treasury bills, he will have dollars in 30 days, whereas if he buys U.K. Treasury bills he will have pounds, and who knows how many dollars a pound will then be worth. Like Acme Spirits in the previous example, our trader can use the forward exchange market to escape this risk, that is, he can sell pounds forward at the same time that he buys U.K. Treasury bills. Suppose he does this. How much will each dollar invested in such a fashion be worth in 30 days?

If the spot price of a pound is R_s, each dollar can buy $1/R_s$ pounds (if a pound costs $2, $1 buys one-half a pound). If this many pounds are invested in U.K. Treasury bills, in 30 days they will become $(1/R_s)$ $(1 + i_{UK})$ pounds. The trader protects himself by *now* selling this many pounds forward. If R_{30} denotes the 30-day forward price of the pound, each dollar invested in this way will be worth (R_{30}/R_s) $(1 + i_{UK})$ dollars in 30 days. This term is called the *covered yield*, to distinguish it from the uncovered yield $1 + i_{UK}$, which exposes the trader to exchange risk. The trader compares this covered yield to $1 + i_{US}$ in order to discover whether the U.S. or U.K. Treasury bills are more attractive. If the yields on the two bills differ, traders will move their funds into the higher-paying bill, a process known as *covered interest arbitrage.*

The process is illustrated in Table 10.3. If, for example, $(1 + i_{US}) < (R_{30}/R_s)(1 + i_{UK})$, then the U.K. Treasury bills yield more. Traders will therefore simultaneously buy pounds in the spot market, use the pounds to buy U.K. Treasury bills, and sell the proceeds in the forward market. They will do this with whatever liquid funds they have available or obtain by selling or redeeming U.S. Treasury bills they own. As many dealers do this, i_{US} will tend to rise and i_{UK} to fall, as the U.S. and U.K. treasuries find it respectively harder and easier to sell their bills to the public. Similarly the increased demand for spot pounds and supply of forward pounds by the dealers causes R_s to rise and R_{30} to fall. As a result the two yields will be driven together.

Table 10.3. COVERED INTEREST ARBITRAGE

If:	$(1 + i_{US}) < \dfrac{R_{30}}{R_s}(1 + i_{UK})$	$(1 + i_{US}) = \dfrac{R_{30}}{R_s}(1 + i_{UK})$	$(1 + i_{US}) > \dfrac{R_{30}}{R_s}(1 + i_{UK})$
Then traders:	(1) Redeem U.S. bills (2) Buy pounds spot (3) Buy U.K. bills (4) Sell pounds forward	continue as they were doing	(1) Redeem U.K. bills (2) Sell pounds spot (3) Buy U.S. bills (4) Buy pounds forward
So that:	(1) U.S. capital account deficit increases (2) The above inequality shrinks	no change	(1) U.S. capital account deficit falls (2) The above inequality shrinks

If international capital mobility is perfect, that is, if dealers are completely unwilling to hold a Treasury bill yielding less than an alternative bill, the yields must be equal so that the middle column of Table 10.3 holds. In this case

$$\frac{R_{30}}{R_s}(1 + i_{UK}) = 1 + i_{US} \tag{10.1}$$

This is known as the *covered interest parity* condition. It is sometimes written an alternative way. Divide both sides of (10.1) by $1 + i_{UK}$ and then subtract unity from both sides. This gives

$$\frac{R_{30} - R_s}{R_s} = \frac{i_{US} - i_{UK}}{1 + i_{UK}} \tag{10.2}$$

The left-hand of this equation is called the *forward premium* (if positive) or *forward discount* (if negative) on the pound. It measures the percentage return a dealer can obtain by simultaneously buying pounds spot and selling them forward (a *swap* transaction). The right-hand side, called the (discounted) *interest differential*, measures the uncovered international difference in yields. With capital mobility perfect, any departure from covered interest parity would immediately induce enough interest arbitrage to force the interest rates and exchange rates back into line; imperfect capital mobility would allow persistent divergence.

SPECULATION

Interest arbitrage supplies one theory of the relationship between spot and forward exchange rates: the forward premium should equal the interest differential. Speculation supplies another theory. The dealer in the above example was not a speculator, but an arbitrageur: he always avoided exchange risk by taking a covered position. But other individuals might actually want to incur such risk in the hope of making a killing. The forward market can be used for speculation as well as for eliminating risk.

Suppose, for example, that the 30-day forward rate for the pound is $2.10, but that a certain trader believes that in 30 days the spot rate will be $2.00/£. If she has the courage of her convictions, the trader will sell pounds forward, hoping to make a profit in 30 days. Suppose that she sells £1 million pounds forward, that is, agrees that in 30 days she will deliver £1 million in return for $2.1 million. By agreeing to deliver pounds that she does not own (taking an *open* position), the trader is assuming exchange risk. If she turns out to be right and in 30 days the spot rate is in fact $2.00, the trader can buy the £1 million in the spot market for $2 million and then execute the forward contract, receiving $2.1 million for the pounds. This gives her a profit of $100,000: not bad for a few minutes' work. Of course, if she guessed wrong and the spot rate actually turns out to be $2.30/£, she loses $200,000, but that is the risk one takes to play the game. Keynes made a fortune for himself—and for King's College, Cambridge—by foreign exchange speculation. But earlier he had suffered losses and had had to be bailed out by a loan from a financier who admired his work and by an advance on royalties of *The Economic Consequences of the Peace*.

Table 10.4 indicates the role of speculation. In the table, R_{30} denotes the 30-day forward rate of the pound in terms of dollars, and E_{30} denotes what people in general believe the spot rate will equal in 30 days. Since speculators buy forward pounds, and thereby force up the rate when the latter is less than E_{30}, the forward rate is driven to equal the expected future spot rate, that is

$$R_{30} = E_{30}.$$

Table 10.4. SPECULATION

If:	$R_{30} > E_{30}$	$R_{30} = E_{30}$	$R_{30} < E_{30}$
Then:	Speculators will sell pounds forward	No reason to speculate	Speculators will buy pounds forward
So that:	R_{30} is forced down	No effect on R_{30}	R_{30} is forced up

Subtracting the current spot rate, R_s, from both sides and dividing R_s into both sides gives

$$\frac{R_{30} - R_s}{R_s} = \frac{E_{30} - R_s}{R_s} \tag{10.3}$$

The left-hand side is, once again, the forward premium on the pound. The right-hand side is the percentage by which people expect the spot rate to appreciate. Thus speculation implies that the forward premium should equal the expected spot appreciation.

CONSISTENCY OF THE EXPLANATIONS

We thus have two theories explaining the relation between spot and forward rates. If international capital mobility is nearly perfect, we would expect interest arbitrage to exert dominant influence on the forward premium; a strong consensus on expected future appreciation should give speculation a dominant influence. The two theories are by no means inconsistant. With both nearly perfect capital mobility and a strong consensus about expectations, the two theories together imply that the expected spot appreciation should equal the interest differential—the same conclusion that we reached in section 7 of Chapter 9.

How do forward premiums actually behave? As pointed out in the preceding chapter, we cannot directly observe the speculation theory because we do not know what people think the future holds in store. But all the variables in the covered interest parity relation (10.2) are observable, as Table 10.5 illustrates with data as of June 1979. In this case the interest parity relation holds quite well. In general, capital mobility between the industrial countries is sufficiently great that interest parity usually exerts a dominating influence, even though there are huge pools of funds able to react to expectations about exchange-rate movements. Interest differentials and forward premiums commonly differ by less than 1 percent, and differences above 2 percent are rather rare. Nevertheless, occasions do arise when interest differentials and exchange-rate expectations markedly diverge, so that at least one of the two theories must fail.

Consider for example Table 10.6, which records the analogous information as Table 10.5 for sometime in February 1973 instead. In this case

Table 10.5. NINETY-DAY FORWARD PREMIUMS AND INTEREST
DIFFERENTIALS, JUNE 1979

	Country			
	U.K.	Canada	Germany	Japan
1. Interest Differential in Favor of the Dollar	− 1.9	− 1.3	4.9	5
2. Forward Premium (+) or Discount (−) Relative to the Dollar	− 1.5	− .5	4.4	5
3. Difference: (1) − (2)	− .4	− .8	.5	0

Table 10.6. NINETY-DAY FORWARD PREMIUMS AND INTEREST
DIFFERENTIALS, FEBRUARY 1973

	Country			
	U.K.	Canada	Germany	Japan
1. Interest Differential in Favor of the Dollar	−2.5	1.5	.7	1.3
2. Forward Premium (+) or Discount (−) Over Dollar	−3.9	1.5	5.7	21.7
3. Difference: (1) − (2)	1.4	0	− 5	− 20.4

interest parity works reasonably well for the United Kingdom and Canada,
but quite badly for Germany and, especially, Japan. In February 1973 the
adjustable-peg system was in its death throes. Fears were widespread of
foreign exchange crises with exchange controls and the closing of markets.
Traders strongly expected the yen and mark to appreciate relative to the
dollar (as in fact they did). Under such conditions capital mobility was far
from perfect. Spot rates were still pegged, and interest rates were heavily
influenced by domestic monetary objectives in the various countries. With
imperfect capital mobility interest arbitrage was simply inadequate to
counter the heavy speculation on appreciation of the mark and yen relative
to the dollar. Examples such as this are, however, quite rare.

PROBLEMS

10.5 In the text, Acme Spirits covered itself against exchange risk by buying
pounds forward. Another way of accomplishing this would be to borrow dollars
from its bank, use the dollars to buy spot pounds, and deposit the pounds in a
British bank until the time came to pay for the whiskey. What would be the cost of
this second method? Which method would probably be cheaper and why?

10.6 Suppose that the U.S. interest rate is 8 percent per annum, the U.K. rate is 12 percent per annum, the spot price of a pound is $2.06, and the 1-year forward price is $2.00. Describe the interest arbitrage this should induce.

10.7 Suppose in Problem **10.6** that the 90-day forward price of a pound is $2.02. Describe the interest arbitrage that should be induced.

10.8 Can you think of any reason why capital movements should be less than perfect if all traders are free to buy and sell spot and forward foreign exchange and the treasury bills of all countries?

10.9 Work out the interest-arbitrage argument in the text if instead the trader is British and is concerned about the value of his assets in pounds rather than dollars. Do the same for the speculation example in the text.

10.10* In section 4 of Chapter 9 we showed that exchange depreciation causes domestic inflation. Suppose Acme Spirits were confident that, should the dollar depreciate relative to the pound, the American price of Scotch whiskey would quickly rise in the same proportion. How should this influence the firm's decision on obtaining forward cover for its obligation to the U.K. distillery? What if Acme Spirits knew that dollar depreciation would raise the U.S. price of the whiskey, but was unsure about how much or how soon?

10.11* Between 1973 and 1979 many controls on international capital movements were removed by the United Kingdom and by Germany. Can you discern any effects of this in Tables 10.5 and 10.6? Explain.

3. *Exploring Further:* Equilibrium in the Forward Exchange Market

THE ARBITRAGE SCHEDULE

Why should capital mobility not be perfect, that is, why should any departure from interest parity not immediately bring about a switch of funds from the lower-yielding to the higher-yielding bill sufficiently massive to restore parity? There are two basic reasons. The first is *transaction cost:* time and expense are involved in selling one asset and assuming a covered position in another. If the difference in covered yields between the two assets is smaller than the transaction cost of switching between them, arbitrage will not ensue. However, this is a minor influence. For one thing, transaction costs are quite small, considerably less than 1 percent of the value of the transaction. In addition, the assets involved have short maturities (from a few days up to a year), so that a substantial amount of the total funds committed to the market are always being redeemed; the cost of reinvesting these funds in one asset is the same as in the other, so that transaction costs are not an issue at all. Sustained departure from interest parity cannot be explained by transaction costs.

The more important consideration is *risk.* If the two investments are perceived as risky, traders will want to protect themselves by diversification and so will not arbitrage without limit. The direct *foreign exchange risk* is of course met by forward cover, but there are other types of risk. *Default risk* on the treasury bills is negligible, as they are the obligations of the governments of wealthy nations. The default risk on the obligations of some governments, such as those of LDCs with large foreign debts, can be significant, but these cases are irrelevant because the respective currencies do not have forward markets. When traders arbitrage the commercial paper issued by U.S. and U.K. corporations, rather than treasury bills, default risk is more significant, but only slightly so. There is one other source of default risk. When a U.S. trader invests in U.S. Treasury bills he has an obligation of the U.S. government alone, but when he invests in U.K. Treasury bills he has an obligation of the U.K. government (the bill) plus an obligation of a private bank (the forward market). The default risk of the latter must be taken account of. This risk is quite small though not zero: several banks have gone bankrupt during the last decade and defaulted on their forward contracts. *Country risk* is potentially more significant. A crisis might conceivably arise that would induce the political authorities to close down the foreign exchange market, impose exchange controls, or take other measures that might prevent the trader from converting the proceeds of maturing foreign bills into domestic currency. This latter sort of risk was probably the most important reason for the failure of interest arbitrage revealed in Table 10.6.

The above considerations govern the shape of the *arbitrage schedule*, drawn in Figure 10.3. This curve shows how many forward pounds will be demanded by interest arbitrageurs at each value of the forward premium on the pound. The distance OI in each panel measures the interest rate differential of the United States over the United Kingdom: $\dfrac{i_{US} - i_{UK}}{1 + i_{UK}}$. The arbitrage schedule goes through I because there is no incentive to perform arbitrage when the forward premium just equals the interest differential.

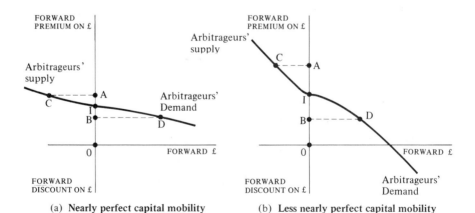

(a) **Nearly perfect capital mobility**   (b) **Less nearly perfect capital mobility**

Figure 10.3. THE ARBITRAGE SCHEDULE

When the forward premium is less than the interest differential, such as at point *B*, arbitrageurs switch from U.K. Treasury bills to U.S. Treasury bills and British dealers therefore demand forward pounds in order to cover their dollar investments. The distance *BD* indicates this demand, and it accordingly equals the total amount that British dealers commit to U.S. bills, plus interest. When the forward premium exceeds the interest differential, arbitrage proceeds in the reverse direction and American dealers cover their purchases of U.K. bills by demanding forward dollars, that is, by supplying forward pounds. Thus the forward premium *OA* in the figure causes arbitrageurs to supply the quantity *AC* of forward pounds.

The more nearly perfect is international capital mobility, the more elastic is the arbitrage schedule, because a given deviation from interest parity causes a greater amount of interest arbitrage. This is illustrated in Figure 10.3 by the contrast between the two panels. The position of the arbitrage schedule depends upon interest rates in the two countries. An increase in the U.S. interest rate increases the interest differential, moves point *I* higher, and shifts the curve up. An increase in the U.K. interest rate has the opposite effect.

THE SPECULATION SCHEDULE

Figure 10.4(a) shows the forward position that will be taken by speculators at each value of the forward premium. The distance *OE* measures the expected appreciation of the spot rate, $\dfrac{E - R_s}{R_s}$. If the forward premium equals *OE*, there is no incentive to speculate. By Table 10.4, when the forward premium exceeds *OE* speculators will sell forward pounds (for example, they sell *FG* when the premium equals *OF*), and when *OE* exceeds the forward premium speculators will buy forward pounds (they buy *JH* at *OH*). The position of the speculation schedule depends upon the actual spot exchange rate and the expected future rate. An increase in the latter moves point *E* higher and shifts the curve upward; an increase in the actual spot rate produces the opposite effect.

Panels (b) and (c) combine the arbitrage and speculation schedules to determine equilibrium. In panel (b), the interest differential exceeds the expected appreciation of the pound. Equilibrium is at point *B*, and the actual forward premium equals *OA*. As this is less than the interest differential, arbitrageurs take a position in U.S. Treasury bills and so cover themselves by purchasing *AB* forward pounds from speculators, who are induced to sell this quantity by the fact that the forward premium exceeds the expected appreciation of the pound, *OE*. Panel (c) shows the opposite possibility.

As discussed in section 2, forward exchange will also be demanded by firms engaged in the international trade of goods and services. Figure 10.4 assumes that such trade is balanced in the sense that the demand for for-

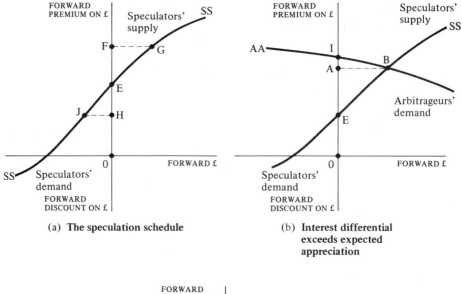

(a) **The speculation schedule**

(b) **Interest differential exceeds expected appreciation**

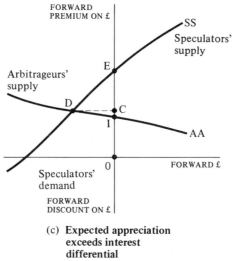

(c) **Expected appreciation exceeds interest differential**

Figure 10.4. Forward Market Equilibrium

ward pounds resulting from U.S. importing equals the supply of forward pounds due to U.K. importing.

CONSISTENCY OF THE INTEREST ARBITRAGE AND SPECULATIVE
THEORIES

Suppose that the interest differential and the expected spot appreciation are unequal. Then the forward premium will be between the two, as shown in Figure 10.4, and, with nearly perfect capital mobility it will almost equal the interest differential. Now the consensus expectation *OE* about spot appreciation may actually turn out to be either right or wrong: the future is uncertain. But there is no reason to err in one direction rather than the other, and speculators who consistently guess wrong will lose their shirts. So, over the long term, the consensus expectation *OE* should *on average* equal the amount by which the spot rate, *on average,* actually does appreciate (more about this in section 6). An individual speculator, though, cannot know what the consensus expectation is, because she has no way of probing the minds of her rivals. But Figure 10.4 shows that the forward premuim exceeds the consensus expectation whenever the interest differential exceeds the forward premium, and is less than the consensus expectation whenever the interest differential is less than the forward premium. Since the consensus expectation turns out, on average, to be correct, this means that a speculator can assure herself of a profit, on average, by selling forward pounds whenever the forward premium is less than the interest differential and by buying forward pounds in the opposite case. If *OE* and *OI* frequently diverge, speculators will become more confident and, armed with the knowledge that they will gain over the long term, they will become more willing to speculate. That is, the speculators' schedule will become more elastic, as shown in Figure 10.5. With capital mobility nearly perfect, and the arbitrage and speculation schedules highly elastic, a small excess of the interest differential over the spot appreciation will induce a very large movement of arbitrage funds from U.K. Treasury bills to U.S. Treasury bills, as shown in Figure 10.6(a). This will put heavy upward pressure on the U.K. interest rate, and heavy downward pressure on the U.S. interest rate and on the spot exchange rate. This tends to shift the arbitrage schedule down and the speculation schedule up, so that the market will tend toward

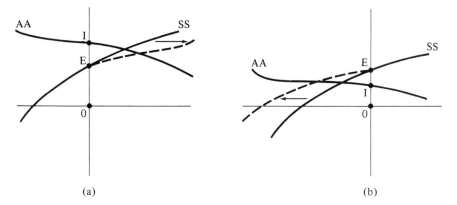

Figure 10.5. AN INCREASE IN SPECULATORS' CONFIDENCE

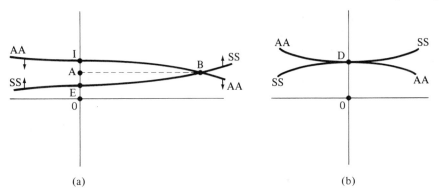

Figure 10.6. CONSISTENCY OF SPECULATIVE AND ARBITRAGE THEORIES

the situation depicted in Figure 10.6(b). So, with nearly perfect capital mobility, there is heavy pressure on national interest rates and on the spot exchange rate to adjust themselves so that the interest differential, the forward premium, and the expected spot appreciation all remain nearly equal to each other.

PROBLEMS

10.12 Show graphically how the forward exchange market would likely react to each of the following events, and describe the consequences in words.
    a An increase in domestic interest rates.
    b An increase in the expected future spot rate.
    c An increased fear that foreign banks may be unable to honor their forward commitments.
Relate this to the situations described in Table 10.6.

10.13 The text assumed that commodity trade between the United States and the United Kingdom was balanced. How would the analysis change if instead the United States had a large trade surplus with the United Kingdom?

10.14 Show geometrically the result of intervention by the Bank of England to support the spot exchange rate of the pound relative to the dollar. Do the same for intervention to support the forward rate.

4. The Eurodollar Market

Banks in New York accept dollar deposits and make dollar loans; London banks deal in pounds sterling, and so on. But recent decades have witnessed the very rapid development of a new type of banking.

EURODOLLARS AND EUROCURRENCIES

Eurodollars are dollars deposited in banks outside the United States, and, more generally, *Eurocurrency* deposits are denominated in currencies other than that of the country in which the bank is located. Institutions that accept deposits and make loans in Eurocurrencies are known as *Eurobanks*. Note that the location of the bank is the determining factor: dollar deposits in London are Eurodollars even if the depositor is an American citizen and the bank accepting the deposit is a London branch of an American bank.

The Eurocurrency market is the major international financial innovation of the postwar period. From virtually nothing in the late fifties, the market grew to over a trillion dollars in size in the early eighties. Almost three-quarters of the total are Eurodollars; Euromarks and Euro-Swiss francs are the most important other Eurocurrencies, and in addition there are large markets in Eurosterling, Euro-French francs, and Euro-yen.

EXAMPLE: EUROCURRENCY MECHANICS

The best way to understand the phenomenon is to consider an example. Suppose that a German firm, say Bayer, has acquired $5 million in the form of a demand deposit in an American bank, say Bank of America. Bayer will not need the funds for thirty days and wishes to earn interest in the meantime. The traditional course of action, as described in section 1, would be to sell the dollars for marks on the foreign exchange market and to invest the marks. But suppose that Bayer wishes to keep dollars because it anticipates making dollar payments in a month. The firm could invest the dollars in New York, or it could use the Eurodollar market. We shall presently discuss some reasons why the latter might be preferable. Suppose Bayer deposits the money in a London Eurobank, say Barclays.

Table 10.7. INITIAL CREATION OF EURODOLLARS

Assets	Liabilities	Assets	Liabilities
Reserves: $1 million Loans: $4 million	Deposits: $5 million	Reserves: $5 million	Deposits: $5 million

(a) Chase Manhattan in New York   (b) Barclays in London

This means that Bayer pays Barclays $5 million and receives a $5 million deposit in return. Barclays then deposits the money received from Bayer into its own account at a correspondent bank in New York, say Chase Manhattan. When the payments clear, Bank of America pays Chase Manhattan the $5 million. This situation is depicted in Table 10.7. Chase Manahattan has the $5 million deposit from Barclays; the table assumes a 20 percent reserve requirement in America, so Chase Manhattan holds $1 mi'lion in reserves at the FED and loans out the remaining $4 million. Barclays has as a liability the $5 million dollar deposit of Bayer, and its reserves are the $5 million Barclays has on deposit with Chase Manhattan. In this example the Eurodollars may be identified as the $5 million Bayer deposit at Barclays in London.

Table 10.7 is, however, only the beginning of the story. Barclays will not sit on its $5 million but will lend it out in order to earn interest. Of course Barclays knows that in 30 days it must repay Bayer. But the money can be put to work until then, and in any case new dollar deposits will be constantly coming in. The Eurodollar market is largely unregulated, so Barclays is under no legal obligation to hold reserves against its dollar deposits, as New York banks must do. Suppose that Barclays nevertheless keeps a small reserve, say $100,000, against an emergency and decides to lend the rest. Perhaps Coagulated Mush, Ltd. borrows $1.9 million from Barclays to pay for imports from the United States. Barclays then gives Coagulated Mush a check for $1.9 million drawn on Chase Manhattan, and Coagulated Mush pays it to the American firm, National Grain, which then deposits it in its own account in New York. Suppose for simplicity (we shall need whatever simplicity we can get) that this is at Chase Manhattan. Then Barclays' deposit at Chase Manhattan goes down by $1.9 million and National Grain's deposit increases by that amount.

If Barclays at the moment has no other customers seeking loans, it will lend the remaining $3 million to some other bank that does. Suppose Credit Suisse in Zurich borrows the money because a Swiss customer, Tick-Tock Watch, wants to borrow funds to meet a payroll. Barclays lends the funds to Credit Suisse by opening a deposit of $3 million in that bank and transferring to it $3 million of its own balance at Chase Manhattan (assume that Credit Suisse also uses Chase Manhattan as its New York correspondent). This interbank deposit is shown in Table 10.8. Suppose that Credit Suisse also keeps a $100,000 reserve in New York and sells the remaining $2.9

Table 10.8.   An Interbank Deposit

Assets	Liabilities		Assets	Liabilities
Reserves:	Deposits:		Reserves:	Deposits:
$1 m (in	$5 million		$3 m (in	$3 m
N.Y.)			N.Y.)	
Loans:				
$1.9 m (to				
Coagulated				
Mush)				
$3 m (to				
Credit				
Suisse)				

(a) Barclays in London   (b) Credit Suisse in Zurich

million on the foreign exchange market for, say, Sfr5 million, which are loaned Tick-Tock. The $2.9 million now leave the Eurodollar market; they will presumably largely be used by their purchasers to buy American goods, services, and assets, and the American sellers will likely hold their deposits in American banks—such as Chase Manhattan.

The final position is summarized in Table 10.9. The *gross* size of the Eurodollar market (total deposits of dollars in banks outside the United States) is $8 million. But this does not take into account the fact that $3 million of this total is used only for an interbank loan between two Eurobanks. Subtracting this amount leaves a *net* size of $5 million.

Table 10.9. FINAL POSITION

Assets	Liabilities	Assets	Liabilities
Reserves: $.42 m	Deposits: $.1 m (Barclays)	Reserves: $.1 m	Deposits: $5 m
Loans: $1.68 m	$1.9 m (National Grain)	Loans: $1.9 m (Coagulated Mush)	
	$.1 m (Credit Suisse)	$3 m (Credit Suisse)	

(a) Chase Manhattan in New York   (b) Barclays in London

Assets	Liabilities
Reserves: $.1 m	Deposits: $3 m (Barclays)
Loans: Sfr 5 m	

(c) Credit Suisse in Zurich

REASONS FOR THE MARKETS

The Eurocurrency markets developed in response to two basic causes. The first was *political:* some individuals who desired to hold dollars did not want to become involved with U.S. financial markets. This motive figured in the early days of the market. In the fifties the Soviet Union increased its trade with the West and accordingly began to acquire and use dollar balances. But the Soviets were reluctant to hold their dollars in U.S. banks: they feared that U.S. authorities could monitor their use or could confiscate or freeze them should the Cold War take a bad turn. (The American assets of Communist China had been frozen.) The Soviets found a Paris bank that was able to find dollar borrowers (the cable address of this bank was EUROBANK—hence the generic term). In recent years the political motive has again become important as Arab governments have placed in the Eurocurrency market huge amounts of funds earned from oil sales.

CASE STUDY: The Iranian Freeze

On November 14, 1979, as part of the deterioration of relations following the Iranian seizure of the U.S. embassy and the holding of embassy personnel as hostages, President Carter ordered the freezing of all official Iranian assets in the United States, estimated to be about $12 billion. Up to half of this amount was not directly in the United States at all but rather consisted of Eurodollar deposits in the overseas branches of American banks. The administration in effect attempted to extend the freeze beyond the United States by virtue of the fact that many Eurobanks are U.S. owned. This action was strongly resented in the banking community (one poll claimed that two-thirds of international bankers—including Americans—disapproved) on the grounds that it struck at one of the basic attractions of a key financial market, that it would place the branches of American banks at a competitive disadvantage relative to other Eurobanks in the competition for Eurodollar deposits, and that it would induce a shift of funds from Eurodollars to other Eurocurrencies. Some commentators blamed the subsequent depreciation of the dollar in part on this action. Also the fact that different national jurisdictions were involved meant that the U.S. action caused an immense legal tangle to begin to develop. A new law journal was founded just to specialize in issues raised by the freeze! The agreement for the return of the hostages, reached early in 1981, also included measures for releasing the frozen assets and for settling private claims against Iran. It remains to be seen to what extent Eurodollars have become less attractive relative to other Eurocurrencies, or whether the bankers' fears will materialize.

The second major impetus to the development of the Eurocurrency markets was furnished by national *controls.* From 1963 until 1974 U.S. exchange controls limited the ability of foreigners to borrow dollars in the United States, and strict U.K. controls seriously limited foreign sterling borrowing until 1978. Such controls had the effect of directing international borrowing and lending toward the Eurocurrency market. National regulation of banking activity has the same effect. All major countries regulate domestic banking in national currencies, but Eurobanking is largely unregulated. U.K. authorities, for example, regulate the sterling activity of British banks because domestic money (sterling) is important to the domestic economy, but they leave British banks essentially free to do what they wish with foreign money (such as dollars) in the belief that such activity has little direct domestic effect but is a source of business for the banking industry. Such regulations often drive a wedge between the rates banks pay depositors and the rates they charge borrowers. The U.S. Fed, for example, requires member banks to hold a portion of their deposits as noninterest earning reserves. Even more significant is Regulation Q, which places ceilings on the interest rates U.S. banks may pay depositors (for example, in the past interest has been prohibited on deposits of less than thirty days). When money is tight and lending rates are high, deposit rates are held down by Regulation Q, and large gaps between the two can arise. Eurobanks are basically unregulated and so are not subject to interest rate ceilings or reserve requirements (and what reserves they choose to hold as a precaution earn interest). All this gives Eurobanking a competitive edge over national banking.

To see how that competitive edge works, suppose that domestic banks have a 25 percent reserve requirement. Then domestic Bank D may lend out only $75 of each $100 received as deposits. If the deposit rate is, say, 5 percent, Bank D must pay $5 interest on the deposit and therefore must charge $6\frac{1}{4}$ percent interest on the $75 loan just to pay for the deposit ($75 \times 6\frac{1}{4}$ percent = $5). If $1\frac{3}{4}$ percent is necessary to cover the other costs of banking, the minimum rate that Bank D can charge on its loans is 8 percent. Since Eurobank E faces no reserve requirement, it can pay $5\frac{1}{2}$ percent on its deposits, thereby luring dollar deposits away from Bank D, and charge $7\frac{1}{2}$ percent for its loans (thereby luring away borrowers) and still cover its costs.

Regulation of domestic U.S. banks was a crucial factor in the very rapid growth the Eurocurrency markets experienced in their formative years during the late sixties and early seventies. When U.S. monetary policy tightened in 1969, for example, foreign subsidiaries of U.S. firms switched their deposits from American banks to the Eurobanks, which paid higher interest. At the same time, corporate borrowers also went to the Eurobanks, where loans were more readily available and the terms attractive. American banks responded by opening many foreign branches to participate in the growing Eurocurrency business (about 40 percent of the activity in London is now actually done through the branches of American banks). The home offices then borrowed dollars from their overseas branches to lend to their domestic customers.

The location of Eurocurrency markets has been determined by national regulations, with the action naturally gravitating toward those countries with the least restrictions. The market is basically unregulated not because no countries regulate such activity, but because the market stays away from those that do. Thus there is little Eurocurrency activity in either the United States or Germany, each a financial colossus, whereas significant centers are in Nassau, Panama, the Cayman Islands, Luxemburg, and Bahrain. (The prefix "Euro" is evidently obsolete). Other important centers include Zurich, Paris, Amsterdam, Hong Kong, and Singapore; activity in the latter two centers is sometimes labeled the "Asia-dollar market." But the most important center, where about a third of all business takes place, is London. In the fifties exchange control prevented London from continuing as the major international financial center that it long had been: specialized institutions and the expertise of the City (London's financial district) were underutilized. Then the Eurodollar market began to develop. The British quickly realized that this offered a way for them to utilize their international banking skills without disturbing domestic monetary arrangements. Accordingly, when in 1958 restrictive regulations were removed, London quickly became the focal point of the new market.

Despite their crucial role in the formative years of the market, and their decisive continuing effect on the location of Eurocurrency activity, national controls are no longer of such importance for the total size of the Euromarkets. These markets have become the conduit for a major part of large-scale international credit transactions, and they function quite efficiently: their continued existence no longer requires a competitive advantage over national money markets. Also the national controls have weakened. American and British exchange controls have been terminated. In the United States Regulation Q is being liberalized; for example, there are no longer interest rate ceilings on large negotiable certificates of deposit, a major competitor of Eurodollar deposits. American banks have been required to hold reserves against Eurodollars they borrow. In recent years the political motive has been more important, rendering the Euromarkets attractive for deposits of Arab oil earnings.

THE NATURE OF CURRENT ACTIVITY

Eurodollar deposits are typically large ($1 million or more) and short term (overnight to six months), though there are exceptions. Loans are also large and short term, but there is also much business in medium-term (three to seven years) loans with the interest rate adjusted every few months. The largest of these loans are typically syndicated (made jointly by a number of banks, so that even the largest credit needs can be met).

In the formative years of the market, large corporations were the most important (nonbank) borrowers and lenders. European central banks deposited part of their dollar reserves in the market, and American banks borrowed from it when money was tight. After the rise in oil prices, the governments of oil-exporting countries also became prominent depositors, and petrodollars (that is, dollars earned by selling oil) an important source of funds. Governments have also become much more important in recent years as borrowers. The communist countries have become important borrowers, and many LDCs have borrowed huge sums to finance large payments deficits. Britain, Canada, and Italy have also made Eurodollar borrowings to augment their official reserves. A good part of the payments deficits prompting these borrowings was in fact due to the increased price of oil. Thus the Eurocurrency markets have played a key role in "recycling" petrodollars from oil exporters to oil importers.

PROBLEMS

10.15 Suppose that Bayer acquires $5 million drawn on an American bank and deposits it in the London branch of Chase Manhattan. Chase's New York office then borrows $4 million from its London branch. Show the balance sheet entries of both the home office and the branch. What are the effects on the sizes of the Eurodollar market and the U.S. and U.K. money supplies?

10.16 The text showed that U.S. reserve requirements gave Eurobanks a competitive edge over domestic banks. But Eurodollars are mostly time deposits, and U.S. reserve requirements for time deposits are quite low, whereas the requirements for demand deposits are much higher. Would you not therefore expect Eurodollars to consist mainly of demand deposits? Why do you think this has not happened?

10.17 The Depository Institutions Deregulation and Monetary Control Act provides that all U.S. ceilings on deposit interest rates are to be phased out by 1986. What will be the likely effects on the Eurocurrency markets?

10.18 Measure what happens to (1) U.S. liabilities to foreign official institutions, (2) German official holdings of dollars, and (3) the size of the Eurodollar market in the following series of transactions:

    a The Bundesbank switches $1 billion from its account at Morgan Guaranty New York to Morgan Guaranty London (MGL) in order to obtain a higher interest rate.

    b MGL lends $900 million to a German firm (which is facing tight monetary conditions inside Germany). The German firm in turn sells the dollars to the Bundesbank for DM in order to invest in Germany. The Bundesbank deposits the $900 million at MGL.

    c Another German firm borrows $810 million from MGL and trades the dollars for DM. In turn the Bundesbank deposits the $810 million at MGL.

    d The Bundesbank lodges a protest with the Federal Reserve Board complaining that it is impossible to maintain an anti-inflationary policy so long as the United States insists on flooding Europe with excess dollars. How should the Fed reply?

10.19* Suppose that Texaco and British Petroleum each make $500 million payments to the Government of Kuwait:

a Texaco makes payment by issuing a draft on its account with First National City Bank/New York (FNCBNY);

b BP sells spot sterling for dollars causing the Bank of England to draw down its dollar reserves held with FNCBNY by $500 million in order to support the spot rate;

c Kuwait deposits the $1 billion with FNCB London.

Show how these transactions affect:

i The U.S. and U.K. money supplies;

ii The size of the Eurodollar market.

In what way would these transactions tend to influence interest rates in the United States, the United Kingdom and the Eurodollar market? How might this alter patterns of borrowing and lending?

10.20* During the mid-sixties many observers worried that the Eurodollar system would collapse in the face of widespread speculation against the dollar. Since that time we have witnessed several speculative episodes, and in each instance not only has the Eurodollar market survived, but it has actually increased in size. Explain why this should have been expected by analyzing the impact of the expectation of a dollar depreciation on:

a Nonbank demand for Eurodollar borrowing;

b Non(commercial)bank supply of Eurodollar deposits.

5. Should the Eurocurrency Markets Be Regulated?

Recommendations that the Eurocurrency markets be regulated are based upon a number of alleged abuses.

1. One alarm is that the rapid growth of Eurocurrencies has created a huge volume of world liquidity in an unmanaged fashion. This is asserted to be highly inflationary. One consequence of the lack of regulation is the absence of uniform reporting requirements for Eurobanks, so we are highly uncertain about the size and composition of the market. But certainly it is huge. The Bank for International Settlements, which collects data on the Euromarkets, estimates their size at the end of 1980 as $981 billion gross ($575 billion net), of which perhaps two-thirds are Eurodollars, 16 percent Euromarks, and 10 percent Euro-Swiss francs. Furthermore, these are surely underestimates, because they do not cover the entire market. Morgan Guaranty Trust Company, for example, estimated the total Eurocurrency market at the end of 1980 at $1470 billion, or $735 billion net of interbank deposits. The net size of the market is greater than any single country's money supply; the number of Eurodollars is greater than the U.S. money supply, the (gross) size of the Euromark market exceeds the German money supply, and likewise for (gross) Euro-Swiss francs and Switzerland's money supply. These figures are mind boggling and seem to give great force to the expressed fears. But detailed considerations result in a much calmer view.

There is, first, the distinction between gross size and net size noted earlier. Second, total net deposits still contain many deposits from central banks and non-Eurobanks. Total nonbank deposits of the public are $300–400 billion, or perhaps three-fourths of the U.S. money supply (M1B). Third, these deposits are time deposits and thus not as analogous to national money supplies as to the much larger totals of commercial bank time deposits, saving and loan shares, and other near-monies. Eurocurrencies are not actually media of exchange. All this makes the problem seem much less ominous. It is still true that the Eurocurrency markets have supplied liquidity services in an unmanaged fashion, but this is a problem with near-monies that central banks have long faced anyway.

2. It has been asserted that the international movement of Eurocurrencies frustrates the attempts of individual countries to control their own money supplies. For example, when the Fed tried to tighten U.S. monetary conditions in the late sixties, American banks were still able to lend by simply borrowing Eurodollars from their foreign branches. But this alarm also loses much of its force when the actual nature of Eurodollars is closely examined. The above example of Eurocurrency mechanics makes it clear that a bank or corporation that borrows Eurodollars receives, not newly created dollars, but already-existing deposits in an American bank. Thus when U.S. banks borrowed Eurodollars from abroad, they did not draw new dollar deposits into the system but merely reallocated existing deposits among themselves. This did not impede the Fed in its efforts to control the total stock of such deposits. Indeed, the Euromarkets contributed to efficiency by allowing credit to be allocated by market-clearing prices (the Eurodollar interest rates) instead of by rationing due to distorted domestic prices. Nevertheless there is again a kernel of truth to the popular alarm. If the authorities do in fact attempt to influence the economy by credit rationing, their efforts could be frustrated by domestic borrowing in the Euromarkets. Or if the Eurodollars borrowed from abroad had originally been deposited in the market as the result of central-bank intervention, they could render control of the money supply more difficult, both at home and abroad. But this is really the basic problem of conducting an effective national monetary policy in the face of a high degree of capital mobility—a problem discussed at length in Chapters 8 and 9. As revealed by that discussion, the crucial considerations are the nature of the exchange-rate regime and the degree of capital mobility. The Eurocurrency markets enter the discussion basically because they are a symptom and a product of highly mobile capital. Only to the extent that they in turn foster even more capital mobility are the Eurocurrency markets candidates for regulation on this score.

3. The Eurocurrency markets have been accused of contributing to international financial instability by weakening the pressures on deficit countries to adjust. As we have seen, in recent years many countries, pri-

marily but not exclusively LDCs, have borrowed in the Eurodollar market to help finance balance of payments deficits. If these countries had been unable to borrow Eurodollars, they would have been forced to take steps to correct their deficits as their international reserves became depleted. These countries might instead have borrowed from other governments or from the International Monetary Fund (taken up in the next chapter), but such lenders, unlike the Eurobanks, would have required corrective action as conditions for the loans. Defenders of the Eurocurrency markets retort that this adds a desirable degree of flexibility to the world economy, and they claim that the official borrowing of Eurodollars was an essential part of the "recycling" of petrodollars in response to the large and sudden increases in oil prices. In any event, what is at issue is again the degree of capital mobility.

4. It is often said that the Eurocurrency markets supply a huge pool of liquid capital that can be moved from currency to currency in search of speculative gain. Once again, what is basically at issue is the desirability of a high degree of capital mobility, of which the Eurocurrency markets are symptoms.

CASE STUDY: What is the Eurodollar Multiplier?

New reserves injected into a national banking system produce a multiplied increase in money: after the reserves are deposited in commercial banks, they are loaned out (except for a fraction kept as reserves) to customers, and after the loans are spent they are also deposited into the banks (except for a fraction that "leaks out"), giving rise to further loans and deposits, and so on. The overall relationship is as follows:

$$\text{(increase in deposits)} = \left[\frac{1}{\text{reserve fraction} + \text{leakage fraction}} \right] \text{(increase in reserves)}$$

The multiplier is the term in square brackets: the smaller the reserve and leakage fractions, the larger the multiplier.

It should be clear from the previous section's example of Eurodollar mechanics that the Eurodollar analogs to reserves in a national banking system are the deposits of Eurobanks in U.S. banks. Economists have wondered how high the Eurodollar multiplier is: if a Eurobank acquires an additional deposit in a U.S. bank, how many more Eurodollars will be created? Since there are no reserve requirements, the reserve fraction is very low, and this led some economists to believe that the multiplier is very high. But it is also true that the leakage fraction is much higher in the Eurodollar market than in a national banking system: when Eurodollars are loaned to a nonbank customer and spent they are not typically redeposited in a Eurobank. Estimates of the actual multiplier have varied enormously, but in recent years a consensus seems to be forming that it is not greatly above unity, and that a high multiplier is thus not a source of instability.

But there have been cases when the multiplier has appeared to be high and where this has mattered. Industrial countries have held some of their dollar reserves as Eurodollar deposits. When there was pressure on the dollar and these countries intervened by selling their currencies, they would deposit the dollars they acquired in the Eurodollar market. Speculators would then borrow these dollars and sell them back to the central banks who would redeposit them, and so on. This so-called *Eurodollar carousel* is an example of a low leakage fraction and a high multiplier. To put a stop to such incidents, the major industrial countries agreed in 1971 not to hold any additional reserves as Eurodollars. But other countries (notably OPEC members) still do, and almost 40 percent of all official reserve dollars are Eurodollar deposits.

5. Eurobanking is often said to be collectively risky because of the absence of regulation. Although the quality of their loans is sometimes criticized, Eurobanks have no reason to be less concerned with the safety of their assets than national banks. But the Eurocurrency system differs in one obvious respect from a national banking system: the latter has a *lender of last resort* (the central bank) that is prepared to supply funds in the event of a crisis to prevent the collapse of the system. It is feared that a serious economic shock could, in contrast, cause the Eurocurrency system to fall apart like a house of cards. If central banks are to collectively supply a lender of last resort to such a market, they must get their act together. They have in fact consulted about the problem, and it seems that this issue will be attacked by continued efforts of central banks to reach a consensus on individual responsibilities, and not by formal regulation.

The various alleged dangers of the Eurocurrency markets reflect to a large extent misunderstanding about the nature of those markets. There are two serious problems to be faced if Eurocurrency regulation is to be used to deal with the alleged dangers.

First, since the basic problem is capital mobility, regulation will be effective only to the degree that it succeeds in limiting such mobility. That is, we are really talking about exchange control with all its problems. Second, the prospects of effectively regulating the Eurocurrency markets are in fact questionable.

CAN THE EUROCURRENCY MARKETS BE REGULATED?

We saw in the previous section that Eurocurrency activity gravitates to those countries where it is not restricted. Should any country attempt to regulate the activity within its borders, the business will simply go elsewhere. Thus there is a strong incentive for those countries where the Euromarkets are located to continue to leave them unregulated, despite the alleged dangers in doing so. Regulation must clearly be multilateral to succeed. Attempts have been made, thus far unsuccessful, to gain agreement for multilateral regulation, with the United States and Germany relatively more enthusiastic than those countries that have the business. Agreement and successful implementation seems unlikely because it would have to be very comprehensive: the market has already demonstrated an ability to locate in obscure places. Thus meaningful regulation of the Eurocurrency markets probably can not be achieved without substantial exchange controls by the major nations.

INTERNATIONAL BANKING FACILITIES

In the United States Eurocurrency regulation has actually been reduced. Since December 1981 U.S. banks have been allowed by the Federal Reserve to set up International Banking Facilities (IBFs), which are free of reserve requirements and interest rate ceilings. The IBFs are allowed to deal only with foreigners, in either dollars or foreign currency, and are excluded from domestic business. The idea is to allow U.S.-based banks to capture part of the business in the Eurocurrency markets. It is too early to tell how successful the attempt will be. The IBFs still have some disadvantages relative to foreign-based Eurobanks; for example IBF deposits must be for at least two days. Also a large gain in the volume of IBF business could in fact be illusory: for years much Eurocurrency business has in effect been conducted in New York but put on the books of Caribbean branches of U.S banks. Transferring all this business to the books of New York IBFs could result in large numbers but not necessarily much practical significance.

PROBLEMS _____

10.21 Describe the Eurodollar carousel in terms of the discussion of sterilization and offset in Chapter 8. Should the decision by the central banks, to deposit no additional reserves in the Eurodollar market, actually have made their job any easier, assuming they wanted to intervene and sterilize? Why?

6. The Efficiency of the Foreign Exchange Markets

Managed floating has been the exchange regime for key industrial countries since March 1973. Since then *exchange rates have indeed fluc-*

tuated. Wide swings and sharp movements of the rates have produced much consternation and have at times strongly influenced national policies. Jacob Frenkel and Michael Mussa have calculated that the dollar/pound, dollar/ mark, and dollar/French franc exchange rates each experienced average monthly fluctuations in excess of 2 percent between June 1973 and February 1979. Such turbulence reduces the usefulness of national currencies as money, as discussed in section 11 of Chapter 9. At the same time, exchange rates have varied much more than relative inflation rates, national economic policies, or other fundamental influences, and so it is not at all clear that this turbulence is simply the price that must be paid to allow individual countries to control their own money supplies. Some commentators accordingly advocate an increased use of adjustable pegs and/or exchange controls. However, we cannot conclude, simply from the pronounced exchange-rate variability, that the foreign exchange markets have not functioned well. The world economy has been subjected to serious shocks since 1973 (for example, oil price increases), and before that foreign exchange crises afflicted, and ultimately destroyed, the adjustable-peg system.

An important criterion for judging the performance of markets is that of efficiency. *A market is efficient if its prices fully reflect all currently available information.* Why is it important that the foreign exchange market be efficient? We saw in Part One that individual consumers and producers base decisions on relative prices; those prices accordingly equal corresponding marginal rates of transformation, marginal rates of substitution, and so on, and cause individuals to make socially "correct" decisions. Exchange rates are used to compare prices expressed in different currencies; therefore, if the exchange rates do not reflect all available information, the decisions of individual consumers and producers will also not be based on all available information and so will not be socially correct.

INTEREST ARBITRAGE

Judging the efficiency of a market is fundamentally difficult because we cannot directly observe whether prices do in fact reflect all available information. An indirect way to try to judge efficiency is to look for unexploited profit opportunities: if some information is not reflected in prices, someone should be able to "beat the market" by utilizing the overlooked information. For example, consider the discussion of interest arbitrage in section 2. The interest-parity condition, equation (10.1) or (10.2), essentially requires that exchange rates (spot and forward) fully reflect the information contained in the interest rates. If this is not so, that is, if interest parity does not hold, you can make a profit by conducting covered interest arbitrage as summarized in Table 10.3. In this case you are exploiting your information about interest rates to beat the market. In fact it is just such activity, or dealers' anticipations of such activity, that will cause the exchange rates to adjust to reflect this information if the markets are in fact efficient.

As Tables 10.5 and 10.6 illustrated, there is a strong tendency toward interest parity, but the tendency is by no means complete. Here we face a problem of interpretation. It is possible that the departures from interest parity reflect a lack of total efficiency in the markets. But it is also possible that these departures instead reflect information *in addition* to interest rates and are, therefore, in a sense consistent with efficiency. For example, the exchange rates could reflect the risk that a bank might default on a forward contract, or that a government might impose exchange controls preventing individuals from repatriating funds placed in foreign assets. We can obtain some perspective on this by examining the activities of Eurobanks, who simultaneously engage in foreign exchange transactions and Eurocurrency borrowing and lending. Tables 10.5 and 10.6 compared forward premiums with differentials in domestic interest rates. If we were to instead go to, say, the Eurocurrency market in London and compare the forward premium on the mark relative to the dollar with the interest rate differential between Euromarks and Eurodollars, we would find interest parity holding almost exactly! Indeed interest arbitrage is so pervasive in the Euromarkets that dealers routinely use the interest parity formula to determine quotes. Why this difference between Euromarkets and national markets? In the former case the risk factor largely washes out. A Eurobank in London could conceivably default on forward contracts, but it would likely do so on both mark and dollar contracts; neither dollars nor marks constitute British money, so the chance of British exchange controls on Eurobank activities in the two currencies is slight and common to both. Also, of course, the Eurocurrency markets are subject to less existing regulation. In summary, *interest arbitrage is virtually complete in the Euromarkets, and is strong, but not comlete, between national markets.*

Figure 10.7 shows the virtual identity between the Euromark interest rate and the covered interest rate of Eurodollars. The Figure also shows how controls influence the relation between Eurocurrency markets and domestic markets. Germany had exchange controls from 1971–1973 that limited foreign purchases of German assets and allowed the domestic (interbank) interest rate to remain considerably above the Euromark rate. When many of these controls were terminated in 1974 the two rates quickly converged, as shown in the figure.

SPECULATION

Interest arbitrage in the Euromarkets furnishes some evidence for market efficiency. The evidence cannot be decisive, however, because interest rates constitute only a portion of all the information that exchange rates should reflect. For example, forward exchange rates should reflect all available information about future spot rates, that is, the forward rate

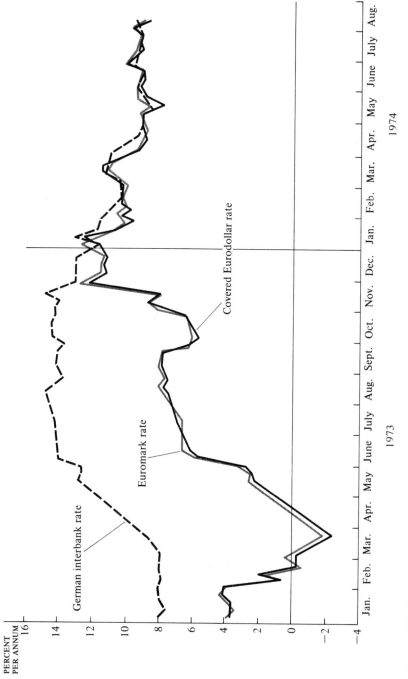

Figure 10.7. Interest Arbitrage in the Eurocurrency Markets (Jan. 1973–Aug. 1974)

source: Money Manager for Euromark rate, and Federal Reserve Board for all other interest and exchange rates.

should be the "best" available forecast of what the spot rate will be. If the market is not efficient in this sense, individuals can utilize the unexploited information to conduct profitable speculation, as described in section 2.

How good a forecast is the forward rate? Not very good, in the sense that the forward premium generally differs from the spot appreciation that subseqently takes place, and often by large amounts. But the errors may not be systematic, so that a speculator need not be able to make money simply by betting against the forward rate in a mechanical way. Figure 10.8 depicts a hypothetical, but typical, relationship between the thirty-day forward premium (indicated by crosses) at various dates and the appreciation (indicated by circles) of the spot rate that actually happens in the thirty days after each date. If the forward rate were a perfectly accurate forecast of the future spot rate, the circle at each date would coincide with the cross at that date. The crosses do not predict the circles very well, but they are not biased in any way either. Many economists have investigated the ability of the forward rate to forecast the future spot rate, and these investigations together strongly indicate that indeed *the forward premium is an inaccurate but almost unbiased predictor of the future spot appreciation*. Recent investigations have cast doubt on whether the forward rate is completely unbiased. For example, Lars Hansen and Robert Hodrick of Carnegie-Mellon University presented data showing that, for several currencies in the seventies and in the twenties, the expected return from speculation was not necessarily zero.

Even if the forward rate is unbiased, there remains the possibility that, by using information not incorporated into the forward rate, it is possible to find another predictor that is also unbiased but more accurate than the

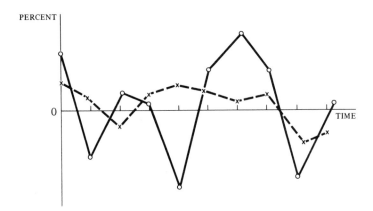

Figure 10.8. HYPOTHETICAL FORWARD PREMIUMS (X) AND SUBSEQUENT SPOT APPRECIATION (O)

forward rate. A number of economists have investigated this possibility, with mixed results. The forward rate is often better, and never very much worse, than proposed alternatives, but there are some indications that a modest improvement on the forward rate could be possible. In recent years a number of firms have gone into the business of forecasting exchange rates and selling their predictions to banks and corporations. That these forecasting firms can earn a profit is interesting, because their customers can presumably learn current forward quotes with a simple phone call. The periodical *Euromoney* recently concluded that corporate treasurers utilize the services of forecasting firms not to obtain forecasts so much as to defuse corporate criticism of their own decisions and to obtain other market information provided by forecasters. It is difficult to know what to make of this. Richard Levich, of New York University, has studied the performance of the forecasters and has found that they may offer some modest benefits relative to forward rates. Overall, research to date indicates that *the forward rate is almost the best available forecast of the future spot rate, but the jury is still out on whether it is in fact the best.*

CASE STUDY: Why It Is So Hard to Test Market Efficiency

Economists often try to test for the efficiency of foreign exchange markets by comparing forward rates and subsequent spot rates; for example the thirty-day forward rate might be compared to the spot rate that actually prevails thirty days later. Such tests are really investigating a joint hypothesis

(a) that individuals use all available information in trying to predict the future behavior of spot rates (for example the hypothesis might be that although people do not know what the future spot rate will actually be, they do discover the probability law that governs its behavior); and

(b) that the forward rate equals what people expect the future spot rate to be (that is, their "best" guess).

There are two fundamental difficulties. The first is that we cannot test (a) and (b) separately because we cannot observe individuals' predictions. Thus if a test should reject the joint hypothesis that (a) and (b) hold, we would not know whether the rejection is due to the fact that (a) is false, that (b) is false, or that both are false. The second problem is that we do not know whether (a) and (b) are in fact necessary for the foreign exchange markets to be efficient (in the general sense that exchange rates rationally reflect all available information). For example, under some circumstances it might be necessary in equilibrium to pay traders a *risk premium* in order to induce them to hold a currency perceived as unusually risky. In such a case hypothesis (b) need not hold but the market could still be efficient: the difference between the forward rate and the expected future spot rate would furnish the required risk premium. Also it is in fact costly to acquire information, and the value of the latter can only be guessed at beforehand. Thus hypothesis (a) need not hold, if people believe that it is not worthwhile to acquire information that is available at a price, but the market could still be efficient. It is a difficult theoretical problem to delineate precisely the circumstances under which (a) and (b) characterize efficiency, and a difficult empirical problem to decide when those circumstances actually hold.

THE EFFECT OF NEW INFORMATION

To the extent that the foreign exchange markets are efficient so that exchange rates do fully reflect all current information, the appearance of new information should immediately cause changes in exchange rates as the market absorbs the news. Any reader of the financial press is aware of the frenetic reception the market accords significant and unexpected news items. Short-term fluctuations in exchange rates seem to be dominated by the receipt of new information because these fluctuations are much larger than what can be explained by continuing influences such as differences in national inflation rates or interest rates. Over longer periods of time the transient information effects tend to cancel each other out, so that the latter continuing influences become more important.

Day-to-day moments in forward rates tend to be accompanied by almost indentical day-to-day movements in current (not future) spot rates. One reason for this is of course interest arbitrage, which as we have seen, links spot and future rates together in the interest parity relationship. But the reciept of new information would also produce such behavior. Suppose, for example, that some development implying a weakening of the pound relative to the dollar suddenly becomes publicly known. The spot pound/dollar exchange rate will quickly adjust as the market absorbs the news. Now the forward rate is a forecast of the future spot rate. As we have seen, it is not a good forecast but it may be an unbiased one. The news item is the *only* change that has taken place and so is the only reason to change the (admittedly bad) forecast of the future spot rate. The forward rate therefore responds in basically the same way as the current spot rate.

In summary, available evidence indicates a high degree of efficiency in the foreign exchange market, and those markets accordingly seem to be quite sensitive to new developments. But the evidence is not conclusive.

PROBLEM _____

10.22 German exchange controls on capital inflows were relaxed on January 30, 1974, but Figure 10.7 shows that the Euromark and German interbank interest rates actually moved together a few months *earlier.* Can you think of any reason for this?

7. International Credit Markets

International borrowing and lending has increased enormously in the last quarter century. Commercial banks are the typical sources of short-term loans. Table 10.10 shows the total outstanding volume of international loans made by commercial banks in the industrial countries as of the end of 1980. Much of this international lending is done by the Eurobanks: of the $903 billion total outstanding international loans by banks located in Europe, $751 billion are Eurocurrency loans and $152 billion are domestic currency loans. As we saw in section 4, the Eurocurrency markets also supply medium-term (three to seven years) credit in the form of loans with an interest rate that adjusts every few months. A survey by the OECD in Paris concluded that about $78 billion of such loans by Eurobank syndicates was outstanding at the end of 1979.

Table 10.10. OUTSTANDING INTERNATIONAL LOANS BY COMMERCIAL BANKS, 1980 *(billions of dollars)*

Europe	$ 903
U.S.	177
U.S. Offshore*	142
Japan and Canada	101
Total	$1323

* U.S. bank branches in Hong Kong, Singapore, and the Caribbean

SOURCE: *Bank for International Settlements,* Annual Report

Long-term international borrowing is typically done, not from banks, but by the sale of bonds to the public. Foreign corporations and governments can borrow American funds for up to twenty-five years by selling bonds in New York, for example.

Foreign bonds are the traditional means of long-term credit. Suppose, for example, that Coagulated Mush, Ltd. wishes to borrow £100,000,000 for twenty years for a plant expansion program. The firm decides to raise the funds in New York. To do so Coagulated Mush issues $200 million of bonds, assuming the exchange rate is $2.00/£, and sells them in New York (through a New York underwriter). The firm may use some of the dollar proceeds of the bond sale to buy equipment in the United States, but probably the dollars will be sold on the foreign exchange market for pounds. Coagulated Mush will have to pay interest on the bonds in dollars and will eventually have to redeem them for dollars upon maturity.

From the point of view of the lenders (in this case the Americans who purchased Coagulated Mush's bonds) there is little difference between foreign bonds and domestic bonds. Both are sold in the local market, are denominated in the local currency, and are subject to local regulations. The only difference is that the foreign bond is the obligation of a foreign resident. But from the borrower's point of view foreign bonds differ in that they establish a long-term obligation to make payments in foreign currency. Coagulated Mush is obligating itself to make dollar payments for twenty years; had the money been raised locally by selling domestic bonds in London the obligation would have been in pounds.

New York is a major market for foreign bonds. Canadian firms and governments annually raise billions of dollars by selling U.S. dollar denominated bonds in New York. Other major centers are in Switzerland (where non-Swiss borrowers sell bonds denominated in Swiss francs), in Germany (mark bonds), and recently in Japan (yen bonds). Both the size of the foreign bond market and its distribution among the centers varies greatly from year to year in response to credit conditions. In 1980 about $16 billion of new foreign bonds were issued. The general trend in recent years has been a declining role for the U.S. market relative to foreign bond issues in Switzerland and Germany; in 1980 the largest volume of borrowing was in fact in Switzerland.

In recent decades international bond markets witnessed an innovation analogous to the Eurocurrency markets in international banking. In addition to the traditional foreign bonds, we now have *Eurobonds*—international bonds denominated in a currency other than that of the country or countries in which they are sold. If Coagulated Mush had wished to go this route, it would have sold its dollar denominated bonds in London, or, perhaps through an international syndicate, in London, Paris, and Amsterdam simultaneously. The purchasers of the bonds would have paid dollars for them, and they would have received dollars for interest. In 1980 about $23 billion of new Eurobonds were issued. During the late sixties over 90 percent of Eurobond issues were denominated in dollars, but this proportion has declined over the years. Recently about 45–55 percent of new issues have been denominated in dollars and about 20–30 percent in marks. The remaining Eurobonds are denominated in many different currencies; there has, for example, been an issue in Kuwaiti dinar. Some Eurobond issues are "currency cocktails": denominated in terms of a basket of different currencies.

Political motives and national regulations were important in the development of Eurobonds, just as they were with Eurocurrencies. The market received a big boost in 1964 when the United States imposed the Interest Equalization Tax on foreign bond sales (except for bonds issued by Canadians). That tax has been repealed, but national regulations still matter. For example, an issue of dollar-denominated Eurobonds would not subject the borrower to the disclosure requirements of the Securities and Exchange Commission that would apply were the bonds issued in New York. Also, individuals buying the Eurobonds could more easily preserve anonymity (for sundry nefarious purposes).

We saw that such regulations were no longer crucial to the survival of the Eurocurrency markets, which have matured to the point that they can compete on equal terms with national markets. The same is not true of Eurobonds. Markets for these bonds are thin, especially the secondary markets, so that a bondholder who wishes to sell out before maturity may have difficulty. Also underwriting costs are higher in the Eurobond markets than in the national markets, and borrowers typically must pay a premium.

8. Summary

1. The monies of different countries are exchanged for each other in the foreign exchange market, which exists to facilitate the international exchange of goods, services, and assets.

2. Spot foreign exchange transactions are settled within two business days; forward transactions are settled at some specified date in the future. Forward markets furnish a way for firms dealing in international markets to escape exchange risk.

3. Two theories explain how spot and forward rates are linked. Covered interest parity asserts that the forward premium equals the interest rate differential, whereas the speculative theory claims that the forward premium equals the expected appreciation of the spot rate.

4. Eurodollars are dollars on deposit in banks outside the United States. The Eurodollar market has grown from nearly nothing in the fifties to its present gigantic size because of the competitive edge over national markets resulting from the lack of Eurodollar regulation, and because of the desire of some governments holding dollars to stay clear of the United States.

5. The foreign exchange market is efficient if exchange rates fully reflect all available information. Research has not yet concluded whether the foreign exchange markets are in fact fully efficient.

6. Foreign banks are domestic currency bonds issued in domestic credit markets by foreign firms or governments. Eurobonds are denominated in a currency other than that of the market in which they are issued.

SUGGESTED READING

Bank for International Settlements. *Annual Report.* Basle, published each June.
   The standard source for information on the Eurocurrency markets.

Dufey, G. and Giddy, I. *The International Money Market.* Englewood Cliffs: Prentice-Hall, 1978. Good treatment.

Einzig, P. *The History of Foreign Exchange.* New York: St. Martin's Press, 1962. Foreign exchange through the ages.

Erdman, P. *The Billion Dollar Sure Thing.* New York, Hutchinson, 1973. An entertaining novel featuring details of the foreign exchange markets; written while the author was in a Swiss jail.

Frenkel, J. A. and Mussa, M. L. "The Efficiency of the Foreign Exchange Market and Measures of Turbulence." *American Economic Review* 70 (May 1980): 374–81. An interpretation of recent market behavior.

Frydl, E. J. "The Debate Over Regulating the Eurocurrency Markets." Federal Reserve Bank of New York, *Quarterly Review* 4, 4 (1979–80): 11–20. The pros and cons.

Hansen, L. P. and Hodrick, R. J. "Forward Exchange Rates as Optimal Predictors of Future Spot Rates: An Econometric Analysis." *Journal of Political Economy* 88 (October 1980): 829–53. Empirical study cited in text.

Keynes, J. M. *A Tract on Monetary Reform.* London: Macmillan, 1923. Section 4 of chapter 3 is the classic description of the forward market.

Kubarych, R. M. *Foreign Exchange Markets in the United States.* New York: Federal Reserve Bank of New York, 1978. A good description of the contemporary foreign exchange market.

Levich, R. M. "On the Efficiency of Markets for Foreign Exchange." In *International Economic Policy.* Edited by R. Dornbusch and J. A. Frenkel. Baltimore: Johns Hopkins, 1979. A survey of investigations of market efficiency.

McKinnon, R. I. "The Eurocurrency Markets." Princeton University, *Essays in International Finance* 125 (1977). A good description and analysis.

Revey, P. A. "Evolution and Growth of the United States Foreign Exchange Market." Federal Reserve Bank of New York, *Quarterly Review* 6, 3 (1981): 32–44. Recent developments.

Roll, R. and Solnik, B. "A Pure Foreign Exchange Asset Pricing Model." *Journal of International Economics* 7 (May 1977): 161–79. A theoretical treatment.

Chapter 11

The International Monetary System

> "It is clear enough in principle that private owners of wealth have no right to the liberty to move funds around the world according to their private convenience, and it is clear that, in the uneasy conditions of modern times, no conceivable international currency system can survive for long if that liberty is granted."
> —JOAN ROBINSON, 1944

> "The doctor found, when she was dead,-
> Her last disorder mortal."
> —OLIVER GOLDSMITH

> "There is closer cooperation among central banks today than there was between the Federal Reserve Bank of Chicago and the Federal Reserve Bank of New York in 1933."
> —E.M. BERNSTEIN, 1965

WE SAW in Chapter 9 that the present international monetary system—if system is the word—is a confusing arrangement with prominent use of managed floating and adjustable pegs. This chapter discusses how this state of affairs came about and the policy issues that it raises. First we describe balance of payments accounting procedures, in order to be able to understand the statistics that follow. Next we describe the development of the international monetary system since the Second World War. In addition to explaining how we got where we are, this discussion will expose the basic problems that need to be faced to fashion a workable system. Finally we examine current proposals for international monetary reform.

1. Balance of Payments Accounts

A country's balance of payments accounts are a record of transactions in a specific time interval between residents of that country and the rest of the world. The time interval is usually a year; some countries, such as the United States, also report quarterly.

The distinction between domestic residents and foreigners is not on the basis of legal citizenship but rather "normal" location of residence. Tourists, military and diplomatic personnel, and temporary migrants are treated as residents of the country from which they come; their transactions while abroad result, in principle, in balance of payments entries, whereas payments they receive from or make to their home countries do not. A permanent migrant, by contrast, is a resident of where she is, even if she still retains the citizenship of the country she has left; in this case transactions in the new country do not involve the balance of payments, but remittances sent to relatives in the old country do. Foreign subsidiaries are regarded as residents of the country in which they are located. Thus sales by a parent firm to a foreign subsidiary result in balance of payments entries, even though the transaction takes place within a single corporation.

GENERAL PRINCIPLES

There are two general principles involved in balance of payments accounting. The first is the distinction between debits and credits. An international transaction involves the export of some good, service, or asset in exchange for the import of an equal-valued good, service, or asset. Thus the total value of all exports always equals the total value of all imports: this is Walras's Law. The balance of payments accounts use a double-entry system in which each transaction gives rise to both a credit entry (the "export") and a debit entry (the "import"). Thus the sum of all credits equals the sum of all debits—balance of payments accounting consists of filling in Walras's Law with numbers. Suppose that Acme Spirits buys two hundred cases of whiskey from a Scottish distillery, paying for it with a $25,000 check. This generates for the U.S. balance of payments a $25,000 debit entry under merchandise trade (the *import* of the whiskey) and a $25,000 credit entry under short-term capital flows (the *export* of the $25,000 demand deposit via the check). What are the effects of the transaction on the U.K. balance of payments? On the French balance of payments?

In some transactions, called *unilateral transfers,* one party gives without receiving anything directly in return. Examples include private gifts, government or private grants, pensions, and remittances sent home by migrants. Separate entries are made for such transfers, debits for unilateral transfers made to foreigners and credits for transfers received from foreigners. Suppose, for example, that $1,000 worth of wheat is given to some Asian nation for famine relief. This results in a $1,000 credit entry for

merchandise trade (the export of wheat) and a $1,000 debit entry for uni-
lateral transfers (making a transfer to foreigners).

To summarize: *each transaction generates two equal entries, a credit
(+) for an export of a good, service, or asset or for the receipt of a unilateral
transfer, and a debit (−) for an import of a good, service, or asset or for
making a unilateral transfer.*

Since the sum of all credits equals the sum of all debits, interest
attaches not to the overall balance of payments—always equal to zero—but
to its constituent parts. The purpose of the accounts is to reveal the structure
of a country's international transactions. The second principle of accounting
is therefore to put the debits and credits in the proper subaccounts. The
overall balance is divided into current and capital accounts, as shown in
Figure 7.4, with the capital account further subdivided, as in Table 7.4. But
countries disaggregate more than this. Table 11.1 shows the U.S. balance of
payments in 1980 broken down to a moderate degree. Each number shows
the excess of credits over debits for entries classified on that line. The
current account is split up into the constituents labeled (1) through (6). Line
(1) shows merchandise trade: evidently U.S. imports of goods exceeded
exports in value by $26.7 billion in 1980. Lines (2), (3), and (4) show net
trade in services disaggregated into three parts. Unilateral transfers are

Table 11.1. THE U.S. BALANCE OF PAYMENTS, 1980 *(billions of
dollars)*

(1)	Merchandise Trade	− 26.7	
(2)	Investment Income	32.5	
(3)	Fees and Royalties	6.2	
(4)	Other Services	− 4.3	
	[Goods and Services	7.7]	
(5)	Private Unilateral Transfers	− 1.2	
(6)	U.S. Government Unilateral Transfers	− 6.4	
	Current Account		.1
(7)	U.S. Government Capital	− 5.1	
(8)	Direct Investment	− 12.4	
(9)	Portfolio Investment	6.9	
(10)	Other Private Capital	− 34.3	
	Non Official Capital Account		− 44.9
(11)	Statistical Discrepancy	35.6	35.6
(12)	Allocation of Special Drawing Rights	1.2	
(13)	U.S. Official Reserve Assets	− 8.2	
(14)	Foreign Official Assets in U.S.	16.2	
	Net Official Reserve Transactions		9.2
	Total	0	0

SOURCE: *Survey of Current Business*

included in the current account in items (5) and (6), with transfers of the U.S. government segregated from the rest. Evidently private unilateral transfers made to the rest of the world exceeded those received from abroad by $1.2 billion in 1980. Since the current account was in surplus by $.1 billion, the total capital account (official plus nonofficial) must have been in deficit by an equal amount.

The nonofficial capital account is split into four parts. The distinction between direct investment, portfolio investment, and short-term capital was explained in Chapter 7. Items (8), (9), and (10) record the respective excesses of credits over debits for transactions involving private U.S. residents; capital transactions involving the U.S. government are segregated into item (7).

Items (12) through (14) show official transactions. The net dealings of U.S. authorities in international reserves are shown in item (13). International reserves include gold and foreign exchange plus two items (Special Drawing Rights and IMF reserve positions), which we shall study in the next section. In 1980 the U.S. authorities increased their holdings of international reserves by $8.2 billion (as always, an "import" of anything is a debit and an "export" a credit). As we saw in Chapter 8, the U.S. dollar is a reserve asset for foreign countries, so that U.S. payments imbalances can cause changes in either U.S. holdings of international reserves or foreign official holdings of dollars. Item (14) records net foreign official transactions in dollar assets, with increases in foreign holdings recorded as credits (an "export" of dollars) and decreases as debits.

The total of items (13) and (14) should normally equal minus the total of the current and (nonofficial) capital accounts. But in 1980 a quantity of a reserve asset—the Special Drawing Right—was artificially created by international agreement and distributed among the world's central banks (we shall discuss this asset later in this chapter). The receipt of this asset added debit entries to item (13), and so the allocation is separately recorded as a credit in line (12).

Items (12), (13), and (14) should in principle now sum to minus the total of items (1) through (10). But in practice this will not be so, because errors are inevitable in compiling the accounts. An additional entry, called the *statistical discrepancy,* is therefore added to balance the books. Item (11) is simply the total of the other thirteen items with the sign reversed. This discrepancy does not measure total errors, because many will cancel out, but only net errors. In particular, if a transaction is missed entirely by the compilers of the accounts, both debits and credits are reduced the same amount. Thus the statistical discrepancy comes from overlooking (or incorrectly measuring) one side of transactions.

Data on merchandise trade comes from customs declarations and, for most countries, is regarded as the most accurate part of the accounts. Trade in services, by contrast, is typically estimated by various sampling techniques; errors are likely substantial but not necessarily volatile year by year. Reporting procedures for capital transactions are likewise highly imperfect, and the volume of such transactions is quite volatile, especially at the short end of the maturity spectrum. Many economists accordingly view the statistical discrepancy as substantially a reflection of unrecorded short-term capital movements.

Balances of payments are typically presented in somewhat greater detail than Table 11.1 with the format varying from country to country in order to isolate what is important to individual countries. Ghana, for example, has a separate entry for exports of cocoa beans and products; the United States isolates military grants and agency sales from other exports and military grants from other transfers (this was not done in Table 11.1).

PROBLEMS _____

11.1 A U.K. distillery sells an American firm 200 cases of whiskey in exchange for a $25,000 check drawn on an American bank. The distillery uses $15,000 of this to buy equipment in France, and the other $10,000 to retire bonds it had issued years ago to a group of wealthy Italian investors. Write all the resulting entries in the balance of payments accounts of the United States, France, U.K., Germany and Italy.

11.2 Write all balance of payments entries resulting from each of the following transactions.

   a The U.S. Army gives $1 million in pay to American soldiers stationed in Germany.

   b Ford Motor Company (U.S.) pays $1 million to Ford's German subsidiary for automobile parts.

   c An American automobile dealer pays $1 million, by check, to the German firm BMW for automobiles.

   d BMW pays $1 million to the Bundesbank for DM1.6 million.

   e Daring Danny of Denver, sky-diving champion of all Colorado west of the Rockies, pays Lloyds of London $10,000 for a life insurance policy.

   f Lloyds of London pays Daring Danny's widow $1 million in settlement of a life-insurance policy claim.

   g A Japanese firm sends the Soviet Union $2 million worth of drilling equipment in return for $2 million worth of oil.

   h A Japanese firm sends the Soviet Union $2 million worth of drilling equipment in return for a promise of $4 million worth of oil in five years.

   i You visit Singapore and have $1,000 stolen by a local pickpocket.

   j You visit Singapore and lose $1,000 worth of American traveler's checks, for which you receive a refund from the local bank.

11.3 Generally, only transactions between American residents and foreign residents generate entries in the American balance of payments. But in one case, transactions between two foreigners result in such entries. What is this case?

11.4* Consider Canada's balance of payments.

CANADIAN BALANCE OF PAYMENTS, 1980 *(billions of Canadian dollars)*

Merchandise Trade		8.6	
Services		−11.4	
[Goods and Services			−2.8]
Private Unilateral Transfers		.8	
Official Unilateral Transfers		.4	
Current Account			−1.6
Direct Investment		− 2.6	
Portfolio Investment		5.4	
Other Non Official Capital		.6	
Non Official Capital			3.4
Net Errors and Omissions		− 2.5	−2.5
Allocation of Special Drawing Rights		.2	
Change in Value of Reserves		.1	
Official Reserve Assets		.4	
Net Official Reserve Transactions		.7	
		0	

SOURCE: *IMF,* Balance of Payments Statistics

a Discuss each line, as the text did for Table 11.1. In what ways do Canada's payments differ from those of the United States? Why?
b What is the item "Change in Value of Reserves"? To what is a positive number due?

2. The Bretton Woods System

As the Second World War drew to a close, the allied powers set about planning a new international order, planning that culminated in the United Nations. The postwar economic system was not ignored in this process. Negotiations over a new international monetary system were centered largely between the United States and Britain, with the former naturally the relatively more influential participant. Final agreement on the new system was reached in 1944 at Bretton Woods, New Hampshire, in a conference of the allied nations. The resulting international monetary arrangement is accordingly often called the Bretton Woods system.

THE BRETTON WOODS CONFERENCE

In July of 1944 over 300 representatives of 44 allied nations met for three weeks at the hamlet of Bretton Woods, New Hampshire, to reach final agreement on details of the postwar international monetary system. The conference was held at the Mt. Washington Hotel, a huge, old-style White Mountains resort that, like the system whose birth it witnessed, fell upon bad times in the seventies. The British delegation was headed by Keynes and the American by Treasury Secretary Morgenthau and his deputy, Harry Dexter White, later a victim of the McCarthy years. The conference had been preceded by several years of preparations and negotiations, notably between the United States and Britain, whose respective positions had been embodied in plans drafted by White and Keynes. The American position reflected the interests of a creditor nation and the British those of a debtor, natural in view of the roles the countries would play after the war. The conference adopted an agreement much closer to the White Plan than to the Keynes Plan, but developments in later years were to move in the direction of the latter (just as the United States developed a persistent deficit position).

THE BRETTON WOODS SYSTEM IN OUTLINE

Two international economic institutions were founded. The International Bank for Reconstruction and Development (IBRD—better known as the World Bank) provides loans for the purposes indicated in its name. The International Monetary Fund (IMF) was designed as the centerpiece of the new international monetary system and will figure prominently in this chapter. Postwar planners subsequently designed a third institution, the International Trade Organization, to deal with commercial policy, but, as we saw in Chapter 6, the ITO never came into being.

Many of the people who helped design the new system had in mind two earlier experiences—or at least caricatures of the experiences. One was the international gold standard in the generation preceding the First World War. This was viewed as a successful international monetary system, but national governments had not pursued economic policies for domestic macroeconomic goals, as they were expected vigorously to do in the postwar world. The second experience was that of the thirties, when national policies were by contrast formulated with domestic goals paramount—but at the expense of the international economy. The experience was perceived to have been characterized by extensive trade and payments restrictions, competitive exchange depreciations, and unstable floating exchange rates. The problem in designing a new system was to capture the international harmony and stable exchange rates associated with the gold standard while also allowing individual countries the freedom to pursue their own macroeconomic policies. This basic problem remains very much with us today.

The planners tried to solve this problem with an exchange-rate compromise between floating and fixed rates: an *adjustable-peg* system. Countries would normally intervene to keep their exchange rates within a narrow band of their pegs; at the same time domestic policies would presumably be directed toward maintaining desirable macroeconomic conditions. Should a country find that its balance of payments was in "fundamental disequilibrium"—a term never defined—it would be able to adjust its peg instead of undergoing a severe deterioration of internal conditions in order to maintain the old peg. The new International Monetary Fund was intended both to help countries with balance of payments difficulties and to prevent competitive depreciation and other aggressive national actions.

THE INTERNATIONAL MONETARY FUND

The IMF is a specialized agency of the United Nations and has 143 member states, nearly all the noncommunist nations of the world. The Soviet Union participated in the Bretton Woods Conference but never became part of the Bretton Woods system. The IMF does have some communist members: Yugoslavia, Rumania, and the People's Republic of China have joined, and Cambodia, Laos, and Vietnam have maintained the memberships of previous regimes (Poland, Czechoslovakia, and Cuba, on the other hand, dropped out, although Poland has asked to rejoin; Hungary has also applied for membership).

The IMF was intended to play two fundamental roles in the Bretton Woods system. The Fund should, first, discourage aggressive exchange-rate behavior by members and help them to manage their balances of payments efficiently and in ways conducive to international harmony. Members accepted general principles, obligations, and rules of conduct by joining the Fund and signing its Articles of Agreement. Chief among these obligations was to maintain an adjustable peg and to allow free convertibility of the national currency for current account transactions, that is, to allow individuals freely to exchange domestic money for foreign money in order to buy and sell goods and services with the rest of the world. (Countries were to be allowed, as a tool of balance of payments policy, to attempt to control foreign exchange dealings associated with capital account transactions.) Also the Fund itself was to oversee and influence member policies (for example, large cumulative peg adjustments were to require IMF approval), to consult periodically with members, and to render them technical advice. To do this, the Fund was given a staff of international civil servants—currently about 1,500 in number—at its headquarters in Washington, D.C. The Fund is managed by an executive board and a managing director (presently J. de Larosière, of France), with ultimate authority resting in a board of governers, which meets annually, representing the member countries.

The second fundamental role assigned the IMF was to supply credit to member states. The Fund was given resources by means of contributions subscripted from members, and was to use these resources to lend international reserves to countries with balance of payments difficulties. Countries would thereby be better able than if they had to rely solely on their own international reserves to finance temporary payments deficits without imposing unwelcome contractionary policies or changing their pegs.

IMF Credit Facilities. Each member country has a quota whose size reflects the relative international economic importance of the country. (The largest quota, that of the United States, is more than 9,000 times the size of the smallest, that of the Maldive Islands.) Its quota equals the subscription payment each country has made to the Fund, and also determines its borrowing privileges from the Fund. In addition, voting power in the IMF is proportional to the quotas, in sharp contrast to the "one-country, one-vote" principle used by the United Nations and its other agencies. Quotas are reviewed every three to five years and have been increased several times in order to enlarge Fund resources; sometimes relative quotas are adjusted to reflect changes in relative country sizes. When new members join the Fund they receive their own quotas, thereby increasing the aggregate total.

Quota subscription payments are generally made 75 percent in the member's own currency and 25 percent in international reserve assets. The latter payments were originally in gold, but now they are in Special Drawing Rights (SDRs)—an international reserve asset created by the IMF in 1969 (SDRs are more fully described below). At present the total of all members' quotas is over SDR 60 billion, worth roughly US$75 billion in early 1981. The Fund may also enlarge its resources by borrowing, has profitably sold gold to the public, and receives fees when members borrow from it.

The Fund operates several borrowing facilities.

(a) *Basic credit facility.* A member technically draws on this facility by using its own currency to purchase from the Fund other currencies or SDRs in order to finance payments deficits. The loan is repaid when the member repurchases its own currency with other currencies or SDRs. Any member may unconditionally borrow in this way until the Fund's holdings of the member's currency equals the member's quota; such unconditional borrowing rights, called the *reserve tranche,* thus originally equal 25 percent of the quota (they can come to equal more than this, if other members borrow a member's currency and so reduce the Fund's holdings to less than 75 percent of the quota). Because reserve tranche positions are unconditional borrowing rights, nations usually

count them as part of their international reserves. This means that a
country does not lose reserves when paying its subscription to the IMF:
the reserves it pays just equal the reserve tranche position it acquires.
Borrowing beyond the reserve tranche may be made under four *credit
tranches,* each equal to 25 percent of the quota. Such borrowings are
conditional, with the member required to implement (increasingly significant) policies to deal with its payments imbalances. If a member
fully utilizes the five tranches of the basic facility, it will have borrowed
125 percent of its quota and the Fund's holdings of the member's currency will equal 200 percent of that quota.

(b) *Extended credit facility.* This provides for additional conditional borrowings beyond the basic facility, up to 140 percent of the quota, for
countries with severe problems.

(c) *Temporary facilities.* The Fund can establish temporary credit facilities
for special purposes. At present there is an *oil facility* to extend credit to
countries with payments difficulties caused by the oil price increases,
and a *supplementary facility* for countries with payments problems that
are largely relative to their present quota sizes.

(d) *Special facilities.* The IMF has two arrangements to aid countries
(chiefly LDCs) with payments problems due to fluctuations in export
earnings (recall our discussion of this in Chapter 2). Such countries may
borrow from the *compensatory facility* to finance payments deficits and
from the *buffer stock facility* to finance contributions to buffer stock
arrangements for the stabilization of primary product prices.

(e) *Trust Fund.* The IMF has sold gold in public auctions at prices greatly
above the price ($35 per ounce) prevailing when the gold was contrib-
uted to the Fund. Part of the difference has been used to establish a
Trust Fund that makes conditional loans to LDCs with payments
problems.

THE SPECIAL ROLE OF THE DOLLAR

It was recognized from the beginning that the United States would
play a special role in the Bretton Woods system, primarily because of the
size of the American economy and the devastation in Europe, but also
partly because the United States owned the bulk of the world's stock of gold
reserves. One important aspect of this special role had to do with the maintenance of the adjustable pegs. Each currency was given a par value in
terms of gold, thereby defining parities between every pair of currencies.
Each country except the United States was obligated to buy and sell its own
currency, in its own foreign exchange market, so as to keep its dollar exchange rate within a band of at most 1 percent on either side of its dollar
parity (the "peg"). The dollar was an *intervention currency:* the currency
most countries exchanged for their own when intervening. The United

States, by contrast, was not obligated to intervene in the exchange market, though it occasionally did so, but was instead obligated to exchange gold for dollars with other central banks on demand, at the par value. (Thus the Bretton Woods system was an example of a *gold-exchange standard.*)

■ *Example: Bretton Woods Obligations.* From 1951 to 1967 the gold parity of the U.K. pound was £12.5 per ounce and that of the U.S. dollar was $35 per ounce, so that sterling's dollar parity was $2.80/£ (= [$35 per ounce]/[£12.5 per ounce]). The Bank of England was thus obligated to exchange dollars for pounds on the London foreign exchange market in whatever quantities necessary to keep the dollar-pound exchange rate between $2.772/£ and $2.828/£—one percent below and above $2.80. (In practice the exchange rate was kept within the narrower band of $2.78–$2.82.) The U.S. Fed was obligated to sell gold at $35 per ounce (plus a small handling charge) to the Bank of England for any dollars acquired through intervention and to buy gold at $35 per ounce (minus the handling charge). ■

If every country that acquired dollars through intervention always redeemed them for gold with the United States, and if every country selling dollars first acquired them by selling gold to the U.S., all payments imbalances (including those of the United States) would be fully reflected in gold movements between central banks. But it was realized that countries would in fact wish to hold some part of their international reserves in the form of dollars (and a few other currencies). Thus the dollar was also a *reserve currency,* as discussed in Chapter 8.

■ *Special Drawing Rights.* Under the Bretton Woods system, countries' international reserves could consist of three assets: gold, IMF reserve tranche positions, and reserve currencies. In 1969 the First Amendment to the Articles of Agreement of the IMF provided for a fourth reserve asset, Special Drawing Rights. Physically, SDRs are simply bookkeeping entries at the IMF in accounts for member countries and the Fund itself. SDRs can be exchanged for national currencies with other central banks and the Fund. If, for example, the Bank of England were to use SDRs to purchase dollars from the U.S. Fed, the Fed would pay the dollars to the Bank of England; at the same time the U.S. SDR account would be increased by an appropriate amount, and the U.K. account decreased. The IMF can create new SDRs from time to time in response to global need for additional international reserves; the newly created SDRs are allocated among member nations in proportion to their IMF quotas. When a member's SDR balance falls below its total allocation, it must pay the IMF interest on the difference; members are paid interest by the Fund on SDR holdings in excess of allocations.

The SDR was initially defined to be equal in value to one-thirty-fifth of an ounce of gold, which at the time made one SDR worth one dollar. But since 1974 the SDR has been valued on the basis of a currency basket; at present the basket is composed of the currencies of the world's five largest exporting countries. Currently one SDR has the value of a basket consisting of .54 U.S. dollar, .46 German mark, .74 French franc, 34 Japanese yen, and .071 pound sterling. This value is calculated daily on the basis of market exchange rates.

SDRs were created and allocated in 1970, 1971, 1972, and again in 1979, 1980, and 1981. There are now SDR 21.3 billion in existence, worth $27.1 billion as of January 2, 1981.

Although there have been proposals to allow private individuals and organizations to hold SDRs, they are now held by, and exchanged among, only central banks, the Fund, and a few other agencies. However, the SDR is used to some extent by others as a unit of account; for example some commercial bank deposits are valued in SDRs, although they cannot consist of SDRs. The IMF intends that at some time in the future the SDR should become the principal international reserve asset, and the Fund uses the SDR as its unit of account. IMF quotas, for example, are now set in terms of SDRs. ■

PROBLEMS

11.5 On January 2, 1981, the dollar exchange rate of the German mark was $.51, of the French franc was $.22, of the Japanese yen was $.005, of the pound sterling was $2.38, and of the Italian lira was $.0011. What was the price of one SDR in terms of U.S dollars? In terms of French francs? In terms of Italian lire?

11.6 Until the creation of SDRs, there were three international reserve assets under the Bretton Woods system. The rapid growth of the world economy and of the volume of international transactions during the years that this system existed certainly made for a substantial increase in the world's need for international reserves. How reasonable do you think it would have been to expect this increased need to actually have been met by increases in each of the three reserve assets?

11.7 In view of the intervention obligations of the Bretton Woods system, what is the maximum percentage by which the market value of the dollar could fluctuate relative to any other currency? What is the maximum percentage by which any two (nondollar) currencies could fluctuate relative to each other?

3. The Bretton Woods System in Operation

The previous section described how the Bretton Woods system was formally supposed to work. But it never in fact functioned in quite that way.

THE POSTWAR TRANSITION, 1947–1958

The IMF and IBRD were formally set up at the end of 1945, and the IMF commenced operations in 1947. But the Fund assumed a basically passive attitude for some years. It was not, for example, a significant source of international credit until the late fifties; this role was instead played by direct dealings between national governments, as with the American Marshall Plan and later foreign aid programs. The Fund also passively approved the initial par values proposed by members, although it did come to be generally accepted that exchange rates were of international concern, and adjustable pegs were generally adopted. A general realignment of exchange rates took place in 1949, resulting in a substantial appreciation of the dollar.

It was generally regarded as unrealistic to expect weakened countries quickly to abandon wartime controls and allow current-account convertibility, and this attitude was subsequently strengthened when Britain, under American pressure, unsuccessfully attempted to restore convertibility in 1947. Thus nations were allowed a transitional period of grace before accepting their convertibility obligations. Except for the United States, and a few Central American states, all IMF members exercised this option. This transitional period was at first expected to last no more than five years, but it was not until the beginning of 1959 that most industrial nations had restored current-account convertibility; to this day only 54 of the 143 IMF members have accepted this obligation, and exchange control remains pervasive among the LDCs.

THE POST-TRANSITIONAL YEARS, 1959–1973

The postwar transition had definitely ended by 1959: the IMF had found itself, its operations had become significant, and a quota increase had bolstered its resources; the currencies of the major industrial countries were convertible for current-account transactions; the days of "dollar scarcity," or fragile European payments positions, were over; European recovery from the war was accomplished; GATT was established; and DC tariff barriers had been significantly reduced. The Bretton Woods system was basically in full swing during the sixties. But these years were hardly calm. They witnessed recurring balance of payments crises, each more serious than the last, culminating in the 1971 crisis, which ended the official gold convertibility of the dollar, and the 1973 crisis in which the Bretton Woods system finally collapsed. The industrial nations responded to these crises with various reforms of the system, some within the IMF and some independently of it. These crises were a reflection of the basic nature of the Bretton Woods system, and their causes can best be analyzed in terms of two essential features of that system: the gold-exchange standard reserve-asset arrangement and the adjustable-peg exchange-rate regime.

Reserve assets

As we have seen, there were originally three types of reserve assets: gold, IMF reserve tranche positions, and reserve currencies. National incomes have grown rapidly since the war, and trade volumes even more so. Also, capital has become much more internationally mobile. Consequently the view has been widely shared that the world has needed a growing stock of international reserves. Consider, then, the possibilities of increasing each of the three reserve assets. Gold reserves were of course limited by the physical amount of the metal in existence. There was some chance of increasing gold reserves by new mining and by coaxing some out of private hoards, but this was quite limited, especially with the price of gold held fixed in an inflationary world. The value of gold stocks could have been increased by a general devaluation (that is, an increase in the price of gold); some economists did recommend such a move, and the French favored it. But most officials were dead set against it. Partly this was for the same reasons that militated against adjustments in exchange-rate pegs—reasons to be examined presently. Also, a rise in the price of gold would substantially benefit the principal gold exporters, who just happened to be South Africa and the USSR.

IMF reserve tranche positions could be increased by raising IMF quotas, and this was done a number of times. But this could not by itself increase the world stock of international reserves—whenever a quota increase boosts a nation's IMF reserve tranche position, its subscription payment reduces its stocks of other reserve assets by an equal amount.

Thus international reserves could in fact be increased only if reserve-currency holdings (in effect, dollar holdings) could be increased, and this is what happened, as is apparent from the first three columns of Table 11.2. This process in turn required American balance of payments deficits—as we saw in Chapter 8, international reserves will be increased by the payments deficits of reserve center countries, provided that other countries do in fact accumulate the reserve currency. This caused two sorts of problems.

The first, diagnosed by Robert Triffin and sometimes called the *confidence problem,* has to do with the value of a reserve currency as an asset. This problem is the simple result of the need for increased reserves: the dollar was as good as gold because the United States would exchange dollars for gold at a fixed price with central banks on demand; the world needed a continually increasing stock of reserves that could be supplied only by continual U.S. payments deficits; if this continued long enough, foreign central banks would eventually have more dollars than the United States had gold. Everyone would then know that all the dollars could not possibly be redeemed for gold, and the United States would be viewed as a country with a chronic deficit. The dollar would thus eventually cease to be attractive. This is the confidence problem—an inherent defect in a reserve-

Table 11.2. INTERNATIONAL RESERVES, END OF YEAR *(billions of dollars)*

	1949	1969	1971	1973	1981
World Reserves*	45.5	78.2	130.1	255.2	773.9
Gold*	33.5	39.1	39.2	114.5	377.6
IMF Positions	1.7	6.7	6.9	7.5	24.8
Foreign Exchange	10.4	32.4	77.6	122.6	352.4
SDRs	—	—	6.4	10.6	19.1
U.S. Reserves*	26	17	13.2	30.1	123.9

* Gold is valued at the official price in 1949, 1969, and 1971, and at the market price in 1973 and 1981.

SOURCE: *International Financial Statistics*

currency system because the only alternative would be to not increase reserves and so strangle world commerce.

The second problem is the *asymmetric position of the reserve-center country.* As we saw in Chapter 8, such countries do not lose international reserves as a result of payments deficits, so long as surplus countries are willing to accumulate the reserve currency. This means that reserve centers are free of the pressure to correct payments deficits faced by other countries, who must worry about running out of reserves. This is apt to be resented by these other countries.

During the fifties the persistent American deficits were generally welcome: the U.S. gold stock was huge, the dollar was at least as good as gold, and the weak European economies faced a "dollar shortage"—they needed reserves. But this changed in the late fifties and sixties. The dollar shortage was over, but the U.S. deficits did not disappear. The remaining American gold stock no longer looked huge compared to the dollar holdings of foreign central banks. During the sixties the latter overtook the former, and all the world knew that the United States could not redeem all those dollars for gold even it wanted to. "We'd better not ask the United States, then," was the inevitable next thought. The dollar would continue to be worth one-thirty-fifth of an ounce of gold only as long as the United States did not have to make good on its promise to actually sell gold at that price.

Any large-scale attempt to redeem dollars for gold would have forced the United States to repudiate its obligation, thereby leaving foreign central banks stuck with devalued dollars. Thus those central banks were loathe to precipitate a run on the dollar by trying to redeem their dollar holdings or by refusing to accept new dollar balances in settlement of payments deficits, thereby making the problem even worse. There continued to be some redemptions of dollars for gold—de Gaulle's France was as troublesome in this regard as in others—but by and large during the sixties the American obligation to maintain central-bank gold convertibility of the dollar ended *de facto,* though it continued *de jure.* More and more, the gold-exchange standard became a dollar standard.

The United States responded to its persistent payments deficit by trying to persuade and induce foreign central banks to hold dollar balances instead of demanding gold in exchange, and by imposing various capital controls in an attempt to stop the outflow. The former was by and large successful, but the latter was not. What the United States did not do was to adjust monetary and fiscal policies to improve the balance of payments. Throughout the period American macroeconomic policies were used for internal objectives. That the country was able to do this was partly due to the relatively closed nature of the American economy, compared to other industrial nations, but no doubt it was also partly due to the reserve-currency role of the dollar and the fact that the *de facto* erosion of the gold-convertibility obligation eliminated the basic source of pressure on the United States to cure a payments deficit.

Naturally many Europeans took a dim view of all this. Countries with a persistent surplus, such as West Germany, had an increasingly difficult time sterilizing the effects of those surpluses, especially when the American deficit worsened in the late sixties in response to the Vietnam War inflation; this German experience was examined in Chapter 8. From this point of view, the American deficits looked as though the United States was using its special position in the international monetary system to export its inflation instead of curing it. Other Europeans pointed out that the persistent American deficits meant that the United States was acquiring goods, services, and

Table 11.3.   U.S. Balance of Payments, Selected Years *(billions of dollars)*

	1960	*1966*	*1971*	*1972*	*1973*	*1978*	*1979*	*1980*
Merchandise Trade	4.9	3.8	−2.3	−6.4	1.0	−33.0	−30.3	−26.7
Current Account	1.8	1.6	−3.9	−9.7	.3	−13.5	−.3	.1
Government and Long-Term Capital	−3.0	−4.3	−6.8	−1.4	−1.3	−10.9	−19.0	−10.6
Private Short-Term Capital	−1.1	2.3	−10.1	2.0	−1.9	−18.3	5.0	−34.3
Statistical Discrepancy	−1.1	.6	−9.7	−1.9	−2.4	10.7	28.7	35.6
SDR Allocation	—	—	.7	.7	—	—	1.1	1.2
Official Reserve Assets	3.4	−.2	29.8	10.4	5.3	32.0	−15.5	8.0
Balance of Payments Surplus	−3.4	.2	−29.8	−10.4	−5.3	−32.0	15.5	−8.0

SOURCE: *Survey of Current Business*

assets from the rest of the world for dollars that the latter had no option but to accept. To such individuals America's unique position allowed her to force Europe to finance both the Vietnam adventure and the acquisition of European industry by American corporations. Charles de Gaulle spoke—as only he could—of America's "exorbitant privilege," and in the early sixties France demanded a rise in the price of gold and insisted on redeeming dollars for gold.

To many Americans the U.S. position seemed like anything but a privilege. The fact that the United States had persistent deficits meant, of course, that other countries on balance had persistent surpluses. If those countries chose not to eliminate those surpluses by currency revaluation or other measures, it must be that the surpluses were actually welcome. When country *A* complained that America should reduce its deficit, country *A* did not mean, so the argument went, that its own surplus should be reduced, but rather that the surpluses of countries *B, C, D,* and so on should shrink, thereby making the dollars acquired by country *A* more attractive. Under this interpretation the United States was in the unique position of having no direct control over its own balance of payments, which was determined by the aggregate desire of foreign central banks to acquire dollars and/or run surpluses. As we have seen, a dollar devaluation (gold price rise) was rejected as a possible policy. Even if it happened, a devaluation, by showing that the gold value of the dollar was indeed subject to change, would make both central banks and private individuals less willing to hold dollars. It therefore would simply make things worse, unless the devaluation caused a sufficient depreciation of the dollar relative to other currencies to cure the American deficit. But dollar devaluation would not produce dollar depreciation if other countries also devalued, and many others presumably would; if they had not revalued on their own, their exchange rates must already be at desired levels. The basic reality was that exchange rates were determined by the intervention policies of countries *other than* the United States.

Two significant reforms attempted to rectify the reserve-asset problems of the Bretton Woods system. In the late sixties confidence in the dollar eroded sufficiently so that private individuals increasingly tended to hoard gold; central banks had then to increase gold sales to the private market in order to maintain the $35/oz. price. Thus central-bank gold holdings started to fall. To stop this, the central banks of the major industrial countries agreed in 1968 to suspend dealings with the private gold market and to exchange the metal only among themselves. This created a two-tier gold market, with one price for central-bank gold (the official price of $35/oz.) and another price on the disjoint private gold market.

The second, and potentially more significant, reform was the creation of SDRs, provided for in 1968 by the first amendment to the IMF Articles of Agreement. The basic idea was to establish a new asset whose quantity could be consciously adjusted in response to the world's need for international reserves. Thus reserve currencies would no longer be needed for this purpose, and the confidence problem and the asymmetric position of reserve centers could be addressed. But the creation of SDRs was not accompanied by provision for exchange rate adjustment or other measures to deal directly with the American deficit, and when SDRs actually began to be allocated in 1970 they turned out to be but a drop in the bucket of liquidity provided by massive U.S. payments deficits.

Adjustable-peg regime

The confidence problem and the asymmetric role of reserve centers were inherent in the original reserve-asset arrangement of the Bretton Woods system. But they need not have been fatal to that system: in principle the problems could have been dealt with by sufficient exchange-rate adjustments, perhaps supplemented by extensive use of the SDR. That this did not in fact happen is due to a second, more fundamental, defect: the inherent deficiency of an adjustable-peg system. At bottom, that deficiency is due to the fact that there is always a latent contradiction between: (a) constant exchange rates, (b) autonomous national macroeconomic policies, and (c) international capital mobility. We saw in Chapter 8 that (a) and (b) are inconsistent in the long run, and that an increased degree of international capital mobility renders the long run more immediate. When capital becomes sufficiently mobile, the latent contradiction becomes a painfully real one. A basic goal of the Bretton Woods system was to sidestep this problem by providing countries with the means of delaying this contradiction until it disappeared, or, if it proved so inhospitable as to stay around, to eliminate it by exchange-rate adjustments. But in the end, the adjustable-peg system could not sidestep the problem; instead it aggravated it.

As we saw in Chapter 9, individuals' decisions on how to allocate wealth between assets denominated in different currencies, say the franc and the mark, is sensitive to the difference between the German interest rate i_G and the French interest rate minus the expected depreciation of the franc relative to the mark, $i_F - d$. If capital is highly mobile, a modest change in the difference between these rates of return can generate a large portfolio shift, and therefore a large payments imbalance. The essence of an adjustable peg system is that the peg should be changed by significant amounts on isolated occasions in response to a "fundamental disequilibrium." Thus if things are working smoothly and there is no reason to expect a parity change, d should equal zero or, more accurately, be constrained by the intervention band about the peg. But consider what happens if things are not working smoothly. Suppose, for example, that France runs a payments deficit that persists long enough so individuals suspect a fundamental disequilibrium. If the market begins to expect a downward adjustment of the French peg, d could become huge. Suppose that, say, a 10 percent devaluation is expected within a week. Expressed as an annual rate of return, d equals 520 percent—since there are fifty-two weeks in the year—a magnitude sufficient to dwarf any conceivable difference between i_F and i_G. This would induce individuals to try to get out of francs before the devaluation, that is, it would cause a flight of short-term capital from France, thereby worsening the French payments deficit and making the devaluation even more likely to take place. An inhibiting consideration is the fact that devaluation is not certain; if the French payments position unexpectedly improves, individuals may not realize their 520 percent profit from switching from francs to marks. But they will not lose much either: the franc will certainly not be revalued. The adjustable-peg system thus presents the market with a *one-way option* in a payments crisis: the market does not know for certain whether the peg will be adjusted or not, but it does know in which direction any adjustment will be.

Instead of allowing the exchange rate to adjust constantly in reponse to market pressure, the adjustable-peg system requires a currency's parity to be defended until it becomes obvious to everyone that a change in some direction is called for, and then to make the change all at once. People will of course realize this and attempt to protect themselves by selling a currency that is expected to be devalued and buying a currency that is expected to be revalued. If capital is sufficiently mobile, these precautionary capital flows will cause the fulfillment of the expectations upon which they are based. Thus parity changes in an adjustable-peg system will be associated with balance of payments crises.

The economics of an adjustable-peg system also generates a political climate that adds more instability. When officials are attempting to defend the peg of a currency associated with a serious payments imbalance, they have little choice, if capital is highly mobile, but to publicly proclaim their confidence that the peg will be maintained. Any expression of doubt will induce capital movements destructive of the efforts to defend the parity. (Even if officials know that a parity change is imminent, they must lie through their teeth until the last moment.) Once officials have nailed the flag to the mast for a given parity, it becomes even more important to them that that parity be defended. If officials change the parity after public declarations that such a thing will never happen, not only will their words be given less credence in the future, but, more ominously, their policy will have failed its own publicly proclaimed test. Richard Cooper has noted that within a year of the devaluation of their currencies nearly 60 percent of the finance ministers lost their jobs. As a result of this political climate, parity adjustments will tend to be avoided as long as possible: the adjustable peg will tend to be not very adjustable after all, and such adjustments as do occur will happen only as climaxes to serious crises. Furthermore, with peg adjustments being made only under the gun of major crises, devaluations are more likely than revaluations because deficit countries, who need worry about running out of reserves, are more vulnerable than surplus countries. With depreciations relative to the dollar (devaluations) more common than appreciations relative to the dollar (revaluations), the dollar will, over time, tend to appreciate relative to other currencies in general. This could worsen the U.S. payments position and help eventually to bring about a dollar crisis.

During the sixties, parity adjustments did in fact take place only in response to currency crises. These crises were recurrent and tended to become steadily more massive as capital became more mobile. In response, officials of the major industrial nations, increasingly conscious of thralldom to a common system, came more and more to cooperate and consult. Major currency crises were met with "rescue operations" in which governments not directly involved jointly extended loans to the central banks of countries with currencies under attack; central bank officials of the major nations met monthly in Basle, Switzerland, to compare notes. It is ironic that the deficiencies of the Bretton Woods system did result in the concrete embodiment of one of that system's major goals: general acceptance of the view that exchange rates are a matter of international concern rather than of nationalistic prerogative.

This cooperation naturally tended to center on the major nations most crucially involved. These came to be organized as the Group of Ten (G-10)—the United States, Canada, Britain, Japan, Sweden, France, Germany, Italy, Belgium, and the Netherlands; Switzerland, not in the IMF, is a *de facto* eleventh member of the G-10. Negotiations within the G-10 have often tended to upstage the more broad-based IMF, which has in fact sometimes been reduced to simply ratifying agreements reached by the smaller group. In 1962 these countries established the General Arrangements to Borrow, under which the G-10 nations stand ready to lend to each other—through the IMF—international reserves to deal with actual or potential payments crises. This agreement has often been utilized.

PROBLEMS

11.8 Discuss how each of the following might be interpreted as evidence in the debate over whether U.S. payments deficits were *supply-determined* (due to a failure of the U.S. to adopt measures to eliminate its deficit) or *demand-determined* (due to the failure of foreign countries to eliminate their surpluses):

    a The U.S. improved its current-account position in the early and mid sixties, but the over-all payments deficits continued.

    b Even as the IMF was allocating a new reserve asset, in the early seventies, the American deficit exploded.

11.9 The text discussed the role of speculative capital movements with an adjustable peg. How would this discussion change in the presence of each of the following alternative exchange regimes: free floating, managed floating, fixed exchange rates.

4. Case Study: The 1969 Devaluation of the Franc

The French franc was strong during the early sixties, but confidence in the currency was shattered by the student-worker strikes in May 1968 and by the subsequent wage settlements, viewed as inflationary. The balance of payments went into deficit and speculative outflows increased during the autumn. The government tightened price controls, imposed temporary exchange control, and then raised taxes. Middle-class French citizens began taking suitcases full of currency to Switzerland for conversion into Swiss francs. It was generally expected that at a November 1968 meeting the franc would be devalued and the Dmark revalued, but President de Gaulle surprised everyone by announcing that national honor made it unthinkable that the franc would ever be devalued. Exchange controls were imposed, a $2 billion credit from the Group of Ten was arranged, and the crisis abated, although the basic position of the franc did not change. In July 1969 the new President Pompidou apparently decided that a devaluation was necessary after all, but he kept the decision a secret from all but a few close advisers and the existing parity was supported in public. A few weeks later the franc was devalued by 11.1 percent, with the surprise announcement made on a weekend—when the exchanges were closed—in August, when all France goes on vacation *("le grand depart")*. In 1970 the balance of payments improved dramatically.

5. Collapse of the Bretton Woods System and After

Although the persistent American payments deficit was regarded as a problem, attention was until the late sixties dramatically focused on the recurring crises of other currencies. In fact, the American current-account position improved in the early sixties. But by the end of the decade there was a widespread feeling that the dollar was overvalued. The dollar appreciation implied by the devaluations of other currencies and the American inflation generated by the deficit financing of the Vietnam War caused America's competitive position to deteriorate. The current account went into deficit in 1968, and in 1971 the United States recorded a merchandise trade deficit for the first time in this century.

THE 1971 CRISIS

The weakness of the American competitive position was briefly masked in 1970, when a combination of an American recession and high economic activity in Europe restored a surplus to the U.S. current account. But relatively loose American monetary policy contributed to a capital outflow, and the payments deficit of $9.8 billion was the largest ever up to that time. Then economic activity began to abate in Europe, the United States began to emerge from her recession, and it became clear that American officials had no intention of aborting the recovery. A flight from the dollar began. In the spring of 1971 the crisis centered on those strong currencies that were especially in demand by individuals selling dollars. Germany and Holland were forced to suspend support of their parities and allow their currencies to float upward; Switzerland and Austria revalued. By summer, the crisis was clearly centered on the dollar, as one foreign currency after another came to be demanded by sellers of dollars. Foreign central banks began to redeem with the United States some of the huge dollar balances they were acquiring.

On August 15, 1971 (the 202nd birthday of Napoleon Bonaparte), President Nixon announced that the United States would no longer redeem dollars from other central banks for gold or other reserve assets. At the same time, a domestic price-and-income freeze was announced, and a temporary 10 percent surcharage was levied on imports. In thus "closing the gold window" the United States was not merely responding to the run on the dollar and to recent dollar redemptions by foreign central banks. After all, the window had already been almost shut anyway, and if the United States had wished to complete the closure in a way consistent with its earlier behavior, it would have simply offered foreign central banks increased incentives to hold dollars and/or told them in private that dollars would not be redeemed. Instead the window was slammed shut in as public and dramatic a manner as possible. The deed was aggressive: the United States had decided on the necessity of new international arrangements, including a realignment of exchange rates, and was determined to force the rest of the world to acquiesce. The president's announcement would greatly increase the flight from the dollar and thereby require any country wishing to maintain its parity to buy huge quantities of dollars publicly proclaimed as officially inconvertible into other assets. Interbank foreign exchange markets were mostly closed for a week—much to the discomfort of many American tourists—and when they opened the major currencies were allowed to float. Only Japan, the industrial nation with the most effective controls on international transactions, attempted to maintain its dollar parity, but before the month of August was out the Japanese, too, were forced to give up and release the yen from its peg. The import surcharge could be defended on the grounds that similar measures had been employed during the sixties by other countries with balance of payments problems. But actually the surcharge was another American weapon, a measure that would be ended once concessions had been gained.

During the autumn of 1971 the currencies of the major industrial nations were allowed to float, with management, while negotiations on reform proceeded. These negotiations culminated in an international conference at the Smithsonian Institute in Washington, D.C., on December 17 and 18. The United States dropped its import surcharge and a realignment of exchange rates was worked out, with the dollar depreciated by an average of about 10 percent. This was done partly by a devaluation of the dollar (to $38 per ounce of gold) and partly by revaluation of various other currencies. But the dollar price of gold was now a nonprice at which the United States would neither buy nor sell gold, for it was widely accepted that America would not resume its covertibility obligation. The deficit of 1971 had itself been more than twice the size of the total American stock of reserve assets.

Besides restoring the adjustable-peg system at a new set of parities, the Smithsonian Agreement provided for a widening of intervention bands from 1 percent on either side of parity to 2.25 percent, and the IMF later established a group, known as the Committee of 20, to develop proposals to reform the international monetary system. But basically the Bretton Woods system was patched together again. The principal formal change, the end of official dollar convertibility, simply made explicit what had been largely implicit since the late sixties. President Nixon described the Smithsonian accord as "the most significant monetary agreement in the history of the world." It was to endure for almost fifteen months.

THE 1973 COLLAPSE OF THE BRETTON WOODS SYSTEM

During 1972 the Smithsonian parities were defended, and the Committee of 20 began its work. A spate of bad economic news in Britain ushered in another crisis for the pound in June, and the United Kingdom abandoned its parity and resumed a managed float.

In February of 1973 another major dollar crisis suddenly materialized, and interbank foreign exchange markets were closed. Negotiations ensued, with American Treasury officials visiting one foreign capital after another over a hectic three-day weekend. Another exchange-rate adjustment was agreed upon. The dollar was devalued by 11 percent (raising the price of gold to $42.22 per ounce); Britain, Italy, Japan, Switzerland, and Canada were to float. But by the end of the month the exchanges were in crisis once more, and in March the major industrial countries abandoned their new dollar parities. This was the end of the Bretton Woods system. At first many people hoped that adjustable pegs might once again be resurrected as soon as the markets calmed down. But these hopes gradually faded with the passage of time, especially after the dramatic oil-price increases of 1973–74 and the subsequent steep world recession.

PRESENT ARRANGEMENTS

The Committee of 20 was meanwhile deliberating. The committee originally hoped to formulate major reforms of the international monetary system that would allow for the return of adjustable pegs. But it soon became apparent that international agreement on major reforms would not be forthcoming, and realization gradually spread that managed floating was not temporary. Thus when the Committee finished its work in July 1974 it presented no major reform proposals but instead concluded that international monetary reform must be a matter of evolution. Some relatively minor changes were made, however, such as changing the valuation basis of the SDR from gold to a basket of currencies. The IMF also established an Interim Committee (to be replaced by a permanent Ministerial Council upon alteration of the Articles of Agreement) to oversee the reform process.

The first order of business was to amend the Articles to allow managed floating, since the actual state of affairs was still quite illegal. The major stumbling block to such an amendment was a disagreement between the United States and some Europeans, notably France. The latter wished to retain a role for gold and to provide for the ultimate return of an adjustable-peg system; the United States was opposed to both ideas and wished to minimize official intervention. In November 1975 a summit meeting at Rambouillet resolved the issue, accepting the essentials of the American position. Agreement was formalized at an Interim Committee meeting in Jamaica during January of 1976, and the Second Amendment of the IMF Articles of Agreement was subsequently ratified and entered into force on April Fool's Day of 1978. This amendment finally legalized the managed float. In fact it legalized practically anything except a gold peg, innocuously describing the international monetary system to be "the kind prevailing on January 1, 1976."

BRETTON WOODS RETROSPECTIVE

How successful was the Bretton Woods system? While the actual date of its demise might have been influenced by exogenous events such as the Vietnam War, there seems to be little doubt that the system carried within itself the seeds of its own destruction. Depending on just how it is defined, the Bretton Woods system lasted for 15 to 27 years, a lifetime roughly comparable to that of the gold standard at the turn of the century. This lifetime was punctuated by recurrent international financial crises. But still there was an unprecedented steady growth of world income and trade and a great liberalization of international transactions between the industrial nations. That the system's inherent flaws ultimately proved decisive was to a large extent the result of that system's own success in fostering (or at least permitting) this great expansion of multilateral economic activity. The repeated crises were troublesome to be sure, but even that cloud has proven to have had its silver lining: the habits and institutions of official international consultation and cooperation, developed in response to the crises, still remain and are of great importance in our present unstructured world. Indeed the timing of the system's death was itself fortuitous, since adjustable pegs could not possibly have handled the oil shock and subsequent events as well as did the more flexible arrangement actually in place.

The Bretton Woods system was unique as history's only example of an international monetary order created largely by conscious human decision rather than evolution. The creation was fatally flawed. But it served its purpose at least adequately, its flaws gathered strength as a result of the system's basic success, and they ultimately shattered that system just as it was about to become seriously inappropriate to changed circumstances.

PROBLEM

11.10 The Smithsonian negotiations included considerable debate over whether the depreciation of the dollar should involve a dollar devaluation or just the revaluation of other currencies. Can you think of any reasons for this, since everyone knew that the United States would not restore official gold convertibility in any case?

6. International Monetary Reform Issues

The international monetary system continues to evolve, and proposals for substantive reform continue to be debated. These can best be discussed relative to the two features so crucial in the breakdown of the Bretton Woods system: reserve assets and the exchange-rate regime.

RESERVE ASSETS

With freely floating currencies, international reserves are unnecessary, so it might be thought that the substitution of widespread managed floating for the adjustable-peg system would reduce the need for reserves. But the huge American payments deficits of 1970–73 greatly expanded international reserves, so that, when the Bretton Woods system collapsed, world reserve-currency holdings were nearly $120 billion, of which about 85 percent were U.S. dollars. These were referred to as the *dollar overhang:* huge holdings of inconvertible dollars that central banks presumably did not want but could not dispose of without cataclysmic effect on the exchange markets.

As it has turned out, however, management of the float has been sufficiently intensive so that the overall amount of intervention since 1973 has not been greatly different from before. Also, since 1973 total international reserves other than gold have grown somewhat more slowly than the value of total world exports. Thus there is no longer much concern that total world reserves are excessive. Policy issues instead center upon the *composition* of those reserves, and relate in particular to the role of currency reserves and the asymmetric position of the United States as a reserve center. The world faced just these problems under the Bretton Woods system, and our discussion of them in section 3 therefore remains relevant to the present day. Additional present-day issues can be discussed by looking separately at various reserve assets.

Gold

For over two decades the French have advocated a monetary role for gold, and today some advocate greater reliance on the metal. The dominant attitude, however, shared by the IMF and the United States, has been to phase out gold as a reserve asset. Recent actions have been consistent with this goal. The IMF will no longer accept gold in Fund transactions, and gold has generally been displaced by the SDR for IMF purposes. The Fund has also disposed of one-third (or fifty million ounces) of its gold holdings, half of this amount being sold to members at the pre-Smithsonian official price and half being auctioned off to the public, with the profits above the old official price used to establish the Trust Fund described in section 2. The U.S. Treasury has also auctioned off a modest part of its gold stock. The two-tier system has been abolished, so that central banks may deal in gold with private markets, and the amended Articles of Agreement do not allow currencies to be pegged to gold (thus there is no official gold price; the United States still values its gold stock at $42.22 per ounce, but this is only a national accounting convention).

Aside from the gold transactions just described, plus some gold that members of the European Monetary System subscribed to that organization, there have been very few central-bank gold dealings in recent years. The metal is basically an inactive asset.

Despite all this, it would be premature to conclude that gold's long, long history as a monetary asset is about to end. The astronomical rise in the metal's price has greatly increased the market value of gold reserves, both absolutely and relative to other reserve assets, as is evident in Table 11.2. Gold has also become the most volatile reserve component, not because of quantity changes, which are negligible, but because of price volatility. This "gold overhang" could conceivably acquire an active role should price fluctuations or large payments imbalances induce central banks to start dealing in the metal.

CASE STUDY: Should the United States Return to the Gold Standard?

Toward the close of the Carter Administration, Congress provided for the establishment of a commission to study the role of gold and make recommendations. Interest in the U.S. Gold Commission increased when some members and supporters of the Reagan administration publicly expressed support for a return to the gold standard. But the issue is controversial even within the administration, which essentially ended foreign exchange market intervention: free floating is the antithesis of the gold standard. In any case the Commission decided against any change in the role of gold, though it did recommend that the U.S. Treasury mint and sell a gold coin (with no fixed dollar value).

SDRs.

We discussed in section 2 how the IMF wishes the SDR to become the principal reserve asset. SDRs have in fact had moderate use in recent years: the United States and the United Kingdom have both been significantly active with their allocations, and the central banks of the LDCs have on balance sold substantial amounts of SDRs to the oil-exporting countries. But attainment of the IMF goal certainly seems to be a long way off. As Table 11.2 showed, SDRs accounted for less than 3 percent of world reserves at the end of 1981. For the SDR to become the principal reserve asset, it is necessary that the role of reserve currencies be formalized and limited (and perhaps also that the same be done to the gold overhang).

A proposed move in this direction is the establishment of an IMF *substitution account*. Such an account would accept dollar deposits from central banks and in return issue an equivalent amount of SDRs. Ideally this would both deal with the dollar overhang and expand the role of the SDR. Consideration of such an account was recommended by the Interim Committee at the 1979 IMF annual meeting in Belgrade, and the proposal has been subject to investigation and negotiation. But agreement has not been forthcoming on how much interest the United States should pay on the dollars held by such a substitution account, nor on the extent to which the United States or other countries should be responsible for losses suffered by the account if exchange-rate changes cause its dollar holdings to become worth less than its SDR liabilities. At present the proposal seems to be in limbo.

Reserve Currencies

The role of the dollar has constantly been at issue since the Second World War. Discussions since 1973 have focused on ways to make the dollar more like other currencies, that is, to moderate the asymmetrical position of the United States. The proposed substitution account could, under certain circumstances, contribute toward this end. So too could proposals for *multicurrency intervention* (various plans under which a basket of currencies would, in effect, replace the dollar as principal intervention currency). These proposals, and others, have made little headway. But while debate on these issues has continued, actual practice has quietly been changing. Central banks have been diversifying their holdings of foreign exchange away from nearly exclusive reliance upon dollars. As Table 11.4 shows, dollars have declined from almost 87 percent of official foreign ex-

Table 11.4.   OFFICIAL FOREIGN EXCHANGE HOLDINGS
            (End of Period)

	March 1973	1976	1980	(1980)*
Total Foreign Exchange Holdings *(billions of SDRs)*	98.5	160.3	293.3	(241.1)
Percentage of Total in:				
U.S. dollar	84.6	86.6	59.0	(73.1)
Pound sterling	7.0	2.1	2.6	(3.0)
Deutsche mark	5.8	7.4	12.1	(14.0)
French franc	1.0	1.0	1.1	(1.3)
Swiss franc	1.2	1.6	3.5	(4.1)
Netherlands guilder	.3	.5	.8	(.9)
Japanese yen	—	.8	3.2	(3.7)
ECU	—	—	17.8	(—)

* What the 1980 figures would be if ECUs were not included in foreign currency holdings.

SOURCES: *IMF,* Annual Report, 1980, *and International Financial Statistics*

change holdings at the end of 1976 to barely 59 percent at the end of 1980. These figures should, it is true, be qualified in two ways. First, when the European Monetary System (EMS) was created, the member states contributed gold and SDRs and recieved in return European Currency Units (ECUs). This will be discussed in greater detail in Chapter 12. The point is that national reserve holdings count as part of international reserves whereas EMS holdings do not. Thus the creation of the EMS necessarily reduced the dollar's share in total foreign currency reserves by adding another (nondollar) currency: the ECU. The effect of this can be seen by comparing the last two columns of Table 11.4. Second, most of the remaining decline in the dollar's relative importance is due to the decisions of a small group of countries, mainly oil exporters, to diversify the currency composition of newly acquired liquid holdings.

But these considerations cannot nullify the trend. The "small group of countries" is part of the world, and the ECU was inaugurated, in part, expressly to reduce the dollar's role. Furthermore, there has in recent years been some increase in the use of nondollar currencies for intervention purposes; many nations now peg to currency baskets rather than to the dollar; and the SDR has in effect displaced the dollar within the IMF in a technical sense.

Thus there is a definite, if modest, tendency for the dollar to increasingly share its hitherto unique position with other currencies. The dollar's role in international reserves greatly exceeds the United States' current role in the world economy. In this sense the tendency is natural, but is it desirable? Two arguments say no. The first claims that, for politico-economic reasons of obscure origin, an efficient international monetary system requires a dominant currency to take a leadership role. This was done by the pound under the gold standard, by the dollar under the Bretton Woods system, and by no one during the terrible thirties. This view may have its merits, but the dominant theme in international monetary negotiations since 1944 has been that the international monetary system is a matter of collective concern.

The second argument is that diversification of official foreign exchange holdings is destabilizing, because central banks will dump their reserve holdings of currencies they expect to depreciate in exchange for currencies they expect to appreciate. Why should central banks act in a more destabilizing way than alternative private holders of the same currencies? Perhaps they should not, if only economic motives matter. But political motives also count, especially once official agencies become involved. The 1979 American freeze of Iranian dollar assets was prompted at least in part by the fear that the Iranians were about to dump their dollars on world markets, and large-scale Arab financial maneuvers have been the subject of two popular novels (Paul Erdman's *The Crash of '79* and Michael Thomas' *Green Monday*). It is clear that large official foreign currency holdings are a source of potential danger. What is not clear, however, is whether that danger is increased by diversification of the currency composition of those holdings.

THE EXCHANGE-RATE REGIME

It was not by conscious design that the world abandoned the adjustable-peg system for widespread managed floating; the former had ceased to be feasible. Of the unstable triumvirate of pegged exchange rates, autonomous national macroeconomic policies, and extensive international transactions, nations are unwilling to dispense with the second and have not wished (fortunately) to impose the Draconian controls necessary to nullify the effects of the third. Thus the first must go. This has come to be widely recognized, and debate is no longer significantly concerned with whether a general system of adjustable pegs should be reintroduced, or with the general merits of fixed versus floating rates (there has, however, been much discussion about whether specific countries or groups of countries—such as the EEC members—should peg). Instead debate has centered over whether, and how, intervention ought to be internationally regulated in a world of managed floating. Recall that a fixed-exchange rate system has two basic advantages: national monies are more useful as money when they can be exchanged for each other at fixed prices, and countries are prevented from aggressively manipulating their exchange rates for nationalistic purposes.

Proposed rules attempt to salvage some of these gains by limiting exchange-rate fluctuations and by subjecting national intervention to international guidelines. The Second Amendment to the IMF Articles of Agreement gave the Fund a vague responsibility for surveillance of members' intervention, and the Fund has on two occasions made general statements on the subject. As a result of the Committee of 20's negotiations, the Fund in 1974 issued its *Guidelines for the Management of Floating Exchange Rates,* and, in preparation for adoption of the Second Amendment, the *Text of Executive Directors' Decisions of Exchange Rate Policy Surveillance* was issued in 1977. But debate continues. Most of the discussion has centered on four types of norms for behavior.

1. *Leaning against the wind.* The basic idea here is that central banks should intervene to resist but not neutralize market forces: exchange-rate fluctuations should be reduced, but long-term trends should be dictated by the market. Some central banks, such as the German Bundesbank, have described their intervention policies as leaning against the wind (or the correction of "disorderly" market conditions). The idea was forwarded in the IMF *Guidelines,* and much actual intervention since 1973 seems to have been of this sort. The principal reason for this prominence is probably the large exchange-rate fluctuations that have in fact been experienced with managed floating.

The wisdom of trying to limit these fluctuations is related to the question of exchange-market efficiency discussed in Chapter 10. If exchange rates do not accurately reflect available information and if their fluctuations are a reflection of distortions, leaning against the wind is much more attractive than if the fluctuations reflect the market's quick absorption of new information.

The most common complaint about such a policy is that countries might lean too heavily and prevent needed exchange-rate adjustments. The Japanese have often been criticized on this score, and in 1977 a number of American officials—in a resurrection of the pre-1971 complaint that only the United States lacked control over its exchange rate—expressed the view that excessive European and Japanese intervention was preventing a desirable (to the Americans) depreciation of the dollar. The IMF *Decisions on Surveillance* in fact warned about excessive leaning. It is even possible that countries might not merely defend inappropriate rates but actually use monetary policy, news leaks, and so forth to induce changes in directions that are desired for nationalistic reasons—and then defend the new rates.

The general practice of leaning against the wind could result in the same sort of speculative capital movements that we discussed in section 3 with respect to adjustable pegs. A depreciation of a currency, for example, could well cause speculators to sell that currency if they felt that authorities were resisting the depreciation and that further downward movements would therefore ensue. It is therefore even conceivable that leaning against the wind could actually magnify exchange-rate fluctuations.

2. *Targets.* A second idea is that target values should be set for the various exchange rates and that the authorities should then intervene so as to move rates toward these targets. This approach has been favored by some individuals who would like a return to adjustable pegs but realize that that is not practicable. The targets are not to be interpreted as pegs that must be maintained, and different advocates of this approach have different views of how forcefully central banks should attempt to attain their targets; the use of targets could involve either more intervention or less than a general policy of leaning against the wind. Indeed some proposals have provided for targets to be altered or abandoned should they entail too heavy a degree of intervention.

The IMF *Guidelines* provided for the use of targets, but the subsequent *Decisions of Surveillance* did not mention them. There is little evidence that central banks have made use of explicit targets in their management of the float, unless one counts under this head those countries that have chosen to peg.

3. *Objective indicators.* Some individuals have recommended that countries be required to alter their intervention policies when objective indicators signal the presence of substantial disequilibrium. Several indicators have been suggested, such as the net amount of intervention in one direction in a specified time interval. A country would be required to cease leaning against the wind, or to alter its exchange-rate target, once the total of such intervention reaches a pre-set limit.

The use of objective indicators was strongly advocated by American negotiators in the early seventies, but foreign governments did not agree. One problem with such indicators is that they could induce speculative capital movements as did the adjustable-peg system. Suppose, for example, that a country is selling its own currency in the foreign exchange market to prevent, or to slow down, an appreciation. If the country accumulates reserves close to the point where an objective indicator would require that intervention cease, speculators would realize this and would increase their purchase of the currency in anticipation of its subsequent appreciation.

4. *Reference rates.* Still another proposal is to set and revise periodically reference rates for the various currencies, at levels consistent with the self-proclaimed national economic policies of the countries involved. Each central bank would then be prohibited from intervening so as to force its exchange rate away from a band about its reference rate. No intervention would be required of any central bank, which could conduct a free float or, if it wished, use its reference rate as a target. The goal of the proposal is not to directly reduce exchange-rate fluctuations (though individual countries might try to do this) but to help prevent aggressively nationalistic interven-

tion policies. A possible danger of the proposal—shared by the other proposals as well—is that the reference rates might come to be regarded as pegs,
despite the quite contrary intention, and therefore bring back some of the
problems associated with an adjustable-peg system.

Thus far the world has not adopted formal rules for managed floating,
and the IMF surveillance has apparently not been conducted so as to have
substantial impact. Meanwhile, exchange rates actively continue to fluctuate. But, despite disagreements and other incidents, the central banks of the
industrial countries have not waged international currency war with each
other. The sense of common interest in the system and the Bretton Woods
legacy of international cooperation and consultation have thus far proved
sufficient. If we could be assured that this would continue, it would probably be better not to have any formal rules, with their potential for the
introduction of destabilizing and inefficient rigidities.

PROBLEMS

11.11 Under what circumstances could the existence of a substitution account lessen the asymmetric position of the United States?

11.12 Discuss the likely consequences of a unilateral U.S. return to the gold
standard, under the assumption that other major countries do not follow suit and
that the IMF's rules and policies are not altered.

11.13 Suppose that the fluctuations of some exchange rates consist of random deviations from a constant equilibrium value. If a central bank then under-
takes to lean against the wind, would its intervention on balance serve to move the
exchange rate toward equilibrium or away from it? Answer the same question if the
exchange-rate fluctuations instead consist of random deviations from a *moving*
equilibrium.

7. Summary

1. A country's balance of payments accounts are a record of transactions in a
specific time interval between residents of that country and the rest of the world.
An export of a good, service, or asset, or the receipt of a unilateral transfer, is
recorded as a credit; the import of a good, service, or asset, or the making of
a unilateral transfer, is recorded as a debit. Since each transaction generates credit
and debit entries of equal value, total credits should in principle always equal total
debits.

2. After the Second World War the international financial order, called the
Bretton Woods system, featured a modified gold-exchange standard in which
countries maintained adjustable pegs vis-à-vis the U.S. dollar, while the United
States undertook to exchange gold for dollars with foreign central banks at a fixed
price. A new institution, the International Monetary Fund, was founded as part of
the system.

3. The Bretton Woods arrangement was subjected to recurrent crises and finally collapsed in March 1973. The system was flawed by a contradiction, latent in an adjustable-peg framework, between constant exchange rates, autonomous national macroeconomic policies, and international capital mobility.

4. The IMF articles have been amended to legalize present practices and to allow countries wide discretion in exchange practices. The major industrial countries basically have managed floats relative to each other, except for the adjustable pegs of the European Monetary System, while the majority of LDCs peg to a currency or to a basket of currencies.

SUGGESTED READING

Coombs, C. A. *The Arena of International Finance*. New York: John Wiley, 1976. An insider's account of central bank policy in the Bretton Woods years.

Cooper, R. N. "Currency Devaluation in Developing Countries." *Princeton Essays in International Finance* 86 (June 1971).

Diaz-Alejandro, C. "Less Developed Countries and the Post-1971 International Financial System." *Princeton Essays in International Finance* 108 (April 1975).

Ethier, W. and Bloomfield, A. I. "The Reference Rate Proposal and Recent Experience." *Banca Nazionale del Lavoro Quarterly Review,* September 1978.

Gardner, R. N. *Sterling-Dollar Diplomacy*. 2nd ed. New York: McGraw-Hill, 1969. The formation of the Bretton Woods system.

IMF. *The International Monetary Fund: Purposes, Structure and Activities*. A descriptive pamphlet available free of charge from the Fund.

IMF. "The Fund under the Second Amendment: A Supplement." *IMF Survey,* September 18, 1978; "Supplement on the Fund," *IMF Survey,* May 18, 1981. Useful descriptions of the Fund.

McKinnon, R. I. "Private and Official International Money: The Case for the Dollar." *Princeton Essays in International Finance* 74 (April 1969).

Plumptre, A. F. W. "Exchange-Rate Policy: Experience with Canada's Floating Rate." *Princeton Essays in International Finance* 81 (June 1970).

Solomon, R. *The International Monetary System, 1945–1976: An Insider's View*. New York: Harper and Row, 1977.

Triffin, R. *Gold and the Dollar Crisis*. New Haven: Yale University Press, 1960. Triffin's diagnosis of the Bretton Woods system.

Williamson, J. *The Failure of World Monetary Reform, 1971–1974*. New York: NYU Press, 1977. A perceptive account of the negotiations accompanying the collapse of the Bretton Woods system.

Yeager, L. B. *International Monetary Relations: Theory, History, and Policy*. 2nd ed. New York: Harper and Row, 1976. Chapters 19–32 give an excellent history of the Bretton Woods system.

Part Five

The Modern World Economy

The concluding part of this book examines some issues that involve the basic ideas of both trade theory and international monetary theory. These issues largely concern *economic integration:* a reduction in barriers to economic transactions between residents of different nations. In a sense, most of this book has been concerned with economic integration, since we have investigated questions such as the welfare consequences of free or liberal trade, the effects of international transactions on domestic macroeconomic policy, and much more. This part, therefore, appropriately closes the book.

Chapter 12

Economic Integration

> "Rich men's clubs take care of their own members and we are told to fend for ourselves." —INDIRA GANDHI

> "The world has narrowed to a neighborhood before it has broadened into a brotherhood." —LYNDON JOHNSON

THIS CHAPTER examines two aspects of integration hitherto ignored in this book. The first, *biased integration,* is a reduction of economic barriers between a group of countries but not between those countries and the rest of the world. Examples include the formation of free-trade areas or customs unions, such as the EEC, the granting of tariff preferences to the LDCs by the DCs, and the GATT-sponsored multilateral tariff negotiations, which reduced trade barriers among the DCs by much more than barriers between the DCs and the LDCs.

We next investigate *asymmetric integration* between nations with different economic systems. An obvious example of this would be an increase in East-West trade, between market and non-market economies.

Although we will be concerned with only the economic aspects of integration, there is usually a political dimension as well. Often political integration brings about economic integration, and achieving the latter may be a significant motive for pushing ahead with the former. Such was the case with the adoption of the United States Constitution, and in Canada, Australia, and Russia political unification preceded or was accompanied by economic unification. The imperfect political union of the Austro-Hungarian Empire, on the other hand, ultimately failed to derive a successful customs union. More rarely, economic union precedes political union and may be intended to help foster the latter. The creation of the German Zollverein in 1818–1834 preceded by decades the unification of Germany, and the South African customs union also antedated political unification. The promotion of European unity was, in many quarters, a significant objective of the formation of the EEC in 1957.

1. The Basic Theory of Biased Integration

Economic integration could involve a reduction in barriers to trade or to factor mobility, or a unification of economic policies. We discuss each in turn.

TRADE INTEGRATION

Suppose that France (*F*), Germany (*G*), and the rest of the world (*R*) all initially trade with each other and all have tariffs. *F* and *G* then abolish all tariffs on each other's products but maintain their tariffs on goods from *R*, whose commerical policy is unchanged. What are the effects of such biased integration? The reduction of tariffs between *F* and *G* is a move toward free trade, which we might expect to be beneficial. But now goods from *R* are subject to a tax in *F* and *G* whereas similar goods from *G* and *F*, respectively, are not. We would expect this *price discrimination* to be harmful. Thus biased integration has on balance replaced one distortion (the tariff on *F-G* trade) with another distortion (geographical price discrimination).

Trade Creation. The elimination of tariffs between *F* and *G* creates trade between these two countries and generates gains, as discussed in Chapter 1. Each country concentrates more on producing the goods in which it has a comparative advantage relative to the other country, and trade expands, causing marginal rates of transformation and of substitution in *F* to equal those in *G*.

Trade Diversion. Since *F* now levies a tariff when goods are imported from *R*, but not when the same goods are imported from *G*, residents of *F* will now buy from *G* some products that were previously purchased from *R*. Similarly, *G* residents will divert their trade from *R* to *F*. This trade diversion is necessarily inefficient, because if *F* residents chose to buy from *R* suppliers when they competed on equal terms with *G* suppliers, it must be that the former could supply the product more favorably.

■ *Example of Trade Diversion.* As hypothesized in Table 12.1, suppose Britain initially imposes a tariff of £.60 on imports of butter, which can be

Table 12.1. A Hypothetical Case of Trade Diversion

	New Zealand Butter	*European Butter*
World Price	£1.00	£1.50
British Tariff	.60	.60
British Price (Pre Union)	£1.60	£2.10
European Tariff	.60	0
British Price (Post Union)	£1.60	£1.50

purchased from either New Zealand or Europe. New Zealand is the more efficient producer and so captures most of the British market; only those British consumers who expressly favor the European product would be willing to pay £2.10 for it when New Zealand butter is available for £1.60. Now Britain and Europe abolish tariffs on each other's products. European butter now enters duty free and, at £1.50, is cheaper than New Zealand butter, which is still subject to the tariff. Many British consumers will now shift from New Zealand butter to European butter. This trade diversion is globally inefficient (because New Zealand can give the world butter at a lower real cost than can Europe) and is also harmful to Britain (because the £.60 tariff on New Zealand butter would not be paid to New Zealand but retained by the British collectively). ∎

Balance of Trade Creation and Trade Diversion. Trade creation is beneficial and trade diversion is harmful. Which one dominates depends upon circumstances; biased integration may or may not be a good thing. If, before integration, most of F's trade is with G, trade creation will likely dominate, because there is not much trade with R to be diverted. Thus the larger the extent of the integration, the more likely it is to be beneficial: integration of the whole world can involve no trade diversion (in the absence of interplanetary trade). If, on the other hand, most of the products that F imports can be produced more cheaply in R than in G, integration with G is likely to be harmful. The situation is reminiscent of the discussion in Chapter 6 of the use of tariffs to cure domestic distortions: one distortion is replaced by another, so that the net effect is ambiguous. This is initially counterintuitive: since integration involves a reduction of tariff protection in the world, one would naturally expect it to be beneficial.

The original intuition is partially resurrected when we realize that, when F and G integrate, they might want also to change the tariffs they levy on imports from R. Suppose that they do in fact do this, and that they do it in such a way that, after integration, F and G together import and export to R exactly what they together did before integration. In this case there is no net trade diversion, and integration is necessarily beneficial.

All of this is amply illustrated by the EEC. When Britain joined in

1973, the basic economic issue was one of weighing the trade creation, stemming from free trade with the continent in manufactures, against the trade diversion of replacing agricultural imports from the Commonwealth and America with more expensive food from Europe. The Kennedy Round of multilateral tariff negotiations in the early sixties was significantly motivated by a desire to reduce tariffs in general to assure that the formation of the EEC not divide the industrial world into distinct trade blocks. In other words, the aim was to alter tariffs between the EEC and the rest of the world in such a way as to minimize trade diversion.

Trade Modification. Integration most often takes place between economies that are relatively similar. Thus it might be that F imports from G an assortment of goods quite different from those that it would import from R under any conceivable circumstances. In this case effective price discrimination is unlikely (because G and R are not competitive suppliers of identical goods to F in any case), and trade diversion will probably not be serious. But integration could still cause a general substitution, by consumers in F, of G products for R products, if they serve broadly similar purposes. Suppose, for example, that in Table 12.1 New Zealand produces butter as before, but that Europe produces only margarine (that is, relabel the right-hand column of the table as "European margarine"). In this case integration does not cause price discrimination because New Zealand and Europe export different goods to Britain. But obviously our earlier conclusions are unchanged, because butter and margarine serve basically the same purposes: they are good *substitutes.* Such trade modification might seem, at this stage, to be essentially the same as trade diversion. But this is not so. For one thing, it might work in the opposite way. To see this, suppose that in Table 12.1 New Zealand once again faithfully exports butter, but that Europe exports bread (once again relabel the right-hand column of the table, this time as "European bread"). The difference now is that people do not consume butter *instead* of bread—the relation between butter and margarine—but rather butter *with* bread. If they have more of one, they will want more of the other; bread and butter are *complements.* In this sense, when integration makes European bread cheaper in Britain, and therefore increases British demand for bread, it will also cause the British to *increase* their demand for New Zealand butter.

Thus trade modification might mean that integration between F and G either increases or decreases trade with R, depending upon the relative importance of complements and substitutes. But there is a more fundamental difference between trade diversion and trade modification. The former results when integration involves a new distortion: price discrimination. This, by itself, is necessarily bad. Trade modification, by contrast, does not involve the introduction of price discrimination but rather the substitution of one pattern of world tariffs by another. This might be good or bad.

The distinction is quite important in the modern world. As we have seen, the most prominent characteristic of post–Second World War commerical policy is the dramatic mutual reduction of DC tariff barriers unaccompanied by any comparable reduction of LDC barriers. Because of the most-favored-nation clause, the reductions in DC tariffs also apply to imports of identical goods from the LDCs. Thus price discrimination, and trade diversion, is of limited relevance here. But the DCs import from each other a significantly different assortment of goods than they import from LDCs, so that trade modification is potentially very significant. An evaluation of the welfare significance of the dominant feature of postwar commerical policy necessarily reduces to weighing trade creation against (or with) trade modification.

Terms of Trade Effects. If the partners of integration are together sizable in the world markets in which they deal, the integration could well alter world prices and thus the terms of trade of partners. There are two aspects to this.

The first involves the trade between the partners, F and G. We saw in Chapter 1 that a country need not benefit by a movement from limited trade to free trade because it could suffer a significant terms-of-trade deterioration. The same applies here: if F and G mutually eliminate their tariffs on each other's goods, the terms of trade between them could conceivably change radically. Thus, even if we completely ignore trade diversion, one country might gain by more than total trade creation while the other country loses. This could be compensated for by a transfer payment from the gainer to the loser that still leaves both better off, since they together have the net benefit of trade creation to divide (remember, we are ignoring trade diversion for now). This sort of thing is not of such practical irrelevance as it might sound: the EEC makes transfers through the community budget, financed by members' contributions, which disburses funds for agricultural support and regional development. Negotiations over Britain's entry involved her relation to that budget (as did renegotiations when the country became convinced it had struck a bad deal).

Integration can also alter the partners' terms of trade with the rest of the world, and this might mitigate the harmful effects of trade diversion. Integration between F and G, which causes those two countries to trade more with each other and less with R (trade diversion), could bring about a reduction in the prices demanded by sellers in R, if F and G together constitute a significant portion of the total market for R's products. Furthermore, if F and G together are significantly more important in world markets than either separately, integration would enable the two to jointly exercise more monopoly power.

National Economies of Scale. We saw in Chapter 1 that, in addition to comparative cost differences, scale economies could serve, in two different ways, as a basis for international trade. Consider first those national economies that follow from geographical concentration of an industry, such as cost reductions due to the adoption of an efficient plant size. By allowing increased specialization by the partner countries, integration can result in gains via such scale economies. Suppose for example, that *F*, *G* and *R* each initially has its own steel industry and automobile industry, each of which is protected and serves its local market. Suppose that the markets for these products in *F* and *G* are too small to support plants of the most efficient size. If these countries now integrate, they can jointly rationalize the two industries, with a single efficient steel plant located in, say, *G* serving both countries and a single efficient automobile plant doing the same from *F*. These gains are clearly analogous to those of trade creation described with reference to comparative costs. There is also an analog to trade diversion: if *R* was initially exporting some steel and automobiles to *F* and *G*, the reduction in those exports could require the industries in *R* to operate at less efficient scales.

The importance of national scale economies is sensitive to country sizes. Large countries are most likely already to have industries composed of firms sizable enough to operate at efficient scales. Gains are accordingly most likely when integration takes place between small countries with inefficiently small plants; furthermore, if the rest of the world is large, it is unlikely to be forced to inefficient scales of operation by a loss of customers. National scale economies have probably not been a significant factor in the EEC, whose member states seem large enough to support efficient-sized industries on their own, but those scale economies are central to many proposals for integration between LDCs, especially LDCs that have adopted vigorous import substitution policies in the past.

International Scale Economies and Product Differentiation. Even economies that are initially large enough to support many firms of efficient size in each industry may benefit from scale economies in another way, as we also saw in Chapter 1. Integration between such economies allows the production process within an industry to be further subdivided, with individual firms concentrating on distinct stages of the process, allowing the realization of any external scale economies due to the further division of labor. Also, different firms can concentrate on different versions of one basic product, giving consumers more choice than they had before. When the integration is between similar countries, who therefore continue to diversify in production, the result will be to expand intra-industry trade: carburetors will be exchanged for cylinder heads, red wine for white wine, and so forth. Such integration may also produce an analog to trade modification, as intermediate goods or differentiated products from the rest of the world become more costly relative to those from the integration partner.

International scale economies and product differentiation appear to be quite important in the EEC, as European integration was followed by a large expansion in intra-industry trade rather than in inter-industry specialization. More generally, the substantial postwar biased integration of the DCs has been accompanied, as we saw in Chapter 1, by the steady increase of intra-industry trade. By contrast, national scale economies are generally thought to be more relevant to potential integration among LDCs. But, even here, there is some evidence that those LDCs that have followed liberal trade policies (that is, biased integration with DCs), and some of those LDCs that have attempted integration among themselves, have expanded intra-industry trade.

Competitive Effects. If national markets are initially characterized by oligopoly or monopoly, integration may increase economic efficiency by subjecting domestic firms to competition with firms in the partner country, thereby reducing market imperfections. Some economists maintain that this has been a significant benefit of the EEC.

FACTOR-MARKET INTEGRATION

Countries sometimes mutually eliminate barriers to factor movements between each other; such is one feature of the EEC. This produces effects analogous to trade integration. For example, productive factors will tend to move from that partner in which their absolute productivities are low to the partner in which they are high; this raises the joint income of the integrating countries. There is even an analog to trade diversion: if the formation of the EEC allows Italian workers to enter Germany more readily than it does Turkish workers, the former will tend to displace the latter. This will be inefficient if labor's productivity in Germany exceeds its productivity in Turkey by more than its productivity in Italy.

INTEGRATION OF MACROECONOMIC POLICIES

Integration sometimes takes the form of a merging or coordination of national economic policies, notably macroeconomic policies. This can have the effect of reducing payments imbalances or exchange-rate fluctuations, and the attainment of fixed exchange rates between the partners is a major consideration in such integration.

Recall the basic inconsistency between (a) fixed exchange rates, (b) autonomous national macroeconomic policies, and (c) free international transactions. The sort of integration we are now considering attempts to attain (a) and forsake (b). The issue is not exactly one of removing policy conflicts between nations: we saw in Chapter 9 that such conflicts are not necessarily eliminated by flexible exchange rates, and, with highly mobile capital, may even be accentuated. Rather, the problem is to coordinate macroeconomic policy internationally to make fixed exchange rates feasible.

We currently have many examples of countries that peg their own currencies to another currency, or currency basket, while floating relative to the rest of the world. Some of these countries do accept the loss of autonomy in macroeconomic policy making; a full monetary union of the EEC countries is in fact an ultimate goal of the European Monetary System (EMS). But many LDCs peg their currencies and maintain fully autonomous national policies by reliance on extensive trade and exchange controls; of the inconsistent triumvirate, it is (c), free international transactions, that is sacrificed. This hardly constitutes economic integration.

Monetary integration of course limits the likelihood of partner countries aggressively manipulating exchange rates for nationalistic purposes, as it produces macroeconomic policy coordination, and it may also constitute a vital step toward a political unification desired for noneconomic reasons. But the primary economic benefit is that the usefulness of each country's money is enhanced, as we discussed in Chapter 9. The principal cost is the loss of autonomy in macroeconomic policy. What circumstances most likely render the benefits more important than the costs?

Monetary integration between two countries is likely to be more attractive the more *open* the economies are relative to each other. If residents of one country make a large proportion of their economic transactions directly or indirectly with residents of the other country, fixed exchange rates can greatly increase the usefulness of that country's money. Also the loss of policy autonomy is not likely to be large, because such countries will be quite interdependent even with a floating exchange rate. A region best suited to an arrangement with fixed exchange rates between countries in the region is sometimes called an *optimum currency area*. Ronald McKinnon, of Stanford, has emphasized the importance of degrees of openness in the delineation of such an area. Earlier Robert Mundell, the originator of the concept of an optimum currency area, had stressed the importance of factor mobility. If such mobility is high, factors will move from areas of high unemployment to areas of low unemployment, and equalization of factor costs will also tend to equalize inflation rates within the region. Thus there will be little need, and little opportunity, for independent macroeconomic policies by countries within the region. According to this criterion, then, an optimum currency area is defined by the extent of free factor mobility between countries. The EMS would seem to score high relative to both criteria: its member countries are quite open *vis-à-vis* each other, and the EEC has eliminated internal barriers to factor movements.

PROBLEMS _____

12.1 In terms of the concepts discussed in this section, speculate about the consequences for the United States of the formation of the EEC.

12.2 Should the existence of the guest-worker system discussed in Chapter 7 prove a help or hindrance in the effort of the EEC to achieve monetary integration?

12.3 Suppose the world is as described in the Heckscher-Ohlin-Samuelson model of Chapter 3, except that there are several countries instead of just two. Is integration more likely to be beneficial to two countries if their relative endowments are similar or if they are different?

12.4 Are those gains from integration that are due to international scale economies and product differentiation more likely to be large if the partners are similar or if they are different?

12.5* Suppose that F and G mutually eliminate tariffs on each other's products and then jointly levy an optimum common tariff on goods from R. Can you say anything about the significance of trade diversion?

2. *Exploring Further:* **Trade Creation and Trade Diversion**

This section uses geometric tools developed earlier in this book to examine in greater detail those aspects of biased trade integration that have to do with comparative costs.

Suppose that a small country, call it Greece (G), integrates with a large country, Europe (E), excluding the rest of the world (R). G is sufficiently small in that this deed produces no change in relative prices in E or R. This assumption means that we ignore terms-of-trade changes (to concentrate more efficiently on trade creation and trade diversion). Also R and E do not trade with each other, so that trade diversion involves only G's trade with R.

Let us start by looking at a simple example of trade creation. In Figure 12.1 the M-axis measures Greece's imports, and the X-axis Greece's exports. OR and OE represent the tariff-ridden offer curves presented to G by R and E respectively, OAG represents Greece's tariff-ridden offer curve, and OE' shows domestic relative prices in E. In this case trade initially takes place at A, putting Greece on the trade indifference curve U_A. No trade takes place with R, who offers G less favorable terms than does E. Now suppose that E and G mutually eliminate tariffs on each other's goods. There can be no trade diversion in this case, because there is no trade with R to divert. Greece's free-trade offer curve is depicted as OBG', and, since G can now trade with Europe at the latter's domestic price, trade is now indicated by B. Greece has moved to the higher indifference curve U_B.

Trade diversion can occur when Greek imports can be produced more cheaply in R than in E. This is shown in Figure 12.2 where OE' is drawn

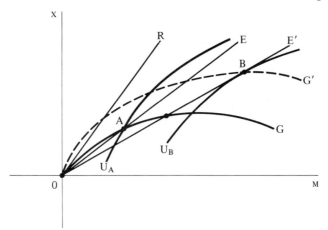

Figure 12.1.   TRADE CREATION

steeper than *OR. OE,* which would be even steeper than *OE',* is not drawn, because before integration *G* trades only with *R,* the low cost supplier. Pre-integration trade is shown by point *A* in each panel, with the tariff-ridden offer curve of *G* depicted by *OAG.* Greece is initially on the trade indifference curve U_A and Greek domestic relative prices are indicated by the slope of U_A at *A.* Now suppose that *G* and *E* integrate. Greece can now trade with *E* along the line *OE';* *G* residents must still buy from *R* at the former price—the slope of U_A through *A,* because there has been no change in tariff relative to *R.* Since *E* offers better terms to *G* residents, trade is diverted, and Greek trade is now indicated by point *B* on Greece's free-trade curve *OBG'.* In all cases the domestic relative price of imports falls, because Greeks no longer pay a tariff, but in panels (a) and (b) the Greek terms of trade deteriorate because of the trade diversion. In panel (a) the new trade indifference curve U_B lies below the old; trade diversion has caused integration to harm *G.* By contrast panel (b) shows a case where *G* gains because the trade diversion is more than offset by the trade creation resulting from the decline in the relative domestic price of imports. Panel (c) differs from the other two panels in that here trade diversion is actually beneficial to Greece, whose terms of trade improve, and therefore reinforces the favorable influence of trade creation. Even in this case, though, trade diversion is harmful from a global perspective, because Greek imports could be supplied more cheaply from the rest of the world (whose free-trade offer curve is *OR'*) than from Europe. But Greece does not have the option of trading on *OR'.*

Trade integration is a *second-best* policy whereby one distortion is replaced by another, as with a tariff for domestic purposes, as discussed in Chapter 6. One might suspect, therefore, that other conclusions of that

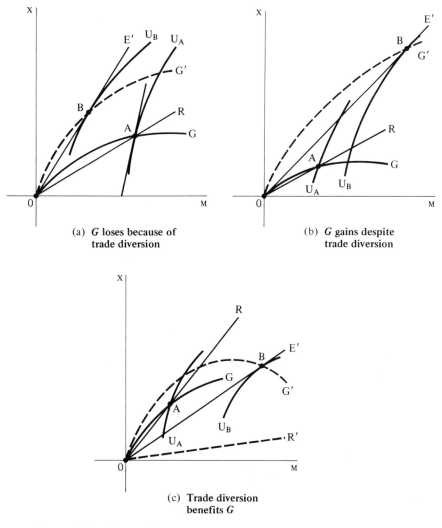

(a) **G** loses because of
trade diversion

(b) **G** gains despite
trade diversion

(c) **Trade diversion**
benefits **G**

Figure 12.2. TRADE DIVERSION

earlier discussion would have their present analogs. Such a suspicion is
correct. Consider the effects of *small* mutual tariff changes by the partners.
From an initial state of nondiscriminatory trade, a small mutual, discriminatory tariff reduction by the partners will necessarily be to their joint
benefit: the advantage of trade creation must outweigh any disadvantage
due to trade diversion. Likewise, if the partners initially have mutual free
trade but restrict trade with the rest of the world, a small retreat from
integration (that is, the introduction of small tariffs on each others' goods)
must be jointly beneficial (the reversal of trade diversion will outweigh

trade destruction), provided that the partners do initially import at least some of the same goods that they trade with each other from the rest of the world.

Consider the first of these statements. In the initial nondiscriminatory state, a country is buying goods from its potential partner at the same price as from the rest of the world. Thus trade diversion can not make much difference unless there is enough discrimination (that is, a large enough tariff reduction) to allow a significant difference in prices between the two sources. But because initially there are (nondiscriminatory) tariffs, imports are initially worth (the domestic prices) significantly more than they cost, so that any trade creation gives a significant benefit.

The second statement is illustrated in Figure 12.3. We no longer assume that Europe is large relative to Greece, so that G can import from E and R simultaneously. OBR shows the terms at which R will trade, and OAE shows E's free-trade offer curve. The slope of OA—equal to that of BC—shows the terms of trade between G and E, while the slope of OBR—equal to that of AC—shows the terms of trade between G and R. Point B shows G's trade with R and point A shows G's trade with E, so point C shows G's total trade. Initially G is on the trade indifference curve U_G, and E is on the trade indifference curve U_E. Now suppose G and E impose a small tariff on each other's goods. This will, first of all, reduce trade between the two partners, as is indicated by the arrow from point A and the parallel arrow from C. Since AE and BC are tangent to the respective indifference curves, movements as indicated by the arrows are not much different from

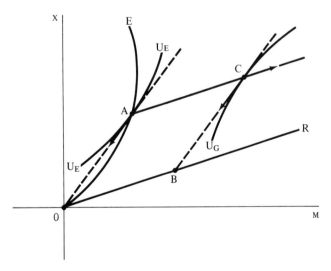

Figure 12.3. A SMALL INTERNAL TARIFF BENEFITS THE PARTNER COUNTRIES

movements along those indifference curves: there will be little effect on each country's welfare. (It is possible that the terms of trade between *G* and *E* might change, but this would only redistribute income between the two partners, and not change their aggregate welfare.) The tariff will also cause *G* to trade more with *R*, that is, trade diversion will fall; this is indicated by the arrow from point *C* along the line *AC*. Since this line cuts through the indifference curve U_G, the effect of this trade movement is to significantly increase Greece's welfare. (In this example the internal tariff benefits only *G*, because *E* has been assumed not to trade with *R*.)

The general conclusion is that any group of countries has an incentive to mutually reduce, but not eliminate, the tariffs they levy on each other's goods, *if* tariff arrangements with the rest of the world cannot be altered.

PROBLEMS _____

12.6 In Figure 12.1, the effect of integration upon Greece can be thought of as consisting of two parts: the expansion of Greek trade resulting solely from *G*'s removal of tariffs on goods from *E*, and the improvement in *G*'s terms of trade resulting from *E*'s removal of tariffs on goods from *G*. Indicate each part in the figure, and show how each part contributes to Greek welfare by drawing in an appropriate Greek trade indifference curve. How can the total change in *E*'s trade likewise be decomposed?

12.7 Draw Figure 12.1 if *E* is no longer large relative to *G*. Answer Problem **12.6** in this case. What do you conclude about the influence of relative partner sizes upon the terms-of-trade portion of the total effect of integration?

12.8 Draw Figure 12.3 if *R* is no longer large relative to *G* and *E*. How does this affect our basic conclusion?

12.9 Try to show geometrically that, starting from nondiscriminatory protection, a small mutual tariff reduction necessarily benefits the partners. How does the argument change if the initial state is not nondiscriminatory?

3. Biased Integration in Practice

Perhaps the most significant postwar exercise in economic integration is the GATT-sponsored multilateral reduction in DC tariffs on manufactured goods. This reduction has been in the context of the most-favored-nation clause and therefore has not introduced price discrimination, but it has brought about biased integration by largely restricting tariff cuts to goods largely traded among the DCs. As mentioned earlier, this means that trade diversion can be ignored, but trade modification must be considered in addition to trade creation. We also saw in Chapter 1 that this integration has been accompanied by a large increase in intra-industry trade, leading one to suspect that international scale economies and product differentiation could be important considerations.

DEFINITIONS

The following are the principal forms of biased integration:

Biased tariff reduction. A group of countries nondiscriminately reduces tariffs on goods largely traded only among themselves and leaves other tariffs unchanged.

Discriminatory tariff preferences. A group of countries reduces tariffs on each other's products and leaves unchanged tariffs on the products of other countries.

Free-trade area. The member countries eliminate tariffs among themselves, and each member maintains its own tariff schedule on goods from outside countries.

Customs union. The member countries eliminate tariffs among themselves and establish a common tariff schedule on goods from outside countries.

Common market. A customs union with the additional removal of all barriers to factor movements between members.

Economic union. The members integrate all economic policies.

Discriminatory tariff preferences—with a group of countries reducing but not eliminating tariffs vis-à-vis each other while leaving unchanged tariffs against third-country products—violate the MFN clause and hence are inconsistent with the GATT. But the postwar world still offers some significant examples. Commonwealth Preferences, between those nations formerly part of the British Empire, were established before the war and allowed by GATT to continue. The United Kingdom, though, largely turned its back on Commonwealth Preference by joining the EEC. Other examples of this type of integration are the preference schemes for LDC products adopted by most DCs. These schemes, however, do not involve reciprocal preferences by the LDCs. Finally, it is possible that one effect of the Tokyo Round could be to significantly increase the importance of this type of integration. As we saw in Chapter 6, codes have been established for various nontariff barriers. These codes need not be signed by all GATT members and may be signed by nonmembers. Thus far some of these codes have attracted a limited number of signatories, who intend to apply the codes only to each other. To the extent that these nontariff barriers are equivalent to tariffs, the Tokyo Round may, therefore, produce the non-tariff equivalent of discriminatory tariff preferences.

The GATT departs from the MFN principle by explicitly allowing free-trade areas and customs unions. These differ in that the latter involves a common tariff relative to the rest of the world, whereas the former does not. A major drawback to a free-trade area is the need to regulate internal trade despite the abolition of internal tariffs. If this were not done, individual members would be unable to maintain their own tariffs on goods from nonmembers, as such goods would enter the free-trade area exclusively through the member with the lowest tariff. Suppose, for example, that Sweden and Finland participate in a free-trade area, with Finland imposing a tariff on steel of $50 a ton, and Sweden one of $30 a ton. Then a Finnish steel importer would, if he could get away with it, import his steel through Sweden, paying the Swedish tariff and then shipping the steel duty free into Finland. This would make it impossible for Finland to effectively impose its higher tariff, and would also cause Finland to lose tariff revenue to Sweden. Trade between Finland and Sweden must be monitored to prevent this sort of evasion, and administration can become quite complex (for example, suppose Finland imports cars made in Sweden using steel imported from outside the free-trade area). A customs union avoids this problem by establishing a common external tariff, but this means that individual members lose the ability to conduct independent trade policies and must reach agreement on a common policy. Also the members must agree on how to distribute among themselves the tariff revenues they jointly collect.

There are many examples of attempted free-trade areas and customs unions. LDCs have formed many such arrangements, lured usually by the hope of realizing scale economies, but the arrangements have in fact achieved little real economic integration. The decisive obstacle has been political disagreement between the governments of would-be partners. Two unions have simply dissolved: the West Indian Federation and the integration of Uganda, Tanzania, and Kenya. The largest arrangement, the Latin American Free Trade Association (LAFTA), including Mexico and most of South America, has made at best modest progress toward the goal embodied in its name. A subgroup, signers of the Andean Pact, hoped to accelerate integration among themselves and establish a customs union within LAFTA, but they have also been balked by political conflicts. The Central American Common Market actually had to endure a 1969 war between two of its members, Honduras and El Salvador, over a soccer game. The LDC union with the most current promise is probably the Association of Southeast Asian Nations (ASEAN), comprising Thailand, Malaysia, Singapore, Indonesia, and the Philippines. It decided in 1976 to try to form a common market.

The most successful attempts have been made in Europe. The 1957 Treaty of Rome created the European Economic Community (EEC) of France, Germany, Italy, Belgium, Luxemburg, and the Netherlands. The United Kingdom, Denmark, and Ireland joined in 1973, Greece in 1981, and Spain and Portugal are currently scheduled to join in 1984. The European Free Trade Association (EFTA) was formed in 1960 by seven European nations desiring a looser form of integration than that planned by the EEC. Both arrangements proved successful in that the EEC has established a true common market, and the EFTA a true free-trade area (in manufactures). In 1977 these two groups of countries eliminated most tariffs on each other's industrial goods, so that the EFTA and the EEC together now comprise a large free-trade area.

THE EEC

As the most prominent postwar example of formal integration, the EEC has been an invitation to economists seeking to quantitatively measure the effects of customs unions. Techniques and specific results have varied, but the strong consensus is that formation of the EEC resulted in substantially more trade creation than diversion. But international scale economies and product differentiation may have been even more significant: studies by Bela Balassa and others have shown that the formation of the EEC was followed by a significant increase in the amount and relative importance of intra-industry trade between all the partners, rather than by an increase in inter-industrial specialization.

But the EEC is more than a customs union. It is something between a common market and an economic union—with the latter the ultimate goal. The EEC followed earlier, more limited, integration measures, and was enthusiastically pushed by those who hoped for a federated European state that would finally end centuries of local wars and establish a new superpower. The federation is yet to be, and the individual countries have certainly not surrendered key aspects of sovereignty such as foreign and defense policies. Still, the EEC is not only an agreement over international economic matters. There is a significant EEC bureaucracy, headquartered at Brussels, with over ten-thousand "eurocrats," and members of the community parliament are now chosen by direct election—prompting speculation that that body may become a power center independent of the national governments. The EEC now conducts much economic policy beyond its customs union and the dreamed-of monetary union. There are community regulations and policies dealing with competition (antitrust), labor, industry, and social affairs, energy, the environment, and consumer issues. But two areas stand out in the community budget: a regional policy aids economically backward parts of the community, and the Common Agricultural Policy (CAP) is now the single most significant activity of the EEC.

This policy makes little sense economically. It is very complex and expensive, and its net effect is to cause the community to produce food at a much higher cost than it could be obtained from abroad (trade diversion again). The CAP harms the external relations of the EEC with those countries, such as the United States, that are thereby deprived of agricultural export markets. It causes even more internal dissension, between those countries who see themselves as net losers (the United Kingdom and Germany) and those who are net gainers (France), and also between community agricultural interests generally and those who object to such a large budget for the benefit of that sector. But in spite of all this the CAP is a concrete integration achievement in a most difficult and sensitive policy area.

PROBLEMS _____

12.10 Why is it necessary for a customs union to negotiate some way of distributing the joint tariff revenues, rather than simply letting each country keep what it collects (hint: consider the geographical position of Luxemburg)?

12.11 Can you think of any reasons why the European attempts at integration were notably more successful than LDC attempts?

12.12 The United States strongly supported formation of the EEC. Why?

12.13 Discuss the implications of the GATT multilateral tariff reduction for the significance of the EEC.

4. Case Study: The European Monetary System

Full monetary union has been a goal of the EEC since at least 1969. The strategy for reaching this goal is one of gradualism. The first step was attempted in 1972, when the EEC established the "snake-in-the-tunnel": a band of exchange-rate fluctuations for members' currencies narrower than the bands adopted by countries in general after the Smithsonian agreement. The arrangement continued after the collapse of the Bretton Woods system in 1973, with the participating countries jointly floating relative to the rest of the world ("the snake out of the tunnel"). But there was no formal structure for the integration or coordination of monetary and fiscal policies, and countries moved into or out of the arrangement as circumstances changed. In the end the snake was basically reduced to a DM currency area, with Germany the only large participant.

A Franco-German initiative in 1978 added new momentum, and the European Monetary System was formed in 1979. Member countries (all the EEC but Greece) have temporarily earmarked for the EMS one-fifth of their reserves of gold and dollars, and have received in return equal-valued quantities of European Currency Units (ECUs). The ECU is a currency composite, something like the SDR, used for official transactions within the EEC. The intention seems to be that, in the hazy future, the EMS should become the EEC central bank with the ECU as the EEC currency. The medium-term goal is to set up a European Monetary Fund to issue ECUs and extend credit to member-country central banks. But for now there are only large stand-by credit arrangements between the banks, plus a new snake: adjustable pegs have been established for the exchange rates of members' currencies relative to each other, and the countries undertake to maintain market rates within 2.25 percent of these pegs (the United Kingdom does not participate in the pegging arrangement, and Italy is committed only to keeping the lira within 6 percent of its peg).

The EMS is an example of what political scientists call the "neofunctionalist" approach to integration: countries are tied together in obscure technical ways in the hope that this will induce more meaningful integration. In this case the hope is that the commitment to exchange-rate pegging will help bring about macroeconomic policy coordination and unification. The contrasting integration approach is to attempt at the outset complete merger (in this case, that could mean agreeing to start the EMS as an EEC central bank). This use of the EMS in the monetary sphere is analogous to the strategy followed by Europeans in the larger context: instead of trying directly to set up a unified European state they established a customs union with the hope that it would lead to political union.

5. Case Study: The Common Agricultural Policy

Most of the nations that combined into the EEC had long histories of protection and support for their agricultural sectors. They did not wish to end this support, but free trade in agriculture within the EEC was a central part of integration; thus a common policy was called for. Under this policy the authorities purchase agricultural products within the EEC as required to maintain prices at target levels. At the same time, the community is protected from world markets, notably by variable-levy tariffs on many products, which assure that EEC farmers will not be undersold within the community no matter how much world prices drop. When harvests are good, the authorities accumulate huge stocks of products bought at high EEC prices (a $14 million "butter mountain," insured with Lloyd's of London, once burned down in the Netherlands). These products are eventually sold abroad at low world prices. This makes the CAP very expensive. This brief description does not begin to do justice to the complexity of the CAP, which uses more than twenty distinct systems of prices.

The CAP has been in operation since 1968. This operation has become more difficult as a result of the increasing currency fluctuations dating from 1969. CAP support prices were set in terms of units of account (defined in varying ways) and translated into national currency prices using exchange rates. If market exchange rates were used for this, the support prices received by a country's farmers and the food prices paid by its consumers would fluctuate directly with the exchange rate. An appreciation of the DM of 10 percent relative to the unit of account, for example, would immediately reduce by 10 percent the mark price of food in Germany. This was politically unacceptable to national governments. As a result, market exchange rates are not used to translate CAP prices into national currencies. Instead this is done with administratively determined exchange rates— called "green currency" rates— which the authorities adjust gradually from time to time. This has had two effects. First, when the market rates and green rates diverge—and they have diverged by up to 40 percent—food prices differ from country to country. If the green rate is two francs per mark while the actual exchange rate is three francs per mark, food prices in Germany are 50 percent higher than in France (why?). Under these circumstances, the CAP would quickly be destroyed by arbitrage between countries. To prevent this, there are border taxes and subsidies, called Monetary Compensatory Amounts (MCAs), which cancel out the price differences. The second effect of this system is that the substantial exchange-rate fluctuations experienced under managed floating imply substantial fluctuations in the relation between market rates and the slowly adjusting green rates. This requires quick and substantial changes in the MCAs. Obviously this system will be much easier to administer if the EMS succeeds in limiting fluctuations in members' relative exchange rates. This consideration was in fact the single most significant technical motive for proceeding with the EMS's snake arrangement.

6. The International Trade of Centrally Planned Economies

Asymmetric integration takes place with every reduction in economic barriers between countries whose governments assume different economic functions. As such, it is an aspect of nearly all international transactions. But it arises in most dramatic form with increased trade between communist countries and the West. To study this trade we must examine the international economics of the communist world.

FOREIGN TRADE IN SOVIET-TYPE ECONOMIES

In soviet-type economies prices are primarily accounting devices and summaries of terms of exchange; only to a very limited degree do they convey information or serve as incentives to allocate resources, as in market economies. These functions are instead subsumed in the planning mechanism. There are two direct implications of this. The first is that such economies cannot allow foreigners to deal directly with domestic consumers and enterprises; such transactions could be very harmful since domestic prices do not reflect opportunity costs. For example, the general tendency in such economies is for consumer goods to have artificially high prices and for capital goods to have artificially low prices—a reflection of the planners' priorities. Were foreigners allowed to do so, they would sell consumer goods and buy capital goods, thereby causing the planned economy to lose by the transaction (and also frustrating the plan objectives that generated the artificial prices in the first place). Thus foreigners are not allowed to buy and sell freely in the economy, nor, for the same reason, can domestic residents buy and sell freely abroad. Instead international trade is conducted solely through a government foreign trade organization. The second implication is that this foreign trade organization has a difficult time in deciding whether to trade or not. It cannot simply compare foreign prices to domestic prices to decide whether to buy or sell, because domestic prices do not reflect true opportunity costs.

Resource allocation is basically planned, and the planning process centers on achieving *material balances.* In order to attain basic goals, the planners attempt to reconcile aggregate demands and supplies of all key commodities. This balancing process involves considerable give-and-take with lower levels of the economic hierachy. The natural tendency is to call upon the Foreign Trade Organization to import those goods for which it turns out especially difficult to balance demands with domestic supplies, and to export those goods for which domestic demands are most easily met. Thus trade tends to follow from the dictates of the planning process. As trade becomes more significant, it cannot be left entirely as a residuum but must begin to be allowed a more central role in planning. This requires some criterion to decide which goods the plan should attempt to provide for export and which to import. To a large degree, such decisions are based on past history, the "sixth-sense" of the planners, and international political objectives. But various formulae are also used to determine those goods in which the country has the greatest comparative advantage and those in which it has the greatest comparative disadvantage.

TRADE AMONG THE COMMUNIST COUNTRIES

As we saw at the beginning of this book, communist nations do not trade much, compared with Western countries with similar characteristics. This is partly due to economic considerations, international trade being more difficult to manage for planned economies than for market economies, but obviously international politics have been crucial. The West has shunned trade with the East, in varying degrees, and the East has shown a decided taste for autarky. (Actually this has not been dramatically different from precommunist practice: Tsarist Russia was highly protectionist, China resisted Western contacts for centuries, and much of Eastern Europe was controlled by the Ottoman and Russian empires). The proliferation of communist regimes after the Second World War introduced the possibility of international trade among communist states just as the Cold War was precluding the possibility of significant East-West trade. The Council for Mutual Economic Assistance (CMEA or COMECON) was set up in 1949 as an Eastern counterpart to Western cooperative efforts and as an instrument for Soviet control. Present members include all the communist states of Eastern Europe except Yugoslavia and Albania, plus Cuba, Mongolia, Vietnam, and, of course, the Soviet Union. China is excluded, for obvious reasons. COMECON apparently had a substantial real influence: at the start considerably less than one-third of its members' trade was with each other: within five years almost three-quarters was.

What does commercial integration between centrally planned economies actually mean? Trade diversion is simple enough: the foreign trade organizations of the various countries simply look to each other for deals and try to ignore market economies. But what about trade creation? The essence of integration between market economies is the reduction of differences between those economies in domestic relative prices, with a consequent increase in specialization and trade. But in centrally planned economies domestic relative prices do not reflect opportunity costs and do not guide the actions of foreign trade organizations. Increased specialization and trade must be planned for. That is, integration means the integration of national planning procedures. COMECON has made several attempts at this, and has even set 1990 as a target date for planning integration. But relatively little has been achieved: even when the will is there, planning is difficult enough at the national level. It appears that the early growth of COMECON trade consisted mainly of trade diversion.

Trade between centrally planned economies is in two ways actually *more* difficult than trade between such economies and the West. The first problem is to decide what prices to trade at. When the Soviet Union trades with the West, it knows that it can buy or sell at Western market prices, and the only problem (a big enough one, to be sure) is to decide whether to do so. But when the Soviet Union and Czechoslovakia trade, neither country's prices reflect opportunity costs or the terms at which either country is willing to trade. The foreign trade organizations of the two countries could resolve this problem on a case-by-case basis if they limit themselves to barter: Czechoslovakia could agree to send the Soviet Union so many tractors for so much oil. But such a cumbersome method of trade would result in little trade taking place. If the two countries are to exchange a range of products they need prices with which to value those products, and the prices must be consistent with the prices used for trade between the Soviet Union and Bulgaria, and so forth. Thus COMECON needs a set of prices to govern the trade between its members. To its not-inconsiderable embarrassment, it gets those prices from the West. COMECON sets its internal prices by computing averages of world prices over the preceding five years and then adjusting them in various ways. (Thus many COMECON prices tend to follow world prices with a lag.) This method works best with standardized products, such as raw materials, and worst with differentiated goods, for which the similarities between Western products and their COMECON counterparts are quite inexact.

The second problem is that of conducting multilateral trade. This difficulty is due to the fact that all the Eastern currencies are inconvertible, and they must be inconvertible to protect the planning process. We saw above that a centrally planned economy can not allow foreigners freely to buy and sell at domestic prices, nor domestic residents freely to buy and sell at foreign prices. This means that Russia, for example, cannot allow foreigners freely to spend rubles or allow Russians freely to use their rubles to buy foreign currency. This lack of convertibility means that there is no medium of exchange for intra-COMECON trade. For example, in a non-monetary economy a barber would have to barter haircuts for cabbages with a grocer, haircuts for taxi-rides with a cabbie, and so forth. The existence of money simplifies things enormously and actually makes a detailed division of labor possible. Convertible currencies do the same thing for international trade: the United States does not need to worry that exports to the United Kingdom are paid for with imports from the United Kingdom, because the dollars or pounds acquired for the exports can easily be used to buy goods elsewhere in the world. But if Czechoslovakia sells tractors to the Soviet Union for rubles, the rubles can only be used to buy what the Czechs can convince the Soviet foreign trade organization to sell. Thus they will not want to part with the tractors before arranging to buy something desirable from the Soviet Union in return. Trade within COMECON accordingly tends to be bilateral, with pairs of countries negotiating so as to balance out their mutual trade over a period of five years or so. Studies of intra-COMECON trade patterns generally show less than 5 percent of this trade to be multilateral. All this reinforces the tendency of COMECON to foster trade diversion rather than trade creation. Multilateral exchanges are actually easier in East-West trade than in East-East trade, since in the former case the convertible Western currency can be used. This is in fact common practice, and East-West trade is rarely conducted with Eastern currencies. Centrally planned economies finance their trade with the West by borrowing and lending in the Eurocurrency markets, where the Soviet Union has earned a reputation as a good credit risk. The Soviets have created banking institutions to deal in these markets.

CASE STUDY: The Transferable Ruble

In an attempt to foster multilateral trade, COMECON has established a central clearinghouse and created "transferable rubles" for intra-COMECON trade. COMECON trading prices are denominated in transferable rubles, and when one country sells goods to another it receives a credit of these transferable rubles that can then be used to buy goods from any other CO-MECON country. It might seem that COMECON now has its medium of exchange, so that extensive multilateral trade is possible. But, alas, no. If Czechoslovakia receives transferable rubles from the Soviet Union for its tractors, it is true that the rubles can be used to buy goods from any other COMECON country. But Czechoslovakia cannot freely shop around in those countries; it must convince some other foreign trade organization to strike a deal. Thus it still has no way of knowing that it will in fact be able to use the rubles to buy goods valuable enough to justify the sale of the tractors. The transferable ruble is not a true medium of exchange, and there has been little success in promoting multilateral trade.

In principal COMECON could solve this problem by using convertible Western currencies (so that intra-COMECON trade would be financed, at least indirectly, by Western banks). Czechoslovakia need have no reluctance in selling the Soviet Union tractors for dollars, because the dollars could be freely used to shop around in the West. But apparently such a solution would be too humiliating to contemplate.

EAST-WEST TRADE

About twenty years ago, East-West trade began to significantly increase, partly in response to the large gains that it promises and partly due to realization of the inadequacies of East-East trade noted above. During the sixties, the USSR and Eastern Europe expanded their trade with the West more rapidly than their trade with each other. As a result, East-West trade now accounts for about 45 percent of total Eastern trade, as shown in Table 12.2. This inter-bloc trade is much more important, relative to total trade, for the East than it is for the West (since the latter has much more total trade), and it is also more important relative to GNP (since the West has a larger GNP). On balance, the East exports raw materials to the West in exchange for manufactured goods and new technology—see Table 12.3. This mutually beneficial trade faces both political and economic obstacles.

The political obstacles of course vary with the general state of international relations between the blocs: trade has grown as the Cold War has thawed. The United States has tended to lag behind other Western nations in this regard. The outlook for Soviet-American trade improved with the 1972 easing of relations—abetted perhaps by an increased feeling that American policy was causing American firms to lose business to European and Japanese rivals. But subsequent developments have not been especially encouraging. Concern about Soviet policy toward Jewish emigration, and human rights generally, has caused American restrictions, such as the 1978 cancellation of a computer sale (the computer had been intended for TASS, who bought a French one instead), and the continued denial of most-

Table 12.2. East-West Trade as a Percentage of Total Trade, 1979

	Exports	Imports
Bulgaria	29	21
Czechoslovakia	32	32
East Germany	29	37
Hungary	36	38
Poland	42	48
Romania	58	61
USSR	53	52
(Above Countries together	44	45)
U.S.	4	1
Japan	7	5
Canada	3	1
EEC	4	4

sources: *IMF*, Direction of Trade, *and GATT*, International Trade

favored-nation status to the USSR and other Eastern nations (Poland, Romania and Hungary are GATT members and have MFN status with the United States). Thus imports from the USSR are generally subject to higher American duties than would be similar goods from other countries (a reason that your bottle of Stolichnaya vodka costs so much). The deterioration in Soviet-American relations following the Soviet intervention in Afghanistan has further worsened commercial relations, most dramatically with the American embargo on exports of grain and high-technology goods. The Reagan administration ended the grain embargo; but it has not encouraged other exchanges and promises redoubled efforts to limit trade in strategic goods.

Table 12.3. USSR Exports Minus Imports, 1979 (*billions of dollars*)

	The West*	Eastern Europe
Machinery and Transport	−6.4	−8
Consumer Goods	−.4	−3.9
Chemicals and Building Materials	−.7	0
Metals and Materials	9.5	13.8
Agricultural Raw Materials	1	1.3
Food	−3.5	−1.8
All Goods	−.6	1.6

* Includes: U.S., Canada, Japan, EEC, EFTA.

source: *GATT*, International Trade

Serious economic obstacles to East-West trade arise from the centrally planned nature of the Eastern economies. These countries have found it difficult to expand their exports to the West fast enough to keep pace with their imports and have consequently contracted substantial debts. To a degree, this would probably happen even if the Eastern countries had market economies, because the West is relatively capital abundant and so would tend to lend. But the tendency has been exacerbated by the actual economic systems. The planning process, together with the practice of trading through the medium of foreign trade organizations, gives individual Eastern enterprises insufficient incentive to develop product varieties or quality standards to compete on world markets. Also goods that do become available for export tend to be tied up in advance by bilateral trade agreements with other COMECON members.

CASE STUDY: The Sorry State of Poland

Poland is probably the COMECON member that has suffered most from the difficulty of building Western export markets. The country is a GATT member and, relative to other Eastern countries, has conducted a high level of trade with the West, borrowing heavily there to finance imports for industrial development and, recently, to maintain consumption levels in the hope of forestalling domestic discontent. By 1981 Poland's accumulated debt to the West exceeded $23 billion, and nearly three-quarters of the country's earnings from exports to the West would be required simply to service this debt, leaving little to pay for imports (which continued to exeed exports). In hope of preventing default, Western banks extended new loans, some of them supplemented and guaranteed by Western governments who wanted to help keep the beleaguered Polish government going. The 1980 worker unrest worsened the situation, both by forcing the government to maintain living standards (and thereby to maintain imports as well) and also by reducing the supply of exports by strike activity. This increased even more the country's financial dependence upon the West. In 1981 Western banks agreed to a four-year postponement of debt repayments originally due in that year, but Poland found it very difficult even to live up to this agreement, and in 1982 a new agreement had to be worked out for the 1981 interest called for in the first agreement.

In an effort to obtain hard currency, Poland—like other Eastern countries—maintains a network of special stores where consumer goods are sold, to Poles and to foreign visitors, for dollars only. These *Pewex* stores offer goods not available in

regular shops, whose shelves had become especially bare by
1981. Dollars are exchanged in a flourishing black market, and
Poles may establish dollar accounts in Polish banks. When such
a depositor wishes to withdraw some of her dollars to make a
purchase at a Pewex store, she receives dollar-denominated certificates called *bony*, which may be used for the purpose.

East-West trade is also hampered by foreign trade organizations' use
of bilateral agreements, although Eastern attempts to get away from this
have, as discussed earlier, been more successful with respect to East-West
trade than with intra-COMECON trade. Also Western firms have proven
adaptable to Eastern practices. Multinational enterprises have joined with
Eastern governments in cooperative arrangements and joint investments,
with the MNE typically supplying capital goods, technology, and perhaps
management, and the Eastern nations contributing labor and raw materials.
These deals—sometimes on a multi-billion-dollar scale—are most often to
establish Eastern manufacturing facilities or to exploit Eastern reserves of
natural resources. Sometimes the deals involve barter (as in Occidental
Petroleum's $20 billion 1972 agreement to export phosphates from Florida
to the USSR for ammonia over a twenty-year period), and often the participating MNEs are paid back with the natural resources or output produced by the project itself. An interesting aspect of such transactions is the
fact that Western MNEs essentially serve as agents "selling" multilateralism
to the centrally planned economy. By utilizing their world-wide organizations and contacts, the MNEs arrange for purchases of goods and credit
from all corners of that world. For example, Control Data Corporation was
able to sell the USSR a computer when it arranged for the Russians to
produce Christmas cards and to market them in Britain in order to obtain
the Western currency to pay for the computer.

Economic integration has always altered life in the integrating countries, and the same is potentially true of East-West trade. As the East for-
sakes autarky for significant Western commercial relations, it subjects itself
to external economic disturbances: Western business cycles, changes in energy prices, and so forth. Pity the poor planner. On the Western side, the
most common fear is that decentralized Western economic agents might be
driven to the wall by monolithic Eastern states exerting monopoly power in
world markets and trading on the exclusive knowledge of what is actually
happening within their own borders. Soviet wheat purchases in the United
States in 1972 are sometimes interpreted in this light. But clear examples
are lacking, and the game could conceivably be played both ways: Western
MNEs who acquired a knowledge of the intricacies of Eastern planning
would realize when to hold out for high prices as Eastern agencies needed

to acquire highly specific goods to meet a deadline to satisfy plan requirements.

PROBLEMS

12.14 Suppose that COMECON makes the transferable ruble convertible into Western currency and pegs the ruble to a currency composite, such as the SDR. Discuss the implications.

12.15 Why does the Polish government go to the trouble of printing up and issuing bony to dollar depositors, instead of simply giving back the dollars that were deposited in the first place?

7. Case Study: The Kama River Plant

A joint East-West effort constructed the world's largest truck plant on the Kama River 600 miles east of Moscow. Principal contractors were three Western firms, one each from the U.S., France, and Germany, and over one hundred firms participated as minor contractors. These firms contributed about $1 billion worth of equipment and technology, half from the United States. The project also illustrates the political dimension to East-West cooperation: when it became known that some trucks produced at the plant were being used by Soviet forces in Afghanistan, a controversy erupted within the American Commerce Department and Congress, with demands that the U.S. embargo spare parts for the project. The administration has attempted to prevent the installation of an additional assembly line at the plant.

8. Case Study: Those Soviet-American Wheat Deals

The USSR is a large grain producer (the world's largest wheat producer for many years), and has traditionally exported grain to Eastern Europe. But the country is also a large consumer, and consumption rises with decisions to improve domestic living standards. Futhermore, Soviet growing conditions are very variable. As a result, the USSR has been a net grain importer since the early seventies, with imports booming whenever the Soviet crop is bad. It was bad in 1972. The U.S. administration had taken steps to encourage grain sales to Russia, and the Soviets made massive American purchases, buying fully one-quarter of the 1972 U.S. wheat crop. These purchases were made quietly, and it was later charged that the Soviets had managed to buy the grain at a low price by keeping their true needs a secret, and subsequent U.S inflation was also popularly blamed on the Russian sales. Neither of these charges seems to have a great deal of merit: the market price of grain would respond directly to increased Russian purchases, regardless of whether the world knows anything about conditions in Russia; world prices depend basically on world demand and supply and not on whether the Russians exercise their demand directly in the U.S. or elsewhere in the world market.

The Soviet deals did unduly disrupt the American economy, but the principal culprit was a perverse American policy. Agricultural policy had restricted the number of acres planted in order to hold up domestic prices and farm incomes. These restrictions were not lifted as it became known that the market was tight. Also, the United States subsidized grain exports, with a subsidy that varied along with the domestic price in order to hold the export price at a target level near the world price (note that this system was the exact opposite of the variable levies used by the EEC in its CAP). These subsidies should have been ended when the Russian sales began; instead the subsidies were allowed to *increase* as Russian purchases drove up the domestic price. As a result, the government in effect subsidized the Russians, by holding down the export price, at the expense of domestic consumers (the domestic price rose more than it would have without the subsidy) and taxpayers.

Soviet crops were good in 1973, and the USSR did not enter the American market again until late 1974. The two countries negotiated a bilateral grain trade agreement for the five years beginning in October of 1976. The USSR agreed to buy at least six million metric tons of wheat and corn each year, and the United States agreed that up to eight million tons a year could be bought through regular commercial channels. Larger purchases were to require negotiations between the two governments.

On January 5, 1980, the United States reacted to Soviet intervention in Afghanistan with an embargo on exports of grain and high-technology goods. The grain purchases provided for in the remainder of the bilateral agreement were allowed, but other contracts were canceled. The United States tried, with some success, to persuade other countries not to fill the gap. But Argentina concluded a five-year agreement with the Russians, who also increased purchases from Canada, France, and other sources. American farmers were able in turn to replace some of their lost Russian sales with sales to the normal customers of those countries who increased sales to Russia. Also the Russians cut back on livestock feeding, and instead increased meat imports the following year. The U.S. government increased its grain purchases from farmers, to make up for lost sales, and thereby put upward pressure on prices. The net result of all this was inconvenience and added cost from the rearrangement of trade patterns, but probably not large damage to either the USSR or to U.S. farmers. President Reagan lifted the grain embargo in 1981, and when the bilateral agreement expired it was extended another year, during which negotiations on a new agreement were to be held.

As relations with China improved, Chinese-American grain trade became more important and, like the Russian trade, tended to fluctuate from year to year. To try to stabilize this trade, the two countries in October 1980 negotiated a four-year bilateral grain agreement along lines similar to the Russian agreement.

PROBLEMS

12.16 The Soviet grain purchases in 1972 raised world grain prices. What was the effect on the welfare of American urban dwellers, American farmers, and America as a whole? How was the welfare of each of these groups affected by the American policies followed at the time?

12.17 Assume that American efforts to persuade other countries not to increase grain sales to the Soviet Union fail. What would be the effect of the American embargo when: (a) world grain supplies are plentiful and the agricultural programs of most grain-producing states are buying grain to keep up prices; (b) grain supplies are tight and agricultural programs are inactive? How do your answers change if U.S. persuasion has some success?

9. Summary

1. Integration can lead to geographical price discrimination resulting in trade creation among the partners and trade diversion from the rest of the world. Domination of either effect depends on circumstances.

2. Integration can lead to trade modification, which could either increase or decrease trade with the rest of the world depending on the substitutibility or complementarity of the goods traded. This effect involves a change in the pattern of world tariffs rather than price discrimination.

3. Integration can influence the terms of trade between the partners. If the partners are big relative to the world market, integration can also alter the terms of trade of the partners vis-à-vis the rest of the world.

4. Integration could lead to greater specialization among partners resulting in reduced costs of production if the industry exhibits national economies of scale. It can also lead to increased product differentiation and division of labor resulting in expanded intra-industry trade if the partners are similar.

5. Monopoly and oligopoly could decrease as integration results in more competition among partners.

6. Integration of macroeconomic policies could lead to decreased payment imbalances or exhange-rate fluctuations or to attainment of a fixed exchange rate between partners.

7. GATT did not lead to price discrimination but did cause biased integra-

tion implying that trade diversion can be ignored but trade modification and creation must be considered.

8. The EEC apparently caused more trade creation than diversion and more importantly allowed realization of international scale economies and increased product differentiation.

9. Prices in a soviet-type economy do not determine resource allocation; therefore foreign trade organizations must decide what goods to trade. They also act as middle agents in carrying out the foreign transaction.

10. Part of foreign trade plays the role of absorbing internal deficits and surpluses that arise during the process of material balancing; an increasing percentage is related to comparative advantage as trade plays an increasing role in the national economy.

11. The creation of the CMEA led to big trade diversion but not much trade creation. This is due to the inconvertibility of Eastern currencies, which results in little multilateral trade and the necessity to decide trading prices on a contract-by-contract basis.

12. East-West trade has been expanding and is easier than intra-CMEA trade because prices are determined in Western markets and transactions take place in Western currency. The planned nature of the economy, coupled with the necessity to use Foreign Trade Organizations, slows the necessary expansion of exports relative to imports causing the East to incur large debts.

SUGGESTED READING

Balassa, B. *European Economic Integration*. Amsterdam: North Holland, 1975. An assessment of the economic impact of the EEC.

Cooper, C. A. and Massell, B. F. "Towards a General Theory of Customs Unions for Developing Countries." *Journal of Political Economy,* October 1965.

Corden, W. M. "Economies of Scale and Customs Union Theory." *Journal of Political Economy,* March 1972.

Corden, W. M. "Monetary Integration." *Princeton Essays in International Finance* 93 (April 1972).

deVries, T. "On the Meaning and Future of the European Monetary System." *Princeton Essays in International Finance* 138 (September 1980).

Holzman, F. D. *International Trade Under Communism: Politics and Economics.* London: Macmillan, 1976. An excellent treatment of the basic issues.

Kemp, M. C. *A Contribution to the General Equilibrium Theory of Preferential Trading.* Amsterdam: North Holland, 1969. The pure theory of the subject.

Krauss, M. B. "Recent Developments in Customs Union Theory: An Interpretive Survey." *Journal of Economic Literature,* June 1972.

Machlup, F. *A History of Thought on Economic Integration.* New York: Columbia University Press, 1977. A useful summary of the literature.

McKinnon, R. I. *Money in International Exchange.* Oxford: Oxford University Press, 1979. Chapter 3 offers an excellent discussion of currency inconvertibility and eastern trade.

Rosefielde, S. "Factor Proportions and Economic Rationality in Soviet International Trade 1955–68." *American Economic Review,* September 1974. There is no Leontief Paradox for the USSR.

Swann, D. *The Economics of the Common Market.* 4th ed. London: Penguin, 1978. A description of the EEC.

Vanek, J. *General Equilibrium of International Discrimination.* Cambridge: Harvard University Press, 1965.

Viner, J. *The Customs Union Issue.* New York: Carnegie Endowment for International Peace, 1950. The classic treatment.

Wilczynski, J. *The Multinationals and East-West Relations.* London: Macmillan, 1976.

Epilogue

"When you get there, there is no there there."
—GERTRUDE STEIN

THREE SETS of global issues have emerged in this book. *East-West* relations, discussed in Chapter 12, involve exchanges between nations with fundamentally different economic systems (and with less-than-cordial political relations). The dominant consideration in *North-South* debate is, by contrast, that of distribution: what should the North concede in order to improve the lot of the South. Finally, the issues confronting the industrial nations in their relations with *each other* (North-North or West-West problems) are strongly colored by the consequences of extensive international interdependence. The interdependence between these essentially similar economies has emerged again and again in the course of our study. We now draw that study to a close by presenting an example of a type of international interdependence not yet mentioned, and with a discussion of a prominent attempt by the largest industrial countries jointly to resolve economic issues.

UNITED STATES ACID RAIN FALLS ON CANADA

This is a good example of a more direct form of international interdependence than those discussed thus far. Emissions of sulfur and of nitrogen oxides from industry in the United States midwest falls on the most populous parts of Canada in what is called "acid rain." The result is significant environmental damage to Canadian farmland and forests and to lakes, rivers, and their fish populations. Canada cannot directly control the actions of the responsible firms, and the United States is reluctant to incur a large financial cost for the benefit of foreign citizens. Thus the matter has become a sensitive political issue between the two nations. They agreed in

1980 to study crossborder pollution, and talks on the problem have begun. The roles of the two countries are reversed with regard to a Canadian decision to open a coal mine in British Columbia near the U.S border: some people fear that the mine will damage Glacier National Park, just over the border in Montana.

These are examples of *external economies and diseconomies,* which we studied in Chapter 6. That chapter discussed how a tariff on imports might be used to deal with externalities involving various groups or institutions *within* an economy. The distinctive feature about the present examples is that the externalities extend across national boundaries. Other examples include radio or television broadcasts that might be picked up in foreign lands and the pollution of bodies of water—such as the Mediterranean Sea—bordered by many countries.

THE ECONOMIC SUMMITS

Since 1975, annual summit meetings dealing with economic matters of mutual concern have been held by the national leaders of seven large industrial countries (the United States, Canada, Japan, Britain, France, West Germany, and Italy). The 1975 meeting in Rambouillet, France, was mentioned in Chapter 11: a compromise was reached on international monetary issues that allowed the present system of managed floating subsequently to be legalized. The London summit in 1977 revived the multilateral trade negotiations that then reached the Tokyo Round agreement discussed in Chapter 6. Energy issues were important during the 1978 Bonn summit, when the United States committed itself to the decontrol of domestic oil prices. Most of the summit meetings have been concerned at least in part with macroeconomic policies; thus the meetings have been addressed to the problems of international policy conflict discussed in Chapters 4, 8, and 9. The 1981 meeting in Ottawa accomplished little, but, with each participating nation having played host once, a second round of summits was decided upon. It commenced with the gathering at Versailles in 1982.

Appendices

Nothing adds such weight and dignity to a
book as an Appendix.

—Herodotus (Mark Twain)

A Survey of the Pure Theory
of International Trade

THIS SURVEY is intended for readers with a year or two of university-level mathematics, and it will be best appreciated by those who have also studied contemporary microeconomics. The corresponding chapter in the main text is indicated in parentheses after the title of each section of the survey, for the benefit of those who wish to coordinate the two. As in the text, an asterisk (*) indicates portions of the appendix—one section and several subsections—that are relatively more advanced and may be skipped without loss of continuity.

A.1. The National Income of a Trading Economy (Chapter 1)

THE TRANSFORMATION CURVE

Suppose that the domestic economy can produce two goods, cloth and wheat. Existing technology and factor supplies determine a production possibility frontier, or *transformation curve*, $S_C = T(S_W)$, where S_C denotes supply of cloth and S_W that of wheat. The curve is shown in Figure A.1. Point C_0 shows the supply of cloth if the home country specializes in it, W_0 is the analogous specialization output of wheat, and the transformation curve connects these two points. The derivative of this curve, $T'(S_W)$, is negative, indicating that producing more wheat requires producing less cloth.

NATIONAL INCOME

Denote world prices of cloth and wheat (in dollars) as P_C and P_W respectively. Then, if our economy produces S_C and S_W, its income will be

$$y = P_C S_C + P_W S_W. \tag{1}$$

The collection of S_C and S_W, which, for given P_C and P_W, all yield a particular level of income y in (1) form a straight line with slope $-P_W/P_C$. Such *budget lines* are shown by the dotted lines in the three panels of Figure A.1. Evidently increasing P_W relative to P_C makes a budget line steeper, whereas increasing y shifts the line away from the origin. Thus in order to maximize

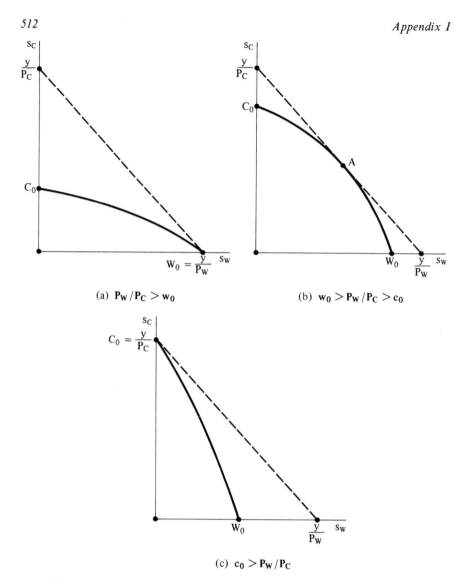

(a) $P_W/P_C > w_0$

(b) $w_0 > P_W/P_C > c_0$

(c) $c_0 > P_W/P_C$

Figure A.1. MAXIMIZING INCOME

its national income y, a trading economy should produce at that point on its transformation curve that pushes as far from the origin as possible a budget line with a slope reflecting actual world prices. This is shown in Figure A.1.

There are evidently three possibilities. Denote by w_0 the slope of $T(S_W)$ at W_0, its steepest spot, and by c_0 the slope at C_0—the flattest spot. Then if $P_W/P_C > w_0$, a budget line will be steeper than every point of the transformation curve, so the country can push its budget line as far out as possible, and so maximize its income, by producing at W_0. This is shown in panel (a) of Figure A.1. Similarly, if $P_W/P_C < c_0$ the budget line is flatter than $T(S_W)$ at every point and the country should specialize in cloth at C_0.

Finally, if $w_o > P_w/P_c > c_o$, the country should produce both goods at that point on its transformation curve just tangent to a budget line, as shown in panel (b).

The *national income function* records the highest income attainable for a country under different circumstances:

$$y(P_c, P_w; \ldots) = P_c S_c + P_w S_w. \tag{2}$$

As we have just seen, this highest income depends upon world prices plus the shape and position of the transformation curve. Thus y is a function of P_c, P_w, and whatever (...) determines $T(S_w)$.

A BASIC PROPERTY

Suppose a country is maximizing its national income by producing both goods, as in Figure A.1.(b). Then for a differential movement along the transformation curve:

$$P_c(dS_c) + P_w(dS_w) = 0. \tag{3}$$

Mathematically, (3) is the first-order condition for the solution to the problem of maximizing y subject to $S_c = T(S_w)$. Geometrically it is obvious from Figure A.1. (b), since at point A, where income is maximized, $dS_c/dS_w = T'(S_w) = -P_w/P_c$.

This property tells us something about our national income function. Differentiate (2):

$$\frac{\partial y}{\partial P_c} = S_c + \left[P_c \frac{dS_c}{dP_c} + P_w \frac{dS_w}{dP_c} \right] = S_c \tag{4}$$

by (3). Similarly, $\partial y/\partial P_w = S_w$.

HOW INCOME DEPENDS ON PRICES

In Figure A.2 below, we arbitrarily fix P_c and let P_w vary, recording how y varies in response. If $P_w < P_c c_o$, then the economy specializes in C, so that $y = P_c C_o$, which does not change as P_w changes. If, on the other hand, $P_w > P_c w_o$, the economy specializes in wheat so that $y = P_w W_o$, a straight line through the origin with slope W_o. Intermediate values of P_w imply production of both goods; since we know that $\partial y/\partial P_w = S_w$, y increases as P_w increases, and the slope of the y curve in Figure A.2 shows what S_w is. Thus if $P_w = P_w^A$ in the figure, $S_w = EB/AB$. Furthermore, between $P_c c_o$ and $P_c w_o$, the y curve increases at an *increasing* rate. This is because $\partial^2 y/\partial P_w^2 = \partial S_w/\partial P_w$, and it is clear from Figure A.1 that an increase in P_w (making the budget line steeper) results in an increase in S_w as the production point moves downward and to the right along the transformation curve.

Suppose that P_w^A is the autarkic equilibrium price, so that D shows

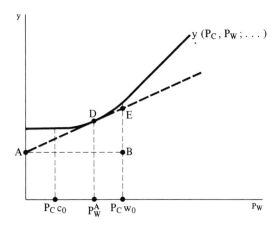

Figure A.2. How Income Depends on Prices

national income in autarky. The straight dashed line tangent to the y curve at D has a slope equal to autarkic production—and therefore consumption—of wheat. Thus this dashed line shows how much income is required, at each P_w, to purchase the goods actually consumed in autarky. Note that the y curve lies above this dashed line everywhere (except at the autarky point D), reflecting the gains from trade.

THE SIMPLE RICARDIAN MODEL

In the simple Ricardian model, $C_o = L/a_c$ and $W_o = L/a_w$ where L, a_c and a_w respectively denote the national labor supply and the amount of labor required to produce one unit of cloth and one unit of wheat. $T(S_w)$ is now a straight line, with slope $(-a_w/a_c)$. The national income curve is drawn in Figure A.3. In autarky $P_w = P_c a_w/a_c$, and y is represented by point D, regardless of where on the transformation curve production takes

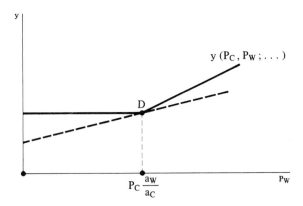

Figure A.3. THE SIMPLE RICARDIAN MODEL

place. The dashed line through D is drawn with a slope to reflect a hypothetical autarkic S_W.

PROBLEMS

A.1.1 Figure A.2 was drawn by holding P_C constant and allowing P_W to vary.
Derive an income curve by instead holding P_W constant and allowing P_C to vary.

A.1.2 Equation (4) holds for small (that is, differential) movements along the
transformation curve, when both goods are being produced. What can you say
about large movements? If only one good is initially produced?

A.2. The National Expenditure of a Trading Economy (Chapter 1)

UTILITY

Represent the tastes of an individual or a community by a set of
indifference curves, as discussed in section 8* of Chapter 1 and illustrated in
Figure A.4. For now we ignore any difficulties in treating a community in
this way. Number the indifference curves in some manner, with curves
further from the origin receiving higher numbers. (For example, draw a ray
through the origin and assign each curve the number equal to its distance
from the origin along this ray.) The *utililty* $u(D_C, D_W)$ of any consumption
combination—the number assigned to the indifference curve passing
through (D_C, D_W)—is a measure of the satisfaction derived from the consumption of D_C cloth and D_W wheat. Combinations with higher utility are
preferred to combinations with lower utility.

NATIONAL EXPENDITURE

If the community faces the prices P_C and P_W and consumes the quantities D_C and D_W, its total expenditure is

$$E = P_C D_C + P_W D_W.$$

Consider the problem of attaining a specified utility level, u_A, with minimum expenditure. Given the commodity prices, the problem is to find that
point on the indifference curve $u(D_C, D_W) = u_A$ that pushes a budget line
with slope $-P_W/P_C$ as close to the origin as possible. This is at point A in
Figure A.4, where the indifference curve and budget line are tangent to
each other; the required minimum expenditure is then determined by the
intersection of the budget line with either axis.

The *national expenditure function* records the minimum expenditure
necessary to achieve various utility levels under various prices:

$$E(P_C, P_W; u) = P_C D_C + P_W D_W \qquad (5)$$

where D_C and D_W are chosen as shown in Figure A.4.

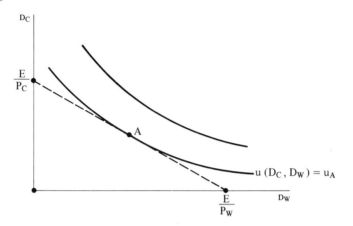

Figure A.4. MAXIMIZING UTILITY–MINIMIZING EXPENDITURE

A BASIC PROPERTY

Suppose that a country is enjoying the utility u_A at minimum expenditure, as shown in Figure A.4. Then for a differential movement along the indifference curve $u(D_C, D_W) = u_A$,

$$P_C(dD_C) + P_W(dD_W) = 0.\tag{6}$$

This is the first-order condition for the problem of minimizing E subject to the constraint $u(D_C, D_W) = u_A$. This condition is obvious from Figure A.4, since at point A, $dD_C/dD_W = -P_W/P_C$. Now differentiate (5):

$$\frac{\partial E}{\partial P_C} = D_C + \left[P_C\frac{dD_C}{dP_C} + P_W\frac{dD_W}{dP_C} \right] = D_C$$

by (6). Similarly, $\partial E/\partial P_W = D_W$.

HOW EXPENDITURE DEPENDS ON PRICES

In Figure A.5 below, we arbitrarily fix P_C, hold u equal to u_A, and let P_W vary, recording how E varies in response. Since $\partial E/\partial P_W = D_W$, E increases as P_W increases and the slope of the E curve always equals the consumption of wheat. Indeed E increases at a decreasing rate, because $\partial E/\partial P_W^2 = \partial D_W/\partial P_W$, and Figure A.4 shows that a rise in P_W, which makes the budget line steeper, reduces D_W, and increases D_C. If $P_W = P_W^A$ in Figure A. 5, $D_W = AD/BD$.

THE GAINS FROM TRADE

In Figure A.5, suppose that P_W^A equals the autarkic price of wine, and u_A is the utility enjoyed in autarky. Then the $E(P_C, P_W; u_A)$ curve shows, for

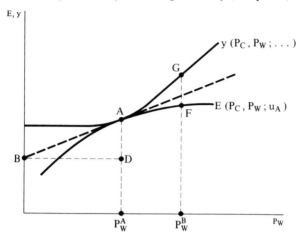

Figure A.5. How Expenditure Varies with Price: Autarkic Equilibrium

each value of P_W, the expenditure necessary to obtain the same utility as that experienced under autarky. The national income function $y(P_C, P_W...)$ shows national income at each price. At the autarkic price P_W^A of course $E = y$. Because of the curvature of the two functions, $y > E$ for every other P_W. This shows the gains from trade: at any price, national income is greater (equal at P_W^A) than the amount that must be spent at that price for the country to be as well off as in autarky. The gap is one way of measuring the gains from trade: at the prices P_W^B the country gains GF. Obviously the gains, according to this measure, are larger the more P_W differs from P_W^A.

MANY GOODS AND MANY CITIZENS*

Suppose that there are n goods. Let $p = (P_1, P_2, ..., P_n)$ denote the *vector* of commodity prices. Then $y(p, ...)$ can be defined as the national income function analogously to section A.1. It is easily seen that $\sum_{i=1}^{n} P_i(dS_i) = 0$ so that $\partial y / \partial P_i = S_i$ as before. In similar fashion, the expenditure function $E(p, u)$ follows as before, $\sum_{i=1}^{n} P_i(dD_i) = 0$ for given utility, and consequently $\partial E / \partial P_i = D_i$.

Of course different individuals have different tastes. This means that we should derive an expenditure function for each individual. Suppose that the community consists of m individuals and let $E^j(p, u^j)$ denote individual

---

* An asterisk indicates material that is relatively more advanced and may be skipped without loss of continuity.

j's expenditure function (derived as above) and u^j his utility. Let $U = (u^1, u^2, \ldots, u^m)$ be the *vector* of utilities of the citizens of this community. All citizens face the same commodity prices. Then we can define the community expenditure function

$$E(p, U) = \sum_{j=1}^{m} E^j(p, u^j).$$

Note that $\partial E/\partial P_i = \sum_{j=1}^{m} \partial E^j/\partial P_i = \sum_{j=1}^{m} D_i^j = D_i$, where D_i^j denotes individual *j*'s demand for good *i* and D_i denotes the total community demand.

THE GAINS FROM TRADE WITH MANY GOODS AND CITIZENS*

Let p^T denote the vector of free-trade prices, S^T and S^A the free trade and autarkic vectors of commodities produced, and D^A the autarkic vector of commodites consumed. Then

$$p^T. S^T = y(p^T, \ldots) \geq p^T. S^A$$

because[1] national income is maximized at price p^T when S^T is produced. But $S^A = D^A$ in autarky. Thus $y(p^T, \ldots) \geq p^T. D^A$. This means that the community *as a whole* can afford at free-trade prices to buy what it would consume under autarky. It does not imply that *each* consumer can afford at free-trade prices what she would buy in autarky. But, since the whole community can, there must be some system of lump-sum taxes and subsidies that, if implemented, would enable each individual citizen to purchase under free trade the same goods that she would consume in autarky. This would ensure that no one would be worse off in free trade; such is the meaning of the gains from trade.

THE LAW OF COMPARATIVE ADVANTAGE

Returning now to an environment of two goods and community indifference curves, point *A* in Figure A.6 below shows autarkic equilibrium, where $P_W^A/P_C^A = -T'(S_W)$. If the country moves to free trade, it will gain (unless the free-trade price equals the autarkic price), as we have seen, so that the community's utility will rise, say from u_A to u_T. This shifts the expenditure function upward as shown in Figure A.6, with $E = y$ at the free-trade equilibrium. If the free-trade relative price of wheat exceeds the autarkic price, this equilibrium will be at a point such as *B* in the figure. At *B* the *y* curve is steeper than the *E* curve, so that $S_W > D_W$, that is, wheat is

---

* An asterisk indicates material that is relatively more advanced and may be skipped without loss of continuity.

[1] Here *p. S* denotes the inner product of the vectors *p* and *S*: $\sum_{i=1}^{n} P_i S_i$.

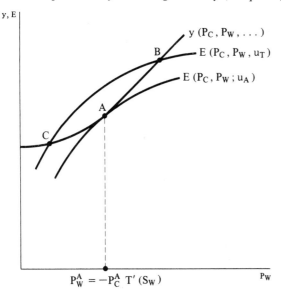

Figure A.6. THE LAW OF COMPARATIVE ADVANTAGE

exported. Also y is steeper at B than at A, so that S_W has risen: resources have shifted from cloth production to wheat production. If, on the other hand, the free-trade relative price of wheat is less than the autarkic price, equilibrium is at a point such as C and these conclusions are reversed. Finally, note that whatever the home country exports in equilibrium the foreign country must import. Thus if the home country is at a point such as B, the foreign country must be at a point such as C in the foreign analog to Figure A.6, and vice versa. This implies that the free-trade relative price lies between the autarkic prices of the two countries, and that the relative sizes of the latter predict the direction of trade.

COMPARATIVE ADVANTAGE WITH MANY GOODS*

Once again allow many goods, but retain community indifference curves (or lump-sum transfers so that no one loses from free trade relative to autarky). Then the vector of commodities consumed under free trade, D^T, yields at least as much satisfaction as obtained under autarky, so that $E(p^A, u_A) \leq p^A . D^T$. Now $E(p^A, u_A) = y(p^A, ...) \geq p^A . S^T$. Thus $p^A . D^T \geq p^A . S^T$ so that

$$p^A . (D^T - S^T) \geq 0.$$

*An asterisk indicates material that is relatively more advanced and may be skipped without loss of continuity.

But in free trade $p^T.(D^T - S^T) = 0$ so that

$$(p^A - p^T).(D^T - S^T) \geq 0. \tag{7}$$

$(D^T - S^T)$ is the vector of imports (positive components) and exports (negative components). Letting an asterisk refer to the foreign country, the same logic establishes the foreign analog of (7).

$$(p^{A*} - p^{T*}).(D^{T*} - S^{T*}) \geq 0. \tag{8}$$

Note that what the home country imports the foreign country exports: $(D^T - S^T) = (S^{T*} - D^{T*})$. Thus subtracting (8) from (7) gives

$$(p^A - p^{A*}).(D^T - S^T) \geq 0. \tag{9}$$

Finally, $p^A. S^A = y(p^A, \dots) \geq p^A. S^T$ and $p^T. S^T = y(p^T, \dots) \geq p^T. S^A$. Thus

$$(p^A - p^T).(S^A - S^T) \geq 0. \tag{10}$$

(7) and (8) say that, in each country, imports are positively *correlated* with lower trade prices relative to autarky; (9) says that imports are positively correlated with lower foreign autarkic prices, relative to domestic, and (10) says that output reductions are positively correlated with lower trade prices relative to autarky. Thus the basic two-commodity conclusions about comparative advantage hold *on average* in the multi-commodity environment. They need not hold on a commodity-by-commodity basis.[2]

AN IMPROVEMENT[3] IN THE TERMS OF TRADE*

We have seen how free trade is better than no trade. As shown in the text, and as we shall see later in this Appendix, free trade need not be as good as restricted trade, from a strictly nationalistic point of view. In what sense does a terms of trade "improvement" make a country better off?

Suppose that a country is freely trading at the price vector p^T and that, for some reason, international prices change to $p^{T'}$. We shall call this a terms of trade improvement if, at the new prices, the value of the country's original production exceeds that of its original consumption: $p^{T'}. S^T \geq p^{T'}. D^T$. What follows from this? At the new equilibrium $E(p^{T'}, u_{T'}) = y(p^{T'}, \dots)$, and of course $y(p^{T'}, \dots) \geq p^{T'}. S^T$. Thus, from our defini-

*An asterisk indicates material that is relatively more advanced and may be skipped without loss of continuity.

[2] The basic results of this subsection may be found in A. Deardoff, "The General Validity of the Law of Comparative Advantage," *Journal of Political Economy, 88* (1980), 941–57, and in Dixit and Norman, *Theory of International Trade,* 1980 (London: Cambridge University Press), 94, 95.

[3] This subsection depends upon Krueger and Sonnenschein, "The Terms of Trade, the Gains from Trade, and Price Divergence," *International Economic Review, 8* (1967), 121–27.

tion of a terms of trade improvement,

$$E(p^{T'}, u_T) > p^{T'}. D^T.$$

Thus after the improvement the country can afford what it consumed before and still have something left over. The country must be better off (as always, this means, if we drop community indifference curves, that some system of lump-sum transfers can make everyone in the community better off: the gainers gain more in this sense than the losers lose).

PROBLEMS

A.2.1 Suppose a country has the utility function $u(D_C, D_W) = D_C{}^\alpha D_W{}^{1-\alpha}$ for some number α between zero and one. Derive a formula for $E(P_C, P_W; u)$. Verify the properties discussed in the text.

A.2.2 Derive $E(P_C, P_W; u)$ if consumers *always* demand wheat and cloth in equal amounts. If $u(D_C, D_W) = D_C + D_W$.

A.3. International Equilibrium (Chapter 2)

EQUILIBRIUM CONDITIONS

Suppose that two countries trade cloth and wheat. Each country's expenditure must equal its income (Walras's Law):

$$P_C D_C + P_W D_W = P_C S_C + P_W S_W \tag{11}$$

$$P_C D_C^* + P_W D_W^* = P_C S_C^* + P_W S_W^*. \tag{12}$$

Call the home country the one that ends up importing wheat and accordingly define domestic import demand and export supply as $M \equiv D_W - S_W$ and $X \equiv S_C - D_C$. The foreign country must have the reciprocal trade pattern, so define $M^* = D_C^* - S_C^*$ and $X^* = S_W^* - D_W^*$. Only relative prices count, so define a unit of cloth to be one dollar's worth. This ensures that P_C always equals unity, and can therefore be dropped, and that P_W—which we now denote simply as P—equals the relative price of wheat in terms of cloth. Making use of the conventions, we can rewrite (11) and (12) as

$$PM = X \tag{13}$$

$$\left(\frac{1}{P}\right) M^* = X^*. \tag{14}$$

In equilibrium the world demand for each good must equal the world supply, or each country's demand for imports must equal the other's supply of exports:

$$M = X^* \tag{15}$$

$$M^* = X . \tag{16}$$

Equations (15) and (16) are the equilibrium conditions in the wheat and cloth markets respectively, but they are in fact redundant: either can be derived from the other by using Walras's Law, (13) and (14). Thus there is only one independent equilibrium condition. This is conventionally expressed by substituting (14) into (15) to obtain

$$PM = M^*. \tag{17}$$

Equation (17) is the algebraic analog to the intersection of two offer curves in the geometry of Chapter 2.

ELASTICITY

By definition, $M(P) = D_W(P, E(P, u)) - S_W(P)$, where $E(P, u) = y(P)$. As usual, demand depends upon relative prices and spending (income) while supply depends upon relative prices. The elasticity of import demand, e, is defined as $- (P/M)(dM/dP)$. Differentiate the definition of $M(P)$, noting that $E = y$,

$$\frac{dM}{dP} = \left.\frac{\partial D_W}{\partial P}\right|_E + \frac{\partial D_W}{\partial E}\frac{\partial y}{\partial P} - \frac{dS_W}{dP} \tag{18}$$

where $\left.\dfrac{\partial D_W}{\partial P}\right|_E$ means that E is kept constant under the differentiation. Now differentiating $D_W(P, E(P, u))$ gives

$$\left.\frac{\partial D_W}{\partial P}\right|_u = \left.\frac{\partial D_W}{\partial P}\right|_E + \frac{\partial D_W}{\partial E}\frac{\partial E}{\partial P}. \tag{19}$$

Substitute (18) into (19) and rearrange to obtain

$$\frac{dM}{dP} = \left[\left.\frac{\partial D_W}{\partial P}\right|_u - \frac{dS_W}{dP} \right] - \frac{\partial D_W}{\partial E}\left[\frac{\partial E}{\partial P} - \frac{\partial y}{\partial P} \right]. \tag{20}$$

The first term in brackets is the *substitution effect*, composed of a demand component and a supply component. As we saw in section A.2, the demand component

$$\left.\frac{\partial D_W}{\partial P}\right|_u = \frac{\partial^2 E}{\partial P^2} < 0, \text{ and section A.1 showed that } dS_W/dP = \partial^2 y/\partial P^2 > 0.$$

Thus the sign of the substitution effect is unambiguous: it causes the demand for imports to fall as they become more expensive.

The rest of the right hand side of (20) is the *income effect*. We know that $\partial E/\partial P = D_W$ and $\partial y/\partial P = S_W$, so the bracketed portion is just M.

Thus the strength and sign of the income effect depends upon the magnitude and direction of trade: near autarky M is almost zero so that the substitution effect necessarily dominates. $\partial D_w/\partial E$ measures how the demand for imports (wheat) increases as expenditure rises. One normally expects this to be positive, so that the income effect will work in the same direction as the substitution effect, but it could be negative for some goods (which are called *inferior*). In the latter case the income and substitution effects work at cross purposes. To put (20) in elasticity terms, multiply both sides by $-(P/M)$:

$$-\frac{P}{M}\frac{dM}{DP} = \left[-\frac{P}{M}\frac{\partial D_w}{\partial P}\bigg|_u + \frac{P}{M}\frac{dS_w}{dP} \right] + P\frac{\partial D_w}{\partial E},$$

which we can represent as

$$e = c + s + m \tag{21}$$

where $c = -\dfrac{P}{M}\dfrac{\partial D_w}{\partial P}\bigg|_u$

is the demand substitution elasticity,

$s = \dfrac{P}{M}\dfrac{dS_w}{dP}$ is the supply substitution elasticity, and

$m = P\dfrac{\partial D_w}{\partial E}$, representing the income effect, is the *marginal propensity to import:* the fraction of an increase in expenditure that is devoted to imports. Note than 1-m, the fraction of an increase in spending that is *not* spent on imports (wheat), is the fraction spent on exportables (cloth). Thus if both wheat and cloth are normal, m will lie between zero and one; it will be negative if wheat is inferior and greater than one if cloth is inferior. (Both goods can not be inferior).

Differentation of (13) yields[4] $\hat{P} + \hat{M} = \hat{X}$, and dividing both sides by $-\hat{P}$ in turn leads to $e - 1 = f$, where $f = -\hat{X}/\hat{P}$, the elasticity of export supply. Thus from (21)

$$f = c + s + (m - 1) \tag{22}$$

The supply elasticity f has the same substitution terms as does e but a different income term. We know that $1 - m$ is the fraction of an increase in expenditure that is spent on exportables. Now any increase in domestic spending on exportables is a *reduction* in exports; thus $m - 1[= -(1 - m)]$ is the *marginal propensity to export*. Note that if neither good is inferior, income and substitution effects reinforce each other in (21) but work at cross purposes in (22).

---

[4] For any variable x, the notation $\hat{x}$ means $(dx)/x$, or $d(\log x)$.

STABILITY OF EQUILIBRIUM

Let P_o denote the equilibrium prices, or solution to (17),

$$P_o M(P_o) = M^* \left(\frac{1}{P_o} \right).$$

We write M^* as a function of $(1/P_o)$ because the latter is the relative price of cloth, the foreign import. If $P \neq P_o$ markets do not clear; we hypothesize that price is rising whenever demand exceeds supply. This disequilibrium hypothesis can be represented by the differential equation (DH):

$$\dot{P} = M(P) - X^* \left(\frac{1}{P} \right). \tag{DH}$$

If $P = P_o$, $\dot{P} = 0$ so the international economy is stationary. The stability question is whether (DH) will move P toward P_o if it is not there initially. The stability condition that assures this is that a rise of P above P_o reduces excess demand, so that in (DH) $\dot{P}$ becomes negative:

$$\frac{dM(P)}{dP} - \frac{dX^* \left(\frac{1}{P} \right)}{dP} < 0. \tag{SC}$$

The role of the stability condition (SC) is demonstrated in Figure A.7. In panel (a), (SC) is satisfied and in panel (b) it is violated. In the former, P is moving toward P_o whenever, as at P_A or P_B, it is not initially there; in panel (b), P is moving away from P_o when not in equilibrium.

We evaluate (SC) at equilibrium P_o and transform it to elasticity terms by multiplying[5] it by $P_o/M(P_o)$:

$$0 > \frac{P_o}{M(P_o)} \left[\frac{dM(P_o)}{dP_o} - \frac{dX^* \left(\frac{1}{P_o} \right)}{dP} \right] = -e - f^*$$

Since $f^* = e^* - 1$, (SC) can be written

$$e + e^* > 1, \tag{23}$$

which is called the *Marshall-Lerner condition*. We can gain some insight into when the condition is likely to hold by substituting the decomposition (21) into (23):

$$(c + c^* + s + s^*) + (m + m^* - 1) > 0. \tag{24}$$

[5] Recall that $M(P_o) = X^* \left(\frac{1}{P_o} \right)$ and that $\left(\frac{\hat{1}}{P} \right) = -\hat{P}$.

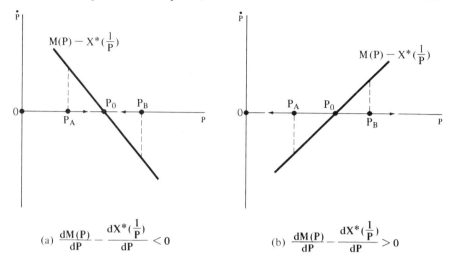

(a) $\dfrac{dM(P)}{dP} - \dfrac{dX^*(\frac{1}{P})}{dP} < 0$ (b) $\dfrac{dM(P)}{dP} - \dfrac{dX^*(\frac{1}{P})}{dP} > 0$

Figure A.7. THE STABILITY CONDITION

1. The substitution elasticities are always positive. Thus a greater consumer willingness to substitute between the two goods (high c's) and a greater ease of altering production patterns (high s's) are conducive to stability.

2. A low volume of trade renders the substitution effects dominant relative to the income effects—this is reflected in the fact that M appears in the denominators of the definitions of the c's and s's but does not enter that of the m's. Again stability is therefore more likely.

3. The home and foreign marginal propensities to spend on wheat, the home import, are m and $1 - m^*$. Thus stability is assured if each country has at least as large a marginal propensity to spend on the good it imports as does the other country on that same good ($m \geq - 1 - m^*$ or, equivalently, $m^* \geq 1 - m$).

4. In particular, (24) must hold if the two countries have identical tastes in the sense of equal marginal propensities to spend on the same good ($m = 1 - m^*$). This assumption is made in the Heckscher-Ohlin-Samuelson model and other cases where international taste differences are deemed unimportant. Thus the Heckscher-Ohlin theorem derived in this way describes a stable equilibrium.

The revelance for stability of the Marshall-Lerner condition depended upon the disequilibrium hypothesis (DH), and the latter is quite arbitrary since it was not derived from any detailed theory of how people behave outside of equilibrium[6]. But the condition is useful in another way. It measures the sensitivity of world excess demand to price fluctuations. Thus one would expect it to be central to an analysis of any problem in which changes in international prices play a significant role. This is indeed the case, as will become apparent when we analyze commerical policy in section A.6.

PROBLEMS

A.3.1 Why can not both cloth and wheat be inferior?

A.3.2 For any variables x and y, show: $\left(\dfrac{\hat{1}}{x}\right) = \hat{x}$, $(\widehat{xy}) = \hat{x} + \hat{y}$, and $(\widehat{x/y}) = \hat{x} - \hat{y}$.

A.3.3 Find an explicit solution to the differential equation (DH) and use this solution to derive the stability condition (SC).

A.3.4 Derive the elasticity formulas for an economy with the tastes of Problem **A.2.1** and a Ricardian technology. If instead S_C and S_W cannot be varied at all.

A.4. Factor Endowments (Chapter 3)

Thus far the transformation curve has been simply a datum for each country. We now move on to the 2×2 Heckscher-Ohlin-Samuelson production structure discussed in Chapter 3.

PRODUCTION COSTS

Each country has a fixed endowment of capital (K) and labor (L) used to produce the two goods. Firms choose the technique of production that costs the least, at the prevailing wage (w) and rent (r). In Figure A.8 point A on the $S_W = 1$ isoquant depicts the least-cost technique for producing each unit of wheat if the factor prices are as indicated by the slope of the budget line that has been drawn. The techique involves using a_{LW} units of labor and a_{KW} units of capital to produce each unit of wheat at the resulting cost $C_W = w a_{LW} + r a_{KW}$, which can be measured off the diagram as indicated.

The *unit cost function* for wheat records the least cost, determined as above, for producing one unit:

$$C_W(w, r) = w a_{LW}(w, r) + r a_{KW}(w, r) \tag{25}$$

---

[6] However it can be shown that the Marshall-Lerner condition is also relevant to several alternative disequilibrium hypotheses.

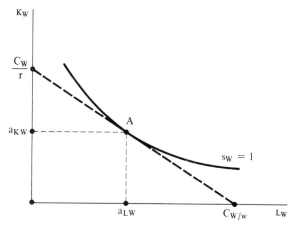

Figure A.8. Minimizing Cost

and analogously for the cloth industry

$$C_C(w, r) = w\,a_{LC}(w, r) + r\,a_{KC}(w, r). \tag{26}$$

The a's are written as functions of the factor prices because the latter determine what the least-cost technique is, as shown in Figure A.8.

A BASIC PROPERTY

Suppose that a wheat firm is operating at minimum cost. Then for a differential movement along the isoquant:

$$w\,(da_{LW}) + r\,(da_{KW}) = 0. \tag{27}$$

This is the first-order condition for minimizing cost subject to $S_W = 1$ and is obvious from Figure A.8, since at A, $da_{KW}/da_{LW} = -(w/r)$. If we now differentiate (25):

$$\frac{\partial C_W}{\partial w} = a_{LW} + \left[w\frac{\partial a_{LW}}{\partial w} + r\frac{\partial a_{KW}}{\partial w} \right] = a_{LW}.$$

Similarly, $\partial C_W/\partial r = a_{KW}, \partial C_C/\partial w = a_{LC}$, and $\partial C_C/\partial r = a_{KC}$.

ISOCOST CURVES

In equilibrium profits are driven to zero, so that the price of each good is no greater than its cost. Figure A.9 below shows isocost curves for each industry (combinations of w and r for which the minimum cost of production is constant) where cost equals price, so that the curves are the graphs of

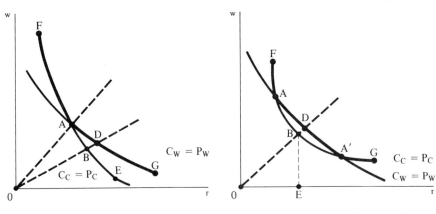

(a) No factor–intensity reversals.   (b) One factor–intensity reversal.

Figure A.9. Isocost Curves

$C_W(w, r) = P_W$ and $C_C(w, r) = P_C$. The slope of such a curve at any point equals minus the capital-labor ratio that that industry would use at the indicated factor prices (proof: the slope of $C_W(w, r) = P_W$ is $(dw)/dr = -(\partial C_W/\partial r)/(\partial C_W/\partial w) = -a_{KW}/a_{LW}$, which is the capital-labor ratio). In panel (a), for each wage-rental ratio–indicated by the slope of a ray through the origin–the cloth curve is steeper than the wheat curve, indicating that cloth is relatively capital intensive. Panel (b) shows a factor intensity reversal. The cloth curve has the same slope at B as does the wheat curve at D. For wage-rental ratios greater than BE/OE cloth is relatively capital intensive; at smaller wage-rental ratios wheat is capital intensive.

PRODUCTION EQUILIBRIUM

If both goods are produced in equilibrium, $P_W = C_W$ and $P_C = C_C$, so that w and r must be given by the intersection of the two isocost curves, as at A in Figure A.9. The slope of each curve at A shows the capital-labor ratio employed in each sector. Now $K = K_W + K_C$ and $L = L_W + L_C$, where K_W is the amount of capital employed in the wheat industry, and so forth. Thus

$$\frac{K}{L} = \frac{L_W}{L_W + L_C}\frac{K_W}{L_W} + \frac{L_C}{L_W + L_C}\frac{K_C}{L_C} = \lambda_{LW}\left(\frac{a_{KW}}{a_{LW}}\right) + \lambda_{LC}\left(\frac{a_{KC}}{a_{LC}}\right) \qquad (28)$$

where $\lambda_{LW} = L_W/L$, the fraction of the total labor force used in the wheat industry, and analogously for λ_{LC}. Clearly $\lambda_{LW} + \lambda_{LC} = 1$, so that (28) says that the economy-wide capital-labor ratio is a *weighted average* of the two factor intensities.

But what if K/L is not a weighted average of the capital-labor ratios employed in the two sectors at A, that is, if K/L is either larger than the slope of both curves at that point or else smaller than both slopes? Suppose that it is smaller, and equal to, say, the slope of C_W at D in Figure A.9 (a) and the slope of C_C at E. If w and r were as indicated by point E, $P_C = C_C$ but $P_W > C_W$, because E is below the $C_W = P_W$ curve so that cost is less than P_W. This means that E cannot be an equilibrium as wheat producers would earn positive profits. But D is an equilibrium because here $P_W = C_W$ and $P_C < C_C$: the economy specializes to wheat, as the unprofitable cloth industry is shut down. In similar manner, high capital-labor endowment ratios result in specialization in cloth, with w and r as indicated by that point (somewhere above A) where the $C_C = P_C$ curve has a slope equal to the endowment ratio.

Thus equilibrium always lies on the portion of the two isocost curves lying furthest from the origin. Such an outer envelope, known as the *factor-price frontier,* is distinguished by thick lines in Figure A.9: *FADG* in panel (a) and *FADA'G* in panel (b). The frontier consists of smooth segments, where only one good is produced, and a kink, where both industries operate. Factor intensity reversals allow the possibility of multiple kinks.

FACTOR-PRICE EQUALIZATION

Suppose that the home and foreign countries have identical technologies and freely trade, so that they also have identical commodity prices. Then the two countries will have the same pair of isocost curves. Assume for a moment that there is no factor intensity reversal. The equilibrium prices that are established for cloth and wheat must imply an intersection of the two isocost curves: otherwise both countries would necessarily specialize to the good represented by the outer curve, and the other good could not be produced at all. Thus both countries are represented by a diagram like Figure A.9(a).

If both countries produce both goods they are both at A and so have identical factor prices. If one or both countries specializes, they cannot both be at A and must have distinct factor prices. Whether or not both countries are at A depends upon whether both have factor-endowment ratios between the slopes of the two isocost curves at A.

Factor-price equalization is basically a matter of similarity in factor endowments. The equilibrium commodity prices that are established must be such as to leave one of the countries on the wheat isocost curve at A or above and the other country on the cloth curve at A or below; otherwise both countries would specialize to the same good and the world would have none of the other. Thus the closer the endowments of the two countries are to each other, the closer the countries must both be to point A.

If we now allow factor intensity reversals and turn to Figure A.9 (b), the above argument still holds. The only change is that factor-price equalization is no longer identified with nonspecialization in both countries, since one country could be at point A and the other at A' with different factor prices. But note that the two countries must in this case have quite different relative factor endowments, emphasizing the crucial role of similarities in the latter.

THE STOLPER-SAMUELSON THEOREM

Suppose that a country produces both goods, with factor prices as indicated by point A in Figure A.10 below. Now suppose that the price of cloth, the capital-intensive good, rises from P_C to P_C'. This shifts the cloth isocost curve outward in the proportion of the price rise; thus the figure shows a price increase in the proportion AB/OA. At B the C_C curve has the same slope as at A and w, r and P_C are all greater by an equal percentage, so that their relative magnitudes are unaltered.

P_W has not changed, so the new equilibrium is at A'. Since the wheat isocost curve slopes down, w is lower at A' than A: the wage has fallen. Since the cloth isocost curve slopes down, r is greater at A' than B: the rent has increased by a greater proportion than has P_C. Thus the rent rises relative to the prices of both goods and the wage falls relative to the prices of both goods.

To see the theorem algebraically, set $P_C = C_C(w, r)$ in (25) and $P_W = C_W(w, r)$ in (26) and differentiate both equations.

$$dP_C = (dw) a_{LC} + (dr) a_{KC} + [w(da_{LC}) + r(da_{KC})]$$

$$dP_W = (dw) a_{LW} + (dr) a_{KW} + [w(da_{LW}) + r(da_{KW})].$$

From (27), and its cloth analog, both bracketed terms vanish. Dividing each equation by its respective commodity price and manipulating just a little gives

$$\hat{P}_C = \theta_{LC}\, \hat{w} + \theta_{KC}\, \hat{r} \tag{29}$$

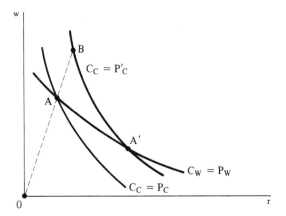

Figure A.10. THE STOLPER-SAMUELSON THEOREM

$$\hat{P}_W = \theta_{LW}\,\hat{w} + \theta_{KW}\,\hat{r} \tag{30}$$

where $\theta_{LC} = w\,a_{LC}/P_C = w\,a_{LC}S_C/P_C S_C$, the share of wages in the total earnings of the cloth industry. The other θ's are defined analogously so that θ_{KC}, for example, denotes the share of capital rents in the cloth industry. Thus $\theta_{LC} + \theta_{KC} = 1$ and $\theta_{LW} + \theta_{KW} = 1$. Equation (29) then says that $\hat{P}_C$ is a *weighted average* of $\hat{w}$ and $\hat{r}$ and thus lies between the two factor price changes. Equation (30) likewise says that $\hat{P}_W$ is bounded by $\hat{w}$ and $\hat{r}$. It is easy to see that cloth is relatively capital intensive if $\theta_{KC} > \theta_{KW}$ (or $\theta_{LW} > \theta_{LC}$). Then (29) and (30) imply that

$$\hat{r} > \hat{P}_C > \hat{P}_W > \hat{w}$$

when cloth becomes relatively more expensive ($\hat{P}_C > \hat{P}_W$), and that

$$\hat{w} > \hat{P}_W > \hat{P}_C > \hat{r}$$

when wheat becomes relatively more expensive. A change in relative commodity prices always increases the real reward of the factor intensive to the good whose relative price has increased and reduces the real reward of the other factor.

The Stolper-Samuelson theorem concerns real factor rewards. It says something about income distribution to the extent that different groups in society derive income from different factors. If every individual supplied capital and labor services in the same proportion, the Stolper-Samuelson analysis would be irrelevant to income distribution.

DUALITY

In section A.1 we wrote the national income function as $y(P_C, P_W \dots)$ to indicate that income was sensitive to whatever determines the transformation curve. But now that curve is determined by a country's factor endowment, so we have $y(P_C, P_W; K, L)$. Since each factor is paid the value of its marginal product, $\partial y/\partial K = r$ (and $\partial y/\partial L = w$).

Recall that $\partial y/\partial P_C = S_C$. Taking second derivatives,

$$\frac{\partial^2 y}{\partial K \partial P_C} = \frac{\partial r}{\partial P_C} \quad \text{and} \quad \frac{\partial^2 y}{\partial P_C \partial K} = \frac{\partial S_C}{\partial K}.$$

But $\partial^2 y/\partial K \partial P_C = \partial^2 y/\partial P_C \partial K$ so that

$$\frac{\partial r}{\partial P_C} = \frac{\partial S_C}{\partial K} \tag{31}$$

and similarly for other combinations of factors and goods. A rise in a commodity price produces the same effect on a factor reward as a rise in the endowment of that factor would produce upon the output of the commodity. The relation between goods prices and factor rewards is the turf of the Stolper-Samuelson theorem, whereas the Rybczynski analysis concerns the relation between endowments and outputs. *Reciprocity relations* such as (31) link the two.

We can also now obtain an alternative interpretation of our national income function $y(P_C, P_W; K, L)$. We defined y as the maximum income obtainable when goods that can be produced from K and L are evaluated at P_C and P_W. But y can also be regarded as the minimum that must be spent on K and L if factor prices are to leave commodity costs no lower than P_C and P_W. To understand this, return to Figure A.9(a) and suppose that, for the given P_C, P_W, K and L, point D denotes equilibrium. Then the slope of the factor-price frontier at D equals $-K/L$. Thus we can think of ourselves as reaching D by pushing a straight line with this slope as close to the origin as possible while still touching the factor-price frontier. In other words, D denotes the combination of w and r that minimizes $wL + rK$ subject to the condition that w and r not lie below the factor-price frontier, that is, that $C_W(w, r) \geq P_W$ and $C_C(w, r) \geq P_C$.

THE RYBCZYNSKI THEOREM

In equilibrium each factor is fully employed by the two industries:

$$K = a_{KC}(w, r) S_C + a_{KW}(w, r) S_W \tag{32}$$

$$L = a_{LC}(w, r) S_C + a_{LW}(w, r) S_W. \tag{33}$$

These relations are drawn in Figure A.11 for given wages and rents, and therefore fixed a's. The line labeled L is the graph of (33) for the given labor force L and the fixed a's. The slope of this line is $-a_{LW}/a_{LC}$. The K line analogously represents (32), and the fact that the L line is steeper reflects an assumption that cloth is relatively capital intensive. Point A shows equilibrium outputs of the two goods. (Since both industries are operating, the assumed capital-labor endowment ratio must be between the slopes of the two isocost curves in the pertinent version of Figure A.10.)

Now suppose that, at unchanged commodity prices, K is increased. If the endowment change is not large enough to induce specialization, w and r will not alter, by the factor-price equalization theorem, and therefore the a's remain fixed. The effect of the increase in K is simply to shift the graph of (32) outward; Figure A.10 shows a rise in K in the proportion AB/OA. If wheat and cloth output were to rise proportionally with K, production would have to shift from point A to B. But instead it shifts to C, the new point of intersection. Since C is above B, the output of cloth, the capital-intensive commodity, has risen in greater proportion than has the stock of capital; since C is to the left of A, the output of wheat has fallen.

To see the situation algebraically, differentiate (32) and (33), remembering that the a's are fixed.

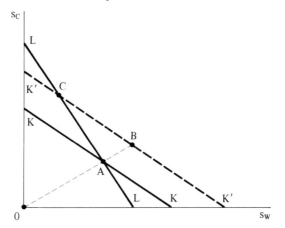

Figure A.11. THE RYBCZYNSKI THEOREM

$$dK = a_{KC}(dS_C) + a_{KW}(dS_W)$$

$$dL = a_{LC}(dS_C) + a_{LW}(dS_W).$$

Dividing each equation by its respective factor endowment and manipulating just a little gives

$$\hat{K} = \lambda_{KC}\,\hat{S}_C + \lambda_{KW}\,\hat{S}_W \tag{34}$$

$$\hat{L} = \lambda_{LC}\,\hat{S}_C + \lambda_{LW}\,\hat{S}_W \tag{35}$$

where $\lambda_{KC} = a_{KC} S_C / K$, the fraction of the nation's capital stock used in the cloth industry, and analogously for the other λ's. Note that $\lambda_{KC} + \lambda_{KW} = 1$, so that (34) says that $\hat{K}$ is a weighted average of $\hat{S}_C$ and $\hat{S}_W$, and similarly for (35). As in the previous subsection, we can easily show that, if cloth is relatively capital intensive,

$$\hat{S}_C > \hat{K} > \hat{L} > \hat{S}_W$$

when $\hat{K} > \hat{L}$, and

$$\hat{S}_W > \hat{L} > \hat{K} > \hat{S}_C$$

when $\hat{L} > \hat{K}$.

THE HECKSCHER-OHLIN THEOREM

Increases in the wage relative to the rent accompany increases in the relative price of the labor intensive good, by the Stolper-Samuelson theorem. Thus if two countries are in autarky, share a common technology, and are not separated by a factor intensity reversal, the country with the lower wage-rental ratio must have the lower relative autarkic price of the labor intensive good. If we define labor abundance to mean a relatively low autarkic wage-rental ratio, this gives us the *price version* of the Heckscher-Ohlin theorem: each country has a comparative advantage in that good relatively intensive in the use of the country's relatively abundant factor. (This is called the price version because factor abundance is defined in terms of autarkic factor prices.)

When can the pattern of trade be predicted on the basis of *physical* factor endowments? Suppose two countries with identical technology and no separating factor intensity reversal enter into free trade. The commodity prices that are established must then yield a situation as illustrated in Figure A.9 (a); since both goods must be produced in equilibrium, prices must be such that the two isocost curves intersect, and also such that one country produces at A or above and the other at A or below. Suppose first that not both countries are nonspecialized, that is, they are not both[7] at point A. Suppose it is because one of the countries is at A or above and specialized to cloth. This must be the capital-abundant country, since each point above A has a steeper slope than all points below. Since this country specializes to cloth it must export it, with the other country exporting wheat. Thus each country exports the good intensive in the country's relatively abundant factor. The argument is similar if we suppose instead that a country is at A or below and specialized to wheat.

Now suppose that both countries produce both goods and are at A. Then factor prices are equalized and the countries employ similar techniques. If, for example, the home country is relatively capital abundant in a physical sense, the Rybczynski theorem tells us that $S_C/S_W > S_C^*/S_W^*$. To proceed further we assume the two countries have similar tastes in the sense that, when they face identical prices they consume the two goods in identical proportions, that is $D_C/D_W = D_C^*/D_W^*$. These ratios in turn must equal $(S_C + S_C^*)/(S_W + S_w^*)$ because the world consumption of each good necessarily equals world supply. Thus

$$S_C/S_W > D_C/D_W = (S_C + S_C^*)/(S_W + S_W^*) = D_C^*/D_W^* > S_C^*/S_W^*.$$

The first inequality says that the home country exports cloth and imports wheat, and the last inequality says the opposite about the foreign country. Thus we have the *quantity* version of the Heckscher-Ohlin theorem: a country will export the good intensive in the factor that is (physically) relatively abundant.

The price version has the disadvantage that it requires knowledge of autarkic prices, whereas the quantity version depends upon physical en-

---

[7] It could be that one of the countries is specialized but nonetheless at A, if its endowment just equals the slope of one of the isocost curves at A. The following argument also applies to such a case.

dowments that can be measured in either free trade or autarky. But the price version says nothing about demands, whereas the quantity version requires international similarity whenever endowment differences are small enough to permit factor-price equalization.

INTERSECTORAL FACTOR IMMOBILITY (SECTION 13* OF CHAPTER 6)

The Heckscher-Ohlin-Samuelson model has dominated trade theory for most of the last thirty years. But for about seventy years before that economists had put great stress on the degrees of factor mobility between sectors when analyzing the internal effects of international trade. This earlier analysis is now being resurrected, and given contemporary expression, largely in response to concern about how people actually perceive their interests to be linked to price changes. This was discussed in sections 4 and 13* of Chapter 6.

The degree of mobility varies between factors and is also sensitive to the relevant time horizon, as pointed out in the text. This variability is often captured in the literature by adding to the H.O.S. model the assumption that one of the factors is sector specific, while the other remains fully mobile between industries. Call the mobile factor labor and the specific factor capital. Since there is still a single labor market there will still be a single wage, in each country, but the market for cloth capital is now disjoint from the market for wheat capital, so rents in the two sectors need not be the same. Let r_C denote the rent of cloth capital and r_W that of wheat capital.

The isocost curves in Figure A.12 below have the same meaning as before: these curves are derived from isoquants independently of factor mobility. The intersection A will be the equilibrium if the capital-labor ratio lies between the slopes of the two curves at A, *and* if the two factors can be allocated as required between the two sectors. We can still regard A as long-run equilibrium, but now we are concerned with a perspective in which intersectoral capital immobility rules A out. Equilibrium will instead be illustrated by a pair of parallel points, such as D and E. In this case OB measures the common wage, $r_C = BE$ and $r_W = BD$.

How does the Stolper-Samuelson theorem change in this environment? Suppose P_C rises in the proportion $EM/OE (= BJ/OB)$ to P_C'; this shifts the $C_C = P_C$ curve outward as shown. If labor, like capital, did not move between sectors, the cloth equilibrium would switch from E to M, where w and r_C rise in proportion to P_C, while wheat stays at D. But this is impossible because the cloth wage, OJ, would exceed the wheat wage, OB. Thus labor will move from the wheat sector to the cloth sector until a common intermediate wage is established. This is illustrated in the figure by the new equilibrium: G and H.

Because G is necessarily to the left of D, r_W has fallen; because H is to

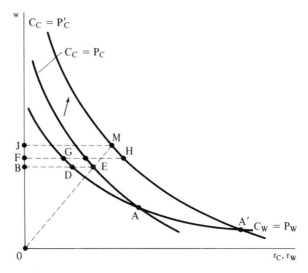

Figure A.12. INTERSECTORAL CAPITAL IMMOBILITY

the right of M, r_C has risen relative to P_C; because F is between J and B, w has risen relative to the unchanged P_W but fallen relative to P_C:

$$\hat{r}_C > \hat{P}_C > \hat{w} > \hat{P}_W > \hat{r}_W \tag{36}$$

A relative price change increases the real reward of the factor specific to the good with the higher price and reduces the real reward of the other specific factor. The reward of the mobile factor rises in terms of one good and falls in terms of the other. Thus the effect on the real wage depends upon how wage income is spent among the two goods and upon just how much the wage changes; the latter depends in turn upon the technological details that determine the slopes of the isoquants and thereby those of the isocost curves.

PROBLEMS

A.4.1 Geometrically demonstrate exactly how an isocost curve can be derived from a given isoquant. Show how an isoquant can be derived from a given isocost curve.

A.4.2 Show how Figure A.11 may alter in the presence of a facor intensity reversal. Trace out the values of S_C and S_W as K varies from zero toward infinity.

A.4.3 Discuss the Rybczynski theorem if capital is immobile between sectors. What can you say about the factor-price equalization and Heckscher-Ohlin theorems?

A.5. Higher-Dimensional Factor-Endowments Theory*
(Section 17* of Chapter 3)

The Heckscher-Ohlin-Samuelson model has been the mainstay of international trade theory for more than thirty years. But empirical work during these years has, on balance, been quite unkind to the model. The basic idea that trade is significantly influenced by relative factor endowments has not fared too badly, but the two-factor, two-commodity H.O.S. model seems decisively inadequate to describe reality. Thus the extension of that model to more goods and factors is actually the key step in understanding the practical significance of the dominant structure of modern trade theory.

ADDITIONAL GOODS

We start by adding more goods while retaining two factors. A third good brings out the important points; adding still more is straightforward but tedious.

Figure A.13 adds an isocost curve for a third good, deckles, to those of wheat and cloth. For given prices of the latter two goods, the price of deckles, P_D, must be just equal to that value which will cause the $P_D = C_D(r, w)$ curve to pass through the intersection of the wheat and cloth curves if production of all three goods is to be possible. This is shown in panel (b). Algebraically, if a deckle equation is added to (25) and (26), and if the costs of the three goods are set equal to exogenously specified prices, we have a system of three equations in two unknowns (w and r). This will be overdetermined unless the prices happen to be set just right to make one of the equations redundant.

This would appear to make diversification highly unlikely. So it would be if commodity prices were chosen at random. But they are not chosen at random: they must clear markets. The importance of this is apparent upon consideration of autarky, where all three goods must be produced, so that their prices must be such as to give a picture like Figure A.13(b).

Now suppose that two countries with the same technology freely trade. It is not now necessary that any individual country be able to produce all three goods, but prices must be such that all three are producible somewhere. This means that the factor-price frontier must include part of each isocost curve, that is, prices cannot be such as to leave any isocost curve entirely below the other two. We have the two possibilities illustrated in Figure A.13. Factor intensity reversals permit additional possibilities, but

---

*An asterisk indicates material that is relatively more advanced and may be skipped without loss of continuity.

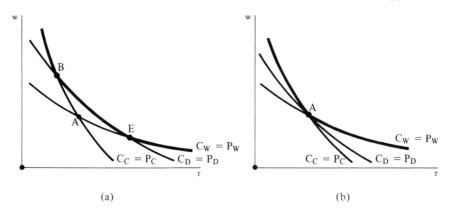

Figure A.13. FACTOR-PRICE FRONTIERS WITH THREE GOODS

we assume them away and suppose that deckles are of intermediate capital intensity.

In panel (a), no country can ever produce all three goods at once, and for the world to do so one country must be on the factor-price frontier at point B or above and the other country at E or below: factor-price equalization is impossible. Neither country can have a factor endowment equal to the slope of the curve BE at any point (other than the endpoints). Thus equilibrium prices cannot be such as to yield panel (a) if the two countries have sufficiently similar endowments. The latter require panel (b), which is consistent with both countries producing all goods if they each have endowments between the slopes of the wheat and cloth isocost curves at A. Thus the factor-price equalization argument is basically unchanged: free trade between countries with sufficiently similar relative factor endowments will equalize factor prices.

Consider next the Heckscher-Ohlin theorem. In Figure A.13(a) one country must be on the frontier at B or above and the other at E or below. It is easy to verify that in this case all the goods exported by the capital abundant country must be more capital intensive than all the goods imported, and analogously for the other country, regardless of which country's techniques are used to make the comparison. In panel (b) it is likewise easy to see that the Heckscher-Ohlin predictions continue to hold if one country produces all three goods while the other specializes to either cloth or wheat. But if both countries produce all goods, problems arise. To see why, rewrite (32) and (33) with the addition of a third good.

$$K = a_{KC}(w, r) S_C + a_{KW}(w, r) S_W + a_{KD}(w, r) S_D \tag{37}$$

$$L = a_{LC}(w, r) S_C + a_{LW}(w, r) S_W + a_{LD}(w, r) S_D. \tag{38}$$

For each country, the endowments K and L are given and the a's are determined by the equalized factor prices. Thus (37) and (38) form a system of two linear equations in three unknowns: S_C, S_W and S_D. The system will likely be underdetermined: if there is one solution with all outputs positive, there must be many such solutions.

A little geometry is useful. In Figure A.14, the *transformation surface* (three-dimensional generalization of the transformation curve) is $AHJGE$. This structure, showing all combinations of the three goods that can be produced from given amounts of the two factors, is a *ruled surface*. It is composed of linear segments, just as an ice cream cone has its tip connected to its rim by linear segments but is smoothly curved in every other direction on its surface. The three commodity prices determine a *budget plane*. The figure shows the budget plane BMF, which reflects relative prices $P_W/P_D = OM/OB$ and $P_W/P_C = OF/OB$. National income is maximized by producing at a point on the transformation surface where the budget plane is as far from the origin as possible. Because the surface is ruled, this occurs not at a unique point of tangency, but anywhere along the line segment HG. Now if the foreign country is also producing all three goods, that country can likewise produce anywhere on a linear segment $H'G'$ in the foreign analog of Figure A.14. Because factor price equalization causes the two economies to use the same techniques, HG and $H'G'$ will be exactly parallel to each other. Thus if the domestic economy were to shift production from, say, N to Q, the foreign economy could switch in exactly the opposite way and world production of all three goods would be unchanged. National production and therefore world trade patterns are indeterminate! Neither

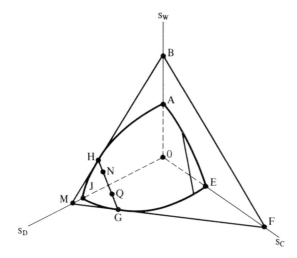

Figure A.14.   TRANSFORMATION SURFACE WITH THREE GOODS AND TWO FACTORS

the Heckscher-Ohlin theorem nor any other statement predicting specific trade flows is valid.

If a country produces just two goods, as at B or E in Figure A.13(a), the logic of the Rybczynski theorem is clearly unchanged. But if all three goods are produced, the exact effects of endowment changes on outputs must be indeterminate, since the outputs themselves are indeterminate both before and after the changes.

With regard to commodity price changes, equations like (29) and (30) hold for all produced goods, so that the Stolper-Samuelson theorem continues to hold for changes in the prices of all goods (either two or three) that are actually produced.

ADDITIONAL FACTORS

Let us now return to two goods but add a third factor, land (T). Then equations (32) and (33) are replaced by

$$K = a_{KC}(w, r, v) S_C + a_{KW}(w, r, v) S_W \tag{39}$$

$$L = a_{LC}(w, r, v) S_C + a_{LW}(w, r, v) S_W \tag{40}$$

$$T = a_{TC}(w, r, v) S_C + a_{TW}(w, r, v) S_W \tag{41}$$

where v denotes the rent paid for land. Suppose we are initially in equilibrium and that there is a small change in endowments, say a slight rise in K. Since T and L do not change, equations (40) and (41) uniquely determine S_C and S_W for fixed factor prices (except in the very special case where (40) and (41) are identical). Thus the increase in K cannot, at the initial factor prices, change the output of either good. But then (39) cannot continue to hold after the rise in K. The conclusion must be that factor prices will change, if all factors are to remain fully employed. Thus the factor-price equalization theorem does not hold. The Rybczynski result also runs into trouble, because employed endowments *can't* be changed independently of prices.

We can see this in another way by adding a third factor to equations (25) and (26):

$$C_W(w, r, v) = w\, a_{LW}(w, r, v) + r\, a_{KW}(w, r, v) + v\, a_{TW}(w, r, v) \tag{42}$$

$$C_C(w, r, v) = w\, a_{LC}(w, r, v) + r\, a_{KC}(w, r, v) + v\, a_{TC}(w, r, v). \tag{43}$$

If costs are set equal to given commodity prices, we have two equations in the three unknowns w, r, and v. The system is underdetermined and cannot be solved without additional information (the factor endowments and their constraints). If we then differentiate these equations to obtain our version of (29) and (30), we have

$$\hat{P}_C = \theta_{LC}\,\hat{w} + \theta_{KC}\,\hat{r} + \theta_{TC}\,\hat{v} \tag{44}$$

$$\hat{P}_W = \theta_{LW}\,\hat{w} + \theta_{KW}\,\hat{r} + \theta_{TW}\,\hat{v}. \tag{45}$$

This leaves open the (non-Stopler-Samuelson) possibility that one of the proportional factor-price changes might fall between $\hat{P}_C$ and $\hat{P}_W$. Indeed in the previous section we had an example where this happened: intersectoral capital immobility. Since cloth capital and wheat capital were distinct this was a special three-factor, two-good model (special because, although there were in effect three factors in the economy, each sector used only two), and we saw that $\hat{w}$ was necessarily between $\hat{P}_C$ and $\hat{P}_W$.

MANY GOODS AND FACTORS: FACTOR-PRICE EQUALIZATION

Let us now turn to the more general case of n goods ($n \geq 2$) and m factors ($m \geq 2$). Consider the factor-price equalization property.

Suppose initially that $n = m$, and let two countries engage in free trade at some equilibrium commodity price *vector p*. If the two countries happen to possess the various factors in identical proportions, they will produce the various goods in identical proportions, have identical factor prices, and use identical techniques (the production sides of such economies will be identical, except for scale, and so they will behave identically). Let W be such a common *vector* of factor prices. Then, if we number the goods from 1 to n and the factors from 1 to m,

$$P_i = \sum_{j=1}^{m} W_j a_{ji}(W) \qquad i = 1, \ldots, n,$$

or

$$p = W A(W) \tag{46}$$

where $A(W) = \begin{bmatrix} a_{11}(W) \ldots a_{1n}(W) \\ a_{m1}(W) \ldots a_{mn}(W) \end{bmatrix}$ is the *matrix* of techniques.

The problem is whether factor prices will continue to be identical if relative endowments cease to be. If, in either country, all goods are produced (as they will be with relatively identical endowments):

$$K = A(W) S \tag{47}$$

where $S = (S_1, \ldots, S_n)$ denotes commodity outputs and $K = (K_1, \ldots, K_m)$ factor endowments. For any non-negative vector S of outputs, equations (47) give some non-negative vector K of factors necessary to produce the outputs. Let K_W denote the collection of *all* vectors K that solve (47) for non-negative Ss. If both countries have factor endowments in K_W, both can produce all goods at factor prices W. Factor-price equalization will therefore be possible, but will it be necessary? Suppose not, that is, suppose that for some other vector of factor rewards, W', the economy can be in equilibrium at the same commodity prices p, so that $p = W'A(W')$ and $K = A(W') S'$. Now, $A(W)$ is the cheapest technique to use at factor prices W but is not the cheapest technique at factor prices W' (since $A(W')$ is); therefore,

$$W A(W) = p < W' A(W)$$ (48)

where "$x < y$" means that no component of the vector x is greater than the corresponding component of the vector y and at least one component is strictly less. Exactly analogous reasoning yields

$$p = W' A(W') < W A(W').$$ (49)

Multiplying both sides of (48) by the vector S yields $WK < W'K$ while multiplying both sides of (49) by S' gives the contradictory result $W'K < WK$. Thus if a country has factor endowments in K_W, that country can have no factor prices other than W.

With an arbitrary number of goods and factors, if the two countries have sufficiently similar factor endowments, that is, if both endowments are in K_W, they must have equal factor prices. The factor-price equalization argument survives basically intact in higher dimensions.

If we now allow unequal numbers of factors and goods, the considerations of the previous subsections arise. When $n > m$ the situation does not substantially change, but $m > n$ reduces factor-price equalization to a fluke. The general conclusion is that factor-price equalization can be expected between countries with similar relative factor endowments if there are at least as many goods as factors[8].

THE STOLPER-SAMUELSON THEOREM

Suppose that some good, say the first, is initially produced in equilibrium, so that $P_1 = C_1(W)$, that its production requires at least two factors, and let its price rise. In the new equilibrium the cost of production of S_1 must rise at least as much as its price, with $\hat{P}_1 = \hat{C}_1$ if the good continues to be produced and $\hat{P}_1 \leq \hat{C}_1$ if it does not. In either case we must have, as a result of by-now-familiar operations:

$$\hat{P}_1 \leq \hat{C}_1 = \theta_{11} \hat{W}_1 + \ldots + \theta_{m1} \hat{W}_m,$$ (50)

where $\theta_{11} + \ldots + \theta_{m1} = 1$. Thus $\hat{C}_1$ is a weighted average of the $\hat{W}_j$. This means that at least one $\hat{W}_j$ must at least equal $\hat{C}_1$ and therefore $\hat{P}_1$ as well: an increase in the price of any good that is initially produced causes some factor reward to rise in at least equal proportion. Now suppose that there is some other good, say the second, whose price has not changed, which uses exactly the same factors in its production as does the first good, and which is produced after the rise in P_1. Then we must have

$$0 = \hat{P}_2 \geq \hat{C}_2 = \theta_{12} \hat{W}_1 + \ldots + \theta_{m2} \hat{W}_m.$$ (51)

[8] The analysis of this subsection depends upon L. W. McKenzie, "Equality of Factor Prices in World Trade," *Econometrica* 23 (1955), 239–57. See also: H. Uzawa, "Prices of the Factors of Production in International Trade," *Econometrica* 27 (1959), 448–68; W. Ethier, "Some of the Theorems of International Trade with Many Goods and Factors," *Journal of International Economics* 4 (1974), 199–206; A. Dixit and V. Norman, *op. cit.*

Now we know that one of the factor rewards W_j has increased. Thus for (51) to be true some factor reward must fall: $\hat{W_i} < 0$ for some i. But good 1 uses the same factors that good 2 does. Thus at least one of the $\hat{W_i}$ on the right hand of (50) must be negative; this means that (50) requires some $\hat{W_i}$ to exceed $\hat{C_1} \geq \hat{P_1}$. Thus the increase in the price of good 1 must cause the reward of *some* factor to rise in even greater proportion (and therefore to unambiguously rise in real terms) and the reward to *some* other factor to fall absolutely (and therefore in real terms). The basic requirements are that the good whose price rises actually be produced in the initial equilibrium, and that this good use a *non-specific assortment* of at least two factors, in the sense that the factors used to produce this good are precisely the same factors used by some other good that is produced after the price change.

> *An increase in the price of an initially produced good using a nonspecific assortment of at least two factors necessarily causes some factor reward to rise in even greater proportion and some factor reward to fall.*

Thus we have the basic Stolper-Samuelson result that a commodity price change produces *conflict:* some factor has an unambiguously higher real reward and some has an unambiguously lower real reward. This proposition does not depend upon the relative sizes of m and n (if they each exceed one), and reduces to the standard Stolper-Samuelson theorem when $n = m = 2$. The proposition says nothing about some factors whenever $m > 2$; this is consistent with our earlier conclusion that some proportional factor rewards could be weighted averages of proportional commodity-price changes when $m > n$.

THE RYBCZYNSKI THEOREM[9]

Suppose that the endowment of some factor, say the first, is used in at least two industries, and that its quantity is increased. If it is fully employed after the endowment increase, we must have, if factor prices do not change,

$$\hat{K_1} \leqq \lambda_{11} \hat{S_1} + \dots + \lambda_{1n} \hat{S_n}. \tag{52}$$

where $\lambda_{11} + \dots + \lambda_{1n} = 1$, so that at least one $\hat{S_i}$ must be at least as large as $\hat{K_1}$. Suppose that K_1 is a *nonspecific factor* in the sense that at least one other factor, say the second, is used in positive amounts by exactly the same sectors that use K_1, and is fully employed initially. Then

$$0 = \hat{K_2} \geqq \lambda_{21} \hat{S_1} + \dots + \lambda_{2n} \hat{S_n}. \tag{53}$$

---

[9] For more on the topic of this and the preceding subsections, see W. Ethier, *op. cit;* M. C. Kemp, *Three Topics in the Theory of International Trade,* 1976 (Amsterdam: North Holland), chapters 4, 7.

Since at least one of the $\hat{S}_i \geq \hat{K}_1 > 0$, (53) requires *some* $\hat{S}_i < 0$. Then (52) requires *some other* $\hat{S}_i > \hat{K}_1$.

> *At constant factor prices, an increase in the endowment of a non-specific factor used in at least two sectors, which leaves that factor fully employed, produces a more than proportional rise in the output of some good and a fall in the output of some other good.*

Once again, this result is independent of the relative magnitudes of m and n. If $n > 2$, some output changes are unaccounted for. This makes the proposition consistent with $n > m$ where outputs are indeterminate: *some* good must increase its output in greater proportion than the factor endowment has risen, but no one can say which.

This proposition applies to cases where factor prices do not change, but we have seen that, if $m > n$, endowment changes *must* generally produce factor-price changes if all factors are to remain fully employed. Thus if $m > n$, our proposition is of practical interest only if unemployment of factors is considered.

DUALITY

Recall that in the previous section we established the *reciprocity relations*

$$\frac{\partial W_j}{\partial P_i} = \frac{\partial S_i}{\partial K_j}. \tag{54}$$

The proof of these relations was not sensitive to the number of goods and factors and is generally valid, but the application of the relations to our propositions becomes tricky when $n \neq m$. With more goods than factors, terms such as $\partial S_i / \partial K_j$ are indeterminate; with more factors than goods, (54) is derived under the assumption that the economy adjusts to keep all factors fully employed, in contrast to our generalized Rybczynski result. It is still possible to derive some conclusions with unequal numbers of goods and factors, but for simplicity we assume $n = m$.

Note, first, that (54) establishes a duality between those parts of the Stolper-Samuelson and Rybczynski propositions relating to reactions in the *opposite* direction: a change in the price of good i will change the reward of factor j in the opposite direction if and only if a change in the endowment of factor j changes the output of good i in the opposite direction. But this duality does not extend to the more-than-proportional reactions in the same direction: $\hat{W}_j > \hat{P}_i$, or $\partial W_j / \partial P_i > W_j / P_i > 0$, implies, from (54), only that $\partial S_i / \partial K_j > 0$; it need not be true that $\partial S_i / \partial K_j > S_i / K_j$.

Second, our Stolper-Samuelson property tells us that a rise in any commodity price reduces the reward of some factor. But is it also true that the real reward of any factor can be changed by the manipulation of just one commodity price? Yes, because the Rybczynski property says that a rise in any factor endowment must reduce the output of some good, and so we can use the duality property (54) to conclude that the reward of any factor can indeed be increased by a fall in some commodity price.

In similar fashion, duality allows us to conclude that the output of any good will fall in response to a rise in the endowment of some factor.

THE HECKSCHER-OHLIN THEOREM[10]

We have left the Heckscher-Ohlin theorem for last because even in the H.O.S. model this is the most fragile of the four central theorems. The assumptions of no factor intensity reversals and of identical tastes, for example, play little or no role in the other three propositions.

We start with a generalization of the price version. Recall that in the 2 $\times$ 2 case this version made no assumptions about demand, but was sensitive to the nature of technology (that is, factor intensity reversals). The same will be true now. Suppose that in free trade a country exchanges the vector $M = D^T - S^T$ of net imports with the rest of the world. Now we know that $p^A D^T \geq p^A D^A$, where the superscript A refers to autarky, because D^T gives higher utility than D^A, so the country would not have consumed the latter in autarky if it could have afforded the former. Next, let M_K denote the factors of production that were *actually used* to produce M, that is

$$M_K = \bar{A}\, M$$

where the i-th column of $\bar{A}$ is the technique used at home to produce S_i if that good is exported ($D_i^T - S_i^T = M_i < 0$) and is the technique used abroad if the good is imported ($M_i > 0$). Then it must be possible for the country to produce the goods D^T from the factors $K + M_K$ simply by no longer producing exports and by producing imports the same way they are produced abroad. But this technique need not be profitable at autarkic prices:

$$W^A(K + M_K) \geq p^A D^T.$$

Thus,

$$W^A M_K \geq p^A D^T - W^A K \geq p^A D^A - W^A K = 0.$$

Therefore,

$$W^A M_K \geq 0. \tag{55}$$

If we apply the same logic to the rest of the world,

$$W^{A*} . M_K^* \geq 0 \tag{56}$$

---

[10] The material of this subsection depends upon: A Deardorff, "The General Validity of the Heckscher-Ohlin Theorem," 1981, processed; A. Dixit and V. Norman, *op. cit.*, 93–102; J. Vanek, "The Factor Proportions Theory: the N-Factor Case," *Kyklos* 21 (1968), 749–56.

where W^{A*} denotes foreign autarkic factor prices. Now foreign imports are home exports, so that $M^* = -M$. Thus $M_K^* = \bar{A} M^* = -\bar{A} M = -M_K$. Substituting this into (56) and subtracting from (55) yields

$$(W^A - W^{A*}). M_K \geq 0. \tag{57}$$

This says that autarkic factor-price differences are positively correlated with the factor content of imports: countries tend to import (via trade) those factors that are relatively expensive in autarky.

   Note two things about this result. First, it is independent of demand, just as is the 2 × 2 price version. Next, factor content is evaluated according to the *country of origin* of each export, instead of using a single country's technique to evaluate all trade flows, or using each country's technique for both imports and exports of that country. Of course, if factor prices are equalized techniques are the same everywhere, so that such distinctions do not matter. But otherwise, when countries have substantially different factor endowments, they will use different techniques and the global nature of the technology will begin to matter. We measure factor content the way we do in order to avoid the problems caused by factor intensity reversals and their higher-dimensional analogs. To see this, consider the 2 × 2 case where a factor intensity reversal separates the two countries. With only two factors, (57) says that each country is a net exporter of its relatively abundant factor. We know that this cannot be true for both countries if each evaluates factor content of trade according to its own techniques (or if both countries use the techniques of just one country), but it is true when the technique of the exporter is used for each good.

   We would expect to have to impose conditions on tastes in order to obtain a general quantity version, since this was necessary in the 2 × 2 case. The two countries will both consume the various goods in similar proportions when facing similar relative prices if the same collection of (n-dimensional) indifference curves can be used to represent tastes in both countries, *and* if these curves are radially symmetric—so that all indifference curves have the same slope along the same ray from the origin. In this case, when we assign a utility value to each indifference curve by measuring its distance from the origin along a ray from there, we obtain the same results, proportionally, no matter which ray is used.

   Now consider what we can conclude about relative factor endowments. Note first that $W^{A*}. K \geq y(p^{A*}; K)$, the maximum income obtainable from *home* factor endowments at *foreign* autarkic prices. This is so because we saw in the last section that $y(p^{A*}; K)$ can also be regarded as the minimum spent on the endowments K at any factor prices that make costs at least as high as p^{A*}, and W^{A*} certainly does this. Next let u_o be the utility level for which $y(p^{A*}; K) = E(p^{A*}, u_o)$. Now u_o must be at least as large as u_A, actual home autarkic utility, because we saw in section A.2 that the opportunity to buy and sell at any prices other than p^A increased utility. Thus $E(p^A, u_o) \geq E(p^A, u_A) = W^A_o K$. Define $\lambda = E(p^{A*}, u_o)/E(p^A, u_o)$. Then putting it all together:

$$W^{A*}_o K \geq y(p^{A*}; K) = E(p^{A*}, u_o) =$$
$$\lambda E(p^A, u_o) \geq \lambda E(p^A, u_A) = \lambda W^A_o K. \tag{58}$$

Using the same logic but reversing the roles of the two countries:

$$W^{A*} \geq \mu W^{A*}_o . K^* \tag{59}$$

where $\mu = E(p^A, u_1)/E(p^{A*}, u_1)$ and u_1 is such that $E(p^{A*}, u_1) = y$ $(p^A; K^*)$. Now, because of the assumption of radially symmetric indifference curves,

$$\frac{E(p^{A*}, u_o)}{E(p^{A*}, u_1)} = \frac{E(p^A, u_o)}{E(p^A, u_1)}$$

(the ratios equal relative distance from the origin of the u_o and u_1 indifference curves along two different rays), so that $\lambda = \dfrac{l}{\mu}$. Thus (58) and (59) can be written

$$(W^{A*} - \lambda W^A) . K \geq 0 \tag{60}$$

$$(\lambda W^A - W^{A*}) . K^* \geq 0 . \tag{61}$$

Subtracting (61) from (60),

$$(W^{A*} - \lambda W^A) . (K - K^*) \geq 0 . \tag{62}$$

The number λ is a measure of the general level of foreign autarkic prices relative to domestic autarkic prices. Thus (62) says that each country tends to have relatively high autarkic prices for its relatively scarce factors, in a physical sense. This gives us an indirect quantity version, in that we already know that each country tends to import those factors with relatively high autarkic prices.

   If there are at least as many goods as factors and if countries' endowments are sufficiently similar so that trade equalizes factor prices, considerably more can be said. Number the m factors in order of decreasing home relative abundance, in the sense that

$$\frac{K_1}{K^W_1} \geq \frac{K_2}{K^W_2} \geq \ldots \geq \frac{K_m}{K^W_m} \tag{63}$$

where K^W_i denotes the total world supply of factor i. Suppose that in free trade home country income is the fraction g of world income. Then, because of our assumption about tastes, the home country must be consuming the fraction g of the total world output of each and every good. Because of factor-price equalization, each good is produced by a single technique, regardless of how many countries actually produce it. Thus the goods consumed at home must, in the aggregate, require for their production the fraction g of the world endowment of each and every factor. Thus the net home import of factor i equals $gK_i^w - K_i$. In the chain (63), all factors with ratios greater than g are exported and all with ratios less than g are imported.

PROBLEMS

A.5.1 Show how the presence of factor intensity reversals can alter Figure A.13. Discuss the implications.

A.5.2 Suppose there are three goods and two factors, that all three goods are being produced in equilibrium, and that the techniques used in the three sectors relate to each other as follows:

$$\frac{K_C}{L_C} > \frac{K_D}{L_D} > \frac{K_W}{L_W}. \tag{64}$$

Now consider the price change: $\hat{P}_D > 0$, $\hat{P}_C = \hat{P}_W = 0$.
What can you say about the consequences for factor rewards and the pattern of production?

A.5.3 Suppose that there are three goods and two factors with relative intensities as in (64) for all wage-rental ratios. If there are two countries, is it possible for one to specialize in deckles in equilibrium? Explain.

A.5.4 How does our general version of the Stolper-Samuelson theorem change if we drop the assumption that the good whose price increases uses a nonspecific assortment of factors?

A.5.5 What can you say about the general version of the Rybczynski theorem in the case of more goods than factors if, instead of holding factor prices constant, we fix commodity prices and suppose that all factors remain fully employed?

A.6. Tariffs (Chapter 5)[11]

TARIFF-RIDDEN EQUILIBRIA

Suppose again that the home country imports wheat from the rest of the world in exchange for cloth, but levies an ad valorem tariff at the rate t on wheat imports, so that the *domestic* relative price of wheat q is given by

$$q = (1 + t) P. \tag{65}$$

---

[11] For more detail on the subject of this section, see R. W. Jones, "Tariffs and Trade in General Equilibrium: Comment," *American Economic Review* 59 (June 1969): 418–24.

International equilibrium is still given by equation (17) from section A.3: $PM = M^*$, where P denotes the relative international price of wheat in terms of cloth. Differentiating this expression, we have across equilibria,

$$\hat{P} + \hat{M} = \hat{M}^* . \tag{66}$$

Now home imports need not equal exports in value at domestic prices. Instead we must have

$$E(q, u_t) = y(q, \ldots) + t P M \tag{67}$$

where u_t is the level of home utility with the tariff. Total expenditure on wheat and cloth at domestic prices must equal the value of production at domestic prices plus the revenue from the tariff.

THE EFFECTS OF TARIFFS AND WORLD PRICES ON HOME IMPORTS

In section A.3 we developed equation (21) showing how the demand for imports responds to changes in the terms of trade. We wish to do the same now with tariffs and also show how import demand responds to changes in these tariffs. This can be done by repeating the earlier analysis leading to (21), while taking note of (65) and (67) where appropriate. To see where such a procedure would take us, rewrite equation (20) as follows.

$$dM = \left[\left. \frac{\partial D_W}{\partial P} \right|_u - \frac{dS_W}{dP} \right] dP - \frac{\partial D_W}{\partial E} \left[\frac{\partial E}{\partial P} dP - \frac{\partial y}{\partial P} dP \right] . \tag{68}$$

This expression, the basic decomposition into income and substitution effects, shows how the economy's agents collectively respond to changes in the relative price they face. To adapt this to cases where tariffs are present, two changes are necessary. First, q must replace P everywhere in (68), because domestic agents respond to domestic prices rather than world prices. Second, tariff revenues must be accounted for: the right-hand side of (67) should replace y in (68). Now the derivative of this right-hand side is

$$\frac{\partial y}{\partial q} dq + t d(PM) + PM(dt)$$

so that (68) becomes

$$dM = \left[\left. \frac{\partial D_W}{\partial q} \right|_u - \frac{dS_W}{dq} \right] dq -$$

$$\frac{\partial D_W}{\partial E} \left[\left(\frac{\partial E}{\partial q} - \frac{\partial y}{\partial q} \right) dq - PM \, dt - t \, d(PM) \right] , \tag{69}$$

---

where, from (65), $dq = (1 + t) dP + P dt$. Now we will simplify things by assuming that initially the country has free trade, so that $t = 0$ or $P = q$, and that dt accordingly represents the imposition of a small tariff. Making this assumption in (69) and also repeating the same substitutions we made earlier to go from (20) to (21), gives

$$\hat{M} = - (c + s) (\hat{P} + dt) - m \, \hat{P}$$

or

$$\hat{M} = - e \, \hat{P} - (c + s) \, dt . \tag{70}$$

This expression has a simple interpretation. Imports may become more expensive either because world prices rise ($\hat{P}$) or because a tariff is imposed (dt). The former case (a movement along the offer curve) affects M as measured in the usual way by e, since initially there is no tariff: substitution effects occur because imports are more expensive relative to exports, and the income effect results from the fact that more must now be spent than before the price rise to purchase the same imports. When import prices instead rise because of the tariff (dt), the offer curve shifts. This causes the same substitution effects as would a rise in P because imports are relatively more expensive than before in either case. But now there is no income effect because domestic residents collectively "pay themselves" the tariff proceeds; the latter are not paid to foreigners and thereby subtracted from domestic income as would be the case with a rise in P.

A TARIFF AND THE TERMS OF TRADE

Suppose that the home country, initially in free trade, imposes a tariff dt. Equation (70) then applies to the home country, while for the foreign country of course

$$\hat{M}^* = e^* \, \hat{P} . \tag{71}$$

For equilibrium (66) must hold. Substitute (70) and (71) into (66) and rearrange to obtain

$$\hat{P} = \frac{- (c + s)}{e + e^* - 1} \, dt . \tag{72}$$

The term $e + e^* - 1$ is necessarily positive if we accept the Marshall-Lerner condition as necessary for stability. Then, since the substitution terms are positive, $\hat{P}$ and dt are of opposite sign: a tariff necessarily improves the terms of trade of any country able to influence world prices (if the home country is "small", $e^* = \infty$ so that $\hat{P} = O$).

A TARIFF AND DOMESTIC PRICES

Equation (72) shows the effect of the tariff on world prices. What about its effect on domestic prices? From (65) we have

$$\hat{q} = \hat{p} + \frac{dt}{1 + t} \, . \tag{73}$$

Letting $t = 0$ initially, substituting (72) into (73) and rearranging, gives

$$\hat{q} = \frac{e^* - (1 - m)}{e + e^* - 1} \, dt \, . \tag{74}$$

Thus a tariff increases the domestic price of importables if and only if the foreign import elasticity exceeds the domestic marginal propensity to spend on the same good (that is, domestic imports). Note that this necessarily holds if the foreign offer curve is elastic. It also holds under the H.O.S. assumption of internationally identical tastes at common relative prices since in that case $1 - m = m^*$, with initial free trade, so that the numerator of (74) equals $c^* + s^*$. But if $e^* < 1 - m$ we must have the *Metzler paradox:* a tariff on imports lowers their relative domestic price.

A TARIFF AND DOMESTIC WELFARE

We know that a tariff, as a price distortion, is inefficient for the world as a whole. Its effect on domestic utility can be determined from (67). Differentiating this expression with respect to t gives

$$\frac{\partial E}{\partial q} \frac{dq}{dt} + \frac{\partial E}{\partial u_t} \frac{du_t}{dt} = \frac{\partial y}{\partial q} \frac{dq}{dt} + t \, P \frac{dM}{dt} + M \frac{d(t \, P)}{dt} \, . \tag{75}$$

Recall that $\partial E / \partial q = D_w$, $\partial y / \partial q = S_w$ and note that, from (65), $dq/dt = dP/dt + d(t \, P)/dt$. Performing these substitutions gives

$$\frac{\partial E}{\partial u_t} \frac{du_t}{dt} = -M \frac{dP}{dt} + t \, P \frac{dM}{dt} \, . \tag{76}$$

Recall that $\partial E / \partial u_t > 0$. Thus a tariff influences domestic utililty in two ways: a terms-of-trade effect alters what the country must pay for its imports, and a change in import volume alters tariff revenue. The latter has welfare significance because $t \, P = q - P$, the excess of how much the domestic economy values an import above what it must pay for it. Four conclusions follow from this analysis.

1. If the country initially has free trade, the right-hand side of (76) reduces to $-M \, (dP/dt)$, which is necessarily positive. Thus a small tariff is better than no tariff for any country able to influence world prices, if foreign retaliation can be ignored.
2. If the country has a prohibitive tariff, $M = 0$ so the right-hand side of (76) reduces to $t \, P \, (dM/dt)$. Thus a reduction in t below the prohibitive level increases u_t: a little trade is better than no trade.
3. If the home country levies an optimum tariff, that is, varies t to maximize u_t, the first-order condition is $du_t/dt = 0$ in (76). Thus

$$t = \frac{M \; (dP/dt)}{P \; (dM/dt)} = \frac{\hat{P}}{\hat{M}} \; .$$

Substituting the equilibrium condition (66) and the definition $\hat{M}^*$ $= e^* \; \hat{P}$ then gives the formula for the optimum tariff:

$$t = \frac{1}{e^* - 1} \; .$$

4. At the optimum tariff $du_t/dt = 0$ and dq/dt is positive since $e^* > 1$. Thus from (75), $d(t \; PM)/dt = t \; P \; (dM/dt) + M \; (d(tp)/dt) > 0$. That is, a further rise in t increases tariff revenue: the optimum tariff is necessarily smaller than the tariff which maximizes tariff revenue.

A TARIFF AND LONG-RUN DOMESTIC INCOME DISTRIBUTION

Discussion of the effects of protection on national welfare in effect concerns the *international* distribution of income, since we know that a tariff is globally inefficient. Turning to the *domestic* income distribution, we now investigate in detail the chain of reasoning behind the basic Stolper-Samuelson argument that a tariff increases the real income accruing to a country's relatively scarce factor and reduces that of its relatively abundant factor.

1. Note first that the argument applies to a two-good, two-factor context in which the Heckscher-Ohlin theorem holds. If the latter fails, the roles of the two factors reverse. With higher dimensions, the results of section A.5 must be used to obtain more general, but weaker, results.

2. For the Stolper-Samuelson argument to relate to income distribution, the income groups we are interested in must depend in substantially different ways upon the rewards of the two factors.

3. The Stolper-Samuelson theorem shows how factor rewards respond to changes in the domestic relative price of imports. The latter is in turn related to the tariff by equation (74). Thus a necessary condition for a tariff to raise, relative to both commodity prices, the reward of that factor used intensively by the import-competing industry is

$$e^* > 1 - m \; . \tag{77}$$

If (77) is violated (the "Metzler Paradox"), the tariff redistributes income in the opposite direction.

4. Suppose the tariff does increase the domestic relative price q of wheat. Then, since wheat is assumed labor intensive, the wage rises

relative to q and the rent falls. But to complete the description of the tariff's effect on factor incomes, we must take account of the tariff revenue. The real income earned by labor must rise in any case, since the wage is higher in terms of both commodities, but it is not clear that capital's real income falls once its share of tariff revenue is considered. To ignore the latter is to tacitly assume that tariff revenues are spent so as to influence income distribution. This would be inconsistent with our discussion thus far, which has treated these revenues just like other income and would also confuse our attempt to isolate the distributional consequences of a tariff-induced price distortion. Thus we assume that tariff revenues are distributed between owners of the two factors in proportion to the latters' shares in national income. The total accruing to owners of capital, y_K, is accordingly

$$y_K = r K + \frac{r K}{y} t PM .$$

Assuming that $t = 0$ initially, we differentiate this expression to obtain:

$$\hat{y}_K = \hat{r} + a \, dt \tag{78}$$

where $a = PM / y$. We can obtain an expression for $\hat{r}$ by setting $\hat{P}_C = 0$ in (29), $\hat{P}_W = \hat{q}$ in (30) and solving.

$$\hat{r} = \frac{\theta_{LC}}{\theta_{KW} - \theta_{KC}} \hat{q} . \tag{79}$$

Substituting (74) and (79) into (78) reveals the effect of a small tariff on the income accruing to owners of capital.

$$\hat{y}_K = \left[\frac{\theta_{LC}}{\theta_{KW} - \theta_{KC}} \frac{e^* - (1 - m)}{e + e^* - 1} + a \right] dt .$$

For capital's income to fall in terms of both goods we require $\hat{y}_K < 0$, which after a little manipulation reduces to:

$$e^* > (1 - m) + a \frac{\theta_{KC} - \theta_{KW}}{\theta_{LC}} (e + e^* - 1) . \tag{80}$$

Note that $\theta_{KC} > \theta_{KW}$ so that (80) is a stronger condition than (77) and so rules out the Metzler paradox. Thus (80) is the basic condition for a tariff to raise the income, in terms of both goods, of the factor intensive to imports and to lower the other factor's income, in terms of both goods.

At this point one might wonder how, if a tariff makes the country as a whole worse off, and if it makes labor better off, capital could possibly avoid a loss. There are two relevant considerations. First, a tariff improves the terms of trade and may therefore make the country better off–indeed a small departure from free trade must do so. This benefit could conceivably allow both factors to be better off. But there is a second consideration as well: even without a terms of trade improvement, capital's income need not fall in terms of both goods even though the wage rises in terms of both and the country as a whole must lose! The reason for this sheds light on the nature of the gains from trade. When we say that a tariff confers a loss on a country we mean that the country's residents cannot afford, with their post-tariff incomes and domestic prices, to purchase the same assortment of goods they purchased before the tariff. Now the total wage income can still clearly buy the same goods it did before, since the wage has risen in terms of both commodities. Thus capital's income can not possibly afford the same bundle of commodities that it was used to purchase before the tariff. The "representative" recipient of capital rents thus finds those rents worth less. But not *every* recipient need do so if capital's income has not fallen in terms of both goods: "unrepresentative" capitalists with a decided preference for exportables might actually be benefitted by the tariff. If we drop the small country assumption and allow a terms-of-trade improvement, even the representative capitalist could benefit.

To illustrate, suppose the home country is indeed small, so that $\hat{q} = dt$ replaces (73). Substituting this and (79) into (78) now leads to the following necessary condition for capital's income to fall in terms of both goods:

$$a < \frac{\theta_{LC}}{\theta_{KC} - \theta_{KW}}.$$

If this condition is violated, as is possible, some recipients of income from capital could indeed find the real value of that income enhanced by a tariff, even with no change in the terms of trade.

To summarize: in the 2×2 environment a tariff will raise in terms of both goods the income accruing to the factor intensive to imports and reduce in terms of both goods the income of the other factor if (80) holds.

DOMESTIC INCOME DISTRIBUTION AND INTERSECTORAL FACTOR
MOBILITY

The Stolper-Samuelson argument applies to a long-run context in which all factors are fully mobile between industries. With a shorter perspective at least some factors will not be fully mobile, and in the very short run few if any will be. We now inquire how the distributional implications of protection consequently vary over time.

Define the short run as a period during which neither capital nor labor is mobile between sectors, and suppose that a tariff on wheat raises its relative domestic price. Wages and rents in the wheat industry need not remain equal to wages and rents in the cloth industry because of the inter-sectoral immobility. Physical marginal productivities of the two factors in the two industries do not change because employment levels do not change. Competition between firms in each industry therefore causes the wages and rents earned in the wheat sector to both rise in equal proportion to wheat's domestic price and wages and rents in the cloth sector to remain un-changed. Thus, if every income recipient purchases at least some of each good, the real rewards of wheat capital and wheat labor rise while those of cloth capital and cloth labor fall. The short-run distributional consequences of protection hinge entirely on the *sector* from which one's income comes and not at all upon the *factor*. (We shall now ignore the effect of tariff revenue investigated in the previous subsection.)

By contrast, in the long run we have the Stolper-Samuelson argument, which implies just the reverse: everything depends upon the factor to which one has title, irrespective of the sector in which that factor is employed.

With a more intermediate perspective, intersectoral mobility will vary from factor to factor. We can capture this consideration by supposing that labor is fully mobile whereas capital is sector specific. Then the analysis of section A.4, culminating in (36), implies that a rise in the relative domestic price of wheat raises the reward of wheat capital in terms of both goods, lowers that of cloth capital in terms of both goods, and causes the wage to rise in terms of cloth but fall in terms of wheat. The fate of owners of the specific factor depends completely and unambiguously upon the sector in which that factor is employed, whereas the real income of the mobile factor is ambiguous but independent of where it is employed.

The distributional consequences of a tariff over time are summarized in the following table.

Table A.1. EFFECTS OF A RISE IN THE DOMESTIC RELATIVE PRICE OF WHEAT ON FACTOR INCOMES

Perspective	*Capital*		*Labor*
Short Run	K_W: up	=	L_W: up
	K_C: down	=	L_C: down
Medium Run	K_W: up		L_W: ?
			$\parallel$
	K_C: down		L_C: ?
Long Run	K_W: down		L_W: up
	$\parallel$		$\parallel$
	K_C: down		L_C: up

W = Wheat; C = Cloth; K_W = real income of capital employed in the wheat sector, etc.

PROBLEMS

A.6.1 Explicitly derive (67).

A.6.2 What will equation (70) look like if we do not assume that $t = 0$ initially?

A.6.3 What does the assumption of internationally identical tastes imply about the relative sizes of $\hat{P}$ and $\hat{q}$?

A.6.4 Condition (77) was derived under the condition that $t = 0$ initially. What can you say if instead the initial tariff is large?

A.6.5 Discuss the role of the distribution of tariff revenue upon the Stolper-Samuelson property if the initial tariff level equals: (a) the optimum tariff; (b) the tariff that maximizes tariff revenue; (c) somewhere between that of (a) and that of (b); (d) larger than that of (b) but less than a prohibitive tariff.

SUGGESTED READING

Bhagwati, J., ed. *International Trade: Selected Readings.* Cambridge: M.I.T. Press, 1981.

Caves, R. E. and Jones, R. W. *World Trade and Payments.* 3rd ed. Boston: Little, Brown, 1981. pp. 489–541.

Chacholiades, M. *International Trade Theory and Policy.* New York: McGraw-Hill, 1978.

Chipman, J. S. "A Survey of the Theory of International Trade." *Econometrica,* July 1965, Oct. 1965, Jan. 1966. In three parts.

Dixit, A. K. and Norman, V. *Theory of International Trade.* London: Cambridge University Press, 1980.

Jones, R. W. *International Trade: Essays in Theory.* Amsterdam: North Holland, 1979.

Kemp, M. C. *The Pure Theory of International Trade and Investment.* Englewood Cliffs: Prentice-Hall, 1969.

Kemp, M. C. *Three Topics in the Theory of International Trade.* Amsterdam: North Holland, 1976.

Mundell, R. A. *International Economics.* New York: Macmillan, 1968.

Pearce, I. F. *International Trade.* London: Macmillan, 1970.

Takayama, A. *International Trade.* New York: Holt, Rinehart and Winston, 1972.

Source Material in International Economics

Annual Report on the Trade Agreements Program, available from the U.S. Government Printing Office. Describes administration actions with regard to international trade during the previous year: countervailing duties, antidumping actions, and so forth.

Bank of England *Quarterly Bulletin,* published in London in March, June, September, and December of each year. One of the most useful of the central bank bulletins. Along with British financial data, contains statistics on the London gold market, Eurodollar activity in London and a selection of exchange rates and external interest rates.

Bank of International Settlements *Annual Report,* published in Basle in June of each year. The standard source for statistics on the Eurocurrency markets. Also contains a useful summary of major financial events in the large industrial countries during the preceding year.

Canada Yearbook, published annually by Statistics Canada in Ottawa. A convenient source for Canadian data.

Canadian Statistical Review, published monthly (with weekly supplements) by Statistics Canada. Contains current data on the Canadian economy plus special articles.

Commodity Trade Statistics, published by the United Nations, gives annual figures on world trade by commodity, by region, and by trading partner.

Direction of Trade, published monthly in Washington by the IMF and the IBRD. Contains a detailed world trade matrix displaying bilateral trade flows among most countries, and also shows trade flows between major country groups. Also a *Yearbook.*

Euromoney, published monthly in London. Features timely articles on developments in the Eurocurrency markets and problems in international lending. Occasionally has special supplements surveying regions that have become the focus of world attention. Statistical section contains an array of national interest rates, Eurodollar rates, and exchange rates.

Federal Reserve Bulletin, published monthly in Washington, D.C. Along with domestic U.S. financial data, contains a selection of balance of payments statistics, gold statistics, and international money market and foreign exchange rates. Features an invaluable quarterly report on "Treasury and Federal Reserve Foreign Exchange Operations," the only systematic and comprehensive description of official intervention available. (This report is published simultaneously in the *Quarterly Review* of the New York Federal Reserve Bank.)

Foreign Statistical Publications, published quarterly in Washington by the U.S. Bureau of the Census. Lists foreign sources classified by country.

Guide to Foreign Trade Statistics, an annual publication of the U.S. Bureau of the Census. Very useful, especially for those without experience with trade data sources.

International Currency Review, published bi-monthly in London, contains analytic articles of contemporary international financial developments as well as reviews of conditions in approximately twenty of the leading currency markets and the gold market.

International Economic Conditions, issued quarterly by the Federal Reserve Bank of St. Louis. Rates of change in important national and international economic variables for ten major countries.

International Financial Statistics, published monthly in Washington by the IMF. A very useful source with a wealth of data on international and domestic finance for most countries of the world. Also a *Yearbook* and special supplements.

International Letter. An interesting newsletter on international economic developments, issued every other week by the Federal Reserve Bank of Chicago.

IMF Annual Report, published in Washington. In addition to a report on Fund activities, contains a discussion of developments in the world economy and the international financial system, with tables and charts.

IMF Balance of Payments Yearbook, issued in monthly installments from Washington. Presents annual balance of payments data and analytic balances (denominated in SDRs) for all IMF members.

IMF Report on Exchange Arrangements and Exchange Restrictions, published annually in Washington. A comprehensive listing of capital controls in each of the member countries.

IMF Survey, published monthly in Washington, D.C. by the International Monetary Fund. Timely reports on Fund activities and current issues in international economic policy.

International Trade, published annually by the General Agreements on Tariffs and Trade in Geneva. Describes developments in international trade and supplies relevant data.

Journal of Economic Literature, published quarterly by the American Economic Association. Lists current professional journal articles by subject and by journal. Also lists new books and contains book reviews, article abstracts, and review articles.

Journal of International Economics, published quarterly by North Holland in Amsterdam. Scholarly articles on the subject.

MacBean, A. I. and P. N. Snowden, *International Institutions in Trade and Finance,* 1981 (London: Allen & Unwin). Useful descriptions and reviews of the basic institutions.

The Money Manager, published weekly in New York by the Bond Trader. Presents a wide variety of international, short-term rates on a timely basis as well as commentary on recent developments. A prime source for nondollar, Euro-currency rates.

Monthly Bulletin of Statistics, published by the United Nations in New York. Contains basic population and economic data and detailed analyses of world trade patterns. Also a *Yearbook.*

Monthly Report of the Deutsche Bundesbank, published in Frankfurt in German and English. In addition to German financial data, contains a good selection of international money market rates and exchange rates. Often includes a timely analysis of international economic events.

OECD Financial Statistics, published by the Organization for Economic Cooperation and Development in Paris once a year with supplements available every two months. A collection of financial data from each member country. Particularly useful as an introduction to individual country sources. Also an important summary of Eurodollar and Eurobond data.

OECD Statistics of Foreign Trade Series A, published monthly, contains detailed trade statistics.

Pick's Currency Yearbook, published annually in New York by Franz Pick. A compendium of unusual financial statistics. Because the data are based solely on personal dealings, this source is less than impeccable; however, nowhere else can one find black market exchange rates and gold price quotations for virtually every leading financial center.

Statistical Abstract of the United States, published annually by the U.S. Bureau of the Census. A good starting point for information about the United States.

Statistical Sources of the U.S. Government, a publication of the U.S. Bureau of the Budget. Lists and evaluates U.S. sources.

Survey of Current Business, published monthly in Washington, D.C., by the Department of Commerce. U.S. balance of payments statistics are presented in the March, June, September, and December issues and the U.S. international investment position in October. Information on the activities of foreign subsidiaries of U.S. firms and on particular categories of balance of payments flows appears throughout the year.

Trade Yearbook, published annually by the U.N. Food and Agriculture Organization. Contains detailed data on trade in agricultural products. The same organization also publishes a *Production Yearbook.*

World Bank Atlas, published annually by the World Bank. A quick reference for population statistics, per capita GNP and growth rates for 183 countries and entities.

World Bank Annual Report, published in Washington. In addition to a summary of IBRD activities and a standard array of economic indicators, contains an analysis of international debt outstanding and debt service ratios for developing countries.

The World Economy, published quarterly for the Trade Policy Research Center by North Holland. Articles on international economic affairs.

World Financial Markets, published monthly in New York by the Morgan Guaranty Trust Company. Contains trade-weighted exchange rates, Eurobond yields, effective Eurodollar rates, money and bond market rates and bank lending rates for twenty-eight countries. In addition, there is a good analysis of contemporary financial events. A highly regarded private source.

Appendix III

Answers to Selected Problems

THIS APPENDIX supplies the answers—sometimes complete and sometimes partial—
to a fraction of the problems that appear in the text. The purpose is to give you an
idea of how well you are doing. Only the answers are given—not the methods of
solution.

Chapter 1
  1.4 (a)

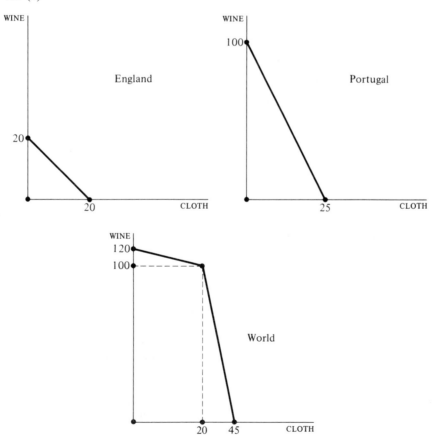

1.5

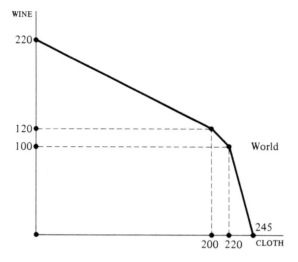

1.8

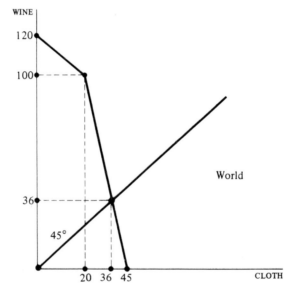

The world price $p = P_W/P_C = \frac{1}{4}$ (Portugal's autarkic price). In *Portugal,* production consists of 36 wine and 16 cloth and consumption consists of 20 units each of wine and of cloth, the same as in autarky. *England's* production is 20 cloth and her consumption is 16 units of each, compared to 10 each in autarky. Thus England exports 4 cloth to Portugal for 16 wine.

1.11 If $p = 1$, the English autarkic price, Portugal must specialize to wine, Portugal exports wine to England for cloth, and all gains go to Portugal. If the English wage $= 1$, then $P_W = 5$ and $P_C = 5$ because England can compete in both goods. The Portuguese wage equals 5 because Portugal can compete in wine. Note that cloth costs 20 to make in Portugal, so that country cannot compete in that good.

Chapter 2

2.2

Price of Wine in Terms of Machines	Excess Demand for Wine	Excess Demand for Machines
1/10	1000	− 100
1/5	400	− 80
1/2	40	− 20
2/3	0	0
1	− 10	10
3/2	− 20	30
2	− 25	50
5	− 20	100
10	− 15	150

2.6 See the statement of Problem **5.12** on p. 178.

2.7 See the statement of Problem **5.11** on p. 177.

2.14 France exports 70 wine to Germany for 30 machines, so that $P_M/P_W = 7/3$.

2.16

P	M	X
100	1000	100,000
99	1030	101,970

$$e = \frac{100}{1000} \cdot \frac{30}{1} = 3; f = \frac{100}{100,000} \cdot \frac{1970}{1} = 1.97 \approx 2 = e\text{-}1;$$

$$g = \frac{1000}{100,000} \cdot \frac{1970}{30} = .66 \approx 2/3 \approx f/e.$$

Chapter 3

3.5

$$\frac{\text{wine cost}}{\text{cloth cost}} = \frac{4w + r}{2w + r} = \frac{4\dfrac{w}{r} + 1}{2\dfrac{w}{r} + 5}, \quad \text{so:}$$

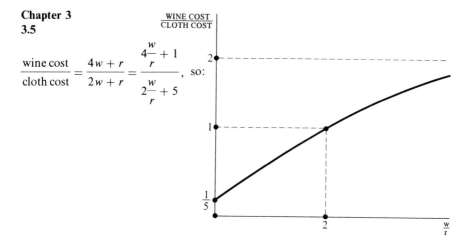

If $w = 1 = r$, then (wine cost/cloth cost) $= 5/7$, which is less than 2, so England would produce only wine.

3.17 In England:

$W + 5C = 160$ (capital) and $4W + 2C = 100$ (labor). These have the solution $W = 10$ and $C = 30$.

In Portugal:

$W + 5C = 70$ (capital) and $4W + 2C = 100$ (labor). These have the solution $W = 20$ and $C = 10$.

Thus

$$\left(\frac{30-10}{10} = 3\right) > \left(\frac{160-70}{70} = \frac{9}{7}\right) > \left(\frac{100-100}{100} = 0\right) > \left(\frac{10-20}{10} = -1\right),$$

which illustrates the Rybczynski theorem.

3.23

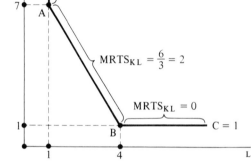

At kinks A and B, $MRTS_{KL}$ is undefined. If $w/r = 5$, A would be used; if $w/r = 1$, B would be used; if $w/r = 2$, any technique between A and B inclusive could be used.

3.25 $4W + C = 6$ (capital) and $2W + 4C - 10$ (labor) have the solution $W = 1$ and $C = 2$.

$4r + 2w = 2$ (price of wine) and $r + 4w = 1$ (price of cloth) have the solution $r = 3/7$, $w = 1/7$.

3.39 He would not have obtained the paradox in either case.

Chapter 4

4.4 $MPM = 1/2$, $APM = 1/2$, $\eta = 1$.

4.9 Multiplier $= 4/3$. $S\text{-}I = X\text{-}M$ because $(1/4) Y - 50 = 100 - (1/2) Y$, which solves for $Y = 200$.

4.10 $-[MPM/(MPM + MPS)]$.

Chapter 5

5.1 Asti Spumante: $t = \dfrac{5.17 - 4.00}{4.00} = .29$

Champagne: $t = \dfrac{31.17 - 30.00}{30.00} = .04$

5.5 $p = 1$ and so $q = 4/3$. Then Germany supplies 110 machines and 30 wine, which are worth 140 wine at $p = 1$. With free trade Germany would supply 100 machines and 50 wine, worth 150 wine. Thus the production cost is 10 wine (or 10 machines).

5.12 With the tariff, France exports 60 wine to Germany for 20 machines. Before the tariff 10 wine were exchanged for 30 machines, so Germany's terms of trade have improved from 3/7 to 1/3. The relative price of wine in Germany is now 1/2.

5.16 A tariff *reduces* the relative domestic price of importables thereby lowering the real income of the relatively scarce factor and raising that of the relatively abundant factor.

Chapter 6

6.8 A tariff is second best from a cosmopolitan perspective because it reduces world income, whereas direct international transfer payments would not, and are thereby first best.

6.14 e_R equals:

$$\left[\frac{P_G b_G}{Q} t_G + \frac{P_A b_A}{Q} t_A \right] +$$

$$\left[\left(\frac{P_G b_G}{Q} t_G + \frac{P_A b_A}{Q} t_A \right) - \left(\frac{P_o a_o}{Q - v} t_o + \frac{P_c a_c}{Q - v} t_c + \frac{P_M a_M}{Q - v} t_M \right) \right] \frac{Q - v}{v}$$

where $Q = P_B b_G + P_A b_A$, so that $Q - v = P_o a_o + P_c a_c + P_M a_M$.

Chapter 7

7.1 The world frontier:

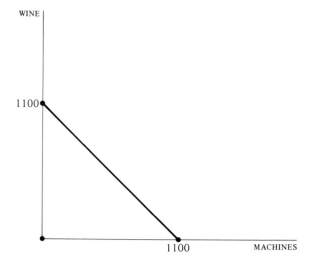

7.11 **(a)** The marginal propensities to import sum to 1/2. Thus the transfer will be undereffected and France's terms of trade will deteriorate.
    (b) C' equals \$5 billion.
    (c) \$5 billion, $-$\$5 billion.

Chapter 8
8.1

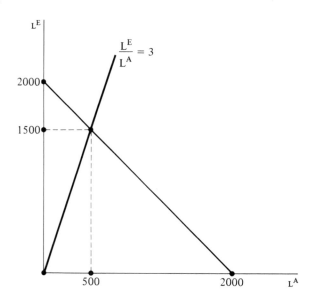

Thus, $L^A = 500$, $L^E = 1500$, $P_W = 1$, $P_C = 5$.
If $L^A + L^E = 4000$, then $L^A = 1000$, $L^E = 3000$, $P_W = 2$ and $P_C = 10$.
If $P_W / P_C = 5/3$, $L^A = 1000 = L^E$.

8.2 A cumulative American deficit (or cumulative European surplus) of 1500.

8.11 $L^S = 80,000$, $L^I = 100,000$. $P_G = 10$ ounces $= 5$ pesetas $= 20$ lire. $P_o = 5$ ounces $= 10$ lire $= 2.5$ pesetas.

8.12 $P_G = 14$ ounces and $P_o = 7$ ounces. The initial Spanish deficit (Italian surplus) is 4000 ounces, so that after one year $L^S = 148,000$ ounces and $L^I = 104,000$.

8.32 The Spanish surplus is 10,000 pesetas or 20,000 ounces. Thus the Spanish gold stock increases to 70,000 ounces and the Spanish money supply to 70,000 pesetas. Italian reserves fall to 30,000 ounces and the Italian money supply falls to 180,000 lire.

Chapter 9
9.1

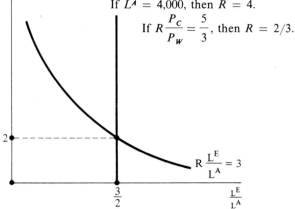

The American exchange rate $R = 3$ dollars per pound.
If $L^A = 4{,}000$, then $R = 4$.

If $R\dfrac{P_C}{P_W} = \dfrac{5}{3}$, then $R = 2/3$.

9.6 France devalues relative to silver but not to gold; France depreciates relative to China but not to England; China appreciates relative to France but not to England. Neither China nor England devalue or revalue.

9.12 Italy's exchange rate equals 1 lira per peseta. $P_G = 10$ pesetas $= 10$ lire; $P_o = 5$ pesetas $= 5$ lire.

9.13 Now the Italian exchange rate is $1/2$. $P_G = 140/9$ lire $= 280/9$ pesetas; $P_o = 35/9$ pesetas $= 35/18$ lire.

Chapter 10
10.6 $1 + i_{us} = 1.08 < (1 + i_{uk})(R_F/R_S) = (1.12)(2/2.06) = 1.09$ so arbitrageurs sell U.S. Treasury bills, buy pounds spot, buy U.K. Treasury bills, and sell pounds forward.

10.7 The 90-day interest rate equals one-fourth of the per annum rate. Thus $1 + i_{us} = 1.02 > (1 + i_{uk})(R_F/R_S) = (1.03)(2.02/2.06) = 1.01$ so arbitrage is in the opposite direction to that in Problem (10.6).

10.15

	New York		*London*	
Reserves: $4 million	Demand Deposits: $4 million		$1 million (deposit in some U.S. bank) Loans: $4 million	Demand Deposits: $5 million

The Eurodollar market increases by $5 million; there is no effect on either money supply.

Chapter 11
11.3 When foreign residents sell U.S. dollar assets to a foreign central bank.

11.5 SDR $1 = \$1.28 = $ fr5.8 $= 1160$ Lire.

Index